W9-BEY-528

Rick Steves'

LONDON

Rick Steves & Gene Openshaw

2010

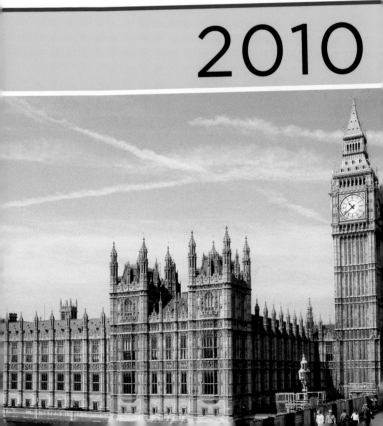

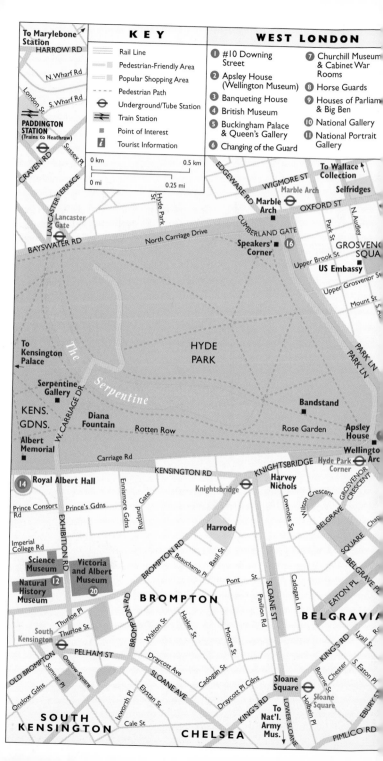

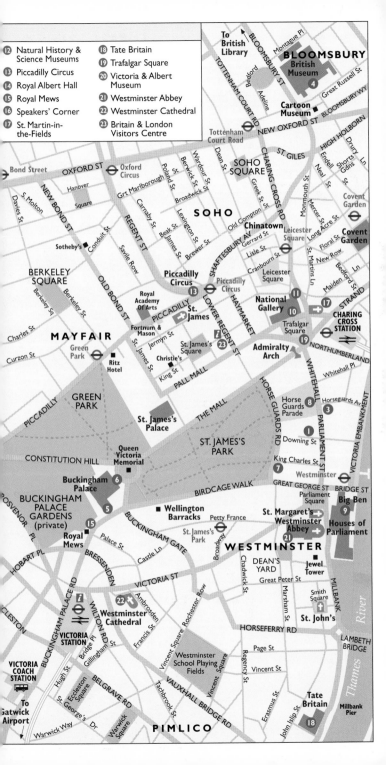

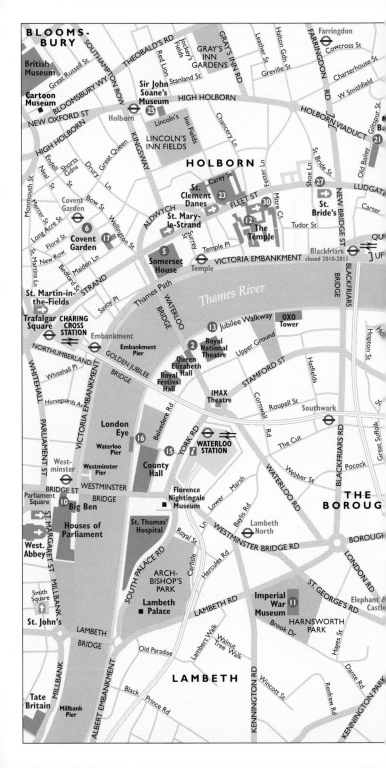

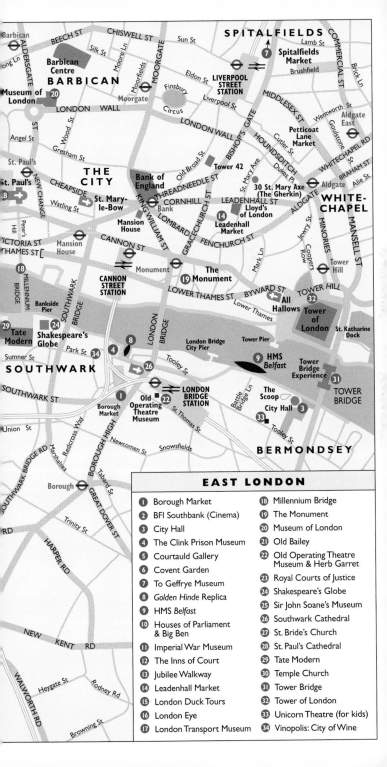

EAST LONDON

1. Borough Market
2. BFI Southbank (Cinema)
3. City Hall
4. The Clink Prison Museum
5. Courtauld Gallery
6. Covent Garden
7. To Geffrye Museum
8. *Golden Hinde* Replica
9. HMS *Belfast*
10. Houses of Parliament & Big Ben
11. Imperial War Museum
12. The Inns of Court
13. Jubilee Walkway
14. Leadenhall Market
15. London Duck Tours
16. London Eye
17. London Transport Museum
18. Millennium Bridge
19. The Monument
20. Museum of London
21. Old Bailey
22. Old Operating Theatre Museum & Herb Garret
23. Royal Courts of Justice
24. Shakespeare's Globe
25. Sir John Soane's Museum
26. Southwark Cathedral
27. St. Bride's Church
28. St. Paul's Cathedral
29. Tate Modern
30. Temple Church
31. Tower Bridge
32. Tower of London
33. Unicorn Theatre (for kids)
34. Vinopolis: City of Wine

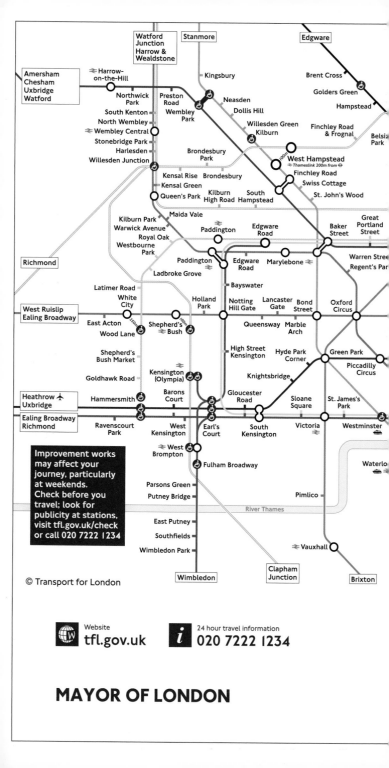

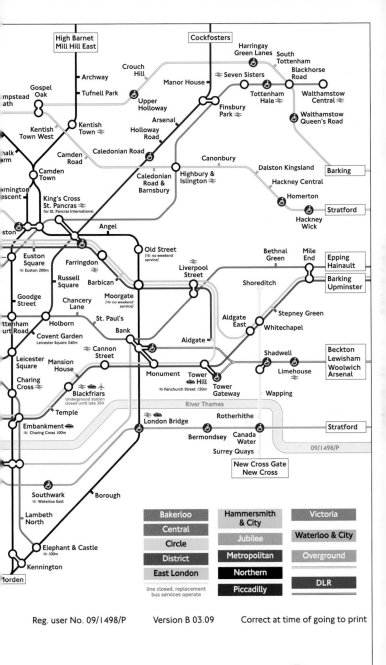

Reg. user No. 09/1498/P   Version B 03.09   Correct at time of going to print

Transport for London UNDERGROUND

Rick Steves'

LONDON

2010

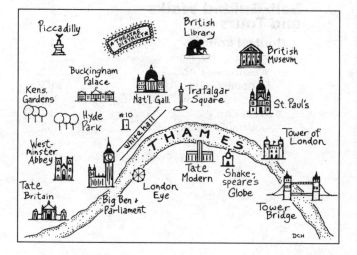

AVALON
TRAVEL

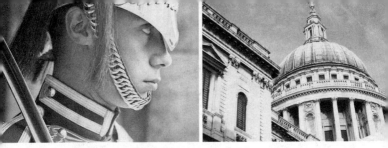

CONTENTS

CITY OF LONDON

London Map Overview

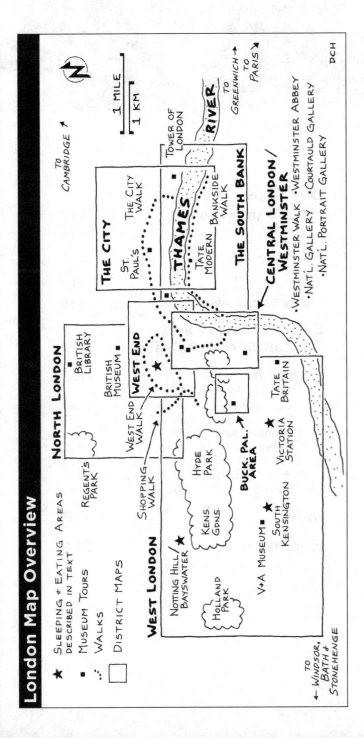

★ SLEEPING + EATING AREAS
  DESCRIBED IN TEXT

■ MUSEUM TOURS

∶∶ WALKS

☐ DISTRICT MAPS

1 MILE
1 KM

NORTH LONDON

REGENT'S PARK

BRITISH LIBRARY

BRITISH MUSEUM

WEST END

WEST END WALK

SHOPPING WALK

WEST LONDON

NOTTING HILL / BAYSWATER ★

HOLLAND PARK

KENS. GDNS.

HYDE PARK

BUCK. PAL. AREA

VICTORIA STATION ★

SOUTH KENSINGTON ★

V+A MUSEUM

TATE BRITAIN

THE CITY

ST. PAUL'S

THE CITY WALK

THAMES

TATE MODERN

BANKSIDE WALK

TOWER OF LONDON

RIVER

TO CAMBRIDGE ↑

TO GREENWICH →
TO PARIS ↘

THE SOUTH BANK

CENTRAL LONDON / WESTMINSTER

• WESTMINSTER WALK • WESTMINSTER ABBEY
• NAT'L. GALLERY   • COURTAULD GALLERY
• NAT'L. PORTRAIT GALLERY

TO WINDSOR, BATH + STONEHENGE ←

DCH

INTRODUCTION

Blow through the city on the open deck of a double-decker orientation tour bus, and take a pinch-me-I'm-in-London walk through the West End. Ogle the crown jewels at the Tower of London, hear the chimes of Big Ben, and see the Houses of Parliament in action. Cruise the Thames River and take a spin on the London Eye. Hobnob with the tombstones in Westminster Abbey, and visit with Leonardo, Botticelli, and Rembrandt in the National Gallery. Enjoy Shakespeare in a replica of the Globe Theatre and marvel at a glitzy, fun musical at a modern-day theater. Whisper across the dome of St. Paul's Cathedral, then rummage through our civilization's attic at the British Museum. And sip your tea with pinky raised and clotted cream dribbling down your scone.

You can enjoy some of Europe's best people-watching at Covent Garden, and snap to at Buckingham Palace's Changing of the Guard. Just sit in Victoria Station, Piccadilly Circus, or a major Tube station and observe. Tip a pint in a pub with a chatty local, and beachcomb the Thames. Spend one evening at a theater and the other nights catching your breath.

London is more than its museums and landmarks. It's a living, breathing, thriving organism...a coral reef of humanity. The city has changed dramatically in recent years, and many visitors are surprised to find how "un-English" it is. White people are now a minority in major parts of the city that once symbolized white imperialism. Arabs have nearly bought out the area north of Hyde Park. Chinese takeouts outnumber fish-and-chips shops. Eastern Europeans pull pints in British pubs. Many hotels are run by people with foreign accents (who hire English chambermaids), while outlying suburbs are home to huge communities of Indians and Pakistanis. London is a city of eight million separate dreams, inhabiting a place that tolerates and encourages them.

With the English Channel Tunnel and discount airlines making travel between Britain and the Continent easier than ever, many locals see even more holes in their bastion of Britishness. London is learning—sometimes fitfully—to live as a microcosm of its formerly vast empire. In anticipation of the 2012 Olympic Games, London is busy spiffing up the place, especially its rapidly developing Olympic Park in East London.

About This Book

Rick Steves' London 2010 is a personal tour guide in your pocket. Better yet, it's actually two tour guides in your pocket: The co-author of this book is Gene Openshaw. Since our first "Europe through the gutter" trip together as high school buddies in the 1970s, Gene and I have been exploring the wonders of the Old World. An inquisitive historian and lover of European culture, Gene wrote most of this book's self-guided museum tours and neighborhood walks. Together, Gene and I keep this book current and accurate (though, for simplicity, from this point "we" will shed our respective egos and become "I"). For any updates that have occurred since our recent research, see www.ricksteves .com/update, and for a valuable list of reports and experiences—good and bad—from fellow travelers, check www.ricksteves.com /feedback.

In this book, you'll find the following chapters:

Orientation includes specifics on public transportation, local tour options, helpful hints, and tourist information (note that tourist information is abbreviated "TI" in this book). The "Planning Your Time" section suggests a day-to-day schedule for how to best use your limited time.

Sights provides a succinct overview of the most important sights, arranged by neighborhood, with ratings:

▲▲▲—Don't miss.

▲▲—Try hard to see.

▲—Worthwhile if you can make it.

No rating—Worth knowing about.

The **Self-Guided Walks** cover Westminster (from Big Ben to Trafalgar Square), the West End (it's the thee-ah-ter district, darling, with restaurants and shops galore, from Leicester Square to Covent Garden, with Piccadilly Circus as the finale), The City (the financial district—banks, churches, and courts busy with barristers and baristas), and Bankside (on the South Bank, through Shakespeare's world to the Tate Modern).

The **Self-Guided Tours** lead you through London's most fascinating museums and sights: Westminster Abbey, National Gallery, National Portrait Gallery, Courtauld Gallery, the British Museum, the British Library, St. Paul's Cathedral, the Tower of

London, Tate Modern, Victoria and Albert Museum, and the Tate Britain.

Sleeping describes my favorite hotels, from budget deals to cushy splurges.

Eating serves up a range of options, from inexpensive pubs to fancier restaurants.

London with Children includes my top recommendations for keeping your kids (and you) happy in London.

Shopping gives you tips for shopping painlessly and enjoyably, without letting it overwhelm your vacation or ruin your budget.

Entertainment is your guide to fun, including theater, music, walks, and cruises.

Connections lays the groundwork for your smooth arrival and departure, covering transportation by train (including the Eurostar to Paris) and by plane (with detailed information on London's major airports).

Day Trips covers nearby sights: Greenwich, Windsor, Cambridge, Stonehenge, Bath, and even Paris.

English History and Contemporary Politics gives the background of this historic city, including a timeline and a *Who's Who* list of British notables.

The **appendix** is a traveler's tool kit, with telephone tips, useful phone numbers, recommended books and films, a festival list, climate chart, handy packing checklist, hotel reservation form, and a fun British–Yankee dictionary.

Throughout this book, when you see a ✪ in a listing, it means that the sight is covered in much more detail in one of the tour chapters.

Browse through this book and select your favorite sights. Then have a brilliant trip! Traveling like a temporary local, you'll get the absolute most out of every mile, minute, and pound. As you visit places I know and love, I'm happy you'll be meeting my favorite Londoners.

Planning

This section will help you get started planning your trip—with notes on trip costs, when to go, and things to know before you take off.

Travel Smart

Your trip to London is like a complex play—easier to follow and really appreciate on a second viewing. While no one does the same trip twice to gain that advantage, reading this book in its entirety before your trip accomplishes much the same thing.

Design an itinerary that enables you to visit the various sights at the best possible times. Make note of festivals, holidays, street market days, and days when sights are closed. Visit The City (London's old center) during the day on weekdays, when it's lively, not at night and on weekends, when it's dead. The two-hour orientation bus tour is best on Sunday morning (when some sights are closed) or evenings (when it's cheaper). There are no plays on Sunday nights, except at Shakespeare's Globe. Treat Saturday as a weekday, except for transportation connections outside of London (which can be less frequent than on Mon–Fri, and downright meager on Sun). A smart trip is a puzzle—a fun, doable, and worthwhile challenge.

Be sure to mix intense and relaxed periods in your itinerary. Every trip (and every traveler) needs at least a few slack days. Pace yourself. Assume you will return.

Plan ahead for laundry and picnics. Get online at Internet cafés or at your hotel to research transportation connections, confirm events, and check the weather. Buy a phone card (or carry a mobile phone) and use it to make reservations, reconfirm hotels, book tours, and double-check hours of sights.

Connect with the culture. Set up your own quest for the best pub, silly sign, or chocolate bar. Slow down and be open to unexpected experiences. You speak the language—use it! Ask questions—most locals are eager to point you in their idea of the right direction. Keep a notepad in your pocket for organizing your thoughts. Wear your money belt, and learn the local currency and how to estimate prices in dollars. Those who expect to travel smart, do.

Trip Costs

Five components make up your trip costs: airfare, surface transportation, room and board, sightseeing and entertainment, and shopping and miscellany.

Airfare: A basic, round-trip, US-to-London flight can cost $700 to $1,200, depending on where you fly from and when (cheaper in winter).

Surface Transportation: For a typical one-week visit, allow about $42 for the Tube and buses (for a Seven-Day Oyster card transportation pass). The cost of round-trip train rides to day-trip destinations is about $25 for Windsor, $7 for Greenwich (two rides on a 1–2-zone Oyster card—see page 26), $46 for Cambridge, $65 for Bath, and $190 (round-trip second-class Passholder ticket) for Paris on the Eurostar (see page 373 for tips on how to get the cheapest Eurostar tickets). You can save money by taking buses instead of trains. Add $75–100 if you plan to take a taxi ride between London's Heathrow Airport and your hotel (or save money by taking the Tube, train, bus, or airport shuttle).

Major Holidays and Weekends

Popular places are even busier on weekends...and inundated on three-day weekends. Plan ahead and reserve your accommodations and transportation well in advance.

A few national holidays jam things up, especially Bank Holiday Mondays (some hotels require you to book the full three-day weekend around Bank Holidays). Mark these dates in red on your travel calendar: New Year's Day, Good Friday through Easter Monday (April 2–5 in 2010), the Bank Holidays that occur on the first and last Mondays in May (May 3 and 31), the last Monday in August (Aug 30, also a Bank Holiday), Christmas, and December 26 (Boxing Day). For more information, check the list of festivals and holidays in the appendix.

Many businesses, as well as many museums, close on Good Friday, Easter, and New Year's Day. On Christmas, virtually everything closes down, even the Tube (and taxi rates are high). Museums are also generally closed December 24 and 26; smaller shops are usually closed December 26. For tips on winter travel, see page 359.

Room and Board: London is one of Europe's most expensive major capitals. But if you're careful, you can manage comfortably in London on $130 a day per person for room and board. A $130-a-day budget allows $15 for lunch, $25 for dinner, and $90 for lodging (based on two people splitting the cost of a basic $180 double room that includes breakfast). That's doable. Students and tightwads can do it on $70 a day ($45 for hostel bed, $25 for groceries).

Sightseeing and Entertainment: You'll pay more in London for sights that charge admission than you will anywhere else in Europe. Fortunately, most of London's best sights are free (although many request a donation), including the British Museum, National Gallery, National Portrait Gallery, Tate Britain, Tate Modern, British Library, and the Victoria and Albert Museum. (For a full list of free museums—and advice on saving money on sightseeing—see "Affording London's Sights," page 56).

Figure on paying roughly $20–30 each for the major sights that charge admission (e.g., Westminster Abbey-$19, Tower of London-$27), $15 for guided walks, and $40 for bus tours and splurge experiences (plays range $20–90). You may be able to save money with a sightseeing pass—for information on the London Pass and other passes, see page 15.

An average of $50 a day works for most. Don't skimp here. After all, this category is the driving force behind your trip—you came to sightsee, enjoy, and experience London.

Shopping and Miscellany: Figure roughly $2 per postcard,

$3 for tea or an ice cream cone, and $6 per pint of beer. Shopping can vary in cost from nearly nothing to a small fortune. Good budget travelers find that this category has little to do with assembling a trip full of lifelong and wonderful memories.

When to Go

July and August are peak season—my favorite time—with long days, the best weather, and the busiest schedule of tourist fun.

Prices and crowds don't go up as dramatically in Britain as they do in much of Europe, except for holidays and festivals (see "Major Holidays and Weekends" sidebar on the previous page). Still, travel during "shoulder season" (May, early June, Sept, and early Oct) is easier and can be a bit less expensive. Shoulder-season travelers usually enjoy smaller crowds, decent weather, and the full range of sights and tourist fun spots. Winter travelers find absolutely no crowds and soft room prices, but shorter sightseeing hours. The weather can be cold and dreary, and nightfall draws the shades on sightseeing well before dinnertime. While England's rural charm falls with the leaves, London sightseeing is fine in the winter, and is especially popular during the Christmas season. For more on planning a winter holiday visit, read "Winter Diversions" (at the end of the Entertainment chapter).

Plan for rain no matter when you go. Just keep traveling and take full advantage of "bright spells." The weather can change several times a day, but rarely is it extreme. As the locals say, "There's no bad weather, only inappropriate clothing." Bring a jacket and dress in layers. Temperatures below 32°F cause headlines, and days that break 80°F—while increasing in recent years—are still rare in London. (For more information, see the climate chart in the appendix.) July and August are not much better than shoulder months. May and June can be lovely. While sunshine may be rare, summer days are very long. The summer sun is up from 6:30 to 22:30. It's not uncommon to have a gray day, eat dinner, and enjoy hours of sunshine afterward.

Know Before You Go

Your trip is more likely to go smoothly if you plan ahead. Check this list of things to arrange while you're still at home.

You need a **passport**—but no visa or shots—to travel in Great Britain. You may be denied entry into certain European countries if your passport is due to expire within three to six months of your ticketed date of return. Get it renewed if you'll be cutting it close. It can take up to six weeks to get or renew a passport. (For more on passports, see www.travel.state.gov.) Pack a photocopy of your passport in your luggage in case the original is lost or stolen.

Book your rooms well in advance, especially if you'll be

traveling during any major **holidays** (see "Major Holidays and Weekends," on page 5). It's smart to reserve rooms in peak season if you'd like to stay in my lead listings, and definitely reserve for your first night.

If you're planning to **stay in Bath** as well as London, consider doing it before London as the ideal small-town jet-lag pillow, then visit London afterward, when you're rested and accustomed to travel in Britain. Heathrow Airport has direct bus connections to Bath and other cities.

To book a **London play,** you can call from the US as easily as from London, using your credit-card number to pay for your tickets. For the current schedule and phone numbers, visit www.officiallondontheatre.co.uk, or check the American magazine *Variety*. For simplicity, I book plays while in London. For more information, see the Entertainment chapter.

If you want to attend the free **Ceremony of the Keys** in the Tower of London, write for tickets at least two months in advance (see page 227).

Call your **debit- and credit-card companies** to let them know the countries you'll be visiting, so that they'll accept (and not deny) your international charges. Confirm your daily withdrawal limit; consider asking to have it raised so you can take out more cash at each ATM stop. Ask about international transaction fees.

If you're interested in travel insurance, do your homework before you buy. Compare the cost of the insurance to the likelihood of your using it and your potential loss if something goes wrong. For details on the many kinds of travel insurance, see www.ricksteves.com/plan/tips/insurance.htm.

If you're bringing an iPod or other MP3 player, take advantage of our free downloadable **audio tours** of London's major sights (coming in early 2010).

If you'll be **renting a car** for travels beyond London, bring your driver's license. It's recommended—but not required—that you also carry an International Driving Permit, available at your local AAA office ($15 plus the cost of two passport photos, www.aaa.com).

If traveling to continental Europe on the **Eurostar train,** consider ordering a ticket in advance (or buy it in Britain); for details, see page 373.

Because **airline carry-on restrictions** are always changing, visit the Transportation Security Administration's website (www.tsa.gov/travelers) for an up-to-date list of what you can bring on the plane with you, and what you have to check. Remember to arrive with plenty of time to get through security. Some airlines may restrict you to only one carry-on (no extras like a purse or daypack); check Britain's website for the latest (www.dft.gov.uk).

Practicalities

Emergency Telephone Numbers: In Britain, dial 999 for police or medical emergencies.

Time: In Britain—and in this book—you'll use the 24-hour clock. It's the same through 12:00 noon, then keep going: 13:00, 14:00, and so on. For anything over 12, subtract 12 and add p.m. (14:00 is 2:00 p.m.)

Britain, which is one hour earlier than most of continental Europe, is five/eight hours ahead of the East/West Coasts of the US. The exceptions are the beginning and end of Daylight Saving Time: Britain and Europe "spring forward" the last Sunday in March (two weeks after most of North America) and "fall back" the last Sunday in October (one week before North America). For a handy online time converter, try www.timeanddate .com/worldclock.

Business Hours: Most stores are open Monday through Saturday (roughly 10:00–17:00), with a late night on Wednesday or Thursday (until 19:00 or 20:00), depending on the neighborhood. On Sunday, when some stores are closed, street markets are lively with shoppers.

Watt's Up? Britain's electrical system is different from North America's in two ways: the shape of the plug (three square prongs—not the two round prongs used in continental Europe) and the voltage of the current (220 volts instead of 110 volts). For your North American plug to work in Britain, you'll need a three-prong adapter plug, sold inexpensively at travel stores in the US, and in British airports and drugstores. As for the voltage, most newer electronics or travel appliances (such as hair dryers, laptops, and battery chargers) automatically convert the voltage—if you see a range of voltages printed on the item or its plug (such as "110–220"), it'll work in Great Britain and Europe. Otherwise, you can buy a converter separately in the US or at a drugstore in Britain (about $20).

Discounts: While discounts (called "concessions" or "concs" in Britain) are not listed in this book, many British sights, buses, and trains are discounted for seniors (loosely defined as those who are retired or willing to call themselves a senior), youths (ages 8–18), students, groups of 10 or more, and families. Always ask. To get a teacher or student ID card, visit www.statravel.com or www .isic.org.

You might see a "Gift Aid" admission price listed at sights (US tourists are not eligible for this).

News: British papers cover global events, and Americans can also peruse the *International Herald Tribune,* published almost daily throughout Europe and online at www.iht.com. Other newsy

Where Do I Find Information On...?

Credit-Card Theft	See page 11.
Packing Light	See the packing list on page 487.
Phoning	See "How to Dial" on page 470.
Making Hotel Reservations	See page 298.
Tipping	See page 12.
Tourist Information Office	See page 24.
Updates to This Book	See www.ricksteves.com/update

sites are http://news.bbc.co.uk and www.europeantimes.com. Every Tuesday, editions of *Time* and *Newsweek* hit the stands with articles of particular interest to European travelers. Sports addicts can get their daily fix online or from *USA Today*. Many hotels have BBC (of course) and CNN television channels.

Money

This section covers how to get cash, using credit and debit cards in London, what to do if your card is lost or stolen, and tips on tipping.

Cash from ATMs

Throughout Britain, cash machines (ATMs) are the standard way for travelers to get local currency. As an emergency backup, bring several hundred US dollars in hard cash (in $20 bills rather than hard-to-exchange $100 bills). Avoid using currency exchange booths (lousy rates and/or outrageous fees); if you have currency to exchange, take it to a bank. Also avoid traveler's checks, which are a waste of time (long waits at banks) and a waste of money in fees.

To use an ATM to withdraw money from your account, you'll need a debit card (ideally with a Visa or MasterCard logo for maximum usability), plus a PIN. Know your PIN in numbers; there are only numbers—no letters—on European keypads. It's smart to bring two cards, in case one gets demagnetized or eaten by a temperamental machine.

Before you go, confirm with your bank that your cards will work overseas, and alert them that you'll be making withdrawals in Europe—otherwise, the bank might freeze your card if it detects unusual spending patterns. (Credit-card companies do the same thing—inform them of your travel plans as well.) Also ask about international fees; see "Credit and Debit Cards," next page.

When using an ATM, try to take out large sums of money to reduce your per-transaction bank fees. If the machine refuses your

Exchange Rate

I list prices in pounds (£) throughout this book.

1 British pound (£1) = about $1.60

While the euro (€) is now the currency of most of Europe, Britain is sticking with its pound sterling. The British pound (£), also called a "quid," is broken into 100 pence (p). Pence means "cents." You'll find coins ranging from 1p to £2 and bills from £5 to £50. Fake pound coins are easy to spot (real coins have an inscription on their outside rims; the fakes look like tree bark).

London is so expensive that some travelers try to kid themselves that pounds are dollars. But when they get home, that £1,000-pound Visa bill isn't asking for $1,000...it wants around $1,600. (To get the latest rate and print a cheat sheet, see www.oanda.com.)

request, try again and select a smaller amount (some cash machines limit the amount you can withdraw—don't take it personally). If that doesn't work, try a different machine.

Even in jolly olde England, you'll need to keep your cash safe. Use a money belt—a pouch with a strap that you buckle around your waist—and wear it under your clothes. Thieves target tourists. A money belt provides peace of mind, allowing you to carry lots of cash safely. Don't waste time every few days tracking down a cash machine—withdraw a week's worth of money, stuff it in your money belt, and travel!

Credit and Debit Cards

For purchases, Visa and MasterCard are more commonly accepted than American Express. Just like at home, credit or debit cards work easily at larger hotels, restaurants, and shops, but smaller businesses prefer payment in local currency (in small bills—break large bills at a bank or larger store). If receipts show your credit-card number, don't toss these thoughtlessly.

Fees: Credit and debit cards—whether used for purchases or ATM withdrawals—often charge additional, tacked-on "international transaction" fees of up to 3 percent plus $5 per transaction. Note that if you use a credit card for ATM transactions, it's technically a "cash advance" rather than a "withdrawal"—and subject to an additional cash-advance fee.

To avoid unpleasant surprises, call your bank or credit-card company before your trip to ask about these fees. If the fees are too high, consider getting a card just for your trip: Capital One (www .capitalone.com) and most credit unions have low-to-no international transaction fees.

If merchants offer to convert your purchase price into dollars (called dynamic currency conversion, or DCC), refuse this "service." You'll pay even more in fees for the expensive convenience of seeing your charge in dollars.

Dealing with "Chip and PIN": Some parts of Europe (especially Great Britain, Ireland, France, the Netherlands, and Scandinavia) are adopting a "chip and PIN" system for their credit and debit cards. These "smartcards" come with an embedded microchip, and cardholders enter a PIN instead of signing a receipt. In most cases, you can still use your credit or debit card at the cashier and sign the receipt the old-fashioned way. A few merchants might insist on the PIN—making it helpful for you to know the PIN for your credit card (ask your credit-card company); in a pinch, use cash or your debit card and PIN instead. Some newer, automated pay-at-the-pump gas stations or ticket machines can no longer read the magnetic strip on American credit cards. But in most of these situations, there's a cashier nearby who can take your credit or debit card and make it work.

Damage Control for Lost Cards

If you lose your credit, debit, or ATM card, you can stop people from using it by reporting the loss immediately to the respective global customer-assistance centers. Call these 24-hour US numbers collect: Visa (410/581-9994), MasterCard (636/722-7111), and American Express (623/492-8427). Diner's Club has offices in Britain (0870-1900-011) and the US (702/797-5532, call collect).

At a minimum, you'll need to know the name of the financial institution that issued you the card, along with the type of card (classic, platinum, or whatever). Providing the following information will allow for a quicker cancellation of your missing card: full card number, whether you are the primary or secondary cardholder, the cardholder's name exactly as printed on the card, billing address, home phone number, circumstances of the loss or theft, and identification verification (your birth date, your mother's maiden name, or your Social Security Number—memorize this, don't carry a copy). If you are the secondary cardholder, you'll also need to provide the primary cardholder's identification-verification details. You can generally receive a temporary card within two or three business days in Europe.

If you promptly report your card lost or stolen, you typically won't be responsible for any unauthorized transactions on your account, although many banks charge a liability fee of $50.

Tipping

Tipping in Britain isn't as automatic and generous as it is in the US, but for special service, tips are appreciated, if not expected. As in the US, the proper amount depends on your resources, tipping philosophy, and the circumstances, but some general guidelines apply.

Restaurants: At pubs where you order at the counter, you don't have to tip. (Regular customers ordering a round sometimes say, "Add one for yourself" as a tip for drinks ordered at the bar—but this isn't expected.) At a pub or restaurant with waitstaff, check the menu or your bill to see if the service is included; if not, tip about 10 percent.

Taxis: To tip the cabbie, round up. For a typical ride, round up to a maximum of 10 percent (to pay a £4.50 fare, give £5; or for a £28 fare, give £30). If the cabbie hauls your bags and zips you to the airport to help you catch your flight, you might want to toss in a little more. But if you feel like you're being driven in circles or otherwise ripped off, skip the tip.

Special Services: It's thoughtful to tip a pound to someone who shows you a special sight and who is not otherwise paid. Tour guides at public sites often hold out their hands for tips after they give their spiel; if I've already paid for the tour, I don't tip extra, though some tourists do give a pound, particularly for a job well done. At hotels, porters expect 50p for each bag they carry (another reason to pack light). Leaving the maid 50p per overnight at the end of your stay is a nice touch. In general, if someone in the service industry does a super job for you, a tip of a pound or two is appropriate, but not required.

When in doubt, ask. If you're not sure whether (or how much) to tip for a service, ask your hotelier or the tourist information office; they'll fill you in on how it's done on their turf.

Getting a VAT Refund

Wrapped into the purchase price of your British souvenirs is a Value-Added Tax (VAT) of about 17.5 percent. If you purchase more than £20 (about $32) worth of goods at a store that participates in the VAT-refund scheme, you're entitled to get most of that tax back. Getting your refund is usually straightforward and, if you buy a substantial amount of souvenirs, well worth the hassle. If you're lucky, the merchant will subtract the tax when you make your purchase. (This is more likely to occur if the store ships the goods to your home.) Otherwise, you'll need to do the following:

Get the paperwork. Have the merchant completely fill out the necessary refund document, called a "Tax-Free Shopping Cheque." You'll have to present your passport at the store.

Get your stamp at the border or airport. Process your

cheque(s) at your last stop in the EU (e.g., at the airport) with the customs agent who deals with VAT refunds. It's best to keep your purchases in your carry-on for viewing, but if they're too large or dangerous (such as knives) to carry on, track down the proper customs agent to inspect them before you check your bag. You're not supposed to use your purchased goods before you leave. If you show up at customs wearing your new Wellingtons, officials might look the other way—or deny you a refund.

Collect your refund. You'll need to return your stamped document to the retailer or its representative. Many merchants work with a service, such as Global Refund (www.globalrefund.com) or Premier Tax Free (www.premiertaxfree.com), which have offices at major airports, ports, or border crossings. These services, which extract a 4 percent fee, can refund your money immediately in your currency of choice or credit your card (within two billing cycles). If the retailer handles VAT refunds directly, it's up to you to contact the merchant for your refund. You can mail the documents from home, or, even quicker, from your point of departure (using a stamped, addressed envelope you've prepared or one that's been provided by the merchant)—and then wait. It could take months.

Customs for American Shoppers

You are allowed to take home $800 worth of items per person duty-free, once every 30 days. The next $1,000 is taxed at a flat 3 percent. After that, you pay the individual item's duty rate. You can also bring in duty-free a liter of alcohol (slightly more than a standard-size bottle of wine; you must be at least 21), 200 cigarettes, and up to 100 non-Cuban cigars. You may take home vacuum-packed cheeses; dried herbs, spices, or mushrooms; and canned fruits or vegetables, including jams and vegetable spreads. Baked goods, candy, chocolate, oil, vinegar, mustard, and honey are OK. Meats (even vacuum-packed or canned) and fresh fruits or vegetables are not permitted. Note that you'll need to carefully pack any bottles of wine and other liquid-containing items in your checked luggage, due to limits on liquids in carry-ons. To check customs rules and duty rates, visit www.cbp.gov, and click on "Travel," then "Know Before You Go."

Sightseeing

Sightseeing can be hard work. Use these tips to make your visits to London's finest sights meaningful, fun, fast, and painless.

Plan Ahead

Set up an itinerary that allows you to fit in all your must-see sights. For a one-stop look at opening hours, see "London at a Glance"

INTRODUCTION

(page 46; also see "Daily Reminder" on page 22). Most sights keep stable hours, but you can easily confirm the latest by checking their website or with the local TI.

If you'll be visiting during a holiday, find out if a particular sight will be open by phoning ahead or checking its website. And don't put off visiting a must-see sight—you never know when a place will close unexpectedly for a holiday, strike, or restoration.

To get the most out of the self-guided tours and sight descriptions in this book, reread them the night before your visit. The British Library is much more entertaining if you've boned up on the Magna Carta beforehand. When you arrive at the sight, use the overview map to get the lay of the land and the basic tour route.

When possible, visit key museums first thing in the day (when your energy is best) and save other activities for the afternoon. Hit the highlights first, then go back to other things if you have the stamina and time. Going at the right time can also help you avoid crowds. This book offers tips on specific sights. Try visiting the sight very early, at lunch, or very late (evening hours are usually peaceful, with fewer crowds). In addition to the London Eye, at least one London sight is open late every night (including the British Library, British Museum, National Portrait Gallery, Victoria and Albert Museum, and Tate Modern; see the "London for Early Birds and Night Owls" sidebar on page 64).

At Sights

All sights have rules, and if you know about these in advance, they're no big deal. At churches—which often offer interesting art (usually free) and a cool, welcome seat—a modest dress code (no bare shoulders or shorts) is encouraged.

Some important sights may have metal detectors or conduct bag searches that will slow your entry, while others require you to check daypacks and coats. They'll be kept safely. If you have something you can't bear to part with, stash it in a pocket or purse. To avoid checking a small backpack, carry it under your arm like a purse as you enter. From a guard's point of view, a backpack is generally a problem though a purse is not.

Photography is sometimes banned at major sights. Look for signs or ask. If cameras are allowed, flashes or tripods usually are not. Flashes damage oil paintings and distract others in the room. Even without a flash, a handheld camera will take a decent picture (or buy postcards or posters at the museum bookstore). Video cameras are generally allowed.

Museums may have special exhibits in addition to their permanent collections. Some exhibits are included in the entry price;

others come at an extra cost (which you may have to pay even if you don't want to see the exhibit).

Many sights rent audioguides, which generally offer excellent recorded descriptions (about £3.50). If you bring along your own pair of headphones and a Y-jack, two people can sometimes share one audioguide and save. To save more money, download my free audio tours of London's major sights (coming in early 2010—see page 477). Guided tours (usually around £3–8, and widely ranging in quality) are most likely to occur during peak season.

Expect changes—artwork can be on tour, on loan, out sick, or shifted at the whim of the curator. Ask museum staff if you can't find a particular piece.

Important sights often have an on-site café or cafeteria (usually a good place to rest and have a snack or light meal). The WCs are free and generally clean. Key sights and museums have bookstores selling postcards and souvenirs. Before you leave, scan the postcards and thumb through the biggest guidebook (or skim its index) to be sure you haven't overlooked something that you'd like to see.

Most sights stop admitting people 30–60 minutes before closing time, and some rooms close early (generally about 45 minutes before the actual closing time). Guards usher people out, so don't save the best for last.

Every sight or museum offers more than what is covered in this book. Use this book as an introduction—not the final word.

Sightseeing Passes

The following three sightseeing passes are sold online and at the Britain and London Visitors Centre on Lower Regent Street (see page 24). Keep in mind that passes can sometimes tempt travelers into seeing so-so sights just because they're "free."

The **London Pass** is only worth considering if you're a whirlwind sightseer (£39/1 day, £52/2 days, £63/3 days, £87/6 days, includes 160-page guidebook, toll tel. 0870-242-9988, www.londonpass.com). It covers plenty of sights that cost £11–17, including the Tower of London, St. Paul's Cathedral, Shakespeare's Globe, Cabinet War Rooms, Kensington Palace, Windsor Castle, and Kew Gardens. But if you saw just these sights without the pass, you'd pay about £90, roughly the cost of a six-day London Pass. Note that busy sightseers can make a short pass work for a longer trip by seeing only covered sights during the validity of the pass, and touring London's many free sights (listed on page 56) before or after the pass' validity period. Think through your sightseeing plans carefully before you buy.

The **Great British Heritage Pass,** which covers your entry fees into more than 600 British Heritage and National Trust properties, doesn't make sense for a London visit, but is worth considering if you'll be traveling extensively throughout Britain (£32/4 days, £45/7 days, £60/15 days, £80/30 days; £72/£99/£135/£180 family pass also available for up to 2 adults and 3 kids aged 5–15, though note that kids already get discounts at sights; tel. 0870-242-9988, www.britishheritagepass.com).

The similar-sounding **English Heritage** society sells passes and memberships that include free entry to its 400 sights (which are exclusive to England but partly overlap the sights covered by the Great British Heritage Pass described above); again, they're worth it only if you'll be thoroughly exploring England, not just London. You can buy passes or memberships at any participating sight. For most travelers, the Overseas Visitor Pass is a better choice than the pricier one-year membership (Visitor Pass: £19.50/7 days, £23.50/14 days, discounts for couples and families, www.english-heritage.org.uk/ovp; Membership: £43 for one person, £75 for two, discounts for seniors and students, children under 19 free, www.english-heritage.org.uk/membership; toll tel. 0870-333-1182).

Transportation

Transportation concerns within London are limited to the Tube (subway), buses, and taxis, all of which are covered in the Orientation chapter. If you have a car, stow it. You don't want to drive in London. If you need convincing, here's one more reason: In order to fight traffic congestion, the London city government charges drivers an £8/day fee to enter central London during peak hours (Mon–Fri 7:00–18:00, no charge Sat–Sun and holidays, fee payable at gas stations, convenience stores, and self-service machines at public parking lots, or online at www.cclondon.com; see website for details). Traffic cameras photograph and identify every vehicle that enters the fee-zone; if you get spotted and don't pay up by midnight that day (or pay £10 until midnight of the following day) you'll get socked with at least a £60 penalty.

Transportation to day-trip destinations is covered in the Day Trips and Connections chapters.

Traveling as a Temporary Local

We travel all the way to Europe to enjoy differences—to become temporary locals. You'll experience frustrations. Certain truths that we find "God-given" or "self-evident," such as cold beer, ice in drinks, bottomless cups of coffee, hot showers, and bigger being better, are suddenly not so true. One of the benefits of travel is the eye-opening realization that there are logical, civil, and even

How Was Your Trip?

Were your travels fun, smooth, and meaningful? If you'd like to share your tips, concerns, and discoveries, please fill out the survey at www.ricksteves.com/feedback. I value your feedback. Thanks in advance—it helps a lot.

better alternatives.

If there is a negative aspect to the image the British have of Americans, it's that we are big, loud, aggressive, impolite, rich, superficially friendly, and a bit naive.

The British (and Europeans in general) place a high value on speaking quietly in restaurants and on trains. Listen while on the bus or in a restaurant—the place can be packed, but the decibel level is low. Try to adjust your volume accordingly to show respect for the culture.

While the British look bemusedly at some of our Yankee excesses—and worriedly at others—they nearly always afford us individual travelers all the warmth we deserve. Judging from all the happy feedback I receive from travelers who have used this book, it's safe to assume you'll enjoy a great, affordable vacation—with the finesse of an independent, experienced traveler.

Thanks, and have a brilliant holiday!

Back Door Travel Philosophy
From *Rick Steves' Europe Through the Back Door*

Travel is intensified living—maximum thrills per minute and one of the last great sources of legal adventure. Travel is freedom. It's recess, and we need it.

Experiencing the real Europe requires catching it by surprise, going casual..."Through the Back Door."

Affording travel is a matter of priorities. (Make do with the old car.) You can eat and sleep—simply, safely, and enjoyably—anywhere in Europe for $120 a day plus transportation costs (although allow more for bigger cities). In many ways, spending more money only builds a thicker wall between you and what you traveled so far to see. Europe is a cultural carnival, and, time after time, you'll find that its best acts are free and the best seats are the cheap ones.

A tight budget forces you to travel close to the ground, meeting and communicating with the people. Never sacrifice sleep, nutrition, safety, or cleanliness to save money. Simply enjoy the local-style alternatives to expensive hotels and restaurants.

Connecting with people carbonates your experience. Extroverts have more fun. If your trip is low on magic moments, kick yourself and make things happen. If you don't enjoy a place, maybe you don't know enough about it. Seek the truth. Recognize tourist traps. Give a culture the benefit of your open mind. See things as different, but not better or worse. Any culture has plenty to share.

Of course, travel, like the world, is a series of hills and valleys. Be fanatically positive and militantly optimistic. If something's not to your liking, change your liking.

Travel can make you a happier American, as well as a citizen of the world. Our Earth is home to six and a half billion equally precious people. It's humbling to travel and find that people don't have the "American Dream"—they have their own dreams. Europeans like us, but, with all due respect, they wouldn't trade passports.

Thoughtful travel engages us with the world. In tough economic times, it reminds us what is truly important. By broadening perspectives, travel teaches new ways to measure quality of life.

Globetrotting destroys ethnocentricity, helping us understand and appreciate other cultures. Rather than fear the diversity on this planet, celebrate it. Among your most prized souvenirs will be the strands of different cultures you choose to knit into your own character. The world is a cultural yarn shop, and Back Door travelers are weaving the ultimate tapestry. Join in!

ORIENTATION

London is more than 600 square miles of urban jungle. With eight million people—who don't all speak English—it's a world in itself and a barrage on all the senses. On my first visit, I felt extremely small. To grasp London more comfortably, see it as the old town in the city center without the modern, congested sprawl.

The Thames River runs roughly west to east through the city, with most of the visitor's sights on the north bank. Mentally, maybe even physically with scissors, trim down your map to include only the area between the Tower of London (to the east), Hyde Park (west), Regent's Park (north), and the South Bank (south). This is roughly the area bordered by the Tube's Circle Line. This four-mile stretch between the Tower and Hyde Park (about a 90-min walk) looks like a milk bottle on its side (see map on next page), and holds 80 percent of the sights mentioned in this book.

Sprawling London becomes much more manageable if you think of it as a collection of neighborhoods:

Central London: This area contains Westminster and what Londoners call the West End. The **Westminster** district includes Big Ben, Parliament, Westminster Abbey, and Buckingham Palace—the grand government buildings from which Britain is ruled. Trafalgar Square, London's gathering place, has many major museums. The **West End** is the center of London's cultural life, with bustling squares: Piccadilly Circus and Leicester Square host cinemas, tourist traps, and nighttime glitz. Soho and Covent Garden are thriving people-zones with theaters, restaurants, pubs, and boutiques.

North London: Neighborhoods in this part of town, such as Bloomsbury, Fitzrovia, and Marylebone, contain major sights such as the British Museum and the overhyped Madame Tussauds Waxworks. Nearby, along busy Euston Road, is the British Library

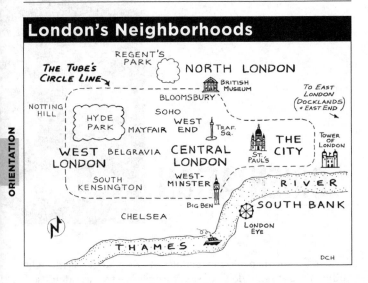

London's Neighborhoods

plus a trio of train stations, including St. Pancras International, the Eurostar launchpad for Paris.

The City: "The City," today's modern financial district, was a walled town in Roman times. Gleaming skyscrapers are interspersed with historical landmarks such as St. Paul's Cathedral, legal sights (Old Bailey), and the Museum of London. The Tower of London and Tower Bridge lie just outside The City's eastern border.

The South Bank: The South Bank of the Thames River offers major sights (Tate Modern, Shakespeare's Globe, London Eye) linked by a riverside walkway. Pedestrian bridges connect the South Bank with The City and Trafalgar Square.

West London: This huge area contains neighborhoods such as Mayfair, Belgravia, Chelsea, South Kensington, and Notting Hill. It's home to London's wealthy, and has many trendy shops and enticing restaurants. Here you'll find a range of museums (Victoria and Albert Museum, Kensington Palace, Tate Britain, and more), recommended hotels, lively Victoria Station, and the vast green expanses of Hyde Park and Kensington Gardens.

East London: London's version of Manhattan—the Docklands—has sprung up far to the east around Canary Wharf. Energized by big businesses and gearing up to host parts of the 2012 Olympics, the Docklands show you London at its most modern. Historic Greenwich lies just south of the Docklands/Canary Wharf area, across the Thames.

With this focus and a good orientation, you'll get a sampling of London's top sights, history, and cultural entertainment, and a good look at its ever-changing human face.

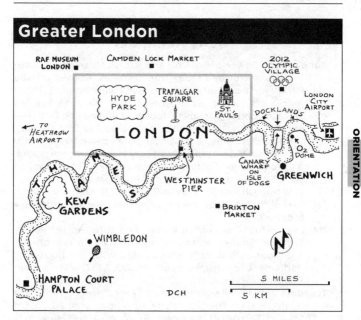

Greater London

Planning Your Time

London's a super one-week getaway. Its sights can keep even the most fidgety traveler well entertained for seven days. After considering London's major tourist desti-
nations, I've covered just my favorites
in this book. You won't be able to
see all of these, so don't try. You'll
keep coming back to London. After
dozens of visits myself, I still enjoy a
healthy list of excuses to return.

Here's a suggested schedule:

Day 1: 9:00–Tower of London
(crown jewels first, then Beefeater
tour, then White Tower); 12:30–
Munch a sandwich on the Thames
while cruising from Tower to
Westminster Bridge; 14:00–Tour
Westminster Abbey; 15:30–Follow
the self-guided Westminster Walk (see the Westminster Walk
chapter). When you're finished, you could return to the Houses of
Parliament and pop in to see the House of Commons in action.

Day 2: 9:00–Take a double-decker hop-on, hop-off London
sightseeing bus tour (start at Victoria Street and hop off for the
Changing of the Guard); 11:30–Buckingham Palace (guards
change most days, but worth confirming); 13:00–Covent Garden

ORIENTATION

Daily Reminder

Sunday: The Tower of London and British Museum are both especially crowded today. The Speakers' Corner in Hyde Park rants from early afternoon until early evening. These places are closed: Banqueting House, Sir John Soane's Museum, and legal sights (Houses of Parliament, City Hall, and Old Bailey; the neighborhood called The City is dead). Westminster Abbey and St. Paul's are open during the day for worship but closed to sightseers. Many stores are closed, and some minor sights don't open until noon. The Camden Lock, Spitalfields, Greenwich, and Petticoat Lane street markets flourish, but Portobello Road and Brixton are closed. Except for the Globe, theaters are quiet, as most actors take today off.

Monday: Virtually all sights are open except for Apsley House, Sir John Soane's Museum, Vinopolis, and a few others. The Courtauld Gallery is free until 14:00. The Houses of Parliament are usually open until 22:30. The Portobello Road market is sparse.

Tuesday: Virtually all sights are open, except for Vinopolis and Apsley House. The British Library is open until 20:00. On the first Tuesday of the month, Sir John Soane's Museum is also open 18:00–21:00. The Houses of Parliament are usually open until 22:30.

Wednesday: Virtually all sights are open, except for Vinopolis.

Thursday: All sights are open, plus evening hours at the British

for lunch, shopping, and people-watching (consider following the self-guided West End Walk); 14:30–Tour the British Museum. Have a pub dinner before a play, concert, or evening walking tour (for ideas, see the Entertainment chapter).

Day 3: Tour British Library, St. Paul's Cathedral (following the self-guided City Walk), and Museum of London. Enjoy a Shakespearean play at Shakespeare's Globe (19:30). Dive into Soho for London's liveliest night scene and a memorable dinner.

Day 4: 10:00–National Gallery and lunch on or near Trafalgar Square and the National Portrait Gallery; 14:00–Follow the self-guided Bankside Walk along the South Bank of the Thames. Cap the day with a ride on the London Eye (open late).

Day 5: Spend the morning at an antique market and visit a famous London department store. In the afternoon, depending on your interests, choose from Tate Britain, Tate Modern, the Imperial War Museum, or Kew Gardens (cruise to Kew, return to London by Tube). Take in a play, go on a guided walk, or watch a concert tonight.

Day 6: Cruise to Greenwich, tour the town's salty sights, then

Museum (selected galleries until 20:30), National Portrait Gallery (until 21:00), and Vinopolis (until 22:00).

Friday: All sights are open, plus evening hours at the British Museum (selected galleries until 20:30), National Gallery (until 21:00), National Portrait Gallery (until 21:00), Vinopolis (until 22:00), Victoria and Albert Museum (until 22:00), and Tate Modern (until 22:00). The Houses of Parliament close early today (15:00). Best street market today: Spitalfields.

Saturday: Most sights are open except legal ones (Old Bailey, City Hall, Houses of Parliament; skip The City). Vinopolis is open until 22:00, the Tate Modern until 22:00. Best street markets today: Portobello, Camden Lock, Greenwich.

Notes: The St. Martin-in-the-Fields church offers **concerts** at lunchtime (free, Mon, Tue, and Fri at 13:00) and in the evening (jazz £5-8, Wed at 20:00; classical £6-25, at 19:30 Thu-Sat, sometimes Tue). **Evensong** occurs daily at St. Paul's (Mon-Sat at 17:00 and Sun at 15:15), Westminster Abbey (Mon-Fri at 17:00—may be spoken on Wed, Sat-Sun at 15:00), and Southwark Cathedral (weekdays at 17:30, Sat at 16:00, Sun at 15:00, no service on Wed or alternate Mon). **London by Night Sightseeing Tour** buses leave from Victoria Station every evening (19:30-21:30, only at 19:30 in winter). The **London Eye** spins nightly (until 20:00-21:30, depending on the season).

Tube back to London (stopping by the Docklands if you're interested). With extra time in the afternoon, drop by the Victoria and Albert Museum.

Day 7: For a one-week visit to London, I'd spend a day or two side-tripping. To keep an English focus, head out to Windsor, Cambridge, Stonehenge, or Bath for one day. For maximum travel thrills, consider a Paris getaway. With the zippy English Channel train, Paris is less than three hours away and can even be worth a long day trip. To pull this off, see the Day Trip to Paris chapter.

For a one-week visit, buy the Seven-Day Oyster card (£25.80, see page 26) and study up on "Affording London's Sights" (see pages 56–57). Armed with this information and your Oyster card, you'll forget the high cost of sightseeing in London and see London with a better attitude.

Arrival in London

By Train: London has nine major train stations, all connected by the Tube (subway). All have ATMs, and many of the larger stations also have shops, fast food, exchange offices, and luggage storage. From any station, you can ride the Tube or taxi to your hotel. For more info on train travel, see the Connections chapter and www.nationalrail.co.uk.

By Bus: The bus ("coach") station is one block southwest of Victoria Station, where you can take the Tube. For more info on bus travel, see www.nationalexpress.com.

By Plane: London has five airports. Most tourists arrive at Heathrow or Gatwick airports, although flights from elsewhere in Europe may land at Stansted, Luton, or London City airports. For specifics on getting from London's airports to downtown London, see the Connections chapter.

Tourist Information

The **Britain and London Visitors Centre,** just a block off Piccadilly Circus, is the best tourist information service in town (June–Sept Mon–Fri 9:30–18:30, Sat 9:00–17:00, Sun 10:00–16:00; Oct–May Mon–Fri 9:30–18:00, Sat–Sun 10:00–16:00; 1 Lower Regent Street, tel. 020/8846-9000, toll tel. 0870-156-6366, www.visitbritain.com, www.visitlondon.com).

This TI has many different departments. It's a great one-stop shopping place to get tourist information, buy advance tickets to big sights, buy sightseeing passes, arrange coach tours, buy theater tickets, plan travel beyond London, even book trains to the Continent. Bring your itinerary and a checklist of questions.

Entering the lobby, check out the various departments and get in the right line for what you need. At the Tourist Information desk handling both London and Britain inquiries, pick up various free publications: the *London Planner* (a great free monthly that lists all the sights, events, and hours), walking tours info, a theater guide, London bus map, and the Thames River Services brochure. The staff sells a good £1 map and all the various sightseeing passes, including the London Pass (described on page 15), Great British Heritage Pass, and English Heritage membership.

The Entertainment and Tickets desk sells tickets to plays (20 percent booking fee). The Hotels and Travel desk sells long-distance bus tickets and passes, train tickets (convenient for reservations), and Fast Track tickets to some of London's attractions. The Fast Track tickets, which allow you to skip the queue at the sights at no extra cost, are worthwhile for places that sometimes have long ticket lines, such as the Tower of London, the London Eye, and Madame Tussauds Waxworks. (If you'll be going to the Waxworks, buy tickets here, since—at £20—they're cheaper than at the sight itself.)

The Visitors Centre reserves hotel rooms, but you can avoid their £5 booking fee by contacting hotels on your own (see the Sleeping chapter). A Rail Europe section books the Eurostar and train travel or train passes on the Continent.

Upstairs, there are even more brochures, Internet access (£1/20 min), and comfy chairs where you can read or get organized. If you visit only one TI, make it this one, the Britain and London Visitors Centre. Unfortunately, London's many Tourist Information Centres (which represent themselves as TIs at major train and bus stations and airports) are now simply businesses, selling advertising space to companies with fliers to distribute.

Helpful Hints

Theft Alert: The Artful Dodger is alive and well in London. Be on guard, particularly on public transportation and in places crowded with tourists, who, considered naive and rich, are targeted. More than 7,500 purses are stolen annually at Covent Garden alone. Wear your money belt.

Pedestrian Safety: Cars drive on the left side of the road, so before crossing a street, I always look right, look left, then look right again just to be sure. Many crosswalks are even painted with instructions, reminding foreign guests to "Look right" or "Look left."

Medical Problems: Local hospitals have good-quality 24-hour-a-day emergency care centers where any tourist who needs help can drop in and, after a wait, be seen by a doctor. Your hotel has details. St. Thomas' Hospital, immediately across the river from Big Ben, has a fine reputation.

Internet Access: The **easyInternetcafé** chain offers dozens of computers per store (generally daily 8:00–22:00, £3/30 min). You'll find branches at Trafalgar Square (456 Strand), Bayswater (Queensway, second floor of Whiteley's Shopping Centre), Oxford Street (#358, opposite Bond Street Tube station), and Kensington High Street (#160–166). Your hotelier can direct you to the nearest Internet café.

Travel Bookstores: Located in Covent Garden, **Stanfords Travel Bookstore** is good and stocks current editions of my books (Mon, Wed, and Fri 9:00–19:30, Tue 9:30–19:30, Thu 9:00–20:00, Sat 10:00–20:00, Sun 12:00–18:00, 12–14 Long Acre, Tube: Covent Garden, tel. 020/7836-1321, www.stanfords .co.uk).

Two impressive **Waterstone's** bookstores have the biggest collection of travel guides in town: on Piccadilly (Mon–Sat 9:00–22:00, Sun 11:30–18:00, 203 Piccadilly, tel. 020/7851-2400) and on Trafalgar Square (Mon–Sat 9:30–21:00, Sun 12:00–18:00, Costa Café on second floor, tel. 020/7839-4411).

Baggage Storage: Train stations have replaced their lockers with more secure baggage storage counters, known locally as "left luggage." Each bag must go through a scanner (just like at the airport), so lines can be slow. Expect long waits in the morning to check in (up to 45 min) and in the afternoon to pick up (each item-£8/24 hours, most stations daily 7:00–23:00). You can also store bags at the airports (similar rates and hours, www.excess-baggage.com). If leaving London and returning later, you may be able to leave a box or bag at your hotel for free—assuming you'll be staying there again.

Time Zone Difference: Remember that Britain is one hour earlier than most of continental Europe. British Summer Time (daylight saving time) springs forward the last Sunday in March and falls back the last Sunday in October.

Getting Around London

To travel smart in a city this size, you must get comfortable with public transportation. London's excellent taxis, buses, and subway (Tube) system make a private car unnecessary. An £8 congestion charge levied on any private car entering the city center has been effective in cutting down traffic jam delays and bolstering London's public transit. The revenue raised subsidizes the buses, which are now cheaper, more frequent, and even more user-friendly than before. Today, the vast majority of vehicles in the city center are buses, taxis, and service trucks. (Drivers can find out more information on the congestion charge at www.cclondon.com.)

Public-Transit Passes: Oyster Cards and Travelcards

London has the most expensive public transit in the world—you will definitely save money on your Tube and bus rides using a multi-ride pass. There are two options: plastic Oyster cards and paper Travelcards (details online at www.tfl.gov.uk, click "Tickets").

Oyster Cards

An Oyster card (a plastic card embedded with a computer chip) is the standard, smart way to economically ride the Tube, buses, and Docklands Light Railway (DLR). You pre-pay an amount, and fares are automatically deducted each time you use your card. On each type of transport, you simply touch the card to the yellow card reader at  the turnstile/entrance, it flashes green, and you've paid your fare. (You'll need the card to exit the Tube and DLR turnstiles, but not to exit buses.)

With an Oyster card, you'll pay only £1.60–2.20 per ride on the Tube (in Zones 1–6 off-peak) instead of £4 per ride with a full-fare ticket. For the bus, it's £1 versus £2. A price cap guarantees you'll never pay more than the One-Day Travelcard price within a 24-hour period (see "One-Day Travelcard," below). An Oyster card is worth considering if you'll be in London for even a few days, and it is especially handy if you're not sure you'll ride enough each day to justify a Travelcard.

You can buy Oyster cards at any Tube station ticket window. With the standard **pay-as-you-go Oyster card,** you load up your Oyster with as much credit you want (there's no minimum, but start with at least £10). When your balance gets low, you simply pay more money (at a ticket window or machine) to keep riding. To see how much credit remains on your card, swipe it at any automatic ticket machine. You can also see a record of all your travels (and what you paid). Try it. Pay-as-you-go Oyster balances never expire (though they need reactivating at a ticket window every two years); you can use the card whenever you're in London, or lend it to someone else. The only downside, and it's minor, is that you pay a £3 one-time refundable deposit for the card itself (you can turn in your card for the £3 refund at any ticket window, but allow 20 minutes for the process).

The **Seven-Day Oyster card** is another good possibility to consider, even for a visit as short as four days. Technically a seven-day Travelcard (see below), this odd hybrid is generally issued on a plastic Oyster card. The least expensive version is £25.80 and covers unlimited, peak-time travel through Zones 1 and 2 (no deposit required, cards covering more zones are also available).

Travelcards

A paper Travelcard works like a traditional ticket: You buy it at any Tube station ticket window or machine, then feed it into a turnstile (and retrieve it) to enter and exit the Tube. On a bus, just show it to the driver when you get on. If you take at least two rides a day, a Travelcard is a better deal than buying individual tickets. Like the Oyster card, Travelcards are valid on the Tube, buses, and Docklands Light Railway. Before you buy a card, estimate where you'll be going; there's a card for Zones 1 and 2, and another for Zones 1–6 (which includes Heathrow Airport).

The **One-Day Travelcard** gives you unlimited travel for a day; cheaper off-peak versions are good for travel after 9:30 on weekdays and anytime on weekends (Zones 1–2: £7.20, off-peak version £5.60; Zones 1–6: £14.80, off-peak version £7.50).

The **Three-Day Travelcard** is good any time of day. It costs about 15 percent less than three One-Day "peak" Travelcards (buying three One-Day off-peak Travelcards will save you a few pence, but you can only travel after 9:30 on weekdays). Most travelers staying three days will easily take enough Tube and bus rides to make this option worthwhile (Zones 1–2: £18.40, no off-peak version; Zones 1–6: £42.40, off-peak version £21.20).

Which Pass to Buy?

Trying to decide between an Oyster and a Travelcard? Here's what I recommend:

- For one to two days, get a One-Day Travelcard each day.
- For three consecutive days, buy a Three-Day Travelcard or a pay-as-you-go Oyster card.
- For four consecutive days, choose among a Three-Day Travelcard plus an extra One-Day Travelcard as needed (total £25.60); a Seven-Day Oyster card (£25.80); or a pay-as-you-go Oyster card.
- For five or more days in a row, a Seven-Day Oyster card is usually your best bet. But if you aren't sure if you'll ride enough each day to justify the expense, get the pay-as-you-go Oyster card instead.
- If your trip involves travel to Heathrow Airport, depending on the time of day you travel, you may be better off just paying £4 for a full-fare ticket to or from Heathrow, and buying a Zones 1–2 Travelcard for the rest of your time in London.

Other Discounts

Groups of 10 or more adults can travel all day on the Tube for £3.70 each (but not on buses). Kids ages 11–17 pay £1 when part of a group of 10.

Families: A paying adult can take up to four kids (aged 10 and under) for free on the Tube and Docklands Light Railway all day, every day. At the Tube station, use the manual gate, rather than the turnstiles, to be waved in. Families with older kids should consider the "Kid for a Quid" promotion: Any adult with a Travelcard can buy an off-peak One-Day Travelcard for up to four kids 15 or younger for only £1 (a "quid") each.

River Cruises: A Travelcard or a Seven-Day Oyster card gives you a 33 percent discount on most Thames cruises (see "Cruises" on page 39).

Sightseeing Deal: Buy a paper Travelcard or rail ticket at a National Rail station and you may qualify for two-for-one discounts at many popular sights (look for brochures with coupons at major train stations or print vouchers at www.daysoutguide .co.uk).

By Tube

London's subway system (called the Tube or Underground, but never "subway," which refers to a pedestrian underpass) is one of this planet's great people-movers and often the fastest long-distance transport in town (runs Mon–Sat about 5:00–24:00, Sun about 7:00–23:00).

Start by studying a Tube map. At the front of this book, you'll find a Tube map with color-coded lines and names. You can also pick up a free Tube map at any station.

Each line has a name (such as Circle, Northern, or Bakerloo) and two directions (indicated by the end-of-the-line stops). Find the line that will take you to your destination, and figure out roughly what direction (north, south, east, or west) you'll need to go to get there.

You can use paper tickets, Travelcards, or an Oyster card to pay for your journey. At the Tube station, feed your paper ticket or Travelcard into the turnstile, reclaim it, and hang on to it—you'll need it to get through the turnstile at the end of your journey. If you're using a plastic Oyster card, touch the card to the yellow card reader both when you enter and exit the station.

Find your train by following signs to your line and the (general) direction it's headed (such as Central Line: east). Since some tracks are shared by several lines, double-check before boarding a train: First, make sure your destination is one of the stops listed on the sign at the platform. Also, check the electronic signboards that announce which train is next, and make sure the destination (the end-of-the-line stop) is the one you want. Some trains, particularly on the Circle and District lines, split off for other directions, but each train has its final destination marked above its windshield.

Trains run roughly every 3–10 minutes. If one train is absolutely packed and you notice another to the same destination is coming in three minutes, wait to avoid the sardine routine. The system can be fraught with construction delays and breakdowns, so pay attention to signs and announcements explaining necessary detours (the Circle Line is notorious for problems). Rush hours (8:00–10:00 and 16:00–19:00) can be packed and sweaty. Bring something to do to make your waiting time productive. If you get confused, ask for advice from a local, a blue-vested staff person, or at the information window located before the turnstile entry.

Remember that you can't leave the system without feeding your ticket or Travelcard into the turnstile or touching your Oyster card to an electronic reader. If you have a single-trip paper ticket, the turnstile will eat your now-expired ticket; if it's a Travelcard, it will spit out your still-valid card. Save walking time by choosing the best street exit—check the maps on the walls or ask any station personnel. For Tube and bus information, visit www.tfl.gov.uk (and check out the journey planner).

Any ride in Zones 1–6 (i.e., the center of town all the way out to Heathrow Airport) costs a steep £4 for adults paying cash. If you plan to ride the Tube and buses more than once in a day, you'll save money by getting a Travelcard (or for visits of four days or more, an Oyster card is a good choice).

If you do buy a single Tube ticket, you can avoid ticket-window lines in stations by using the coin-op machines; practice on the punchboard to see how the system works (hit "Adult Single" and your destination). These tickets are valid only on the day of purchase.

Tube Etiquette

- When waiting at the platform, get out of the way of those exiting the train. Board only once everyone is off.
- Avoid using the hinged seats near the doors of some trains when the car is jammed; they take up valuable standing space.
- In a crowded train, try not to block the exit. If you're blocking the door when the train stops, step out of the car and to the side, let others off, then get back on.
- Talk softly in the cars. Listen to how quietly Londoners communicate and follow their lead.
- On escalators, stand on the right and pass on the left (even though Brits do the opposite behind the wheel). But note that in some passageways or stairways, you might be directed to walk on the left (same as car direction).
- When leaving a station, it's polite to hold the door for the person behind you.
- Flash photos are not allowed on the Tube or in any of the stations because they can affect the drivers' vision.
- Discreet eating and drinking are fine (nothing smelly); drinking alcohol and smoking are not.

By Bus

If you figure out the bus system, you'll swing like Tarzan through the urban jungle of London. Pick up a free bus map at a TI, transport office, or some major museums; it will list the bus routes best for sightseeing. Also see "Handy Bus Routes" on pages 32–33.

The first step in mastering the London bus system is learning how to decipher the bus stop signs. Find a bus stop and study the signs mounted on the pole next to the stop. You'll see a chart listing (alphabetically) the destinations served by buses that pick up at this spot or nearby; the names of the buses; and alphabet letters

O		
Oakwood ⊖	N91	Ⓞ Ⓞ
Old Coulsdon	N68	Aldwych
Old Ford	N8	Oxford Circus
Old Kent Road Canal Bridge	53, N381	Ⓞ
	453	Ⓞ Ⓞ
	N21	Ⓞ
Old Street ⊖ ≊	243	Aldwych
Orpington	N47	Ⓞ
Oxford Circus ⊖	Any bus	Ⓞ
	N18	Ⓞ

P		
Paddington ⊖ ≊	23, N15	Ⓞ Ⓞ Ⓞ
Palmers Green ≊	N29	Ⓞ
Park Langley	N3	Ⓞ Ⓞ
Peckham	12	Ⓞ Ⓞ
	N89, N343	Ⓞ Ⓞ
	N136	Ⓞ Ⓞ
	N381	Ⓞ
Penge Pawleyne Arms	176	Ⓞ Ⓞ
	N3	Ⓞ Ⓞ
Petts Wood ≊	N47	Ⓞ
Pimlico Grosvenor Road	24	Ⓞ Ⓞ
Plaistow Greengate	N15	Ⓞ Ⓞ
Plumstead ≊	53	Ⓞ
Plumstead Common	53	Ⓞ

that identify exactly where the buses pick up. After locating your destination, remember or write down the bus name and bus stop letter. Next, refer to the neighborhood map (also on the pole) to find your bus stop. Just match your letter with a stop on the map. Make your way to that stop—you'll know it's yours because it will have the same letter on its pole—and wait for the bus with the right name to arrive. Some fancy stops have electric boards indicating the minutes until the next bus arrives, but remember to check the name on the bus before you hop on. Crack the code and you're good to go.

On almost all buses, you'll pay at a machine at the bus stop (no change given), then show your ticket or pass as you board. You can also use Travelcards and Oyster cards (see page 26). If you're using an Oyster card, touch it to the electronic card reader as you board; no need to do so when you hop off. On "Heritage Routes" #9 and #15 (which use older double-decker buses), you still pay a conductor; take a seat, and he or she will come around to collect your fare or verify your pass.

Any bus ride in downtown London costs £2 for those paying cash; £1 if using an Oyster card. An all-day bus pass costs £3.80. If you're staying longer, consider the £13.80 Seven-Day bus pass. If you have a Travelcard or Oyster card, save your feet and get in the habit of hopping buses for quick little straight shots, even just to get to a Tube stop. During bump-and-grind rush hours (8:00–10:00 and 16:00–19:00), you'll usually go faster by Tube.

By Taxi

London is the best taxi town in Europe. Big, black, carefully regulated cabs are everywhere. (While historically known as "black cabs," some of London's official taxis are now covered with wildly colored ads.)

I've never met a crabby cabbie in London. They love to talk, and they know every nook and cranny in town. I ride in one each day just to get my London questions answered (drivers must pass a rigorous test on "The Knowledge" of London geography to earn their license). Rides start at £2.20. Connecting downtown sights is quick and easy, and will cost you about £6–8 (for example, St. Paul's to the Tower of London). For a short ride, three adults in a cab generally travel at close to Tube prices, and groups of four or five adults should taxi everywhere. Telephoning a cab will get you one in a few minutes (toll tel. 0871-871-8710; £2 surcharge,

Handy Bus Routes

Since London instituted a congestion charge for cars, the bus system has gotten faster, easier, and cheaper than ever. Tube-oriented travelers need to get over their tunnel vision, learn the bus system, and get around fast and easy. The best views are upstairs on a double-decker.

Here are some of the most useful routes:

Route #9: Knightsbridge (Harrods) to Hyde Park Corner to Piccadilly Circus to Trafalgar Square. This is one of two "Heritage Routes," using old-style double-decker buses.

Routes #11 and #24: Victoria Station to Westminster Abbey to Trafalgar Square (#11 continues to St. Paul's and Liverpool Street Station).

Route #RV1: Tower of London to Tower Bridge to Tate Modern/Shakespeare's Globe to London Eye/Waterloo Station/County Hall Travel Inn accommodations to Aldwych to Covent Garden (a scenic South Bank joyride).

Route #15: Paddington Station to Oxford Circus to Regent Street/TI to Piccadilly Circus to Trafalgar Square to Fleet Street

Handy Bus Routes

to St. Paul's to Tower of London. This is the other "Heritage Route," using old-style double-decker buses.

Route #168: Waterloo Station/London Eye to Covent Garden and then near British Museum and British Library.

In addition, several buses (including #6, #13, #15, #23, #139, and #159) make the corridor run from Trafalgar, Piccadilly Circus, and Oxford Circus to Marble Arch. Check the bus stop closest to your hotel—it might be convenient to your sightseeing plans.

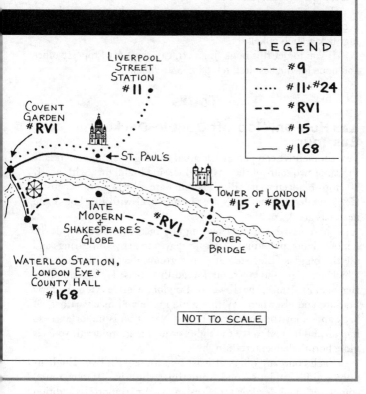

LIVERPOOL STREET STATION
#11

COVENT GARDEN
#RVI

ST. PAUL'S

TOWER OF LONDON
#15 + #RVI

TATE MODERN + SHAKESPEARE'S GLOBE

#RVI

TOWER BRIDGE

WATERLOO STATION, LONDON EYE + COUNTY HALL
#168

LEGEND
--- #9
..... #11+#24
--- #RVI
— #15
— #168

NOT TO SCALE

ORIENTATION

plus extra fee to book ahead by credit card), but it's generally not necessary; hailing a cab is easy and costs less. If a cab's top light is on, just wave it down. Drivers flash lights when they see you wave. They have a tight turning radius, so you can hail cabs going in either direction. If waving doesn't work, ask someone where you can find a taxi stand.

Don't worry about meter cheating. Licensed British cab meters come with a sealed computer chip and clock that ensures you'll get the regular tariff #1 most of the time (Mon–Fri 6:00–20:00), tariff #2 during "unsociable hours" (Mon–Fri 20:00–22:00 and Sat–Sun 6:00–22:00), and tariff #3 at night (nightly 22:00–6:00) and on holidays. (Rates go up about 15–20 percent with each higher tariff.) All extra charges are explained in writing on the cab wall. The only way a cabbie can cheat you is by taking a needlessly long route. Another pitfall is taking a cab when traffic is bad to a destination efficiently served by the Tube. On a recent trip to London, I hopped in a taxi at South Kensington for Waterloo Station and hit bad traffic. Rather than spending 20 minutes and £2–4 on the Tube, I spent 40 minutes and £16 in a taxi.

Tip a cabbie by rounding up (maximum 10 percent). If you overdrink and ride in a taxi, be warned: Taxis charge £40 for "soiling" (a.k.a., pub puke).

If you forget this book in a taxi, call the Lost Property office and hope for the best (toll tel. 0845-330-9882).

Tours

▲▲▲Hop-on, Hop-off Double-Decker Bus Tours

Two competitive companies (Original and Big Bus) offer essentially the same two tours of the city's sightseeing highlights, with nearly 30 stops on each route. Big Bus tours are a little more expensive (£25), while Original tours are cheaper (£21 with this book) and nearly as good.

These two-hour, once-over-lightly bus tours drive by all the famous sights, providing a stress-free way to get your bearings and see the biggies. They stop at a core group of sights regardless of which overview tour you're on: Piccadilly Circus, Trafalgar Square, Big Ben, St. Paul's, the Tower of London, Marble Arch, Victoria Station, and elsewhere. With a good guide and nice weather, sit back and enjoy the entire two hours. Narration is important—so hop on and hop off to see the sights or to change guides (if yours is more boring than entertaining).

Each company offers at least one route with live (English-only) guides, and a second (sometimes slightly different route) comes with tape-recorded, dial-a-language narration. In addition to the overview tours, both Original and Big Bus include river cruises and three walking tours.

Pick up a map from any flier rack or from one of the countless salespeople, and study the complex system. Note: If you start at Victoria Station at 9:00, you'll finish near Buckingham Palace in time to see the Changing of the Guard at 11:30; ask your driver for the best place to hop off. Sunday morning—when the traffic is light and many museums are closed—is a fine time for a tour. Unless you're using the bus tour mainly for hop-on, hop-off transportation, consider saving money by taking a night tour (described on the next page).

Buses run about every 10–15 minutes in summer, every 20 minutes in winter, and operate daily. They start at about 8:00 and run until early evening in summer, until late afternoon in winter. The last full loop usually leaves Victoria Station about 17:00 (confirm by checking the schedule or asking the driver).

You can buy tickets from drivers or from staff at street kiosks (credit cards accepted at kiosks at major stops such as Victoria, ticket good for 24 hours).

Original London Sightseeing Bus Tour: For a live guide on the city highlights tour, look for a yellow triangle on the front of the

bus. A red triangle means a longer, tape-recorded multilingual tour that includes Madame Tussauds—avoid it, unless you have kids who'd enjoy the entertaining recorded kids' tour. A blue triangle connects far-flung museums, while green, black, and purple triangle routes link major train stations to the central routes. All routes are covered by the same ticket. Keep it simple and just take the city highlights tour (£24, £21 after £3 discount with this book, limit two discounts per book, they'll rip off the corner of this page—raise bloody hell if the staff or driver won't honor this discount; also online deals, info center at 17 Cockspur Street, tel. 020/8877-1722, www.theoriginaltour .com). Your ticket includes a City Cruises "River Red Rover" all-day river cruise ticket (normally £11.50; for details see "Cruises: To Greenwich," later in this chapter), as well as three free 90-minute walking tours.

Big Bus London Tours: For £25 (£20 online if you pick a specific date; requires printer), you get the same basic overview tours: Red buses come with a live guide, while the blue route has a recorded narration and a longer path around Hyde Park. Your ticket includes three silly one-hour London walks, as well as river cruises on the Thames (similar to "Rover" ticket mentioned above;

cruises operated by City Cruises). These pricier tours tend to have better, more dynamic guides than Original, and more departures as well—meaning shorter waits for those hopping on and off (daily 8:30–18:00, winter until 16:30, info center at 48 Buckingham Palace Road, tel. 020/7233-9533, www.bigbustours.com).

At Night: The **London by Night Sightseeing Tour** offers a two-hour circuit, but after hours, with no extras (e.g., walks, river cruises), and at a lower price. While the narration can be pretty lame, the views at twilight are grand—though note that it stays light until late on summer nights (£15, £11 online, drivers take cash only; May–late Sept departs 19:30, 20:30, and 21:30 from Victoria Station, Jan–April and late Sept–late Dec departs 19:30 only, no tours between Christmas and New Year; Taxi Road, at front of station near end of Wilton Road; or board at any stop, such as Paddington Station, Marble Arch, Trafalgar Square, London Eye, or Tower of London; tel. 020/8545-6109, www.london-by-night .net). For a memorable and economical evening, munch a scenic picnic dinner on the top deck. There are plenty of take-away options within the train stations and near the various stops.

▲▲Walking Tours

Several times a day, top-notch local guides lead (sometimes big) groups through specific slices of London's past. Look for brochures at TIs or ask at hotels, although the latter usually push higher-priced bus tours. *Time Out,* the weekly entertainment guide (£3 at newsstands), lists some, but not all, scheduled walks. Check with the various tour companies by phone or online to get their full picture.

To take a walking tour, you simply show up at the announced location and pay the guide. Then enjoy two chatty hours of Dickens, Harry Potter, the Plague, Shakespeare, Legal London, the Beatles, or whatever is on the agenda.

London Walks: This leading company lists its extensive daily schedule in a beefy, plain *London Walks* brochure. Pick it up at St. Martin-in-the-Fields on Trafalgar Square, or access it on their website. Their two-hour walks cost £7 (cash only, walks offered year-round—even Christmas, private tours for groups-£100, tel. 020/7624-3978, for a recorded listing of today's walks call 020/7624-9255, www.walks.com). They also run Explorer day trips, a good option for those with limited time and transportation (£12 plus £10–40 for transportation and any admission costs, cash only, trips change most days: Stonehenge/Salisbury, Oxford/Cotswolds, Cambridge, Bath, and so on; fewer trips offered in winter).

Sandemans New London Tours: This company employs English-speaking students to give three-hour London tours. The fast-moving, youthful tours are light, irreverent, entertaining, and fun. Best of all, one of their tours—Royal London—is free (daily at 11:00, meet at Wellington Arch, Tube: Hyde Park Corner, Exit 2; they push for tips at the end and cross-promote their evening pub crawl). Their other tours include Old City (£9, daily at 10:00, meet at sundial opposite the Tower Hill Tube station exit); Grim Reapers (£9, daily at 14:00, also meets at Tower Hill Tube sundial); and a Pub Crawl (£12, Tue–Sat at 19:30, meet at Belushi's at 9 Russell Street, Tube: Covent Garden). Look for the guides in their red T-shirts (www.newlondon-tours.com).

The Beatles: Fans of the still–Fab Four can take one of three Beatles walks (London Walks, above, has two that run 5/week; Big Bus, above, includes a daily walk with their bus tour). For a photo op, go to Abbey Road and walk the famous cross-walk (at intersection with Grove End Road, Tube: St. John's Wood). The Beatles Store is at 231 Baker Street (daily 10:00–18:30, next to Sherlock Holmes Museum, Tube: Baker Street, tel. 020/7935-4464, www.beatlesstorelondon.co.uk).

Jack the Ripper: Each walking tour company seems to make most of its money with "haunted" and Jack the Ripper tours. Many guides are historians and would rather not lead these lightweight tours—but tourists pay more for gore (the ridiculously juvenile London Dungeon is one of the city's top sights). You'll find plenty of Ripper tours, but for a little twist, you might consider the scary walk given by Ripping Yarns, guided by Yeoman Warders of the Tower of London (£7, pay at end, 2.5 hours, nightly at 18:45 at Tower Hill Tube station, no tours between Christmas and New Year, mobile 07813-559-301, www.jack-the-ripper-tours.com).

Local Guides—Standard rates for London's registered "Blue Badge" guides usually run about £120 for four hours, and £190 or more for nine hours (tel. 020/7780-4060, www.touristguides.org.uk, www.blue-badge.org.uk). Consider Sean Kelleher (£120/half-day, £200/day, also conducts tours about the history of transportation in London, tel. 020/8673-1624, mobile 07764-612-770, seankelleher@btinternet.com) or Britt Lonsdale (£150/half-day, £220/day, great with families, tel. 020/7386-9907, mobile 07813-278-077, brittl@btinternet.com).

Drivers: Robina Brown leads small group tours in her Toyota Previa minivan (with car £270/half-day, £410–600/day; without car £120/half-day, £200/day; prices vary by destination, tel. 020/7228-2238, www.driverguidetours.com, robina@driverguidetours.com). Janine Barton provides a similar driver-and-guide

tour and similar prices (tel. 020/7402-4600, http://seeitinstyle
.synthasite.com, jbsiis@aol.com). Robina's and Janine's services are
particularly helpful for travelers with disabilities who want to see
more of London.

London Duck Tours

A bright-yellow amphibious WWII-vintage vehicle (the model
that landed troops on Normandy's beaches on D-Day) takes a gang
of 30 tourists past some famous sights on land—Big Ben, Trafalgar
Square, Piccadilly Circus—then splashes into the Thames for a
cruise. All in all, it's good fun at a rather steep price. The live guide
works hard, and it's kid-friendly to the point of goofiness (£20, 2/
hr, daily 10:00–17:00, 75 min—45 min on land and 30 min in the
river, £2.50 booking fee online, these book up in advance, departs
from Chicheley Street—you'll see the big, ugly vehicle parked 100
yards behind the London Eye, Tube: Waterloo or Westminster,
tel. 020/7928-3132, www.londonducktours.co.uk).

Bike Tours

London, like Paris, is committed to making more bike paths, and
many of its best sights can be laced together with a pleasant pedal
through its parks.

London Bicycle Tour Company: Three tours covering
London are offered daily from their base at Gabriel's Wharf on the
south bank of the Thames. Sunday is the best, as there is less car
traffic (Central Tour—£15.95, April–Oct daily at 10:30, 6 miles,
2.5 hours, includes Westminster, Covent Garden, and St. Paul's;
West Tour—£18.95, April–Oct Sat–Sun at 12:00, Nov–March
only on Sun, 9 miles, 3.5 hours, includes Westminster, Hyde Park,
Buckingham Palace, and Covent Garden; East Tour—£18.95,
April–Oct Sat–Sun at 14:00, Nov–March only on Sat, 9 miles,
3.5 hours, includes south side of the river to Tower Bridge, then
The City to the East End). They also rent bikes (office open daily
10:00–18:00, west of Blackfriars Bridge on the South Bank, 1a
Gabriel's Wharf, tel. 020/7928-6838, www.londonbicycle.com).

Fat Tire Bike Tours: Daily bike tours cover the highlights of
downtown London. The spiel is light and irreverent rather than
scholarly, but the price is right. This is a fun way to see the sights
and enjoy the city on two wheels (£16, daily June–Aug at 11:00 and
15:30, March–May and Sept–Nov at 11:00, Dec–Feb by reservation only, covers 7 miles in 4 hours, pay when you show up—no
reservations needed except for kids' bikes or in winter, Queensway
Tube station, mobile 078-8233-8779, www.fattirebiketours
london.com).

ORIENTATION

▲▲Cruises

Boat tours with entertaining commentaries sail regularly from many points along the Thames. It's a bit confusing, since several companies offer essentially the same trip. Your basic options are to use the boats to go downstream to the Tower and Greenwich, upstream to Kew Gardens and Hampton Court, or just enjoy a round-trip scenic tour cruise. Most people depart from the Westminster Pier (at the base of Westminster Bridge across the street from Big Ben). You can catch many of the same boats (with less waiting) from Waterloo Pier at the London Eye across the river. For pleasure and efficiency, consider combining a one-way cruise (to Kew, Greenwich, or wherever) with a Tube or train ride back.

Buy boat tickets at the small ticket offices on the docks. While individual Tube and bus tickets don't work on the boats, a Travelcard or Seven-Day Oyster card can snare you a 33 percent discount on most cruises (just show the card when you pay for the cruise, not valid with pay-as-you-go Oyster cards). Children and seniors get discounts. You can purchase drinks and scant, pricey snacks on board. Clever budget travelers pack a picnic and munch while they cruise.

Here are some of the most popular cruise options:

To the Tower of London: City Cruises boats sail 30 minutes to the Tower from Westminster Pier (£6.90 one-way, £8.70

round-trip, one-way included with Big Bus London tour; covered by £11.50 "River Red Rover" ticket that includes Greenwich; daily April–Oct roughly 10:00–21:00, until 18:00 in winter, every 20 min).

To Greenwich: Two companies—City Cruises and the Thames River Services—head to Greenwich from Westminster Pier. The cruises are usually narrated by the captain, with most commentary given on the way to Greenwich. The companies' prices are the same, though **City Cruises** offers a few more alternatives (£8.40 one-way, £11 round-trip; or get their £11.50 all-day, hop-on, hop-off "River Red Rover" ticket to have the option of getting off at the London Eye and Tower of London—included with Original London bus tour; daily April–Oct generally 10:00–17:00, less off-season, about every 40 min, 75 min to Greenwich; also departs for Greenwich from the pier at the Tower of London for less: £6.90 one-way, £8.70 round-trip, 30 min; tel. 020/7740-0400, www.citycruises.com). The **Thames River Services** goes to Greenwich from Westminster

Thames Boat Piers

While Westminster Pier is the most popular, it's not the only dock in town. Consider all the options:

Westminster Pier, at the base of Big Ben, offers round-trip sightseeing cruises and lots of departures in both directions.

Waterloo Pier, at the base of the London Eye, is a good, less-crowded alternative to Westminster, with many of the same cruise options.

Embankment Pier is near Covent Garden, Trafalgar Square, and Cleopatra's Needle (the obelisk on the Thames). You can take a round-trip cruise from here, or catch a boat to the Tower of London and Greenwich.

Tower Pier is at the Tower of London. Boats sail west to Westminster Pier or east to Greenwich.

Bankside Pier (near Tate Modern and Shakespeare's Globe) and **Millbank Pier** (near Tate Britain) are connected to each other by the Tate Boat ferry service.

Pier a bit more frequently and a little quicker (£8.40 one-way, £11 round-trip, April–Oct 10:00–16:00, July–Aug until 17:00, daily 2/hr; Nov–March shorter hours and runs every 40 min; 1 hour to Greenwich, tel. 020/7930-4097, www.thamesriverservices.co.uk).

To Kew Gardens: Boats run by the Westminster Passenger Services Association leave for Kew Gardens from Westminster Pier (£11 one-way, £17 round-trip, cash only, 4/day, April–Oct daily 10:30–14:00, 90 min, narrated for 45 min, tel. 020/7930-2062, www.wpsa.co.uk). Some boats continue on to **Hampton Court Palace** for an additional £3 (and 90 min). Because of the river current, you'll sometimes save 30 minutes cruising from Hampton Court back into town (depends on the tide).

Round-Trip Cruises: The London Eye operates its own "River Cruise," offering a 40-minute live-guided circular tour from Waterloo Pier (£12, reservations recommended, departures daily generally at 45 past the hour, April–Oct 10:45–18:45, Nov–March 11:45–16:45, closed mid-Jan–mid-Feb, toll tel. 0870-500-0600, www.londoneye.com).

From Tate to Tate: The Tate Boat service for art-lovers connects the Tate Modern and Tate Britain on a sleek, 220-seat catamaran (£5 one-way or £12 for a day ticket, discounted with Travelcard, buy ticket at gallery desk or on board, runs daily every 40 min, from Tate Modern 10:10–16:50, from Tate Britain 10:30–17:10, 18-min trip, tel. 020/7887-8888, www.tate.org.uk).

On Regent's Canal: Consider exploring London's canals by taking a cruise on historic Regent's Canal in north London. The good ship *Jenny Wren* offers 90-minute guided canal boat cruises from Walker's Quay in Camden Town through scenic Regent's Park to Little Venice (£8.50, Aug daily at 10:30, 12:30, 14:30, and 16:30, April–July and Sept–Oct daily at 12:30 and 14:30, Sat–Sun also at 16:30; Walker's Quay, 250 Camden High Street, 3-min walk from Tube: Camden Town; tel. 020/7485-4433, www.walkers quay.com). While in Camden Town, stop by the popular, punky Camden Lock Market to browse through trendy arts and crafts (daily 10:00–18:00, busiest on weekends, a block from Walker's Quay, www.camdenlock.net).

ORIENTATION

SIGHTS IN LONDON

These sights are arranged by neighborhood for handy sightseeing. When you see a ✪ in a listing, it means the sight is covered in much more depth in a self-guided walk or in one of the tours.

For advice on keeping down your costs, see "Affording London's Sights" on page 56.

Central London

Westminster

These sights are listed roughly in geographical order from Westminster Abbey to Trafalgar Square, and are linked in the ✪ Westminster Walk chapter.

▲▲▲**Westminster Abbey**—The greatest church in the English-speaking world, Westminster Abbey is the place where England's kings and queens have been crowned and buried since 1066. Like a stony refugee camp huddled outside St. Peter's Pearly Gates, Westminster Abbey has many stories to tell. The steep admission includes an excellent audioguide, worthwhile if you have the time and interest. To experience the church more vividly, take a live tour, or attend evensong or an organ concert.

Cost: £15, £30 family ticket for three, includes cloisters, audioguide, and Abbey Museum.

Hours and Information: Abbey open Mon–Fri 9:30–16:30, Sat 9:30–14:30, last entry one hour before closing, closed Sun to sightseers but open for services; Abbey Museum open daily 10:30–16:00; cloisters open daily 8:00–18:00;

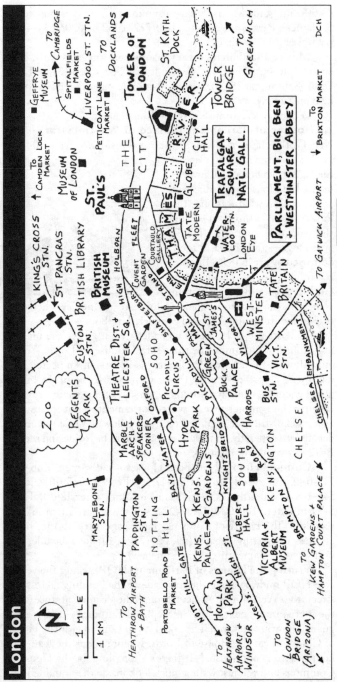

London

£3 90-min guided tours, 5/day in summer; Tube: Westminster or St. James's Park. Info desk tel. 020/7222-5152 or 020/7654-4834, www.westminster-abbey.org.

Music: The church hosts **evensong** performances daily, sung every night but Wednesday, when it may be spoken (Mon–Fri at 17:00; Sat–Sun at 15:00). A free 30-minute **organ recital** is often held on Sunday at 17:45.

✪ See the Westminster Abbey Tour chapter.

▲▲**Houses of Parliament (Palace of Westminster)**—This Neo-Gothic icon of London, the royal residence from 1042 to 1547, is now the meeting place of the legislative branch of government. The Houses of Parliament are located in what was once the Palace of Westminster—long the palace of England's medieval kings—until it was largely destroyed by fire in 1834. The palace was rebuilt in the Victorian Gothic style (a move away from Neoclassicism back to England's Christian and medieval heritage, true to the Romantic Age) and completed in 1860.

Tourists are welcome to view debates in either the bickering House of Commons or the genteel House of Lords. You're only allowed inside when Parliament is in session, indicated by a flag flying atop the Victoria Tower at the south end of the building (generally Mondays through Thursdays, plus some Fridays). During the summer recess, when Parliament is not in session, visitors can still take a guided tour (see below). While the actual debates are generally quite dull, it is a thrill to be inside and see the British government inaction.

Cost and Hours: Free, both Houses usually open Mon–Tue 14:30–22:30, Wed–Thu 11:30–17:50, Fri 9:30–15:00, closed Sat–Sun, generally less action and no lines after 18:00, Tube: Westminster. Tel. 020/7219-4272, see www.parliament.uk for schedule. The House of Lords has more pageantry, shorter lines, and less interesting debates (tel. 020/7219-3107 for schedule, and visit www.parliamentlive.tv for a preview).

Visiting the Houses of Parliament (HOP): Enter the venerable HOP midway along the west side of the building (across the street from Westminster Abbey) through the Visitor Entrance (with the tourist ramp, next to the St. Stephen's Entrance—if lost, ask a guard). As you enter, you'll be asked if you want to visit the House of Commons or the House of Lords. Inquire about the wait—an hour or two is not unusual. If there's a long line for the House of Commons and you just want a quick look inside the grand halls of

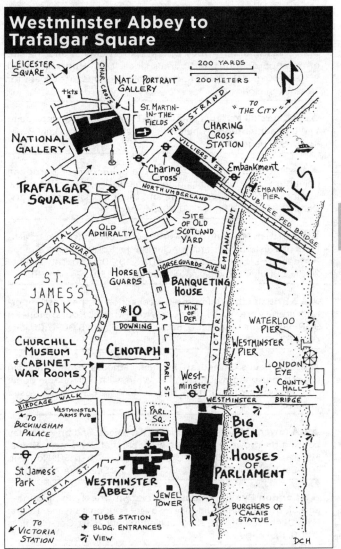

Westminster Abbey to Trafalgar Square

LEICESTER SQUARE

+kts

NAT'L PORTRAIT GALLERY

ST. MARTIN-IN-THE-FIELDS

CHAR. CROSS

THE STRAND

TO "THE CITY"

200 YARDS
200 METERS

CHARING CROSS STATION

NATIONAL GALLERY

VILLIERS ST.

Embankment

TRAFALGAR SQUARE

Charing Cross

NORTHUMBERLAND

EMBANK. PIER
JUBILEE PED. BRIDGE

THAMES

OLD ADMIRALTY

SITE OF OLD SCOTLAND YARD

THE MALL

GUARDS ROAD

HORSEGUARDS AVE.

ST. JAMES'S PARK

Horse Guards

BANQUETING HOUSE

EMBANKMENT

VICTORIA

WATERLOO PIER

#10 DOWNING

MIN. OF DEF.

WESTMINSTER PIER

CHURCHILL MUSEUM & CABINET WAR ROOMS

WHITEHALL

CENOTAPH

PARL. ST.

LONDON EYE

COUNTY HALL

BIRDCAGE WALK

WESTMINSTER ARMS PUB

Westminster

WESTMINSTER BRIDGE

TO BUCKINGHAM PALACE

PARL. SQ.

BIG BEN

St James's Park

VICTORIA ST.

WESTMINSTER ABBEY

JEWEL TOWER

HOUSES OF PARLIAMENT

TO VICTORIA STATION

BURGHERS OF CALAIS STATUE

DCH

- ⊖ TUBE STATION
- → BLDG. ENTRANCES
- 7i VIEW

this majestic building, start with the House of Lords. Once inside, you can switch if you like.

Just past security, you enter the vast and historic **Westminster Hall,** which survived the 1834 fire. The hall was built in the 11th century, and its famous self-supporting hammer-beam roof was added in 1397. Racks of brochures here explain how the British government works, and plaques describe the hall. The Jubilee Café, open to the public, has live video feeds showing exactly what's

London at a Glance

▲▲▲Westminster Abbey Britain's finest church and the site of royal coronations and burials since 1066. **Hours:** Mon-Fri 9:30-16:30, Sat 9:30-14:30, closed Sun to sightseers except for worship. See page 42.

▲▲▲Churchill Museum and Cabinet War Rooms Underground WWII headquarters of Churchill's war effort. **Hours:** Daily 9:30-18:00. See page 49.

▲▲▲National Gallery Remarkable collection of European paintings (1250-1900), including Leonardo, Botticelli, Velázquez, Rembrandt, Turner, Van Gogh, and the Impressionists. **Hours:** Daily 10:00-18:00, Fri until 21:00. See page 51.

▲▲▲British Museum The world's greatest collection of artifacts of Western civilization, including the Rosetta Stone and the Parthenon's Elgin Marbles. **Hours:** Daily 10:00-17:30, Thu-Fri until 20:30, but only a few galleries open after 17:30. See page 61.

▲▲▲British Library Impressive collection of the most important literary treasures of the Western world. **Hours:** Mon-Fri 9:30-18:00, Tue until 20:00, Sat 9:30-17:00, Sun 11:00-17:00. See page 62.

▲▲▲St. Paul's Cathedral The main cathedral of the Anglican Church, designed by Christopher Wren, with a climbable dome and daily evensong services. **Hours:** Mon-Sat 8:30-16:30, closed Sun except for worship. See page 68.

▲▲▲Tower of London Historic castle, palace, and prison, today housing the crown jewels and a witty band of Beefeaters. **Hours:** March-Oct Tue-Sat 9:00-17:30, Sun-Mon 10:00-17:30; Nov-Feb Tue-Sat 9:00-16:30, Sun-Mon 10:00-16:30. See page 70.

▲▲London Eye Enormous observation wheel, dominating—and offering commanding views over—London's skyline. **Hours:** Daily June-Sept 10:00-21:00, July-Aug until 21:30, Oct-May until 20:00. See page 72.

▲▲Tate Modern Works by Monet, Matisse, Dalí, Picasso, and Warhol displayed in a converted powerhouse. **Hours:** Daily 10:00-18:00, Fri-Sat until 22:00. See page 75.

▲▲Houses of Parliament London's famous Neo-Gothic landmark, topped by Big Ben and occupied by the Houses of Lords and Commons. **Hours** (both Houses): Generally Mon–Tue 14:30–22:30, Wed–Thu 11:30–17:50, Fri 9:30–15:00, closed Sat–Sun. See page 44.

▲▲**National Portrait Gallery** A *Who's Who* of British history, featuring portraits of this nation's most important historical figures. **Hours:** Daily 10:00–18:00, Thu–Fri until 21:00. See page 52.

▲▲**Victoria and Albert Museum** The best collection of decorative arts anywhere. **Hours:** Daily 10:00–17:45, Fri until 22:00. See page 83.

▲▲**Imperial War Museum** Examines the military history of the bloody 20th century. **Hours:** Daily 10:00–18:00. See page 74.

▲▲**Shakespeare's Globe** Timbered, thatched-roofed reconstruction of the Bard's original wooden "O." **Hours:** Theater complex, museum, and actor-led tours generally daily May–Sept 9:00–17:00, Oct–April 10:00–17:00; in summer, morning theater tours only. Plays are also held here. See page 76.

▲▲**Tate Britain** Collection of British painting from the 16th century through modern times, including works by William Blake, the Pre-Raphaelites, and J. M. W. Turner. **Hours:** Daily 10:00–17:50, first Fri of the month until 21:40. See page 80.

▲**Courtauld Gallery** Fine collection of paintings filling one wing of the Somerset House, a grand 18th-century palace. **Hours:** Daily 10:00–18:00. See page 55.

▲**Buckingham Palace** Britain's royal residence with the famous Changing of the Guard. **Hours:** Palace—Aug–Sept only, daily 9:45–18:00; Guard—May–July daily at 11:30, Aug–April every other day. See page 58.

▲**Old Operating Theatre Museum** 19th-century hall where surgeons performed amputations for an audience of aspiring med students. **Hours:** Daily 10:30–17:00. See page 79.

Vinopolis Offering a breezy history of wine with plenty of tasting opportunities. **Hours:** Thu–Fri 12:00–22:00, Sat 11:00–22:00, Sun 12:00–18:00, closed Mon–Wed. See page 78.

SIGHTS IN LONDON

Winston Churchill
(1874–1965)

As the 20th century dawned, 25-year-old Winston Churchill became famous. Working as a newspaper reporter embedded with British troops in South Africa, his train was attacked by Boers. Churchill was captured and held as a POW. Meanwhile, back home, the London papers were praising the young man's heroism for saving fellow train passengers. After two weeks, Churchill escaped from the Boer camp—he slipped through a bathroom window, scaled a wall, walked nonchalantly through an enemy town, hopped a freight train, and was smuggled out of the country. He emerged to find himself famous.

Churchill entered politics. He first followed in his father's (Lord Randolph Churchill) Conservative Party footsteps, but his desire for social reform drove him to switch to the Liberal Party. (He would later flip-flop back to Conservative.) For three decades, Churchill held numerous government posts, serving as Chancellor of This, Undersecretary of That, and Minister of The Other. He earned praise for prison reform and for developing newfangled airplanes for warfare; he was criticized for heavy-handedly crushing strikes and bungling the pacification of Iraq. During World War I, he took a break

going on in each house. Just seeing the café video is a fun experience (and can help you decide which house—if either—you'd like to see). Walking through the hall and up the stairs, you'll enter the busy world of government with all its high-powered goings-on.

Houses of Parliament Summer Recess Tours: Though Parliament is in recess during much of August and September, you can get a behind-the-scenes peek at the royal chambers of both houses with a tour (£13, 75 min, tours generally Tue–Thu, times vary, so confirm in advance; book ahead through Keith Prowse ticket agency—toll tel. 0870-906-3773, www.keithprowse.com, no booking fee).

Jewel Tower: Across the street from the Parliament building's St. Stephen's Gate, the Jewel Tower is a rare remnant of the old Palace of Westminster used by kings until Henry VIII. The crude stone tower (1365–66) was a guard tower in the palace wall, overlooking a moat. It contains a fine little exhibit on Parliament and the tower. Next to the tower (and free) is a quiet courtyard from politics to personally command British troops on the Western Front.

In 1929, Churchill-the-career-bureaucrat retired from politics. He wrote books *(History of the English Speaking Peoples)* and spoke out about the growing threat of fascist Germany. When World War II broke out, Prime Minister Chamberlain's appeasement policies were discredited, and—on the day when Germany invaded the Netherlands—the king appointed Churchill as prime minister. Churchill guided the nation through its darkest hour (see "St. Paul's, the Blitz, and the Battle of Britain," page 222). His greatest contribution may have been his stirring radio speeches that galvanized the will of the British people.

Despite the Allies' victory over the Nazis, Churchill lost the 1945 election. Though considered the ideal man to lead Britain during war, many believed he and his Conservative Party colleagues were not the best choice to lead the country in peace and during rebuilding. Never one to be idle, he continued to be active in politics (especially in world affairs) as Leader of the Opposition. In 1946 he gave a speech at a Missouri college, which included the famous Cold War line, "From Stettin in the Baltic to Trieste in the Adriatic, an Iron Curtain has descended across the Continent." In 1951 Churchill was again elected prime minister, and served for four years before he retired in 1955. When he died at the age of 90 in 1965, his state funeral in St. Paul's attracted leaders from around the world. Churchill, a legend in his own time, was buried northwest of Oxford in Bladon, two miles from Blenheim Palace, the place of his birth.

with picnic-friendly benches (£3, daily March–Oct 10:00–17:00, Nov–Feb 10:00–16:00, tel. 020/7222-2219).

Big Ben: The clock tower (315 feet high) is named for its 13-ton bell, Ben. The light above the clock is lit when the House of Commons is sitting. The face of the clock is huge—you can actually see the minute hand moving. For a good view of it, walk halfway over Westminster Bridge.

▲▲▲**Churchill Museum and Cabinet War Rooms**—This is a fascinating walk through the underground headquarters of the British government's fight against the Nazis in the darkest days of the Battle for Britain. The 27-room nerve center of the British war effort was used from 1939 to 1945. Churchill's room, the map room, and other rooms are just as they were in 1945. For details on all the blood, sweat, toil, and tears, pick up the excellent, essential, and included audioguide at the entry and follow the 60-minute tour. Be patient—it's well worth it.

Don't bypass the Churchill Museum (entrance is a half-dozen

rooms into the exhibit), which shows the man behind the famous cigar, bowler hat, and V-for-victory sign—allow an hour for that museum alone. It shows his wit, irascibility, work ethic, American ties, writing talents, and drinking habits. A long touch-the-screen time-line lets you zero in on events in his life from birth (November 30, 1874) to his appointment as prime minister in 1940. It's all the more amazing considering that, in the 1930s, the man who would become my vote for greatest statesman of the 20th century was once considered a washed-up loony ranting about the growing threat of fascism.

Cost, Hours, Location: £13, daily 9:30–18:00, last entry one hour before closing; on King Charles Street, 200 yards off Whitehall, follow the signs, Tube: Westminster. Tel. 020/7930-6961, www.iwm.org.uk. The museum's gift shop is great for anyone nostalgic for the 1940s. Note that this wonderful museum is far superior to the Winston Churchill's Britain at War Experience (next to the London Dungeon on the South Bank); give that one—and the London Dungeon—a miss.

Nearby: If you're hungry, get your rations at the Switch Room café (in the museum) or, for a nearby pub lunch, try the Westminster Arms (food served downstairs, on Storey's Gate, a couple of blocks south of Cabinet War Rooms).

Horse Guards—The Horse Guards change daily at 11:00 (10:00 on Sun), and there's a colorful dismounting ceremony daily at 16:00. The rest of the day, they just stand there—terrible for video cameras (on Whitehall, between Trafalgar Square and #10 Downing Street, Tube: Westminster, www.changing-the-guard.com). Buckingham Palace pageantry is canceled when it rains, but the horse guards change regardless of the weather.

▲**Banqueting House**—England's first Renaissance build-ing was designed by Inigo Jones around 1620. It's one of the few London landmarks spared by the 1698 fire and the only surviving part of the original Palace of Whitehall. Don't miss its Rubens ceiling, which, at Charles I's request, drove home the doctrine of the legitimacy of the divine right of kings. In 1649—divine right ignored—Charles I was beheaded on the balcony of this building by order of a Cromwellian Parliament. Admission includes a restful 20-minute audiovisual history, which shows the place in banqueting action; a 30-minute audio tour—interesting only to history buffs; and a look at the exquisite banqueting hall.

Cost, Hours, Location: £4.80, includes audioguide, Mon-Sat 10:00–17:00, closed Sun, last entry at 16:30, subject to closure for government functions, aristocratic WC, immediately across Whitehall from the Horse Guards, Tube: Westminster. Tel. 020/3166-6154 or 020/3166-6155, www.hrp.org.uk. Just up the street is Trafalgar Square.

On Trafalgar Square

▲▲**Trafalgar Square**—London's recently renovated central square, the climax of most marches and demonstrations, is a

thrilling place to simply hang out. Lord Nelson stands atop his 185-foot-tall fluted granite column, gazing out toward Trafalgar, where he lost his life but defeated the French fleet. Part of this 1842 memorial is made from his victims' melted-down cannons. He's surrounded by spraying fountains, giant lions, hordes of people, and—until recently—even more pigeons. A former London mayor decided that London's "flying rats" were a public nuisance and evicted Trafalgar Square's venerable seed salesmen (Tube: Charing Cross).

▲▲▲**National Gallery**—Displaying Britain's top collection of European paintings from 1250 to 1900—including works by Leonardo, Botticelli, Velázquez, Rembrandt, Turner, Van Gogh, and the Impressionists—this is one of Europe's great galleries.

Although the collection is huge, following the route suggested in my self-guided tour will give you my best quick visit. The audioguide (suggested £3.50 donation) is one of the finest I've used in Europe.

Cost, Hours, Location: Free, but suggested donation of £1–2; daily 10:00–18:00, Fri until 21:00; last entry to special exhibits 45 min before closing, free one-hour overview tours daily at 11:30 and 14:30; no photography, on Trafalgar Square, Tube: Charing Cross or Leicester Square. Recorded info tel. 020/7747-2885, switchboard tel. 020/7839-3321, www.nationalgallery.org.uk. The excellent-but-pricey museum restaurant called the National Dining Rooms is a good spot to split afternoon tea (see page 335).

○ See the National Gallery Tour chapter.

▲▲**National Portrait Gallery**—Put off by halls of 19th-century characters who meant nothing to me, I used to call this "as interesting as someone else's yearbook." But a selective walk through this 500-year-long *Who's Who* of British history is quick and free, and puts faces on the story of England.

Some highlights: Henry VIII and wives; portraits of the "Virgin Queen" Elizabeth I, Sir Francis Drake, and Sir Walter Raleigh; the only real-life portrait of William Shakespeare; Oliver Cromwell and Charles I with his head on; portraits by Gainsborough and Reynolds; the Romantics (William Blake, Lord Byron, William Wordsworth, and company); Queen Victoria and her era; and the present royal family, including the late Princess Diana.

The collection is well-described, not huge, and in historical sequence, from the 16th century on the second floor to today's royal family on the ground floor.

Cost, Hours, Location: Free, but suggested donation of £3; daily 10:00–18:00, Thu–Fri until 21:00, last entry to special exhibits 45 min before closing, excellent themed audioguides—£2 suggested donation; entry 100 yards off Trafalgar Square, around corner from National Gallery, opposite Church of St. Martin-in-the-Fields; Tube: Charing Cross or Leicester Square. Tel. 020/7306-0055, recorded info tel. 020/7312-2463, www.npg.org.uk.

○ See the National Portrait Gallery Tour chapter.

▲**St. Martin-in-the-Fields**—The church, built in the 1720s with a Gothic spire atop a Greek-type temple, is an oasis of peace on the wild and noisy Trafalgar Square. St. Martin cared for the poor. "In the fields" was where the first church stood on this spot (in the 13th century), between Westminster and The City. Stepping inside, you still feel a compassion for the needs of the people in this neighborhood— the church serves the homeless and houses a Chinese community center. The modern east window—with grillwork bent into the shape of a warped cross—was installed in 2008 to replace one damaged in World War II.

A new freestanding glass pavilion to the left of the church serves as the entrance to the church's underground areas. There you'll find the concert ticket office, a gift shop, brass-rubbing center, and the fine support-the-church Café in the Crypt (listed on page 324).

Cost, Hours, Information: Church entry free, donations welcome, audioguide available, open daily, Tube: Charing Cross. Tel. 020/7766-1100, www2.stmartin-in-the-fields.org.

Music: The church is famous for its concerts. Consider a free lunchtime concert (Mon, Tue, and Fri at 13:00), an evening concert (£6–25, at 19:30 Thu–Sat and on some Tue), or live jazz in the church's café (£5–8, Wed at 20:00). See the church's website for the concert schedule.

West End and Nearby

These sights are linked in the ♻ West End Walk chapter.

▲▲**Piccadilly Circus**—London's most touristy square got its name from the fancy ruffled shirts—*picadils*—made in the neigh-

borhood long ago. Today, the square (Tube: Piccadilly), while pretty grotty, is surrounded by fascinating streets swimming with youth on the rampage. Look no further than the gargantuan **Ripley's Believe-It-Or-Not Museum** to capture the gimmicky flavor of today's Piccadilly. For overstimulation in a grimy mall that smells like teen spirit, drop by the extremely trashy **Trocadero Center** for its Funland arcade games, 9-screen cinema, and 10-lane bowling alley (admission to Trocadero is free; individual attractions cost £2–10; located between Piccadilly and Leicester Squares on Coventry Street). Chinatown, to the east, swelled when the former British colony of Hong Kong was returned to China in 1997, but is now threatened by developers. Nearby Shaftesbury Avenue and Leicester Square teem with fun-seekers, theaters, Chinese restaurants, and street singers.

Soho—North of Piccadilly, seedy Soho has become seriously trendy and is well worth a gawk (see the West End Walk chapter). But Soho is also London's red light district (especially near Brewer and Berwick Streets), where "friendly models" wait in tiny rooms up dreary stairways, and voluptuous con artists sell strip shows. Though venturing up a stairway to check out a model is interesting, anyone who goes into any one of the shows will be ripped off. Every time. Even a £5 show in a "licensed bar" comes with a £100 cover or minimum (as it's printed on the drink menu) and a "security man." You may accidentally buy a £200 bottle of bubbly. And suddenly, the door has no handle.

SIGHTS IN LONDON

West End and Nearby

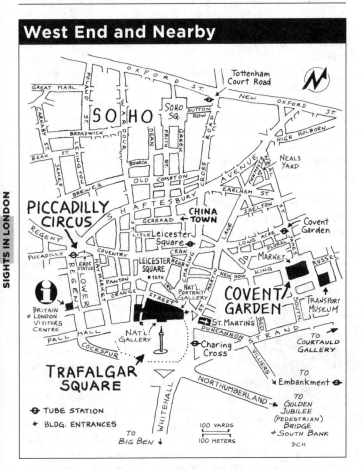

Telephone sex ads are hard to avoid these days in London. Phone booths are littered with racy fliers of busty ladies "new in town." Some travelers gather six or eight phone booths' worth of fliers and take them home for kinky wallpaper.

▲▲**Covent Garden**—The centerpiece of this boutique-ish shop-ping district is an iron-and-glass arcade. The opera house borders the square, and venerable theatres are nearby. The area is a people-watcher's delight, with cigarette eaters, Punch-and-Judy acts, food that's good for you (but not your wallet), trendy crafts, sweet whiffs of marijuana, two-tone hair (nei-ther natural), and faces that could

set off a metal detector (Tube: Covent Garden). For better Covent Garden lunch deals, walk a block or two away from the eye of this touristic hurricane (check out the places north of the Tube station along Endell and Neal Streets).

▲**London Transport Museum**—This newly renovated museum is fun for kids and thought-provoking for adults. Whether you're cursing or marveling at the buses and Tube, the growth of Europe's third-biggest city (after Moscow and Istanbul) has been made possible by its public transit system. An elevator transports you back to 1800, when horse-drawn vehicles ruled the road. London invented the notion of a public bus traveling a set route that anyone could board without a reservation. Next, you descend to the first floor and the world's first underground Metro system, which used steam-powered locomotives (the Circle Line, c. 1865). On the ground floor, horses and trains are quickly replaced by motorized vehicles (cars, taxis, double-decker buses, streetcars), resulting in 20th-century congestion. How to deal with it? In 2003, car drivers were slapped with a congestion charge. Today, a half-billion people ride the Tube every year. Learn how city planners hope to improve efficiency with better tracks and more coverage of the expanding East End. Finally, an exhibit lets you imagine four different scenarios for the year 2055 depending on the choices you make today. Will fresh strawberries in December destroy the planet?

Cost, Hours, Location: £10, includes optional £2 donation, Sat–Thu 10:00–18:00, Fri 11:00–18:00, some Fri until 21:00, last entry 45 min before closing, pleasant upstairs café with Covent Garden view, in southeast corner of Covent Garden courtyard, Tube: Covent Garden. Switchboard tel. 020/7379-6344 or recorded info tel. 020/7565-7299, www.ltmuseum.co.uk.

▲**Courtauld Gallery**—While less impressive than the National Gallery, this wonderful collection of paintings is still a joy. The gallery is part of the Courtauld Institute of Art, and the thoughtful description of each piece of art reminds visitors that the gallery is still used for teaching. You'll see medieval European paintings and works by Rubens, the Impressionists (Manet, Monet, and Degas), Post-Impressionists (such as Cézanne), and more. Besides the permanent collection, a quality selection of loaners and temporary exhibits are often included in the entry fee.

Cost, Hours, Location: £5, free Mon until 14:00, open daily 10:00–18:00, last entry at 17:30; downstairs cafeteria, lockers, and WC; bus #6, #9, #11, #13, #15, or #23 from Trafalgar Square; Tube: Temple or Covent Garden. Tel. 020/7848-1194 or 020/7848-2777, recorded info tel. 020/7848-2526, www.courtauld.ac.uk.

Somerset House: The Courtauld Gallery is located at Somerset House, a grand 18th-century civic palace that offers a marvelous public space (housing temporary exhibits) and a riverside

Affording London's Sights

London is, in many ways, Europe's most expensive city, with the dubious distinction of having some of the world's most expensive admission prices. Fortunately, many of its best sights are free.

Free Museums: Many of the city's biggest and best museums won't cost you a dime. Free sights include the British Museum, British Library, National Gallery, National Portrait Gallery, Tate Britain, Tate Modern, Wallace Collection, Imperial War Museum, Victoria and Albert Museum, Natural History Museum, Science Museum, National Army Museum, Sir John Soane's Museum, the Museum of London, the Geffrye, and on the outskirts of town, the Royal Air Force Museum London.

Several museums, such as the British Museum, request a donation of a few pounds, but whether you contribute or not is up to you. If I spend money for an audioguide, I feel fine about not otherwise donating. If that makes you uncomfortable, donate.

Free Churches: Smaller churches let worshippers (and tourists) in free, although they may ask for a donation. The big sightseeing churches—Westminster Abbey and St. Paul's—charge steep admission fees, but offer free evensong services daily. Westminster Abbey offers free organ recitals most Sundays at 17:45.

Other Freebies: There are plenty of free performances, such as lunch concerts at St. Martin-in-the-Fields (see page 357) and summertime movies at The Scoop amphitheater near City Hall (Tube: London Bridge, schedule at www.morelondon.com—click on "The Scoop"). For other freebies, check out www.freelondonlistings.co.uk. There's no charge to enjoy the pageantry of the Changing of the Guard, rants at Speaker's Corner in Hyde Park, displays at Harrods, and the people-watching scene at Covent Garden. It's free to view the legal action at the Old Bailey and the legislature at work in the Houses of Parliament. And you can get  into a bit of the Tower of London by attending Sunday services in the Tower's chapel (chapel access only).

Sightseeing Deals: If you buy a paper Travelcard or rail ticket at a National Rail station (such as Paddington or Victoria), you may be eligible for two-for-one discounts at many popular sights, such as the Tower of London, Westminster Abbey, and Madame Tussauds Waxworks. Get details and print vouchers at www.daysoutguide.co.uk, or look for brochures with coupons at major train stations.

Good-Value Tours: The £7–9 city walking tours with professional guides are one of the best deals going. And with the free Royal London walking tour, you always get at least your money's worth (see page 36; www.newlondon-tours.com). Hop-on, hop-off big-bus tours (£15–25), while expensive, provide a great overview, and include free boat tours as well as city walks. A one-hour Thames ride to Greenwich costs £8.40 one-way, but generally comes with an entertaining commentary. A three-hour bicycle tour is about £16–19.

Pricey...But Worth It?: Big-ticket sights worth their admission fees are Kew Gardens (£13), Shakespeare's Globe (£10.50), and the Cabinet War Rooms, with its fine Churchill Museum (£13). The London Eye has become a London must-see (£17).

While Kensington Palace (£12.50) and Hampton Court Palace (£14) are expensive, they are well-presented and a reasonable value if you have an interest in royal history. The Queen charges big time to open her palace to the public: Buckingham Palace (£16.50, Aug–Sept only) and her art gallery and carriage museum (adjacent to the palace, about £8 each, £14.50 for both) are expensive but interesting. Madame Tussauds Waxworks is pricey but still fun and popular (£25, drops to £16 after 17:00 if booked online). The Vinopolis wine museum provides a way to get a buzz and call it museum-going (from £25, entry includes five small glasses of wine).

Many smaller museums cost only around £5. My favorites include the Courtauld Gallery (free on Mon until 14:00) and the Wellington Museum at Apsley House (£5.70).

Not Worth It: Gimmicky, overpriced, bad-value enterprises include the London Dungeon (£20) and the Dalí Universe (great location next to the popular London Eye, but for £14.50, skip it).

Theater: Compared with Broadway's prices, London theater is a bargain. Seek out the freestanding "tkts" booth at Leicester Square to get discounts from 25 to 50 percent (though not necessarily for the hottest shows; see page 355). A £5 "groundling" ticket for a play at Shakespeare's Globe is the best theater deal in town (see page 356). Tickets to the Open Air Theatre at north London's Regent's Park start at £10 (see page 357).

London doesn't come cheap. But with its many free museums and affordable plays, this cosmopolitan, cultured city offers days of sightseeing thrills without requiring you to pinch your pennies (or your pounds).

terrace with several eateries (between the Strand and the Thames). The palace once held the national registry that recorded Britain's births, marriages, and deaths: "...where they hatch 'em, match 'em, and dispatch 'em." Step into the courtyard to enjoy the fountain. Go ahead...walk through it. The 55 jets get playful twice an hour. In the winter, this becomes a popular ice-skating rink with a toasty café for viewing (www.somerset-house.org.uk).

○ See the Courtauld Gallery Tour chapter.

Buckingham Palace

There are three palace sights that require admission: the State

Rooms, Queen's Gallery, and Royal Mews. You can pay for each separately, or buy a combo-ticket. The combo-ticket for £29.50 admits you to all three sights; a cheaper version for £14.50 covers the Queen's Gallery and Royal Mews. Many tourists are more interested in the Changing of the Guard, which costs nothing at all to view.

▲**State Rooms at Buckingham Palace**—This lavish home has been Britain's royal residence since 1837. When the Queen's at home, the royal standard flies (a red, yellow, and blue flag); otherwise, the Union Jack flaps in the wind. Recently, the Queen has opened her palace to the public—but only in August and September, when she's out of town.

Cost, Hours, Location: £16.50 for lavish State Rooms and throne room, includes audioguide, Aug–Sept only, daily 9:45–18:00, last admission 15:45; only 8,000 visitors a day by timed entry; come early to the palace's Visitor Entrance (opens 9:15) or book ahead in person or by phone or online (£1.25 extra); Tube: Victoria. Tel. 020/7766-7300, www.royalcollection.org.uk.

▲**Queen's Gallery at Buckingham Palace**—Queen Elizabeth's personal collection of art is on display in a wing adjoining the palace. Her 7,000 paintings make up the finest private art collection in the world, rivaling Europe's biggest national art galleries. It's actually a collection of collections, built on by each successive monarch since the 16th century. She rotates her paintings, enjoying some privately in her many palatial residences while sharing others with her subjects in public galleries in Edinburgh and London. Small, thoughtfully presented, and always exquisite displays fill the handful of rooms open to the public. As you're in "the most important building in London," security is tight. In addition to the permanent collection, you'll see temporary exhibits and a room full of the Queen's personal jewelry. Compared to the crown jewels at the Tower, it may be Her Majesty's bottom drawer—but it's still a dazzling pile of diamonds. Temporary exhibits change about twice a year, and are lovingly described by the included audioguide. While admission tickets come with an entry time, this is only enforced during rare days when crowds are a problem.

Cost, Hours, Location: £8.50, daily 10:00–17:30, last entry one hour before closing, Tube: Victoria. Tel. 020/7766-7301, but Her Majesty rarely answers. Men shouldn't miss the mahogany-trimmed urinals.

Royal Mews—Located to the left of Buckingham Palace, the Queen's working stables, or "mews," are open to visitors. The visit is likely to be disappointing unless you follow the included guided tour, in which case it's thoroughly entertaining—especially if you're interested in horses and/or royalty. The 40-minute tours show off a few of the Queen's 30 horses, a fancy car, and a bunch of old carriages, finishing with the Gold State Coach (c. 1760, 4 tons, 4 mph). Queen Victoria said absolutely no cars. When she died, in 1901, the mews got its first Daimler. Today, along with the hay-eating transport, the stable is home to five Rolls-Royce Phantoms, with one on display.

Cost, Hours, Location: £7.50, April–July and Oct Sat–Thu 11:00–16:00, Aug–Sept 10:00–17:00, last entry 45 min before closing, closed Fri and Nov–March, 2 tours/hr, Buckingham Palace Road, Tube: Victoria. Tel. 020/7766-7302.

▲▲Changing of the Guard at Buckingham Palace—This is the spectacle every visitor to London has to see at least once: stone-

faced, red-coated, bearskin-hatted guards changing posts with much fanfare, in an hour-long ceremony accompanied by a brass band.

It's 11:00 at Buckingham Palace, and the on-duty guards are ready to finish their shift. Nearby at St. James's Palace (a half-mile northwest), a second set of guards is also ready for a break. In a third location, fresh replacement guards gather for a review and inspection at Wellington Barracks, 500 yards east of the palace (on Birdcage Walk).

At 11:15, the tired St. James's guards head out to the Mall, and then take a right turn for Buckingham Palace. At 11:30, the replacement troops, led by the band, also head for Buckingham Palace. Meanwhile, a fourth group—the Horse Guard—passes by along the Mall en route to their own changing-of-the-guard ceremony on Whitehall.

At 11:45, the tired and fresh guards converge on Buckingham

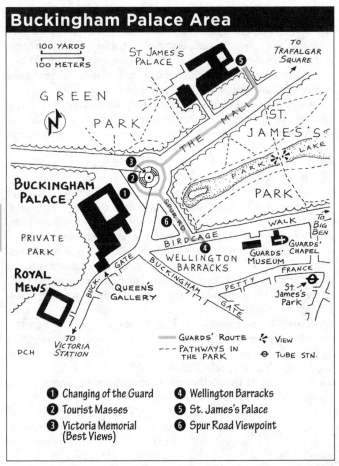

Buckingham Palace Area

100 YARDS
100 METERS

ST JAMES'S PALACE

TO TRAFALGAR SQUARE

GREEN PARK

N

THE MALL

ST. JAMES'S PARK

LAKE

BUCKINGHAM PALACE

VIEW

PARK

PRIVATE PARK

SPUR RD.

WALK

TO BIG BEN

BIRDCAGE

WELLINGTON BARRACKS

GUARDS' MUSEUM

GUARDS' CHAPEL

ROYAL MEWS

GATE

BUCK.

BUCKINGHAM

FRANCE

PETTY

ST. James's Park

QUEEN'S GALLERY

GATE

TO VICTORIA STATION

DCH

——— GUARDS' ROUTE   ↙ VIEW
- - - PATHWAYS IN THE PARK   ⊖ TUBE STN.

❶ Changing of the Guard   ❹ Wellington Barracks
❷ Tourist Masses   ❺ St. James's Palace
❸ Victoria Memorial (Best Views)   ❻ Spur Road Viewpoint

Palace in a perfect storm of Red Coat pageantry. Everyone parades around, the guard changes (passing the regimental flag, or "color") with much shouting, the band plays a happy little concert, and then they march out. A few minutes later, the fresh guards set up at St. James's Palace, the tired ones dress down at the barracks, and the tourists disperse.

Cost, Hours, Location: Free, daily May–July at 11:30, every other day Aug–April, no ceremony in very wet weather; exact schedule subject to change—call 020/7766-7300 for the day's plan, or check www.changing-the-guard.com or www.royalcollection .org.uk (click "Visit," then "Changing the Guard"); Buckingham Palace, Tube: Victoria, St. James's Park, or Green Park. Or hop into a big black taxi and say, "Buck House, please" (a.k.a. Buckingham Palace).

Sightseeing Strategies: Most tourists just show up and get lost in the crowds, but those who know the drill will enjoy the event more. The action takes place in stages over the course of an hour, at several different locations. The main event is in the forecourt right in front of Buckingham Palace (between Buckingham Palace and the fence) from 11:30 to 12:00. To see it close up, you'll need to get here no later than 10:30 to get a place right next to the fence.

But there's plenty of pageantry elsewhere. Get out your map and strategize. You could see the guards mobilizing at Wellington Barracks or St. James's Palace (11:00–11:30). Or watch them parade with bands down The Mall and Spur Road (11:30). After the ceremony at Buckingham Palace is over (and many tourists have gotten bored and gone home), the parades march back along those same streets (12:10).

Pick one event and find a good, unobstructed place from which to view it. The key is to either get right up front along the road or fence, or find some raised elevation to stand or sit on—a balustrade or a curb—so you can see over people's heads.

For the best overall view, stake out the high ground on the circular Victoria Memorial (come before 11:00 to get a place). From the Memorial, you have good views of the palace as well as the arriving and departing parades along The Mall and Spur Road. The actual changing of the guard in front of the palace is a nonevent. It is interesting, however, to see nearly every tourist in London gathered in one place at the same time. Afterward, stroll through nearby St. James's Park.

SIGHTS IN LONDON

North London

▲▲▲**British Museum**—Simply put, this is the greatest chronicle of civilization...anywhere. A visit here is like taking a long hike through *Encyclopedia Britannica* National Park. While the

vast British Museum wraps around its Great Court (the huge entrance hall), the most popular sections of the museum fill the ground floor: Egyptian, Assyrian, and ancient Greek, with the famous Elgin Marbles from the Athenian Parthenon. The museum's stately Reading Room—famous as the place where Karl Marx hung out while formulating his ideas on communism and writing *Das Kapital*—sometimes hosts special exhibits.

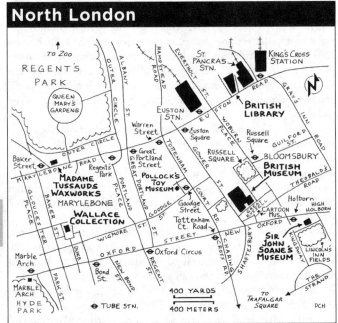

North London

Cost, Hours, Location: Museum free but a £3, $5, or €5 donation requested; temporary exhibits extra, daily 10:00–17:30, Thu–Fri until 20:30—but not all galleries open after 17:30, £8 90-min guided tours, free 30–40 min tours of select rooms generally every 30 min 11:00–15:30, three £3.50 audioguides, least crowded weekday late afternoons, Great Russell Street, Tube: Tottenham Court Road. Switchboard tel. 020/7323-8000, general info tel. 020/7323-8299, collection questions tel. 020/7323-8838, www.britishmuseum.org.

○ See the British Museum Tour chapter.

▲▲▲**British Library**—Here, in just two rooms, are the literary treasures of Western civilization, from early Bibles to the Magna Carta to Shakespeare's *Hamlet* to Lewis Carroll's *Alice's Adventures in Wonderland*. You'll see the Lindisfarne Gospels transcribed on an illuminated manuscript, as well as Beatles lyrics scrawled on the back of a greeting card. The British Empire built its greatest monuments out of paper, and it's with literature that England made her lasting contribution to civilization and the arts.

Cost, Hours, Location: Free but donations appreciated, temporary exhibits extra, Mon–Fri 9:30–18:00, Tue until 20:00, Sat 9:30–17:00, Sun 11:00–17:00; helpful free computers give you extra info; ground-floor café, self-service cafeteria upstairs; Tube: King's Cross St. Pancras, walk a block west to 96 Euston Road; Euston

Tube station is also close; bus #10, #30, #73, #91, #205, or #390.
Library tel. 020-7412-7332, www.bl.uk.

○ See the British Library Tour chapter.

▲**Wallace Collection**—Sir Richard Wallace's fine collection of
17th-century Dutch Masters, 18th-century French Rococo, medieval armor, and assorted aristocratic fancies fills the sumptuously
furnished Hertford House on Manchester Square. From the rough
and intimate Dutch life-scapes of Jan Steen to the pink-cheeked
Rococo fantasies of François Boucher, a wander through this little-
visited mansion makes you nostalgic for the days of the empire.

Cost, Hours, Location: Free, daily 10:00–17:00, £3 audioguide, free guided tours or lectures almost daily—call to confirm
times, just north of Oxford Street on Manchester Square, Tube:
Bond Street. Tel. 020/7563-9500, www.wallacecollection.org.

▲**Madame Tussauds Waxworks**—This is gimmicky and expensive but dang good. The original Madame Tussaud did wax casts
of heads lopped off during the French Revolution (such as Marie-

Antoinette's). She took her show
on the road and ended up in
London in 1835. Now it's much
easier to be featured. The gallery
is one big photo-op—a huge
hit with the kind of travelers
who skip the British Museum.
After looking a hundred famous
people in their glassy eyes and
surviving a silly hall of horror, you'll board a Disney-type ride
and cruise through a kid-pleasing "Spirit of London" time trip.
Your last stop is the auditorium for a 12-minute stage show (runs
every 15 min). They've dumped anything really historical (except
for what they claim is the blade that beheaded Marie-Antoinette)
because "there's no money in it and we're a business." Now it's all
about squeezing Brad Pitt's bum, gambling with George Clooney,
and partying with Beyoncé, Britney, and Bill Clinton. The unpop-
ular Gordon Brown is the first British prime minister in 150 years
not to be immortalized in wax—but President Obama has already
joined the club.

Cost, Hours, Location: £25, £37 combo-ticket with London
Eye, cheaper for kids. From 17:00 to closing, it's £16 if you buy
online, kids £11 (does not include London Eye). Children under 5
are always free. Open Mon–Fri 9:30–17:30, Sat–Sun 9:00–18:00,
mid-July–Aug and school holidays daily 9:00–18:00; Marylebone
Road; Tube: Baker Street. Toll tel. 08709-990-046, www
.madametussauds.com. Check the website for discounts on this
pricey waxtravaganza.

SIGHTS IN LONDON

London for Early Birds and Night Owls

Most sightseeing in London is restricted to the hours between 10:00 and 18:00. Here are a few exceptions:

Sights Open Early

Every day several sights open at 9:30 or earlier.

Shakespeare's Globe: May–Sept daily at 9:00.

Churchill Museum and Cabinet War Rooms: Daily at 9:30.

Kew Gardens: Daily at 9:30.

Madame Tussauds Waxworks: Mon–Fri at 9:30, Sat–Sun at 9:00 (opens daily at 9:00 mid-July–Aug).

Westminster Cathedral: Daily at 7:00.

Buckingham Palace: Aug–Sept daily at 9:45.

St. Paul's Cathedral: Mon–Sat at 8:30.

Westminster Abbey: Mon–Sat at 9:30.

British Library: Mon–Sat at 9:30.

Tower of London: Tue–Sat at 9:00.

Houses of Parliament: Fri at 9:30.

Sights Open Late

Every night in London at least one sight is open late, in addition to the London Eye. Here's the scoop from Monday through Sunday:

London Eye: July–Aug daily until 21:30, June and Sept until 21:00, otherwise until 20:00.

Vinopolis: Thu–Sat until 22:00, Sun until 18:00.

Houses of Parliament (when in session): Mon–Tue until 22:30.

British Library: Tue until 20:00.

Sir John Soane's Museum: First Tue of month until 21:00.

National Gallery: Fri until 21:00.

British Museum (some galleries): Thu–Fri until 20:30.

National Portrait Gallery: Thu–Fri until 21:00.

London Transport Museum: Some Fri until 21:00.

Victoria and Albert Museum: Fri until 22:00.

Tate Modern: Fri–Sat until 22:00.

Clink Prison Museum: Sat–Sun until 21:00 in summer.

Sir John Soane's Museum—Architects and fans of eclectic knickknacks love this quirky place, as do fans of interior décor and lovers of Back Door sights. Tour this furnished home on a bird-chirping square and see 19th-century chairs, lamps, and carpets, wood-paneled nooks and crannies, and stained-glass skylights. The townhouse is cluttered with Soane's (and his wife's) collection of ancient relics, curios, and famous paintings, including Hogarth's series on *The Rake's Progress* (read the fun plot) and

several excellent Canalettos. In 1833, just before his death, Soane established his house as a museum, stipulating that it be kept as nearly as possible in the state he left it. If he visited today, he'd be entirely satisfied. You'll leave wishing you'd known the man.

Cost, Hours, Location: Free but donations much appreciated, Tue–Sat 10:00–17:00, last entry 30 min before closing, first Tue of the month also 18:00–21:00, closed Sun–Mon, long entry lines on Sat and first Tue, good £1 brochure, £5 guided tours Sat at 11:00, 13 Lincoln's Inn Fields, quarter-mile southeast of British Museum, Tube: Holborn. Tel. 020/7405-2107.

Cartoon Museum—This humble but interesting museum is located in the shadow of the British Museum. While its three rooms are filled with British cartoons unknown to most Americans, the satire of famous bigwigs and politicians—from Napoleon to Margaret Thatcher, the Queen, and Tony Blair—shows the power of parody to deliver social commentary. Upstairs, you'll see pages spanning from *Tarzan* to *Tank Girl, Andy Capp* to the British *Dennis the Menace*—interesting only to comic-book diehards.

Cost, Hours, Location: £5; Tue–Sat 10:30–17:30, Sun 12:00–17:30, closed Mon; 35 Little Russell Street—go one block south of the British Museum on Museum Street and make a right; Tube: Tottenham Court Road. Tel. 020/7580-8155, www.cartoon museum.org.

Pollock's Toy Museum—This rickety old house, with glass cases filled with toys and games lining its walls and halls, is a time-warp experience that brings back childhood memories to people who grew up without batteries or computer chips. Though the museum is small, you could spend a lot of time here, squinting at the fascinating toys and dolls that entertained the children of 19th- and early 20th-century England. The included information is great. The story of Theodore Roosevelt refusing to shoot a bear cub while on a hunting trip was celebrated in 1902 cartoons, resulting in a

SIGHTS IN LONDON

Harry Potter's London

Harry Potter's story is set in a magical Britain, and all of the places mentioned in the books, except London, are fictional, but you can visit many real film locations. Many of the locations are closed to visitors, though, or are an un-magical disappointment in person, unless you're a huge fan. For those diehards, here's a list.

Spoiler Warning: Information in this sidebar will ruin surprises for the three of you who haven't yet read or seen any of the Harry Potter books or movies.

Harry's story begins in suburban London, in the fictional town of Little Whinging. In the first film, the gentle-giant Hagrid on his flying motorcycle touches down at #4 Privet Drive. There, baby Harry—who was orphaned by the murder of his wizard parents—is left on the doorstep to be raised by an anti-magic aunt and uncle. The scene was shot in the town of **Bracknell** (pop. 50,000, 10 miles west of Heathrow) on a street of generic brick rowhouses called Picket Close. Later, 10-year-old Harry first realizes his wizard powers when talking with a boa constrictor, filmed at the **London Zoo's Reptile House** in Regent's Park (Tube: Great Portland Street). Harry soon gets invited to Hogwarts School of Witchcraft and Wizardry, where he'll learn the magical skills he'll need to eventually confront his parents' murderer, Lord Voldemort.

Big Ben and **Parliament,** along the Thames, welcome Harry to the modern city inhabited by Muggles (nonmagic folk). London bustles along oblivious to the parallel universe of wizards. Hagrid takes Harry shopping for school supplies. They enter the glass-roofed **Leadenhall Market** (Tube: Bank), and approach a **storefront** in Bull's Head Passage—the entrance to The Leaky Cauldron pub (which, in the books, is placed among the bookshops of Charing Cross Road). The pub's back wall parts, opening onto the magical Diagon Alley (filmed on a set at Leavesden Studios, north of London), where Harry shops for wands, cauldrons, and wizard textbooks. He pays for them with gold Galleons from goblin-run Gringotts Wizarding Bank, filmed in the marble-floored and chandeliered Exhibition Hall of **Australia House** (Tube: Temple), home of the Australian Embassy.

new, huggable toy: the Teddy Bear. It was popular for good reason: it could be manufactured during World War I without rationed products; it coincided with the new belief that soft toys were good for a child's development; it was an acceptable "doll for boys"; and it's *the* toy children keep long after they've grown up.

Cost, Hours, Location: £5, kids-£2, Mon–Sat 10:00–17:00, closed Sun, last entry 30 min before closing, 1 Scala Street, Tube: Goodge Street. Tel. 020/7636-3452, www.pollockstoymuseum .com. Call before you go to make sure it's open.

PLATFORM 9¾

Harry catches the train to Hogwarts at **King's Cross Station.** (The fanciful exterior shot from film #2 is actually nearby **St. Pancras Station.**) Inside the glass-roofed train station, on a **pedestrian sky bridge** over the tracks, Hagrid gives Harry a train ticket. Harry heads to platform 9¾, where he and his new buddy Ron magically push their luggage carts through a brick pillar between the platforms, emerging onto a hidden platform. (For a fun photo-op, find the *Platform 9¾* sign and the luggage cart that appears to be disappearing into the wall. They're located on the way to platform 9—walk toward the pedestrian bridge and make a left at the arch.)

A red steam train—the Hogwarts Express—speeds the boys through the (Scottish) countryside to Hogwarts, where Harry will spend the next seven years. Harry is taught how to wave his wand by tiny Professor Flitwick in a wood-paneled classroom filmed at **Harrow School** in Harrow on the Hill, eight miles northwest of London (Tube: Harrow on the Hill).

In film #3, Harry careens through London's lamp-lit streets on a purple three-decker bus that dumps him at the Leaky Cauldron. In this film, the pub's exterior was shot on rough-looking Stoney Street at the southeast edge of **Borough Street Market,** by The Market Porter pub, with trains rumbling overhead (Tube: London Bridge). In the "Half-Blood Prince" film, the **Millennium Bridge** collapses into the Thames.

Other scenes from the books are set in London—Sirius Black and the Order reside at Twelve Grimmauld Place and Harry plumbs the depths of the Ministry of Magic—but these places are fictional.

Finally, cinema buffs can visit **Leicester Square** (Tube: Leicester Square), where Daniel Radcliffe and other stars strolled past paparazzi and down red carpets to the Odeon Theater to watch the movies' premieres.

The City

When Londoners say "The City," they mean the one-square-mile business center in East London that 2,000 years ago was Roman Londinium. The outline of the Roman city walls can still be seen in the arc of roads from Blackfriars Bridge to Tower Bridge. Within The City are 23 churches designed by Sir Christopher Wren, mostly just ornamentation around St. Paul's Cathedral. Today, while home to only 5,000 residents, The City thrives with nearly

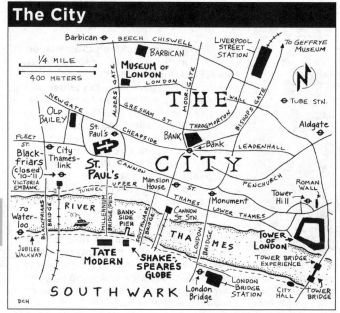

The City

SIGHTS IN LONDON

500,000 office workers coming and going daily. It's a fascinating district to wander on weekdays, but since almost nobody actually lives there, it's dull in the evenings and on Saturday and Sunday.

○ See The City Walk chapter.

St. Paul's Cathedral and Nearby

▲▲▲**St. Paul's Cathedral**—Wren's most famous church is the great St. Paul's, its elaborate interior capped by a 365-foot dome. Since World War II, St. Paul's has been Britain's symbol of resistance. Despite 57 nights of bombing, the Nazis failed to destroy the cathedral, thanks to the St. Paul's volunteer fire watchmen, who stayed on the dome. Today you can climb the dome for a great city view. The crypt (included with admission) is a world of historic bones and memorials, including Admiral Nelson's tomb and interesting cathedral models.

Cost, Hours, Location: £11, includes church entry and dome climb; Mon–Sat 8:30–16:30, last church entry 16:00, last dome entry 16:15, closed Sun except for worship, £3 tours and £4 audioguides, no photography allowed, cheery café and pricier restaurant in crypt, Tube: St. Paul's; bus #4, #11, #15, #23, #26, or #100. Recorded info tel. 020/7246-8348, office tel. 020/7236-8350, www.stpauls.co.uk.

Music: The evensong services are free, but nonpaying visitors are not allowed to linger afterward (Mon–Sat at 17:00, Sun at 15:15, 40 min).

✪ See the St. Paul's Tour chapter.

▲**Old Bailey**—To view the British legal system in action—lawyers in little blond wigs speaking legalese with a British accent—spend a few minutes in the visitors' gallery at the Old Bailey, called the "Central Criminal Court." Don't enter under the dome; signs point you to the two visitors' entrances.

Cost, Hours, Location: Free, generally Mon–Fri 10:00–13:00 & 14:00–17:00 depending on caseload, closed Sat–Sun, reduced hours in Aug; no kids under 14; no bags, mobile phones, cameras, or food, but small purses OK; Eddie at Bailey's Café across the street at #30 stores bags for £2; 2 blocks northwest of St. Paul's on Old Bailey Street, follow signs to public entrance, Tube: St. Paul's. Tel. 020/7248-3277.

▲**Museum of London**—London, a 2,000-year-old city, is so littered with ruins that when a London builder finds Roman antiquities, he simply documents the finds, moves the artifacts to a museum, and resumes building. If you're asking, "Why did the Romans build their cities underground?" a trip to the creative and entertaining Museum of London is a must.

The museum features London's distinguished citizens through history—from Neanderthals to Romans to Elizabethans to Victorians to Mods to today. The museum's displays are chronological, spacious, and informative without being overwhelming. Scale models and costumes help you visualize everyday life in the city at different periods. There are enough whiz-bang multimedia displays (including the Plague and the Great Fire) to spice up otherwise humdrum artifacts. This regular stop for the local school kids gives the best overview of London history in town.

London's Story at the Museum of London: Here, you can walk through London's history from prehistory to the present. First, zip quickly through a half-million years, when Britain morphed from peninsula to island, Neanderthals speared mammoths, and Stone Age humans huddled in crude huts on the South Bank of the Thames.

In 54 B.C., Julius Caesar invaded, and the Romans built "Londinium" on the North Bank. The settlement quickly became the hub of Britain and a river-trade town, complete with arenas, forums, baths, a bridge across the Thames, and a city wall. That wall—arcing from the present Tower of London to St. Paul's—defined the city's boundaries for the next 1,500 years. The Museum of London sits on the northwest perimeter of the city wall, and you can look out the windows to see a crumbling remnant along the street, now called "London Wall."

When Rome could no longer defend the city (A.D. 410), it fell to the Saxons (becoming "Lundenburg") and, later, the Normans (in 1066), who built the Tower of London. Medieval London was devastated by the Black Death plague of 1348. As the city recovered and grew even bigger, it became clear to wannabe kings that whoever controlled London controlled Britain.

When Queen Elizabeth I brought peace to the land, London thrived as a capital of theaters (the Globe and Rose), arts, and ideas. Then, just when things were going so well, the city was disintegrated by the Great Fire of 1666, which left London a blank slate.

The exhibits covering 1666 to the present have been closed for years, but they're scheduled to reopen in spring 2010 with great fanfare. You'll see the opulence of rebuilt Georgian London in the Museum's prized possession—the Lord Mayor's Coach, a golden carriage pulled by six white horses that looks right out of Cinderella. Next, stroll through a multimedia "pleasure garden" and take a "Victorian Walk," experiencing what it was like to live in the world's greatest city.

Two world wars and the car changed 20th-century London into a concrete jungle. But it remained a cultural capital of elegance (see an Art Deco elevator from Selfridge's) and a global trendsetter (Beatles-era memorabilia).

Finally, displays on the 21st century—including the terrorist bombings of July 7, 2005—weave contemporary London into the tapestry of history.

Cost, Hours, Location: Free, daily 10:00–18:00, until 21:00 first Thu of month, last entry 30 min before closing, Tube: Barbican or St. Paul's plus a five-minute walk. Tel. 020/7814-5530, recorded info tel. 020/7001-9844, www.museumoflondon.org.uk.

Tower of London and Nearby

▲▲▲**Tower of London**—The Tower has served as a castle in wartime, a king's residence in peace time, and, most notoriously, as the prison and execution site of rebels. You can see the crown jewels, take a witty Beefeater tour, and ponder the executioner's block that dispensed with troublesome heirs to the throne and a couple of Henry VIII's wives.

Cost, Hours, Location: £17, family-£47; audioguide-£4; March–Oct Tue–Sat 9:00–17:30, Sun–Mon 10:00–17:30; Nov–

Feb Tue–Sat 9:00–16:30, Sun–Mon 10:00–16:30; last entry 30 min before closing; the long but fast-moving ticket lines are worst on Sun; no photography allowed of jewels, in chapels, or in the White Tower; Tube: Tower Hill. Switchboard toll tel. 0844-482-7777, booking toll tel. 0844-482-7799.

Avoid long lines by buying your ticket online (www.hrp.org .uk), at any London TI, at the Trader's Gate gift shop down the steps from the Tower Hill Tube stop, or at the Welcome Centre to the left of the normal ticket line (credit card only). After your visit, consider taking the boat to Greenwich from here (see cruise info on page 39).

✪ See the Tower of London Tour chapter.

Tower Bridge—The iconic Tower Bridge (often mistakenly called London Bridge) has been freshly painted and is undergoing restoration. The hydraulically powered drawbridge was built in 1894 to accommodate the growing East End. While fully modern, its design was a retro Neo-Gothic look.

You can tour the bridge at the **Tower Bridge Experience**, with a history exhibit and a peek at the Victorian engine room that lifts the span (£6, family £14, daily 10:00–18:30 in summer, 9:30–18:00 in winter, last entry 30 min before closing, good view, poor value, enter at the northwest tower, tel. 020/7403-3761, Tube: Tower Hill, www.towerbridge.org.uk). The visit is most interesting when the drawbridge lifts to let ships pass, as it does a thousand times a year; for the bridge-lifting schedule, call 020/7940-3984.

More Sights near the Tower—The best remaining bit of London's **Roman Wall** is just north of the Tower (at the Tower Hill Tube station). The chic **St. Katharine Dock,** just east of Tower Bridge, has private yachts, mod shops, and the classic Dickens Inn, fun for a drink or pub lunch. Across the bridge is the South Bank, with the upscale Butlers Wharf area, City Hall, museums, and the Jubilee Walkway.

Northeast of The City

▲**Geffrye Museum**—This low-key but well-organized museum —housed in an 18th-century almshouse—is located north of Liverpool Street Station in the trendy Shoreditch area. Walk past a dozen English living rooms, furnished and decorated in styles from 1600 to 2000, then descend the circular stairs to see changing

exhibits on home decor. In summer, explore the fragrant herb garden.

Cost, Hours, Location: Free, Tue–Sat 10:00–17:00, Sun 12:00–17:00, closed Mon, garden open April–Oct, 136 Kingsland Road, Tube: Liverpool Street, then 10-min ride north on bus #149 or #242 north. When the new Hoxton Tube station opens in mid-2010, you'll be able to take the East London line directly to the museum. Tel. 020/7739-9893, www.geffrye-museum.org.uk.

The South Bank

▲**Jubilee Walkway**—The South Bank is a thriving arts and cultural center tied together by this riverside path, a popular, pub-crawling pedestrian promenade called the Jubilee Walkway. Stretching from Tower Bridge past Westminster Bridge, it offers grand views of the Houses of Parliament and St. Paul's. On a sunny day, this is the place to see London out strolling. The Walkway hugs the river except just east of London Bridge,

where it cuts inland for a couple of blocks. Plans are underway to expand the path into a 60-mile "Greenway" encircling the city, scheduled to open in 2012 for the Olympic Games and Elizabeth's 60th year as queen (www.jubileewalkway.org.uk).

The following sights (described below) are connected by the ✪ Bankside Walk on page 235: Shakespeare's Globe, Tate Modern, Millennium Bridge, Old Operating Theatre Museum, and Vinopolis.

▲▲**London Eye**—This giant Ferris wheel, towering above London opposite Big Ben, is the world's highest observational wheel and London's answer to the Eiffel Tower. While the experience is memorable, London doesn't have much of a skyline and the price is borderline outrageous. But whether you ride or not, the wheel is a sight to behold. Designed like a giant bicycle wheel, it's a pan-European undertaking: British steel and Dutch engineering, with Czech, German, French, and Italian mechanical parts. It's also very "green," running extremely efficiently and virtually silently. You start with a short "pre-flight" exhibit in the ticket

The South Bank

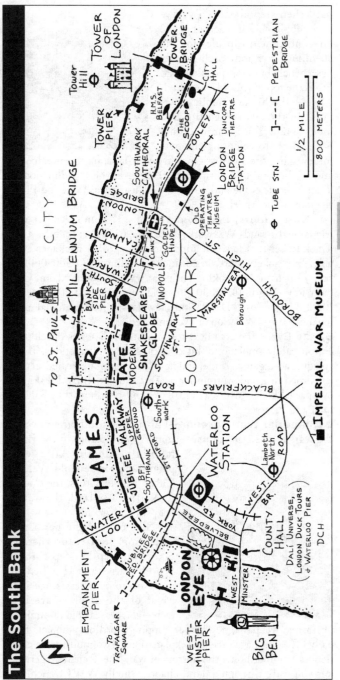

hall, then step aboard. Twenty-five people ride in each of its 32 air-conditioned capsules for the 30-minute rotation. Each capsule has a bench, but most people stand. From the top of this 443-foot-high wheel—the highest public viewpoint in the city—even Big Ben looks small. You go around only once. Built to celebrate the new millennium, the Eye's original five-year lease has been extended, and it's becoming a permanent fixture on the London skyline. Thames boats come and go from here using the Waterloo Pier at the foot of the wheel.

Cost, Hours, Location: £17, or £37 combo-ticket with Madame Tussauds Waxworks—see page 63, £10 extra buys a Fast Track ticket that lets you jump the queue, other packages available. Buy tickets there, in advance by calling 0870-500-0600, or save 10 percent by booking online at www.londoneye.com. Open daily July–Aug 10:00–21:30, June and Sept 10:00–21:00, Oct–May 10:00–20:00, closed Dec 25 and a few days in Jan for annual maintenance, Tube: Waterloo or Westminster.

By the Eye—The area next to the London Eye has developed a cotton-candy ambience of kitschy, kid-friendly attractions. There's an aquarium, game arcade, and new "Movieum" dedicated to movies filmed in London, from *Harry Potter* to *Star Wars*. I'd skip the overpriced Dalí Universe (£14.50) of mind-bending art by Salvador Dalí and Picasso.

▲▲Imperial War Museum—This impressive museum covers the wars of the last century—from WWI biplanes to the rise of

fascism to Monty's Africa campaign tank to the Cold War, the Cuban Missile Crisis, the troubles in Northern Ireland, the wars in Iraq, and terrorism.

The core of the permanent collection, located downstairs, takes you step by step through World Wars I and II. Then you move on to conflicts since 1945. Most of the displays are low-tech—glass cases hold dummies in uniforms, weapons, newspaper clippings, ordinary objects from daily life—but have excellent explanations. Two multimedia experiences hammer home the horrors of war. The Trench Experience lets you walk through a dark, chaotic, smelly WWI trench. The

Blitz Experience film assaults the senses with the noise and intensity of a WWII air raid on London. Also, the cinema shows a rotating selection of films.

In the entry hall are the large exhibits—including Montgomery's tank, several field guns, and, dangling overhead, vintage planes. Imagine the awesome power of the 50-foot V-2 rocket, the kind the Nazis rained down on London, which could arrive silently and destroy a city block. Its direct descendant is the Polaris missile, capable of traveling nearly 3,000 miles in 20 minutes and obliterating an entire city.

Besides exhibits on the world wars, the museum has several other permanent sections. The "Secret War" peeks into the intrigues of espionage in World Wars I and II. The section on the Holocaust is one of the best on the subject anywhere, and there are always several temporary exhibitions that are top-notch.

War wonks will love the place, as will general history buffs who enjoy patiently reading displays. For the rest, there are enough multimedia exhibits and submarines for the kids to climb in to keep it interesting.

Rather than glorify war, the museum does its best to shine a light on the 100 million deaths of the 20th century. It shows everyday life for people back home and never neglects the powerful human side of one of humankind's most persistent traits.

The museum is housed in what was the Royal Bethlam Hospital. Also known as "the Bedlam asylum," the place was so wild it gave the world a new word for chaos. Back in Victorian times, locals—without reality shows and YouTube—paid admission to visit the asylum on weekends for entertainment.

Cost, Hours, Location: Free, daily 10:00–18:00, temporary exhibits extra, often guided tours on weekends—ask at info desk, £4 audioguide, Tube: Lambeth North or bus #12 or bus #159. Tel. 020/7416-5000, www.iwm.org.uk.

▲▲**Tate Modern**—Dedicated in the spring of 2000, the striking museum across the river from St. Paul's opened the new century with art from the old one. Its powerhouse collection of Monet, Matisse, Dalí, Picasso, Warhol, and much more is displayed in a converted powerhouse. Of equal interest are the many temporary exhibits featuring cutting-edge art. Each year, the main hall features a different monumental installation by a prominent artist.

Cost, Hours, Location: Free but £3 donations appreciated, fee for special exhibitions, daily 10:00–18:00, Fri–Sat until

SIGHTS IN LONDON

Crossing the Thames on Foot

You can cross the Thames on any of the bridges that carry car traffic over the river, but London's two pedestrian bridges are

more fun. The Millennium Bridge (see photo) connects the sedate St. Paul's Cathedral with the great Tate Modern. The Golden Jubilee Bridge, well-lit with a sleek, futuristic look, links bustling Trafalgar Square on the North Bank with the London Eye and Waterloo Station on the South Bank.

22:00—a good time to visit, last entry 45 min before closing, audioguide-£2, children's audioguide-£1; free guided tours at 11:00, 12:00, 14:00, and 15:00—confirm at info desk; view restaurant on top floor; cross the Millennium Bridge from St. Paul's; Tube: Southwark, London Bridge or Mansion House plus a 10–15 min walk; or connect by Tate Boat ferry from Tate Britain for £5 one-way, discounted with Travelcard. Switchboard tel. 020/7887-8888, recorded info tel. 020/7887-8008, www.tate.org.uk.

○ See the Tate Modern Tour chapter.

▲**Millennium Bridge**—The pedestrian bridge links St. Paul's Cathedral and the Tate Modern across the Thames. This is London's first new bridge in a century. When it first opened, the $25 million bridge wiggled when people walked on it, so it promptly closed for an $8 million, 20-month stabilization; now it's stable and open again (free). Nicknamed the "blade of light" for its sleek minimalist design (370 yards long, four yards wide, stainless steel with teak planks), its clever aerodynamic handrails deflect wind over the heads of pedestrians.

▲▲**Shakespeare's Globe**—A replica of the original Globe Theatre has been built, half-timbered and thatched, as it was in Shakespeare's time. (This is the first thatched roof in London since they were outlawed after the Great Fire of 1666.) The Globe originally accommodated 2,200 seated and another 1,000 standing. Today, slightly smaller and leaving space for reasonable aisles,

the theater holds 800 seated and 600 groundlings. Its promoters brag that the theater melds "the three A's"—actors, audience, and architecture—with each contributing to the play. The working theater hosts authentic performances of Shakespeare's plays with actors in period costumes, modern interpretations of his works, and some works by other playwrights (generally all summer at 14:00 and 19:30—but confirm). For details on seeing a play, see page 356.

The complex has three parts: the theater itself, the box office, and the "Globe Exhibition" museum.

The **Globe Exhibition** ticket (£10.50) includes both a tour of the theater and a museum. First, you browse on your own through displays of Elizabethan-era costumes, music, script-printing, and special effects. There are early folios and objects that were dug up on the site. A video and scale models help put Shakespearean theater within the context of the times. (The Globe opened one year after England mastered the seas by defeating the Spanish Armada. The debut play was Shakespeare's *Julius Caesar*.)

Next comes the tour of the theater—you must take the tour at the time stamped on your ticket, but you can come back to the museum afterward; tickets are good all day. The guide (usually an actor) leads you into the theater to see the stage and the different seating areas for the different classes of people. You take a seat and learn how the new Globe is similar to the old Globe (open-air performances, standing-room by the stage, no curtain) and how it's different (female actors today, lights for night performances, concrete floor). It's not a backstage tour—you don't see dressing rooms or costume shops or sit in on rehearsals, though you may see workers building sets for a new production. You mostly sit and listen. The guides are energetic, theatrical, and knowledgeable, bringing the Elizabethan period to life.

When performances are going on, you can't tour the theater. But you can see the museum, then tour the nearby (and less interesting) Rose Theatre instead.

Cost, Hours, Location: £10.50 includes museum and 60-min tour, £7.50 on Rose Theater days; tickets good all day; complex open daily 9:00–17:00; exhibition and tours May–Sept 9:00–17:00—Globe tours offered mornings only in summer with Rose tours in afternoon, Oct–April daily 10:00–17:00—Globe tours run all day in winter; tours start every 15–30 min; on the South Bank directly across Thames over Southwark Bridge from St. Paul's; Tube: Mansion House or London Bridge plus a 10-min walk. Tel. 020/7902-1400 or 020/7902-1500, www.shakespeares-globe.org.

The Swan at the Globe café is open daily (11:00–1:00 in the morning, tel. 020/7928-9444).

Vinopolis: City of Wine—While it seems illogical to have a huge wine museum in beer-loving London, Vinopolis makes a good case. Built over a Roman wine store and filling the massive vaults of an old wine warehouse, the museum offers an excellent audioguide with a light yet earnest history of wine to accompany your sips of various mediocre reds and whites, ports, and champagnes. Allow some time, as the audioguide takes 90 minutes—and the sipping can slow things down pleasantly. This place is popular. Booking ahead for Friday and Saturday nights is a must.

Cost, Hours, Location: Various tour options range from £25 to £75 (save 20 percent by booking online at www.vinopolis.co.uk). Each includes about five wine tastes and an audioguide. Some packages also include whiskey (the new wine), other spirits, or a meal (Thu–Fri 12:00–22:00, Sat 11:00–22:00, Sun 12:00–18:00, closed Mon–Wed, last entry 2.5 hours before closing, between the Globe and Southwark Cathedral at 1 Bank End, Tube: London Bridge. Tel. 020/7940-8300 or toll tel. 0870-241-4040).

Southwark

The next three sights are in Southwark, on the South Bank. The area stretching from the Tate Modern to London Bridge, known as Southwark (SUTH-uck), was for centuries the place Londoners would go to escape the rules and decency of the city and let their hair down. Bearbaiting, brothels, rollicking pubs, and theater—you name the dream, and it could be fulfilled just across the Thames. A run-down warehouse district through the 20th century, it's been gentrified with classy restaurants, office parks, pedestrian promenades, major sights (such as the Tate Modern and Shakespeare's Globe—described on page 76), and this colorful collection of lesser sights. The area is easy on foot and a scenic—though circuitous—way to connect the Tower of London with St. Paul's. You'll find more information on these sights in the ✪ Bankside Walk chapter.

The Clink Prison Museum—Proudly the "original clink," this was, until 1780, where law-abiding citizens threw Southwark troublemakers. Today, it's a low-tech torture museum filling grotty old rooms with papier-mâché gore. Unfortunately, there's little that seriously deals with the fascinating problem of law and order in Southwark, where 18th-century Londoners went for a good time.

Cost, Hours, Location: Overpriced at £5, Mon–Fri 10:00–18:00, Sat–Sun until 21:00, 1 Clink Street, Tube: London Bridge. Tel. 020/7403-0900, www.clink.co.uk. Call before you come to make sure it's open.

Golden Hinde **Replica**—This is a full-size replica of the 16th-century warship in which Sir Francis Drake circumnavigated the globe from 1577 to 1580. Commanding this ship, Drake earned the reputation as history's most successful pirate. The original is long gone, but this boat has logged more than 100,000 miles, including a voyage around the world. While the ship is fun to see, its interior is not worth touring.

Cost, Hours, Location: £7, Mon–Sat 10:00–17:30, Sun 10:30–17:00; may be closed if rented out for pirate birthday parties, school groups, or weddings; Tube: London Bridge. Tel. 020/7403-0123, www.goldenhinde.org.

Southwark Cathedral—While made a cathedral only in 1905, it's been the neighborhood church since the 13th century, and comes with some interesting history. The enthusiastic docents give impromptu tours if you ask.

Cost, Hours, Location: Free but £4 suggested donation, daily 10:00–18:00, last entry 30 min before closing, £2.50 audio-guide, £2.50 guidebook, no photos without permission, Tube: London Bridge. Tel. 020/7367-6700, http://cathedral.southwark.anglican.org.

Music: The cathedral hosts evensong services (weekdays at 17:30, Sat at 16:00, Sun at 15:00, no service on Wed or alternate Mon).

▲**Old Operating Theatre Museum and Herb Garret**—Climb a tight and creaky wooden spiral staircase to a church attic where you'll find a garret used to dry medicinal herbs, a fascinating exhibit on Victorian surgery, cases of well-described 19th-century medical paraphernalia, and a special look at "anesthesia, the defeat of pain." Then you stumble upon Britain's oldest operating theater, where limbs were sawed off way back in 1821.

Cost, Hours, Location: £5.60, daily 10:30–17:00, closed Dec 15–Jan 5, 9a St. Thomas Street, Tube: London Bridge. Tel. 020/7188-2679, www.thegarret.org.uk.

✪ See the Bankside Walk chapter.

HMS *Belfast*—"The last big-gun armored warship of World War II" clogs the Thames just upstream from the Tower Bridge. This huge vessel—now manned with wax sailors—thrills kids who always dreamed of sitting in a turret shooting off their imaginary guns. If you're into WWII warships, this is the ultimate. Otherwise, it's just lots of exercise with a nice view of Tower Bridge.

Cost, Hours, Location: £10.70, daily March–Oct 10:00–18:00, Nov–Feb 10:00–17:00, last entry one hour before closing,

Tube: London Bridge. Tel. 020/7940-6300, www.hmsbelfast.iwm .org.uk.

City Hall—The glassy, egg-shaped building near the south end of Tower Bridge is London's City Hall, designed by Sir Norman

Foster, the architect who worked on London's Millennium Bridge and Berlin's Reichstag. City Hall is where London's mayor works, the blonde, flamboyant, conservative, former journalist and author Boris Johnson. He consults here with the Assembly representatives of the city's 25 districts. An interior spiral ramp allows visitors to watch and hear the action below in the Assembly Chamber—ride the lift to the second floor (the highest visitors can go) and spiral down. On the lower ground floor is a large aerial photograph of London, an information desk, and a handy cafeteria. Next to City Hall is the outdoor amphitheatre called the Scoop.

Cost, Hours, Location: City Hall is free and open to visitors Mon–Fri 8:00–17:30, Tube: London Bridge station plus 10-min walk, or Tower Hill station plus 15-min walk. Tel. 020/7983-4000, www.london.gov.uk/gla/city_hall.

West London

▲▲**Tate Britain**—One of Europe's great art houses, Tate Britain specializes in British painting from the 16th century through modern times. The museum has a good representation of William Blake's religious sketches, the Pre-Raphaelites' realistic art, and J. M. W. Turner's swirling works.

Cost, Hours, Location: Free, £2 donation requested, temporary exhibits extra; daily 10:00–17:50, first Fri of the month until 21:40, last entry 50 min before closing; fine and necessary £3.50 audioguide; free tours offered daily—see page 279; no photography allowed without advance permission; café and restaurant; Tube: Pimlico, then 7-min walk; or arrive directly at museum by taking the Tate Boat ferry from Tate Modern; or take bus #87 from National Gallery or bus #88 from Oxford Circus. Recorded info tel. 020/7887-8008, switchboard tel. 020/7887-8888, www.tate.org.uk.

West London

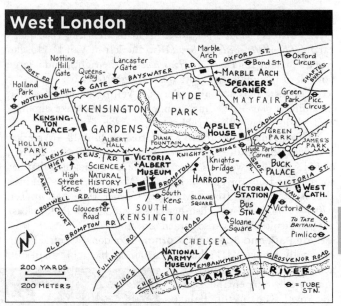

✪ See the Tate Britain Tour chapter.

▲**Apsley House (Wellington Museum)**—Having beaten Napoleon at Waterloo, Arthur Wellesley, the First Duke of Wellington, was once the most famous man in Europe. He was given London's ultimate address, #1 London. His newly refurbished mansion offers a nice interior, a handful of world-class paintings, and a glimpse at the life of the great soldier and two-time prime minister. Those who know something about Wellington ahead of time will appreciate the place much more than those who don't, as there's scarce biographical background.

An 11-foot-tall marble statue of Napoleon, clad only in a fig leaf, greets you. Napoleon commissioned the sculptor Canova to make it for him but didn't like it, and after Napoleon's defeat, it was eventually sold to Wellington as a war trophy. It's one of several images Wellington acquired of his former foe to have in his home. The two great men were polar opposites—Napoleon the daring general and champion of revolution, Wellington the play-it-safe strategist and conservative politician—but they're forever linked in history.

The core of the collection is a dozen first-floor rooms decorated with fancy wallpaper, chandeliers, a few pieces of furniture, and wall-to-wall paintings from Wellington's collection. You'll see fancy dinnerware and precious objects given to the Irish-born general by the crowned heads of Europe, who were eternally grateful to him for saving their necks from the guillotine. The highlight is the large ballroom, the Waterloo Gallery, decorated with Van Dyck's *Charles I on Horseback* (over the main fireplace), Velazquez's earthy *The Water-Seller of Seville* (to the left of Van Dyck), Jan Steen's playful *The Dissolute Household* (to the right), and a large portrait of Wellington by Goya (farther right).

Downstairs is a small gallery of Wellington memorabilia, including a pair of Wellington boots, which the duke popularized—Brits today still call rubber boots "wellies."

Cost, Hours, Location: £5.70, free on June 18—Waterloo Day, Wed–Sun 11:00–17:00 April–Oct, until 16:00 Nov–March, closed Mon–Tue, well-described by included audioguide that has sound bites from the current Duke of Wellington who still lives at Apsley, 20 yards from Hyde Park Corner Tube station. Tel. 020/7499-5676, www.english-heritage.org.uk. Hyde Park's pleasant and picnic-friendly rose garden is nearby.

▲**Hyde Park and Speakers' Corner**—London's "Central Park," originally Henry VIII's hunting grounds, has more than 600 acres of lush greenery, the huge man-made Serpentine Lake, the royal Kensington Palace and Orangery (see page 83), and the ornate Neo-Gothic Albert Memorial across from the Royal Albert Hall. The western half of the park is known as Kensington Gardens. On Sundays, from just after noon until early evening, Speakers' Corner offers soapbox oratory at its best (northeast corner of the park, Tube: Marble Arch). Characters climb their stepladders, wave their flags, pound emphatically on their sandwich boards, and share what they are convinced is their wisdom. Regulars have resident hecklers who know their lines and are always ready with a verbal jab or barb. "The grass roots

of democracy" is actually a holdover from when the gallows stood here and the criminal was allowed to say just about anything he wanted to before he swung. I dare you to raise your voice and gather a crowd—it's easy to do.

The **Princess Diana Memorial Fountain** honors the "People's Princess," who once lived in nearby Kensington Palace. The low-key circular stream, great for cooling off your feet on a hot day, is in the south central part of the park, near the Albert Memorial and Serpentine Gallery. (Don't be confused by signs to the Diana, Princess of Wales Memorial Playground, in the northwest corner of the park.)

▲▲**Victoria and Albert Museum**—The world's top collection of decorative arts (vases, stained glass, fine furniture, clothing, jewelry, carpets, and more) is a surprisingly interesting assortment of crafts from the West, as well as Asian and Islamic cultures. The British Galleries are grand, but there's much more to see, including Raphael's tapestry cartoons and a cast of Trajan's Column that depicts the emperor's conquests.

Cost, Hours, Location: Free, £3 donation requested, possible pricey fee for special exhibits, daily 10:00–17:45, Fri until 22:00; free 60-min tours daily on the half-hour from 10:30–15:30; Tube: South Kensington, a long tunnel leads directly from the Tube station to museum. Tel. 020/7942-2000, www.vam.ac.uk.

✪ See the Victoria and Albert Museum Tour chapter.

▲**Natural History Museum**—Across the street from Victoria and Albert, this mammoth museum is housed in a giant and wonderful Victorian, Neo-Romanesque building. Built in the 1870s specifically for the huge collection (50 million specimens), it has two halves: the Life Galleries (creepy-crawlies, human biology, "our place in evolution," and awesome dinosaurs) and the Earth Galleries (meteors, volcanoes, earthquakes, and so on). Exhibits are wonderfully explained, with lots of creative, interactive displays. Pop in, if only for the wild collection of dinosaurs and the roaring *Tyrannosaurus rex.*

Cost, Hours, Location: Free, fees for special exhibits, daily 10:00–17:50, last entry at 17:30, occasional tours, a long tunnel leads directly from South Kensington Tube station to museum. Tel. 020/7942-5000, www.nhm.ac.uk.

▲**Science Museum**—Next door to the Natural History Museum, this sprawling wonderland for curious minds is kid-perfect. It offers hands-on fun, from moonwalks to deep-sea exploration, with trendy technology exhibits, an IMAX theater (£8, kids-£6.25), and cool rotating themed exhibits, including "Cosmos and Culture: How Astronomy Has Shaped Our World," on display through 2010.

Cost, Hours, Location: Free entry, daily 10:00–18:00, Exhibition Road, Tube: South Kensington. Toll tel. 0870-870-4868, www.sciencemuseum.org.uk.

▲▲**Kensington Palace**—In 1689, King William and Queen Mary moved from Whitehall in central London to the more pristine and peaceful village of Kensington (now engulfed by London). Sir Christopher Wren renovated an existing house into Kensington Palace, which became the center of English court life until 1760, when the royal family moved into Buckingham Palace. Since then, lesser royals have bedded down in Kensington Palace. Princess Diana lived here from her 1981 marriage to Prince Charles until her death in 1997. Today it's home to three of Charles' cousins and to employees of the royal family. The palace, while still functioning as a royal residence, also welcomes visitors with an impressive string of royal apartments and a few rooms of royal dresses. Enjoy a re-created royal tailor and dressmaker's workshop, the 17th-century splendor of the apartments of William and Mary, and the bed where Queen Victoria was born (fully clothed, it is said).

Cost, Hours, Location: £12.50, includes excellent audioguide, daily 10:00–18:00, until 17:00 in winter, last entry one hour before closing, a 10-min hike through Kensington Gardens from either Queensway or High Street Kensington Tube station. Toll tel. 0870-751-5170 or 0844-482-7777, www.hrp.org.uk.

Nearby: Garden enthusiasts enjoy popping into the secluded Sunken Garden, 50 yards from the exit. Consider afternoon tea at the nearby Orangery (see page 335), built as a greenhouse for Queen Anne in 1704.

Victoria Station—From underneath this station's iron-and-glass canopy, trains depart for the south of England and Gatwick Airport. While Victoria Station is famous and a major Tube stop, few tourists actually take trains from here—most just come to take in the exciting bustle. It's a fun place to just be a "rock in a river" teeming with commuters and services. The station is surrounded by big red buses and taxis, travel agencies, and lousy eateries. It's next to the main bus station (National Express) and the best inexpensive lodgings in town.

Westminster Cathedral—This, the largest Catholic church in England, just a block from Victoria Station, is striking, but not very historic or important to visit. Opened in 1903, it has a brick Neo-Byzantine flavor (surrounded by glassy office blocks). While it's definitely not Westminster Abbey, half the tourists wandering around inside seem to think it is. The highlight is the lift to the viewing gallery atop its 273-foot bell tower (£3 for the lift, tower open daily 9:30–12:30 & 13:00–17:00 in summer, Thu–Sat 9:00–17:00 in winter).

Cost, Hours, Location: Free entry, daily 7:00–19:00; 5-min walk from Victoria Station or take bus #11, #24, #148, #211, or #507 to museum's door; just off Victoria Street, Tube: Victoria; www.westminstercathedral.org.uk.

National Army Museum—This museum is not as awe-inspiring as the Imperial War Museum, but it's still fun, especially for kids into soldiers, armor, and guns. And while the Imperial War Museum is limited to wars of the 20th century, the National Army Museum tells the story of the British army from 1415 through the

Bosnian conflict and Iraq, with lots of Redcoat lore and a good look at Waterloo. Kids enjoy trying on a Cromwellian helmet, seeing the skeleton of Napoleon's horse, and peering out from a WWI trench through a working periscope.

Cost, Hours, Location: Free, daily 10:00–17:30, Royal Hospital Road, Chelsea, Tube: Sloane Square. Tel. 020/7730-0717 or 020/7881-2455, www.national-army-museum.ac.uk.

East London

A visit to the Docklands is easy to combine with an excursion to Greenwich; you can catch a boat (or the Tube) to Greenwich, then stop by Docklands on the way back in the afternoon, when it's especially lively at the end of the workday (see page 379 for details).

▲▲**The Docklands**—Survey the skyline or notice the emergence of an entire new Tube network, and it becomes clear that London is shifting east. This vibrant city center will become even more important in the near future, as it will host several events during the 2012 Olympics. The heart of this new London is the Docklands, filling the Isle of Dogs—a peninsula created by a hairpin bend in the Thames—with gleaming skyscrapers springing out of a futuristic, modern art–filled people zone below.

By the late 1700s, 13,000 ships a year were loaded and unloaded in London, congesting the Thames. In 1802 the world's largest-of-its-kind harbor was built here in the Docklands, organizing shipping for the capital of the empire upon which the sun never set. When Britannia ruled the waves, the Isle of Dogs hosted the world's leading harbor. But with the advent of container shipping in the 1960s, London's shipping industry moved to deep-water ports. The Docklands became a derelict and dangerous wasteland—the perfect place to host a new and vibrant economic center. Over the past few decades, Britain's new Information Age industries—banking, finance, publishing, and media—have vacated downtown London and set up shop here.

Those 1802 West India warehouses survive, but rather than trading sugar and rum, today they house the Museum of London Docklands (see below) and a row of happening restaurants. And where sailors once drank grog while stevedores unloaded cargo, today thousands of office workers populate a forest of skyscrapers, towering high above the remnants of the Industrial Age. If you simply stroll around, you'll find this one of the most exciting hours of free entertainment London has to offer. This is today's London—there's not a tourist in sight.

The Tube and Docklands Light Railway stations themselves are awe-inspiring. Explore sprawling underground malls and delightfully peaceful, green parks with pedestrian bridges looping over the now-tranquil canals. Though you can't get up the skyscrapers, the ground-floor levels are welcoming with fun art. Photographers can't help but catch jumbo jets gliding past gleaming towers, goofy pose-with-me statues, and trendy pubs filled with trendier young professionals. Jubilee Park is an oasis of green in this Manhattan of Britain.

The Canary Wharf Tower (with its pyramid cap), once the tallest in Europe, remains the tallest in the UK—for now. Like its little sister skyscrapers, owned by HSBC (Hong Kong Shanghai Banking Corporation) and Citigroup, it's filled with big banks, finance, and media companies. The stubby building just to one side, occupied by an American bank, is a painfully truthful metaphor.

This pedestrian-friendly district is well-served by signs. Follow them over the pedestrian bridge to the **Museum of London Docklands,** which tells the story of the world's leading 19th-century port (£5, daily 10:00–18:00, last entry 30 min before closing, West India Quay, Canary Wharf, tel. 020/7001-9844, www.museumindocklands.org.uk). Between the bridge and the museum is a line of fun, mod eateries (£10 main courses, huge variety of cuisines).

Getting There: Ride the Tube's Jubilee Line (just 15 min from Westminster, frequent departures) to its Canary Wharf stop, or take the Docklands Light Railway from Bank to Canary Wharf (this makes a good stop en route to or from Greenwich). At Canary Wharf, the Jubilee Line station and DLR station are a short walk apart.

Greater London

▲▲**Kew Gardens**—For a fine riverside park and a palatial greenhouse jungle to swing through, take the Tube or the boat to every botanist's favorite escape, Kew Gardens. While to most visitors the Royal Botanic Gardens of Kew are simply a delightful opportunity to wander among 33,000 different types of plants, to the hardworking organization that runs the gardens, it's a way to promote understanding and preservation of  the botanical diversity of our planet. The Kew Tube station drops you in an herbal little business community, a two-block walk from Victoria Gate (the main garden entrance). Pick up a map brochure and check at the gate for a monthly listing of best blooms.

Garden lovers could spend days exploring Kew's 300 acres. For a quick visit, spend a fragrant hour wandering through three buildings: the Palm House, a humid Victorian world of iron, glass, and tropical plants built in 1844; a Waterlily House that Monet would swim for; and the Princess of Wales Conservatory, a modern greenhouse with many different climate zones growing countless cacti, bug-munching carnivorous plants, and more. The latest addition to the gardens is the Rhizotron and

Xstrata Treetop Walkway, a 200-yard-long scenic steel walkway that puts you high in the canopy 60 feet above the ground.

Cost, Hours, Location: £13, discounted to £11 45 min before closing, kids under 17 free, £5 for Kew Palace only; April–Aug Mon–Fri 9:30–18:30, Sat–Sun 9:30–19:30; closes earlier Sept–March, last entry to gardens 30 min before closing, galleries and conservatories close at 17:30 in high season—earlier off-season; free 60-min walking tours daily at 11:00 and 14:00; £4 narrated floral 40-min hop-on, hop-off joyride on little tram departs on the hour from 11:00 from near Victoria Gate; Tube: Kew Gardens, boats run April–Oct between Kew Gardens and Westminster Pier—see page 40. Switchboard tel. 020/8332-5000, recorded info tel. 020/8332-5655, www.kew.org.

Nearby: For a sun-dappled lunch, walk 10 minutes from the Palm House to the Orangery (£6 hot meals, daily 10:00–17:30).

▲**Hampton Court Palace**—Fifteen miles up the Thames from downtown (£15 taxi ride from Kew Gardens) is the 500-year-old

palace of Henry VIII. Actually, it was the palace of his minister, Cardinal Wolsey. When Wolsey, a clever man, realized Henry VIII was experiencing a little palace envy, he gave the mansion to his king. The Tudor palace was also home to Elizabeth I and Charles I. Sections were updated by Christopher Wren for William and Mary. The stately palace stands overlooking the Thames and includes some impressive Tudor rooms, including a Great Hall with a magnificent hammer-beam ceiling. The industrial-strength Tudor kitchen was capable of keeping 600 schmoozing courtiers thoroughly—if not well—fed. The sculpted garden features a rare Tudor tennis court and a popular maze.

The palace, fully restored after a 1986 fire, tries hard to please, but it doesn't quite sparkle. From the information center in the main courtyard pick up audioguides for self-guided tours of various wings of the palace (free). The Tudor kitchens, Henry VIII's apartments, and the King's apartments are most interesting. The Georgian rooms are pretty dull. The maze in the nearby garden is a curiosity some find fun (maze free with palace ticket, otherwise £3.50).

Cost and Hours: The palace costs £14, or £38 for families, daily April–Oct 10:00–18:00, Nov–March 10:00–16:30, last entry one hour earlier. Toll tel. 0870-751-5175, recorded info toll tel. 0870-752-7777, www.hrp.org.uk.

Getting There: The train (2/hr, 30 min) from London's Waterloo station drops you across the river from the palace (just walk across the bridge). Note that there are often discounts available for people riding the train from London to the palace. Check online or at the ticket office at Waterloo station for the latest offers.

Consider arriving at or departing from the palace by boat (connections with London's Westminster Pier, see page 40); it's a relaxing and scenic three-hour cruise past two locks and a fun new/old riverside mix.

Royal Air Force Museum London—A hit with aviation enthusiasts, this huge aerodrome and airfield contain planes from World War II's Battle of Britain up through the Gulf War. You can climb inside some of the planes, try your luck in a cockpit, and fly with the Red Arrows in a flight simulator.

Cost, Hours, Location: Free, daily 10:00–18:00, last entry 30 min earlier, café, shop, parking, Grahame Park Way, Tube: Colindale—top of Northern Line Edgware branch. Tel. 020/8205-2266, www.rafmuseum.org.uk.

WESTMINSTER WALK

From Big Ben to Trafalgar Square

London is the L.A., D.C., and N.Y.C. of Britain. This walk starts with London's "star" attraction, continues to its "Capitol," passes its "White House," and ends at its "Times Square"...all in about an hour.

Just about every visitor to London strolls along historic Whitehall from Big Ben to Trafalgar Square. This quick nine-stop walk gives meaning to that touristy ramble. Under London's modern traffic and big-city bustle lie 2,000 fascinating years of history. You'll get a whirlwind tour as well as a practical orientation to London.

Orientation

Length of This Tour: Allow one hour for a leisurely walk, but figure on two or three hours if you drop by the Churchill Museum and Cabinet War Rooms, and the Banqueting House. (Other nearby sights include the Houses of Parliament, Westminster Abbey, National Gallery, National Portrait Gallery, and St. Martin-in-the-Fields.)

Getting There: Take the Tube to Westminster, then take the Westminster Pier exit. The walk ends at Trafalgar Square (nearest Tube stop: Charing Cross).

WCs: You'll find several WCs along this walk, at Westminster Pier (50p), at the intersection of Bridge Street and Whitehall (underground, 50p), and at Trafalgar Square (the National Gallery and St. Martin-in-the-Fields both have free WCs).

Churchill Museum and Cabinet War Rooms: £13, daily 9:30–18:00, last entry one hour before closing.

Banqueting House: £4.80 includes audioguide, Mon–Sat 10:00–17:00, closed Sun, last entry at 16:30, may close for government functions, aristocratic WC, immediately across Whitehall from the Horse Guards.

The Walk Begins

• *Start halfway across Westminster Bridge.*

❶ On Westminster Bridge
Views of Big Ben and Parliament

• *First look upstream, toward the Parliament.*

Ding dong ding dong. Dong ding ding dong. Yes, indeed, you are in London. **Big Ben** is actually "not the clock, not the tower, but the bell that tolls the hour." However, since the 13-ton bell is not visible, everyone just calls the whole works Big Ben. Named for a fat bureaucrat, Ben is scarcely older than my great-grandmother, but it has quickly become the city's symbol. The tower is 320 feet high, and the clock faces are 23 feet across. The 13-foot-long minute hand sweeps the length of your body every five minutes. For fun, call home from a pay phone near Big Ben at about three minutes before the hour, to let your loved one hear the bell ring. You'll find four red phone booths lining the north side of Parliament Square (along Great George Street).

Big Ben hangs out in the north tower of a long building, the Houses of Parliament, stretching along the Thames. Britain is ruled from this building, which for five centuries was the home of kings and queens. Then, as democracy was foisted on tyrants, a parliament of nobles was allowed to meet in some of the rooms. Soon, commoners were elected to office, the neighborhood was shot, and the royalty moved to Buckingham Palace. While most of the current building looks medieval with its prickly flamboyant spires, it was actually built after a fire gutted the old Westminster Palace in 1834.

Today, the House of Commons, which is more powerful than the Queen and prime minister combined, meets in one end of the building. The rubber-stamp House of Lords grumbles and snoozes in the other end of this 1,000-room complex, and provides a tempering effect on extreme governmental changes. The two houses are very much separate: Notice the riverside tea terraces with the color-coded awnings—royal red for lords, common green for commoners. Alluding to the traditional leanings of the two chambers,

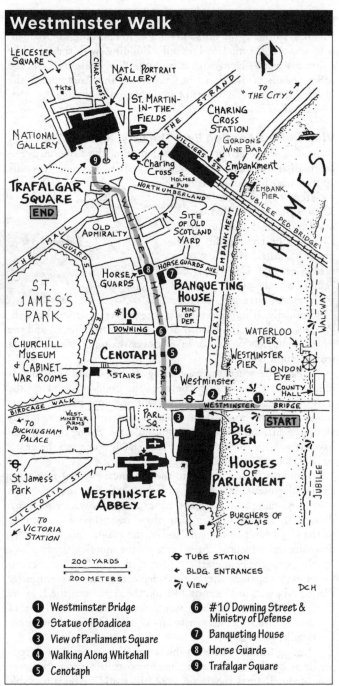

Westminster Walk

LEICESTER SQUARE

+tkts

CHAR. CROSS

NAT'L PORTRAIT GALLERY

ST. MARTIN-IN-THE-FIELDS

THE STRAND

TO "THE CITY"

CHARING CROSS STATION

GORDON'S WINE BAR

VILLIERS ST.

Embankment

NATIONAL GALLERY

9

Charing Cross

S. HOLMES PUB

NORTHUMBERLAND

EMBANK. JUBILEE PIER

EMBANKMENT

THAMES

JUBILEE PED BRIDGE

TRAFALGAR SQUARE

END

OLD ADMIRALTY

SITE OF OLD SCOTLAND YARD

THE MALL

GUARDS

THE

ROAD

ST. JAMES'S PARK

8 HORSE GUARDS AVE

HORSE GUARDS

7

BANQUETING HOUSE

MIN. OF DEF.

#10 DOWNING

6

WHITEHALL

WATERLOO PIER

CHURCHILL MUSEUM & CABINET WAR ROOMS

CENOTAPH

STAIRS

5

4

PARL. ST.

VICTORIA

WESTMINSTER PIER

LONDON EYE

COUNTY HALL

Westminster

BIRDCAGE WALK

WESTMINSTER ARMS PUB

2

1

WESTMINSTER BRIDGE

START

TO BUCKINGHAM PALACE

PARL. SQ.

3

BIG BEN

St James's Park

VICTORIA ST.

WESTMINSTER ABBEY

HOUSES OF PARLIAMENT

JUBILEE

TO VICTORIA STATION

BURGHERS OF CALAIS

200 YARDS
200 METERS

⊖ TUBE STATION
← BLDG. ENTRANCES
⃝ VIEW

DCH

1 Westminster Bridge
2 Statue of Boadicea
3 View of Parliament Square
4 Walking Along Whitehall
5 Cenotaph

6 #10 Downing Street & Ministry of Defense
7 Banqueting House
8 Horse Guards
9 Trafalgar Square

WESTMINSTER WALK

locals say, "Green for go...red for stop." If a flag is flying from the Victoria Tower, at the far south end of the building, Parliament is in session. The modern Portcullis Building (with the tube-like chimneys), across Bridge Street from Big Ben, holds offices for the 659 members of the House of Commons. They commute to the Houses of Parliament by way of an underground passage.

• *Now look north (downstream).*

Views of the London Eye, The City, and the Thames

Built in 2000 to celebrate the millennium, the London Eye—originally nicknamed "the London Eyesore," but now generally appreciated by locals—stands 443 feet tall. It slowly spins 32 capsules, each filled with a maximum of 25 visitors, up to London's best viewpoint (with up to 25 miles' visibility on a rare clear day). Call the Eye a "Ferris wheel," and Londoners will set you straight, saying,

"Technically, it's an *observation* wheel." Aside from Big Ben, Parliament, St. Paul's Cathedral (not visible from here), and the wheel itself, London's skyline is not overwhelming; it's a city that wows from within.

Next to the wheel sprawls the huge former County Hall building, now a hotel and tourist complex. The London Eye marks the start of the Jubilee Walkway, a pleasant one-hour riverside promenade along the South Bank of the Thames, through London's vibrant, gentrified new arts-and-cultural zone. Along the way, you have views across the river of St. Paul's stately dome and the financial district, called The City.

London's history is tied to the **Thames,** the 210-mile river linking the interior of England with the North Sea. The city got its start in Roman times as a trade center along this watery highway. As recently as a century ago, large ships made their way upstream to the city center to unload. Today, the major port is 25 miles downstream and tourist cruise boats ply the waters.

Look for the **boat piers** on either bank of the Thames. Several tour-boat companies offer regular departures from Westminster Pier (on the left) or Waterloo Pier (on the right, near the London Eye). This is an efficient, scenic way to get from here to the Tower of London or Greenwich (downstream) or Kew Gardens (upstream). For details, see page 39.

Lining the river, beneath the lampposts, are little green copper **lions' heads** with rings for tying up boats. Before the construction of the Thames Barrier in 1982 (the world's largest movable flood barrier, downstream near Greenwich), high tides from the nearby North Sea made floods a recurring London problem. The police kept an eye on these lions: "When the lions drink, the city's at risk."

Until 1750, only London Bridge crossed the Thames. Then a bridge was built here. Early in the morning of September 3, 1802, William Wordsworth stood where you're standing and described what he saw:

> *This City now doth, like a garment, wear*
> *The beauty of the morning; silent, bare,*
> *Ships, towers, domes, theatres, and temples lie*
> *Open unto the fields, and to the sky;*
> *All bright and glittering in the smokeless air.*

• *Near Westminster Pier is a big statue of a lady on a chariot (nicknamed "the first woman driver"...no reins).*

❷ Statue of Boadicea, Queen of the Iceni

Riding in her two-horse chariot, daughters by her side, this Celtic Xena leads her people against Roman invaders. Julius

Caesar was the first Roman to cross the Channel, but even he was weirded out by the island's strange inhabitants, who worshipped trees, sacrificed virgins, and went to war painted blue. Later, Romans subdued and civilized them, building roads and making this spot on the Thames—"Londinium"—into a major urban center.

But Boadicea refused to be Romanized. In A.D. 60, after Roman soldiers raped her daughters, she rallied her people and "liberated" London, massacring its 60,000 Romanized citizens. However, the brief revolt was snuffed out, and she and her family took poison rather than surrender.

• *There's a civilized public toilet down the stairs behind Boadicea. Cross the street to just under Big Ben and continue one block inland to the busy intersection of Parliament Square.*

❸ View of Parliament Square

To your left are the sandstone-hued **Houses of Parliament.** If Parliament is in session, the entrance (midway down the building) is lined with tourists, enlivened by political demonstrations, and staked out by camera crews interviewing Members of Parliament (MPs) for the evening news. Only the core part, Westminster

Hall, survives from the circa-1090s original. While the Houses of Parliament are commonly described as "Neo-Gothic" (even in this book), this uniquely English style is more specifically called Neo-Perpendicular Gothic. For a peek at genuine Perpendicular Gothic (the fanciest and final stage of that style), simply look across the street at the section of Westminster Abbey closest to the Houses of Parliament—it dates from 1484.

Kitty-corner across the square, the two white towers of **Westminster Abbey** rise above the trees. The broad boulevard of Whitehall (here called Parliament Street) stretches to your right up to Trafalgar Square.

This is the heart of what was once a suburb of London—the medieval City of Westminster.

Like Buda and Pest (later Budapest), London is two cities that grew into one. The City of London, centered near St. Paul's Cathedral and the Tower of London, was the place to live. But King Edward the Confessor decided to build a church (minster) and monastery (abbey) here, west of the city walls—hence Westminster. And to oversee its construction, he moved his court to this spot and built a palace, which gradually evolved into a meeting place for debating public policy. To this day, the Houses of Parliament are known to Brits as the "Palace of Westminster."

Across from Parliament, the cute little church with the blue sundials, snuggling under the Abbey "like a baby lamb under a ewe," is **St. Margaret's Church.** Since 1480, this has been *the* place for politicians' weddings, including Winston and Clementine Churchill.

Parliament Square, the expanse of green between Westminster Abbey and Big Ben, is filled with statues of famous Brits. The statue of **Winston Churchill,** the man who saved Britain from Hitler, shows him in the military overcoat he was fond of wearing. According to tour guides, the statue has a current of electricity running through it to honor Churchill's wish that if a statue were made of him, his head wouldn't be soiled by pigeons.

In 1868, the world's first traffic light was installed on the corner where Whitehall now spills double-decker buses into the square. Another reminder of a bygone era is the little yellow "Taxi" lantern atop the fence on the street corner closest to Parliament. In pre-mobile phone days, when an MP needed a taxi, this lit up to hail one.

• Consider touring Westminster Abbey (✪ see the Westminster Abbey Tour chapter). Otherwise, turn right (north), walk away from the

WESTMINSTER WALK

Houses of Parliament and the Abbey, and continue up Parliament Street, which becomes Whitehall.

❹ Walking Along Whitehall

Today, Whitehall is choked with traffic, but imagine the effect this broad street must have had on out-of-towners a century ago. In your horse-drawn carriage, you'd clop along a tree-lined boulevard past well-dressed lords and ladies, dodging street urchins. Gazing left, then right, you'd try to take it all in, your eyes dazzled by the bone-white walls of this man-made marble canyon.

Whitehall is now the most important street in Britain, lined with the ministries of finance, treasury, and so on. You may see limos and camera crews as an important dignitary enters or exits. Political demonstrators wave signs and chant slogans—sometimes about issues foreign to most Americans (Britain's former colonies still resent the empire's continuing influence), and sometimes about issues very familiar to us. (In recent years, the war in Iraq has been the catalyst for protest marches here.) Notice the security measures. Iron grates seal off the concrete ditches between the buildings and sidewalks for protection against explosives. The city has been on "orange alert" since long before September 2001, but Londoners refuse to be terrorized, as shown by their determination to continue with life as normal after the July 2005 Tube and bus bombings.

The black, ornamental arrowheads topping the iron fences were once colorfully painted. In 1861, Queen Victoria ordered them all painted black when her beloved Prince Albert ("the only one who called her Vickie") died. Possibly the world's most determined mourner, Victoria wore black for the standard two years of mourning—and tacked on 38 more.

• *Continue toward the tall, square, concrete monument in the middle of the road. On your right is a colorful pub, the Red Lion. Across the street, a 700-foot detour down King Charles Street leads to the Churchill Museum and Cabinet War Rooms, the underground bunker of 27 rooms that was the nerve center of Britain's campaign against Hitler (see page 49 for details).*

❺ Cenotaph

This big, white stone monument (in the middle of the boulevard) honors those who died in the two events that most shaped modern Britain—World Wars I and II. The monumental devastation of these wars helped turn a colonial superpower into a cultural colony of an American superpower.

The actual cenotaph is the slab that sits atop the pillar—a tomb. You'll notice no religious symbols on this memorial. The dead honored here came from many creeds and all corners of

Britain's empire. It looks lost in a sea of noisy cars, but on each Remembrance Sunday (closest to November 11), Whitehall is closed off to traffic, the royal family fills the balcony overhead in the foreign ministry, and a memorial service is held around the cenotaph.

It's hard for an American to understand the impact of the Great War (World War I) on Europe. It's said that if the roughly one million WWI dead from the British Empire were to march four abreast past the cenotaph, the sad parade would last for seven days.

Eternally pondering the cenotaph is an equestrian statue up the street. Field Marshal Douglas Haig, commander-in-chief of the British army from 1916 to 1918, was responsible for ordering so many brave and not-so-brave British boys out of the trenches and onto the killing fields of World War I.

In 2005, a memorial honoring the women who fought and died in World War II was constructed just beyond the cenotaph. Its empty uniforms evoke the often-overlooked sacrifices of Britain's female war heroes.

• *Just past the cenotaph, on the other (west) side of Whitehall, is an iron security gate guarding the entrance to Downing Street.*

❻ #10 Downing Street and the Ministry of Defense

Britain's version of the White House is where the prime minister and his family live, at #10 (in the black-brick building 300 feet

down the blocked-off street, on the right).

Like the White House's Rose Garden, the black door marked #10 is a highly symbolic point of power, popular for photo ops to mark big occasions. This is where suffragettes protested in the early 20th century, where Neville Chamberlain showed off his regrettable peace treaty with Hitler, and where Winston Churchill made famous the V-for-Victory sign. In 2008, new Prime Minister Gordon Brown and US President George W. Bush posed here to bolster US–UK solidarity, and in 2009, the new US President Barack Obama huddled here with Brown to consider solutions to the economic downturn.

Prime Minister Gordon Brown

Gordon Brown (b. 1951) succeeded Tony Blair as prime minister in June of 2007. As is the practice in the UK, he was not elected by popular vote but appointed by party leaders. Brown lives at #10 Downing Street with his wife, Sarah, and their two young sons, John and Fraser.

Brown, who hails from a humble fishing village in Scotland, is the yin to Tony Blair's yang. Unlike the gregarious Blair, Brown comes across as a staid and gruff policy wonk. While Blair was enjoying a successful decade at #10, Brown and his family lived next door at #11 as finance minister.

The British media lampoon Brown mercilessly as gloomy, plodding, and boring, with shifty eyes (actually, from a rugby accident) and Darth Vader breathing. His wife refuses to do media interviews, making the couple less approachable than showman Tony and his lawyer-wife Cherie.

As prime minister, Brown heads the Labour Party, which controls the most seats in Parliament. The main opposition is the Conservative Party, or "Tories." (A third party, the Liberals, often sides with Labour.) Blair had tried to bridge the gap between Labour and Conservatives, but his popularity was undermined by his decision to join the US invasion of Iraq. Brown has refused to disavow Britain's Iraq involvement, further damaging Labour's image. As Britain's financial woes continue, it's uncertain how long Brown will hold power. The next general election must be held by June of 2010.

It looks modest, but #10's entryway does open up into fairly impressive digs—the prime minister's offices (downstairs), his residence (upstairs), and two large formal dining rooms. The PM's staff has offices here, and the cabinet meets here on Tuesday mornings. This is where foreign dignitaries come for official government dinners, where the prime minister receives honored school kids and victorious soccer teams, and where he gives monthly addresses to the nation. Next door, at #11, the chancellor of the exchequer (finance minister) lives with his family, and #12 houses the PM's press office.

This has been the traditional home of the prime minister since the position was created in the early 18th century. But even before that, the neighborhood (if not the building itself) was a center of power, where Edward the Confessor and Henry VIII had palaces. The facade is, frankly, quite cheap, having been built as part of a middle-class cul-de-sac of homes by American-born George Downing in the 1680s. When the first PM moved in, the humble interior was combined with a mansion in back. During a major upgrade in the 1950s, they discovered that the facade's black bricks were actually yellow—but had been stained by centuries of Industrial Age soot. To keep with tradition, they now paint the bricks black.

The guarded metal gates were installed in 1989 to protect against Irish terrorists. Even so, #10 was hit and partly damaged in 1991 by an Irish Republican Army mortar launched from a van. These days, there's typically not much to see unless a VIP happens to drive up. Then the bobbies snap to and check credentials, the gates open, the car is inspected for bombs, the traffic barrier midway down the street drops into its bat cave, the car drives in, and... the bobbies go back to mugging for the tourists.

The huge building across Whitehall from Downing Street is the **Ministry of Defense** (MOD), the "British Pentagon." This bleak place looks like a Ministry of Defense should. In front are statues of illustrious defenders of Britain. "Monty" is **Field Marshal Bernard Law Montgomery** of World War II, who beat the Nazis in North Africa (defeating Erwin "the Desert Fox" Rommel at El Alamein), giving the Allies a jumping-off point to retake Europe. Along with Churchill, Monty breathed confidence back into a demoralized British army, persuading them they could ultimately beat Hitler.

You may be enjoying the shade of London's **plane trees.** They do well in polluted London: roots that work well in clay, waxy leaves that self-clean in the rain, and bark that sheds and regenerates so the pollution doesn't get into their vascular systems.

• *At the equestrian statue, you'll be flanked by the Welsh and Scottish government offices. At the corner (same side as the Ministry of Defense), you'll find the Banqueting House.*

❼ Banqueting House

This two-story building in the Georgian style (the English version of Neoclassical) is just about all that remains of what was once the

biggest palace in Europe—Whitehall Palace, stretching from Trafalgar Square to Big Ben. Henry VIII started it when he moved out of the Palace of Westminster (now the Parliament) and into the residence of the archbishop of York. Queen Elizabeth I and other monarchs added on as England's worldwide prestige grew. Finally, in 1698, a roaring fire destroyed everything at Whitehall except the name and the Banqueting House.

The monarchs held their parties and feasts in the Banqueting

House's grand ballroom on the first floor. At 112 feet wide by 56 feet tall and 56 feet deep, the Banqueting House is a perfect double cube. Today, the exterior of Greek-style columns and pediments looks rather ho-hum, much like every other white, marble, Georgian building in London. But in 1620, it was the first—a highly influential building by architect Inigo Jones that sparked London's distinct Georgian look. (For details on visiting the Banqueting House, see page 50).

On January 30, 1649, a man dressed in black appeared at one of the Banqueting House's first-floor windows and looked out at a huge crowd that surrounded the building. He stepped out the window and onto a wooden platform. It was King Charles I. He gave a short speech to the crowd, framed by the magnificent backdrop of the Banqueting House. His final word was "Remember." Then he knelt and laid his neck on a block as another man in black approached. It was the executioner—who cut off the King's head.

Plop—the concept of divine monarchy in Britain was decapitated. But there would still be kings after Oliver Cromwell, the Protestant anti-monarchist who brought about Charles I's death and then became England's leader. Soon after, the royalty was restored, and Charles' son, Charles II, got his revenge here in the Banqueting Hall...by living well. His elaborate parties under the chandeliers celebrated the Restoration of the monarchy. But, from then on, every king knew that he ruled by the grace of Parliament.

Charles I is remembered today with a statue at one end of Whitehall (in Trafalgar Square at the base of the tall column), while his killer, Oliver Cromwell, is given equal time with a statue at the other end (at the Houses of Parliament).

• *Just up Whitehall on the left (west) side is the building known as Horse Guards, which is guarded by traditionally dressed soldiers who are also called Horse Guards.*

❽ Horse Guards

For 200 years, soldiers in cavalry uniforms have guarded this arched entrance along Whitehall that leads to Buckingham Palace and its predecessor as royal residence, St. James's Palace.

Two different squads alternate, so depending on the day you visit, you'll see soldiers in either red coats with white plumes in their helmets (the Life Guards), or blue coats with red plumes (the Blues and Royals). Together, they constitute the Queen's personal bodyguard. Besides their ceremonial duties here in old-time uniforms, these elite troops have fought in Iraq and Afghanistan. Both Prince William and Prince Harry have served in the Blues and Royals.

The Horse Guards building was the headquarters of the British army from the time of the American Revolution until the Ministry of Defense was created in World War II. Back when this archway was the only access point to The Mall (the street leading to Buckingham Palace), it was a security checkpoint. Anyone on horseback had to dismount before passing through. Today, by tradition, you must dismount your bicycle, Vespa, or Segway and walk it through (Changing of the Guard Mon–Sat at 11:00, Sun at 10:00, dismounting ceremony daily at 16:00). The Horse Guards Museum offers a glimpse at the stables and a collection of uniforms and weapons.

• *Continue up Whitehall, passing the* **Old Admiralty** *(#26), headquarters of the British navy that once ruled the waves. Across the street, behind the old Clarence Pub, stood the original Scotland Yard, headquarters of London's crack police force in the days of Sherlock Holmes. Finally, Whitehall opens up into the grand, noisy, traffic-filled...*

❾ Trafalgar Square

London's Times Square bustles around the world's biggest Corinthian column, where **Admiral Horatio Nelson** stands 170 feet tall, looking over London in the direction of one of the greatest naval battles in history. Nelson saved England at a time as dark as World War II. In 1805, Napoleon was poised on the other side of the Channel, threatening to invade England. Meanwhile, more than 900 miles away, the one-armed, one-eyed, and one-minded Lord Nelson attacked the French fleet off the coast of Spain at Trafalgar. The French were routed, Britannia ruled the waves,

Trafalgar Square

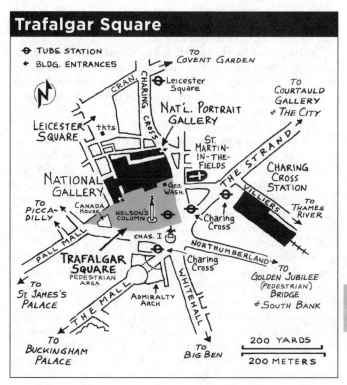

- TUBE STATION
- BLDG. ENTRANCES

TO COVENT GARDEN

CRAN.

CHARING CROSS

Leicester Square

NAT'L. PORTRAIT GALLERY

LEICESTER SQUARE   tkts

TO COURTAULD GALLERY & THE CITY

ST. MARTIN-IN-THE-FIELDS

THE STRAND

CHARING CROSS STATION

NATIONAL GALLERY

VILLIERS

GEO. WASH.

TO PICCADILLY

CANADA HOUSE

NELSON'S COLUMN

Charing Cross

TO THAMES RIVER

CHAS. I

NORTHUMBERLAND

PALL MALL

TRAFALGAR SQUARE PEDESTRIAN AREA

Charing Cross

TO ST. JAMES'S PALACE

THE MALL

ADMIRALTY ARCH

WHITEHALL

TO GOLDEN JUBILEE (PEDESTRIAN) BRIDGE & SOUTH BANK

TO BUCKINGHAM PALACE

TO BIG BEN

200 YARDS

200 METERS

WESTMINSTER WALK

and the once-invincible French army was slowly worn down, then defeated at Waterloo. Nelson, while victorious, was shot by a sniper in the battle. He died, gasping, "Thank God, I have done my duty."

At the top of Trafalgar Square (north) sits the domed **National Gallery** with its grand staircase, and, to the right, the steeple of **St. Martin-in-the-Fields,** built in 1722, inspiring the steeple-over-the-entrance style of many town churches in New England (free lunch concerts—see page 357).

At the base of Nelson's column are bronze reliefs cast from melted-down enemy cannons, and four huggable lions dying to

have their photo taken with you. In front of the column, Charles I sits on horseback, with his head still on his shoulders. In the pavement just behind the statue is a plaque marking the center of London, from which all distances are measured. Of the many statues that dot the square, the empty

pedestal on the northwest corner (the "fourth plinth") is periodically topped with contemporary art.

Trafalgar Square is indeed the center of modern London,
connecting Westminster, The City, and the West End. A recent
remodeling of the square has rerouted some car traffic, helping
reclaim the area for London's citizens. Spin clockwise 360 degrees
and survey the city:

To the south (down Whitehall) is the center of government,
Westminster. Looking southwest, down the broad boulevard
called The Mall, you see Buckingham Palace in the distance.
(Down Pall Mall is St. James's Palace, where Prince Charles lives
when in London.) A few blocks northwest of Trafalgar Square
is Piccadilly Circus. Directly north (a block behind the National
Gallery) sits Leicester Square, the jumping-off point for Soho,
Covent Garden, and the West End theater district (**۞** see the West
End Walk chapter).

The boulevard called the Strand takes you past Charing Cross
Station, then eastward to The City, the original walled town of
London and today's financial center. In medieval times, when peo-
ple from The City met with the Westminster government, it was
here. And finally, Northumberland Street leads southeast to the
Golden Jubilee pedestrian bridge over the Thames. Along the way,
you'll pass the Sherlock Holmes Pub (just off Northumberland
Street, on Craven Street), housed in Sir Arthur Conan Doyle's
favorite watering hole, with an upstairs replica of 221-B Baker
Street.

Soak it in. You're smack-dab in the center of London, a
thriving city atop two millennia of history.

WESTMINSTER ABBEY TOUR

Westminster Abbey is the greatest church in the English-speaking world, where the nation's kings and queens have been crowned and buried since 1066. The histories of Westminster Abbey and England are almost the same. A thousand years of English history—3,000 tombs, the remains of 29 kings and queens, and hundreds of memorials to poets, politicians, and warriors—lie within its stained-glass splendor and under its stone slabs.

Orientation

Cost: £15, £30 family ticket (for 3 people), both include fine audioguide and admission to the cloisters and Abbey Museum. Praying is free, thank God.

Worshippers: Although the Abbey is wise to tourists who fold their hands reverently so they can get in for free, serious worshippers are welcome to attend any number of services without paying. You'll sit in the nave, and while you won't get to look at the many historic tombs, you will have the chance to experience this great church in action (four services Mon–Fri—7:30 morning prayer, 8:00 Holy Communion, 12:30 Holy Communion, 17:00 evensong; Sat evensong at 15:00; full day of services on Sun).

Hours: Abbey—Mon–Fri 9:30–16:30, Sat 9:30–14:30, last entry one hour before closing, closed Sun to sightseers but open for services; Abbey Museum—daily 10:30–16:00; cloisters—daily 8:00–18:00, free access to cloisters through Dean Court (near west entrance). Special events can shut down all or part of the Abbey.

Crowd Control: The main entrance, on the Parliament Square side, often has a sizable line. Visit early, during lunch, or late to avoid tourist hordes. Midmornings are most crowded, while weekdays after 14:30 are less congested; come then and stay for the 17:00 evensong (but note that on Wed the service may be spoken; for more info, see "Music," below).

Getting There: Near Big Ben and the Houses of Parliament (Tube: Westminster or St. James's Park).

Information: Because events and services can shut out sightseers, call ahead to confirm that the Abbey is open, and ask about the schedule for guided tours, concerts, or services, depending on your interest (tel. 020/7222-5152 or 020/7654-4834, www.westminster-abbey.org). If you have questions about the cathedral, ask a marshal in red, or any of the green-cloaked volunteer vergers (who also lead tours—see below).

Music: Evensong, a stirring experience in a nearly empty church, is Mon–Fri at 17:00, and Sat–Sun at 15:00. On Wed the evensong may be spoken (without music). Free organ recitals are often held Sun at 17:45 (30 min, look for posted signs with schedules).

Tours: The included **audioguide** is excellent. If you take advantage of it, you'll find the steep admission to be a much better value. To add to the experience, you can take an entertaining **guided tour** from a verger—the church equivalent of a museum docent (£3, see schedule just inside entry, up to 5/day in summer, 4/day in winter, 90 min).

Length of This Tour: Allow 90 minutes.

Photography: Photos are prohibited.

WCs: The nearest public WCs (50p) are in front of Methodist Central Hall, the domed building across the street from the Abbey's west entrance.

Cuisine Art: In good weather, there are sandwich-soup-and-drink kiosks in the cloister courtyard. Or find reasonably priced cafeteria-style lunches in the basement of Methodist Central Hall (Wesley's Café, Mon–Fri 8:00–16:00, good free WC). The Westminster Arms pub (£9 fish and chips, food served daily 12:00–20:00, eat downstairs) is near Methodist Central Hall on Storey's Gate. Picnickers can find benches at the nearby Jewel Tower, a half-block south of the Abbey.

Starring: Edwards, Elizabeths, Henrys, Annes, Marys, and poets.

The Tour Begins

You'll have no choice but to follow the steady flow of tourists circling clockwise through the church—in through the north entrance, behind the altar, into Poets' Corner in the south transept, detouring through the cloisters, and, finally, back out through the

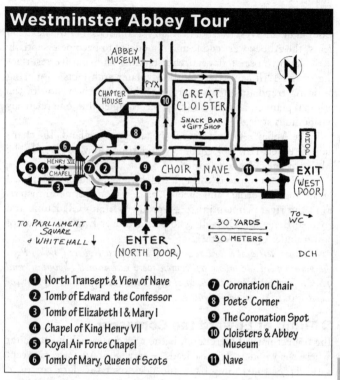

Westminster Abbey Tour

❶ North Transept & View of Nave
❷ Tomb of Edward the Confessor
❸ Tomb of Elizabeth I & Mary I
❹ Chapel of King Henry VII
❺ Royal Air Force Chapel
❻ Tomb of Mary, Queen of Scots
❼ Coronation Chair
❽ Poets' Corner
❾ The Coronation Spot
❿ Cloisters & Abbey Museum
⓫ Nave

west end of the nave. It's all one-way, and the crowds can be a real crush. Here are the Abbey's top 10 (plus one) stops.

• *Walk straight in, entering the north transept. Pick up the map flier that locates the most illustrious tombs, and belly up to the barricade in the center of the church.*

❶ North Transept and View of Nave

You're standing at the center of a cross-shaped church. The main altar (with cross and candlesticks) sits on the platform up the five stairs in front of you. To the right stretches the long, high-ceilinged nave. Nestled in the nave is the elaborately carved wooden seating of the choir (or "quire"), where monks once held intimate services and where, today, the Abbey boys' choir sings the evensong.

Lean over the rail and look down the long and narrow center aisle of the church. Lined with the praying hands of the Gothic arches, glowing with light from the stained glass, it's clear that this is more than a museum. With saints in stained glass, heroes in carved stone, and the bodies of England's greatest citizens under the floor stones, Westminster Abbey is the religious heart of England.

The Abbey was built in 1065. Its name, Westminster, means Church in the West (west of St. Paul's Cathedral). For the next 250 years, the Abbey was redone and remodeled to become essentially the church you see today, notwithstanding an extensive resurfacing in the 19th century. Thankfully, later architects—ignoring building trends of their generation—honored the vision of the original planner, and the building was completed in one relatively harmonious style.

The Abbey's 10-story nave is the tallest in England. The chandeliers, 10 feet tall, look small in comparison (16 were given to the Abbey by the Guinness family).

The north transept (through which you entered) is nicknamed "Statesmen's Corner" and specializes in famous prime ministers. Find the rival prime ministers—proud William Gladstone and goateed Benjamin Disraeli, who presided over England's peak of power under Queen Victoria.

• *Now turn left and follow the crowd. Walk past Robert ("Bob") Peel, the prime minister whose policemen were nicknamed "bobbies," and stroll a few yards into the land of dead kings and queens. Stop at the wooden staircase on your right.*

❷ Tomb of Edward the Confessor

The holiest part of the church is the raised area behind the altar (where the wooden staircase leads—sorry, no tourist access except with verger tour). Step back and peek over the dark coffin of Edward I to see the tippy-top of the green-and-gold wedding-cake tomb of King Edward the Confessor—the man who built Westminster Abbey.

God had told pious Edward to visit St. Peter's Basilica in Rome. But with the Normans thinking conquest, it was too dangerous for him to leave England. Instead, he built this grand church and dedicated it to St. Peter. It was finished just in time to bury Edward and to crown his foreign successor, William the Conqueror, in 1066. After Edward's death, people prayed at his tomb and, after getting fine results, Pope Alexander III canonized him. This elevated, central tomb—which lost some of its luster when Henry VIII melted down the gold coffin-case—is surrounded by the tombs of eight kings and queens.

• *Continue on. At the top of the stone staircase, veer left into the private burial chapel of Queen Elizabeth I.*

❸ Tomb of Queen Elizabeth I and Mary I

Although there's only one effigy on the tomb (Elizabeth's), there are actually two queens buried beneath it, both daughters of Henry VIII (by different mothers). Bloody Mary—meek, pious, sickly, and Catholic—enforced Catholicism during her short reign

(1553–1558) by burning "heretics" at the stake.

Elizabeth—strong, clever, and Protestant—steered England on an Anglican course. She holds a royal orb symbolizing that she's queen of the whole globe. When 26-year-old Elizabeth was crowned in the Abbey, her right to rule was questioned (especially by her Catholic subjects) because she was the bastard seed of Henry VIII's unsanctioned marriage to Anne Boleyn. But Elizabeth's long reign (1559–1603) was one of the greatest in English history, a time when England ruled the seas and Shakespeare explored human emotions. When she died, thousands turned out for her funeral in the Abbey. Elizabeth's face, modeled after her death mask, is considered a very accurate take on this hook-nosed, imperious "Virgin Queen."

The two half-sisters disliked each other in life—Mary even had Elizabeth locked up in the Tower of London for a short time. Now they lie side by side for eternity—with a prayer for Christians of all persuasions to live together peacefully.

• *Continue into the ornate, flag-draped room behind the main altar.*

❹ Chapel of King Henry VII (a.k.a. the Lady Chapel)

The light from the stained-glass windows; the colorful banners overhead; and the elaborate tracery in stone, wood, and glass give this room the festive air of a medieval tournament. The prestigious Knights of the Bath meet here, under the magnificent ceiling studded with gold pendants. The ceiling—of carved stone, not plaster (1519)—is the finest English Perpendicular Gothic and fan vaulting you'll see (unless you're going to King's College Chapel in Cambridge). The ceiling was sculpted on the floor in pieces, then jigsaw-puzzled into place. It capped the Gothic period and signaled the vitality of the coming Renaissance.

The knights sit in the wooden stalls with their coats of arms on the back, churches on their heads, their banner flying above, and the graves of dozens of kings beneath their feet. When the Queen worships here, she sits in the southwest corner chair under the carved wooden throne with the lion crown.

Behind the small altar is an iron cage housing tombs of the old warrior Henry VII of Lancaster and his wife, Elizabeth of York. Their love and marriage finally settled the Wars of the Roses between the two clans. The combined red-and-white rose symbol decorates the top band of the ironwork. Henry VII, the first

Tudor king, was the father of Henry VIII and the grandfather of Elizabeth I. This exuberant chapel heralds a new optimistic, post-war era as England prepares to step onto the world stage.

• *Go to the far end of the chapel and stand at the banister in front of the modern set of stained-glass windows.*

❺ Royal Air Force Chapel

Saints in robes and halos mingle with pilots in parachutes and bomber jackets. This tribute to WWII flyers is for those who earned their angel wings in the Battle of Britain (July–Oct 1940). Hitler's air force ruled the skies in the early days of the war, bombing at will, and threatening to snuff Britain out without a fight. But while determined Londoners hunkered down underground, British pilots in their Spitfires took advantage of newly invented radar to get the jump on the more powerful Luftwaffe. These were the fighters about whom Churchill said, "Never...was so much owed by so many to so few."

The Abbey survived the Battle and the Blitz, but this window did not. As a memorial, a bit of bomb damage has been preserved—the little glassed-over hole in the wall below the windows in the lower left-hand corner. The book of remembrances lists each of the 1,497 airmen (including one American) who died in the Battle of Britain.

You're standing on the grave of Oliver Cromwell, leader of the rebel forces in England's Civil War. Or, rather, Cromwell was buried here from 1658 to 1661. Then his corpse was exhumed, hanged, drawn, quartered, and decapitated, and the head displayed on a stake as a warning to anarchists.

• *Exit the Chapel of Henry VII. Turn left into a side chapel with the tomb (the central one of three in the chapel).*

❻ Tomb of Mary, Queen of Scots

Historians get dewy-eyed over the fate of Mary, Queen of Scots (1542–1587). The beautiful, French-educated queen was held under house arrest for 19 years by Queen Elizabeth I, who considered her a threat to her sovereignty. Elizabeth got wind of an assassination plot, suspected Mary was behind it, and had her beheaded. When Elizabeth—who was called the "Virgin Queen"—died heirless, Mary's son James I became king of England. James buried his mum here (with her head sewn back on) in the Abbey's most sumptuous tomb.

• *Exit Mary's chapel. Ahead of you, at the foot of the stairs, is the Coronation Chair. Behind the chair, again, is the tomb of the church's founder, Edward the Confessor.*

❼ Coronation Chair

The gold-painted wooden chair waits here—with its back to the high altar—for the next coronation. For every English coronation since 1308 (except two), it's been moved to its spot before the high altar to receive the royal buttocks. The chair's legs rest on lions, England's symbol. The space below the chair originally held a big rock from Scotland called the Stone of Scone (pronounced "skoon"), symbolizing Scotland's unity with England's monarch. Recently, however, Britain gave Scotland more sovereignty, its own Parliament, and the Stone, which Scotland has agreed to loan to Britain for future coronations.

• *Continue on. Turn left into the south transept. You're in Poets' Corner.*

❽ Poets' Corner

England's greatest artistic contributions are in the written word. Here lie buried the masters of arguably the world's most complex and expressive language. (Many writers are honored with plaques and monuments; relatively few are actually buried here.)

• *Start with Chaucer, buried in the wall under the blue windows, marked with a white plaque reading* Qui Fuit Anglorum...

Geoffrey Chaucer (c. 1343–1400) is often considered the father of English literature. Chaucer's *Canterbury Tales* told of earthy people speaking everyday English. He was the first great writer buried in the Abbey (thanks to his job as a Westminster clerk). Later, it became a tradition to bury other writers here, and Poets' Corner was built around his tomb. The blue windows have blank panels awaiting the names of future poets.

• *The plaques on the floor before Chaucer are gravestones and memorials to other literary greats.*

Lord Byron, the great lover of women and adventure: "Though the night was made for loving,/And the day returns too soon,/Yet we'll go no more a-roving/By the light of the moon."

Dylan Thomas, alcoholic master of modernism, with a Romantic's heart: "Oh as I was young and easy in the mercy of his means,/Time held me green and dying/Though I sang in my chains like the sea."

W. H. Auden, Brit-turned-American modernist on love, politics, and religion: "He was my North, my South, my East and West/My working week and Sunday rest/My noon, my midnight, my talk, my song/I thought that love would last forever: I was wrong."

Lewis Carroll, creator of *Alice's Adventures in Wonderland* and *Through the Looking-Glass:* "'Twas brillig, and the slithy toves/Did gyre and gimble in the wabe..."

T. S. Eliot, American-turned-British author of the influential *The Waste Land:* "April is the cruellest month, breeding/Lilacs out of the dead land, mixing/Memory and desire, stirring/Dull roots with spring rain."

Alfred, Lord Tennyson, conscience of the Victorian era: "'Tis better to have loved and lost/Than never to have loved at all."

Robert Browning: "Oh, to be in England/Now that April's there."

• *Farther out in the south transept, you'll find a statue of...*

William Shakespeare: Although he's not buried here, this greatest of English writers is honored by a fine statue that stands near the end of the transept, overlooking the others: "Life's but a walking shadow, a poor player that struts and frets his hour upon the stage and then is heard no more."

George Frideric Handel: High on the wall opposite Shakespeare is the German immigrant famous for composing the *Messiah* oratorio: "Hallelujah, hallelujah, hallelujah." The statue's features are modeled on Handel's death mask. Musicians can read the vocal score in his hands for "I Know That My Redeemer Liveth." His actual tomb is on the floor, next to...

Charles Dickens, whose serialized novels brought literature to the masses: "It was the best of times, it was the worst of times."

On the floor near Shakespeare, you'll also find the tombs of **Samuel Johnson** (who wrote the first English dictionary) and the great English actor **Laurence Olivier.** (Olivier disdained the "Method" style of experiencing intense emotions in order to portray them. When co-star Dustin Hoffman stayed up all night in order to appear haggard for a scene, Olivier said, "My dear boy, why don't you simply try acting?")

And finally, near the center of the transept, find the small, white floor plaque of **Thomas Parr** (marked "THO: PARR"). Check the dates of his life (1483–1635) and do the math. In his (reputed) 152 years, he served 10 sovereigns and was a contemporary of Columbus, Henry VIII, Elizabeth I, Shakespeare, and Galileo.

• *Walk to the center of the church in front of the high altar.*

❾ The Coronation Spot

Here is where every English coronation since 1066 has taken place. Imagine the day when Prince William becomes king:

The nobles in robes and powdered wigs look on from the carved wooden stalls of the choir. The Archbishop of Canterbury stands at the high altar (table with candlesticks, up five steps). The coronation chair is placed before the altar on the round, brown pavement stone representing the earth. Surrounding the whole area are temporary bleachers for 8,000 VIPs, going halfway up the rose windows of each transept, creating a "theater."

Long silver trumpets hung with banners sound a fanfare as the monarch-to-be enters the church. The congregation sings, "I will go into the house of the Lord," as William parades slowly down the nave and up the steps to the altar. After a church service, he sits in the chair, facing the altar, where the crown jewels are placed. William is anointed with holy oil, then receives a ceremonial sword, ring, and cup. The royal scepter is placed in his hands, and—dut, dutta dah—the archbishop lowers the Crown of St. Edward the Confessor onto his royal head. Finally, King William stands up, descends the steps, and is presented to the people. As cannons roar throughout the city, the people cry, "God save the king!"

Royalty are also given funerals here. Princess Diana's coffin lay here before her funeral service. She was then buried on her family estate. The "Queen Mum" (mother of Elizabeth II) had her funeral here, and this is also where Prince Andrew married Sarah Ferguson.

• *Exit the church (temporarily) at the south door, which leads to the...*

⑩ Cloisters and Abbey Museum

The buildings that adjoin the church housed the monks. (The church is known as the "abbey" because it was the headquarters of the Benedictine Order until Henry VIII kicked them out in 1540.) Cloistered courtyards gave them a place to meditate on God's creations.

The Chapter House, where the monks had daily meetings, features fine architecture and stained glass with faded but well-described medieval art.

The small Abbey Museum, formerly the monks' lounge, is worth a peek for its fascinating and well-described exhibits. Look into the impressively realistic eyes of Henry VII, Elizabeth I, Charles II, Admiral Nelson, and a dozen others, part of a compelling series of wax-and-wood statues that, for three centuries, graced coffins during funeral processions. Also see exhibits on royal coronations, funerals, Abbey history, a close-up look at medieval stained glass, and replicas of the crown jewels used for coronation practice. The exquisite Westminster Retable, which decorated the high altar in 1270, is the oldest surviving altarpiece in England. Beyond the Abbey Museum, passageways lead to the picturesque College Garden (open on certain days).

As you return to the church, look back through the cloister courtyard to the church exterior, and meditate on the flying buttresses. These stone bridges that push in on the church walls allowed Gothic architects to build so high.

• *Go back into the church for the last stop.*

⓫ Nave

On the floor near the west entrance of the Abbey is the flower-lined Tomb of the Unknown Warrior, one ordinary WWI soldier buried in soil from France with lettering made from melted-down weapons from that war. Think about that million-man army from the empire and commonwealth, and all those who gave their lives. Hanging on a column next to the tomb is the US Congressional Medal of Honor, presented by General Pershing in 1921 to honor England's WWI dead. Closer to the door is a memorial to the hero of World War II, Winston Churchill.

To the left of the choir screen is so-called "Scientists' Corner," with memorials to Isaac Newton, Michael Faraday, Charles Darwin, and others.

On that side of the nave, find the stained-glass window of St. Edward the Confessor (third bay from the end, marked *S: Edwardus rex...*), with crown, scepter, and ring. Thank him for the Abbey.

Finally, grab a seat in the center and look down the nave. Listen to and ponder this place, filled with the remains of the people who made Britain a world power—saints, royalty, poets, musicians, scientists, soldiers, politicians. Now step back outside into a city filled with modern-day poets, saints, and heroes who continue to make Britain great.

NATIONAL GALLERY TOUR

The National Gallery lets you tour Europe's art without ever crossing the Channel. With so many exciting artists and styles, it's a fine overture to art if you're just starting a European trip, and a pleasant reprise if you're just finishing. The "National Gal" is always a welcome interlude from the bustle of London sightseeing.

Orientation

Cost: Free, but suggested donation of £1–2. Temporary (optional) exhibits require an admission fee.

Hours: Daily 10:00–18:00, Fri until 21:00, last entry to special exhibits 45 minutes before closing.

Getting There: It's central as can be, overlooking Trafalgar Square, a 15-minute walk from Big Ben and 10 minutes from Piccadilly. The closest Tube stop is Charing Cross or Leicester Square.

Information: The information desk in the lobby offers a free, handy floor plan and a schedule of upcoming events and lunchtime lectures (info tel. 020/7747-2885, switchboard tel. 020/7839-3321, www.nationalgallery.org.uk).

Tours: Free one-hour overview tours are offered daily at 11:30 and 14:30. The excellent audioguide—one of the best I've found in Europe—lets you dial up info on any painting in the museum (£3.50). The Gallery's ArtStart computer terminals help you study any artist, style, or topic in the museum, and print out a tailor-made tour map (one computer room is located on the first floor of the Sainsbury Wing; the other is in the comfy Espresso Bar near the Getty Entrance).

Length of This Tour: Allow 90 minutes.

Cloakroom: Cloakrooms are at each entrance (free, but £1–2 suggested donation). You can take a small bag into the museum.

Photography: Photos are strictly forbidden.

Cuisine Art: There are three eateries in the Gallery. The National Dining Rooms—located on the first floor of the Sainsbury Wing—are cool and classy, though pricey, for a sit-down meal (£15–20 entrées, £15 afternoon tea). The National Café—located near the Getty Entrance—is easier on the budget, with both a casual sandwich/soup/salad/pastry area and a table-service restaurant. The Espresso Bar, also near the Getty Entrance, has soft couches, sandwiches, and ArtStart computers. Outside the Gallery, there are several options on or near Trafalgar Square (recommended in "Eating").

Starring: You name it—Leonardo da Vinci, Raphael, Titian, Rembrandt, Monet, and Van Gogh.

Overview

The newly remodeled National Gallery feels fresh and elegant, giving visitors a grand first impression of Britain's greatest collection of paintings. This tour gives you a quick overview of European art history. We'll stay on one floor, working chronologically through medieval holiness, Renaissance realism, Dutch detail, Baroque excess, British restraint, and the colorful French Impressionism that leads to the modern world. Cruise like an eagle with wide eyes for the big picture, seeing how each style progresses into the next.

The Gallery has three entrances facing Trafalgar Square: The main Portico Entrance (under the dome, in the center), the low-key Getty Entrance (to the right), and the Sainsbury Entrance (to the left—in the smaller building to the left of the main entrance).

The Tour Begins

• *Enter through the Sainsbury Entrance. Pick up the free map and climb the stairs. At the top, turn left, then left again, entering Room 52.*

Medieval and Early Renaissance (1260–1440)

In Rooms 52 and 53, you see shiny gold paintings of saints, angels, Madonnas, and crucifixions floating in an ethereal gold never-never land. One thing is very clear: Medieval heaven was different from medieval earth. The holy wore gold plates on their heads. Faces were serene and generic. People posed stiffly, facing directly out or to the side, never in between. Saints are recognized by the symbols they carry (a key, a sword, a book), rather than by their human features.

Art in the Middle Ages was religious, dominated by the Church. The illiterate faithful could meditate on an altarpiece and visualize heaven. It's as though they couldn't imagine saints and angels inhabiting the dreary world of rocks, trees, and sky we live in.

• *One of the finest medieval altarpieces is in a glass case in Room 53.*

Anonymous—*The Wilton Diptych* (c. 1395)

Three kings (left panel) come to adore Mary and her rosy-cheeked baby (right panel), surrounded by flame-like angels. Despite the gold-leaf background, a glimmer of human realism peeks through.

The kings have distinct, down-to-earth faces. And the backside shows not a saint, not a god, not a symbol, but a real-life deer lying down in the grass of this earth.

Still, the anonymous artist is struggling with reality. John the Baptist (among the kings) is holding a "lamb of God" that looks more like a Chihuahua. Nice try. Mary's exquisite fingers hold an anatomically impossible little foot. The figures are flat, scrawny, and sinless, with cartoon features—far from flesh-and-blood human beings.

• *Walking straight through Room 54 into Room 55, you'll leave this gold-leaf peace and find...*

Uccello—*Battle of San Romano* (c. 1450)

This colorful battle scene shows the victory of Florence over Siena—and the battle for literal realism on the canvas. It's an

early Renaissance attempt at a realistic, nonreligious, three-dimensional scene.

Uccello challenges his ability by posing the horses and soldiers at every conceivable angle. The background of farmyards, receding hedges, and tiny soldiers creates an illusion of distance. The artist actually constructs a grid of fallen lances in the foreground, then places the horses and warriors within it. Still, Uccello hasn't quite worked out the bugs—the figures in the distance are far too big, and the fallen soldier on the left isn't much larger than the fallen shield on the right.

• *In Room 56, you'll find...*

National Gallery Highlights

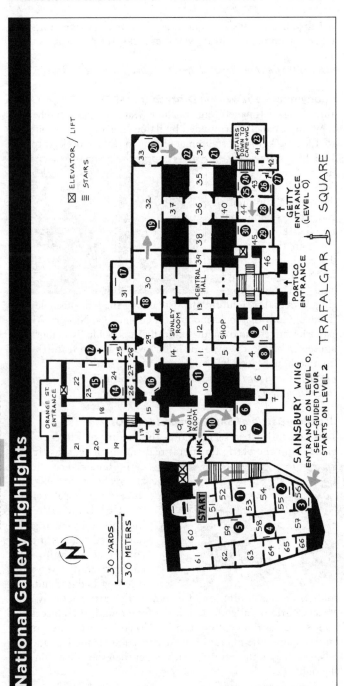

⊠ ELEVATOR / LIFT
☰ STAIRS

30 YARDS
30 METERS

ORANGE ST. ENTRANCE

SUNLEY ROOM

CENTRAL HALL

SHOP

WOHL ROOM

LINK

START

SAINSBURY WING
ENTRANCE ON LEVEL 0,
SELF-GUIDED TOUR
STARTS ON LEVEL 2

GETTY ENTRANCE
(LEVEL 0)

PORTICO ENTRANCE

STAIRS DOWN TO
CAFE + WC

TRAFALGAR SQUARE

MEDIEVAL & EARLY RENAISSANCE

1. ANONYMOUS – The Wilton Diptych
2. UCCELLO – Battle of San Romano
3. VAN EYCK – The Arnolfini Marriage

ITALIAN RENAISSANCE

4. BOTTICELLI – Venus and Mars
5. CRIVELLI – The Annunciation, with Saint Emidius

HIGH RENAISSANCE

6. MICHELANGELO – Entombment
7. RAPHAEL – Pope Julius II
8. HOLBEIN – The Ambassadors
9. DA VINCI – The Virgin of the Rocks; Virgin and Child with St. Anne and St. John the Baptist

VENETIAN RENAISSANCE

10. TINTORETTO – The Origin of the Milky Way
11. TITIAN – Bacchus and Ariadne

NORTHERN PROTESTANT ART

12. VERMEER – A Young Woman
13. "A Peepshow"
14. REMBRANDT – Belshazzar's Feast
15. REMBRANDT – Self-Portrait

BAROQUE & ROCOCO

16. RUBENS – The Judgment of Paris
17. VAN DYCK – Equestrian Portrait of Charles I
18. VELÁZQUEZ – The Rokeby Venus
19. CARAVAGGIO – The Supper at Emmaus
20. BOUCHER – Pan and Syrinx

BRITISH

21. CONSTABLE – The Hay Wain
22. TURNER – The Fighting Téméraire
23. DELAROCHE – The Execution of Lady Jane Grey

IMPRESSIONISM & BEYOND

24. MONET – Gare St. Lazare
25. MONET – The Water-Lily Pond
26. MANET – Corner of a Café-Concert (a.k.a. The Waitress)
27. RENOIR – Boating on the Seine
28. SEURAT – Bathers at Asnières
29. VAN GOGH – Sunflowers
30. CÉZANNE – Bathers

Van Eyck—*The Arnolfini Marriage* (1434)

Called by some "The Shotgun Wedding," this painting of a simple ceremony (set in Bruges, Belgium) is a masterpiece of down-to-earth details. The solemn, well-dressed couple take their vows, their hands joined in the center.

Van Eyck has built a medieval dollhouse, inviting us to linger over the furnishings. Feel the texture of the fabrics, count the terrier's hairs, trace the shadows generated by the window. Each object is painted at an ideal angle, with the details you'd see if you were standing directly in front of it. So the strings of beads hanging on the back wall are as crystal clear as the bracelets on the bride.

To top it off, look into the round mirror on the far wall—the whole scene is reflected backward in miniature, showing the loving couple and a pair of mysterious visitors. Is it the concerned parents? The minister? Van Eyck himself at his easel? Or has the artist painted you, the home viewer, into the scene?

The surface detail is extraordinary, but the painting lacks true Renaissance depth. The tiny room looks unnaturally narrow, cramped, and claustrophobic.

In medieval times (this was painted only a generation after *The Wilton Diptych*), everyone could read the hidden meaning of certain symbols—the chandelier with its one lit candle (love), the fruit on the windowsill (fertility), the dangling whisk broom (the bride's domestic responsibilities), and the terrier (Fido—fidelity).

By the way, the bride may not be pregnant. The fashion of the day was to wear a pillow to look pregnant in hopes she'd soon get that way. At least, that's what they told their parents.

• *Return to Room 55, turn left into Room 57, then turn right into Room 58.*

The Italian Renaissance (1400–1550)

The Renaissance—or "rebirth" of the culture of ancient Greece and Rome—was a cultural boom that changed people's thinking about every aspect of life. In politics, it meant democracy. In religion, it meant a move away from Church dominance and toward the assertion of man (humanism) and a more personal faith. Science and secular learning were revived after centuries of superstition and ignorance. In architecture, it was a return to the balanced columns and domes of Greece and Rome.

In painting, the Renaissance meant realism. Artists rediscovered the beauty of nature and the human body. With pictures of beautiful people in harmonious, 3-D surroundings, they expressed the optimism and confidence of this new age.

Botticelli—*Venus and Mars* (c. 1485)

Mars takes a break from war, succumbing to the delights of love (Venus), while impish satyrs play innocently with the discarded tools of death. In the early spring of the Renaissance, there was an optimistic mood in the air—the feeling that enlightened Man could solve all problems, narrowing the gap between mortals and the Greek gods. Artists felt free to use the pagan Greek gods as symbols of human traits, virtues, and vices. Venus has sapped man's medieval stiffness, and the Renaissance is coming.

• *Continue to Room 59.*

Crivelli—*The Annunciation, with Saint Emidius* (1486)

Mary, in green, is visited by the dove of the Holy Ghost, who beams down from the distant heavens in a shaft of light.

Like Van Eyck's wedding, this is a brilliant collection of realistic details. Notice the hanging rug, the peacock, the architectural minutiae that lead you way, way back, then bam!—you have a giant pickle in your face.

It combines meticulous detail with Italian spaciousness. The floor tiles and building bricks recede into the distance. We're sucked right in, accelerating through the alleyway, under the arch, and off into space. The Holy Ghost spans the entire distance, connecting heavenly background with earthly foreground. Crivelli creates an Escheresque labyrinth of rooms and walkways that we want to walk through, around, and into—or is that just a male thing?

Renaissance Italians were interested in—even obsessed with—portraying 3-D space. Perhaps they focused their spiritual

NATIONAL GALLERY TOUR

passion away from heaven and toward the physical world. With such restless energy, they needed lots of elbowroom. Space, the final frontier.

• *Just two rooms ahead is Room 51, where we first entered. From Room 51, cross to the main building (the West Wing) and enter the large Room 9. We'll return to these big, colorful canvases—but first, turn right in to Room 8.*

The High Renaissance (1500)

With the "Big Three" of the High Renaissance—Leonardo, Michelangelo, and Raphael—painters had finally conquered realism. But these three Florence-trained artists weren't content just to copy nature, cranking out photographs-on-canvas. Like Renaissance architects (which they also were), they carefully composed their figures on the canvas, "building" them into geometrical patterns that reflected the balance and order they saw in nature.

Michelangelo—*Entombment* (unfinished, c. 1500-1501)

Michelangelo, the greatest sculptor ever, proves it here in this "painted sculpture" of the crucified Jesus being carried to the tomb.

Like a chiseled Greek god, the muscle-head in red ripples beneath his clothes. Christ's naked body, shocking to the medieval Church, was completely acceptable in the Renaissance world, where classical nudes were admired as an expression of the divine.

Renaissance balance and symmetry reign. Christ is the center of the composition, flanked by two equally leaning people who support his body with strips of cloth. They, in turn, are flanked by two others.

The painting is not damaged, but unfinished. Michelangelo, 25 years old at the time, moved on to other projects before he got around to adding crucial details, even leaving a blank space in the lower right where Mary would have been.

Regardless of the lack of detail, Michelangelo lets the bodies do the talking. The two supporters strain to hold up Christ's body, and in their tension we, too, feel the great weight and tragedy of their dead god. Michelangelo expresses the divine through the human form.

Raphael—*Pope Julius II* (1511)

The new worldliness of the Renaissance even reached the Church. Pope Julius II, who was more a swaggering conquistador than a pious pope, set out to rebuild Rome in Renaissance style, hiring

Michelangelo to paint the ceiling of the Vatican's Sistine Chapel.

Raphael gives a behind-the-scenes look at this complex leader. On the one hand, the pope is an imposing pyramid of power, with a velvet shawl, silk shirt, and fancy rings boasting of wealth and success. But at the same time, he's a bent and broken man, his throne backed into a corner, with an expression that seems to say, "Is this all there is?"

• *Exit Room 8 (opposite where you entered), and pass through several rooms until you reach Room 4.*

Holbein—*The Ambassadors* (1533)

Italian 3-D even shows up in this work by German-born Hans Holbein, who settled in England to create portraits for Henry

VIII. Two well-dressed, suave men flank a shelf full of books, globes, navigational tools, and musical instruments—objects that symbolize the secular knowledge of the Renaissance. Almost forgotten is the tiny crucifix in the upper-left corner. So what's with the gray, slanting blob at the bottom? If you view the blob from the right-hand edge of the painting (get real close, right up to the frame), the blob suddenly becomes...a skull. In painting terms, the optical illusion is called an anamorphic projection. (For another example, see page 136.) Symbolically, the skull is a *memento mori*, a reminder that—despite the fine clothes, proud poses, and worldly knowledge—we will all die.

• *Continue into Room 2, with two works by Leonardo.*

Leonardo da Vinci—*The Virgin of the Rocks* (1508)

In this painting—under restoration until spring of 2010—Mary, the mother of Jesus, plays with her son and little Johnny the Baptist (with cross, at left) while an androgynous angel looks on. Leonardo brings this holy scene right down to earth by setting it among rocks, stalactites, water,

Painting: From Tempera to Tubes

The technology of painting has evolved over the centuries.

1400s   Artists used tempera (pigments dissolved in egg yolk) on wood.

1500s   Still painting on wood, artists mainly used oil (pigments dissolved in vegetable oil, such as linseed, walnut, or poppy).

1600s   Artists applied oil paints to canvases stretched across wooden frames.

1850   Paints in convenient, collapsible tubes are invented, making open-air painting feasible.

The Frames: Although some frames are original, having been chosen by the artist, most are selected by museum curators. Some are old frames from another painting, others are Victorian-era reproductions in wood, and still others are recent reproductions made of a composition substance to look like gilded wood.

and flowering plants. But looking closer, we see that Leonardo has deliberately posed his people into a pyramid shape, with Mary's head at the peak, creating an oasis of maternal stability and serenity amid the hard rock of the earth. Leonardo, who was illegitimate, may have sought in his art the young mother he never knew. Freud thought so.

• *Also in Room 2, you'll find...*

Leonardo da Vinci—*Virgin and Child with St. Anne and St. John the Baptist* (c. 1499–1500)

At first glance, this chalk drawing, or cartoon, looks like a simple snapshot of two loving moms and two playful kids. The two chil-

dren play—oblivious to the violent deaths they'll both suffer—beneath their mothers' Mona Lisa smiles.

But follow the eyes: Shadowy-eyed Anne turns toward Mary, who looks tenderly down to Jesus, who blesses John, who gazes back dreamily. As your eyes follow theirs, you're led back to the literal and psychological center of the composition—Jesus—the Alpha and Omega. Without resorting to heavy-handed medieval symbolism, Leonardo drives home a theological concept in a natural, human way. Leonardo the perfectionist rarely finished paintings. This sketch—pieced together from two separate papers (see the line down the middle)—gives us an inside peek at his genius.

• *The Renaissance—born in Florence and nurtured in Rome—soon shifted to Venice. Backtrack to the long Room 9.*

Venetian Renaissance (1510–1600)

Big change. The canvases are bigger, the colors brighter. Goddesses and heroes replace Madonnas and saints. And there are nudes—not Michelangelo's lumps of noble, knotted muscle, but smooth-skinned, sexy, golden centerfolds.

Venice got wealthy by trading with the luxurious and exotic East. Its happy-go-lucky art style shows a taste for the finer things in life.

Tintoretto—*The Origin of the Milky Way* (c. 1575)

In this scene from a classical myth, the god Jupiter places his illegitimate son, baby Hercules, at his wife's breast. Juno says, "Wait a minute. That's not my baby!" Her milk spurts upward, becoming the Milky Way.

Tintoretto places us right up in the clouds, among the gods, who swirl around at every angle. Jupiter appears to be flying almost right at us. An X composition unites it all—Juno slants one way while Jupiter tilts the other.

• *Find a colorful, raucous parade in the adjoining Room 10.*

Titian—*Bacchus and Ariadne* (1523)

Bacchus, the god of wine, leaps from his leopard-drawn chariot, his red cape blowing behind him, to cheer up Ariadne (far left), who has been jilted by her lover. Bacchus' motley entourage rattles

cymbals, bangs on tambourines, and literally shakes a leg.

Man and animal mingle in this pre-Christian orgy, with leopards, a snake, a dog, and the severed head and leg of an ass ready for the barbecue. Man and animal also literally "mix" in the satyrs—part man, part goat. The fat, sleepy guy in the background has had too much.

Titian (see his "Ticianus" signature on the gold vase, lower left) uses a pyramid composition to balance an otherwise chaotic scene. Follow Ariadne's gaze up to the peak of Bacchus' flowing cape, then down along the snake handler's spine to the lower-right corner. In addition, he balances the picture with harmonious colors—blue sky on the left, green trees on the right, while the two main figures stand out with loud splotches of red.

• *Return to Room 9 and turn right. Exit this room at the far end and turn right, entering the long Room 29 (with mint-green wallpaper). Midway through Room 29, turn left, and go into Room 25.*

Northern Protestant Art (1600–1700)

We switch from CinemaScope to a tiny TV—smaller canvases, subdued colors, everyday scenes, and not even a bare shoulder.

Money shapes art. While Italy had wealthy aristocrats and the powerful Catholic Church to purchase art, the North's patrons were middle-class, hardworking, Protestant merchants. They wanted simple, cheap, no-nonsense pictures to decorate their homes and offices. Greek gods and Virgin Marys were out, hometown folks and hometown places were in—portraits, landscapes, still lifes, and slice-of-life scenes. Painted with great attention to detail, this art meant not to wow or preach at you, but to be enjoyed and lingered over. Sightsee.

Vermeer—*A Young Woman Standing at a Virginal* (c. 1670)

Inside a simple Dutch home, a prim virgin plays an early piano called a "virginal." We've surprised her, and she pauses to look up at us.

By framing off such a small world to look at—from the blue chair in the foreground to the wall in back—Vermeer forces us to appreciate the tiniest details, the beauty of everyday things. We can meditate on the tiles lining the floor, the subtle shades of the white wall, and the pale, diffused light that seeps in from the window. Amid straight lines and rectangles, the woman's billowing dress adds a soft touch. The painting of a nude cupid on the back wall only strengthens this virgin's purity.

• *Also in Room 25 you'll find...*

A Peepshow

Look through the holes at the ends of this ingenious device to make the painting of a house interior come to three-dimensional life. Compare the twisted curves of the painting with the illusion it creates and appreciate the painstaking work of dedicated artists.

• *Enter the adjoining Room 24.*

Rembrandt—*Belshazzar's Feast* (c. 1635)

The wicked king has been feasting with God's sacred dinnerware when the meal is interrupted. Belshazzar turns to see the hand of

God, burning an ominous message into the wall that Belshazzar's number is up. As he turns, he knocks over a goblet of wine. We see the jewels and riches of his decadent life.

Rembrandt captures the scene at the most ironic moment. Belshazzar is about to be ruined. We know it, his guests know it, and, judging by the

look on his face, he's coming to the same conclusion.

Rembrandt's flair for the dramatic is accentuated by the strong contrast between light and dark. Most of his canvases are a rich, dark brown, with a few crucial details highlighted by a bright light.

• *Enter the adjoining Room 23.*

Rembrandt—*Self-Portrait* (1669)

Rembrandt throws the light of truth on...himself. This craggy self-portrait was done the year he died, at age 63. Contrast it with one

done three decades earlier (hanging directly opposite). Rembrandt, the greatest Dutch painter, started out as the successful, wealthy young genius of the art world. But he refused to crank out commercial works. Rembrandt painted things that he believed in but no one would invest in—family members, down-to-earth Bible scenes, and self-portraits like these.

Here, Rembrandt surveys the wreckage of his independent life.

He was bankrupt, his mistress had just died, and he had also buried several of his children. We see a disillusioned, well-worn, but proud old genius.

• *Backtrack to the long, mint-green Room 29.*

Baroque (1600–1700)

Rubens

This room holds big, colorful, emotional works by Peter Paul Rubens and others from Catholic Flanders (Belgium). While

Protestant and democratic Europe
painted simple scenes, Catholic
and aristocratic countries turned
to the style called Baroque.
Baroque art took what was flashy
in Venetian art and made it flash-
ier, gaudy and made it gaudier,
dramatic and made it shocking.

Rubens painted anything that
would raise your pulse—battles,
miracles, hunts, and, especially, fleshy women with dimples on all
four cheeks. For instance, *The Judgment of Paris* (one of two versions in this museum that Rubens did of the subject) is little more
than an excuse for a study of the female nude, showing front, back,
and profile all on one canvas.

• *Exit Room 29 at the far end. In Room 30 (with red wallpaper), turn
left into the big, red Room 31, where you'll see a large canvas.*

Van Dyck—*Equestrian Portrait of Charles I* (c. 1637–1638)

King Charles sits on a huge horse, accentuating his power. The
horse's small head makes sure that little Charles isn't dwarfed.

Charles was a soft-on-Catholics king
in a hard-core Protestant country
until England's Civil War (1648),
when his genteel head was separated
from his refined body by Cromwell
and company.

Kings and bishops used the grandiose Baroque style to impress the
masses with their power. Van Dyck's
portrait style set the tone for all the
stuffy, boring portraits of British aristocrats who wished to be portrayed as
sophisticated gentlemen—whether they were or not.

• *For the complete opposite of a stuffy portrait, backpedal into Room 30
for...*

Velázquez—*The Rokeby Venus* (c. 1647–1651)

Like a Venetian centerfold, she
lounges diagonally across the
canvas, admiring herself, with
flaring red, white, and gray fabrics
to highlight her rosy-white skin
and inflame our passion. Horny
Spanish kings loved Titianesque

NATIONAL GALLERY TOUR

nudes, despite that country's strict Inquisition. This work by the king's personal court painter is the first (and, for over a century, the only) Spanish nude. About the sole concession to Spanish modesty is the false reflection in the mirror—if it really showed what the angle should show, Velázquez would have needed two mirrors... and a new job.

• *Turning your left cheek to hers, tango into Room 32.*

Caravaggio—*The Supper at Emmaus* (1601)

After Jesus was crucified, he rose from the dead and appeared without warning to some of his followers. Jesus just wants a quiet meal,

but the man in green, suddenly realizing who he's eating with, is about to jump out of his chair in shock. To the right, a man spreads his hands in amazement, bridging the distance between Christ and us by sticking his hand in our face.

Baroque took reality and exaggerated it. Most artists amplified the prettiness, but Caravaggio exaggerated the grittiness, using real, ugly, unhaloed people in Bible scenes. Caravaggio's paintings look like how a wet dog smells. Reality.

We've come a long way since the first medieval altarpieces that wrapped holy people in gold foil. From the torn shirts to the five o'clock shadows, from the blemished apples to the uneven part in Jesus' hair, we are witnessing a very human miracle.

• *Leave Room 32 at the far end, and enter Room 33.*

French Rococo (1700–1800)

As Europe's political and economic center shifted from Italy to France, Louis XIV's court at Versailles became its cultural hub. Every aristocrat spoke French, dressed French, and bought French paintings. The Rococo art of Louis' successors was as frilly, sensual, and suggestive as the decadent French court. We see their rosy-cheeked portraits and their fantasies: lords and ladies at play in classical gardens, where mortals and gods cavort together.

• *One of the finest examples is the tiny...*

Boucher—*Pan and Syrinx* (1739–1759)

Curious Pan seeks a threesome, but Syrinx eventually changes to reeds, leaving him all wet.

Rococo art is like a Rubens that got shrunk in the wash—

smaller, lighter pastel colors, frillier, and more delicate than the Baroque style. Same dimples, though.

• *Enter Room 34. Take a hike around and enjoy the English-country-garden ambience.*

British (1800–1850)
Constable—*The Hay Wain* (1821)

The more reserved British were more comfortable cavorting with nature than with the lofty gods. Come-as-you-are poets like Wordsworth found the same ecstasy just being outside.

John Constable set up his easel out-of-doors, painstakingly capturing the simple majesty of billowing clouds, billowing trees,

and everyday rural life. Even British portraits (by Thomas Gainsborough and others) placed refined lords and ladies amid idealized greenery.

This simple style—believe it or not—was considered shocking in its day. The rough, thick, earth-toned paint and crude country settings scandalized art lovers used to the highfalutin, prettified sheen of Baroque and Rococo.

Turner—*The Fighting Téméraire* (before 1839)

Constable's landscape was about to be paved over by the Industrial Revolution. Soon, machines began to replace humans, factories belched smoke over Constable's hay cart, and cloud-gazers had to punch the clock. Romantics tried to resist it, lauding the forces of nature and natural human emotions in the face of technological "progress." But alas, here a modern steamboat symbolically drags a famous but obsolete sailing battleship off into the sunset to be destroyed.

Turner's messy, colorful style gives us our first glimpse into the modern art world—he influenced the Impressionists. Turner takes an ordinary scene (like Constable), captures the play of light with messy paints (like Impressionists), and charges it with mystery (like, wow).

• *To view more Constables and an enormous collection of Turner's work, visit London's Tate Britain (see the Tate Britain Tour). For now, enter Room 41.*

NATIONAL GALLERY TOUR

Delaroche—*The Execution of Lady Jane Grey* (1833)

It's 1554. The teenage queen's nine-day reign has reached its curfew. This innocent girl, manipulated into power politics by

cunning advisors, is now sent to the execution site in the Tower of London. As her friends swoon with grief, she's blindfolded and forced to kneel at the block. Legend has it that the confused, humiliated girl was left kneeling on the scaffold. She crawled around, groping for the chopping block, crying out, "Where is it? What am I supposed to do?" The executioner in scarlet looks on with as much compassion as he can muster.

Britain's distinct contribution to art history is this Pre-Raphaelite style, showing medieval scenes in luminous realism with a mood of understated tragedy.

• *Exit Room 41 and enter Room 43. The Impressionist paintings are scattered throughout Rooms 43–46.*

Impressionism and Beyond (1850–1910)

For 500 years, a great artist was someone who could paint the real world with perfect accuracy. Then along came the camera and, click, the artist was replaced by a machine. But unemployed artists refused to go the way of *The Fighting Téméraire*.

They couldn't match the camera for painstaking detail, but they could match it—even beat it—in capturing color, the fleeting moment, the candid pose, the play of light and shadow, the quick impression a scene makes on you. A new breed of artists bursts out of the stuffy confines of the studio. They donned scarves and berets and set up their canvases in farmers' fields or carried their notebooks into crowded cafés, dashing off quick sketches in order to catch a momentary...impression.

• *Start with the misty Monet train station.*

Monet—*Gare St. Lazare* (1877)

Claude Monet, the father of Impressionism, was more interested in the play of light off his subject than the subject itself. He uses smudges of white and gray paint to capture how sun filters through the glass roof of the train station and is refiltered through the clouds of steam.

Monet—*The Water-Lily Pond* (1899)

We've traveled from medieval spirituality to Renaissance realism to Baroque elegance and Impressionist colors. Before you spill out into the 21st century hubbub of London, relax for a second in Monet's garden at Giverny, near Paris. Monet planned an artificial garden, rechanneled a stream, built a bridge, and planted these water lilies—a living work of art, an oasis of order and calm in a hectic world.

Manet—*Corner of a Café-Concert* (a.k.a. *The Waitress*, 1878–1880)

Imagine just how mundane (and therefore shocking) Manet's quick "impression" of this café must have been to a public that was raised on Greek gods, luscious nudes, and glowing Madonnas.

Renoir—*Boating on the Seine* (1879–1880)

It's a nice scene of boats on sun-dappled water. Now move in close. The "scene" breaks up into almost random patches of bright colors. The "blue" water is actually separate brushstrokes of blue, green, pink, purple, gray, white, etc. The rower's hat is a blob of green, white, and blue. Up close, it looks like a mess, but when you back up to a proper distance, *voilà!* It shimmers. This kind of rough, coarse brushwork (where you can actually see the brushstrokes) is one of the telltale signs of Impressionism. Renoir was not trying to paint the water itself, but the reflection of sky, shore, and boats off its surface.

• *In Room 44, you'll find...*

Seurat—*Bathers at Asnières* (1883–1884)

Viewed from about 15 feet away, this is a bright, sunny scene of people lounging on a riverbank. Up close it's a mess of dots, showing the Impressionist color technique taken to its logical extreme. The "green" grass is a shag rug of green, yellow, red, brown, purple, and white brushstrokes. The boy's "red" cap is a collage of red, yellow, and blue.

Seurat has "built" the scene dot by dot, like a newspaper photo, using small points of different, bright colors. Only at a distance do the individual brushstrokes blend together. Impressionism is all about color. Even people's shadows are not dingy black, but warm blues, greens, and purples.

• *In Room 45...*

Van Gogh—*Sunflowers* (1888)

In military terms, Van Gogh was the point man of his culture. He went ahead of his cohorts, explored the unknown, and caught a bullet young. He added emotion to Impressionism, infusing his love of life even into inanimate objects. These sunflowers, painted with characteristic swirling brushstrokes, shimmer and writhe in either agony or ecstasy—depending on your own mood.

Van Gogh painted these during his stay in southern France, a time of frenzied creativity, when he hovered between agony and ecstasy, bliss and madness. A year later, he shot himself.

In his day, Van Gogh was a penniless nobody, selling only one painting in his whole career. In 1987, a different *Sunflowers* painting (he did a half-dozen versions) sold for $40 million (a salary of about $2,500 a day for 45 years), and that's not even his highest-priced painting. Hmm.

Cézanne—*Bathers (Les Grandes Baigneuses,* c. 1900–1906)

These bathers are arranged in strict triangles à la Leonardo—the five nudes on the left form one triangle, the seated nude on the

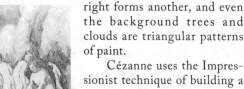

right forms another, and even the background trees and clouds are triangular patterns of paint.

Cézanne uses the Impressionist technique of building a figure with dabs of paint (though his "dabs" are often larger-sized "cube" shapes) to make solid, 3-D geometrical figures in the style of the Renaissance. In the process, his cube shapes helped inspire a radical new art style—

Cubism—bringing art into the 20th century.

• *Exiting Room 45, you find yourself in the stairwell of the Gallery's main entrance (under the dome) on Trafalgar Square. If you want to return to the Sainsbury Entrance, cross the stairwell and pass through several familiar rooms (with Leonardo,* The Ambassadors, *etc.); in Room 9, turn left to reach the Sainsbury Wing.*

After perusing 700 years of art—from gold-backed Madonnas to Cubistic bathers—you've earned a well-deserved break.

NATIONAL PORTRAIT GALLERY TOUR

Rock groupies, book lovers, movie fans, gossipmongers, and even historians all can find at least one favorite celebrity here. From Elizabeth I to Elizabeth II, Byron to Bowie, the National Portrait Gallery puts a face on 500 years, making "history" the simple story of flesh-and-blood people. It's a great rainy-day museum for serious students, or a quick (and free) peek at the islands' eccentric inhabitants.

Orientation

Cost: Free, but suggested donation of £3. Temporary (optional) exhibits require an admission fee.

Hours: Daily 10:00–18:00, Thu–Fri until 21:00, last entry to special exhibits 45 minutes before closing.

Getting There: It's at St. Martin's Place, 100 yards off Trafalgar Square (around the corner from the National Gallery and opposite the Church of St. Martin-in-the-Fields). The closest Tube stops are Charing Cross and Leicester Square.

Information: Tel. 020/7306-0055, recorded info tel. 020/7312-2463, www.npg.org.uk.

Tours: Choose from various audioguides (£2) with different themes such as "Highlights," "Kings and Queens," and "Writers."

Length of This Tour: Allow 90 minutes.

Photography: Photos are not allowed.

Cuisine Art: The elegant Portrait Restaurant on the top floor is pricey but has a fine view of Trafalgar Square (£15–20 entrées, reservations smart, tel. 020/7312-2490). The Portrait Café in the basement (take the lift down) is cheaper and offers sandwiches, salads, and pastries.

Starring: Royalty (Henry VIII, Elizabeth I, Victoria), writers (Shakespeare, the Brontës), scientists (Newton, Darwin), politicians (Churchill), and musicians (Handel, McCartney).

Overview

The Gallery covers 500 years of history from top to bottom—literally. Start on the top (second) floor and work chronologically down to modern times on the ground floor. Historians should linger at the top; celebrity hunters will lose elevation quickly to the contemporary section. There are many, many famous people from all walks of life, so use this chapter as an overview, then follow your interests, either with an audioguide or by reading the museum's informative labels.

The Tour Begins

• *Ride the long escalator up to the second floor and start in Room 1, marked* The Early Tudors. *Find the large black-and-white sketch (cartoon) of Henry VIII with his hands on his hips.*

Second Floor

1500s—Debut

The small, isolated island of Britain (pop. four million) enters onto the world stage. The Tudor kings—having already settled family feuds (the Wars of the Roses), balanced religious factions, and built England's navy—bring wealth from abroad.

• *Enter Room 1.*

❶ Henry VIII (1491-1547), The Whitehall Mural Cartoon

Young, athletic, intense, and charismatic, with jeweled hands, gold dagger, and bulging codpiece (the very image of kingly power), Henry VIII carried England on his broad shoulders from political isolation to international power.

In middle age, he divorced his older, dull-eyed, post-childbearing queen, Catherine of Aragon (see her portrait opposite Henry), for younger, shrewd, sparkling-eyed Anne Boleyn (near Catherine to the left), in search of love, sex, and a male heir. Nine months later, the future Elizabeth I was born, and the pope excommunicated adulterous Henry. Defiant, Henry started the (Protestant) Church of England, sparking a century-plus of religious strife between the country's Protestants and Catholics.

NAT'L PORTRAIT GALLERY

National Portrait Gallery—Second Floor

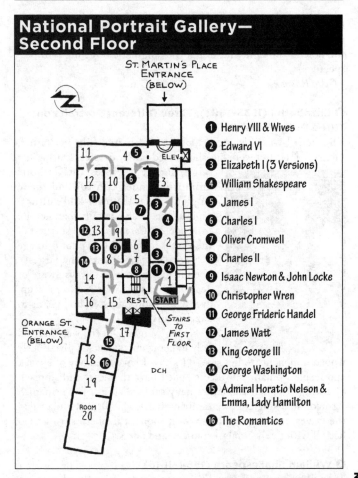

ST. MARTIN'S PLACE ENTRANCE (BELOW)

ELEV.

11 4 ⑤
12 10 ⑥
⑪ ⑩ 3
5 ③
⑦ ④
12 13 9 ③ 2
⑫ ⑬ ⑨ 6 ③
⑭ 8 ⑦
14 ⑧ ① ②
START
16 15
REST.
ORANGE ST. ENTRANCE (BELOW)
STAIRS TO FIRST FLOOR
17
⑮
18 ⑯
DCH
19
ROOM 20

❶ Henry VIII & Wives
❷ Edward VI
❸ Elizabeth I (3 Versions)
❹ William Shakespeare
❺ James I
❻ Charles I
❼ Oliver Cromwell
❽ Charles II
❾ Isaac Newton & John Locke
❿ Christopher Wren
⓫ George Frideric Handel
⓬ James Watt
⓭ King George III
⓮ George Washington
⓯ Admiral Horatio Nelson & Emma, Lady Hamilton
⓰ The Romantics

By the time Henry died—400 pounds of stinking, pus-ridden paranoia—he had wed six wives (see the sixth, sweet young Catherine Parr, opposite Henry), executed several of them (including Anne Boleyn), killed trusted advisors, pursued costly wars, and produced one male heir, Edward VI.

• *Also in Room 1 is the lo-o-o-ong picture of...*

NAT'L PORTRAIT GALLERY

❷ Edward VI (1537–1553)

Nine-year-old Edward (son of Henry's third wife, Jane Seymour) ruled for only six years before dying young, leaving England in religious and economic turmoil. (View the optical illusion through the hole at the right end to put the enigmatic boy king into perspective.)

• *Go to Room 2.*

❸ Elizabeth I (1533–1603), Three Different Portraits on Three Different Walls

Elizabeth I was pale, stern-looking, red-haired (like her father, Henry VIII), and wore big-shouldered power dresses. During her

reign, she kept Protestant/Catholic animosity under control and made England a naval power and cultural capital. The three portraits span her life from age 26 (*Coronation,* the smallest of the three) to age 42 (see photo) to age 60 (*The Ditchley Portrait,* the largest). Yet she looks ageless, always aware of her public image, resorting to makeup, dye, wigs, showy dresses, and pearls to dazzle courtiers.

The "Virgin Queen" was married only to her country, but she flirtatiously wooed opponents to her side. ("I know I have the body of a weak and feeble woman," she'd coo, "but I have the heart and stomach of a king.") When England's navy sank 72 ships of the Spanish Armada in a single, power-shifting battle (1588), Britannia ruled the waves, feasting on New World spoils. Elizabeth surrounded herself with intellectuals, explorers, and poets.

❹ William Shakespeare (1564–1616)

Though famous in his day, Shakespeare's long hair, beard, earring, untied collar, and red-rimmed eyes make him look less the celebrity and more the bohemian barfly he likely

was. This unassuming portrait (reportedly one of only two done in his lifetime) captures 45-year-old Shakespeare just before he retired from his career as actor, poet, and world's greatest playwright. The shiny, domed forehead is a beacon of intelligence. (I suspect Shakespeare liked this plain-spoken portrait.)

Using borrowed plots, outrageous puns, and poetic language, Shakespeare wrote comedies (c. 1590—*Taming of the Shrew, As You Like It*), tragedies

(c. 1600—*Hamlet, Othello, Macbeth, King Lear*), and fanciful combinations (c. 1610—*The Tempest*), exploring the full range of human emotions and reinventing the English language.

The museum attributes this portrait to a Shakespeare contemporary, John Taylor, but other scholars insist it was done long after the writer's death. One recently discovered portrait (not in the museum) depicts a 46-year-old Shakespeare looking like a matinee idol, with a full head of hair. The search goes on for the "real" Will.

• *Pass through Room 3, through the stairwell, and into Room 4.*

1600s—Religious and Civil Wars

Catholic kings bickered with an increasingly vocal Protestant Parliament until civil war erupted (1642–1651), killing thousands, decapitating the king, and eventually establishing Parliament as the main power.

❺ James I (1566–1625) of England and VI of Scotland

When the "Virgin Queen" died childless, her cousin—a rough, unkempt, arrogant Scotsman—moved to genteel London and donned the royal robes. Deeply religious, he launched the "King James" translation of the Bible, but he alienated Anglicans (Church of England), harder-line Protestants (Puritans), and democrats everywhere by insisting that he ruled by divine right, directly from God. He passed on this attitude to his son, Charles.

• *Enter Room 5, with portraits of Civil War veterans.*

❻ Charles I (1600–1649)

Picture Charles' sensitive face (with scholar's eyes and artist's long hair and beard) severed from his elegant body (in horse-riding finery), and you've arrived quickly at the heart of the Civil War.

The short, shy, stuttering Charles angered Protestants and democrats by dissolving Parliament, raising taxes, and marrying a Catholic. Parliament formed an army, fought the king's supporters, arrested and tried Charles, and—outside the Banqueting House on Whitehall—beheaded him.

• *The man responsible was...*

❼ Oliver Cromwell (1599–1658)

Cromwell, with armor, sword, command baton, and a determined look, was the Protestant champion and military leader. The

Civil War pitted Parliamentarians (Parliament, Protestant Puritans, industry, and urban areas) against Royalists (King, Catholics, nobles, traditionalists, and rural areas). After Charles' execution, Cromwell led kingless England as "Lord Protector."

Stern Cromwell hated luxury and ordered a warts-and-all portrait (see wart on his left temple and scar between his eyebrows). He has a simple, bowl-cut hairstyle adorning his 82-ounce brain (49 is average). Speaking of heads, after Cromwell's death, vengeful Royalists exhumed his body, cut off the head, stuck it on a stick, and placed it outside Westminster Abbey, where it rotted publicly for 24 years.

• *Pass through Room 6 and into Room 7. Facing you is...*

❽ Charles II (1630–1685)

After two decades of wars, Cromwell's harsh rule, and Puritanical excesses (no dancing, theater, or political incorrectness), Parliament welcomed the monarchy back (with tight restrictions) under Charles II. England was ready to party.

Looking completely ridiculous, with splayed legs, puffy face, big-hair wig, garters, and ribbons on his shoes, Charles II became a king with nothing to do, and he did it with grace and a sense of humor. Charles' picture is sandwiched between portraits of his devoted wife, Catherine of Braganza, and one of his well-known mistresses.

• *Make a U-turn right, entering Room 8. In the right corner are the bewigged and unamused...*

❾ Isaac Newton (1642–1727) and John Locke (1632–1704)

The 1600s, the Age of Enlightenment, saw scientific discoveries suggesting that the world operates in an orderly, rational way. Isaac Newton explained the universe's motion with the simplest of formulas ($f = ma$, etc.), and John Locke used human reason to plan a democratic utopia, coining phrases like "life, liberty..." that would inspire America's revolutionaries.

NAT'L PORTRAIT GALLERY

• *Walk straight ahead to Room 10. Along the right wall, find...*

❿ Christopher Wren (1632–1723)

Christopher Wren—leaning on blueprints with a compass in hand—designed St. Paul's Cathedral, a glorious demonstration of mathematics in stone.

• *In Room 11, make a U-turn left, entering Room 12, with painters, writers, actors, and musicians of the 1700s.*

1700s—Domestic Stability, Wars with France

Blossoming agriculture, the first factories, overseas colonization, and political stability from German-born kings (George I, II, III) allowed the arts to flourish. Overseas, England financed wars against Europe's No. 1 power, France.

⓫ George Frideric Handel (1685–1759)

In London, an old form of art became something new—modern theater. Handel, a German writing Italian operas in England, had several smash hits in London (especially with the oratorio *Messiah*, on his desk), making musical theater popular with ordinary folk. Hallelujah.

• *Walk on, to Room 13, for the portrait of...*

⓬ James Watt (1736–1819)

Deep-thinking Watt pores over plans to turn brainpower into work power. His steam engines (with a separate condenser to capture formerly wasted heat energy) soon powered gleaming machines, changing England's economy from grain and ships to iron and coal.

• *Head to Room 14, where you'll find George III over your left shoulder and George Washington along the right wall.*

⓭ King George III (1738–1820) and
⓮ George Washington (1732–1799)

Just crowned at 23, King George III gives little hint in this portrait that he will lead England into the drawn-out, humiliating "American War" (Revolutionary War) against a colony demanding independence. George III, perhaps a victim of an undiagnosed disease, closed out the stuffy "Georgian" era (in Percy Shelley's words) "an old, mad, blind, despised, dying king."

Perhaps it was the war that drove him mad, or perhaps it was that his enemy, George Washington (portrait nearby), had the same hairdo. Washington was born in British-ruled Virginia, and fought for Britain in the French and Indian War, but sided with the colonies in what the British called the American War. This famous portrait of Washington is one of several versions of a 1796 portrait by Gilbert Stuart.

1800s—Colonial and Industrial Giant

Britain defeated France (Napoleon) and emerged as the top power. With natural resources from overseas colonies (Australia, Canada, India, West Indies, China), good communications, and a growing population of seven million, Britain became the first industrial power, dotted with smoke-belching factories and laced with railroads.

· *Exit Room 14 into Room 8 and turn right, ending up in the bright aqua Room 17.*

⓮ Admiral Horatio Nelson (1758–1805); Emma, Lady Hamilton (1761–1815)

While the Duke of Wellington fought Napoleon on land (the final victory at Waterloo, near Brussels, 1815), Admiral Nelson battled

France at sea (Battle of Trafalgar, off Spain, 1805).

At Nelson's side is Emma, Lady Hamilton, dressed in white with her famously beautiful face turned coyly. She first met dashing Nelson on his way to fight the French in Egypt. She used the influence of her husband, Lord Hamilton, to restock Nelson's ships. Nelson's daring victory made him an instant celebrity, though the battle cost him an arm and an eye. The hero—a married man—returned home to woo, bed, and impregnate Lady H., with sophisticated Lord Hamilton's patriotic tolerance.

· *Go to Room 18.*

⓯ The Romantics

Not everyone worshipped industrial progress. Romantics questioned the clinical detachment of science, industrial pollution, and the personal restrictions of modern life. They reveled in strong emotions, non-Western cultures, personal freedom, opium, and the beauties of nature.

· *Scattered around the room, you'll see...*

John Keats (1795–1821) broods over his just-written "Ode to a

Nightingale." ("My heart aches, and a drowsy numbness pains/My sense, as though of hemlock I had drunk.")

Samuel Taylor Coleridge (1772–1834), at 23, is open-eyed, open-mouthed, and eager. ("And all should cry, Beware! Beware!/His flashing eyes, his floating hair!/...For he on honey-dew hath fed,/And drunk the milk of Paradise."—from "Kubla Khan")

Mary Wollstonecraft (1797–1851), in telling ghost stories with husband Percy Shelley and friend Lord Byron, conceived a tale of science run amok—*Frankenstein*—imitated by many. ("Ahhhhhhh, sweet mystery of life, at last I've found you!")

William Wordsworth (1770–1850): "The world is too much with us.../Little we see in Nature that is ours;/We have given our hearts away, a sordid boon!"

Percy Bysshe Shelley (1792–1822), political radical, sexual explorer (involving Mary and Claire Clairmont), traveler, and poet. ("O wild West Wind, thou breath of Autumn's being,.../If Winter comes, can Spring be far behind?")

George Gordon, **Lord Byron** (1788–1824), was athletic, exotic, and passionate about women and freedom. Famous and scandalous in his day, he became a Kerouacian symbol of the Romantic movement. ("She walks in beauty, like the night/Of cloudless climes and starry skies...")

• *After browsing Rooms 19 and 20, backtrack to Room 15 and head downstairs one flight to the first floor. Turn right at the bottom of the stairs, and enter a long hall lined with busts (Room 22). Go to the far end of the hall to Room 21, where you'll find a statue of a happy couple, titled* Queen Victoria and Prince Albert in Anglo-Saxon Dress.

First Floor

1837–1901—The Victorians

As the wealthiest nation on earth with a global colonial empire, Britain during Queen Victoria's long reign embraced modern technology, contributing to the development of power looms, railroads, telephones, motorcars, and electric lights. It was a golden age of science, literature, and middle-class morality, though pockets of

National Portrait Gallery—
First Floor

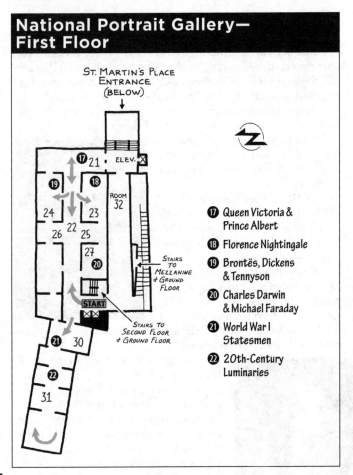

ST. MARTIN'S PLACE
ENTRANCE
(BELOW)

ELEV. ✕

17 21

19   **18**

ROOM
32

24   23

26   **22**   25

27

20

STAIRS
TO
MEZZANINE
& GROUND
FLOOR

START
✕✕

STAIRS TO
SECOND FLOOR
& GROUND FLOOR

21   30

22

31

17 Queen Victoria &
Prince Albert

18 Florence Nightingale

19 Brontës, Dickens
& Tennyson

20 Charles Darwin
& Michael Faraday

21 World War I
Statesmen

22 20th-Century
Luminaries

extreme poverty and vice lurked in the heart of London itself.

• *In Room 21, on either side of the statue of* Queen
Victoria and Prince Albert in Anglo-Saxon
Dress, *you'll find paintings of...*

17 Queen Victoria (1819–1901)
and Prince Albert (1819–1861)

Crowned at 18, the short (5 feet), plump, bug-
eyed, quiet girl inherited a world empire. The
next year, she proposed marriage (the custom)
to the German Prince Albert. They were a perfect match—lovers, friends, and partners—a
model for middle-class couples. (See the white
statue of the pair as genteel knight and ador-

ing lady.) Albert co-ruled, especially when "Vickie" was pregnant with their nine kids. "Bertie" promoted education, science, public works, and the Great Exhibition of 1851 in Hyde Park. When Albert died at 42, a heartbroken Victoria moped for 40 years.

• *Double back through the long hall lined with stuffy busts of starched shirts (Room 22), browsing around the rooms branching off it. These rooms are filled with many prominent Victorians. Start with Room 23 and...*

⓲ Florence Nightingale *(The Mission of Mercy: Florence Nightingale Receiving the Wounded at Scutari)*

Known as "the Lady with the Lamp" for her nightly nursing visits (though she's standing lampless here, in the center, with a piece

of paper), Nightingale traveled to Turkey to tend to Crimean War victims. In fact, her forte was not hands-on nursing but efficient hospital administration (sanitation, keeping supplies stocked, transporting wounded), which ended up saving lives and raising public awareness about health issues. To learn more about her, you can visit the Florence Nightingale Museum, just across the Thames from Big Ben (in Gassiot House at 2 Lambeth Palace Road, Tube: Westminster, Waterloo, or Lambeth North).

• *Across the hall, in Room 24, you'll find several...*

⓳ Writers

Anne, Emily, and Charlotte Brontë (left to right, youngest to oldest, painted by brother Branwell), three teenage country girls, grew up to write novels such as *Wuthering Heights* (Emily) and *Jane Eyre* (Charlotte), about the complex family and love lives of England's rural gentry.

To the left of the Brontës is **Charles Dickens** (1812–1870). Only 12 years old when his dad was sent to a debtor's prison, young Charles was forced to work in a factory. The experience gave him a working-class perspective on British society. He became phenomenally successful writing popular novels (*Oliver Twist, A Tale of Two Cities, A Christmas Carol*) for Britain's educated middle class.

To the right of the Brontës is **Alfred, Lord Tennyson** (1809–1892), the poet laureate of Victorian earnestness. ("Theirs not to reason why,/Theirs but to do and die;/Into the Valley of Death/ Rode the six hundred.")

• *Head to Room 27.*

⑳ Science and Technology
Charles Darwin, with basset-hound eyes and long white beard, looks tired after a lifetime of reluctantly defending his controversial theory of evolution that shocked an entire generation. **Michael Faraday,** across from Darwin, shocked himself from time to time, harnessing electricity as the work force of the next century.

• *The long hall (Room 22) leads into Room 30, dedicated to World War I.*

1900s—World Wars
Two devastating world wars and an emerging US superpower shrank Britain from global empire to island nation. But the country remained a cultural giant, producing writers, actors, composers, painters, and Beatles.

㉑ World War I Statesmen
Fighting Germans from trenches in France, Britain sent a million-man army to the grave. In the big group portrait titled *Some Statesmen of the Great War,* find a bored-looking Winston Churchill.

• *The large Room 31 contains 20th-century portraits.*

⓰ 20th-Century Luminaries

Find the painting of the **Duchess of Windsor** and the small statue of **Edward, Duke of Windsor.** The Duchess' smug smile tells us she got her man. (Note that these displays change frequently, and some of the portraits mentioned here may not be on display during your visit.)

Edward VIII (1894–1972), great-grandson of Queen Victoria, became king in 1936 as a bachelor dating a common-born (gasp), twice-divorced (double gasp) American (oh no!) named Wallis Simpson (1896–1986). Rather than create a constitutional stink, Edward quietly abdicated, married Wallis, and the two moved to the Continent, living happily ever after. They hosted cocktail parties, played golf, and listened to servants call them "Your Majesty"—though they were now just plain Duke and Duchess of Windsor. (Edward's brother took over as King

George VI, married the "Queen Mum"—who died in 2002—and their daughter became Queen Elizabeth II. Elizabeth snubbed her disgraceful aunt and uncle.)

George Bernard Shaw (bust)—playwright, critic, and political thinker—brought socialist ideas into popular discussion with plays such as *Man and Superman* and *Major Barbara*. **Virginia Woolf** (1882–1941) wrote feminist essays ("A woman must have money and a room of her own if she is to write fiction") and experimental novels (*Mrs. Dalloway* jumps back and forth in time) before filling her pockets with stones and drowning herself in a river to silence the voices in her head.

In the darkest days at the beginning of the war, with Nazi bombs raining on a helpless London, **Sir Winston Churchill** (1874–1965) rallied his people with stirring radio speeches from an underground bunker. ("We will fight them on the beaches.... We will never surrender!") Britain's military chief, Field Marshall **Bernard Montgomery, 1st Viscount** (1887–1976, known as "Monty") points out the D-Day beaches of the decisive Allied assault.

Laurence Olivier (bust), movie and stage actor, played everything from romantic leads and Shakespeare heavies to character parts with funny accents. **Noel Coward** (bust) continued the British tradition of writing witty, sophisticated comedies about the idle rich. **Henry Moore** (bust), the most famous 20th-century sculptor, combined the grandeur of Michelangelo, the raw stone

of primitive carvings, and the simplified style of abstract art. **Dylan Thomas** wrote abstract imagery with a Romantic's heart ("Do not go gentle into that good night..."). American-born poet **T. S. Eliot** (bust and Cubist-style portrait) captured the quiet banality of modern life: "This is the way the world ends/ Not with a bang but a whimper."

• *Backtrack to the stairs, and head down to the ground floor.*

Ground Floor

1990 to the Present

London since the Swinging '60s has been a major exporter of pop culture. The contemporary collection, located in Rooms 32–42,

changes often depending on who's hot, but you'll likely find royalty (Queen Elizabeth II, Prince Charles, Princess Diana), politicians (Tony Blair), entrepreneurs (Sir Richard Branson), classic-rock geezers (Sir Paul McCartney, Sir Elton John, David Bowie), and actors (Sir Michael Caine, Dame Judi Dench), as well as those in lower-profile professions—writers (Sir Salman Rushdie, Doris Lessing, Germaine Greer), scientists (Stephen Hawking), composers, painters, and intellectuals.

We've gone from battles to Beatles, seeing Britain's history in the faces of its major players.

WEST END WALK

From Leicester Square to Piccadilly Circus

The West End, the area just west of the original walled City of London, is London's liveliest neighborhood. Theaters, pubs, restaurants, bookstores, ethnic food, markets, and boutiques attract rock stars, gays, punks, tourists, and ladies and gentlemen stepping from black cabs for a night on the town.

Allow an hour for this one-mile orientation walk through the neighborhood called "W1" by Londoners. You'll thread through the heart of the West End and the neighborhood of Soho. From Leicester Square (Tube: Leicester Square), we'll head east to Covent Garden, then north on shop-lined Neal Street, then west along Soho's Old Compton Street, ending at Piccadilly Circus. Use the walk to get the lay of the land, then go explore—especially in the evening, when the neon glitters and London gets funky.

The Walk Begins

❶ Leicester Square

Orient yourself from the top (north) end of sloping Leicester (LES-ter) Square. A few blocks to the west is Piccadilly, to the south is Trafalgar Square (and way beyond that, Big Ben), and to the east is Covent Garden. The neighborhood north of the square is trendy Soho. Chinatown is just two blocks north of Leicester Square, with decent-quality, inexpensive Chinese (mostly Cantonese) restaurants.

Leicester Square itself is, by day, the central clearinghouse for theater tickets. Check out the half-price "tkts" kiosk (see page 355) and ignore all the other establishments that bill themselves as "half-price," though they're just normal booking agencies. When the neon ignites after dark, the square hosts red-carpet movie

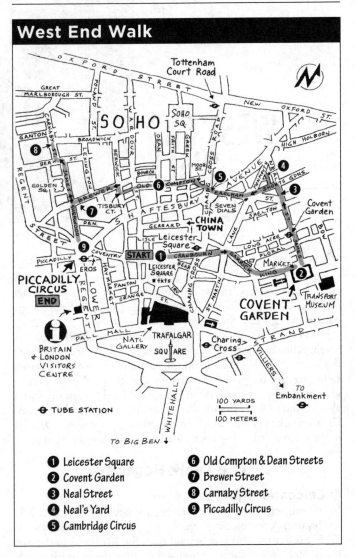

West End Walk

❶ Leicester Square
❷ Covent Garden
❸ Neal Street
❹ Neal's Yard
❺ Cambridge Circus
❻ Old Compton & Dean Streets
❼ Brewer Street
❽ Carnaby Street
❾ Piccadilly Circus

premieres (with publicity appearances by, for example, Angelina Jolie and Brad Pitt), clubs, and partying teens in town from the suburbs.

• *To get to Covent Garden, follow street signs east on Cranbourn Street. Veer right on Garrick Street, then take your second left onto King Street, which leads to a large square teeming with people (and pickpockets) with a covered marketplace in the center.*

❷ Covent Garden

London's chief produce market was built in 1830. Picture it in full Dickensian color, lined with fruit and vegetable stalls. It func-

tioned as a produce market until the 1980s, when Covent Garden's iron-and-glass arcades were converted to boutiques, cafés, and antiques shops. Be sure to step inside, under the iron-and-glass structure so typical of the Industrial Age. If you catch a whiff of marijuana smoke, don't call the cops—Britain is moving to decriminalize the substance. When it comes to possession of small amounts for personal use, the British have learned to live and let live.

The area is festive and theatrical. You'll see a variety of street performers—jugglers, human statues, sword swallowers, and guitar players. St. Paul's Church (not the famous cathedral), with its Greek temple–like entrance, is known as the Actors' Church. It's long been a favorite of nervous performers praying for success. The Royal Opera House (with entrances on the square and on Bow Street) showcases top-notch opera and ballet. There's also the recently refurbished London Transport Museum (see page 55). And two short blocks east down Russell Street is one of London's oldest, biggest, and most historic theaters, the Theatre Royal, on Drury Lane.

• *Head north (uphill) on James Street, which becomes Neal Street.*

❸ Neal Street

This busy pedestrian-only street is lined with clothing shops and boutiques. Look to the left down Earlham Street, with the **Belgo Centraal** restaurant (recommended in "Eating"), cut-flower stands (by day), theaters, and shops.

• *Where Neal Street intersects with Short's Garden Street, you'll find a small courtyard called...*

❹ Neal's Yard

For fun and earthy food, check out the restaurants here and nearby (see "Near Covent Garden" in the Eating chapter). Next door is Neal's Yard Dairy, carrying on the process of traditional cheese-making into the 21st century. Farther west down Short's Garden Street is the "Seven Dials" intersection, where seven sundials atop a pole mark the meeting of seven small streets.

• *Head west on Short's Garden Street to the Seven Dials. Continue past the intersection, following Earlham Street into the heavy traffic of the busy, round intersection called…*

❺ Cambridge Circus

This intersection, surrounded by fine, red-brick Victorian architecture, is the center of the theater district, where Shaftesbury Avenue (running east–west) crosses Charing Cross Road (north–south). The Palace Theatre is the first of five big theaters stretching west along Shaftesbury. Book-lovers browse Charing Cross Road, traditional home of bookstores.

• *Cross kitty-corner to the other side of the intersection. Continue west (keeping to the right of the Palace Theatre) on Moor Street, which becomes Old Compton Street.*

❻ Old Compton and Dean Streets

Welcome to Soho, which stretches from Charing Cross Road westward to Regent Street, and from Leicester Square and Piccadilly in the south to Oxford Street in the north. ("Soho" was a hunting cry back when this area consisted of fields.) The restaurants and boutiques here and on adjoining streets (e.g., Greek, Dean, and Wardour Streets) are trendy and gay, the kind that attract high society when they feel like slumming it. Bars with burly, well-dressed bouncers abound. Private clubs, like the low-profile Groucho Club (45 Dean Street), cater to the late-night rock crowd. A right on Frith Street leads to the green lawn of Soho Square (charming by day, somewhat seedy after dark).

Where Old Compton Street meets Dean Street is perhaps the center of the neighborhood. Just stand and observe the variety of people going by. You're surrounded by the buzz of Soho. South of here, on the other side of Shaftesbury Avenue (see the pagoda-style arch), is Gerrard Street, the center of Chinatown.

• *Continue west, to where Old Compton Street squeezes down into a narrow alley (Tisbury Court). Penetrate this sleazy passage of sex shows and blue-video shops, then jog a half-block right and continue west on Brewer Street.*

❼ Brewer Street

Sex shops, video arcades, and prostitution mingle with upscale restaurants as we enter lower-class west Soho. While it's illegal to sell sex on the street, well-advertised "models" entertain (profitably) in their tiny apartments. Berwick Street hosts a daily produce market.

• *At Sherwood Street (also called Lower James Street), a left turn takes you south to Piccadilly Circus, a block away. But aging boomers may consider taking a detour right (north on Upper James Street) and walk-ing two blocks. Then jog left to find...*

❽ Carnaby Street

In the Swinging '60s, when Pete Townsend needed a paisley shirt, John Lennon a Nehru jacket, or Twiggy a miniskirt, they came here—where those mod fashions were invented.

Today, there's not a hint of hippie. The street looks like everything else from the '60s—sanitized and co-opted by upscale franchises. From Carnaby Street, it's another block north to the Oxford Circus Tube station.

• *Back at the intersection of Brewer and Sherwood Streets, head south on Sherwood Street one block to...*

❾ Piccadilly Circus

The famous circular intersection spins around the tipsy-but-perfectly-balanced Eros statue in the center. At night, when neon pulses, the 20-foot-high Coke ads paint the classic Georgian facades pink. Black cabs honk, people crowd the attractions, and Piccadilly shows off big-city London at its glitziest.

COURTAULD GALLERY TOUR

The Courtauld Gallery (part of the Courtauld Institute of Art) is just small enough that you can see it all in a single visit, which makes for a pleasant experience. The collection spans the history of Western painting, from medieval altarpieces through Italian Renaissance to the 20th century. But its highlight is Impressionist and Post-Impressionist works, some of which you'll recognize. Besides the pieces I've featured, you'll likely see many other well-known Post-Impressionist, Fauvist, and early modern paintings, part of the museum's rotating collection of loaners. For some, the Van Gogh self-portrait alone is worth the price of admission.

Orientation

Cost: £5 (free on Mon until 14:00).

Hours: Daily 10:00–18:00 (last entry at 17:30).

Getting There: The Courtauld is part of the museum/temporary exhibit complex at Somerset House along the Strand. It's a 10-minute walk from Trafalgar Square. Tube: Temple or Covent Garden, or catch bus #6, #9, #11, #13, #15, or #23 from Trafalgar Square.

Information: Tel. 020/7848-1194 or 020/7848-2777, recorded info at 020/7848-2526, www.courtauld.ac.uk.

Length of This Tour: Allow one hour.

Cloakroom: Free coin-op lockers (you get your £1 coin back), and WCs are in the basement.

Photography: Permitted without flash.
Cuisine Art: The café (serving soups, salads, sandwiches, pastries, and drinks), with the same hours as the gallery, is in the basement.
Starring: Van Gogh, Manet, Cézanne, Degas, and many other artists spanning the centuries.

Overview

The museum is not arranged chronologically, but by collector—namely the wealthy people who created this museum by donating their personal collections. Samuel Courtauld (1876–1947), a philanthropist, industrialist, and wealthy great-nephew of a textile magnate, gave his paintings (Van Gogh, Manet, Cézanne, and others on the first floor) and his name to the budding museum.

Occasionally, the paintings described in this tour are lent out to other museums. If there's a piece you really want to see, check with a guard or at the front desk (the ticket seller has a notebook that lists which pieces are currently out on loan).

This tour covers just enough to introduce you to the wide range of art in the collection. Take time to explore the gallery's many more masterpieces.

The Tour Begins

• *Start on the ground floor, in Room 1 (a.k.a. Gallery I, directly across from the ticket counter), filled with religious paintings.*

Master of Flémalle (Robert Campin?)—*Triptych with the Entombment, the Resurrection and a Donor* (c. 1420)

As the earliest known work of this pioneering artist, the altarpiece is a mix of medieval piety and proto-Renaissance techniques. Christ's followers prepare to lower him into the tomb. In medieval fashion, it's set on a gold-leaf background with intricate vines and flowers hammered in. Christ's body is spindly, weightless, and presented at an unnatural angle. But the faces! With knit brows, they bear their sorrow solemnly. Even the angels are choked up. The man kneeling at left (who donated the money for the altarpiece) has a day's growth of beard that's spot-on realism.

• *Upstairs on the first floor, in Room 3, you'll find...*

Edouard Manet—*A Bar at the Folies-Bergère* (1881–1882)

While we look at the barmaid and her wares, Manet also shows us the barmaid's-eye view of the crowded nightclub, reflected in the (slightly tilted) mirror behind her. We see the glittering chandeliers rendered in Impressionist smudges, the bottles of wine, the swirl of activity, and even a trapeze artist (upper left). From the barmaid's own reflection, we see that she's facing a moustached man in a top hat. This may be a self-portrait, but whoever he is, he's standing right where we are.

Manet, in his last major painting, places us in the center of the scene, surrounded with glitter. Reflected in the mirror, the gaiety all looks a bit fake, and, judging from her blank expression, that's the way the barmaid sees it.

Edouard Manet—*Le Dejeuner sur l'Herbe* (1863)
This is a smaller, cruder version Manet did of his famous painting (now in Paris' Orsay Museum) that launched the Impressionist rev-

olution. The nude woman in a classical pose wasn't shocking. It was the presence of the fully clothed men in everyday dress that suddenly made the nude naked. Manet and the Impressionists rejected goddesses and romance for the landscapes, café scenes, and still lifes of the real world.

Paul Cézanne—*La Montagne Sainte-Victoire* (c. 1887)
Cézanne could look out his studio window at this 3,300-foot-high mountain in Provence. Over a 20-year span, he painted the same mountain 60 different ways, each with its own color scheme and mood. This one—with a windblown branch framing the mountain from above—may reflect the turmoil of the fortysomething's life (father's death, stalled Impressionist career, shuttling between Paris and hometown Provence, the recent humiliation of having his childhood friend Emile Zola parody him in a novel).

The mountain is realistic, but the scene is carefully composed. The tree branch echoes the curving ridgeline, uniting foreground and background. A patch of paint forming a house (in the foreground) is the same size as a patch depicting a rock formation (in the background), further flattening this "distant" scene into a wall of brushstrokes. (Cézanne's "cube"-shaped brushstrokes inspired the Cubists, a decade later, to build figures using geometric shapes, to mix foreground and background, and to emphasize style over realism.) Cézanne juggles many technical balls of modern painting—a roughed-up surface texture done with thick brush-work, a self-imposed color scheme, abstract composition—and still manages to stay true to his Impressionist roots, painting the mountain he sees.

Paul Gauguin—*Nevermore* (1897)

A nude Tahitian woman lies daydreaming. The curves of her body and of the headboard soften the horizontal lines of the bed and the verticals of the wall.

Gauguin—who quit his stockbroker job, abandoned his wife and family, and moved to Tahiti—paints in the "primitive" style he found there. Like a child, he draws the girl with a thick outline (so different from Impressionists who "built" a figure with a mosaic of brushstrokes) and then fills it in with solid Crayola colors. Gauguin emphasizes only the two dimensions of height and width, so that the women and clouds in the "background" blend into the flowery wallpaper in the "foreground." Gauguin rejected the camera-eye literalness of Western art. His is a simpler style that requires the viewer's imagination to fill in the blanks, perhaps evoking the romance of a bygone world that is...nevermore.

By the way, Gauguin insisted that the title and the raven were not from Poe's poem, but "a bird of the devil who watches." Hmm.
• *In Room 4, you'll see...*

Vincent van Gogh—*Self-Portrait with Bandaged Ear* (1888-1889)

On the night of December 23, 1888, Vincent van Gogh went ballistic. Drunk, self-doubting, clinically insane, and enraged at his friend Gauguin's smug superiority, he waved a knife in Gauguin's face, then cut off a piece of his own ear and gave it to a prostitute. Gauguin hightailed it back to Paris, and the locals in Arles persuaded the mad Dutchman to get help. A week later, just released from the hospital, Vincent stood in front of a blank canvas and looked at himself in the mirror.

What he saw looking back was a calm man with an unflinch-ing gaze, dressed in a heavy coat (painted with thick, vertical strokes of blue and green) and fur-lined hat. The slightly stained bandage over his ear is neither hidden in shame nor worn as a badge of honor—it's just another accessory. The scene is evenly lit with no melodramatic shadows.

Vincent must have been puzzled and unnerved by his "artist's fit," as he called it. Does this man suspect it was only the first of many he'd suffer over the next year and a half before finally taking his own life?

• *Pass through Room 5 and into Room 6.*

Lucas Cranach the Elder—*Adam and Eve* (1526)

Eve takes a bite of Knowledge, gazes into the distance, and passes the forbidden fruit to a puzzled Adam, standing in a lush garden amid peaceful animals. Strategic branches fuzz their genitals, but otherwise they're nude, with the pale, thin bodies of the aristocrats for whom Cranach painted. (Adam, beware of antlers.) Though the subject is biblical, it captures the worldly spirit of Germany's Renaissance. The northern version of humanism saw humans not as noble Greek gods (as the Italian Renaissance did), but as fallible, lusty, and even a bit cynical.

Peter Paul Rubens—*The Family of Jan Brueghel the Elder* (c. 1613–1615)

Rubens paints his close friend and occasional collaborator, along with his wife and two kids. Rubens and Brueghel, Antwerp's two best painters, tag-teamed a couple of dozen works. Brueghel would focus on his specialty—background, flowers, animals, and garlands—and Rubens did the people. Also in Room 6 is Rubens' dreamy *Landscape by Moonlight* (c. 1637–1638).

• *Upstairs on the second floor is the sculpture gallery in Room 8.*

Edgar Degas—*Study in the Nude for Dressed Ballet Dancer* (1879–1917)

The naked 14-year-old girl splays her feet out (fourth position), bends her arms back, and turns her face up, exuding the sheer joy of dancing. Like a stripped Barbie doll, this is a smaller-scale, nude version of the famous statue Edgar Degas exhibited in Paris in 1881. The original was made of wax and plaster over a wire frame. (The Courtauld's version is a bronze cast of a wax statue, done after Degas' death.) Degas dressed his original wax statue in a cloth tutu and ballet slippers and attached real human hair to the wax head, creating a modern collage of materials that shocked and intrigued the Parisians. Critics of the day both praised its modernism and lambasted the angular, adolescent body and "ugly" face.

The model for the statue was an aspiring dancer who, like so many adolescent girls then and now, dreamed of finding a career on stage. Degas sketched and painted her many times. But this well-known painter was also a closet sculptor, fashioning dozens of small-scale statues in the privacy of his studio, especially in his later years as his eyesight failed and painting became more difficult. Only *The Little Fourteen-Year-Old Dancer* was exhibited.

The Rest of the Courtauld

Rooms 9–14 contain late 19th- and early 20th-century paintings by Derain, Dufy, Jawlensky, and more. Many have the bright, bold colors and thick brushstrokes of the Fauvist style, from the time when Impressionism was merging into abstract. Temporary exhibits also occupy the second floor.

You'll also see works by members of Britain's own Bloomsbury Group—Roger Fry, Vanessa Bell, and Duncan Grant. This group of intellectual friends also included Virginia Woolf (Bell's sister), E. M. Forster, and the economist John Maynard Keynes. During the 1910s and 1920s, they met for cocktails, flirting, and high-minded discussions in their Bloomsbury neighborhood (east of the British Museum), and went on to fame in their respective fields.

BRITISH MUSEUM TOUR

In the 19th century, the British flag flew over one-fourth of the world. London was the world's capital, where women in saris walked the streets with men in top hats. And England collected art as fast as it collected colonies.

The British Museum is *the* chronicle of Western civilization. History is a modern invention. Three hundred years ago, people didn't care about crumbling statues and dusty columns. Nowadays, we value a look at past civilizations, knowing that "those who don't learn from history are condemned to repeat it."

The British Museum is the only place I can think of where you can follow the rise and fall of three great civilizations—Egypt, Assyria, and Greece—in a few hours with a coffee break in the middle. And, while the sun never set on the British Empire, it will on you, so on this tour we'll see just the most exciting two hours.

Orientation

Cost: Free (but a £3, $5, or €5 donation is requested). If you can afford it, donate. Interesting temporary exhibits often require a separate admission.

Hours: The **British Museum** is open daily 10:00–17:30, plus Thu–Fri until 20:30 (but not all galleries are open after 17:30). Rainy days and Sundays always get me down, because they're most crowded. (The museum is least crowded late on weekday afternoons.)

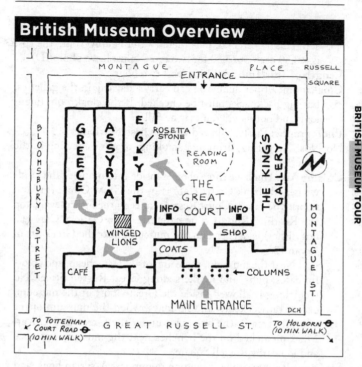

British Museum Overview

The **Great Court**—the grand entrance with eateries, gift shops, an exhibit gallery, and the Reading Room—has longer opening hours than the museum (daily 9:00–18:00, Thu–Sat until 23:00).

Getting There: The main entrance is on Great Russell Street. Take the Tube to Tottenham Court Road, take exit #3, turn right, and follow the brown signs four blocks to the museum. The Holborn and Russell Square Tube stops are also nearby.

Information: The information desks just inside the Great Court have museum maps—one is free but blurry; another is £2 and highlights important pieces (switchboard tel. 020/7323-8000, general info tel. 020/7323-8299; for questions on the collection, call 020/7323-8838; www.britishmuseum.org).

The main bookstore is tucked behind the Reading Room. The "Visitor's Guide" (£3.50) offers 15 different tours and skimpy text.

Tours: The 90-minute **Highlights tours,** led by licensed guides, are expensive but meaty, giving an introduction to the museum's masterpieces (£8, 90 min, daily at 10:30, 13:00, and 15:00). The free 30-minute **eyeOpener tours** focus on select rooms (daily 11:00–15:30, generally running every half-hour).

There are three **audioguide tours:** Museum Highlights

(90 min) and Parthenon Sculptures (60 min) are both substantial and cerebral, plus there's a fun Family Tour. The cost is £3.50 each or £5.50 for two tours (must leave photo ID).

Length of This Tour: Allow at least two hours.

Cloakroom: £1 per item. You can carry a day bag in the galleries, but big backpacks must be checked. If the cloakroom line is long and not moving, it may be full.

Photography: Photos allowed without flash or tripod.

No-Nos: No eating, drinking, smoking, or gum-chewing in the galleries.

Cuisine Art: You have three choices inside the complex. The sandwich-and-drink Court Café is in the Great Court (ground floor). The pricier Court Restaurant is on the upper level (atop the Reading Room). The cafeteria-style Gallery Café (£8 hot dishes) is deeper into the museum, near the Greek art in Room 12.

Near the museum, there are lots of fast, cheap, and colorful cafés, pubs, and markets along Great Russell Street. No picnicking is allowed inside the Great Court or the museum, except on weekends and holidays, when the museum opens a family area in the basement under the Great Court. Karl Marx picnicked on the benches near the museum entrance and in nearby Russell Square.

Starring: Rosetta Stone, Egyptian mummies, Assyrian lions, and Elgin Marbles.

The Tour Begins

The main entrance on Great Russell Street spills you into the Great Court, a glass-domed space with the round Reading Room in the center. From the Great Court, doorways lead to all wings.

To the left are the exhibits on Egypt, Assyria, and Greece—our tour. You'll notice that this tour does not follow the museum's numbered sequence of rooms. Instead, we'll try to hit the highlights as we work chronologically.

Enjoy the Great Court, Europe's largest covered square, bigger than a football field. This people-friendly court—delightfully spared from the London rain—was for 150 years one of London's great lost spaces...closed off and gathering dust. Since the year 2000, it's been the 140-foot-wide hub

The Ancient World

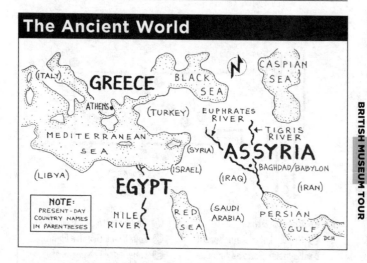

GREECE
ATHENS
(ITALY)
BLACK SEA
(TURKEY)
CASPIAN SEA
EUPHRATES RIVER
TIGRIS RIVER
MEDITERRANEAN SEA
(SYRIA)
ASSYRIA
(LIBYA)
(ISRAEL)
EGYPT
(IRAQ)
BAGHDAD/BABYLON
(IRAN)
NILE RIVER
RED SEA
(SAUDI ARABIA)
PERSIAN GULF

NOTE:
PRESENT-DAY COUNTRY NAMES IN PARENTHESES

of a two-acre cultural complex.

When the stately Reading Room is not being used for special exhibitions, it's open free to the public. In years past, it was a study hall for Oscar Wilde, Arthur Conan Doyle, Rudyard Kipling, T. S. Eliot, Virginia Woolf, W. B. Yeats, Mark Twain, V. I. Lenin, and for Karl Marx while formulating his ideas on communism and writing *Das Kapital*.

• *The Egyptian Gallery is in the West Wing, to the left of the round Reading Room. Enter the Egyptian Gallery. The Rosetta Stone is directly in front of you.*

Egypt (3000 B.C.– A.D. 1)

Egypt was one of the world's first "civilizations"—that is, a group of people with a government, religion, art, free time, and a written language. The Egypt we think of—pyramids, mummies, pharaohs, and guys who walk funny—lasted from 3000 to 1000 B.C. with hardly any change in the government, religion, or arts. Imagine two millennia of Eisenhower.

❶ The Rosetta Stone (196 B.C.)

When this rock was unearthed in the Egyptian desert in 1799, it was a sensation in Europe. This black slab caused a quantum leap in the evolution of history. Finally, Egyptian writing could be decoded.

The writing in the upper

British Museum—Egypt

ASSYRIA
WINGED LIONS
CLOAKROOM
DCH
To ⑤ ⑥
⑧
⑦ ① ② ④
⑩ ⑨ ③
⑪

GREAT COURT + READING ROOM

❶ Rosetta Stone
❷ Upper Half of Ramesses II
❸ Egyptian Gods as Animals
❹ Monumental Granite Scarab
❺ Up to Nebamun Hunting in the Marshes
❻ Up to Mummies, Coffins, Etc.

❼ Red Granite Head
❽ Four Black Granite Figures
❾ Limestone Fragment of Sphinx Beard
❿ Limestone False Door & Architrave of Ptahshepses
⓫ Statue of Nenkheftka

part of the stone is known as hieroglyphics, indecipherable for a thousand years. Did a picture of a bird mean "bird"? Or was it a sound, forming part of a larger word, like "burden"? As it turned out, hieroglyphics are a complex combination of the two, surprisingly more phonetic than symbolic. (For example, the hieroglyph that looks like a mouth or eye is the letter "R.")

The Rosetta Stone allowed scientists to break the code. It contains a single inscription repeated in three languages. The bottom third is plain old Greek (find your favorite frat or sorority), while the middle is medieval Egyptian. By comparing the two known languages with the one they didn't know, translators figured out the hieroglyphics.

The breakthrough came when they discovered that the large ovals (e.g., in the sixth line from the top) represented the name of the ruler, Ptolemy. Simple.

• *The Rosetta Stone sits in the middle of the long Egyptian Gallery. In the gallery to the right of the Stone, find the huge head of Ramesses.*

❷ Upper Half of Colossal Statue of Ramesses II of Granite (c. 1270 B.C.)

When Moses told the king of Egypt, "Let my people go!" this was the stony-faced look he got. Ramesses II ruled for 67 years

(c. 1290–1223 B.C.) and may have been in power when Moses cursed Egypt with plagues, freed the Israeli slaves, and led them out of Egypt to their homeland in Israel (according to the Bible, but not exactly corroborated by Egyptian chronicles).

This seven-ton statue, made from two different colors of granite, is a fragment from a temple in Thebes. Ramesses was a great builder of temples, palaces, tombs, and statues of himself. There are probably more statues of him in the world than there are cheesy fake *David*s. He was so concerned about achieving immortality that he even chiseled his own name on other people's statues. Very cheeky.

Picture what the archaeologists saw when they came upon this: a colossal head and torso separated from the enormous legs and toppled into the sand—all that remained of the works of a once-great pharaoh. Kings, megalomaniacs, and workaholics, take note.

• *Say, "Ooh, heavy," and climb the ramp behind Ramesses, looking for animals.*

❸ Egyptian Gods as Animals

Before technology made humans the alpha animal on earth, it was easier to appreciate our fellow creatures. Animals were stronger, swifter, or fiercer than puny *Homo sapiens*. The Egyptians worshipped animals as incarnations of the gods.

The powerful ram is the god Amun (king of the gods), protecting a puny pharaoh under his powerful chin. The falcon is Horus, the god of the living. The speckled, standing hippo (with lion head) is Tawaret, protectress of childbirth. Her stylized breasts and pregnant belly are supported by ankhs, symbols of life. (Is Tawaret grinning or grimacing in labor?) Finally, the cat (with ear- and nose-rings) served Bastet, the popular goddess of stress relief.

Scattered around the floor are huge stone boxes. The famous mummies of ancient Egypt were wrapped in linen, and then encased in finely decorated wooden coffins, which were then placed in these massive stone outer coffins.

• *At the end of the Egyptian Gallery is a big stone beetle.*

❹ Monumental Granite Scarab (c. 200 B.C.)

This species of beetle would burrow into the ground, then reappear—like the sun rising and setting, or dying and rebirth, a sym-

bol of resurrection. Scarab amulets were placed on mummies' chests to protect the spirit's heart from acting impulsively.

Like the scarab, Egyptian culture was buried—first by Greece, then by Rome. Knowledge of the ancient writing died, condemning the culture to obscurity. But since the discovery of the Rosetta Stone, Egyptology has boomed, and Egypt has come back to life.

• *You can't call Egypt a wrap until you visit the mummies upstairs. Continue to the end of the gallery past the giant stone scarab and up the West Stairs (four flights). At the top, take a left into Room 61, with objects and wall-paintings from the tomb of Nebamun.*

❺ Painting of Nebamun Hunting in the Marshes (c. 1425 B.C.)

Nebamun stands in a reed boat, gliding through the marshes. He raises his arm, ready to bean a bird with a snakelike hunting stick.

On the right, his wife looks on, while his daughter crouches between his legs, a symbol of fatherly protection.

This nobleman walks like Egyptian statues look—stiff and flat, like he was just run over by a pyramid. We see the torso from the front and everything else—arms, legs, face—in profile, creating the funny walk that has become an Egyptian cliché. (Like an early version of Cubism, we see various perspectives at once.)

But the stiffness is softened by a human touch. It's a family snapshot of loved ones from a happy time. The birds, fish, and plants are painted realistically, like encyclopedia entries. (The first "paper" came from papyrus plants like the bush on the left.) The only unrealistic element is the house cat (thigh-high, in front of the man) acting as a retriever—possibly the only cat in history that ever did anything useful.

When Nebamun passed into the afterlife, his awakening soul

could look at this painting on the tomb wall and think of his wife and daughter—doing what they loved for all eternity.

• *Browse through Rooms 61–64, filled with displays in glass cases.*

❻ Rooms 61–64: Mummies, Coffins, Canopic Jars, and Statuettes—The Egyptian Funeral

To mummify a body, disembowel it (but leave the heart inside),

pack the cavities with pitch, and dry it with natron, a natural form of sodium carbonate (and, I believe, the active ingredient in Twinkies). Then carefully bandage it head to toe with hundreds of yards of linen strips. Let it sit 2,000 years, and...*voilà!* Or just dump the corpse in the desert and let the hot, dry, bacteria-killing Egyptian sand do the work—you'll get the same results.

The mummy was placed in a wooden coffin, which was put in a stone coffin, which was placed in a tomb. (The pyramids were super-sized tombs for the rich and famous.) The result is that we now have Egyptian bodies that are as well preserved as Joan Rivers.

The internal organs were preserved alongside in canopic jars, and small-scale statuettes of the deceased *(shabtis)* were scattered around. Written in hieroglyphs on the coffins and the tomb walls were burial rites from the Book of the Dead. These were magical spells to protect the body and crib notes for the waking soul, who needed to know these passwords to get past the guardians of eternity.

Many of the mummies here are from the time of the Roman occupation, when they painted a fine portrait in wax on the wrapping. X-ray photos in the display cases tell us more about these people.

Don't miss the animal mummies. Cats (Room 62) were popular pets. They were also considered incarnations of the goddess Bastet. Worshiped in life as the sun god's allies, preserved in death, and memorialized with statues, cats were given the adulation they've come to expect ever since.

• *Linger in Rooms 62 and 63, but remember that eternity is about the amount of time it takes to see this entire museum. In Room 64, in a glass case, you'll find what's left of a visitor who tried to see it all. (Actually, it's the body of a man called...)*

"Ginger" (Typical Egyptian Grave Containing a Naturally Preserved Body)

This man died 5,400 years ago, a thousand years before the pyramids. His people buried him in the fetal position, where he could "sleep" for eternity. The hot sand naturally dehydrated and protected the body. With him are a few of his possessions: bowls, beads, and the flint blade next to his arm. His grave was covered with stones. Named "Ginger" by scientists for his wisps of red hair, this man from a distant time seems very human.

• *Backtrack to Room 61 and head back down the stairs to the Egyptian Gallery and the Rosetta Stone. Just past the Rosetta Stone, find a huge head (facing away from you) with a hat like a bowling pin.*

❼ Red Granite Head from a Colossal Figure of a King (c. 1350 B.C.)

Art also served as propaganda for the pharaohs, kings who called themselves gods on earth. Put this head on top of an enormous

body (which still stands in Egypt), and you have the intimidating image of an omnipotent ruler who demands servile obedience. Next to the head is, appropriately, the pharaoh's powerful fist—the long arm of the law.

The crown is actually two crowns in one. The pointed upper half is the royal cap of Upper Egypt. This rests on the flat, fez-like crown symbolizing Lower Egypt. A pharaoh wearing both crowns together is bragging that he rules a combined Egypt. As both "Lord of the Two Lands" and "High Priest of Every Temple," the pharaoh united church and state.

• *Along the wall to the left of the red granite head (as you're facing it) are four black lion-headed statues.*

❽ Four Black Granite Figures of the Goddess Sakhmet (1400 B.C.)

This lion-headed goddess looks pretty sedate here, but she could spring into a fierce crouch when crossed.

The gods ruled the Egyptian cosmos like dictators in a big banana republic (or the US Congress). Egyptians bribed their gods for favors, offering food, animals, or money, or by erecting statues like these to them.

Sakhmet holds an ankh. This key-shaped cross was the hieroglyph meaning "life" and was a symbol of eternal life. Later, it was adopted as a Christian symbol because of its cross shape and religious overtones.

• *Continuing down the Egyptian Gallery, a few paces directly in front of you and to the left, find a glass case containing a...*

❾ Limestone Fragment of the Beard of the Sphinx

The Great Sphinx—a statue of a pharaoh-headed lion—crouches in the shadow of the Great Pyramids in Cairo. Time shaved off the sphinx's soft-sandstone, goatee-like beard, and it's now preserved here in a glass case. The beard gives an idea of the scale of the six-story-tall, 200-foot statue.

The Sphinx is as old as the pyramids (c. 2500 B.C.), built during the time known to historians as the Old Kingdom (2686–2181 B.C.), but this beard may have been added later, during a restoration (c. 1420 B.C., or perhaps even later under Ramesses II).

• *Ten steps past the Sphinx's "soul patch" is a 10-foot-tall, red-tinted "building" covered in hieroglyphics.*

❿ Limestone False Door and Architrave of Ptahshepses (c. 2400 B.C.)

This "false door" was a ceremonial entrance (never meant to open) for a sealed building called a *mastaba* that marked the grave of a

man named Ptahshepses. The hieroglyphs of eyes, birds, and rabbits serve as his epitaph, telling his life story, how he went to school with the pharaoh's kids, became an honored vizier, and married the pharaoh's daughter.

The deceased was mummified, placed in a wooden coffin that was encased in a stone coffin, then in a stone sarcophagus (like the **red-granite sarcophagus with paneled exterior surfaces** in front of Ptahshepses' door), and buried 50 feet beneath the *mastaba* in an underground chamber (see the diagram of "Old Kingdom Tombs," on a nearby wall).

Mastabas like Ptahshepses' were decorated inside and out with statues, stelas, and frescoes like those displayed nearby. These pictured the things that the soul could find useful in the next life—magical spells, lists of the deceased's accomplishments, snapshots of the deceased and his family while alive, and secret passwords from the Egyptian Book of the Dead. False doors like this allowed the soul (but not grave robbers) to come and go.

• *Just past Ptahshepses' false door is a glass case with a statue.*

⓫ Statue of Nenkheftka (2400 B.C.)

Originally standing in a "false door" of his *mastaba,* this statue represented the soul of the deceased still active, going in and out of the burial place. This was the image of the departed that greeted

his loved ones when they brought food offerings to the *mastaba* to place at his feet to nourish his soul. (In the mummification rites, the mouth was ritually opened, to prepare it to eat soul food.)

In ancient Egypt, you *could* take it with you. They believed that after you died, your soul lived on, enjoying its earthly possessions—sometimes including servants, who might be walled up alive with their master. (Remember that even the great pyramids were just big tombs for Egypt's most powerful.)

Statues functioned as a refuge for the soul on its journey after death. The rich scattered statues of themselves everywhere, just in case. Statues needed to be simple and easy to recognize, mug shots for eternity: stiff, arms down, chin up, nothing fancy. But this one does have all the essential features, like the simplified human figures on international traffic signs. To a soul caught in the fast lane of astral travel, this symbolic statue would be easier to spot than a detailed one.

With their fervent hope for life after death, Egyptians created calm, dignified art that seems built for eternity.

• *Near the end of the gallery are two huge, winged Assyrian lions (with bearded human heads) standing guard over the Assyrian exhibit halls.*

Assyria (900–600 B.C.)

Long before Saddam Hussein, Iraq was home to other palace-building, iron-fisted rulers—the Assyrians.

Assyria was the lion, the king of beasts of early Middle Eastern civilizations. This Semitic people from the agriculturally challenged hills of northern Iraq became traders and conquerors, not farmers. They conquered their southern neighbors and dominated the Middle East for 300 years (c. 900–600 B.C.).

Their strength came from a superb army (chariots, mounted cavalry, and siege engines), a policy of terrorism against enemies ("I tied their heads to tree trunks all around the city," reads a royal inscription), ethnic cleansing and mass deportations of the vanquished, and efficient administration (roads and express postal service). They have been called "The Romans of the East."

Two Human-Headed Winged Lions (c. 865–860 B.C.)

These lions guarded an Assyrian palace. With the strength of a lion, the wings of an eagle, the brain of a man, and the beard of ZZ Top, they protected the king from evil spirits and scared the heck out of foreign ambassadors and left-wing newspaper reporters. (What has five legs and flies? Take a close look. These quintupeds, which appear complete from both the front and the side, could guard both directions at once.)

Carved into the stone between the bearded lions' loins, you can see one of civilization's most impressive achievements—writing. This wedge-shaped (cuneiform) script is the world's first written language, invented 5,000 years ago by the Sumerians (of southern Iraq) and passed down to their less-civilized descendants, the Assyrians.

• *Walk between the lions, glance at the large reconstructed wooden gates from an Assyrian palace, and turn right into the long, narrow red gallery (Room 7) lined with brown relief panels.*

⑫ Nimrud Gallery (Ninth Century B.C.)—Palace of Ashurnasirpal II

This gallery is a mini version of the throne room of King Ashurnasirpal II's palace at Nimrud. Entering, you'd see the king on his throne at the far end, surrounded by these pleasant, sand-colored, gypsum relief panels (which were, however, originally painted and varnished).

That's Ashurnasirpal himself in the **first panel on your right,** with braided beard, earring, and fez-like crown, flanked by his supernatural hawk-headed henchmen, who sprinkle incense on him with pine cones. The bulging forearms tell us that Ashurnasirpal II (r. 883–859 B.C.) was a conqueror's conqueror who enjoyed his reputation as a merciless warrior, using torture and humiliation as part of his distinct management style. The room's panels chronicle his bloody career.

Under Ashurnasirpal's reign, the Assyrians dominated the Mideast from their capital at Nineveh (near modern Mosul).

British Museum—Assyria

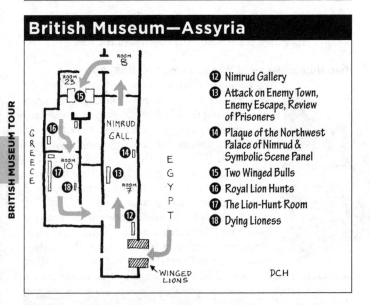

12 Nimrud Gallery

13 Attack on Enemy Town, Enemy Escape, Review of Prisoners

14 Plaque of the Northwest Palace of Nimrud & Symbolic Scene Panel

15 Two Winged Bulls

16 Royal Lion Hunts

17 The Lion-Hunt Room

18 Dying Lioness

DCH

Ashurnasirpal II proved his power by building a brand-new palace in nearby Nimrud (called "Calah" in the Bible).

The cuneiform inscription running through the center of the panel is Ashurnasirpal's résumé: "The king who has enslaved all mankind, the mighty warrior who steps on the necks of his enemies, tramples all foes and shatters the enemy; the weapon of the gods, the mighty king, the King of Assyria, the king of the world, B.A., M.B.A., Ph.D., etc...."

• *A dozen paces farther down, on the left wall, you'll find an upper panel labeled...*

13 Attack on an Enemy Town

Many "nations" conquered by the Assyrians consisted of little more than a single walled city. Here, the Assyrians lay siege with a crude "tank" that shields them as they advance to the city walls to smash down the gate with a battering ram. The king stands a safe distance away

behind the juggernaut and bravely shoots arrows.
• *In the next panel to the right, you'll find...*

Enemy Escape

Soldiers flee the slings and arrows of outrageous Assyrians by swimming across the Euphrates, using inflated animal bladders as life preservers. Their friends in the castle downstream applaud their ingenuity.
• *Below, you'll see...*

Review of Prisoners

The Assyrian economy depended on booty. Here, a conquered nation is paraded before the Assyrian king, who is shaded by a parasol. Ashurnasirpal II sneers and tells the captured chief, "Drop and give me 50." Above the prisoners' heads, we see the rich spoils of war—elephant tusks, metal pots, and so on. The Assyrians depopulated conquered lands

by slavery and ethnic cleansing, then repopulated with Assyrian settlers.
• *On the opposite wall, a few steps farther along, is an artist's rendering of what the palace would have looked like.*

⓮ Plaque of the Northwest Palace of Nimrud, and Symbolic Scene Panel

The plaque shows the king at the far end of the throne room, shaded by a parasol and flanked by winged lions. (In the diagram of the palace's floor plan, the throne room is Room B.) The 30,000-square-foot palace was built atop a 50-acre artificial

mound. The new palace was inaugurated with a 10-day banquet (according to an inscription), where the king picked up the tab for 69,574 of his closest friends.

The relief panel (immediately to the right) labeled **Symbolic Scene** stood behind the throne. It shows the king (and his double) tending the tree of life while reaching up to receive the ring of kingship from the winged sun god.

• *Exit the Nimrud Gallery at the far end, then hang a U-turn left. Pause at the entrance of Room 10c to see the impressive...*

⑮ Two Winged Bulls from Khorsabad, the Palace of Sargon (c. 710–705 B.C.)

These marble bulls guarded the entrance to the city of Dur-Sharrukin ("Sargonsburg"), a new capital (near Nineveh/Mosul) with vast palaces built by Sargon II (r. 721–705 B.C.). The 30-ton bulls were cut from a single block, tipped on their sides, then dragged to their place by POWs. (In modern times, when the British transported them here, they had to cut them in half; you can see the horizontal cracks through the bulls' chests.)

Sargon II gained his reputation as a general by subduing the Israelites after a three-year siege of Jerusalem (2 Kings 17:1–6). He solidified his conquest by ethnically cleansing the area and deporting many Israelites (inspiring legends of the "Lost" Ten Tribes).

In 710 B.C., while these bulls were being carved for his palace, Sargon II marched victorious through the streets of Babylon (near modern Baghdad), having put down a revolt there against him. His descendants would also have to deal with the troublesome Babylonians.

• *Sneak between these bulls and veer right (into Room 10), where horses are being readied for the big hunt.*

⑯ Royal Lion Hunts from the Palace of Ashurbanipal

Lion hunting was Assyria's sport of kings. On the right wall are horses, on the left are the hunting dogs. And next to them, lions, resting peacefully in a garden, unaware that they will shortly be rousted, stampeded, and slaughtered.

Lions lived in Mesopotamia up until modern times, and it was the king's duty to keep the lion population down to protect farmers and herdsmen. This duty soon became sport, with staged hunts and zoo-bred lions, as the kings of men proved their power by taking on the king of beasts.

• *Continue ahead into the larger lion-hunt room. Reading the panels like a comic strip, start on the right and gallop counterclockwise.*

⓱ The Lion-Hunt Room (c. 650 B.C.)

They release the lions from their cages, then soldiers on horseback

herd them into an enclosed arena. The king has them cornered. Let the slaughter begin. The chariot carries King Ashurbanipal, the great-grandson of Sargon II (not to be confused with Ashurnasirpal II, who ruled 200 years earlier, mentioned previously).

The last of Assyria's great kings, Ashurbanipal has reigned now for 50 years. Having left a half-dozen corpses in his wake, he moves on, while spearmen hold off lions attacking from the rear.

• *At about the middle of the long wall...*

The fleeing lions, cornered by hounds, shot through with arrows, and weighed down by fatigue, begin to fall. The lead lion carries on even while vomiting blood.

This low point of Assyrian cruelty is, perhaps, the high point of their artistic achievement. It's a curious coincidence that civilizations often produce their greatest art in their declining years. Hmm.

• *On the wall opposite the vomiting lion is the...*

⓲ Dying Lioness

A lioness roars in pain and frustration. She tries to run, but her body is too heavy. Her muscular hind legs, once the source of her

power, are now paralyzed.

Like these brave, fierce lions, Assyria's once-great warrior nation was slain. Shortly after Ashurbanipal's death, Assyria was conquered, and their capital at Nineveh was sacked and looted by an ascendant

Babylon (612 B.C.). The mood of tragedy, dignity, and proud struggle in a hopeless cause makes this dying lioness simply one of the most beautiful of human creations.

• *Exit the lion-hunt room at the far end and make your way back to the huge, winged lions at the start of the Assyrian exhibit. To reach the Greek section, exit Assyria between the winged lions and make a U-turn to the right, into Room 11.*

You'll walk past (⓳) early Greek Barbie and Ken dolls from the Cycladic period (2500 B.C.). Continue into Room 12 (the hungry can go

straight to the Gallery Café), and turn right, into Room 13, filled with
Greek vases in glass cases.

Greece (600 B.C.–A.D. 1)

The history of ancient Greece could be subtitled "making order
out of chaos." While Assyria was dominating the Middle East,
"Greece"—a gaggle of warring tribes roaming the Greek peninsula—was floundering in darkness. But by about 700 B.C., these
tribes began settling down, experimenting with democracy,
forming self-governing city-states, and making ties with other
city-states. Scarcely two centuries later, they would be a united
community and the center of the civilized world.

During its Golden Age (500–430 B.C.), Greece set the tone for
all of Western civilization to follow. Democracy, theater, literature,
mathematics, philosophy, science, gyros, art, and architecture, as
we know them, were virtually all invented by a single generation of
Greeks in a small town of maybe 80,000 citizens.

• *Roughly in the middle of Room 13 is a Z-shaped glass case marked #8.*
On the upper shelf, find a...

⑳ Black-Figured Amphora (Jar): Achilles and Penthesileia (540–530 B.C.)

Greeks poured wine from jars like this one, painted with a man
stabbing a woman, a legend from the Trojan War. The Trojan War
(c. 1200 B.C.)—part fact but mostly legend—symbolized Greece's
long struggle to rise above war and chaos.

Achilles of Greece faces off against the
Queen of the Amazons, Penthesileia, who
was fighting for Troy. (The Amazons were
a legendary race of warrior women who
cut off one breast to facilitate their archery
skills.) Achilles bears down, plunging a spear
through her neck, as the blood spurts. In her
dying moment, Penthesileia looks up and her
gaze locks on Achilles. His eyes bulge wide,
and he falls instantly in love with her. She
dies, and Achilles is smitten.

Pottery like this (and many others in the room), usually painted
red and black, was a popular export product for the sea-trading
Greeks. The earliest featured geometric patterns (eighth century
B.C.), then a painted black silhouette on the natural orange clay,
then a red figure on a black background. On this jar, see the names
of the two enemies/lovers ("AXILEV" and "PENOESIIEA") as
well as the signature of the craftsman, Exekias.

• *Continue to Room 15, then relax on a bench and read, surrounded by*
statues and vases in glass cases. On the entrance wall, find a...

British Museum—Greece

⑲ Cycladic Figures
⑳ Black-Figured Amphora
㉑ Map of the Greek World
㉒ Idealized Youth
㉓ Wine Cooler
㉔ Nereid Monument
㉕ Elgin Marbles

㉑ Map of the Greek World (500–430 B.C.)

After Greece drove out Persian invaders in 480 B.C., the city of Athens became the most powerful of the city-states and the center of the Greek world. Golden Age Greece was never really a full-fledged empire, but more a common feeling of unity among Greek-speaking people.

A century after the Golden Age, Greek culture was spread still farther by Alexander the Great, who conquered the Mediterranean world and beyond (including Persia). By 300 B.C., the "Greek" world stretched from Italy and Egypt to India (including most of what used to be the Assyrian Empire). Two hundred years later, this Greek-speaking "Hellenistic Empire" was conquered by the Romans.

• *There's a nude male statue on the left side of the room.*

㉒ Idealized Youth (Kouros, 490 B.C.)

The Greeks saw their gods in human form...and human beings were godlike. With his perfectly round head, symmetrical pecs, and navel in the center, the youth exemplifies the divine orderliness of the universe. The ideal man was geometrically perfect, a balance of opposites, the "Golden Mean." In a statue, that meant finding the right balance between movement and stillness,

between realistic human anatomy (with human flaws) and the perfection of a Greek god. He's still a bit uptight, stiff as the rock from which he's carved. But—as we'll see—in just a few short decades, the Greeks would cut loose and create realistic statues that seemed to move like real humans.

• *Two-thirds of the way down Room 15 (on the left) is a glass case containing a vase.*

㉓ Wine Cooler (Psykter) Signed by Douris as Painter (490 B.C.)

This clay vase, designed to float in a bowl of cooling water, shows satyrs at a symposium, or drinking party. These half-man/half-animal creatures (notice their tails) had a reputation for lewd behavior, reminding the balanced and moderate Greeks of their rude roots.

The reveling figures painted on this jar (red on black) are more realistic, more three-dimensional, and suggest more natural movements than even the literally three-dimensional but quite stiff kouros. The Greeks are beginning to conquer the natural world in art. The art, like life, is more in balance. And speaking of "balance," if that's a Greek sobriety test, revel on.

• *Carry on into Room 17 and sit facing the Greek temple at the far end.*

㉔ Nereid Monument from Xanthos (c. 390–380 B.C.)

Greek temples (like this reconstruction of a temple-shaped tomb) housed a statue of a god or goddess. Unlike Christian churches, which serve as meeting places, Greek temples were the gods' homes. Worshippers gathered outside, so the most impressive part of the temple was its exterior. Temples were rectangular buildings surrounded by rows of columns and topped by slanted roofs.

The triangle-shaped roof, filled in with sculpture, is called the "pediment." The cross beams that support the pediment are called "metopes" (MET-uh-pees). Now look through the columns to the building itself. Above the doorway is another set of relief panels running around the building (under the eaves), called the "frieze."

The statues between the columns (and three more facing the monument) are dubbed Nereids—friendly sea nymphs—because of their dramatic wave-like poses and wind-blown clothes, and because some appear to be borne aloft by sea animals. Notice the sculptor's delight in capturing the body in motion, and the way the wet clothes cling to the figures' anatomy.

Next, we'll see pediment, frieze, and metope decorations from Greece's greatest temple.

• *Leave the British Museum. Take the Tube to Heathrow and fly to Athens. In the center of the old city, on top of the high, flat hill known as the Acropolis, you'll find...*

The Parthenon (447–432 B.C.)

The Parthenon—the temple dedicated to Athena, goddess of wisdom and the patroness of Athens—was the crowning glory

of an enormous urban-renewal plan during Greece's Golden Age. After Athens was ruined in a war with Persia, the city—under the bold leadership of Pericles—constructed the greatest building of its day. The Parthenon was a model of balance, simplicity, and harmonious elegance, the symbol of the Golden Age. Phidias, the greatest Greek sculptor, decorated the exterior with statues and relief panels.

While the building itself remains in Athens, many of the Parthenon's best sculptures are right here in the British Museum—the so-called Elgin Marbles (pronounced with a hard "g"), named for the shrewd British ambassador who hammered, chiseled, and sawed them off the Parthenon in the early 1800s. Though the Greek government complains about losing its marbles, the Brits feel they rescued and preserved the sculptures. The often-bitter controversy continues.

• *Enter through the glass doors labeled* The Parthenon Galleries. *(The rooms branching off the entryway usually have helpful exhibits that reconstruct the Parthenon and its once-colorful sculpture.)*

㉕ Elgin Marbles (450 B.C.)

The marble panels you see lining the walls of this large hall are part of the frieze that originally ran around the exterior of the Parthenon (under the eaves). The statues at either end of the hall once filled the Parthenon's triangular-shaped pediments. Near the pediment sculptures, we'll also find the relief panels known as metopes. Let's start with the frieze.

British Museum—Elgin Marbles

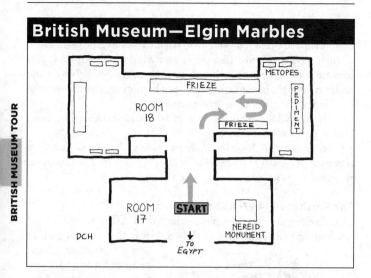

METOPES

FRIEZE

ROOM 18

PEDIMENT

FRIEZE

ROOM 17

START

↓ TO EGYPT

DCH

NEREID MONUMENT

The Frieze

These 56 relief panels show Athens' "Fourth of July" parade, celebrating the birth of the city. On this day, citizens marched up the Acropolis to symbolically present a new robe to the 40-foot-tall gold-and-ivory statue of Athena housed in the Parthenon.

• *Start at the panels by the entrance (#136) and work counterclockwise.*

Men on horseback, chariots, musicians, children, animals for sacrifice, and young maidens with offerings are all part of the grand parade, all heading in the same direction—uphill. Prance on.

Notice the muscles and veins in the horses' legs and the intricate folds in the cloaks and dresses. Some panels have holes drilled in them, where gleaming bronze reins were fitted to heighten the festive look. Of course, all these panels were originally painted in realistic colors. As you move along, notice that, despite the bustle of figures posed every which way, the frieze has one unifying element—all the people's heads are at the same level, creating a single ribbon around the Parthenon.

• *Cross to the opposite wall.*

A three-horse chariot (#67), cut out of only a few inches of marble, is more lifelike and three-dimensional than anything the Egyptians achieved in a freestanding statue.

Enter the girls (five yards to the left, #61), the heart of the procession. Dressed in pleated robes, they shuffle past the parade marshals, carrying incense burners and jugs of wine and bowls to pour out an offering to the thirsty gods.

The procession culminates (#35) in the presentation of the robe to Athena. A man and a child fold the robe for the goddess while the rest of the gods look on. There are Zeus and Hera (#29), the king and queen of the gods, seated, enjoying the fashion show and wondering what length hemlines will be this year.

• *Head for the set of pediment sculptures at the far right end of the hall.*

The Pediment Sculptures

These statues were originally nestled nicely in the triangular pediment above the columns at the Parthenon's main (east) entrance.

The missing statues at the peak of the triangle once showed the birth of Athena. Zeus had his head split open, allowing Athena, the goddess of wisdom, to rise from his brain fully grown and fully armed, inaugurating the Golden Age of Athens.

The other gods at this Olympian banquet slowly become aware of the amazing event. The first to notice is the one closest to them, Hebe, the cup-bearer of the gods (tallest surviving fragment). Frightened, she runs to tell the others, her dress whipping behind her. A startled Demeter (just left of Hebe) turns toward Hebe.

The only one who hasn't lost his head is laid-back Dionysus (the cool guy farther left). He just raises another glass of wine to his lips. Over on the right, Aphrodite, goddess of love, leans back in to her mother's lap, too busy admiring her own bare shoulder to even notice the hubbub. A chess-set horse's head screams, "These people are nuts—let me out of here!"

The scene had a message. Just as wise Athena rose above the lesser gods, who were scared, drunk, or vain, so would her city, Athens, rise above her lesser rivals.

This is amazing workmanship. Compare Dionysus, with his natural, relaxed, reclining pose, to all those stiff Egyptian statues standing eternally at attention.

Appreciate the folds of the clothes on the female figures (on the right half), especially Aphrodite's clinging, rumpled robe.

Centaurs Slain Around the World

Dateline 500 B.C.—Greece, China, India: Man no longer considers himself an animal. Bold new ideas are exploding simultaneously around the world. Socrates, Confucius, Buddha, and others are independently discovering a nonmaterial, unseen order in nature and in man. They say man has a rational mind or soul. He's separate from nature and different from the other animals.

Some sculptors would first build a nude model of their figure, put real clothes on it, and study how the cloth hung down before actually sculpting in marble. Others found inspiration at the *taverna* on wet T-shirt night.

Even without their heads, these statues, with their detailed anatomy and expressive poses, speak volumes.

Wander behind. The statues originally sat 40 feet above the ground. The backs of the statues, which were never intended to be seen, are almost as detailed as the fronts.

• *The metopes are the panels on the walls to either side. Start with "South Metope XXXI" on the right wall, center.*

The Metopes

In #XXXI, a centaur grabs a man by the throat while the man pulls his hair. The humans have invited some centaurs—wild half-man/half-horse creatures—to a wedding feast. All goes well until the brutish centaurs, the original party animals, get too drunk and try to carry off the women. A battle ensues.

The Greeks prided themselves on creating order out of chaos. Within just a few generations, they went from nomadic barbarism to the pinnacle of early Western civilization. These metopes tell the story of this struggle between the forces of human civilization and animal-like barbarism.

In #XXVIII (opposite wall, center, see photo at right), the centaurs start to get the upper hand as one rears back and pre-pares to trample the helpless man. The leopard skin draped over the centaur's arm roars a taunt. The humans lose face.

BRITISH MUSEUM TOUR

In #XXVII (to the left—see photo in sidebar opposite), the humans finally rally and drive off the brutish centaurs. A cen-taur tries to run, but the man grabs him by the neck and raises his right hand (missing) to run him through. The man's folded cloak sets off his smooth skin and graceful figure.

The centaurs have been defeated. Civilization has triumphed over barbarism, order over chaos, and rational man over his half-animal alter ego.

Why are the Elgin Marbles so treasured? The British of the 19th century saw themselves as the new "civilized" race, subduing "barbarians" in their far-flung empire. Maybe these rocks made them stop and wonder—will our great civilization also turn to rubble?

The Rest of the Museum

You've toured only the foundations of Western civilization on the ground floor, West Wing. Upstairs you'll find still more artifacts from these ancient lands, plus Rome and the medieval civilization that sprang from it. Pick up the free map, locate the rooms with themes you find interesting (Etruscan, Persian, Roman Britain, Dark Age Europe, and so on) and explore. Some highlights:

- Lindow Man (a.k.a. the "Bog Man") in Room 50 (upper floor, via east stairs). This victim of a Druid human-sacrifice ritual, with wounds still visible, was preserved for 2,000 years in a peat bog.
- The seventh-century Anglo-Saxon Sutton Hoo Burial Ship (Room 41, upper floor, via East Stairs).
- Treasures of the Persian civilization. The collection here is far better than what remains to be seen in Iran (Room 52, upper floor).
- The only existing, complete cartoon (preliminary sketch) by Michelangelo (Room 90, Level 4, accessed via the North

Stairs or from the top of the Reading Room).
• The King's Library—which once held the British Library's treasures—now houses the delightful Enlightenment Gallery, created to give you the feeling of this grand museum when it was founded in 1753. Back then it was a place of both learning and wonder (Room 1; the long hall to the right of the main entry).

And, of course, history doesn't begin and end in Europe. Look for remnants of the sophisticated, exotic cultures of Asia and the Americas (in North Wing, ground floor) and Africa (lower floor)—all part of the totem pole of the human family.

BRITISH LIBRARY TOUR

The British Empire built its greatest monuments out of paper. It's with literature that England has made her lasting contribution to history and the arts. These national archives of Britain include more than 12 million books, 180 miles of shelving, and the deepest basement in London.

But everything that matters for your visit is in a delightful room labeled "Sir John Ritblat Gallery: Treasures of the British Library" and an adjacent room containing the Magna Carta. We'll concentrate on a handful of documents—literary and historical—that changed the course of history. Start with these top stops, then stray according to your interests.

Orientation

Cost: Free (donations appreciated); admission charged for some temporary exhibits.

Hours: Mon–Fri 9:30–18:00 (until 20:00 on Tue), Sat 9:30–17:00, Sun 11:00–17:00.

Getting There: Take the Tube to King's Cross St. Pancras. Exit to Euston Road, turn right, and walk a block west to 96 Euston Road, where you'll see a humble brick building dating from 1998. Euston Tube station is also nearby. Buses #10, #30, #73, #91, #205, and #390 also stop nearby.

Information: Tel. 020/7412-7332, www.bl.uk. Exhibits rotate often: If your heart's set on seeing that one particular rare Dickens book or letter penned by Gandhi, call ahead to make sure it's on display.

Tours: There are no guided tours or audioguides for "The Treasures." There are, however, guided tours of the building itself—the archives and reading rooms (£8, 75 min, usually offered Mon, Wed, and Fri at 15:00; Sat at 10:30 and 15:00; Sun at 11:30 and 15:00; tel. 020/7412-7639). Touch-screen computers in the Sir John Ritblat Gallery let you virtually page through some of the rare books in the collection.

Length of This Tour: Allow one hour.

Cloakroom: Free. Lockers require £1 coin deposit (no large bags). For security, bags may be searched at the library entrance.

No-Nos: No photography, smoking, or chewing gum.

Cuisine Art: The upper-level, self-service cafeteria has good hot meals. The ground-floor café (sandwiches and drinks) is next to the vast and fun pull-out stamp collection. From either café, you'll see the 50-foot-tall wall of 65,000 books, a present to the people from King George IV in 1823. The high-tech bookshelf is behind glass and has movable lifts.

Starring: Bibles, Shakespeare, English Lit 101, Magna Carta, and—ladies and gentlemen—the Beatles.

The Tour Begins

Entering the library courtyard, you'll see a big statue of a naked Isaac Newton bending forward with a compass to measure the universe. The statue symbolizes the library's purpose: to gather all knowledge and promote our endless search for truth.

Stepping inside, you'll find the information desk and shop. The cloakroom and WC are down a short staircase to the right. The reading rooms upstairs are not open to the general public. The Pearson Gallery, down a few steps to the left, houses temporary exhibits (sometimes requiring an admission charge).

Our tour is of the tiny but exciting area to the left. It's variously labeled "The Sir John Ritblat Gallery," "Treasures of the British Library," or just "The Treasures." This priceless literary and historical collection is held all in one large, carefully designed, dimly lit room.

Enter and let your eyes adjust. The room has display cases grouped according to themes: maps to your left, sacred texts straight ahead, music to your right, and so on. Focus on the big picture, and don't be too worried about locating every specific exhibit in this tour.

❶ Maps

The historic maps on the wall show how humans' perspective of the world expanded over the centuries. These pieces of paper, encoded with information gleaned from travelers, could be passed along to future generations—each building upon the knowledge

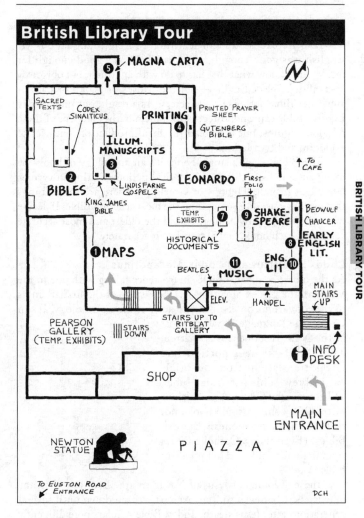

British Library Tour

MAGNA CARTA

❺

SACRED TEXTS

Codex SINAITICUS

PRINTED PRAYER SHEET

PRINTING

❹

GUTENBERG BIBLE

ILLUM. MANUSCRIPTS

❸

→ TO CAFÉ

❷

BIBLES

LINDISFARNE GOSPELS

KING JAMES BIBLE

LEONARDO

❻

FIRST FOLIO

BEOWULF CHAUCER

SHAKE-SPEARE

❾

TEMP. EXHIBITS

❼

HISTORICAL DOCUMENTS

EARLY ENGLISH LIT.

❽

❿

❶ MAPS

BEATLES

MUSIC

❶❶

ENG. LIT

HANDEL

MAIN STAIRS UP

ELEV.

STAIRS UP TO RITBLAT GALLERY

PEARSON GALLERY (TEMP. EXHIBITS)

STAIRS DOWN

❶ INFO DESK

SHOP

MAIN ENTRANCE

NEWTON STATUE

PIAZZA

To EUSTON ROAD ENTRANCE

DCH

BRITISH LIBRARY TOUR

of the last. A crude 13th-century map of Britain put medieval man in an unusual position—looking down on his homeland from 50 miles in the air. A few centuries later, maps of Britain were of such high quality they could be used today to plan a trip. By the 17th century (post-Columbus), the entire globe was fairly well-mapped, except for the mysterious "Terre Incognita" that lay beyond America's east coast.

• *Move into the area dedicated to sacred texts from several cultures— the Hebrew Torah, Muslim Quran, Buddhist sutras, and Hindu Upanishads. Start by browsing the different versions of the sacred text of Christians, the Bible.*

❷ Bibles

My favorite excuse for not learning a foreign language is "If English was good enough for Jesus Christ, it's good enough for me!" I don't know what that has to do with anything, but obviously Jesus didn't speak English—nor did Moses or Isaiah or Paul or any other Bible authors or characters. As a result, our present-day English Bible came not directly from the mouths and pens of these religious figures, but is instead the fitful product of centuries of evolution and translation.

The Bible is not a single book; it's an anthology of books by many authors from different historical periods writing in various languages (usually Hebrew or Greek). So there are three things that editors must do in compiling the most accurate Bible: 1) decide which books actually belong, 2) find the oldest and most accurate version of each book, and 3) translate it accurately.

Codex Sinaiticus and Codex Alexandrinus

As the oldest complete "Bible" in existence (along with one in the Vatican), the Codex Sinaiticus (c. 350) is one of the first attempts to collect various books into one authoritative anthology. It's in Greek, the language in which most of the New Testament was written. The Old Testament portions are Greek translations from the original Hebrew. This particular Bible, and the nearby Codex Alexandrinus (A.D. 425), contain some books not included in most modern English Bibles. (Even today, Catholic Bibles contain books not found in Protestant Bibles.)

These accounts of Jesus of Nazareth are about as old as any in existence, but even so, they weren't written down until several generations after Jesus' death. Today, Bible scholars pore diligently over every word in the New Testament, trying to separate Jesus' authentic words from those that seem to have been added later.

Early English Bibles—King James Version, Wycliffe Bible, etc.

These Bibles are written in the same language you speak, but try reading them. The strange letters and archaic words clearly show how quickly languages evolve.

Jesus spoke Aramaic, a form of Hebrew. His words were written down in Greek. Greek manuscripts were translated into Latin, the language of medieval monks and scholars. By 1400, there was still no English version of the Bible, though only a small percentage of the population understood Latin. A few brave reformers risked death to translate the books into English and print them using Gutenberg's new invention, the printing press. Within two centuries, English translations were both legal and popular.

The King James version (made during his reign) has been the most widely used English translation. Fifty scholars worked for four years, borrowing heavily from previous translations, to produce the work. Its impact on the English language was enormous, making Elizabethan English something of the standard, even after all those *thee*s and *thou*s fell out of fashion in everyday speech.

Many of the most recent translations are not only more accurate (based on better scholarship and original manuscripts), but more readable, using modern speech patterns. The late 20th-century debates over God's gender highlight the problems of translating old phrases to fit contemporary viewpoints.

❸ Lindisfarne Gospels (A.D. 698) and Other Illuminated Manuscripts

Throughout the Middle Ages, Bibles had to be reproduced by hand. This was a painstaking pro-

cess, usually done by monks for a rich patron. This beautifully illustrated ("illuminated") collection of the four Gospels is the most magnificent of medieval British monk-uscripts. The text is in Latin, the language of scholars ever since the Roman Empire, but the illustrations—with elaborate tracery and interwoven decoration—mix Irish, classical, and even Byzantine forms. (Read an electronic copy using the touch-screen computers.)

These Gospels are a reminder that Christianity almost didn't make it in Europe. After the fall of Rome (which had established Christianity as the official religion), much of Europe reverted to its pagan ways. This was the time of *Beowulf*, when people worshipped woodland spirits and terrible Teutonic gods. It took dedicated Irish missionaries 500 years to reestablish the faith on the Continent. Lindisfarne, an obscure monastery of Irish monks on an island off the east coast of England, was one of the few beacons of light after the fall of Rome, tending the embers of civilization through the long night of the Dark Ages.

Browse through more illuminated manuscripts (in the cases behind the Lindisfarne Gospels). This is some of the finest art from what we call the Dark Ages. The little intimate details offer a rare and fascinating peek into medieval life.

❹ Printing

Printing was invented by the Chinese (what wasn't?). The **Printed Prayer Sheet** (c. 618–907) was made seven centuries before the printing press was "invented" in Europe. A bodhisattva (an incarnation of Buddha) rides a lion, surrounded by a prayer in Chinese characters. The faithful gained a blessing by saying the prayer, and so did the printer by reproducing it. Texts such as this were printed using wooden blocks carved with Chinese characters, then dipped into paint or ink.

The Gutenberg Bible (c. 1455)

It looks like just another monk-made Latin manuscript, but it was the first book printed in Europe using movable type. Printing is one of the most revolutionary inventions in history.

Johann Gutenberg (c. 1397–1468), a German silversmith, devised a convenient way to reproduce written materials quickly, neatly, and cheaply—by printing with movable type. You scratch each letter onto a separate metal block, then arrange them into words, ink them up, and press them onto paper. When one job was done you could reuse the same letters for a new one.

This simple idea had immediate and revolutionary consequences. Suddenly, the Bible was available for anyone to read, fueling the Protestant Reformation. Knowledge became cheap and accessible to a wide audience, not just the rich. Books became the mass medium of Europe, linking people by a common set of ideas.

❺ Magna Carta (1215)

Duck into the Magna Carta Room to answer this question: How did Britain, a tiny island with a few million people, come to rule a quarter of the world? Not by force, but by law. The Magna Carta was the basis for England's constitutional system of government. Though historians talk about *the* Magna Carta, several different versions of the document exist, some of which are kept in this room.

The Articles of the Barons: In 1215, England's barons rose in revolt against the slimy King John. (Remember, John appears as a villain in the legends of Robin Hood.) After losing London, John was forced to negotiate. The barons presented him with this list of demands. John, whose rule was worthless without the barons' support, had no choice but to affix his seal to it.

Magna Carta: A few days after John agreed to this original document, it was rewritten in legal form, and some 35 copies of the final version of the "Great Charter" were distributed around the kingdom.

This was a turning point in the history of government. Before, kings had ruled by God-given authority, above the laws of men. Now, for the first time, there were limits—in writing—on how a king could treat his subjects. More generally, it established the idea of "due process"—the notion that a government can't infringe on citizens' freedom without a legitimate legal reason. This small step became the basis for all constitutional governments, including yours.

So what did this radical piece of paper actually say? Not much, by today's standards. The specific demands had to do with things such as inheritance taxes, the king's duties to widows and orphans, and so on. It wasn't the specific articles that were important, but the simple fact that the king had to abide by them as law.

• *Now return to the main room to find...*

❻ Leonardo da Vinci's Notebook

Books also spread secular knowledge. During the Renaissance, men turned their attention away from heaven and toward the nuts and bolts of the material world around them. These pages from Leonardo's notebook show his powerful curiosity, his genius for invention, and his famous backward and inside-out handwriting, which makes sense only if you know Italian and have a mirror. Leonardo's restless mind pondered diverse subjects, from how birds fly to the flow of the Arno River to military fortifications to an early helicopter to the "earthshine" reflecting onto the moon.

One person's research inspired another's, and books allowed knowledge to accumulate. Galileo championed the counter-commonsense notion that the earth spun around the sun, and Isaac Newton later perfected the mathematics of those moving celestial bodies.

❼ Historical Documents

Nearby are many more historical documents. The displays change frequently, but you may see letters by Queen Elizabeth I, Thomas More, Florence Nightingale, Gandhi, and others. But for now, let's trace the evolution of...

❽ Early English Literature

Four out of every five English words have been borrowed from other languages. The English language, like English culture (and

London today), is a mix derived from foreign invaders. Some of the historic ingredients that make this cultural stew:

- The original Celtic tribesmen
- Latin-speaking Romans (A.D. 1–500)
- Germanic tribes called Angles and Saxons (making English a Germanic language and naming the island "Angle-land"—England)
- Vikings from Denmark (A.D. 800)
- French-speaking Normans under William the Conqueror (1066–1250)

Beowulf (c. 1000)

Ponder this first English literary masterpiece. The Anglo-Saxon epic poem, written in Old English (the earliest version of our language), almost makes the hieroglyphics on the Rosetta Stone look easy. The manuscript is from A.D. 1000, although the story itself dates to about 750. In this epic story, the young hero Beowulf defeats two half-human monsters threatening the kingdom. Beowulf symbolizes England's emergence from the chaos and barbarism of the Dark Ages.

The Canterbury Tales (c. 1410)

Six hundred years later, England was Christian, but it was hardly the pious, predictable, Sunday-school world we might imagine. Geoffrey Chaucer's bawdy collection of stories, told by pilgrims on their way to Canterbury, gives us the full range of life's experiences—happy, sad, silly, sexy, and devout. (Late in life, Chaucer wrote an apology for those works of his "that tend toward sin.")

While most serious literature of the time was written in scholarly Latin, the stories in *The Canterbury Tales* were written in Middle English, the language that developed after the French invasion of 1066 added a Norman twist to Old English.

❾ Shakespeare (1564–1616)

William Shakespeare is the greatest author in any language. Period. He expanded and helped define modern English. In one fell swoop, he made the language of everyday people as important as Latin. In the process, he gave us phrases like "one fell swoop," which we quote without knowing it's Shakespeare.

Perhaps as important was his insight into humanity. With his stock of great characters—Hamlet, Othello, Macbeth, Falstaff, Lear, Romeo, Juliet—he probed the psychology of human beings 300 years before Freud. Even today, his characters strike a familiar chord.

William Shakespeare and Some Contemporaries

Some scholars have wondered if maybe Shakespeare had help on several of his plays. After all, they reasoned, how could a journeyman actor, with little education, have written so many masterpieces? And he was surrounded by other great writers, such as his friend and fellow poet, Ben Jonson. Most modern scholars, though, agree that Shakespeare did indeed write the plays and sonnets attributed to him.

The Shakespeare First Folio (1623)

Shakespeare wrote his plays to be performed, not read. He published a few, but as his reputation grew, unauthorized "bootleg" versions began to circulate. Some of these were written by actors who were trying (with faulty memories) to re-create plays they had appeared in years before. Publishers also put out different versions of his plays.

It wasn't until seven years after his death that this complete collection of Shakespeare's plays was published. The editors were friends and fellow actors.

The engraving of Shakespeare on the title page is one of only two portraits done during his lifetime. Is this what he really looked like? No one knows. The best answer probably comes from Ben Jonson, in the introduction on the facing page. Jonson concludes, "Reader, look not on his picture, but his book."

⑩ Other Greats in English Literature

The rest of the "*Beowulf*/Chaucer wall" is a greatest-hits sampling of British literature, featuring works that have enlightened and brightened our lives for centuries. The displays rotate frequently,

but there's always a tasty selection of famous works, from Dickens to Austen to Kipling to Woolf to Joyce. Often on display is the original *Alice's Adventures in Wonderland* by Lewis Carroll. Carroll (whose real name was Charles L. Dodgson) was a stutterer, which made him uncomfortable around everyone but children. For them he created a fantasy world, where grown-up rules and logic were turned upside-down.

BRITISH LIBRARY TOUR

⓫ Music

The Beatles

Future generations will have to judge whether this musical quartet ranks with artists such as Dickens and Keats, but no one can deny their historical significance. The Beatles burst onto the scene in the early 1960s to unheard-of popularity. With their long hair and loud music, they brought counterculture and revolutionary ideas to the middle class, affecting the values of a whole generation. Touring the globe, they served as a link between young people everywhere. Look for photos of John Lennon, Paul McCartney, George Harrison, and Ringo Starr before and after their fame.

Most interesting are the manuscripts of song lyrics written by Lennon and McCartney, the two guiding lights of the group. "I Want to Hold Your Hand" was the song that launched them to superstardom. "A Hard Day's Night" and "Help" were title songs of two films capturing the excitement and chaos of their hectic touring schedule. Some call "A Ticket to Ride" the first heavy-metal song. In "Here, There, and Everywhere," notice the changes Paul made while searching for the perfect rhyme. "Yesterday," by Paul, was recorded with guitar and voice backed by a string quartet—a touch of sophistication by producer George Martin. Also, glance at the rambling, depressed, and cynical but humorous "untitled verse" by a young John Lennon. Is that a self-portrait at the bottom?

Handel's *Messiah* (1741) and Other Music Manuscripts

Kind of an anticlimax after the Fab Four, I know, but here are manuscripts by Mozart, Beethoven, Schubert, and others. George Frideric Handel's famous oratorio, the *Messiah*, was written in a flash of inspiration—three hours of music in 24 days. Here are the final bars of its most famous tune. Hallelujah.

THE CITY WALK

From Trafalgar Square to London Bridge

In Shakespeare's day, London consisted of a one-square-mile area surrounding St. Paul's. Today, that square mile, the neighborhood known as "The City," is still the financial heart of London, densely packed with history and bustling with business.

This two-mile walk from Trafalgar Square to London Bridge parallels the Thames, on the same main road used for centuries. Along the way, you'll see sights from The City's storied past, such as St. Paul's Cathedral, the steeples of other Wren churches, historic taverns, a Crusader church, and narrow alleyways with faint remnants of the London of Shakespeare and Dickens.

But you'll also catch The City in action today, especially if you visit on a weekday at lunchtime, when workers spill out onto the streets and The City is at its liveliest. See lawyers and judges in robes and wigs taking cigarette breaks, brokers in pin-striped power suits buying newspapers from Cockneys, and the last of a dying breed—elderly gentlemen with bowler hats and brollies (umbrellas) browsing for tailored shirts and Cuban cigars. Sip a pint in the same pub where Dickens did, and eavesdrop on a power lunch. Use this walk to help resurrect the London that was, then let The City of today surprise you with what is.

Orientation

Length of This Tour: Allow three or more hours, depending on what you visit.

Getting There: Start at Trafalgar Square (Tube: Charing Cross or Embankment). You'll head east on the Strand and end at London Bridge (where the Bankside Walk begins).

Tourist Information: A TI is across the street from St. Paul's, toward the river (daily 9:30–17:00, tel. 020/7332-1456).

Courtauld Gallery: £5, free Mon until 14:00, daily 10:00–18:00, last entry at 17:30, in Somerset House. ◑ See the Courtauld Gallery Tour chapter.

St. Clement Danes: Free, Mon–Fri 9:00–16:00, Sat 9:30–15:00, Sun 9:30–15:00 but closed to sightseers during worship.

Royal Courts of Justice: Free, Mon–Fri 10:00–16:30, closed Sat–Sun, no photos, located on the Strand.

Temple Church: Free, hours vary, generally Sun–Thu 14:00–16:00, closed most Fri–Sat.

Dr. Johnson's House: £4.50, Mon–Sat 11:00–17:30, closed Sun, closes 30 min early Oct–April, 17 Gough Square.

St. Bride's Church: Free, Mon–Fri 8:00–18:00, Sun 10:00–13:00 & 17:00–19:30, closed Sat, free lunch concerts generally Tue, Wed, or Fri at 13:15, Sun choral Eucharist at 11:00 and evensong at 18:30, just off Fleet Street.

Old Bailey: Free, public galleries only; opening hours depend on court schedule, but are generally Mon–Fri 9:45–12:45 & 14:00–16:30, closed Sat–Sun, reduced hours in Aug; no kids under 14; no cameras, mobile phones, or bags allowed—Eddie at Bailey's Café across the street at #30 stores bags for £2.

St. Paul's Cathedral: £11 includes church entry and dome climb; Mon–Sat 8:30–16:30, last church entry 16:00, last dome entry 16:15, closed Sun except for worship (when it's free); free evensong Mon–Sat at 17:00, Sun at 15:15. ◑ See the St. Paul's Tour chapter.

St. Mary-le-Bow: Free, Mon–Thu 7:00–18:00, Fri 7:00–16:00, closed Sat–Sun, Cheapside, tel. 020/7248-5139, www.stmarylebow.co.uk.

The Monument: £3 to climb the steps for the view, daily 9:30–17:30, last entry at 17:00.

Overview

The City stretches from Temple Church (near Blackfriars Bridge) to the Tower of London. This was the London of the ancient Romans, William the Conqueror, Henry VIII, Shakespeare, and Elizabeth I.

But The City has been stripped of its history by the Great Fire (1666), the WWII Blitz (1940–1941), and modern economic realities. Today, it's a neighborhood of modern bank buildings and retail stores. Only about 7,000 people actually live here, but on work days it's packed with hundreds of thousands of commuting bankers, legal assistants, and coffee-shop baristas. By day, The City is a hive of business activity. At night and on weekends, it's a ghost town.

The route is simple—a two-mile walk east along a single street that changes names as you go. The Strand becomes Fleet Street, which becomes Cannon Street.

The Walk Begins

• *From Trafalgar Square (Tube: Charing Cross or Embankment), head east on the Strand. (Some may wish to skip a mile's worth of the Strand by taking the Tube directly to Temple, picking up the walk at St. Clement Danes.)*

The Strand—From Trafalgar Square to The City

This busy boulevard, home to theaters and retail stores, was formerly a high-class riverside promenade, back before the Thames was tamed with retaining walls in the 19th century.

The venerable **Charing Cross Station** still has a terminus hotel (a standard part of station design in the early days of rail travel) and remains a busy transportation hub.

The station is named for the **Charing Cross monument,** which stands quietly out of place amid all the commotion in front of the station. This monument is a Victorian Age replacement of the original, medieval "Eleanor Cross." When Queen Eleanor died in 1290, her body was carried from Nottingham to Westminster Abbey. King Edward I had a memorial "Eleanor Cross" built at each of the 12 places his wife's funeral procession spent the night during that long, sad trek. Charing Cross marks the final overnight stop. A few blocks up the Strand on the left is Southampton Street, which leads to **Covent Garden** (described on page 54).

Ahead on the right is the drive-up entrance to the **Savoy Hotel and Savoy Theatre.** The renovated hotel is scheduled to reopen in winter 2009 or spring 2010. The shiny gold knight represents the Earl of Savoy, who built the original riverside palace here in 1245. This is one of London's ritziest locales, with Rolls-Royces, fancy shops, Simpson's Restaurant, Donald Trump luxury, and the doorman in top hat and tails. Everyone has stayed here. Monet painted the Thames at the Savoy; Oscar Wilde romanced Lord Douglas; Chaplin, Sinatra, and Burton-and-Taylor made the scene; as did The Beatles, The Who, and Bob Dylan, who filmed his cue-card-flipping film for *Subterranean Homesick Blues* in an alley around back. If the Savoy's

THE CITY WALK

The City Walk

⊕ Tube Station
⚜ View

STREET WIDTH IS
EXAGGERATED
FOR CLARITY

400 YARDS
400 METERS

FETTER LANE

FARRING.

Covent Garden

COVENT GARDEN

ALDWYCH

SOUTH

STRAND

Temple

EMBANK- MENT

FLEET

Black-friars
(closed 10-11)

BLACKFRIARS BRIDGE

TO TRAFALGAR SQUARE

START

Embankment

VICTORIA

WATERLOO BRIDGE

COURTAULD GALLERY

THE TEMPLE

THAMES

Charing Cross

EMB. PIER

JUBILEE --- WALKWAY

❶ Savoy Hotel & Theatre
❷ Courtauld Gallery
❸ St. Mary-le-Strand
❹ St. Clement Danes
❺ Royal Courts of Justice
❻ Twinings Tea
❼ Temple Bar Monument
❽ Prince Henry's Room
❾ Temple Church
❿ The Inns of Court
⓫ St. Dunstan-in-the-West
⓬ Dr. Johnson's House
⓭ Ye Olde Cheshire Cheese Tavern
⓮ View of St. Paul's
⓯ St. Bride's Church

open, step inside the spiffy new lobby under the pretext of asking about their afternoon tea (about £27, often booked up a week in advance).

At the next intersection, a side-trip out onto **Waterloo Bridge** affords one of the best London views, overlooking the city in both directions.

A half-block farther is **Gibraltar House** (at 150 Strand), a quasi-embassy and visitors center for one of Britain's last little "colonies," located on the southern tip of Spain.

Next up is **Somerset House,** the last of the many great riverside mansions that once lined the Strand. Today, it has a people-friendly courtyard with playful fountains, a riverside terrace, an exhibition hall, and the **Courtauld Gallery**—a fine art collection including Impressionist and Post-Impressionist gems (✪ see the Courtauld Gallery Tour chapter).

THE CITY WALK

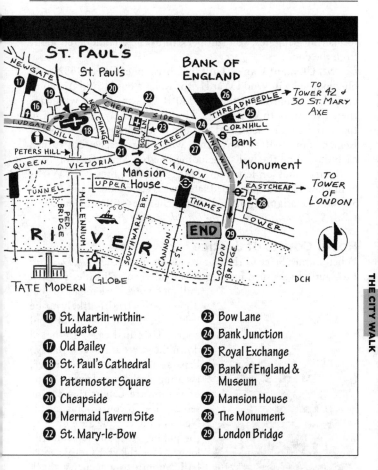

16 St. Martin-within-
   Ludgate
17 Old Bailey
18 St. Paul's Cathedral
19 Paternoster Square
20 Cheapside
21 Mermaid Tavern Site
22 St. Mary-le-Bow

23 Bow Lane
24 Bank Junction
25 Royal Exchange
26 Bank of England &
   Museum
27 Mansion House
28 The Monument
29 London Bridge

You'll encounter two different churches left Strand-ed in the middle of traffic when the road was widened around them. **St. Mary-le-Strand,** with its clean, white interior lit by blue-and-green stained glass, is an oasis of quiet. Charles Dickens' parents got married here. To the right of the church is **King's College,** one of the world's top universities, with 20,000 students.

To the left is **Bush House,** home of BBC's World Service. And just past Bush House is **Australia House,** a kind of embassy for that member of the British Commonwealth. It's most famous for its role as the goblin-run Gringotts

Wizarding Bank in the *Harry Potter* movies. (Though it's not open to visiting Muggles, you can peek in to the chandeliered lobby from the door.)

St. Clement Danes, built by Christopher Wren (1682), was blitzed heavily in World War II. Today, it's a busy Royal Air Force chapel, a memorial to the 125,000 RAF servicemen who gave their lives in both world wars. Hundreds of gray medallions in the pavement are dedicated to various squadrons, and Books of Remembrance—10 thick volumes, with a page respectfully turned each day—line the walls, including one for Americans (on back wall, first book on left side). This is the first of several Wren-built churches (steeple added later) we'll see on the walk. Of the 50-some he originally built, 23 Wren churches still dot London.

• *Past St. Clement Danes, on the left side of street are the...*

Royal Courts of Justice

When former Spice Girls sue tabloids for libel, when *The Da Vinci Code* author gets sued for plagiarism, or when ex-Beatles pay $50

million divorce settlements to gold diggers, the trial is likely to be held here, at Britain's highest civil court. (Criminal cases are heard down the street at the Old Bailey.) Paparazzi often litter the entrance, awaiting a celeb or a lawyer (many of whom are celebrities themselves). The 76 courtrooms in this Neo-Gothic complex are open to the public. At least step into the lobby to see the vast Gothic entry hall. Submit to a security check to go farther in. This is just one of several legal buildings in the neighborhood.

• *Across the street is...*

Twinings Tea (216 Strand)

When this narrow store first opened its doors ("established 1706"), tea was an exotic concoction from newly explored lands. (The Chinese statues at the entrance remind us that tea came first from China, then India.) This store has been in the Twining family for nearly 300 years (Mon–Fri 9:30–17:00, Sat 10:00–16:00, closed Sun, tel. 020/7353-3511). The Twinings shop is narrow, but

THE CITY WALK

explore its depths—there's a tea-tasting room in the back (sessions by appointment, so call ahead).

In the 1700s, London was in the grip of a coffee craze, and "coffee houses" were everywhere. These were rather seedy places, where "gentlemen" went for coffee, tobacco, and female companionship. Tea offered a refreshing change of pace, and the late-in-the-day "cuppa" (as well as "afternoon tea") soon became a national institution. These days—as you'll see on this walk—coffee is making a comeback in London in the form of modern Starbucks-style coffee shops.

• *Up ahead, in the middle of the street, is a small statue of a winged dragon.*

Temple Bar Monument

A statue of a griffin, a mythological beast with wings and lion's body, marks the official border between the City of Westminster and The City of London. The Queen, who presides over Westminster, does not pass this point without ceremonial permission of The City's Lord Mayor. The relief at its base shows Queen Victoria submitting to this ritual in 1837.

• *Cross the border, leaving Westminster and entering The City. Ahead on the left (194 Fleet Street) is The Old Bank of England pub—a former bank with a lavish late Victorian interior that serves lunches to the 9-to-5 crowd. (To imagine a fancy 19th-century bank, pop inside.) Up a few storefronts, on the right side of the street, look above a beauty shop to find an old building with black-framed, stained-glass bay windows.*

Prince Henry's Room (17 Fleet Street)

This half-timbered, three-story, Tudor-style building (1610) is one of the few to survive the Great Fire. In Shakespeare's day, the entire City was packed, rooftop to rooftop, with wood and plaster buildings like this. Many were five and six stories high, with narrow frontage. Little wonder that a small fire could spread so quickly and become the Great Fire of 1666.

The top floor of the house is "Prince Henry's Room," once an

The Da Vinci Code in London

Readers of Dan Brown's famous novel—a work of fiction encrusted with many real and many fictional facts—will recognize scenes set in London. "In London lies a knight a Pope interred...You seek the orb that ought to be on his tomb." This is one of the cryptic clues Robert Langdon, an American art historian, must follow to solve a murder and, ultimately, find the "Holy Grail." Here are some stops along his Grail trail (including details that may spoil the plot for those who haven't read the book):

Temple Church: The church's stone knights from the secret society of Templars seem to be exactly what Langdon seeks. But he finds that there's no "orb," and the knights aren't even "tombs" (containing bodies), but merely effigies. (This isn't the only red herring in the book.) For the film version, some footage was actually shot in Temple Church.

Westminster Abbey: At the tomb of Isaac Newton (in the nave, see page 112), they find an "orb." But then Langdon is summoned to the Chapter House, where he's surprised to find that a friend is the enemy. (The film was not shot in Westminster Abbey, but with a re-creation of Newton's tomb set inside another church.)

King's College: Langdon gets research assistance at the building along the Strand, by Somerset House.

Opus Dei Centre: The conservative Catholic organization (also searching for the Grail) has an office near Kensington Gardens.

Alas for Langdon, the Grail isn't in London after all, but farther afield.

office for King Charles I's son (undergoing renovation but may reopen in 2010; likely open Mon–Fri 11:00–14:00, closed Sat–Sun). An exhibit inside tells about a onetime neighborhood resident, Samuel Pepys (1633–1701). Though not a famous man in his day, Pepys (pronounced "peeps") kept a diary chronicling London life and the Great Fire that, even today, makes that time come alive. Pepys was baptized in nearby St. Bride's Church, and he drank in this room when it was a tavern.

• *Pass underneath the house, through the passageway called Inner Temple Lane that leads a half-block to the exotic...*

Temple Church

Exterior: The round, crenellated, castle-turret roof and tiny statue of a knight on horseback (on a pillar in the courtyard) mark this as a Crusader church (1185) from the days of King Richard the Lionhearted. The church was the headquarters of the Knights Templar, a band of heavily armed, highly trained monks who dressed in long white robes (decorated with red crosses) beneath heavy armor. In their secret rituals, the knights were sworn to chastity and to the protection of pilgrims on their way to the Muslim-held Holy Land.

Interior: Inside, some honored knights lie face-up on the floor under the rotunda of the circular "nave," patterned after the

Church of the Holy Sepulchre in Jerusalem. A knight's crossed legs indicate that he probably died peacefully at home. Surrounding the serene knights are grotesque faces, perhaps the twisted expressions seen in distant wars.

By 1300, the Knights Templar's mission of protecting pilgrims had become a corrupt "protection" racket, and they'd grown rich loaning money to kings and popes. Those same kings and popes condemned the monks as heretics and sodomites, and confiscated their lands (1312). The Temple Church was rented to lawyers, who built the Inns of Court around it.

• *Abutting, surrounding, and extending from the Temple Church is a vast complex of buildings covering a full city block between the Strand/ Fleet Street and the Thames, known collectively as...*

The Inns of Court

Wander through the peaceful maze of buildings, courtyards, narrow lanes, nooks, gardens, fountains, and century-old gas lamps, where lawyers take a break from the Royal Courts. The complex is a self-contained city of lawyers, with offices, lodgings, courtrooms, chapels, and dining halls. Law students must live here (and are even required to eat a number of meals on the premises) to complete their legal internship.

You'll see barristers in modern business suits and ties, plus a few in traditional wigs and robes, as they prepare to do legal battle.

The Great Fire

The stones of St. Paul's flew from the building, the lead melting down the streets in a stream…. God grant mine eyes may never behold the like…. Above 10,000 homes all in one flame, the noise and crackling and thunder of the impetuous flames, the shrieking of women and children, the hurry of the people, the fall of the towers, houses, and churches was like an hideous storm.

—John Evelyn, eyewitness

THE CITY WALK

The wigs are a remnant of French manners of the 1700s, when every European gentleman wore one.

• *Get lost. Don't worry—you'll eventually spill back out onto the busy street. Return to Prince Henry's Room, which marks the spot where the Strand becomes…*

Fleet Street

"The Street" was the notorious haunt of a powerful combination—lawyers and the media. (You just passed a pub called "The Wig and Pen.") In 1500, Wynkyn de Worde moved here with a newfangled invention, a printing press, making this area the center of an early Information Age. In 1702, the first daily newspaper appeared. Soon you had the *Tatler*, the *Spectator*, and many others pumping out both hard news and paparazzi gossip for the hungry masses. Just past St. Dunstan Church, you'll see a building decorated with mosaic signs with the names of some bygone newspapers: the *Dundee Evening Telegraph*, the *People's Journal*, and so on.

London became the nerve center of a global, colonial empire, and Fleet Street was where every twitch found expression. Hard-drinking, ink-stained reporters gathered in taverns and coffeehouses, pumping lawyers for juicy pretrial information, scrambling for that choice bit of must-read gossip that would make their paper number one. They built an industry that still thrives—Britain supports some dozen national newspapers, selling 14 million papers a day.

Today, busy Fleet Street bustles with almost every business *except* newspapers. The industry made a mass exodus in the 1980s for offices elsewhere, replaced by financial institutions. As you walk along, you'll see the former offices of the *Daily Telegraph* (135 Fleet Street) and the *Daily Express* (#121–28—peek in to the lobby to see its classic 1930s Art Deco interior). The last major institution to leave (in the summer of 2005) was the Reuters news agency (#85, opposite the *Daily Express*).

• *Heading east along Fleet Street, you'll find...*

St. Dunstan-in-the-West— The Great Fire of 1666

This church stands where the Great Fire of September 1666 finally ended. The fire started near London Bridge. For three days it swept westward, fanned by hot and blustery weather, leveling everything in its path. As it approached St. Dunstan, 40 theology students battled the blaze, holding it off until the wind shifted, and the fire slowly burned itself out.

From here to the end of our walk (1.5 miles), we'll be passing through the fire's path of destruction. It left London a Sodom-and-Gomorrah wasteland so hot it couldn't be walked on for weeks. (For more on the fire, see the end of the Bankside Walk chapter.)

Today, St. Dunstan is one of the few churches with a thriving congregation (of Orthodox Romanians) in this now depopulated and secularized district. An unbroken line of vicars dating back to 1237 is listed in the vestibule. The clock on the bell tower outside (1670) features London's first minute hand and has two slaves gonging two bells four times an hour.

Alongside the church is a rare contemporary statue of Queen Elizabeth. Surviving from her reign, this 1586 depiction of Elizabeth is as accurate as anything we have. The scepter and orb symbolize her religious and secular authority.

THE CITY WALK

• *Continue east on Fleet Street. A half-block past Fetter Lane, turn left through a covered alleyway (at #167, immediately across from #54). Follow signs through the narrow lanes directing you to* Dr. Johnson's House.

Narrow Lanes—1700s London

"Sir, if you wish to have a just notion of the magnitude of this city, you must...survey the innumerable little lanes and courts," said the writer Samuel Johnson in 1763 to his young friend and biographer, James Boswell. These twisting alleyways and cramped buildings that house urban hobbits give a faint glimpse of rebuilt 1700s London, a crowded city of half a million people. After the Great Fire, London was resurrected in brick and stone instead of wood, but they stuck to the same medieval street plan, resulting in narrow lanes of brick buildings like these.

• *The narrow lanes eventually spill out onto Gough Square, about a block north of Fleet Street, where you'll find...*

Dr. Johnson's House (17 Gough Square)

"When a man is tired of London, he is tired of life," wrote Samuel Johnson, "for there is in London all that life can afford." Johnson (1709–1784) loved to wander these twisting lanes, looking for pungent slices of London street life that he could pass along in his weekly columns called "The Rambler" and "The Idler."

At age 28, Johnson arrived in London with one of his former students, David Garrick, who went on to revolutionize London theater. Dr. Johnson prowled the pubs, brothels, coffeehouses, and illicit gaming pits where terriers battled cornered rats while men bet on the outcome. Johnson—described as "tall, stout," and "slovenly in his dress"—became a well-known eccentric and man-about-town, though he always seemed to live on the fringes of poverty.

Johnson inhabited this house from 1748 to 1759. He prayed at St. Clement Danes, drank in Fleet Street pubs, and, in the attic of the house, produced his most famous work, *A Dictionary of the English Language*. Published in 1755, it was the first great English-language dictionary, starring Johnson's 42,773 favorite words culled from all the books he'd read. It took Johnson and six assistants more than six years to sift through all the alternate spellings and Cockney dialects of the world's most complex language. He standardized spelling and pronunciation, explained the word's etymology, and occasionally put his own droll spin on words. ("Oats: a grain, which is generally given to horses, but in Scotland supports the people.")

Today, the house is a museum. While the exhibits are fascinating for hard-core Johnson fans (I met one once), the old house is interesting in itself, even for the casual visitor. See a video and climb four stories through period furniture, passing a first edition of Johnson's dictionary and pictures of Johnson, Garrick, and Boswell. Nothing is roped off or behind glass, and you can browse at will, finally arriving in the top-floor garret where literary history was made.

• *At the other end of Gough Square, turn right at the statue of Johnson's cat Hodge and head back toward Fleet Street, noticing the lists of barristers (trial lawyers) on the doorways (e.g., at 9 Gough Square). They work not as part of a firm, but as freelancers sharing offices and clerks. Stay to the left as you wind downhill through the alleys, and look near Fleet Street for the entrance of...*

Ye Olde Cheshire Cheese Tavern

Johnson often—and I do mean often—popped 'round here for a quick one, sometimes with David Garrick and his sleazy actor friends.

"The Cheese" dates from 1667, when it was rebuilt after the Great Fire, but it's been a tavern since 1538. It's a four-story warren of small, smoky, wood-lined rooms, each offering different menus, from pub grub to white-tablecloth meals. A traditional "chop house," it serves hearty portions of meats to power-lunching businessmen.

Sit in Charles Dickens' favorite seat, next to a coal fireplace (in the "Chop Room," main floor) and order a steak-and-kidney pie and some spotted dick (sponge pudding with currants). Sip a pint of Samuel Smith (the house beer of the current owners) and think of Samuel Johnson, who drank here pondering various spellings: "pint" or "pynte," "color" or "colour," "theater" or "theatre." Immerse yourself in a world largely unchanged for centuries, a world of reporters scribbling the news over lunch, of Alfred Lord Tennyson inventing rhymes and Arthur Conan Doyle solving crimes, of W. B. Yeats, Teddy Roosevelt, and Mark Twain.

• *Back out on Fleet Street, you're met with a cracking...*

THE CITY WALK

View of St. Paul's—the Blitz, the Great Fire, the Plague, and Christopher Wren

If you were standing here on December 30, 1940, the morning after a German Luftwaffe firebomb raid, you'd see nothing but a flat, smoldering landscape of rubble, with St. Paul's rising above it almost miraculously intact. (For more on the Blitz, see the sidebar on page 222.)

Standing here in September 1666, you'd see nothing but smoke and ruins. The Great Fire razed everything, including the original St. Paul's Cathedral. And standing here in September 1665, you'd hear "Bring out yer dead!" as they carted away 70,000 victims of bubonic plague. After the double-whammy of plague and fire, the architect Christopher Wren was hired to rebuild St. Paul's and The City.

Even today, we see the view that Wren intended—a majestic dome hovering above the hazy rooftops, surrounded by the thin spires of his lesser churches. In the foreground below St. Paul's is the slender, lead-covered steeple of St. Martin-within-Ludgate, perfectly offsetting the more massive dome. Wren's 23 surviving churches are more than plenty for today's secular ghost town of a City.

• *A half-block east of Ye Olde Cheshire Cheese, and a half-block down St. Bride's Avenue, is the stacked-tier steeple of...*

St. Bride's Church (1671–1675)

The 226-foot steeple, Wren's tallest, is said to have inspired a local baker to invent the wedding cake. St. Bride's was one of the first of Wren's churches to open its doors after the Fire. Inside, the church gleams since its post-Blitz reconstruction, re-creating the squares, circles, and rosettes of Wren's original vision.

St. Bride's is nicknamed both "The Cathedral of Fleet Street" and "The Printer's

London's Great Plague of 1665

The Grim Reaper—in the form of the bacteria *Yersinia pestis* (bubonic plague)—rode through London on fleas atop a black rat. It killed one in six people, while leaving the buildings standing. (The next year, the buildings burned.) It started in the spring as "the Poore's Plague," neglected until it spread to richer neighborhoods. During the especially hot summer, 5,000 died each week. By December, St. Bride's congregation was 2,111 souls fewer.

Victims passed through several days of agony: headaches, vomiting, fever, shivering, swollen tongue, and swollen buboes (lumps) on the groin glands. After your skin turned blotchy black (the "Black Death"), you died. "Searchers of the Dead" carted them off to mass graves, including one near St. Bride's. Both the victims and their families were quarantined under house arrest, with a red cross painted on the door and a guard posted nearby, and denied access to food, water, or medical attention for 40 days—a virtual death sentence even for the uninfected.

The disease was blamed on dogs and cats, and paid dog-killers destroyed tens of thousands of pets, bringing even more rats. People who didn't die tried to leave. The Lord Mayor quarantined the whole city within the walls, so the only way out was to produce (or afford) a "certificate of health."

By fall, London was a ghost town, and throughout England, people avoided Londoners like the Plague. It took the Great Fire of 1666 to fully cleanse the city of the disease. Some scholars have suggested that a popular nursery rhyme refers to the dreaded disease (while others brush this off as bunk):

Ring around the rosie (flower garlands to keep the
   Plague away)
A pocket full of posies (buboes on the groin)
Ashes, ashes (your skin turns black)
We all fall down (dead).

Church." It has been home to journalists, scholars, and literati ever since 1500, when Wynkyn de Worde set up his printing press here on church property, in a neighborhood dominated by de Worde's best customers: the literate clergy. The pews bear the names of departed journalists.

Thanks to Hitler's bombs, St. Bride's was instantly excavated down to its sixth-century Saxon foundations, revealing previously unknown history, open to visitors today in the Museum of Fleet Street (free, downstairs on the excavated floor level of the 11th-century church). You'll see layers of history from six previous churches, including Roman coins, medieval

Christopher Wren
(1632–1723)

When London burned, King Charles II turned to his old child-hood friend, Christopher Wren, to rebuild it. The 33-year-old Wren was not an architect, but he'd proven his ability in every field he touched: astronomy (mapping the moon and build-ing a model of Saturn), medicine (using opium as a general anesthetic, making successful blood transfusions between animals), mathematics (a treatise on spherical trigonom-etry), and physics (his study of the laws of motion influenced Newton's "discovery" of gravity). Wren also invented a language for the deaf, studied refraction and optics, and built weather-watching instruments.

Though domed St. Paul's is Wren's most famous church, the smaller churches around it better illustrate his distinctive style: a steeple over the west entrance; an uncluttered, well-lit inte-rior; Neoclassical (Greek-style) columns; a curved or domed plaster ceiling; geo-metrical shapes (e.g., round rosettes inside square frames); and fine carved woodwork, often by his favorite whittler, Grinling Gibbons.

stained glass, and 17th-century tobacco pipes.

Also in the crypt is the wedding dress of the wife of the Fleet Street baker, Mr. Rich, who supposedly gazed out his shop win-dow and made the first many-tiered wedding cake—inspired by St. Bride's steeple. (The word "Bride" is only coincidental, since the church was dedicated to St. Bridgit—or Bride—of Kildare long before the steeple, wedding cakes, or Mrs. Rich's wedding dress.)

• *A block past St. Bride's Church on Fleet Street is The Punch Tavern, draped with memories of the venerable London political magazine famous for its satirical cartoons. Peek in to see Punch and his twin wife Judy looking down on a perfectly Victorian scene. These figures from a popular puppet show gave the magazine its name, and the pub became the magazine staff's hangout (good lunches, 99 Fleet Street). The valley between St. Bride's and St. Paul's is the...*

Fleet River and Ludgate

The Fleet River—now covered over by Farringdon Road—still flows southward, crossing underneath Fleet Street on its way to the Thames at Blackfriars Bridge. In medieval times, the river formed the western boundary of the walled city. Between you and the towering dome of St. Paul's stands Wren's steeple-topped church of **St. Martin-within-Ludgate.** It actually incorporates the old city wall into its west wall, at the old city entrance known as Ludgate.

• *After crossing Farringdon Road, look left down Old Bailey Street to see a dome crowned by a golden statue of justice, which marks the...*

Old Bailey—Central Criminal Court

England's most infamous criminals—from the king-killers of the Civil War to the radically religious William Penn, from the "criminally homosexual" Oscar Wilde to the Yorkshire Ripper—were tried here, in Britain's highest criminal court. On top of the copper dome stands the famous golden Lady who weighs and executes Justice with scale and sword. The Old Bailey is built on the former site of Newgate Prison, with its notorious execution-by-hanging site. Inside, you can visit courtrooms and watch justice doled out the old-fashioned way (see page 69). Bewigged barristers argue before stern judges while the accused sits in the dock.

• *Continue up Ludgate Hill to...*

St. Paul's Cathedral

The greatest of Wren's creations is the rebuilt St. Paul's, England's national church and the heart of The City. After laboring for over

40 years on the church (and what was then the second-largest dome in the world), an elderly Wren got to look up and see his son place the cross on top of the dome, completing the masterpiece. There's been a church on this spot since 604. St. Paul's was the symbol of London's rise from the Great Fire of 1666 and of the city's survival of the Blitz of 1940. (● See the St. Paul's Tour chapter.)

If you're not paying to enter the great church, you can pop into the basement (entry to left of front) for a café, fine WCs, a shop, and a peek at the memorials in the crypt. Belly up to the iron Churchill Gates. Standing on a plaque honoring Churchill, you can see the tomb of Admiral Lord Nelson directly below the dome.

• *A right turn at St. Paul's would take you to the Millennium Bridge, leading across the Thames. Instead, look for the Temple Bar gate—a white stone archway—directly to the left of the church. The gate was once the west entrance to the city of London. Relocated here, it now welcomes you to...*

Paternoster Square

The original Temple Bar gate was built of stone by St. Paul's architect, Christopher Wren, in 1672. But given the increase in traffic and new construction around it, the gate didn't "fit" at Temple Bar anymore. It was disassembled in 1878 and carted off to ornament the rural estate of a brewery owner. Finally, in 2004, the 2,700 stones were brought back to The City and painstakingly rebuilt a half-mile away, here in Paternoster Square.

Enjoy a view of the dome from behind the church's red-brick Chapter House (a good example of Wren's Neoclassicism). This square was designed in the early 21st century to save views of the church, while allowing maximum modern development here in the city center.

• *Stride right past the Shepherd and Sheep statue to the pedestrian walkway behind the statue, which eventually leads to noisy...*

Cheapside—Shakespeare's London

This was the main east–west street of Shakespeare's London, which had a population of about 200,000. The wide street hosted The City's marketplace ("cheap" meant market), seen today in the names of the streets that branch off from it: Bread, Milk, Honey. Rebuilt after the war, Cheapside is now the home of cheap mobile phones, concrete-and-glass offices, clothing stores, and Ye Olde Starbucks. It's also swamped in construction projects, as redeveloping London tears down the cheap buildings of its postwar decades.

If you were to detour two blocks south on Bread Street (to the corner of Bread and Cannon streets), you would not see even a trace of the **Mermaid Tavern,** Shakespeare's favorite haunt—but that's where it stood. In the early 1600s, "Sweet Will" would meet Ben Jonson, Sir Walter Raleigh, and John Donne at the Mermaid for food, ale, and literary conversation. Francis Beaumont, one of the group, wrote: "What things have we seen/Done at the Mermaid! heard words that have been/So nimble, and so full of subtle flame..."

• *A little farther east along Cheapside is...*

St. Mary-le-Bow

From London's earliest Christian times, a church has stood here. The steeple of St. Mary-le-Bow, rebuilt after the Fire, is one of Wren's most impressive. He incorporated the ribbed-arch design of the former church (a "bow" is an arch) in the steeple's midsection. In the courtyard is a statue of a smiling Captain John Smith, who in 1607 established an English colony in Jamestown, Virginia, USA, before retiring here near the church. Inside the church, see not one but two pulpits, used today for point-counterpoint debate of moral issues.

This is the very center of old London, where, in medieval times, the church's bells rang each evening, calling Londoners safely back in to the walled town before the gates were locked. To be born "within the sound of Bow bells" long defined a true local, or "Cockney."

This is also the "Cockney" neighborhood of plucky streetwise urchins, where a distinctive Eliza Doolittle dialect is sometimes still spoken. Today's Cockney is the hard accent of rough-and-tumble, working-class Londoners—and the Geico gecko on American TV ads. There are no Hs. "Are you 'appy, 'arry?" "Where's your 'orse? ...'urry up now." Nineteenth-century social climbers added extra Hs in order not to sound Cockney. "I hunderstand you are hinterested in renting my hattic."

These days, few people actually live within the sound of Bow bells. The City's population, while 300,000 during working hours, falls to about 7,000 at night.

• *Just past St. Mary-le-Bow is...*

Bow Lane

Today, pedestrian-only Bow Lane features smart clothing shops, sandwich bars, and pubs. The entire City once had narrow lanes like Bow, Watling, and Bread Streets. Explore this area between Cheapside and Cannon Street.

When Shakespeare bought his tights and pointy shoes in Bow Lane, the shops were wooden, the streets were dirt, and the bathroom was a ditch down the middle of the road. (The garbage brought rats, and rats brought plagues, like the one in 1665.) You bought your water in buckets carted up from the Thames. And at night, the bellman walked the streets, ringing the hour.

(For more Shakespearean ambience, it's a three-block walk south from St. Paul's to the river, where the Millennium Bridge crosses the Thames to Shakespeare's Globe, a reconstruction of the theater where many of Shakespeare's plays premiered. See page 76.)

• *Continue east on Cheapside a few blocks to the long, wide intersection where nine streets meet, called Bank Junction (Tube: Bank). Looking east, survey the buildings before you. There may be a historical plaque at the street corner with a helpful diagram of Bank Junction's buildings. A good place to view it all is from the front of Mansion House, the building with the six-columned (not eight-columned) entrance, standing where Victoria Street empties onto Bank Junction.*

Bank Junction

You're at the center of financial London. The Square Mile hosts 500 foreign and British banks. London, centrally located amid the globe's time zones, can find some-one around the world to trade with 24 hours a day. In 2009, thousands of protesters packed this square, smashing bank windows in anger over Britain's severe financial downturn.

• *Look across the square at the eight-columned entrance to the...*

Royal Exchange: When London's original stock exchange opened, "stock" meant whatever could be loaded and unloaded onto a boat in the Thames. Remember, London got its start as a river-trading town. Soon, they were gathering here, trading slips of paper and "futures" in place of live goats and chickens. Traders needed money-changers, who needed bankers...and London's financial district boomed. Today, you can step inside under the *Trading Since 1571* sign to a skylight-covered courtyard lined with traders in retail goods.

• *To the left of the Royal Exchange is the city block–sized Bank of England (main entrance just across Threadneedle Street from the Royal Exchange entrance).*

Bank of England: This 3.5-acre, two-story complex houses the country's national bank. In 1694, it loaned £1.2 million to King William III at 8 percent interest to finance a war with France; it's managed the national debt ever since. It's an investment bank (a banker's bank), loaning money to other financial institutions. Working in tandem with the government (nationalized 1946, independent 1997), "The Old Lady of Threadneedle Street" sets interest rates, prints pound notes, and serves as the country's Fort Knox, housing stacks of gold bars.

The complex has a **Bank Museum** inside (free, enter from far side, on St. Bartholomew Lane). See banknotes from 1699, an old safe, account books, and mannequins of CPAs in powdered wigs. Also see current pound notes—with a foil hologram and numbers visible under UV light (to stay one step ahead of counterfeiters). The museum's highlight is under the rotunda, displaying 59 fake gold bars and one real one. The real gold is worth more than

$350,000 (check today's rates nearby) and weighs 28 pounds. Try lifting it.

• *Rising up behind the Bank of England is...*

Tower 42: The black-capped skyscraper at 600 feet is The City's tallest (but not London's tallest, which is Canary Wharf, far to the east of here).

• *Rising to the right is the tip of the bullet-shaped, spiral-ribbed, glass building called...*

30 St. Mary Axe: Built in 2003, the 40-story building houses the London office of a Swiss re-insurance company (an insurer's insurer). The building, nicknamed "The Gherkin" (pickle), is ventilated by natural air entering the balconies spiraling around the perimeter.

• *You're standing in front of...*

Mansion House: As the official residence of The City's Lord Mayor, Mansion House carries on centuries of tradition. Until recently, when an all-London mayor was elected, each district was self-governing. Even today, the Lord Mayor holds a prestigious office, presiding from this palatial building.

• *From Bank Junction, turn right on Lombard Street, which turns into King William Street, and head southeast toward London Bridge. Near the northeast corner of the bridge, look to your left and find a lone column poking its bristly bronze head above the modern rooftops.*

The Monument

The 202-foot hollow column is Wren's tribute to the Great Fire that gave him a blank canvas on which to create modern London.

At 2:00 in the morning of September 2, 1666, a small fire broke out in a baker's oven in nearby Pudding Lane. Supposedly, if you tipped the Monument over (to the east), its top would fall on the exact spot. Fanned by hot, blustery weather, the fire swept westward, leaping from house to house until The City was a square mile of flame.

You can climb the Monument's 311 steps for a view that's still pretty good, despite modern buildings.

• *From here, hike out over the river on...*

London Bridge

End our walk at The City's beginning. (For the history of London Bridge, see page 238.)

The City was born as a river-trading town. The Thames flows

east to west, from the interior of England to the open sea. It's a tidal river from here to the sea, so ancient boats hitched rides on the tide in either direction. London Bridge, first built by the ancient Romans, established a north–south axis. Soon, goods from every corner of the world were pouring into this, one of the modern world's first great urban centers. Surviving plagues, fires, blitzes, economic changes, and even Thatcherism, with its world-wide financial network and cultural heritage, The City thrives.

• *From here, the Tower of London (✪ see the Tower of London Tour chapter) is a seven-minute walk east, down either Eastcheap or Lower Thames Street. The Bankside Walk begins across London Bridge. You can return to Trafalgar Square on the Tube (Monument stop nearby) or bus #15 (from Cannon Street).*

THE CITY WALK

ST. PAUL'S TOUR

No sooner was Sir Christopher Wren selected to refurbish Old St. Paul's Cathedral than the Great Fire of 1666 incinerated it. Within a week, Wren had a plan for a whole new building...and for the city around it, complete with some 50 new churches. For the next four decades he worked to achieve his vision—a spacious church, topped by a dome, surrounded by a flock of Wrens.

St. Paul's is England's national church. There's been a church on this spot since 604. It was the symbol of London's rise from the Great Fire of 1666 and of the city's survival of the Blitz of 1940. Today, it's the center of the Anglican faith. Military buffs will find memorials to many great wars and their war heroes. Dome-climbers will be rewarded with expansive views over London's skyline.

Orientation

Cost: £11 (includes church entry and dome climb). Free on Sun but officially open only to worshippers.

Hours: Mon–Sat 8:30–16:30, last church entry at 16:00, last dome entry at 16:15, closed Sun except for worship. Sometimes closed for special events.

Getting There: Located in The City, Tube: St. Paul's (Mansion House and Cannon Street Tube stops also work; Blackfriars Tube stop is also nearby, but closed until 2011 for renovation). You can take bus #4, #11, #15, #23, #26, or #100. Careful: Don't head for St. Paul's Church near Covent Garden; your destination is St. Paul's Cathedral, in The City.

Information: Recorded info tel. 020/7246-8348, office tel. 020/7236-8350, www.stpauls.co.uk.

Music and Services: Weekday communion is at 8:00 and 12:30. Sunday services are held at 8:00, 10:15 (Matins), 11:30 (sung Eucharist), 15:15 (evensong), and 18:00. Additional evensong services are held Mon–Sat at 17:00 (40 min, free to anyone, though visitors who haven't paid the £11 church admission aren't allowed to linger after the service).

Tours: Guided 90-minute "super tours" (£3) of the cathedral and crypt are offered Mon–Sat at 10:45, 11:15, 13:30, and 14:00 (confirm schedule at church or call 020/7236-8350). Audioguide tours cost £4 (one hour, available Mon–Sat 9:00–15:30).

Climbing the Dome: There are no elevators, and it's 530 steps to the top. Allow an hour to go up and down. There are three levels, called Galleries. The climb gets steeper, narrower, and more claustrophobic as you go higher. It's a one-way system, so you can't come back down until you reach the next level.

Length of This Tour: Allow one hour, two if you climb the dome.

Photography: No photography allowed.

Cuisine Art: Good café in the crypt (free access from north side of church).

Starring: Sir Christopher Wren, Wellington, and World War II.

The Tour Begins

Even now, as skyscrapers encroach, the 365-foot-high dome of St. Paul's rises majestically above the rooftops of the neighborhood. The tall dome is set on classical columns, capped with a lantern, topped by a six-foot ball, and iced with a cross. As the first Anglican cathedral built in London after the Reformation, it is Baroque: St. Peter's in Rome filtered through clear-eyed English reason.

Viewing St. Paul's facade from in front of the church, you can see the story of Paul's conversion told in the stone pediment. A blinding flash leaves Saul sightless on the road to Damascus (see cityscape, lower left). When his sight was restored he became Paul, the Christian. This was the pivotal moment in the life of the man who established Christianity as a world religion through his travels, writing, and evangelizing.

While Paul stands on the top, Peter (with the annoying cock that crowed three times, symbolizing his betrayal of Jesus) is to the left and James is on the right. The four evangelists each carry the gospel they wrote. As Queen Anne was on the throne when the church was finished in 1710, the statue in front portrays her.

• *Enter, buy your ticket, and stand at the far back of the nave.*

St. Paul's Tour

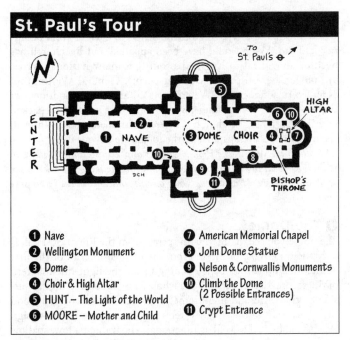

1. Nave
2. Wellington Monument
3. Dome
4. Choir & High Altar
5. HUNT – The Light of the World
6. MOORE – Mother and Child
7. American Memorial Chapel
8. John Donne Statue
9. Nelson & Cornwallis Monuments
10. Climb the Dome (2 Possible Entrances)
11. Crypt Entrance

❶ Nave

Look down the nave through the choir stalls to the stained glass at the far end. This big church feels big. At 515 feet long and 250 feet wide, it's Europe's fourth-largest, after Rome (St. Peter's), Sevilla, and Milan. The spaciousness is accentuated by the relative lack of decoration. The simple, cream-colored ceiling and the clear glass in the windows light everything evenly. Wren wanted this: a simple, open church with nothing to hide. Unfortunately, only this entrance area keeps his original vision—the rest was encrusted with Victorian ornamentation from the 19th century.

A plaque on the floor honors the guards who worked so valiantly from 1939 until 1945 to save the church from WWII destruction. On the wall next to the door a dirty panel of stone remains, reminding visitors how dark the entire church was before undergoing a huge cleaning (2004–2008) in preparation for the 300th anniversary of the first service held in the church. Remarkably, this is the first great church completed in the lifetime of its architect (built 1675–1710).

• Glance up and behind. The organ trumpets say, "Come to the evensong and hear us play." Ahead and on the left is the towering, black-and-white...

❷ Wellington Monument

It's so tall that even Wellington's horse has to duck to avoid bumping its head. Wren would have been appalled, but his church has become so central to England's soul that many national heroes are buried here (in the basement crypt). General Wellington, Napoleon's conqueror at Waterloo (1815) and the embodiment of British stiff-upper-lippedness, was honored here in a funeral packed with 13,000 fans. The church is littered with memorials. While all the monuments are upstairs, all the tombs are downstairs.

• *Stroll up the same nave Prince Charles and Lady Diana walked on their 1981 wedding day. Imagine how they felt making the hike to the altar with the world watching. Grab a chair underneath the impressive dome.*

❸ The Dome

The dome you see, painted with scenes from the life of St. Paul, is only the innermost of three. From the painted interior of the first dome, look up through the opening to see the light-filled lantern of the second dome. Finally, the whole thing is covered on the outside by the third and final dome, the shell of lead-covered wood that you see from the street. Wren's ingenious three-in-one design was psychological as well as functional—he wanted a low, shallow inner dome so worshippers wouldn't feel diminished.

You'll see tourists walking around the base of the dome in the Whispering Gallery. The dome is constructed with such acoustic precision that secrets whispered from one side of the dome are heard on the opposite side, 170 feet away.

Christopher Wren (1632–1723) was the right man at the right time. Though the 31-year-old astronomy professor had never built a major building in his life when he got the commission for St. Paul's, his reputation for brilliance and his unique ability to work with others carried him through. The church has the clean lines and geometric simplicity of the age of Newton, when reason was holy and God set the planets spinning in perfect geometrical motion.

For more than 40 years, Wren worked on this site, overseeing every detail of St. Paul's and the 65,000-ton dome. At age 75, he got to look up and see his son place the cross on top of the dome, completing the masterpiece.

On the floor directly beneath the dome is a brass grate—part of a 19th-century attempt to heat the church. Encircling it is Christopher Wren's name and epitaph, written in Latin: *Lector, si monumentum requiris circumspice* (Reader, if you seek his monument, look around you).

Now review the ceiling: Behind is Wren simplicity and ahead is Victorian ornateness.

• *The choir area blocks your way, but you can see the altar at the far end under a golden canopy.*

❹ The Choir and High Altar

English churches, unlike most in Europe, often have a central choir area (or "quire" or "chancel"), where church officials and the sing-

ers sit. St. Paul's—a cathedral since 604—is home to the local Anglican bishop, who presides in the chair nearest the altar on the south or right side (the carved bishop's hat hangs over the chair).

The ceiling above the choir is a riot of glass mosaic representing God (above the altar) and his creation. The mosaics are very Victorian. In fact, Queen Victoria complained that the earlier ceiling was "dreary and undevotional." The Dean and chapter wisely took note and had it spiffed up with this brilliant mosaic work...textbook late

Victorian. In separate spheres eight "Angels of the Morning" hold up creatures of the earth, seas, and sky.

The altar (the marble slab with crucifix and candlesticks—you'll get a close look later) sits under a huge canopy with cork-screw columns. The canopy looks ancient, but it dates from 1958, when it was rebuilt after being heavily damaged in October 1940 by the bombs of Hitler's Luftwaffe.

• *In the north transept (to your left as you face the altar), find the big painting of Christ, in a golden wood altarpiece. Glare? Try walking side-to-side to find the best viewing angle.*

❺ *The Light of the World* (1904), by William Holman Hunt

In the dark of night, Jesus—with a lantern, halo, jeweled cape, and crown of thorns—approaches an out-of-the-way home in the woods, knocks on the door, and listens for an invitation to come in. A Bible passage on the picture frame says: "Behold, I stand at the door and knock..." (Revelation 3:20).

In his early twenties, William Holman Hunt (1827–1910) was in the dark night of a spiritual crisis when he heard this verse knocking in his head. He opened his soul to Christ, his life changed forever, and he tried to capture the experience in paint. As one of the Pre-Raphaelites who adored medieval art, he used symbolism, but only images the average Brit-on-the-street could understand. The door is the closed mind, the weeds the neglected soul, the darkness is malaise, while Christ carries the lantern of spiritual enlightenment.

ST. PAUL'S TOUR

The Anglican Communion

St. Paul's Cathedral is the symbolic (but not official) nucleus of earth's 70 million Anglicans. The Anglican Communion is a loose association of churches—including the Church of England and the Episcopal Church in the US—with common beliefs. The rallying point is *The Book of Common Prayer,* their handbook for worship services.

Forged in the fires of Europe's Reformation, Anglicans see themselves as a "middle way" between Catholics and Protestants. They retain much of the pomp and ceremony of traditional Catholic worship but with Protestant elements such as married priests (and, recently, female priests); attention to Scripture; and a less hierarchical, more consensus-oriented approach to decision making. Among Anglicans there are divisions, from Low Church congregations (more evangelical and "Protestant") to High Church (more traditional and "Catholic").

The Church of England, the largest single body, is still the official religion of the state, headed by the Archbishop of Canterbury (who presides in Canterbury but lives in London). In 1982, Pope John Paul II and the then Archbishop of Canterbury met face to face, signaling a new ecumenical spirit.

In 1854, Hunt debuted *The Light of the World* (not this version, but a smaller one now at Oxford). The critics savaged it—"syrupy," "too Catholic," "simple"—but the masses lapped it up. It became the most famous painting in Victorian England, a pop icon that inspired sermons, poems, hymns, and countless Christ-at-the-door paintings in churches and homes. Hunt's humble-hippie image of Christ was stamped forever on the minds of generations of school kids. It was so popular that late in life Hunt was asked to do this larger version specifically for St. Paul's. Nearly blind, he needed an assistant. (*The Guardian* newspaper recently published a list of "Britain's Ten Worst Paintings." They honored *The Light of the World* as number seven, comparing it to a plastic crucifix.)

• *Return to the area underneath the dome and walk toward the altar, along the left side of the choir, pausing at a modern statue.*

❻ *Mother and Child,* by Henry Moore

Britain's (and the world's?) greatest modern sculptor, Henry Moore, rendered a traditional subject in an abstract, minimalist way. This Mary and baby Jesus was inspired by the sight of British moms nursing babies in WWII bomb shelters. Moore intended the viewer to touch and interact with the art. It's OK.

• *Continue to the altar at the far end of the church. The area behind it has three bright and modern stained-glass windows.*

❼ American Memorial Chapel

This special spot in St. Paul's honors the Americans who sacrificed their lives to save Britain in World War II.

Each of the three windows has a central core of religious scenes, but the brightly colored panes that arch around them have some unusual iconography: American. Spot the American eagle (center window, to the left of Christ), George Washington (right window, upper-right corner), and symbols of all 50 states (find your state seal). In the carved wood beneath the windows, you'll see birds and foliage native to the US. And at the very far right of the paneling, check out the tiny tree "trunk" (amid foliage, below the bird)—it's a US rocket ship circa 1958, shooting up to the stars.

Britain is very grateful to its WWII saviors, the Yanks, and remembers them religiously with the Roll of Honor (immediately behind the altar). This 500-page book under glass lists the names of 28,000 US servicemen and women based in Britain who gave their lives during the war.

• *Take a close look at the high altar and the view back to the entrance from here. Look up and enjoy the Victorian mosaic ceiling above the choir. Then continue around the altar and head back toward the entrance. On the left wall of the aisle, standing white in a black niche, is a statue of...*

❽ John Donne (1573-1631)

This statue survived the Great Fire of 1666. John Donne, shown here wrapped in a burial shroud, was a passionate preacher in old St. Paul's (1621-1631), as well as a great poet.

Imagine hearing Donne deliver a funeral sermon here, with the huge church bell tolling in the background: "No man is an island....Any man's death diminishes me, because I am involved in Mankind. Therefore, never wonder for whom the bell tolls—it tolls for thee."

• *And also for dozens of people who lie buried beneath your feet, in the crypt where you'll end your tour. But first, in the south transept, find the...*

❾ Horatio Nelson Monument and Charles Cornwallis Monument

Admiral Horatio Nelson (1758-1805) leans on an anchor, his coat draped discreetly over the arm he lost in battle.

In October 1805, England trembled in fear as Napoleon—bent

St. Paul's, the Blitz, and the Battle of Britain

Nazi planes firebombed a helpless London in 1940. While the city around it burned to the ground, St. Paul's survived, giving hope to the citizens. The church took two direct hits, crumbling the altar and collapsing the north transept. On December 29, 1940, some 28 bombs fell on the church. The surrounding neighborhood was absolutely flattened, while the church rose above it, nearly intact. Some swear that many bombs bounced miraculously off Wren's dome, while others credit the heroic work of local firefighters. (There's a memorial chapel to the firefighters who kept watch over St. Paul's with hoses cocked.) Still, it's clear from the damage that St. Paul's was not fully Blitz-proof.

Often used synonymously, the Blitz and the Battle of Britain are actually two different phases of the Nazi air raids of 1940–1941. The Battle of Britain (June–Sept 1940) pitted Britain's Royal Air Force against German planes trying to soften up Britain for a land-and-sea invasion. The Blitz (Sept 1940–May 1941) was Hitler's punitive terror campaign against civilian London.

In the early days of World War II, the powerful, technologically superior Nazi army quickly overran Poland, Belgium, and France. The British army hightailed it out of France, crossing the English Channel from Dunkirk, and Britain hunkered down, waiting to be invaded. Hitler bombed

on world conquest—prepared to invade from across the Channel. Meanwhile, hundreds of miles away, off the coast of Spain, the daring Lord Nelson sailed the HMS *Victory* into battle against the French and Spanish navies. His motto: England expects that every man shall do his duty.

Nelson's fleet smashed the enemy at Trafalgar, and Napoleon's hopes for a naval invasion of Britain sank. Unfortunately, Nelson took a sniper's bullet in the spine and died, gasping, "Thank God I have done my duty." The lion at Nelson's feet groans sadly, and two little boys gaze up—one at Nelson, one at Wren's dome. You'll find Nelson's tomb directly beneath the dome, downstairs in the crypt.

Opposite Nelson is a monument to another great military man, Charles Cornwallis (1738–1805), honored here for his service as Governor General of Bengal (India). Yanks know him better as the general who lost the "American War" (the American

R.A.F. airfields while his ground troops massed along the Channel. Britain was hopelessly outmatched, but Prime Minister Winston Churchill vowed, "We shall fight on the beaches...we shall fight in the fields and in the streets....We shall never surrender."

Britain fought back. Though greatly outgunned, they had a new and secret weapon—radar—that allowed them to get the jump on puzzled Nazi pilots. Speedy Spitfires flown by a new breed of young pilots shot down 1,700 German planes. By September 1940, the German land invasion was called off, Britain counterattacked with a daring raid on Berlin...and the Battle of Britain was won.

A frustrated Hitler retaliated with a series of punishing air raids on London itself, known as the Blitz. All through the fall, winter, and spring of 1940–1941, including 57 consecutive nights, Hermann Göring's Luftwaffe pummeled a defenseless London, killing 20,000 and leveling half the city (mostly from St. Paul's eastward). Residents took refuge deep in the Tube stations. From his Whitehall bunker, Churchill made radio broadcasts exhorting his people to give their all, their "blood, toil, sweat, and tears."

Late in the war (1944–1945), Hitler ordered another round of terror-inducing attacks on London (sometimes called the "second Blitz") using car-sized V-1 and V-2 bombs, an early type of cruise missile. But Britain's resolve had returned, the United States had entered the fight, and the pendulum shifted. Churchill could say that even if the empire lasted a thousand years, Britons would look back and say, "This was their finest hour."

After the war, Churchill's state funeral was held at St. Paul's in a bittersweet remembrance of Britain's victory.

Revolutionary War) when George Washington—aided by French ships—forced his surrender at Yorktown in 1780.

• *There are several entrances to the dome and its Galleries, but only one is open to the public at any given time, so check the free visitor's map.*

⑩ Climb the Dome

The 530-step climb is worthwhile, and each level (or Gallery) offers something different.

First you get to the Whispering Gallery (259 steps, with views of the church interior). Whisper sweet nothings into the wall, and your partner (and anyone else) standing far away can hear you. Exactly how it works is debated (some even question *if* it works). Most likely, the sound does not travel up and over the dome to the diametrically opposite side (as it would in a perfect sphere). Rather, it goes around the curved wall horizontally, so you don't have to stand in any particular spot. For best effects, try whispering (not talking) with your mouth close to the wall, while your partner stands a few dozen yards away with his or her ear to the wall.

After another set of stairs, you're at the Stone Gallery, with views of London. If you're exhausted, claustrophobic, or wary of heights, this middle level might be high enough. (The top level has very little standing room for tourists.)

Finally a long, tight, metal staircase takes you to the very top of the cupola, the Golden Gallery. (Just before the final dozen stairs to the top, there's a tiny window at your feet that allows you to peek directly down—350 feet— to the church floor.) Once at the top, you emerge to stunning unobstructed views of the city. Looking west, you'll see the London

Eye and Big Ben. To the south, across the Thames, is the rectangular smokestack of the Tate Modern, with Shakespeare's Globe nestled nearby. To the east is the 600-foot-tall, black-topped Tower 42 and the bullet-shaped 30 St. Mary Axe building (nicknamed "The Gherkin"). Looking farther into the distance, you'll see London's future—the teeming, fast-growing expanse of the East End and the Docklands. The cluster of skyscrapers marks Canary Wharf. Just north of that is the area under construction for the 2012 Olympic Games.

• *Descend the dome to church level, then follow signs directing you downstairs to the...*

⓫ Crypt

There are many famous people buried here. Start by locating the central tomb of Horatio Nelson, who wore down Napoleon. It's

a big coffin-on-a-pedestal in a round alcove at the center of the crypt, directly beneath the dome. Nearby is the tomb of the Duke of Wellington (who finished Napoleon off).

Continuing up the central axis of the crypt, you enter a chapel. At the chapel's altar, turn right to reach Christopher Wren's tomb—a simple black slab with no statue. ("If you seek his monument..." you'll be disappointed.) Next to it is a hunk of rough Portland stone quarried but unused by Wren while building St.

Paul's; see his triangle brand on the left end.

Use the free visitor's map to find the tombs of painters Turner, Reynolds, and others (near Wren), and that of Florence Nightingale (near Wellington). Look for memorials to many others (including George Washington, who lies buried back in old Virginny).

Temporary exhibits (they change frequently) often chronicle important events that have been held at the cathedral—for instance, Queen Victoria's funeral, services for the victims of the tsunami in 2004, or remembrances of the "7/7" terrorist bombings in London in 2005. There's also a model of the church on display.

The crypt contains a fine gift shop, a WC, and the grim-sounding Crypt Café, which nevertheless serves tasty food.

TOWER OF LONDON TOUR

William I, still getting used to his new title of "the Conqueror," built the stone "White Tower" (1077–1097) to keep the Londoners in line. The Tower also served as an effective lookout for seeing invaders coming up the Thames. His successors enlarged it to its present 18-acre size. Because of the security it provided, it served over the centuries as the Royal Mint, the Royal Jewel House, and, most famously, as the prison and execution site of those who dared oppose the Crown.

The Tower's hard stone and glittering jewels represent the ultimate power of the monarch. So does the executioner's block. You'll find more bloody history per square inch in this original tower of power than anywhere else in Britain. Today, though its military purpose is history, it's still home to a Beefeating community of 120 (the 25 Yeoman Warders and their families), who host three million visitors a year. While these men (and one woman) are no longer expected to protect the monarch, the Beefeaters have evolved into great entertainers, leading groups of tourists through the Tower.

Your visit has four parts: the lively "Beefeater" tour (included in admission price, 1 hour), the White Tower (a serious museum and armory worth ▲▲, which many rush and underrate), the crown jewels (best in Europe, generally with a bit of a wait), and the grounds and walls (a simple and enjoyable stroll).

Orientation

Cost: £17, family ticket £47.

Hours: March–Oct Tue–Sat 9:00–17:30, Sun–Mon 10:00–17:30; Nov–Feb Tue–Sat 9:00–16:30, Sun–Mon 10:00–16:30; last entry 30 min before closing.

Advance Tickets: To avoid the long ticket-buying lines at the Tower of London, you have several options. The easiest is to buy your ticket at the Trader's Gate gift shop, located at the Tower Hill Tube stop (as you exit the station, go down a flight of steps, and you'll find the low-profile souvenir store tucked away at the foot of the stairs). You can also buy tickets in advance, at no extra cost, at any London TI or at the Welcome Centre to the left of the normal ticket lines (credit card only). It's also easy to book online (www.hrp.org.uk) or by phone (tel. 0844-482-7799 within UK or tel. 020-3166-6000 from overseas), then pick up your tickets at the Tower.

More Crowd-Beating Tips: Everyone wants to see the crown jewels—the best on earth. The line for the jewels can be just as long as the line for tickets (worst on Sun). For fewer crowds, arrive before 10:00 and go straight for the jewels, then tour the rest of the Tower—or see the gems after 16:30 in summer.

Getting There: The Tower is located in East London (Tube: Tower Hill). For speed, take the Tube there; for romance, take the boat. City Cruises boats make the trip between the Tower of London and Westminster Pier near Big Ben in 30 minutes; the boat continues on to Greenwich from the Tower Pier. For details about these cruises, see page 39. Buses #15 and #RV1 make the trip from Trafalgar Square (see map on page 32).

Information: Upon arrival, pick up the free map/guide and monthly program, and check the schedule for a list of events and special demonstrations (such as knights in armor explaining medieval fighting techniques). Everything inside is well-described, so skip the audioguide (£4, plus £40 deposit or ID) and the Tower guidebook. Switchboard toll tel. 0844-482-7777, booking toll tel. 0844-482-7799, www.hrp.org.uk.

Special Ceremonies: On Sunday morning, visitors are welcome on the grounds for free to **worship in the Royal Chapel.** You get in without the lines, but you can only see the chapel—no sightseeing (9:15 Communion or 11:00 service with fine choral music, meet at west gate 30 minutes early, dress for church).

The pageantry-filled **Ceremony of the Keys** is held every night at precisely 21:30, when the Tower of London is locked up (as it has been for the last 700 years). To attend this free 30-minute event, you need to request an invitation at least two months before your visit. For details, go to www.hrp.org.uk and select "Tower Of London," then "What's On" and "The Ceremony of the Keys." (Every year, some readers report that it's difficult getting the required International Reply Coupons from their local US post office.)

Yeoman Warder (Beefeater) Tours: The free, worthwhile, 1-hour Beefeater tours leave every 30 minutes from inside the gate

(first one usually at 9:30, last one usually at 15:30, 14:30 in winter, they take a lunch break midday). The boisterous Beefeaters are great entertainers. While groups can be huge, the guides are easy to hear. Their talks include lots of bloody anecdotes about the Tower and its history. Check the clock inside the gate. If you just missed a tour, you can join it in progress (just a bit ahead). Tips are not expected, but if you want, slip your Beefeater a coin (not a bill) at the end of the tour.

Length of This Tour: Allow two hours.

Photography: Photos are allowed, except of the jewels or inside the White Tower or chapels.

Cuisine Art: The New Armouries Café, inside the Tower, is a big, efficient cafeteria (large, splittable meals for £7). You can also grab a lite bite at places outside—along the river or at the big, modern EAT, uphill from the ticket lines. Picnicking is allowed on Tower grounds but not inside the buildings.

Starring: Crown jewels, Beefeaters, William the Conqueror, and Henry VIII.

Also Starring: Ravens. According to goofy tradition, London is only safe as long as the ravens are at the Tower. Their wings were clipped so they'd stay. But with clipped wings, the birds had trouble mating, so a slide was built to help them get a bit of lift to mate. Happily, that worked, and a baby raven was born. A children's TV show sponsored a nationwide contest to come up with a name. The winner: "Ronald Raven." As you leave through the riverside exit, look into the moat on the right for the tiny raven graveyard. There lie Cedric (2003), Gundolf (2005), and Hardey (2006). RIP.

The Tour Begins

❶ Entrance Gate

Even an army the size of the ticket line couldn't storm this castle. After the drawbridge was pulled up and the iron portcullis slammed down, you'd have to swim a moat; cross an island prowled by wild animals; then swim a second, 40-yard-wide inner moat (eventually drained to be a military parade ground); and, finally, toss a grappling hook onto the wall and climb up while the enemy poured boiling oil on you. Yes, it was difficult to get into the Tower (when it protected the monarchs)...but it was almost impossible to get out (when it imprisoned enemies).

• *The entertaining one-hour tours by the Yeoman Warders (nicknamed Beefeaters) begin just inside the entrance gate (see above). The information booth is nearby, and WCs are 100 yards in front of you. Otherwise, go 50 yards straight ahead to the...*

❷ Traitor's Gate

This entrance to the Tower was a waterway from the Thames. Princess Elizabeth I, who was a prisoner here before she became queen, was poled through this gate on a barge, thinking about her mom, Anne Boleyn, who had been decapitated inside just a few years earlier. Many English leaders who fell from grace entered through here—Elizabeth was one of the lucky few to walk out.

• *Pass underneath the "Bloody Tower" into the inner courtyard. The big, white tower in the middle is the...*

❸ White Tower

This is the tower that gives this castle complex of 20 towers its name. William the Conqueror built it more than 900 years ago to

put 15 feet of stone between himself and those he conquered. Over the centuries, the other walls and towers were built around it. Again, don't overlook this museum. It really is a great, well-done collection that's worth some time.

The keep was a last line of defense. The original entry (on south side) is above ground level so that the wooden approach (you'll climb its modern successor to get in, and lots more stairs once you're inside) could be removed, turning the tower into a safe refuge. Originally, there were even fewer windows—the lower windows were added during a Christopher Wren-ovation in 1660. In the 13th century, the tower was painted white.

Standing high above the rest of old London, the White Tower provided a gleaming reminder of the monarch's absolute power over subjects. If you made the wrong move here, you could be feasting on roast boar in the banqueting hall one night and chained to the walls of the prison the next. Torture ranged from stretching on the rack to the full monty: hanging by the neck until nearly dead, then "drawing" (cut open to be gutted), and finally quartering, with your giblets displayed on the walls as a warning. (Guy Fawkes, who tried to blow up Parliament with 36 barrels of gunpowder, got this treatment.) Any cries for help were muffled by the thick stone walls—15 feet at the base, a mere 11 feet at the top.

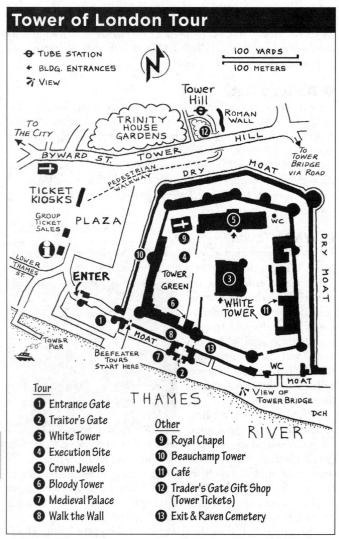

Tower of London Tour

⊕ TUBE STATION
← BLDG. ENTRANCES
ᐅⅰ VIEW

100 YARDS
100 METERS

TRINITY HOUSE GARDENS

Tower Hill

ROMAN WALL

BYWARD ST.   TOWER   HILL

TO THE CITY

TO TOWER BRIDGE VIA ROAD

PEDESTRIAN WALKWAY

DRY   MOAT

TICKET KIOSKS

GROUP TICKET SALES

PLAZA

LOWER THAMES ST.

ENTER

TOWER GREEN

WHITE TOWER

DRY MOAT

WC

TOWER PIER

BEEFEATER TOURS START HERE

MOAT

WC

MOAT

THAMES   RIVER

VIEW OF TOWER BRIDGE

DCH

Tour
1 Entrance Gate
2 Traitor's Gate
3 White Tower
4 Execution Site
5 Crown Jewels
6 Bloody Tower
7 Medieval Palace
8 Walk the Wall

Other
9 Royal Chapel
10 Beauchamp Tower
11 Café
12 Trader's Gate Gift Shop (Tower Tickets)
13 Exit & Raven Cemetery

Inside, you'll follow a one-way path to models of the tower and exhibits re-creating medieval life. You'll see suits of armor in the **Royal Armory** (including one belonging to Henry VIII—with his bigger-is-better codpiece, as well as the armor of other kings and of a 6' 9" giant), along with guns, swords, and the actual execution ax and chopping block.

The rare and lovely **Norman chapel** (St. John's Chapel, 1080)—where Lady Jane Grey (see below) offered up a last unanswered prayer—is simple, plain, and moving. The round

Romanesque arches of this treasured little church evoke the age of William the Conqueror.

• *Left of the White Tower is the Tower Green, where you'll find a granite-paved square marked* Site of Scaffold.

❹ Execution Site

The actual execution site looks just like a lawn today; the chopping block has been moved (inside the White Tower). It was here that enemies of the crown would kneel before the king for the final time. With their hands tied behind their backs, they would say a final prayer, then lay their heads on a block, and—*shlit*—the blade would slice through their necks, their heads tumbling to the ground.

The headless corpses were buried in unmarked graves in the Tower Green or under the floor of the stone church ahead of you. The heads were stuck on a stick and displayed at London Bridge. Passersby did not see heads, but spheres of parasites.

Henry VIII axed a couple of his ex-wives here—Anne Boleyn, whom he called a witch and an adulteress, and the forgettable Catherine Howard. Next.

Henry even beheaded his friend Thomas More (a Catholic) because he refused to recognize (Protestant) Henry as head of the Church of England. (Thomas died at the less-prestigious Tower Hill site just outside the walls—near the Tube stop—where most Tower executions took place.)

The most tragic victim was 17-year-old Lady Jane Grey, who  was manipulated into claiming the crown for nine days during the scramble for power after Henry's death and the short six-year reign and death of his sickly young son, Edward VI. When Bloody Mary took control, she forced her Protestant cousin Jane to kneel at the block. Jane's young husband, locked in the nearby Beauchamp Tower and executed earlier the same day, vented his despair by scratching "Jane" into the tower's stone (in the upstairs room find graffiti #85—"IANE"). Cynics claim he was actually pining for his mother, who was also named Jane.

A Beefeater, tired of what he called "Hollywood coverage" of the Tower, grabbed my manuscript, read it, and told me that in more than 900 years as a fortress, palace, and prison, the place held 8,500 prisoners. But only 120 were executed, and, of those, only six were executed inside it. Stressing the hospitality of the Tower, he added, "Torture was actually quite rare here."

• *Look past the White Tower on the left to the line leading to the crown jewels. Like a Disney ride, the line is still very long once you get inside. But great videos help pass the time pleasantly. First, you'll pass through a room of wooden chairs and coats of arms—one for every monarch who wore jewels like these, from William the Conqueror (1066), to Elizabeth I (with her lion-and-dragon crest), to Elizabeth II. Next, you'll see a film of the latter Elizabeth's 1953 coronation, which gives you a chance to see the jewels (including the world's largest diamond, in the scepter) in use. You'll also see video close-ups of the jewels. If you are not finished with the warm-up videos, don't let the crowd flow rush you. Just step aside and enjoy the entire show. (Even if there's no crowd, take your time watching these videos.) Finally, you pass into a huge vault and reach...*

❺ The Crown Jewels

In the first display case, notice the 12th-century coronation spoon for anointing (last used in 1953). Because most of the original crown jewels were lost during the 1648 revolution, this is the most ancient object here. After scepters, robes, trumpets, and wristlets, a moving sidewalk takes you past the most precious of the crown jewels.

• *Ride the nearest walkway. The crowns and the most impressive stones are all facing forward. You're welcome to circle back and glide by again (I did, several times), then glide by the back side. Stand and study the jewels using the stationary platform, or hang out on the elevated viewing area with the guard. Chat with the guards—they're actually here to provide information. Remember that you're not allowed to take photos of the jewels.*

The most important pieces are in cases #1, #2, #3, #4, and #5:

Case #1: St. Edward's Crown, in the first glass case, is placed by the archbishop upon the head of each new monarch on coronation day in Westminster Abbey. It's worn for 20 minutes, then locked away until the next coronation. The original crown, destroyed by Cromwell, was older than the Tower itself and dated back to 1061, the time of King Edward the Confessor, "the last English king" before William the Conqueror invaded (1066). This 1661 remake is said to contain some of the original's gold amid its 443 precious and semiprecious stones. Because the crown weighs nearly five pounds, weak or frail monarchs have opted not to wear it.

Case #2: The **Sovereign's Scepter,** in the second case, is encrusted with the world's largest cut diamond—the 530-carat Star of Africa, beefy as a quarter-pounder. This was one of nine stones cut from the original 3,106-carat diamond. The **orb** (in the same case) symbolized how Christianity rules over the earth; it's a reminder that even a "divine monarch" is not above God's law. The coronation is a kind of marriage between the church and the state in Britain, since the king or queen is head of both, and the ceremony celebrates the monarch's power to do good for the whole of the nation.

Case #3: Here you see several crowns that illustrate a bit of regalia symbolism. Kings and queens get four arches on their crowns, emperors get eight arches (e.g., the Imperial Crown of India you'll see in the case at the exit), and princes get only two (Charles has a two-arch crown that he keeps in Wales).

Case #4: The **Queen Victoria Small Diamond Crown,** on the second pillow, is tiny. Victoria suffered from migraine headaches, and the last thing someone with a migraine needs is a big crown. This four-ounce job was made in 1870 for £50,000—personally paid for by the queen.

The **Crown of the Queen Mother** (Elizabeth II's famous mum, who died in 2002), the highest crown in the case, has the 106-carat Koh-I-Noor diamond glittering on the front. The Koh-I-Noor diamond is considered unlucky for male rulers and, therefore, only adorns the crown of the king's wife. If Charles becomes king, Camilla might wear this. This crown was remade in 1937 and given an innovative platinum frame.

Case #5: The **Imperial State Crown,** in the last case, is for coronation festivities and the annual opening of Parliament. On those occasions when Victoria wore her small crown, this piece legally had to accompany her (it was carried next to her on a pillow), as it represents the sovereign. Among its 3,733 jewels are Queen Elizabeth I's former earrings (the hanging pearls, top center), a stunning 13th-century ruby look-alike in the center, and Edward the Confessor's ring (the blue sapphire on top, in the center of the Maltese cross of diamonds). When Edward's tomb was exhumed—a hundred years after he was buried—his body was "incorrupted." The ring on his saintly finger featured this sapphire and ended

up on the crown of all future monarchs. This is the stylized crown you see representing the royalty on Britain's coins and stamps. It's even depicted on the pavement at the end of the sliding walk.

• *Leave the jewels. Back near the Traitor's Gate you'll find sights #6 and #7.*

❻ Bloody Tower

Not all prisoners died at the block. The 13-year-old future king Edward V and his kid brother were kidnapped in 1483 during the Wars of the Roses by their uncle Richard III ("Now is the winter of our discontent...") and locked in the Bloody Tower, never to be seen again (until two centuries later, when two children's skeletons were discovered).

Sir Walter Raleigh—poet, explorer, and political radical—was imprisoned here for 13 years. In 1603, the English writer and adventurer was accused of plotting against King James and sentenced to death. The king commuted the sentence to life imprisonment in the Bloody Tower. While in prison, Raleigh wrote the first volume of his *History of the World*. Check out his rather cushy bedroom, study, and walkway (courtesy of the powerful tobacco lobby?). Raleigh promised the king a wealth of gold if he would release him to search for El Dorado. The expedition was a failure. Upon Raleigh's return, the displeased king had him beheaded in 1618.

More recent prisoners in the complex include Rudolf Hess, Hitler's henchman, who parachuted into Scotland in 1941 (kept in the bell tower). Hess claimed to have dropped in to negotiate a separate peace between Germany and Britain. Hitler denied any such plan.

❼ Medieval Palace

The Tower was a royal residence as well as a fortress. These well-described rooms are furnished as they might have been during the reign of Edward I in the 13th century, and come with an actor in medieval garb who explains lifestyles of the medieval rich and royal.

• *Near where you leave the Medieval Palace, enter to...*

❽ Walk the Wall

The Tower was defended by state-of-the-art walls and fortifications in the 13th century. This walk offers a good look. From the walls, you also get a fine view of the famous bridge straddling the Thames, with the twin towers and blue spans. It's not London Bridge (which is the nondescript bridge just upstream), but **Tower Bridge**. Although it looks medieval, this drawbridge was built in 1894 of steel and concrete. Sophisticated steam

engines raise and lower the bridge, allowing tall-masted ships to squeeze through.

Gaze out at the bridge, the river, City Hall (the egg-shaped glass building across the river, see page 80), and life-filled London. Turn back and look at the stern stone walls of the Tower. Be glad you can leave.

BANKSIDE WALK

*Along the South Bank
of the Thames*

Bankside—the neighborhood between London Bridge and Blackfriars Bridge—is the historic heart of the newly revamped southern bank of the Thames. In ancient times "greater London" consisted of two Roman settlements straddling the easiest place to ford the river: one settlement was here, and the other was across the river—in the financial district known today as "The City."

From the Roman era until recently, the south side of the river was the wrong side of the tracks. For centuries, it was London's red light district. In the 20th century, it became an industrial wasteland of empty warehouses and street crime. Today, the prostitutes and pickpockets are gone, replaced by a riverside promenade dotted with pubs, cutesy shops, and historic tourist sights.

This half-mile Bankside walk gives you plenty of history and sights to choose from—you can see it all, design your own plan, or just enjoy the view of London's skyline across the river.

Orientation

Length of This Tour: One hour (or up to an entire day if you tour Vinopolis, Shakespeare's Globe, and the Tate Modern).

Getting There: Take the Tube to the London Bridge stop to begin the walk. (The Monument stop, on the Circle Line, is also nearby.)

The walk ends near Blackfriars Bridge (closest Tube stop: Southwark, several blocks south of the bridge on the South Bank; the Blackfriars Tube stop is closed for renovation until 2011).

Old Operating Theatre Museum and Herb Garret: £5.60, daily 10:30–17:00, 9a St. Thomas Street.

Southwark Cathedral: Free but £4 donation requested (you'll likely be approached about the donation, so be prepared with at least £1 or a simple "No"); daily 10:00–18:00, last entry 30 min before closing; evensong services weekdays at 17:30, Sat at 16:00, Sun at 15:00, no service on Wed or alternate Mon; audioguide £2.50; no photos without permission.

Borough Market: Retail sales Thu 11:00–17:00, Fri 12:00–18:00, Sat 9:00–16:00. A few shops are open on other days (www.boroughmarket.org.uk).

Golden Hinde **Replica:** £7, Mon–Sat 10:00–17:30, Sun 10:30–17:00, sometimes closed for private events.

The Clink Prison Museum: Overpriced at £5, Mon–Fri 10:00–18:00, Sat–Sun until 21:00, 1 Clink Street.

Vinopolis: £25–75 tour options, save 20 percent by booking online; includes five wine tastes, Thu–Fri 12:00–22:00, Sat 11:00–22:00, Sun 12:00–18:00, closed Mon–Wed, last entry 2.5 hours before closing, between Shakespeare's Globe and Southwark Cathedral at 1 Bank End.

Shakespeare's Globe: The complex is open daily 9:00–17:00. To see the theater interior, you must either take a 60-minute guided tour (£10.50, includes "Globe Exhibition" museum; see page 77) or buy a ticket to a performance (see Entertainment chapter).

Tate Modern: Free but £3 donations appreciated (fee for special exhibitions), daily 10:00–18:00, Fri–Sat until 22:00, last entry 45 min before closing, audioguide-£2, view café on top floor. ⊙ See the Tate Modern Tour chapter.

Starring: Shakespeare's world, London Bridge, historic pubs, and views of the London skyline.

The Walk Begins

• *Start at the south end of London Bridge. From the London Bridge Tube stop, take the "Borough High Street east" exit and turn right (north), walking 100 yards to the bridge.*

❶ London Bridge

The City across the river is to the north, Tower Bridge is east, and the Thames flows from west to east (left to right). Looking to the east (downstream) and turning counterclockwise, you'll see the following:

Downstream

- Tower Bridge (the Neo-Gothic-towered drawbridge that many Americans mistakenly call London Bridge).
- The HMS *Belfast* (in the foreground, docked on the southern bank), a WWII cruiser open for tourists.

- Canary Wharf Tower (the distant 800-foot skyscraper with pyramid top and blinking light), built in 1990 on the Isle of Dogs. This is the tallest building in the UK, at least until the planned "Shard of Glass"—a futuristic 1,000-foot-tall super skyscraper slated to open in 2012—rises a block south of the London Bridge Tube station.
- The "Pool of London." This is the stretch of river between Tower Bridge (a drawbridge) and London Bridge, which marks the farthest point seagoing vessels can sail inland. In the 18th century this was the busiest port in the world.

North Bank
- The Tower of London (four domed spires and a flag rising above the trees on the North Bank).
- The Monument (north end of London Bridge but almost completely buried among modern buildings), a column topped with a shiny bronze knob, marking the start of the 1666 Great Fire.
- St. Paul's Cathedral (to the northwest, with a dome like a state capitol and twin spires).
- St. Bride's Church, the pointed, stacked steeple (nestled among office buildings) that supposedly inspired the wedding cake.
- A radio/TV tower.
- Southwark Bridge (the next bridge upstream).

South Bank
- The Tate Modern art museum (square brick smokestack tower on the South Bank).
- Southwark Cathedral (on South Bank, 100 yards away, may not be visible from where you're standing).
- Borough High Street, the busy street that London Bridge spills onto.
- The small griffin statues (winged lions holding shields) at the south end of London Bridge guard the entrance to The City. They marked the jurisdiction of The City to include both sides of the all-important river. For centuries, they said, "Neener neener" to late-night partiers who got locked out of town when the gates shut tight at curfew.

- *The best view of London Bridge is not from the bridge itself, but*

Bankside Walk

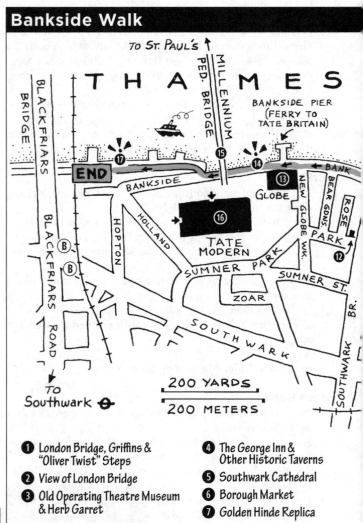

TO ST. PAUL'S

PED. BRIDGE

MILLENNIUM BRIDGE

T H A M E S

BLACKFRIARS BRIDGE

BANKSIDE PIER (FERRY TO TATE BRITAIN)

END

BANKSIDE

⑰

⑮

⑭

⑬ GLOBE

⑯ TATE MODERN

HOPTON

HOLLAND

BLACKFRIARS ROAD

Ⓑ

Ⓑ

SUMNER PARK

ZOAR

NEW GLOBE WK.

BEAR GDNS.

ROSE PARK

⑫

SUMNER ST.

S O U T H W A R K

SOUTHWARK BR.

TO Southwark ⊖

200 YARDS

200 METERS

❶ London Bridge, Griffins & "Oliver Twist" Steps

❷ View of London Bridge

❸ Old Operating Theatre Museum & Herb Garret

❹ The George Inn & Other Historic Taverns

❺ Southwark Cathedral

❻ Borough Market

❼ Golden Hinde Replica

BANKSIDE WALK

from the riverbank, 50 yards west, reached by a staircase leading down from the bridge. Find the staircase next to the southwest griffin, by the building marked Two London Bridge. These stairs will impress fans of Charles Dickens' Oliver Twist—they're the setting of the infamous "Meeting on the Bridge."

❷ View of London Bridge

The bridge of today—three spans of boring, traffic-clogged concrete, built in 1972—is (at least) the fourth incarnation of this

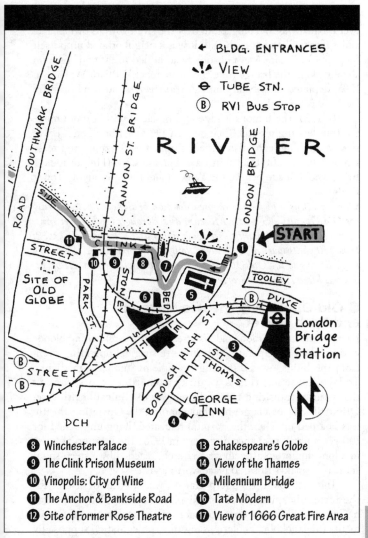

Legend:
- ← BLDG. ENTRANCES
- ↘! VIEW
- ⊖ TUBE STN.
- Ⓑ RVI BUS STOP

RIVER

START

❽ Winchester Palace
❾ The Clink Prison Museum
❿ Vinopolis: City of Wine
⓫ The Anchor & Bankside Road
⓬ Site of Former Rose Theatre

⓭ Shakespeare's Globe
⓮ View of the Thames
⓯ Millennium Bridge
⓰ Tate Modern
⓱ View of 1666 Great Fire Area

2,000-year-old river crossing. The Romans (A.D. 50) built the first wooden footbridge to Londinium (rebuilt many times), which was pulled down by boatmen in 1014 to retake London from Danish invaders. (They celebrated with a song passed down to us as "London Bridge is falling down, my fair lady.")

The most famous version—crossed by everyone from Richard the Lionhearted to Henry VIII to Shakespeare to Newton to Darwin—was built around 1200 and stood for more than six centuries, the only crossing point into this major city. Built of stone on many thick pilings, stacked with houses and shops that arched over the roadway and bulged out over the river, with its own chapel and a fortified gate at each end, it was a neighborhood unto itself (pop. 300). Picture Mel Gibson's head boiled in tar and stuck on a spike along the bridge (like the Scots rebel William Wallace in 1305, depicted in Gibson's movie *Braveheart*), and you'll capture the local color of that time.

In 1823, the famous bridge was replaced with a more modern (but less impressive) brick one. In 1967, that brick bridge was sold to an American, dismantled, shipped to Arizona, and reassembled (all 10,000 bricks) in Lake Havasu City. (Humor today's Brits, who'd like to believe the Yank thought he was buying Tower Bridge.)

• *This walk is a pick-and-choose collection of sights. Those visiting the Old Operating Theatre Museum and Borough High Street inns, described next, will want to see those sights first before heading west: Hike 150 yards south of the bridge (along the left-hand side of Borough High Street) to the Old Operating Theatre Museum (turn left on St. Thomas Street) and The George Inn.*

❸ Old Operating Theatre Museum and Herb Garret

Back when the common cold was treated with a refreshing bloodletting, the Old Operating Theatre—a surgical operating room from the 1800s—was a shining example of "modern" medicine. Today a museum, this is a quirky, sometimes gross, look at that painful transition from folk remedy to clinical health care. Originally part of a larger hospital complex, the Operating Theatre was boarded up when the hospital relocated, lying untouched for 100 years until its chance discovery in 1956. The location alone—in a long-forgotten attic above a church, reached by a steep spiral staircase—makes this odd place worth a visit.

The first room, the Herb Garret, was used to dry herbs for the former hospital. Today, it displays healing plants used for millennia—different ones for each of the traditional four ailments (melancholic, choleric, sanguine, phlegmatic), supposedly caused by an imbalance in the body's traditional four substances, or "humours" (black bile, yellow bile, blood, and phlegm), corresponding to the earth's traditional four elements (earth, wind, fire, and Ringo). You'll also learn that Florence Nightingale, the nurse famed for saving so many Crimean War soldiers wounded in Russia, worked here to improve sanitation and to turn nurses from low-paid domestics into trained doctors' assistants.

The small hallway displays crude anesthetics (ether, chloroform, three pints of ale), surgical instruments by Black & Decker (knives, saws, drills), and a glaring lack of antiseptics—that is, until young Dr. Joseph Lister discovered carbolic acid, which reduced the high rates of mortality and halitosis.

The Operating Theatre is the highlight—a semicircular room surrounded by railings for 150 spectators (truly a "theater"), where doctors operated on patients while med students observed.

The patients were often poor women, blindfolded for their own modesty. The doctors donated their time to help, practice, and teach (see the motto *Miseratione non Mercede:* "Out of compassion, not for profit"). The surgeries, usually amputations, were performed under very crude working conditions—under the skylight or by gaslight, with no sink, and only sawdust to sop up blood. The wood still bears bloodstains. Nearly one in three patients died. There was a fine line between Victorian-era surgeons and Jack the Ripper.

• *Farther down Borough High Street (on the left-hand side), you'll find...*

❹ The George Inn and (Faint Echoes of) Other Historic Taverns

The George is the last of many "coaching inns" that lined the main highway from London to all points south. Like Greyhound bus stations, each inn was a terminal for far-flung journeys, since coaches were forbidden inside The City. They offered food, drink, beds, and entertainment for travelers—Shakespeare, as a young actor, likely performed in The George's courtyard.

Along Borough High Street are plaques locating the alleyway ("yard") of long-gone taverns known to book lovers. **The Queen's Head** (north of The George) was owned by the mother of John Harvard, of university fame. **The White Hart** (also north of The George) was where Shakespeare and Dickens drank and set scenes. At **The Tabard** (now called "Talbot," south of The George), Chaucer's band began its fictional trip south in *The Canterbury Tales*—"Befell that in that season on a day/In Southwark at The Tabard as I lay/Ready to wander on my pilgrimage/To Canterbury with full courage."

• *Walk back toward the bridge. Southwark Cathedral is near the south-west corner of the structure.*

❺ Southwark Cathedral

This neighborhood parish church is where Shakespeare prayed while brother Edmund rang the bells. The Southwark (SUTH-uck) church dates back to 1207, though the site has had a church

Southwark Cathedral

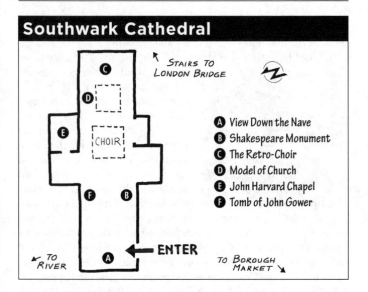

STAIRS TO
LONDON BRIDGE

CHOIR

A View Down the Nave
B Shakespeare Monument
C The Retro-Choir
D Model of Church
E John Harvard Chapel
F Tomb of John Gower

← ENTER

TO
RIVER

TO BOROUGH
MARKET ↘

for at least a thousand years and inhabitants for 2,000.

A **View down the Nave:** Clean and sparse, with warm golden stone, the church was recently revamped, a symbol of the urban renewal of the whole Bankside/Southwark area. Its WWII damage has been repaired, with new unstained glass windows on the right side. The nave bends slightly to the left (the chandelier, ceiling arches, and altar don't line up until you take two baby steps left) as a medieval tribute to Christ's bent body on the cross.

B **Shakespeare Monument:** William reclines in front of a backdrop of the 16th-century Bankside skyline (view looking north). Find (left to right) the original Globe Theatre, Winchester Palace, Southwark Cathedral, and the old London Bridge with its arched gate. Shakespeare seems to be dreaming about the many characters of his plays, depicted in the stained-glass window above

(see Hamlet addressing a skull, right window). To the right is a plaque to the American actor Sam Wanamaker, who spearheaded the building of a replica of Shakespeare's Globe Theatre (explained later in this chapter). Shakespeare's brother Edmund is buried in the church, possibly under a marked slab on the floor of the choir area, near the very center of the church. (The Bard lies buried in his hometown of Stratford-upon-Avon.)

BANKSIDE WALK

❸ The Retro-Choir: The 800-year-old crisscross arches and stone tracery in the windows are some of the oldest parts of this historic church. Located in the heart of the industrial district, the church was heavily bombed during World War II.

❹ Model of Church: Near a reclining stone corpse and a reclining wooden knight, find a model (marked *Church and Priory of St. Mary Overy*) of the church and old Winchester Palace—a helpful reconstruction before we visit the paltry Winchester Palace ruins.

❺ John Harvard Chapel: The Southwark-born son of an innkeeper (see the record of baptism near the window) inherited money from the sale of The Queen's Head tavern, got married, and sailed to Boston (1637), where he soon died. The money and his 400-book library funded the start of Harvard University.

❻ Tomb of John Gower: The poet and friend of Chaucer (c. 1400) rests his head on his three books, one written in Middle English, one in French, and one in Latin—the three languages from which modern English soon emerged.

• *Just south of Southwark Cathedral, you'll find the...*

❼ Borough Market

The first trading starts at 2:00 in the morning at this open-air wholesale produce market. Workers can knock off by sunrise for a

pint at the specially licensed Market Porter tavern (on Park Street). On Thursday and Friday afternoons and all day Saturday, the colorful market opens for retail sales to Londoners seeking trendy specialty and organic foods. It's a great place to get a picnic on a sunny day. Of the many market stalls, the Ginger Pig is *the* place for serious English sausage and bacon, while Maria's Market Café is a colorful eatery popular with market workers.

First started a thousand years ago on London Bridge, where country farmers brought fresh goods to the city gates, the market now sits here under a Victorian arcade. The railroad rumbling overhead, knifing right through dingy apartment houses (and the Globe Tavern), only adds to the color of London's oldest vegetable market and public gathering spot.

A detour westward through the market leads to Park Street, a popular film set for its old 19th-century ambience. Check out the fragrant cheese shop at Neal's Yard Dairy and the colorful pub.

• *Walk to the river along Cathedral Street, veering left at the Y.*

❼ *Golden Hinde* Replica

As we all learned in school, "Sir Francis Drake circumcised the globe with a hundred-foot clipper." Or something like that...

Imagine a hundred men on a boat this size (yes, this replica is full-size) circling the globe on a three-year voyage, sleeping on the wave-swept decks, suffering bad food, flog-gings, doldrums, B.O., and attacks from for-eigners. They explored unknown waters and were paid only from whatever riches they could find or steal along the way. (I took a bus tour like that once.)

The *Golden Hinde* (see the female deer, or hind, on the prow and stern) was Sir Francis Drake's flagship as he circumnavi-gated the globe (1577–1580). Drake, a farm-er's son who followed the lure of the sea, hated Spaniards. So did Queen Elizabeth I, who hired him to plunder rich Spanish vessels and New World colonies in England's name.

With 164 men on five small ships (the *Hinde* was the largest, at 100 tons and 18 cannons), he sailed southwest, dipping around South America, raiding Spanish ships and towns in Chile, and inching up the coast perhaps as far as Canada. By the time it con-tinued across the Pacific to Asia and beyond, the *Hinde* was so full of booty that its crew replaced the rock ballast with gold ingots and silver coins. Three years later, Drake—with only one remain-ing ship and 56 men—sailed the *Hinde* up the Thames, unloading a fabulously valuable hoard of gold, silver, emeralds, diamonds, pearls, silks, cloves, and spices before the Queen. A grateful Elizabeth knighted Drake on the main deck and kissed him on his *Golden Hinde*.

The *Hinde* was retired gloriously, but rotted away from neglect. Drake received a large share of the wealth, became enor-mously famous, and later gained more glory defeating the Spanish Armada (aided by "the winds of God") in the decisive battle in the English Channel, off Plymouth (1588), making England ruler of the waves.

The galleon replica, a working ship that has itself circled the globe, is berthed at St. Mary Overie Dock ("St. Mary's over the river"), a public dock available for free to all Southwark residents. The Thames river trade that used to thrive even this far upstream is now concentrated east of Tower Bridge, a victim of WWII bomb-ing and container ships that require big berths and deep water. Only a few brick warehouses remain (just west of here), waiting to be leveled or yuppified.

• *There's a fine view (with a handy chart to identify things) from the riverside. The beach below is fun for beachcombing—old red roof tiles and little chunks of disposable clay tobacco pipes litter the rocks at low tide. From here, The Monument is visible across London Bridge, poking its bristly bronze head above the ugly postwar buildings. Beyond that is the bullet-shaped tip of the modern 30 St. Mary Axe Tower (also known as the "Swiss Re Tower" as well as "The Gherkin" and "Towering Innuendo" for its unusual design). Now turn left, and head west along Pickfords Wharf. About 25 yards ahead on the left are the excavated ruins of...*

❽ Winchester Palace

All that remains today is a wall with a medieval rose window, but this was once a lavish 80-acre estate stretching along 200 feet of waterfront. It had a palace, gardens, fountains, stables, tennis courts, a working farm, and a fish-stocked lake. The wall marks the west end of the Great Hall (134 feet by 29 feet), the banquet room for receptions held by the palace's owner, the Bishop of Winchester.

Bishops from 1106 to 1626 lived here as wealthy, worldly rulers of the Bankside area, outside the jurisdiction of The City. They profited from activities illegal across the river, such as prostitution and gambling. They were a law unto themselves, with their own courts and prisons. One famous prison built by the bishops remained, even after its creators were ousted by a Puritan Parliament—the Clink.

• *Fifty yards farther west (along what is now called Clink Street) is...*

❾ The Clink Prison Museum

The prison—now an overpriced and disappointing museum—gave us our expression "thrown in the Clink" from the sound of prisoners' chains. It burned down in 1780, but the underground cells remain, featuring historical information on wall plaques, many torture devices, and a generally creepy, claustrophobic atmosphere.

Originally part of Winchester Palace, it housed troublemakers who upset the smooth running of the bishop's 22 licensed brothels (called "the stews"), gambling dens, and taverns. Bouncers delivered drunks who were out of control, johns who couldn't pay, and prostitutes ("women living by their bodies") who tried to go freelance or cheated loyal customers. Offending prostitutes had their heads shaved and breasts bared, and were carted through the streets and whipped while people jeered. They might share cells side by side with "heretics"—namely, priests who crossed their bishops.

In 1352, debtors (who'd maxed out their Visa cards) became criminals, housed here among harder criminals in harsh conditions. Prisoners were not fed. They had to bribe guards to get food, to avoid torture, or even to gain their release. (The idea was that you'd brought this on yourself.) Prisoners relied on their families for money, prostituted themselves to guards and other inmates, or reached through the bars at street level, begging from passersby. Murderers, debtors, Protestants, priests, and many innocent people experienced this strange brand of justice...all part of the rough crowd that gave Bankside such a seedy reputation.

• *Continuing west and crossing under the Cannon Street Bridge, you'll find...*

❿ Vinopolis: City of Wine

This warehouse of wine—with a splash of France, a dash of ancient Rome, and a taste of Italian *vino*—seems out of place in London, but no one's complaining. For more on this wine tasters' Disneyland, see page 78.

• *Switching from wine to beer, across the street is...*

⓫ The Anchor and Bankside Road

The Anchor is the last of the original 22 licensed "inns" (tavern/brothel/restaurant/nightclub/casino) of Bankside's red light district heyday in the 1600s. A tavern has

ANCHOR TAP

stood here for 800 years. The big brick buildings behind the inn were once part of the mass-producing Anchor brewery, with the inn as its brew pub. (Even back in the 1300s, Chaucer wrote, "If the words get muddled in my tale/Just put it down to too much Southwark ale.")

In the cozy, maze-like interior are memories of greats who've drunk here (I did) or indulged in a new drug that hit London in the 1560s—tobacco.

Shakespeare, who may have lived along Clink Street, may have tippled here, especially because the original Globe Theatre was right behind The Anchor (see map on page 238). Dr. Samuel Johnson also worked here while writing the famous dictionary that helped codify the English language and spelling. For more on Dr. Johnson, see page 204.

The Anchor marks the start of once-notorious Bankside Road that runs along a river retaining wall. In Elizabethan times (16th century), the street was lined with "inns" offering one-stop shopping for addictive personalities. The streets were jammed with sword-carrying punks in tights looking for a fight, prostitutes, gaping tourists from the Borough High Street coaching inns, pickpockets, river pirates, highwaymen, navy recruiters kidnapping drunks, and many proper ladies and gentlemen who ferried across from The City for an evening's entertainment. And then there were the really seedy people—yes, actors.

• *Crossing under the green-and-yellow Southwark Bridge, notice the metal reliefs depicting London's "Frost Fair" of 1564. Because the old London Bridge was such a wall of stone, the swift-flowing Thames would back up and even freeze over during cold winters.*

Emerging from under the bridge, head farther west on Bankside to Shakespeare's Globe ⓑ.

Possible Detour: Die-hard theater fans may wish to detour inland to the site of the former Rose Theatre. It's not recommended, since the Rose is rarely open (though tours are offered through Shakespeare's Globe), and, if it is, there's not much to see. But if I can't talk you out of it, here's how to get there: Emerging from under the bridge, turn at the first left (Bear Gardens Lane), then go left on Park Street. Go one block to the gray-granite modern building located on the site of the former Rose Theatre.

⓬ Site of the Former Rose Theatre and Bear Gardens

When the 2,200-seat Rose first raised its curtain in 1587, it signaled four decades of phenomenal popularity (centered in Bankside) for a rapidly evolving form of entertainment—theater. Soon there were four great theaters in the area: the Rose, the Hope, the Swan, and the Globe. (Theatrical types can find the unimpressive plaque marking the site of the original Globe Theatre—a half-block east of the Rose—and be as disappointed as Sam Wanamaker, who was inspired to build the Shakespeare's Globe replica. More on the Globe when we arrive at the replica.)

It's thought that the young Will Shakespeare, recently arrived from the country, got his start at the Rose tending theatergoers' horses ("What?" he said, "and give up show business?!"). Soon, though, the struggling actor saw his first play *(Henry VI, Part I)* come to life on the Rose stage.

Closer to the river was a theatrical venue called the Bear Gardens (only a plaque marks the spot today). Bankside theaters presented everything from serious drama to light comedy to vaudeville to circus acts to...animal fights. Bearbaiting was the most popular. A bear was chained to a stake while a pack of dogs (mastiffs) attacked, and spectators bet on the winner. The bears, often with teeth filed down or jaws wired shut, fought back with their paws, sweeping dogs into the crowd. Now, that's entertainment.

BANKSIDE WALK

⓭ Shakespeare's Globe—1997 Replica of the Original Globe Theatre

All the world's a stage,
And all the men and women merely players.
They have their exits and their entrances,
And one man, in his time, plays many parts.

—As You Like It

By 1599, 35-year-old William Shakespeare was a well-known actor, playwright, and businessman in the booming theater trade.

His acting company, the Lord Chamberlain's Men, built the 3,000-seat Globe Theatre, by far the largest of its day (200 yards from today's replica, where only a plaque stands now). The Globe premiered Shakespeare's greatest works—*Hamlet, Othello, King Lear, Macbeth*—in open-air summer afternoon performances, though occasionally at night by light of torches and buckets of tar-soaked ropes.

In 1612, it featured Shakespeare's *All Is True (Henry VIII).* During Scene 4, a stage cannon boomed, announcing the arrival of King Henry, who started flirting with Anne Boleyn. As the two actors generated sparks onstage, play-watchers smelled fire. Some stray cannon wadding had sparked a real fire offstage. Within an hour, the wood-and-thatch building had burned completely to the ground, but with only one injury: A man's pants caught fire and were quickly doused with a tankard of ale.

Built in 1997, the new Globe—round, half-timbered, thatched, with wooden pegs for nails—is a quite realistic replica, though slightly smaller (seating 1,500 spectators), located a block away from the original site, and constructed with fire-repellent materials. Performances are staged almost nightly in summer—check at the box office (at the east end of the complex).

Bankside's theater scene vanished in the 1640s, closed by a Parliament dominated by Puritans (hard-line Protestants, like America's Pilgrims). Drama seemed to portray and promote immoral behavior, and actors—men who also played women's roles—parodied and besmirched fair womanhood. Bearbaiting was also outlawed by the outraged moralists (to paraphrase the historian Thomas Macaulay)—not because it caused bears pain, but because it gave people pleasure.

⓮ View of the Thames

From the Cotswolds to the North Sea, the river winds eastward a total of 210 miles. London is close enough to the estuary to be

affected by the North Sea's tides, so the river level does indeed rise and fall twice a day. In fact, one of the reasons Romans found this a practical location—even though it was about 40 miles inland—was that their boats could hitch a free ride with the tides between the sea and the town twice a day. But tides also mean floods. After centuries of periodic flooding (spring rains plus high tides), barriers to regulate the tides were built in 1982, east of Tower Bridge. The barriers also slow down the once fast-moving river.

The Thames is still a major commercial artery (again, east of Tower Bridge). In the previous two centuries, it ran brown with Industrial Revolution pollution. Today it's brown because of estuary silt, and the Thames is one of the cleanest rivers in the industrialized world.

• *Fifty yards west of the Globe, spanning the river, is the...*

⓯ Millennium Bridge

This pedestrian bridge was built in 2000 to connect the Tate Modern with St. Paul's Cathedral and The City. For two glorious

days, Londoners made the pleasant seven-minute walk across... before the $25 million "bridge to the next millennium" started wobbling dangerously (insert your own ironic joke here) and was closed for rethinking. After much work, 20 months, and $8 million, the bridge reopened. Nicknamed the "blade of light," it was designed (partly by Lord Norman Foster, who also did the 30 St. Mary Axe Tower and City Hall downstream) to allow a wide-open view of St. Paul's. Now stabilized, it links two revitalized sections of London.

⓰ Tate Modern

London's large, impressive modern art collection is housed in a former power station—typical of the whole South Bank's move to renovate empty, ugly Industrial Age hulks. Even if you don't tour

the collection, pop inside the north entrance (free) to view the spacious interior, decorated each year with a new industrial-sized sculptural installation by one of the world's top contemporary artists.

  ◐ See the Tate Modern Tour chapter.

• *Bankside—maybe at The Founder's Arms pub along the river—is a great place to contemplate...*

⓱ The Great Fire of 1666

On Sunday, September 2, 1666, stunned Londoners quietly sipped beers in Bankside pubs and watched The City across the river go up in flames. ("When we could endure no more upon the water," wrote Samuel Pepys in his diary, "we went to a little alehouse on the Bankside.") Started in a bakery shop near the Monument (north end of London Bridge) and fanned by strong winds, the fire swept westward, engulfing the mostly wooden city, devouring Old St. Paul's, and moving past what is now Blackfriars Bridge and St. Bride's to Temple Church (near the pointy, black, gold-tipped steeple of the Royal Courts of Justice).

In four days, 80 percent of The City was incinerated, including 13,000 houses and 89 churches. The good news? Incredibly, only nine people died, the fire cleansed a plague-infested city, and Christopher Wren was around to rebuild London's skyline.

The fire also marked the end of Bankside's era as London's naughty playground. Having recently been cleaned up by the Puritans, it now served as a temporary refugee camp for those displaced by the fire. And, with the coming Industrial Age, businessmen demolished the inns and replaced them with brick warehouses, docks, and factories to fuel the economy of a world power.

• *From here, the closest Tube stops are Southwark (a several-block walk to the south) and Blackfriars (closed for renovation until 2011). The Jubilee Walkway continues along the South Bank of the Thames to the London Eye and Big Ben. (The 20-minute stroll is particularly enjoyable in the evening.) Or you can cross the Thames on the Millennium Bridge, where a pedestrian mall leads past the glassy Salvation Army headquarters (good café and small, free Salvation Army history display in daylight basement) to St. Paul's Cathedral and Tube station.*

TATE MODERN TOUR

Remember the 20th century? Accelerated by technology and fragmented by war, it was an exciting and chaotic time, with art as turbulent as the world that created it. The Tate Modern lets you walk through the last hundred years with a glimpse at the brave new art of this explosive century.

The Tate Modern is (controversially) displayed by concept—"Poetry and Dream," for example—rather than by artist and chronology. Unlike the museum, this chapter is neatly chronological. It's not intended as a painting-by-painting tour. Read through this chapter for a general introduction, use it as a reference, then take advantage of the Tate's excellent audioguides to focus on specific works.

Orientation

Cost: Free for the permanent collection (but £3 donations are appreciated). Varying costs for temporary exhibits.

Hours: Daily 10:00–18:00, plus Fri–Sat until 22:00, last entry 45 min before closing. This popular place is especially crowded on weekend days (crowds thin out on Fri and Sat evenings).

Getting There: Located on the South Bank, across from St. Paul's and near the Globe Theatre. You can get here by Tube, ferry, and foot:

 By Tube: Take the Tube to Southwark, London Bridge, or Mansion House; then walk 10–15 minutes. ✪ See the Bankside Walk chapter.

 By Ferry: Catch the Tate Boat ferry service from the Tate Britain (£5 one-way or £12 for day ticket, discounted with Travelcard, buy ticket on board and pick up *Tate Boat* pamphlet for departure times, departs every 40 min from 10:10–17:10, 18-min trip).

By Foot: Walk across the Millennium Bridge from St. Paul's Cathedral.

Information: On the ground floor, you'll find the info desk, baggage check, audioguide rentals, and tickets for temporary exhibits. The helpful staff at the info desk can tell you the location of specific works. Switchboard tel. 020/7887-8888, recorded info tel. 020/7887-8008, www.tate.org.uk.

Tours: Audioguide tours include the Collections Tour (£2, covers all of the permanent collection) and a Children's Tour (£1, geared for kids ages 8–12), among others. Free guided tours are offered daily on the third floor at 11:00 and 12:00, and on the fifth floor at 14:00 and 15:00 (confirm at info desk). In addition, several touch-screen computers are scattered throughout the museum (particularly on the fifth floor).

Length of This Tour: Read this chapter ahead of time, then browse according to your tastes.

Cloakroom: Ground floor (free, £2 suggested donation).

Photography: Photos are only permitted in the entrance hall.

Cuisine Art: View coffee shops with food are on the second and

fourth floors. On the seventh floor, there's a table-service restaurant (plus a few stools at the casual bar), with stunning views of St. Paul's—see photo. Some trendy restaurants are several blocks southwest of the Tate, along the street named "the Cut" (near Southwark Tube stop).

Starring: Picasso, Matisse, Dalí, and all the "classic" modern artists, plus the Tate Modern's specialty—British and American artists of the last half of the 20th century.

Overview

To see the core of the permanent collection—and the artwork described in this tour—visit the third and fifth floors. Paintings are arranged according to theme, not artist. Paintings by Picasso, for example, are scattered all over the building. Temporary exhibits are on the fourth floor.

Even though the layout of the Tate Modern changes constantly, the collection's focus is the same:

TATE MODERN TOUR

the postwar period. Don't just come to see the Old Masters of modernism (Matisse, Picasso, Kandinsky, and so on). Push your mental envelope with works by Pollock, Miró, Bacon, Picabia, Beuys, Twombly, and others.

More modern art from British artists is on display at the Tate Britain museum (see the Tate Britain Tour chapter).

The Tour Begins

Entrance Hall

The grandest entry is from the west entrance. The massive empty space of the former industrial powerhouse dwarfs the art it houses. (A metaphor for the triumph of 20th-century technology, perhaps?) The Turbine Hall displays major art installations by contemporary artists—always one of the highlights of the art world. From winter of 2009 through spring of 2010, the hall's decoration is by Polish sculptor Miroslaw Balka, known for his austere gray-and-white cubes and coffin-like rectangles.

From the Turbine Hall, you can reach the third floor (start of permanent collection) via the escalator near the ground floor cloakroom.

Reminder: The following is not a painting-by-painting tour but rather a chronological overview of modern art.

1900—Victoria's Legacy

Anno Domini 1900, a new century dawns. Europe is at peace, Britannia rules the world. Technology is about to usher in a golden age.

Claude Monet (1840-1926)

Monet captures the relaxed, civilized spirit of belle époque France and Victorian England with Impressionist snapshots of peaceful landscapes and middle-class family picnics. But the true subject is the shimmering effect of reflected light, rendered with rough brushstrokes and bright paints that look messy up close but blend at a distance. The newfangled camera made camera-eye realism obsolete. Artists began placing more importance on *how* something was painted than on *what* was painted.

1905—Colonial Europe

Europe ruled a global empire, tapping its dark-skinned colonials for raw materials, cheap labor, and bold new ways to look at the world. The cozy Victorian world was shattering. Nietzsche murdered God. Darwin stripped off Man's robe of culture and found a naked ape. Primitivism was modern. Ooga-booga.

Henri Matisse (1869–1954)

Matisse was one of the Fauves, or "wild beasts," who tried to inject a bit of the jungle into civilized European society. Inspired by

"primitive" African and Oceanic masks and voodoo dolls, the Fauves made modern art that looked primitive: long, mask-like faces with almond eyes; bright, clashing colors; simple figures; and "flat," two-dimensional scenes.

Matisse simplifies. A man is a few black lines and blocks of paint. A snail is a spiral of colored paper. A woman's back is an outline. Matisse's colors are unnaturally bright. The "distant" landscape is as crisp and clear as close objects, and the slanted lines meant to suggest depth are crudely done.

Traditionally, the canvas was like a window that you looked "through" to see a slice of the real world stretching off into the horizon. With Matisse, you look "at" the canvas, like wallpaper, to appreciate the decorative pattern of colors and shapes.

Though his style is modern, Matisse builds on 19th-century art—the bright colors of Van Gogh, the primitive figures of Gauguin, the colorful designs of Japanese wood-block prints, and the Impressionist patches of paint that blend together only at a distance.

Paul Cézanne (1839–1906)

Cézanne brings Impressionism into the 20th century. Whereas Monet uses separate dabs of different-colored paint to "build" a figure, Cézanne "builds" a man with somewhat larger slabs of paint, giving him a kind of 3-D chunkiness. It's not hard to see the progression from Monet's dabs to Cézanne's slabs to Picasso's cubes—Cubism.

1910—The Moderns

The modern world was moving fast, with automobiles, factories, and mass communication. Motion pictures captured the fast-moving world, while Einstein explored the fourth dimension: time.

Cubism: Pablo Picasso (1881–1973)

Picasso's Cubist works show the old European world shattering to bits. He pieces the fragments back together in a whole new way, showing several perspectives at once (looking up the left side of a

TATE MODERN TOUR

woman's body and down at her right at the same time, for example).

Whereas newfangled motion pictures capture several perspectives in succession, Picasso achieves it on a canvas with overlapping images. A single "cube" might contain both an arm (in the foreground) and the window behind (in the background), both painted the same color. The foreground and background are woven together so that the subject dissolves into a pattern.

Born in Spain, Picasso moved to Paris as a young man. He worked with Georges Braque in poverty so dire they often didn't know where their next bottle of wine was coming from.

Picasso, the most famous and—OK, I'll say it—the greatest artist of the 20th century, constantly explored and adapted his style to new trends. He made collages, tried his hand at "statues" out of wood, wire, or whatever, and even made art out of everyday household objects. These multimedia works, so revolutionary at the time, have become stock-in-trade today. Scattered throughout the museum are works from the many periods of Picasso's life.

Futurism: Férnand Leger (1881–1955) and Umberto Boccioni (1882–1916)

The Machine Age is approaching, and the whole world gleams with promise in cylinder shapes ("Tubism"), like an internal-combustion engine. Or is it the gleaming barrel of a cannon?

1914—World War I

A soldier—shivering in a trench, ankle-deep in mud, waiting to be ordered "over the top," to run through barbed wire, over fallen comrades, and into a hail of machine-gun fire, only to capture a few hundred yards of meaningless territory that would be lost the next day. This soldier was not thinking about art.

World War I left nine million dead. (England sometimes lost more men in a single month than America lost during the entire Vietnam War.) The war also killed the optimism and faith in humankind that had guided Europe since the Renaissance.

Expressionism: Grosz, Kirchner, Beckmann, Soutine, Dix, and Kokoschka

Cynicism and decadence settled over postwar Europe. Artists "expressed" their disgust by showing a distorted reality that emphasized the ugly. Using the lurid colors and simplified figures of the Fauves, they slapped paint on in thick brushstrokes, depicting a hypocritical, hard-edged, dog-eat-dog world, a civilization watching its Victorian moral foundations collapse.

Dada: Duchamp's Urinal (1917)

When they could grieve no longer, artists turned to grief's giddy twin, laughter. The war made all old values a joke, including artistic ones. The Dada movement, choosing a purposely childish name, made art that was intentionally outrageous: a moustache on the *Mona Lisa,* a shovel hung on the wall, or a modern version of a Renaissance "fountain"—a urinal (by Marcel Duchamp...or was it I. P. Freeley?).

It was a dig at all the pompous prewar artistic theories based on the noble intellect of Rational Women and Men. While the experts ranted on, Dadaists sat in the back of the class and made cultural fart noises.

Hey, I love this stuff. My mind says it's sophomoric, but my heart belongs to Dada.

1920s—Anything Goes

In the Jazz Age, the world turned upside-down. Genteel ladies smoked cigarettes. Gangsters laid down the law. You could make a fortune in the stock market one day and lose it the next. You could dance the Charleston with the opposite sex, and even say the word "sex" while talking about Freud over cocktails. It was almost...surreal.

Surrealism: Dalí, Ernst, and Magritte

Artists caught the jumble of images on a canvas. A telephone made from a lobster, an elephant with a heating-duct trunk, Venus sleepwalking among skeletons. Take one mixed bag of reality, jumble it in a blender, and serve on a canvas—Surrealism.

The artist scatters seemingly unrelated things on the canvas, leaving us to trace the connections in a kind of connect-the-dots without numbers.

Further complicating the modern world was Freud's discovery of the "unconscious" mind that thinks dirty thoughts while we sleep. Surrealists let the id speak. The canvas is an uncensored, stream-of-consciousness "landscape" of these deep urges, revealed in the bizarre images of dreams.

Salvador Dalí (1904–1989)

Salvador Dalí, the most famous Surrealist, combines an extraordinarily realistic technique
with an extraordinarily
twisted mind. He paints
"unreal" scenes with pho-
tographic realism, making
us believe they could really
happen. Dalí's images—
crucifixes, political and
religious figures, and
naked bodies—pack an emotional punch.

1930s—Depression

As capitalism failed around the world, governments propped up
their economies with vast building projects. The architecture
style was modern, stripped-down (i.e., cheap), and functional.
Propagandist campaigns championed noble workers in the heroic
Social Realist style.

Piet Mondrian (1872–1944)

Like blueprints for modernism, Mondrian's T-square style boils
painting down to its basic building blocks: a white canvas, black

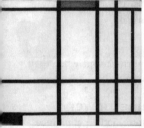

lines, and the three primary colors—red,
yellow, and blue—arranged in orderly
patterns. (When you come right down
to it, that's all painting ever has been. A
schematic drawing of, say, the *Mona Lisa*
shows that it's less about a woman than
about the triangles and rectangles she's
composed of.)

Mondrian started out painting
realistic landscapes of the orderly fields in his native homeland of
Holland. Increasingly, he simplified his style into horizontal and
vertical patterns. For Mondrian, who was heavily into Eastern
mysticism, "up versus down" and "left versus right" were the perfect metaphors for life's dualities: good versus evil, body versus
spirit, fascism versus communism, man versus woman. The canvas
is a bird's-eye view of Mondrian's personal landscape.

1940s—World War II

World War II was a global war (involving Europe, the Americas,
Australia, Africa, and Asia) and a total war (saturation bombing of
civilians and ethnic cleansing). It left Europe in ruins.

Abstract Art

Abstract art simplifies. A man becomes a stick figure. A squiggle is a wave. A streak of red expresses anger. Arches make you want a cheeseburger. These are universal symbols that everyone from a caveman to a banker understands. Abstract artists capture the essence of reality in a few lines and colors, boldly capturing objects and ideas even a camera can't—emotions, abstract concepts, musical rhythms, and spiritual states of mind.

With abstract art, you don't look "through" the canvas to see the visual world, but "at" it to read the symbolism of lines, shapes, and colors. Most 20th-century paintings are a mix of the real world (representation) and colorful patterns (abstraction).

Alberto Giacometti (1901–1966)

Giacometti's skinny statues have the emaciated, haunted, and faceless look of concentration-camp survivors. In the sweep of world war and overpowering technology, man is frail and fragile. All he can do is stand at attention and take it like a man.

Francis Bacon (1909–1992)

Bacon's caged creatures speak for all of war-torn Europe when they scream, "Enough!" (For more on Bacon, see page 291.)

1950s—America, the Global Superpower

As converted war factories turned swords into kitchen appliances, America helped rebuild Europe while pumping out consumer goods for a booming population. Prosperity, a stable government, national television broadcasts, and a common fear of Soviet communism threatened to turn America into a completely homogeneous society.

Some artists, centered in New York, rebelled against conformity and superficial consumerism. (They'd served under Eisenhower in war and now had to in peace, as well.) They created art that was the very opposite of the functional, mass-produced goods of the American marketplace.

Art was a way of asserting your individuality by creating a completely original and personal vision. The trend was toward bigger canvases, abstract designs, and experimentation with new materials and techniques. It was called "Abstract Expressionism"—expressing emotions and ideas using color and form alone.

Jackson Pollock (1912–1956)

"Jack the Dripper" attacks convention with a can of paint, dripping and splashing a dense web onto the canvas. Picture Pollock in his studio, jiving to the hi-fi, bouncing off the walls, throwing paint in a moment of enlightenment. Of course, the artist loses some control this way—over the paint flying in midair and over himself in an ecstatic trance. Painting becomes a whole-body activity, a "dance" between the artist and his materials.

The intuitive act of creating is what's important, not the final product. The canvas is only a record of that moment of ecstasy.

Big, Empty Canvases

With all the postwar prosperity, artists could afford bigger canvases. But what reality are they trying to show?

In the modern world, we find ourselves insignificant specks in a vast and indifferent universe. Every morning, each of us must confront that big, blank, existential canvas, and decide how we're going to make our mark on it.

Another influence was the simplicity of Japanese landscape painting. A Zen master studies and meditates for years to achieve the state of mind in which he can draw one pure line. These canvases, again, are only a record of that state of enlightenment. (What is the sound of one brush painting?)

On more familiar ground, postwar painters were following in the footsteps of artists such as Mondrian. The geometrical forms here reflect the same search for order, but these artists painted to the musical 5/4 asymmetry of the Dave Brubeck Quartet's jazzy *Take Five.*

Patterns and Textures

Enjoy the lines and colors, but also a new element: texture. Some works have very thick paint piled on, where you can see the brushstrokes clearly. Some have substances besides paint applied to the canvas, or the canvas is punctured so the fabric itself (and the hole) becomes the subject. Artists show their skill by mastering new materials. The canvas is a tray, serving up a delightful buffet of different substances with interesting colors, patterns, shapes, and textures.

Mark Rothko (1903–1970)

Rothko makes two-toned rectangles, laid on their sides, that seem to float in a big, vertical canvas. The edges are blurred, so if you get close enough to let the canvas fill your field of vision (as Rothko intended), the rectangles appear to rise and sink from the cloudy depths like answers in a Magic 8-Ball.

Serious students appreciate the subtle differences in color between the rectangles. Rothko experimented with different bases for the same color and used a single undercoat (a "wash") to unify them. His early works are warmer, with brighter reds, yellows, and oranges; the later works are maroon and brown, approaching black.

Still, these are not intended to be formal studies in color and form. Rothko was trying to express the most basic human emotions in a pure language. (A "realistic" painting of a person is inherently fake because it's only an illusion of the person.) Staring into these windows onto the soul, you can laugh, cry, or ponder, just as Rothko did when he painted them.

Rothko, the previous century's "last serious artist," believed in the power of art to express the human spirit. When he found out that his nine large Seagram canvases were to be hung in a corporate restaurant, he refused to sell them (and they ended up in the Tate).

In his last years, Rothko's canvases—always rectangles—got bigger, simpler, and darker. When Rothko finally slashed his wrists in his studio, one nasty critic joked that what killed him was the repetition. Minimalism was painting itself into a blank corner.

1960s—The Sixties

The decade began united in idealism—young John F. Kennedy pledged to put a man on the moon, newly launched satellites signaled a united world, the Beatles sang exuberantly, peaceful race demonstrations championed equality, and the Vatican II Council preached liberation. By decade's end, there were race riots, assassinations, student protests, and America's floundering war in distant Vietnam. In households around the world, parents screamed, "Turn that down...and get a haircut!"

Culturally, every postwar value was questioned by a rising wealthy and populous baby-boom generation. London—producer of rock-and-roll music, film actors, mod fashions, and Austin Powers' joie de vivre—once again became a world cultural center.

20th-Century British Artists

Since 1960, London has rivaled New York as a center for the visual arts. You'll find British artists displayed in both the Tate Modern and the Tate Britain. Check out the Tate Britain Tour chapter for more on the following artists: David Hockney, Stanley Spencer, Jacob Epstein, Gilbert and George, Henry Moore, Francis Bacon, and Barbara Hepworth.

Though government-sponsored public art was dominated by big, abstract canvases and sculptures, other artists pooh-poohed the highbrow seriousness of abstract art. Instead, they mocked lowbrow, popular culture by embracing it in a tongue-in-cheek way (Pop Art), or they attacked authority with absurd performances to make a political statement (conceptual art).

Pop Art: Andy Warhol (1928–1987)

America's postwar wealth made the consumer king. Pop Art is created from the popular objects of that throw-away society—soup can, car fender, tacky plastic statues, movie icons. Take a Sears product, hang it in a museum, and you have to ask, Is this art? Are mass-produced objects beautiful? Or crap? Why do we work so hard to acquire them? Pop Art, like Dadaism before it, questions our society's values.

Andy Warhol (who coined "15 minutes of fame") concentrated on another mass-produced phenomenon: celebrities. He took publicity photos of famous people and reproduced them. The repetition—like the constant bombardment we get from repeated images on TV—cheapens even the most beautiful things.

Roy Lichtenstein (1923–1997)

Take a comic strip, blow it up, hang it on a wall, and charge a million bucks—wham, Pop Art. Lichtenstein supposedly was inspired by his young son, who challenged him to do something as good as

Mickey Mouse. The huge newsprint dots never let us forget that the painting—like all commercial art—is an illusionistic fake. The work's humor comes from portraying a lowbrow subject (comics and ads) on the epic scale of a masterpiece.

Op Art: Bridget Riley (b. 1931)
Optical illusions play tricks with your eyes, the way a spiral starts to spin when you stare at it. These obscure scientific experiments in color, line, and optics suddenly became trendy in the psychedelic '60s.

1970s—The "Me Decade"
All forms of authority—"The Establishment"—seemed bankrupt. America's president resigned in the Watergate scandal, corporations were polluting the earth, and capitalism nearly ground to a halt when Arabs withheld oil.

Artists attacked authority and institutions, trying to free individuals to discover their full human potential. Even the concept of "modernism"—that art wasn't good unless it was totally original and progressive—was questioned. No single style could dictate in this postmodern period.

Earth Art
Fearing for the health of earth's ecology, artists rediscovered the beauty of rocks, dirt, trees, even the sound of the wind, using them to create natural art. A rock placed in a museum or urban square is certainly a strange sight.

Joseph Beuys (1921–1986)
The Tate Modern's collection of "sculptures" by Beuys—assemblages of steel, junk, wood, and, especially, felt and animal fat—only hint at his greatest artwork: Beuys himself.

Imagine Beuys ("boyss") walking through the museum, carrying a dead rabbit, while he explains the paintings to it. Or taking off his clothes, shaving his head, and smearing his body with fat.

This charismatic, ex-Luftwaffe art shaman did ridiculous things to inspire others to break with convention and be free. He choreographed "Happenings"—spectacles where people did absurd things while others watched—and pioneered performance art, in which the artist presents himself as the work of art. Beuys inspired a whole generation of artists to walk on stage, cluck like a chicken, and stick a yam up themselves. Beuys will be Beuys.

New Media
Minimalist painting and abstract sculpture were old hat, and there was an explosion of new art forms. Performance art was the most controversial, combining music, theater, dance, poetry, and the visual arts. New technologies brought video, assemblages, installations, artists' books (paintings in book form), and even (gasp!) realistic painting.

Conceptual Art
Increasingly, artists are not creating an original work (painting a canvas or sculpting a stone) but assembling one from premade objects. The *concept* of which object to pair with another to produce maximum effect ("Let's stick a crucifix in a jar of urine," to cite one notorious example) is the key.

1980s—Material Girl
Ronald Reagan in America, Margaret Thatcher in Britain, and corporate executives around the world ruled over a conservative and materialistic society. On the other side were starving Ethiopians, gays with the new disease of AIDS, people of color, and women—all demanding power. Intelligent, peaceful, straight white males assumed a low profile.

The art world became big business, with a Van Gogh fetching $54 million. Corporations paid big bucks for large, colorful, semi-abstract canvases. Marketing became an art form. Gender and sexual choice were popular themes. Many women picked up paintbrushes, creating bright-colored abstract forms hinting at vulva and penis shapes. Visual art fused with popular music, bringing us installations in dance clubs and fast-edit music videos. The crude style of graffiti art demanded to be included in corporate society.

1990s—Multicultural Diversity
The communist-built Berlin Wall was torn down, ending four decades of a global Cold War between capitalism and communism. The new battleground was the "Culture Wars," the struggle to include all races, genders, and lifestyles within an increasingly corporate-dominated, global society.

Artists looked to Third World countries for inspiration and

championed society's outsiders against government censorship and economic exclusion. A new medium arose, the Internet, allowing instantaneous multimedia communication around the world through electronic signals carried by satellites and telephone lines.

2000—?
A new millennium dawned, with Europe and America at a peak of prosperity unmatched in human history....

VICTORIA AND ALBERT MUSEUM TOUR

With one of the biggest, most eclectic collections of objects anywhere, the Victoria and Albert (V&A) has something for everyone. It bills itself as a museum for the decorative arts, and Martha Stewart types will be in hog heaven. Think of it as two museums. The British Galleries offer a survey of British style, taste, and design from 1500 to 1900. The rest of the museum collects decorative arts from around the world—furniture, glassware, clothing, jewelry, and carpets. Throw in historical artifacts, a few fine-arts masterpieces (painting and sculpture), and a bed that sleeps seven, and you have a museum built for browsing. I've selected a dozen or so objects that I find interesting, but don't limit yourself to those.

The V&A grew out of the Great Exhibition of 1851, that ultimate celebration of the Industrial Revolution. Now "art" could be brought to the masses through modern technology and mass production. The museum was founded on the idealistic Victorian notion that anyone can be continually improved by education and example. After much support from Queen Victoria and Prince Albert, the museum was renamed for the royal couple, and its present building was opened in 1909.

In 2004, the V&A received several grants for refurbishment projects to take place over the next 10 years. Changes so far include a new café, renovated sculpture gallery, and reopened Islamic room. The refurbished Medieval and Renaissance galleries reopen in late 2009. During this chaotic time, exhibits will likely be rearranged, so check with the information desk for current room closures, carry a copy of the museum's detailed map, and ask a nearby guard if you can't find one of the objects in this tour.

British history fans with short attention spans may want to hit the British Galleries first (see the end of this tour for highlights) and do the rest of the self-guided tour afterward.

Orientation

Cost: Free (£3 donation requested), sometimes pricey fees for special exhibits.

Hours: Daily 10:00–17:45, some galleries open Fri until 22:00 (note that Tube tunnel will be closed at this time).

Getting There: It's on Cromwell Road in the South Kensington neighborhood (Tube: South Kensington; a 5-min walk through a tunnel leads directly from the Tube station to a lower level of the museum—follow signs upstairs to the shop to begin this tour).

Information: Pick up the much-needed museum map (£1 suggested donation). The fine £5 *V&A Guide Book* outlines five self-guided, speedy tours. The V&A's helpful website lists its current exhibitions (tel. 020/7942-2000, www.vam.ac.uk).

Tours: Free one-hour orientation tours are offered daily on the half-hour 10:30 to 15:30. Additional tours and lectures are offered sporadically; check the website for details.

Length of This Tour: Allow 90 minutes (not counting the British Galleries).

Cloakroom: Free, mandatory for large bags.

Photography: Permitted without flash or tripod (except for special exhibits and works on loan).

Cuisine Art: The V&A Café serves cafeteria-style lunch and tea in the elegant Morris, Gamble, and Poynter rooms. In summer, an inexpensive self-service café is set up in the Madejski Garden—grab a bite there or bring a picnic.

Overview

The museum is large and gangly, with 150 rooms and more than 12 miles of corridors. Our tour highlights just a few displays, chosen mostly because of their location near the ground-floor entrance (on Cromwell Road). It's a sample of the V&A's range, covering fine art, historical objects, interior design, fashion, and beautiful objects from around the globe. Look at what's offered, survey a museum map, and see what you want in any order you like.

The new Medieval and Renaissance collection (A.D. 300–1600, open from Nov 2009) fills 10 rooms to the right of the lobby. Don't miss the British Galleries upstairs—a one-way tour stretching through 400 years of British lifestyles, almost a museum in itself. You could spend days in this place beyond our quick tour. The museum's free index of displays allows you to survey art in alphabetical order, from the Ardabil Carpet to woven textiles, and track down whatever is of personal interest.

The Tour Begins

• *Enter from Cromwell Road into the Grand Entrance lobby, on the ground floor under the rotunda. If you wish to skip ahead to the British Galleries, go upstairs to the left from the entrance lobby to Room 58. Otherwise, in the lobby, look up.*

❶ Dale Chihuly Chandelier

This modern chandelier/sculpture by an American glass artist epitomizes the spirit of the V&A's collection—beautiful manufactured

objects that demonstrate technical skill and innovation, wedding the old with the new, and blurring the line between arts and crafts.

Each blue-and-yellow strand of the chandelier is tied with a wire to a central spine. When the chandelier first went up in 2001, Chihuly said "Too small," had it disassembled, and fired up still more glass bubbles.

Dale Chihuly (b. 1941)—face-famous for the eye-patch he's worn since a car accident—studied glassmaking in Venice, then set up his own studio/factory in Seattle, creating art as the director of a team effort. He makes an old medium seem fresh and modern, and the V&A keeps his chandelier looking fresh with a long feather duster.

• *From the lobby, look up to the balcony and see the pointed arches of the...*

❷ Hereford Screen (1862)

In the 1800s, just as Britain was steaming into the future on the

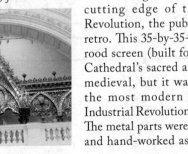

cutting edge of the Industrial Revolution, the public's taste went retro. This 35-by-35-foot, eight-ton rood screen (built for the Hereford Cathedral's sacred altar area) looks medieval, but it was created with the most modern materials the Industrial Revolution could produce. The metal parts were not hammered and hand-worked as in olden days,

VICTORIA AND ALBERT

Victoria and Albert Museum Tour

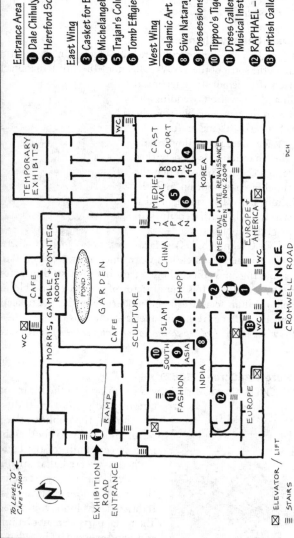

Entrance Area
1. Dale Chihuly Chandelier
2. Hereford Screen (Above Lobby)

East Wing
3. Casket for Becket's Relics
4. Michelangelo Casts
5. Trajan's Column Casts
6. Tomb Effigies

West Wing
7. Islamic Art
8. Siva Nataraja Statue
9. Possessions of Shah Jahan
10. Tippoo's Tiger
11. Dress Gallery & Stairs to Musical Instruments
12. RAPHAEL – Tapestry Cartoons
13. British Galleries Entrance (Upstairs)

☒ ELEVATOR / LIFT
≡ STAIRS

but are made of electroformed copper. The parts were first cast in plaster, then bathed in molten copper with an electric current running through it, leaving a metal skin around the plaster. The entire project—which might have taken years in medieval times—was completed in five months.

George Gilbert Scott (1811–1878), who built the screen, redesigned all of London in the Neo-Gothic style, restoring old churches such as Westminster Abbey, renovating the Houses of Parliament, and building new structures like St. Pancras Station and the Albert Memorial—some 700 buildings in all.

The world turns, and a century later (1960s), the Gothic style was "out" again, modernism was in, and this screen was neglected and ridiculed. Considering that the V&A was originally called the Museum of Manufactures (1857), it's appropriate that the screen was brought here, where it shows off the technical advances of the Industrial Revolution.

• *Look for the following exhibit in the new Medieval and Renaissance rooms. If you can't find it, ask the helpful staff where it's currently displayed...or just skip it and move on to the Michelangelo casts.*

❸ Casket for Relics of St. Thomas Becket (c. 1180)

Look along one side of the blue-and-gold box, where Thomas Becket—the Archbishop of Canterbury—is about to grab a chalice from the altar, when knights tiptoe up, draw their swords, and

slice off his head. Two shocked priests throw up their hands.

Becket's soul (upper right) is borne aloft on a sling by two angels. His body is laid to rest (upper left) and blessed by the new bishop. Mourners kneel at the tomb, just as the man behind Becket's murder—King Henry II—is said to have done in remorse.

Henry II had handpicked his good friend Thomas Becket (1118–1170) for the job of archbishop, assuming he'd follow the king's orders. In two days, Thomas was made a priest, a bishop, then archbishop—the head of all England's Christians. But when Becket proved loyal to the Church and opposed Henry's policies, the king, in a rash fit of anger, said he wanted Becket dead. Remorseful after his knights murdered the archbishop, Henry had 80 monks whip him, and then he spent all night at the foot of the tomb.

Just three years after his death, Becket was made a saint. Pieces of Becket's DNA—valuable relics—were conserved in this enamel-and-metal work box, a specialty of Limoges, France.

• *Head into the East Wing of the museum (to the right).*

East Wing

• *At the far end of the hall, find the long Room 46. Along either side of Room 46 are the Cast Courts in Rooms 46A and 46B. Room 46B, to the right, may be closed until 2010 (if so, you can peek down into it from the upper mezzanine). This room contains plaster-cast replicas of many famous statues, including some...*

❹ Michelangelo Casts

These plaster-cast versions of famous Renaissance statues by Michelangelo and others allowed 19th-century art students who

couldn't afford a railpass to go study the classics.

The statues were made by coating the original with a nonstick substance, then laying wet plaster strips over it that dried to form a mold, from which a plaster cast was made. They look solid but are very fragile. In a

single glance, you can follow Michelangelo's career, from youthful optimism *(David)*, to his never-finished masterpiece (statues from the tomb of Julius II, including *Moses* and two *Slaves*), to full-blown mid-life crisis (while sculpting the brooding Medici Tomb statues of Lorenzo and Giuliano). Compare Michelangelo's monumental *David* with Donatello's girlish *David*, and see Ghiberti's bronze Baptistery doors that inspired the Florentine Renaissance.

David was a gift from Tuscany to Queen Victoria, who immediately donated it to the museum. Circle behind *David* to see the clip-on fig leaf (this was "the Victorian Age") that was hung on him when modest aristocrats visited.

• *In Room 46A, you can't miss...*

❺ Trajan's Column Casts

Rising 140 feet and decorated with a spiral relief of 2,500 figures trumpeting the exploits of the Roman Emperor Trajan (c. A.D. 100), this is a copy of the world's grandest column from antiquity. The original column still stands in Rome, but the V&A's version was cast from a copy in Paris. In fact, they had to cut it in half to fit it here.

The column's relief unfolds like a scroll, telling the story of Trajan's conquest of Dacia (modern-day Romania). It starts at the bottom (the half with the pedestal) with a trickle of water that

becomes a river and soon picks up boats full of supplies. Then come the soldiers themselves, who spill out from the gates of the city. A river god surfaces to bless the journey. Along the way (second band), they build roads and forts to sustain the vast enterprise. Trajan himself (fourth band, in military skirt with toga over his arm) mounts a podium to fire up the troops. They hop into a Roman galley ship (fifth band) and head off to fight the valiant Dacians in the middle of a forest (eighth band). Finally, at the very top, the Romans hold a sacrifice to give thanks for the victory, while the captured armor is displayed on the pedestal.

Originally, the entire story was painted in bright colors. If you unwound the scroll, it would stretch the length of two football fields—it's far longer than the frieze around the Greek Parthenon.

• *Near Trajan's column, find several casts of knights and ladies on their backs, staring at the ceiling (in faded hues of red, gold, and blue). Some of these are the...*

❻ Tomb Effigies of Henry II and Family
(Plaster cast, French, Fontevrault)

This was a remarkable and dysfunctional royal family. King Henry II (1133–1189)—Becket's murderer—lies alongside his wife and their children. Henry's wife, Eleanor of Aquitaine (the one reading a book while dead), was the ex-wife of the King of France and was renowned as Europe's most sophisticated lady. When Henry and Eleanor wed, it united their two families' large land holdings, creating an "England" that stretched as far down as southern France. It would eventually take a "Hundred Years' War" (1336–1453) to sort out the current border between England and France.

As king, Henry placed church courts under secular control, causing the rift that led to Becket's bloody murder. In Henry's old age, his children rebelled, taking arms against him for their slice of the royal pie. Henry's heir, Richard the Lionhearted, famous as the good guy in the Robin Hood legend, was actually an absentee monarch—a French-speaking dandy allied with the King of France. Younger son John, the "evil" King John of the Robin Hood legend, became a tyrant, prompting English nobles to make him sign the document called the Magna Carta, which established the principle that even kings must follow the law. (The British Library has a copy of the Magna Carta. See British Library Tour.)

• *Backtrack toward the entrance lobby. Continue down the hall into the West Wing.*

West Wing

• *Turn right into Room 42, which contains art of the Islamic Middle East.*

❼ Islamic Art (c. 8th and 9th Centuries)

Rather than making paintings and statues, Islamic artists expressed themselves with beautiful but functional objects.

In the center of the room is the 630-square-foot Ardabil Carpet (1539–1540). Its silk-thread underpinnings are topped by a dense wool pile made of 304 knots per square inch. (Carpet connoisseurs will nod approvingly at this impressively high KPI number.) Woven on a huge standing loom, it likely took a dozen workers years to make. In the center of the design is a yellow medallion ringed with ovals, supporting two hanging lamps. If you sat on the carpet near the smaller of the two lamps, you'd have the illusion of a symmetrical pattern.

Also in the room are more carpets, ceramics (mostly blue-and-white or red-and-white), and glazed tile—all covered top to bottom in similarly complex patterns. The intricate interweaving, repetition, and unending lines suggest the complex, infinite nature of God (Allah).

You'll likely see only a few pictures of humans or animals—the Islamic religion is wary of any "graven images" or idols forbidden by God. However, secular for homes and palaces was not bound by this, and you may see realistic depictions of men and women enjoying a garden paradise, a symbol of the Muslim heaven.

Notice floral patterns (twining vines, flowers, arabesques) and geometric designs (stars, diamonds). But the most common pattern is calligraphy—elaborate lettering of an inscription in Arabic, the language of the Quran (and the lettering used even in non-Arabic languages). A quote from the Quran on a vase or lamp combines the power of the message with the beauty of the calligraphy.

• *Return to the hall and continue on. In the hallway (technically "Room" 47B) is a glass case with a statue of...*

❽ Siva Nataraja (12th Century)

Life is a dance.

The Hindu god Siva (SHEE-vah)—one of the hundreds, if not thousands, of godlike incarnations of Hinduism's eternal being, Brahma—steps lively and creates the world by dancing. His four arms are busy creating, and he treads on the sleepy dwarf of ignorance.

This bronze statue, one of Hinduism's most popular, is loaded with symbolism, summing up where humans came from and where we're going. Surrounded by a ring of fire, he crosses a leg

The British in India

December 31, 1600—The British East India Company—a multi-national trading company owned by stockholders—is founded with a charter from Queen Elizabeth I. They're given a virtual monopoly on trade with India.

1600s—The British trade peacefully with Indian locals on the coast, competing with France, Holland, and Portugal for access to spices, cotton, tea, indigo, and jute (for rope-making).

1700s—As the Mughal (Islamic) Empire breaks down, Britain and France vie for trade ports and inland territory. By the 1750s, Britain is winning. Britain establishes itself in Bombay, Madras, and Calcutta. First they rule through puppet Mughal leaders, then dump local leaders altogether.

1800s—By mid-century, two-thirds of the subcontinent is under British rule, exporting opium and tea (transplanted from its native China) and importing British-made cloth. Britain tries to reform Indian social customs (e.g., outlawing widow suicides) with little long-lasting effect. They build railways, roads, and irrigation systems.

1857–1858—The "Indian Mutiny"—sparked by high taxes, British monopoly of trade, and a chafing against foreign rule—is the first of many uprisings that slowly erode British rule.

1900s—Two world wars drain and distract Britain while Indians lobby for self-rule.

August 15, 1947—After a decade of peaceful protests led by Mahatma Gandhi, India gains its independence.

in time to the music. Smiling serenely, he blesses with one hand, while another beats out the rhythm of life with a hand drum. The

cobra draped over his arm symbolizes the *Kundalini Sakti*, the cosmic energy inside each of us that can, with the right training, uncoil and bring us to enlightenment.

As long as Siva keeps dancing, the universe will continue. But Siva also holds a flame, a reminder that, at the end of time, he will transform into his female alter ego, Kali, and destroy the world by fire, clearing the slate for another round of existence.

• *Head through the doorway into the adjoining Room 41 (labeled* South Asia*). You'll run right into a glass case in the center of the room containing small items that were the...*

❾ Possessions of Emperor Shah Jahan (r. 1628–1658)

Look at the cameo portrait, thumb ring, and wine cup (made of white nephrite jade, 1657) that belonged to one of the world's most powerful men.

Shah Jahan—or "King of the World"—ruled the largest empire of the day, covering northern India, Pakistan, and Afghanistan. His Mughal Empire was descended from Genghis Khan and the Mongol horde, who conquered and then settled in central Asia and converted to Islam.

Shah Jahan was known for his building projects, especially the Taj Mahal (see a watercolor of it nearby), built as a mausoleum for his favorite wife, Mumtaz, who bore him 14 children before dying in childbirth.

His unsuccessful attempts to expand the empire drained the treasury. In his old age, his sons quarreled over the inheritance. Imprisoned by his sons in the Agra fort, Shah Jahan died gazing across the river at the Taj Mahal, where he, too, would be buried. India's glory days were ending.

Then came the British.

• *At the far end of Room 41 is the huge wood-carved...*

❿ Tippoo's Tiger (1790s)

This life-size robotic toy, once owned by an oppressed Indian sultan (see Tipu's portrait and belongings nearby), is perhaps better called "India's revenge." The Bengal tiger has a British redcoat down, sinking its teeth into his neck. When you turned the crank, the Brit's left arm would flail, and both he and the tiger would roar through organ pipes. (The mechanism still works.)

Tipu, the Sultan of Mysore (1750–1799), called himself "The Tiger of Mysore." He was well educated in several languages and collected a library of 2,000 books. An enlightened ruler, he built roads and dams and promoted new technology. Tipu could see that India was being swallowed up by the all-powerful British East India Company. He allied himself with France and fought several successful wars against the British, but he was eventually defeated and forced to give up half his kingdom to them. Tipu was later killed by the Brits in battle (1799), his palace ransacked, and his possessions—including this toy—now owned, like much of India, by the British East India Company.

• *Backtrack out of Room 41 and turn right, then right again into Room 40. Here you'll find the...*

⓫ Dress Gallery and Musical Instruments

Nearly 400 years of English fashion are corseted into 40 display cases. The cases around the perimeter show the evolution of a particular article of clothing: formal wear, underwear, men's suits, etc. The inner ring of displays contains designer dresses, and the four freestanding cases in the corners have wedding dresses. For more on old English fashion, visit the British Galleries (described on next page).

Up a staircase in the middle of Room 40, you'll find the Musical Instruments section (Room 40A, not always open), with lutes, harpsichords, early flutes, big violins, and strange, curly horns. Some instruments are recognizable, some obsolete.

• *Directly across the hall from Room 40 is Room 48A, filled with...*

⓬ Raphael's Tapestry Cartoons

For Christmas, 1519, Pope Leo X unveiled 10 new tapestries in the Sistine Chapel, designed by the famous artist Raphael. The

project was one of the largest ever undertaken by a painter—it cost far more than Michelangelo's Sistine ceiling—and when it was done, the tapestries were a hit, inspiring princes across Europe to decorate their palaces in masterpieces of cloth.

The V&A owns seven of the full-size designs by Raphael that were used to produce the tapestries (approximately 13' x 17', done in tempera on paper, now mounted on canvas). The cartoons were sent to factories in Brussels, cut into strips (see the lines), and placed on the looms. The scenes are the reverse of the final product—lots of left-handed saints.

Raphael (1483–1520) chose scenes from the Acts of the Apostles—particularly of Peter and Paul, the two early saints most associated with Rome, the seat of the popes. Knowing where the tapestries were to be hung, Raphael was determined to top Michelangelo's famous Sistine ceiling, with its huge, dramatic figures and subtle color effects. He matched Michelangelo's bodybuilder muscles (e.g., the fishermen in *The Miraculous Draught of Fishes*), dramatic gestures, and reaction shots (e.g., the busy crowd scenes in *St. Paul Preaching in Athens*), and he exceeded

Michelangelo in the subtleties of color.

Unfortunately, it was difficult to reproduce Raphael's painted nuances in the tapestry workshop. Traditional tapestries were simple, depicting either set patterns or block figures on a neutral background. Raphael challenged the Flemish weavers. Each brush stroke had to be reproduced by a colored thread woven horizontally. The finished tapestries (which are still in the Vatican) were glorious, but these cartoons capture Raphael's original vision.

• *In Room 48A, a staircase leads up (turn left at top of stairs) into Room 57, in the heart of the British Galleries, featuring the Great Bed of Ware and Elizabethan miniatures. But to see the complete British Galleries chronologically, return to the entrance lobby and take the stairs to the first floor (Level 2), beginning in Room 58.*

⑬ British Galleries

The "other half" of the V&A consists of beautifully described exhibits laid out along a series of corridors on two floors, sweep-

ing you through 400 years of British high-class living. The theme is "taste, fashion, and design from 1500 through 1900." It's all very impressive, but because the exhibit descriptions are already so thorough, I've included very few specifics here. Wander the entire route,

taking time to read up on whatever you find interesting.

You'll see:

- At the entrance to Room 58 is Henry VIII's writing box, with his quill pens, ink, and sealing wax.
- Next is a couple of rooms with Tudor-era tapestries.
- A room dedicated to "Birth, Marriage and Death" displays swaddling clothes, a wedding portrait, and a casket pall.
- Room 57 covers the era of Queen Elizabeth I. Find rare miniature portraits, a popular item of the day, including Hilliard's

oft-reproduced *Young Man Among Roses* miniature, capturing the romance of a Shakespeare sonnet. Also in the room is the Great Bed of Ware. Built as a tourist-attracting gimmick by an English inn around 1600, this four-poster bed still wows. You and six of your favorite friends could bed down here, taking a well-earned rest after this eclectic tour.

If you're not ready for a nap yet, there's oh-so-much more in the V&A. The new Theatre and Performance galleries (Level 3, get out your map) feature sets and costumes. Or head back out to London's bustling streets for more sightseeing (the Natural History Museum is just across the street), shopping (Harrods is an easy 10-min walk), or dining (see recommended eateries on page 334).

TATE BRITAIN TOUR

The "National Gallery of British Art" (a.k.a. the Tate Britain) features the world's best collection of British art—sweeping you from 1500 until today. This is people's art, with realistic paintings rooted in the people, landscape, and stories of the British Isles. You'll see Hogarth's stage sets, Gainsborough's ladies, Blake's angels, Constable's clouds, Turner's tempests, the swooning realism of the Pre-Raphaelites, and the camera-eye portraits of Hockney and Freud. Even if these names are new to you, don't worry. I'll guarantee that you'll see a few "famous" works you didn't know were British and exit the Tate Britain with at least one new favorite artist.

Because the collection is constantly in motion (visit www.tate
.org.uk for the latest), a painting-by-painting tour is impossible. This chapter covers British art chronologically, presenting the essence of each artist and style. Read it beforehand to get the big picture, and then let the Tate surprise you with its ever-changing wardrobe of paintings.

Orientation

Cost: Free (£2 donation requested), but temporary exhibits require separate admission.

Hours: Daily 10:00–17:50, first Fri of each month until 21:40, last entry 50 min before closing.

Getting There: It's on the Thames River, south of Big Ben and north of Vauxhall Bridge. The museum has two entrances: on Millbank, facing the Thames, and on Atterbury Street (wheelchair-accessible).

You can reach the museum by Tube, ferry, bus, or on foot:

By Tube: Take the Tube to Pimlico, then walk seven minutes.

By Ferry: Hop on the Tate Boat ferry from the Tate Modern (£5 one-way, £12 day ticket, discounted with a Travelcard, buy ticket on board, departs every 40 min 10:10–16:50, 18-min trip).

By Bus: Take bus #87 (leaves from National Gallery, arrives in front of museum on Millbank) or bus #88 (leaves from Oxford Circus, arrives behind museum on Erasmus Street).

By Foot: Walk 25 minutes south along the Thames from Big Ben.

Information: Pick up a free map at the information desk (recorded info tel. 020/7887-8008, switchboard tel. 020/7887-8888, www.tate.org.uk). The bookshop is great.

Tours: Free tours are offered Mon–Fri at 11:00 (art from 1500 to 1800), 12:00 (art from 1800 to 1900), 14:00 (Turner), and 15:00 (art from the 20th century). Weekend tours feature the collection's highlights (Sat–Sun 12:00 and 15:00); call to confirm schedule. The £3.50 audioguide tours are useful. The museum also hosts games, activities, and art projects for children (Sat–Sun 11:00–17:00 plus other times as scheduled).

Length of This Tour: Allow one hour.

Cloakroom: Bag and coat check are free (£2 suggested donation).

Photography: Photos are not allowed, unless you've requested permission at least a week in advance.

Cuisine Art: Your two options are a café with an affordable gourmet buffet line or a pricey-but-delightful restaurant (£20 fixed-price lunch, kids eat free; lunch daily 11:30–15:00, afternoon tea daily 15:15–17:00).

Starring: Hogarth, Gainsborough, Reynolds, Blake, Constable, Pre-Raphaelites, and Turner.

Orien-Tate: Gallery in Motion

The Tate Britain's large collection of paintings changes every year, but the basic layout stays the same: a roughly chronological walk through British paintings from 1500 to 1901 in the west half of the building, the 20th century in the east, and the works of J. M. W. Turner in the adjoining Clore Gallery. In addition, temporary exhibitions (usually requiring an entrance fee) are located in the east wing and in the basement.

Note: There are two separate Tate museums in London. The Tate Britain, which this chapter describes, features British art. The Tate Modern (at Bankside, on the South Bank of the Thames across from St. Paul's Cathedral) features modern art.

❂ See the Tate Modern Tour chapter.

The Tour Begins

British artists painted people, countrysides, and scenes from daily life, realistically and without the artist passing judgment (substance over style). What you won't see here are the fleshy goddesses, naked baby angels, and Madonna-and-child altarpieces so popular elsewhere in Europe. The largely Protestant English abhorred the "graven images" of the wealthy Catholic world. Many were even destroyed during the 16th-century Reformation. They preferred portraits of flesh-and-blood English folk.

• *Start in Room 1, in the far left corner (west half) of the museum, and head to Rooms 2–3 to find some family portraits.*

1500-1700—Portraits of Lord and Lady Whoevertheyare

Stuffy portraits of a beef-fed society try to turn crude country nobles into refined men and delicate women. Men in ruffled collars clutch symbols of power. Women in ruffled collars, puffy sleeves, and elaborately patterned dresses display their lily-white complexions, turning their pinkies out.

English country houses often had a long hall built specially to hang family portraits. You could stroll along and see your noble forebears looking down their noses at you. Britain's upper crust had little interest in art other than as a record of themselves along with their possessions—their wives, children, jewels, furs, ruffled collars, swords, and guns.

You'll see plenty more portraits in the Tate Britain, right up to modern times. Each era had its own style. Portraits from the 1500s are stern and dignified. The 1600s brought a more relaxed and elegant style and more décolletage.

• *Go to Rooms 4–7, where the paintings improve.*

1700s—Art Blossoms

With peace at home (under three King Georges), a strong overseas economy, and a growing urban center in London, England's artistic life began to bloom. As the English grew more sophisticated, so did their portraits. Painters branched out into other subjects, capturing slices of everyday life. The Royal Academy added a veneer of classical Greece to even the simplest subjects.

William Hogarth (1697-1764)

Hogarth loved the theater. "My picture is my stage," he said, "and my men and women my players." The curtain goes up, and

Tate Britain Overview

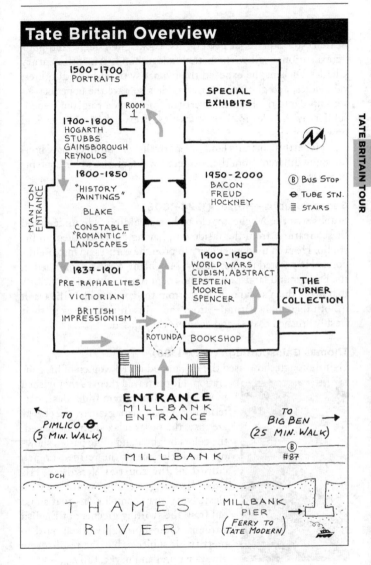

we see one scene that tells a whole story, often satirizing English high society. The London theater scene came into its own (after post-Shakespeare censorship) during Hogarth's generation. He often painted series based on popular plays of the time.

A born Londoner, Hogarth loved every gritty aspect of the big city. You'd find him in seedy pubs and brothels, at the half-price ticket booth in Leicester Square, at prizefights, cockfights, duels, and public executions—all with sketchbook in hand. An 18th-century Charles Dickens, he exposed the hypocrisy of fat-bellied squires, vain ladies, and gluttonous priests. He also gave the upper classes a glimpse into the hidden poverty of "merry olde England"—poor soldiers with holes in their stockings, overworked servants, and unwed mothers.

Hogarth's portraits (and self-portraits) are unflinchingly honest, quite different from the powdered-wig fantasies of his contemporaries.

George Stubbs—Horses (1724–1806)

Stubbs was the Michelangelo of horse painters. He understood these creatures from the inside out, having dissected them in his studio. He even used machinery to prop the corpses up into lifelike poses. He painted the horses first on a blank canvas, then filled in the background landscape around them (notice the heavy outlines that make them stand out clearly from the countryside). The result is both incredibly natural—from the veins in their noses to their freshly brushed coats—and geometrically posed.

Thomas Gainsborough (1727–1788)

Gainsborough showcased the elegant, educated women of his generation. He portrayed them as they wished to see themselves: a feminine ideal, patterned after fashion magazines. The cheeks are rosy, the poses relaxed and S-shaped, the colors brighter and more pastel, showing the influence of the refined French culture of the court at Versailles. His ladies tip-toe gracefully toward us, with clear, Ivory-soap complexions that stand out from the swirling greenery of English gardens. Gainsborough worked hard to prettify his subjects, but the results were always natural and never stuffy.

Sir Joshua Reynolds and the "Grand Manner" (1723–1792)

Real life wasn't worthy of a painting. So said Sir Joshua Reynolds, the pillar of Britain's Royal Academy. Instead, people, places, and things had to be gussied up with Greek columns, symbolism, and great historic moments, ideally from classical Greece.

In his portraits, he'd pose Lady Bagbody like the Medici Venus, or Lord Milquetoast like Apollo Belvedere. In landscapes you get Versailles-type settings of classical monuments amid

perfectly manicured greenery. Inspired by Rembrandt, Reynolds sometimes used dense, clotted paint to capture the look of the Old Masters.

This art was meant to elevate the viewer, to appeal to his rational nature and fill him with noble sentiment. Sir Joshua Reynolds, the pillar of England's art establishment, stood for all that was upright, tasteful, rational, brave, clean, reverent, and...and you'll find me in the next room.

TATE BRITAIN TOUR

History Paintings

Paintings depicting great moments in history—from ancient Greece to medieval knights to Napoleon to Britain's battles abroad—were seen as the classiest form of art, combining the high drama of heroic acts with refined technique.

1800–1850—The Industrial Revolution

Newfangled inventions were everywhere. Railroads laced the land. You could fall asleep in Edinburgh and wake up in London, a trip that used to take days or weeks. But along with technology came factories coating towns with soot, urban poverty, regimentation, and clock-punching. Machines replaced honest laborers, and once-noble Man was viewed as a naked ape.

Strangely, you'll see little of the modern world in paintings of the time—except in reaction to it. Many artists rebelled against "progress" and the modern world. They escaped the dirty cities to commune with nature (Constable and the Romantics). Or they found a new spirituality in intense human emotions (dramatic scenes from history or literature). Or they left the modern world altogether.

• *Duck into the William Blake Room (usually Room 8, to the left).*

William Blake (1757–1827)

At the age of four, Blake saw the face of God. A few years later, he ran across a flock of angels swinging in a tree. Twenty years later, he was living in a run-down London flat with an illiterate wife, scratching out a thin existence as an engraver. But even in this squalor, ignored by all but a few fellow artists, he still had his heavenly visions, and he described them in poems, paintings, drawings, and prints.

One of the original space cowboys, Blake also was a unique artist, often classed with the Romantics because he painted in a fit of ecstatic inspiration rather than by studied technique. He painted angels, not the dull material world. While Britain was conquering the world with guns and nature with machines, and while his fellow Londoners were growing rich, fat, and self-important, Blake turned his gaze inward, illustrating the glorious visions of the soul.

Blake's work hangs in a darkened room to protect his water-colors from deterioration. Enter his mysterious world and let your pupils dilate opium-wide.

His pen and watercolor sketches glow with an unearthly aura. In visions of the Christian heaven or Dante's hell, his figures have superhero musculature. The colors are almost translucent.

Blake saw the material world as bad, trapping the divine spark inside each of our bodies and keeping us from true communion with God. Blake's prints illustrate his views on the ultimate weakness of material, scientific man. Despite their Greek-god anatomy, his men look noble but tragically lost.

A famous poet as well as painter, Blake summed up his distrust of the material world in a poem addressed to "The God of this World"—that is, Satan:

> *Tho' thou art Worship'd by the Names Divine*
> *Of Jesus and Jehovah, thou art still*
> *The Son of Morn in weary Night's decline,*
> *The lost Traveller's Dream under the Hill.*

• *Return to the real world, which you'll find in Room 11.*

John Constable (1776–1837)

Although the Royal Academy thought Nature needed makeup, Constable thought she was just fine. He painted the English landscape as it was—realistically, without idealizing it. With simple earth tones he caught leafy green trees, gathering gray skies, brown country lanes, and rivers the color of the clouds reflected in them.

Clouds are Constable's trademark. Appreciate the effort involved in sketching ever-changing cloud patterns for hours on end—the mix of dark clouds and white clouds, cumulus and stratus, the colors of sunset. A generation before the Impressionists, he actually set up his easel outdoors and painted on the spot, a painstaking process before the invention of ready-made paints-in-a-tube in about 1850.

It's rare to find a Constable (or any British) landscape that doesn't have the mark of man in it—a cottage, hay cart, field hand, or a country road running through the scene. For him, the English countryside and its people were one.

In his later years, Constable's canvases became bigger, the style more "Impressionistic" (messier brushwork), and he worked more from memory than observation.

Constable's commitment to unvarnished nature wasn't fully recognized in his lifetime, and he was forced to paint portraits for his keep. The neglect caused him to ask a friend, "Can it therefore be wondered at that I paint continual storms?"

Other Landscapes

Compare Constable's unpretentious landscapes with others in the Tate Britain. Some artists mixed landscapes with intense human

emotion to produce huge, colorful canvases of storms, burning sunsets, towering clouds, and crashing waves, all dwarfing puny humans. Others made supernatural, religious fantasy-scapes. Artists in the Romantic style saw the most intense human emotions reflected in the drama and mystery in nature. God is found within nature, and nature is charged with the grandeur and power of God.

• *Continue on to Room 12.*

Pre-Raphaelites: Millais, Rossetti, Holman Hunt, Waterhouse, Burne-Jones, etc.

You'll see medieval damsels in dresses and knights in tights, legendary lovers from poetry, and even a very human Virgin Mary as a delicate young woman. The women wear flowing dresses and have long, wavy hair and delicate, elongated, curving bodies. Beautiful.

Overdosed with the gushy sentimentality of their day, a band of 20-year-old artists said "Enough!" and dedicated themselves to less saccharine art. Their "Pre-Raphaelite Brotherhood" (you may see the initials P. R. B. by the artist's signature) returned to a style "pre-Raphael"—that is, "medieval" in its simple style, in the melancholy mood, and often in subject matter.

"Truth to Nature" was their slogan. Like the Impressionists who followed, they donned their scarves, barged out of the stuffy studio, and set up outdoors, painting trees, streams, and people, like scientists on a field trip. Still, they often captured nature with such a close-up clarity that it's downright unnatural. And despite the Pre-Raphaelite claim to paint life just as it is, this is so beautiful it hurts.

This is art from the cult of femininity, worshipping Woman's

haunting beauty, compassion, and depth of soul (proto-feminism or nouveau-chauvinism?). The artists' wives and lovers were their models and muses, and the art echoed their love lives. The people are surrounded by nature at its most beautiful, with every detail painted crystal clear. Even without the people, there is a mood of melancholy.

The Pre-Raphaelites hated overacting. Their subjects—even in the face of great tragedy, high passions, and moral dilemmas—barely raise an eyebrow. Outwardly, they're reflective, accepting their fate. But sinuous postures—with lovers swooning into each other, and parting lovers swooning apart—speak volumes. These volumes are footnoted by the small objects with symbolic importance placed around them: red flowers denoting passion, lilies for

purity, pets for fidelity, and so on.

The colors—greens, blues, and reds—are bright and clear, with everything evenly lit, so that we see every detail. To get the luminous color, some painted a thin layer of bright paint over a pure white, still-wet undercoat, which subtly "shines" through. These canvases radiate a pure spirituality, like stained-glass windows.

• *Continue on to Rooms 14–15.*

1837–1901—The Victorian Era

In the world's wealthiest nation, the prosperous middle class dictated taste in art. They admired paintings that were realistic (showcasing the artist's talent and work ethic), depicting Norman Rockwell–style slices of everyday life.

We see families and ordinary people eating, working, and relaxing. Some paintings tug at the heartstrings, with scenes of parting couples, the grief of death, or the joy of families reuniting. Dramatic scenes from classical (Chaucer and Shakespeare) and popular literature get the heart beating. There's the occasional touching look at the plight of the honest poor, reminiscent of Dickens. And many paintings warn us to be good little boys and girls by showing the consequences of a life of sin. Then there are the puppy dogs with sad eyes.

Stand for a while and enjoy the exquisite realism and human emotions of these Victorian-era works...real people painted realistically. Get your fill, because beloved Queen Victoria is about to check out, the modern world is coming, and, with it, new art to express modern attitudes.

British Impressionism

Realistic British art stood apart from the modernist trends in France, but some influences drifted across the Channel. John Singer Sargent (American-born) studied with Parisian Impressionists, learning the thick, messy brushwork and play of light at twilight. James Tissot used Degas' snapshot technique to capture a crowded scene from an odd angle. And James McNeill Whistler (also born in the United States) composed his paintings like music (see some of his paintings' titles), as collages of shapes and colors that please the eye like a song tickles the ear.

• *To help ease the transition to modern art (in the east half of Tate Britain), first visit the Turner Collection. Pass through the rotunda to the east side of the gallery (near the bookshop) and just keep going through a few rooms (Rooms 19–20) till you enter The Clore Gallery/The Turner Collection.*

The Turner Collection—J. M. W. Turner (1775–1851)

The Tate Britain has the world's best collection of Turners. Walking through his life's work, you can trace his progression from a painter of realistic historical scenes, through his wandering years, to Impressionist paintings of color-and-light patterns.

• *Start a few rooms into the collection, in Room T-7. This room and the adjoining rooms usually contain biographical info on Turner, some of his early works, and a display of his paints and brushes. From Room T-7, explore the rest of the collection, watching Turner's style evolve from clear-eyed realism to hazy proto-Impressionism. You'll also see how Turner dabbled in different subjects: landscapes, seascapes, Roman ruins, snapshots of Venice, and so on.*

Self-Portrait as a Young Man

At 24, Turner has just been elected the youngest Associate of the Royal Academy. The barber's son now dresses like a gentleman. His full-frontal pose and intense gaze show a young man ready to take on the world.

The Royal Academy Years

Trained in the Reynolds school of grandiose epics, Turner painted the obligatory big canvases of great moments in history—*The Destruction of Sodom, Hannibal and His Army Crossing the Alps, The Lost ATM Card, Jason and the Argonauts,* and various shipwrecks. Not content to crank them out in the traditional staid manner, he sets them in expansive landscapes. Nature's stormy mood mirrors the human events, but is so grandiose it dwarfs them.

This is a theme we'll see throughout his works: The forces of nature—the burning sun, swirling clouds, churning waves, gathering storms, and the weathering of time—overwhelm men and wear down the civilizations they build.

Travels with Turner

Turner's true love was nature—he was a born hobo. Oblivious to the wealth and fame that his early paintings gave him, he set out traveling—mostly on foot—throughout England and the Continent, with a rucksack full of sketch pads and painting gear. He sketched the English countryside—not green, leafy, and placid as so many others had done, but churning in motion, hazed over by a burning sunset.

He found the "sublime" not in the studio or in church, but in the overwhelming power of nature. The landscapes throb with life and motion. He sets Constable's clouds on fire.

Italy's Landscape and Ruins

With a Rick Steves guidebook in hand, Turner visited the great museums of Italy, drawing inspiration from the Renaissance masters. He painted the classical monuments and Renaissance architecture. He copied masterpieces and learned, assimilated, and fused a great variety of styles—a true pan-European vision. Turner's Roman ruins are not grand; they're dwarfed by the landscape around them and eroded by swirling, misty, luminous clouds.

Stand close to a big canvas of Roman ruins, close enough so that it fills your whole field of vision. Notice how the buildings seem to wrap around you. Turner was a master of using multiple perspectives to draw the viewer in. On the one hand, you're right in the thick of things, looking "up" at the tall buildings. Then again, you're looking "down" on the distant horizon, as though standing on a mountaintop.

Venice

I know what color the palazzo is. But what color is it at sun-

set? Or through the filter of the watery haze that hangs over Venice? Can I paint the glowing haze itself? Maybe if I combine two different colors and smudge the paint on....

Venice stoked Turner's lust for reflected, golden sunlight. You'll see both finished works and unfinished sketches...uh, which is which?

Seascapes

The ever-changing sea was his specialty, with waves, clouds, mist, and sky churning and mixing together, all driven by the same forces.

Turner used oils like many painters use watercolors. First, he'd lay down a background (a "wash") of large patches of color, then he'd add a few dabs of paint to suggest a figure. The final product lacked photographic clarity, but showed the power and constant change in the forces of nature. He was perhaps the most prolific painter ever, with some 2,000 finished paintings and 20,000 sketches and watercolors.

Late Works

The older Turner got, the messier both he and his paintings became. He was wealthy, but he died in a run-down dive, where he'd set up house with a prostitute. Yet the colors are brighter and the subjects less pessimistic than in the dark and brooding early canvases. His last works—whether landscape, religious, or classical scenes—are a blur and swirl of colors in motion, lit by the sun or a lamp burning through the mist. Even Turner's own creations were finally dissolved by the swirling forces of nature.

These paintings are "modern" in that the subject is less important than the style. You'll have to read the title to "get" it. You could argue that an Englishman helped invent Impressionism a generation before Monet and his ilk boxed the artistic ears of Paris in the 1880s. Turner's messy use of paint to portray reflected light "Chunneled" its way to France to inspire the Impressionists.

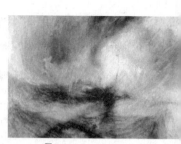

• *The 20th century, found in the east half of the Tate building, starts in Room 19. The following is not a room-by-room tour, but touches on some of the highlights of modern British art.*

1900–1950—World Wars

As two world wars whittled down the powerful British Empire, it still remained a major cultural force.

British art mirrored many of the trends and "-isms" pioneered in Paris. You'll see Cubism like Picasso's, abstract art like Mondrian's, and so on. But British artists also continued the British tradition of realistic paintings of people and landscapes. (Note: You'll find 20th-century artists' work both here in the Tate Britain and in the Tate Modern—see also the Tate Modern Tour chapter.)

World War I, in which Britain lost a million men, cast a long shadow over the land. Artists expressed the horror of war, particularly of dehumanizing battles pitting powerful machines against puny human pawns. **Jacob Epstein's** (1880–1959) gleaming, abstract statues suggest mangled half-human/half-machine forms.

Henry Moore (1898–1986)

Twice a week, young Henry Moore went to the British Museum to sketch ancient statues, especially reclining ones (as in the Parthenon pediment or the Mayan god Chac Mool he saw in a photo). His statues—mostly female, mostly reclining—catch the primitive power of carved stone. Moore almost always carved with his own hands (unlike, say, Rodin, who modeled a small clay figure and let assistants chisel the real thing), capturing the human body in a few simple curves, with minimal changes to the rock itself.

The statues do look vaguely like what their titles say, but it's the stones themselves that are really interesting. Notice the texture and graininess of these mini-Stonehenges; feel the weight, the space they take up, and how the rock forms intermingle.

During World War II, Moore passed time in the bomb shelters sketching mothers with babes in arms, a theme found in later works.

Moore carves the human body with the epic scale and restless poses of Michelangelo but with the crude rocks and simple lines of the primitives.

Stanley Spencer (1891–1959)

Spencer paints unromanticized landscapes, portraits, and hometown scenes. Even the miraculous *Resurrection of the Dead* is portrayed absolutely literally, with the dead climbing out of their Glasgow graves. In fully modern times, Spencer carried on the British tradition of sober realism.

Francis Bacon (1909–1992)

With a stiff upper lip, Britain survived the Blitz, World War II, and the loss of hundreds of thousands of men—but at war's end, the bottled-up horror came rushing out. Bacon's 1945 exhibition, opening just after Holocaust details began surfacing, stunned London with its unmitigated ugliness.

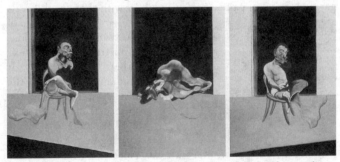

His deformed half-humans/half-animals—caged in a claustrophobic room, with twisted hunk-of-meat bodies and quadriplegic, smudged-mouth helplessness—can do nothing but scream in anguish and frustration. The scream becomes a blur, as though it goes on forever.

Bacon, largely self-taught, uses "traditional" figurativism, painting somewhat recognizable people and things. His subjects express the existential human predicament of being caught in a world not of your making, isolated and helpless to change it.

Lucian Freud (b. 1922)

Sigmund's grandson (who emigrated from Nazi Germany as a boy) puts every detail on the couch for analysis, then reassembles them into works that are still surprisingly realistic. His subjects look you right in the eye, slightly on edge. Even the plants create an ominous mood. Everything is in sharp focus (unlike in real life, where you concentrate on one thing while your peripheral vision is blurred). Thick brushwork is especially good at capturing the pallor of British flesh.

In the great tradition of British portrait painting, Freud recently did an unflinching (and controversial) portrait of Queen Elizabeth.

1950–2000—Modern World

No longer a world power, Britain in the Swinging '60s became a major exporter of pop culture. British art's traditional strengths—realism, portraits, landscapes, and slice-of-life scenes—were redone in the modern style.

David Hockney (b. 1937)

The "British Andy Warhol"—who is bleach-blonde, horn-rimmed, gay, and famous—paints "pop"-ular culture with photographic realism.

Large, airy canvases of L.A. swimming pools, double portraits of his friends in their stylish homes, or mundane scenes from the artist's own life capture the superficial materialism of the 1970s and 1980s. (Is he satirizing or glorifying it by painting it on a monumental scale with painstaking detail?)

Hockney saturates the canvas with bright (acrylic) paint, eliminating any haze, making distant objects as clear and bright as close ones. This technique, combined with his slightly simplified "cutout" figures, gives the painting the flat look of a billboard.

Bridget Riley (b. 1931)

The pioneer of Op Art paints patterns of lines and alternating colors that make the eye vibrate (the way a spiral will "spin") when you stare at them. These obscure, scientific experiments in human optics suddenly became trendy in the psychedelic, cannabis-fueled 1960s. Like, wow.

Barbara Hepworth (1903-1975)

Hepworth's small-scale carvings in stone and wood—like "mini-Moores"—make even holes look interesting. Though they're not exactly realistic, it isn't hard to imagine them being inspired by, say, a man embracing a woman (she called it "sex harmony"), or the shoreline encircling a bay near her Cornwall-coast home, or a cliff penetrated by a cave—that is, two forms intermingling.

Gilbert (b. 1943) and George (b. 1942)

The Siegfried and Roy of art satirize the "Me Generation" and its shameless self-marketing by portraying their nerdy, three-piece-suited selves on the monumental scale normally dedicated to kings, popes, and saints.

The Rest of the Museum

We've covered 500 years, with social satire from Hogarth to Hockney, from Constable's placid landscapes to Turner's churning scenes, from Blake's inner visions to Pre-Raphaelite fantasies, from realistic portraits to...realistic portraits.

But the Tate's great strength is championing contemporary British art in special exhibitions. There are two exhibition spaces: one in the northeast corner of the main floor, and another downstairs (each usually requiring separate admission). Explore the cutting-edge art from one of the world's thriving cultural capitals: London.

Enough Tate? Great. It's late.

SLEEPING IN LONDON

I've chosen several favorite neighborhoods (Victoria Station, South Kensington, and Notting Hill, among others) convenient to your sightseeing activities and recommended the best accommodations values for each. I've also listed big, good-value, modern hotels scattered throughout London.

I look for places that are friendly; clean; a good value; located in a central, safe, quiet neighborhood; and not mentioned in other guidebooks. I'm more impressed by a handy location and a fun-loving philosophy than by hair dryers and shoeshine machines.

London is perhaps Europe's most expensive city for rooms. Cheaper rooms are relatively dumpy. Don't expect £130 cheeriness in an £80 room. For £70, you'll get a double with breakfast in a safe, cramped, and dreary place with minimal service and the bathroom down the hall. For £90, you'll get a basic, clean, reasonably cheery double in a usually cramped, cracked-plaster building with a private bath, or a soulless but comfortable room without breakfast in a huge Motel 6–type place. My London splurges, at £150–260, are spacious, thoughtfully appointed places good for entertaining or romancing. Off-season, it's possible to save money by arriving late without a reservation and looking around. Competition softens prices, especially for multinight stays. Check hotel websites for special deals. All of Britain's accommodations are now nonsmoking.

Hearty English or generous buffet breakfasts are included unless otherwise noted, and TVs are standard in rooms, but may come with only the traditional five British channels (no cable).

London's Hotel Neighborhoods

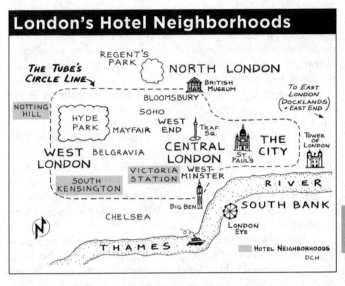

Types of Accommodations

I've described my recommended hotels and B&Bs using a Sleep Code (see sidebar later in this section). Prices listed are for one-night stays in peak season and assume you're booking directly and not through a TI. Some fancy £120 rooms rent for a third off if you arrive late on a slow day and ask for a deal. Official "rack rates" (the highest rates a hotel charges) can be misleading, because they often omit cheaper oddball rooms and special clearance deals. Always mention that you found the place through this book—many of the hotels listed offer special deals to our readers.

"Twin" means two single beds, and "double" means one double bed. If you'll take either one, let them know, or you might be needlessly turned away. Most hotels offer family deals, which means that parents with young children can easily get a room with an extra child's bed or a discount for larger rooms. Call to negotiate the price. Teenagers are generally charged as adults. Kids under five sleep almost free.

Most places listed have three floors of rooms and steep stairs. Elevators are rare except in the larger hotels. If you're concerned about stairs, call and ask about ground-floor rooms or pay for a hotel with a lift (elevator). In this big city, street noise is a fact of life. If concerned, request a room on the back side.

Be careful of the terminology: An "en suite" room has a bathroom (toilet and shower/tub) actually inside the room; a room with a "private bathroom" can mean that the bathroom is all yours, but it's across the hall; and a "standard" room has access to a bathroom down the hall that's shared with other rooms. Figuring there's little difference between "en suite" and "private" rooms, some places charge the same for both. If you want your own bathroom inside the room, request "en suite."

If money's tight, ask for a standard room. You'll almost always have a sink in your room. And, as more rooms go "en suite," the hallway bathroom is shared with fewer standard rooms.

Note that to be called a "Hotel," a place technically must have certain amenities, including a 24-hour reception (though this rule is loosely applied). A place called "townhouse" or "house" (such as "London House") is like a big B&B or a small family-run hotel—with fewer amenities but more character than a "hotel." Places named "B&B"—rare in big and bustling London—typically have six rooms or fewer.

Staying in B&Bs and small hotels can sometimes be a great way to save money over sleeping in a bigger, pricier hotel, but lately the big, impersonal chain hotels are offering rooms even cheaper than the mom-and-pop places (but without breakfast); see "Big, Good-Value, Modern Hotels" on page 301. When considering the price of a B&B or small hotel, remember you're getting two breakfasts (a £25 value) for each double room.

B&Bs and small hotels come with their own etiquette and quirks. Keep in mind that owners are at the whim of their guests—if you're getting up early, so are they; and if you check in late, they'll wait up for you. Be considerate. It's polite to call ahead to confirm your reservation the day before, and give them a rough estimate of your arrival time.

Small places usually serve a hearty fried breakfast of eggs and much more. Because your B&B or small hotel owner is often also the cook, there's usually a quite limited time span when breakfast is served (typically about an hour—make sure you know when it is). It's an unwritten rule that guests shouldn't show up at the very end of the breakfast period and expect a full cooked breakfast—instead, aim to arrive at least 10–15 minutes before breakfast ends. If you do arrive late (or if you need to leave before breakfast is served), most establishments are happy to let you help yourself to cereal, fruit, and coffee; ask politely if it's possible.

Some places stock rooms with a hot-water pot, cups, tea bags, and coffee packets (if you prefer decaf, buy a jar at a grocery and dump it into a baggie for easy packing). Electrical outlets sometimes have switches that turn the current on or off; if your electrical appliance isn't working, flip the switch at the outlet.

Many B&Bs and small hotels come with thin walls and doors that can make for a noisy night. If you're a light sleeper, bring earplugs. And please be quiet in the halls and in your rooms (talk softly, and keep the TV volume low)...those of us getting up early will thank you for it.

You're likely to encounter unusual bathroom fixtures. The "pump toilet" has a flushing handle or button that doesn't kick in unless you push it just right: too hard or too soft, and it won't go. Be decisive but not ruthless. There's also the "dial-a-shower," an electronic box under the shower head where you'll turn a dial to select the heat of the water and (sometimes with a separate dial or button) turn on or shut off the flow of water. If you can't find the switch to turn on the shower, it may be just outside the bathroom.

Hostels and Dorms

London hostels charge about £18–30 per bed. Travelers of any age are welcome if they don't mind sleeping in dorm-style accommodations and meeting other travelers. Cheap meals are sometimes available, and kitchen facilities are usually provided for do-it-yourselfers. Hostelling International hostels (also known as official hostels and run by the YHA in Britain) require a hostel membership and charge a few extra pounds for nonmembers. If you'll be staying for several days in an official hostel, consider buying a membership card before you go (www.hihostels.com). Hostels that have no such requirements are called independent hostels.

Many London colleges rent out their dorms during school holidays, most notably during July and August. Types of accommodation vary, but are usually somewhat spartan (no phones or TVs in the rooms) and come with single or twin beds. Some are en suite while others may share communal bathrooms (bring flip-flops for the shower).

Apartments

It's easy, though not necessarily cheap, to rent a furnished apartment in London. Consider this option if you're traveling with a family or staying at least a week or longer. For listings, see "For Longer Stays" at the end of this chapter.

Practicalities

Calling London

To phone London, you'll need to know Britain's country code: 44. To call from the United States or Canada, dial 011-44-20 (includes London's area code without its initial zero) plus the local number. If making the call from another European country, dial 00-44-20-local number. If calling from within Britain but outside London, dial 020-local number. To call a London phone number from within London, drop the area code (020) and dial only the local number. For more information on calling, see page 470.

Making Reservations

Given the quality of the accommodations I've found for this book, I recommend that you reserve your rooms in advance, particularly if you'll be traveling during peak season. Book several months ahead, or as soon as you've pinned down your travel dates. Note that some national holidays merit your making reservations far in advance (see "Major Holidays and Weekends" on page 5). Just like at home, holidays that fall on a Monday, Thursday, or Friday can turn the weekend into a long holiday, so book the entire weekend well in advance.

Requesting a Reservation: To reserve, contact hotels directly by email, phone, or fax. Email is the clearest and most economical way to make a reservation. Or you can go straight to the hotel website—many have secure online reservation forms and can instantly inform you of availability and any special deals. But be sure you use the hotel's official site and not a booking agency's site—otherwise you may pay higher rates than you should. If you're phoning from the US, be mindful of time zones (see page 26).

The hotelier wants to know these key pieces of information (also included in the sample request form on page 488 and at www .ricksteves.com/reservation):

- number and type of rooms
- number of nights
- date of arrival
- date of departure
- any special needs (e.g., bathroom in the room or down the hall, twin beds vs. double bed, air-conditioning, quiet, view, ground floor, etc.)

When you request a room, use the European style for writing dates: day/month/year. For example, for a two-night stay in July, I would request: "1 double room for 2 nights, arrive 16/07/10, depart 18/07/10." (Consider carefully how long you'll stay; don't just assume you can extend your reservation for extra days when you arrive.)

If you don't get a reply to your email or fax, it usually means the hotel is already fully booked (but you can try sending the message again, or call to follow up).

Confirming a Reservation: If the hotel's response tells you its room availability and rates, it's not a confirmation. You must tell them that you want that room at the given rate. The hotelier will sometimes request your credit-card number for a one-night deposit to hold the room. Although you can email your credit-card information (I do), it's safer to share that personal info by phone call, fax, or secure online reservation form (if the hotel has one on its website).

If you'll be traveling beyond London, you may want to make

Sleep Code

(£1 = about $1.60, country code: 44, area code: 020)
To help you sort through these listings easily, I've divided the rooms into three categories, based on the price for a double room with bath:

$$$ Higher Priced—Most rooms £115 or more.
 $$ Moderately Priced—Most rooms between £70-115.
  $ Lower Priced—Most rooms £70 or less.

To give maximum information in a minimum of space, I use the following code to describe accommodations listed in this book. Prices are listed per room, not per person. When a price range is given for a type of room (such as "Db-£80-120"), it means the price fluctuates with the season, size of room, or length of stay.

 S = Single room, or price for one person in a double.
 D = Double or twin room. (I specify double- and twin-bed rooms only if they are priced differently, or if a place has only one or the other. You should specify when reserving.)
 T = Three-person room (often a double bed with a single).
 Q = Four-person room (adding an extra child's bed to a T is usually cheaper).
 b = Private bathroom with toilet and shower or tub.
 s = Private shower or tub only. (The toilet is down the hall.)

According to this code, a couple staying at a "Db-£90" hotel would pay a total of £90 per night for a room with a private toilet and shower (or tub). Unless otherwise noted, you can assume that breakfast is included and credit cards are accepted.

If I say "Internet access," there's a public terminal in the lobby for guests to use. If I say "Wi-Fi," you can access it in your room, but only if you have your own laptop.

reservations as you go, calling hotels or B&Bs a few days to a week before your visit. If you prefer the flexibility of traveling without any reservations at all, you'll have greater success snaring rooms if you arrive at your destination early in the day. When you anticipate crowds (weekends are worst), call hotels at about 9:00 on the day you plan to arrive, when the hotel clerk knows who'll be checking out and just which rooms will be available.

Canceling a Reservation: If you must cancel your reservation, it's courteous to do so with as much advance notice as possible—at least three days. Simply make a quick phone call or send an email.

Family-run hotels and B&Bs lose money if they turn away customers while holding a room for someone who doesn't show up. Understandably, many hotels bill no-shows for one night.

Hotels in larger cities like London sometimes have strict cancellation policies: For example, you might lose a deposit if you cancel within two weeks of your reserved stay, or you might be billed for the entire visit if you leave early. Ask about cancellation policies before you book.

If canceling in an email, request confirmation that your cancellation was received to avoid being billed accidentally.

Reconfirm Your Reservation: Always call to reconfirm your room reservation a day or two in advance from the road. Smaller hotels and B&Bs appreciate knowing your time of arrival. If you'll be arriving after 17:00, always let your hotelier know, to make sure the room is held for you and not given away. On the small chance that a hotel loses track of your reservation, bring along a hard copy of their emailed or faxed confirmation.

Looking for Hotel Deals Online

Given the high hotel prices and relatively weak dollar, consider using the Internet to help score a hotel deal. Various websites list rooms in high-rise, three- and four-star business hotels. You'll give up the charm and warmth of a family-run establishment, and breakfast will probably not be included, but you might find that the price is right.

Start by checking the websites of several chains to get an idea of typical rates and to check for online-only deals. Big London hotel chains include the following: Millennium/Copthorne (www.millenniumhotels.com), Thistle (www.thistle.com), Intercontinental/Holiday Inn (www.ichotelsgroup.com), Radisson (www.radisson.com), Hilton (www.hilton.com), and Red Carnation (www.redcarnationhotels.com). For information on no-frills, Motel 6–type chains, see "Big, Good-Value, Modern Hotels," below.

Auction-type sites (such as www.priceline.com or www.hotwire.com) can be great for matching flexible travelers with empty hotel rooms, often at prices well below the hotel's normal rates.

Other favorite accommodation discount sites mentioned by my readers include www.londontown.com (an informative site with a discount booking service), http://athomeinlondon.co.uk and www.londonbb.com (both list central B&Bs), www.lastminute.com, www.visitlondon.com, http://roomsnet.com, and www.eurocheapo.com. Read candid reviews of London hotels at www.tripadvisor.com. And check the "Graffiti Wall" at www.ricksteves.com for the latest tips and discoveries.

For a good overview on finding London hotel deals, go to

www.smartertravel.com and click on "Travel Guides," then "London."

Big, Good-Value, Modern Hotels

These places—popular with budget tour groups—are well-run and offer elevators, 24-hour reception, and all the modern comforts in a no-frills, practical package. With the notable exception of my second listing, they are often located on busy streets in dreary train-station neighborhoods, so use common sense after dark and wear your money belt. The doubles for £90–100 are a great value for London. Midweek prices are generally higher than weekend rates. Breakfast is always extra. Online bookings are often the easiest way to make reservations and will generally net you a discount.

$$ Jurys Inn Islington rents 200-plus compact, comfy rooms near King's Cross station (Db/Tb-£89–139, some discounted rooms available online, 2 adults and 2 kids under age 12 can share one room, 60 Pentonville Road, Tube: Angel, tel. 020/7282-5500, fax 020/7282-5511, www.jurysinns.com).

$$ Premier Inn London County Hall, literally down the hall from a $400-a-night Marriott Hotel, fills one end of London's massive former County Hall building. This family-friendly place is wonderfully located near the base of the London Eye and across the Thames from Big Ben. Its 313 efficient rooms come with all the necessary comforts (Db-£109–119 for 2 adults and up to 2 kids under age 16, book in advance, no-show rooms released at 15:00, some easy-access rooms, 500 yards from Westminster Tube stop and Waterloo Station, Belvedere Road, central reservations toll tel. 0870-242-8000, reception desk toll tel. 0870-238-3300, easiest to book online at www.premierinn.com).

$$ Premier Inn London Southwark, with 59 rooms, is near Shakespeare's Globe on the South Bank (Db for up to 2 adults and 2 kids-£99–110, Bankside, 34 Park Street, toll tel. 0870-990-6402, www.premierinn.com).

$$ Premier Inn King's Cross St. Pancras, with 276 rooms, is just east of King's Cross and St. Pancras stations (Db-£90–114, 26–30 York Way, toll tel. 0870-990-6414, www.premierinn.com).

Other **$$ Premier Inns** charging £87–114 per room include **London Euston** (big, blue Lego-type building packed with vacationing families, on handy but noisy street at corner of Euston Road and Dukes Road, Tube: Euston, toll tel. 0870-238-3301), **London Kensington Earl's Court** (11 Knaresborough Place, Tube: Earl's Court or Gloucester Road, toll tel. 0870-238-3304), and **London Putney Bridge** (£79–89, farther out, 3 Putney Bridge Approach, Tube: Putney Bridge, toll tel. 0870-238-3302). Avoid the **Tower Bridge** location, which is an inconvenient 15-minute walk from the nearest Tube stop. For any of these, call 0870-242-8000 or—the best option—book online at www.premierinn.com.

$$ Hotel Ibis London Euston St. Pancras, which feels a bit classier than a Premier Inn, rents 380 rooms on a quiet street a block behind and west of Euston Station (Db-£90–115, up to £150 during special events, no family rooms, 3 Cardington Street, tel. 020/7388-7777 or 020/7304-7712, fax 020/7388-0001, www.ibishotel.com, h0921@accor.com).

$$ Travelodge London Kings Cross is another typical chain hotel with lots of cookie-cutter rooms, just 200 yards south of King's Cross Station (Db-£52–98, family rooms, can be noisy, Grays Inn Road, toll tel. 0871-984-6256). Other convenient Travelodge London locations are nearby **Kings Cross Royal Scot, Euston, Marylebone, Covent Garden, Liverpool Street,** and **Farringdon.** For details on all Travelodge hotels, see www.travelodge.co.uk.

Victoria Station Neighborhood (Belgravia)

The streets behind Victoria Station teem with little, moderately-priced-for-London B&Bs. It's a safe, surprisingly tidy, and decent area without a hint of the trashy, touristy glitz of the streets in front of the station. West of the tracks is Belgravia, where the prices are a bit higher and your neighbors include Andrew Lloyd Webber and Margaret Thatcher (her policeman stands outside 73 Chester Square). Decent eateries abound (see page 330).

All the recommended hotels are within a five-minute walk of the Victoria Tube, bus, and train stations. On hot summer nights, request a quiet back room. Nearby is the 400-space Semley Place NCP **parking garage** (£32/day, possible discounts with hotel voucher, just west of the Victoria Coach Station at Buckingham Palace Road and Semley Place, toll tel. 0845-050-7080, www.ncp.co.uk). The handy **Pimlico Launderette** is about five blocks southwest of Warwick Square (daily 8:00–19:00, self- or full service, south of Sutherland Street at 3 Westmoreland Terrace, tel. 020/7821-8692). **Launderette Centre** is a block northeast of Warwick Square (Mon–Fri 8:00–22:00, Sat–Sun until 19:00, about £7 wash and dry, £11 full-service, 31 Churton Street, tel. 020/7828-6039).

$$$ Lime Tree Hotel, enthusiastically run by Charlotte and Matt, comes with 28 spacious and thoughtfully decorated rooms and a fun-loving breakfast room (Sb-£85–95, Db-£120–150, Tb-£150–180, family room-£170–195, free Internet access and

Victoria Station Neighborhood

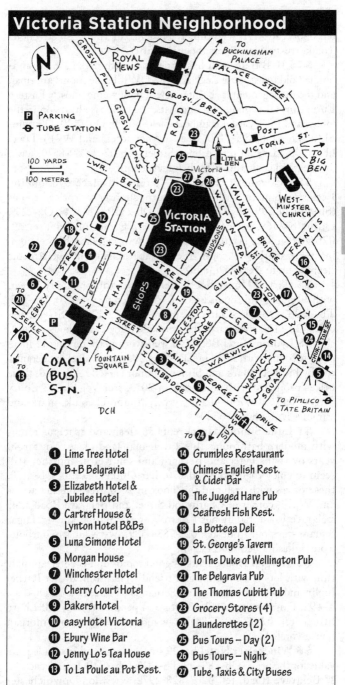

1. Lime Tree Hotel
2. B+B Belgravia
3. Elizabeth Hotel & Jubilee Hotel
4. Cartref House & Lynton Hotel B&Bs
5. Luna Simone Hotel
6. Morgan House
7. Winchester Hotel
8. Cherry Court Hotel
9. Bakers Hotel
10. easyHotel Victoria
11. Ebury Wine Bar
12. Jenny Lo's Tea House
13. To La Poule au Pot Rest.
14. Grumbles Restaurant
15. Chimes English Rest. & Cider Bar
16. The Jugged Hare Pub
17. Seafresh Fish Rest.
18. La Bottega Deli
19. St. George's Tavern
20. To The Duke of Wellington Pub
21. The Belgravia Pub
22. The Thomas Cubitt Pub
23. Grocery Stores (4)
24. Launderettes (2)
25. Bus Tours – Day (2)
26. Bus Tours – Night
27. Tube, Taxis & City Buses

Wi-Fi, small lounge opens onto quiet garden, 135 Ebury Street, tel. 020/7730-8191, www.limetreehotel.co.uk, info@limetreehotel .co.uk, trusty Alan covers the night shift).

$$$ B+B Belgravia has done its best to make a tight-and-tangled old guesthouse sleek and mod. While the rooms are small and the management is absentee, the staff of young, mostly Eastern Europeans takes good care of guests, the coffee is always on in the lobby, and the location is unbeatable (Sb-£99, Db-£120, Db twin-£130, Tb-£150, Qb-£160, free Internet access and Wi-Fi, DVD library, loaner bikes, 64 Ebury Street, tel. 020/7259-8570, www .bb-belgravia.com, info@bb-belgravia.com).

$$$ Elizabeth Hotel is a stately old place overlooking Eccleston Square, with 37 well-worn, slightly overpriced rooms (Sb-£99, D-£99, small Db-£119, big Db-£129, Tb-£149, Qb-£159, Quint/b-£169, air-con-£9, Wi-Fi, 37 Eccleston Square, tel. 020/7828-6812, fax 020/7828-6814, www.elizabethhotel.com, info@elizabethhotel.com). The Elizabeth also rents apartments sleeping up to six (£259/night).

$$ Cartref House B&B offers rare charm on Ebury Street, with 10 delightful rooms and a warm welcome (Sb-£70, Db-£95, Tb-£126, Qb-£155, fans, free Wi-Fi, 129 Ebury Street, tel. 020/7730-6176, www.cartrefhouse.co.uk, info@cartrefhouse.co.uk).

$$ Lynton Hotel B&B is a well-worn place renting 12 inexpensive rooms with small prefab WCs. It's a fine value, exuberantly run by brothers Mark and Simon Connor (D-£80, Db-£90, these prices promised with this book in 2010, free Wi-Fi, 113 Ebury Street, tel. 020/7730-4032, www.lyntonhotel.co.uk, mark-and -simon@lyntonhotel.co.uk).

$$ Luna Simone Hotel rents 36 fresh and spacious rooms with modern bathrooms. It's a well-managed place, run for 40 years by twins Peter and Bernard and son Mark, and they still seem to enjoy their work (Sb-£70, Db-£100, Tb-£120, Qb-£150, these prices with cash and this book in 2010, free Internet access and Wi-Fi, corner of Charlwood Street and Belgrave Road at 47 Belgrave Road, handy bus #24 to Victoria Station and Trafalgar Square stops out front, tel. 020/7834-5897, www.lunasimonehotel .com, lunasimone@talk21.com).

$$ Morgan House rents 11 good rooms and is entertainingly run, with lots of travel tips and friendly chat from owner Rachel Joplin and her staff, Danilo and Fernanda (S-£52, D-£72, Db-£92, T-£92, family suites-£112–132 for 3–4 people, Wi-Fi, 120 Ebury Street, tel. 020/7730-2384, www.morganhouse.co.uk, morgan house@btclick.com).

$$ Winchester Hotel has 19 small rooms and is an adequate value for the price (Db-£89–99, Tb-£115, Qb-£140, Internet access, 17 Belgrave Road, tel. 020/7828-2972, www.londonwinchester

hotel.co.uk, info@londonwinchesterhotel.co.uk). If you need a cab, call your own to avoid excessive fares. They also rent a few apartments around the corner (£125–230, see website for details).

$ Cherry Court Hotel, run by the friendly and industrious Patel family, rents 12 very small, basic, incense-scented rooms in a central location (Sb-£48, Db-£55, Tb-£80, Qb-£95, Quint/b-£110, these prices promised with this book through 2010, 5 percent fee to pay with credit card, fruit-basket breakfast in room, air-con, laundry, free Internet access and Wi-Fi, peaceful garden patio, 23 Hugh Street, tel. 020/7828-2840, fax 020/7828-0393, www.cherry courthotel.co.uk, info@cherrycourthotel.co.uk).

$ Jubilee Hotel is a well-run slumber mill with 24 tiny rooms and many tiny beds. It's a bit musty and its windows only open a few inches, but the price is right (S-£39, Sb-£59, tiny D-£59, tiny Db-£65, Db-£69, Tb-£89, Qb-£105, ask for the 5 percent Rick Steves discount when booking, pay Internet access and Wi-Fi, 31 Eccleston Square, tel. 020/7834-0845, www.jubileehotel.co.uk, stay@jubileehotel.co.uk, Bob Patel).

$ Bakers Hotel is a well-worn cheapie, with 10 tight rooms, but it's well-located and offers youth hostel prices and a small breakfast (S-£30–35, D-£50–55, Db-£60–65, T-£60–65, Tb-£70–75, family room-£70–75, 126 Warwick Way, tel. 020/7834-0729, www.bakershotel.co.uk, reservations@bakershotel.co.uk, Amin Jamani).

$ easyHotel Victoria is a radical concept—offering what you need to sleep well and safe—and no more. Their 77 rooms fit the old floor plan, so some rooms are tiny windowless closets, while others are quite spacious. All rooms are well-ventilated and come with an efficient "bathroom pod"—just big enough to take care of business. Prices are the same for one person or two. You get two towels, soap and shampoo, and a clean bed—no breakfast, no fresh towels, and no daily cleaning. Rooms range from £25 to 65, depending on their size and when you book: "The earlier you book, the less you pay" (reserve only through website, 36 Belgrave Road, tel. 020/7834-1379, www.easyHotel.com, enquiries@victoria.easy Hotel.com). They also have branches at South Kensington, Earl's Court, Paddington, and Heathrow and Luton airports (see their website for details; Heathrow location described on page 312).

"South Kensington," She Said, Loosening His Cummerbund

To stay on a quiet street so classy it doesn't allow hotel signs, surrounded by trendy shops and colorful restaurants, call "South Ken" your London home. Shoppers like being a short walk from Harrods and the designer shops of King's Road and Chelsea. When I splurge, I splurge here. Sumner Place is just off Old Brompton

South Kensington Neighborhood

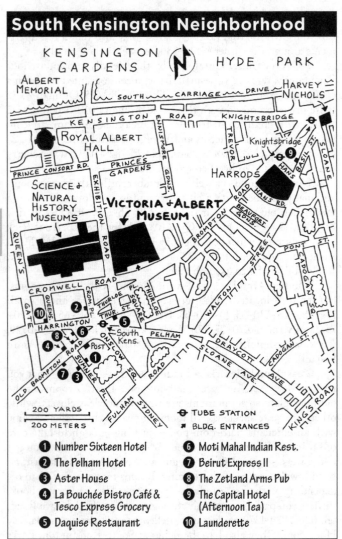

SLEEPING IN LONDON

Map labels:
KENSINGTON GARDENS — HYDE PARK
ALBERT MEMORIAL
SOUTH CARRIAGE DRIVE
HARVEY NICHOLS
KENSINGTON ROAD — KNIGHTSBRIDGE
ROYAL ALBERT HALL
ENNISMORE GDNS.
TREVOR
Knightsbridge
PRINCE CONSORT RD.
PRINCES GARDENS
HARRODS
HANS RD.
SCIENCE & NATURAL HISTORY MUSEUMS
EXHIBITION ROAD
VICTORIA & ALBERT MUSEUM
BROMPTON ROAD
HANS RD.
BEAUFORT GDNS.
SLOANE
BASIL ST.
QUEEN'S GATE
CROMWELL ROAD
WALTON STREET
PONT ST.
CADOGAN ST.
QUEENS GATE
CROM PL.
THURLOE PL.
THURLOE SQUARE
THUR. ST.
PELHAM
HARRINGTON ROAD
South Kens.
ONSLOW SQ.
Post
SUMNER PL.
DRAYCOTT AVE.
SLOANE AVE.
CADOGAN ST.
OLD BROMPTON ROAD
ONSLOW ROAD
FULHAM ROAD
SYDNEY
KING'S ROAD

200 YARDS
200 METERS

⊖ TUBE STATION
✦ BLDG. ENTRANCES

1 Number Sixteen Hotel
2 The Pelham Hotel
3 Aster House
4 La Bouchée Bistro Café & Tesco Express Grocery
5 Daquise Restaurant
6 Moti Mahal Indian Rest.
7 Beirut Express II
8 The Zetland Arms Pub
9 The Capital Hotel (Afternoon Tea)
10 Launderette

Road, 200 yards from the handy South Kensington Tube station (on Circle Line, two stops from Victoria Station, direct Heathrow connection). There's a handy **launderette** on the corner of Queensberry Place and Harrington Road (Mon–Fri 7:30–21:00, Sat 9:00–20:00, Sun 10:00–19:00, bring 50p and £1 coins).

$$$ Number Sixteen, for well-heeled travelers, packs over-the-top formality and class into its 42 rooms, plush lounges, and tranquil garden. It's in a labyrinthine building, with modern decor—perfect for an urban honeymoon (Db-£200—but soft, ask for discounted "seasonal rates," especially in July–Aug—subject to availability, breakfast buffet in the garden-£17, elevator, Wi-Fi, 16 Sumner Place, tel. 020/7589-5232, fax 020/7584-8615, US tel. 800-553-6674, www.firmdalehotels.com, sixteen@firmdale.com).

$$$ The Pelham Hotel, a 52-room business-class hotel with a pricey mix of pretense and style, is not quite sure which investment company owns it. It's genteel, with low lighting and a pleasant drawing room among the many perks (Db-£180–260, breakfast extra, lower prices Aug and weekends, Web specials can include free breakfast, air-con, pay Internet access and Wi-Fi, elevator, gym, 15 Cromwell Place, tel. 020/7589-8288, fax 020/7584-8444, US tel. 1-888-757-5587, www.pelhamhotel.co.uk, reservations @pelhamhotel.co.uk).

$$$ Aster House, run by friendly and accommodating Simon and Leonie Tan, has a cheerful lobby, lounge, and breakfast room. Its rooms are comfy and quiet, with TV, phone, and air-conditioning. Enjoy breakfast or just lounging in the whisper-elegant Orangery, a Victorian greenhouse (Sb-£120, Db-£180, bigger Db-£225, 20 percent discount with this book through 2010 if you book three or more nights, additional 5 percent off for five or more nights with cash, check website for specials, VAT not included, pay Internet access and Wi-Fi, 3 Sumner Place, tel. 020/7581-5888, fax 020/7584-4925, www.asterhouse.com, asterhouse@btinternet.com). Simon and Leonie offer free loaner mobile phones to their guests.

Notting Hill and Bayswater Neighborhoods

Residential Notting Hill has quick bus and Tube access to downtown, and, for London, is very "homely" (Brit-speak for cozy). It's also peppered with trendy bars and restaurants, and is home to the famous Portobello Road Market (see Shopping chapter).

Popular with young international travelers, Bayswater's Queensway street is a multicultural festival of commerce and eateries (see Eating chapter). The neighborhood does its dirty clothes at **Galaxy Launderette** (£6 self-service, £8–10 full-service, daily 8:00–20:00, staff on hand with soap and coins, 65 Moscow Road, at corner of St. Petersburgh Place and Moscow Road, tel. 020/7229-7771). For **Internet access,** you'll find several stops along busy Queensway, and a self-serve bank of easyInternetcafé computer terminals on the food circus level of the Whiteleys Shopping Centre (daily 8:30–24:00, corner of Queensway and Porchester Gardens).

Near Kensington Gardens Square

Several big, old hotels line the quiet Kensington Gardens Square (not to be confused with the much bigger Kensington Gardens adjacent to Hyde Park), a block west of bustling Queensway,

Notting Hill and Bayswater Neighborhoods

SLEEPING IN LONDON

⊖ TUBE STN.

1/4 MILE

400 METERS

SUNDAY MARKET

KENSINGTON GARDENS SQUARE

Post

PRINCE'S PORCH.

Bayswater

Queensway

Notting Hill Gate

PLAYGROUND

KENSINGTON GARDENS

KENSINGTON PALACE

HOLLAND PARK

High Street Kensington

1 Phoenix Hotel
2 Vancouver Studios & Princes Square Guest Accommodation
3 Kensington Gardens Hotel
4 Westland Hotel
5 London Vicarage Hotel
6 To Norwegian YWCA
7 Maggie Jones Restaurant
8 The Churchill Arms Pub & Thai Kitchens

9 The Prince Edward Pub
10 Café Diana
11 Royal China Restaurant
12 Whiteleys Mall (Food Court, Grocery, Internet)
13 Tesco Grocery
14 Spar Market
15 The Orangery (Afternoon Tea)
16 Launderette

north of Bayswater Tube station. These hotels are quiet for central London.

$$$ Phoenix Hotel, a Best Western modernization of a 130-room hotel, offers American business-class comforts; spacious, plush public spaces; and big, fresh, modern-feeling rooms. Its prices—which range from fine value to rip-off—are determined by a greedy computer program, with huge variations according to expected demand. Book online to save money (Db-£90–165, elevator, free Wi-Fi, impersonal staff, 1–8 Kensington Gardens Square, tel. 020/7229-2494, fax 020/7727-1419, US tel. 800-528-1234, www.phoenixhotel.co.uk, info@phoenixhotel.co.uk).

$$$ Vancouver Studios offers 45 modern rooms with fully equipped kitchenettes (utensils, stove, microwave, and fridge) rather than breakfast (small Sb-£79, Db-£125, Tb-£170, extra bed-£15, 10 percent discount for week-long stay or more, welcoming lounge and garden, near Kensington Gardens Square at 30 Prince's Square, tel. 020/7243-1270, fax 020/7221-8678, www.vancouverstudios.co.uk, info@vancouverstudios.co.uk).

$$ Kensington Gardens Hotel laces 17 pleasant rooms together in a tall, skinny building with lots of stairs and no elevator (Ss-£57, Sb-£64, Db-£86, Tb-£105; book by phone or email for these special Rick Steves prices, rather than through the pricier website; continental breakfast served at sister hotel next door, Wi-Fi, 9 Kensington Gardens Square, tel. 020/7221-7790, fax 020/7792-8612, www.kensingtongardenshotel.co.uk, info@kensingtongardenshotel.co.uk, Rowshanak).

$$ Princes Square Guest Accommodation is a big, impersonal 50-room place that's well-located, practical, and a good value, especially with its online discounts (Sb-£65–115, Db-£85–150, Tb-£110–175, elevator, 23–25 Princes Square, tel. 020/7229-9876, www.princessquarehotel.co.uk, info@princessquarehotel.co.uk).

Near Kensington Gardens

$$$ Westland Hotel is comfortable, convenient (5-min walk from Notting Hill neighborhood), and feels like a wood-paneled hunting lodge with a fine lounge. The rooms are spacious, recently refurbished, and quite plush. Their £130 doubles (less your 10 percent discount—see below) are the best value, but check their website for specials (Sb-£110, Db-£130, deluxe Db-£152, cavernous deluxe Db-£172, sprawling Tb-£165–193, gargantuan Qb-£186–220, Quint/b-£234, 10 percent discount with this book in 2010—claim upon booking or arrival; elevator, garage-£12/day, pay Wi-Fi, between Notting Hill Gate and Queensway Tube stations at 154 Bayswater Road, tel. 020/7229-9191, fax 020/7727-1054, www.westlandhotel.co.uk, reservations@westlandhotel.co.uk, Jim and Nora ably staff the front desk).

$$$ **London Vicarage Hotel** is family-run, understandably popular, and elegantly British in a quiet, classy neighborhood. It has 17 rooms furnished with taste and quality, a TV lounge, and facilities on each floor. Mandy and Monika maintain a homey and caring atmosphere (S-£55, Sb-£93, D-£93, Db-£122, T-£117, Tb-£156, Q-£128, Qb-£172, 20 percent less in winter—check website, free Wi-Fi; 8-min walk from Notting Hill Gate and High Street Kensington Tube stations, near Kensington Palace at 10 Vicarage Gate; tel. 020/7229-4030, fax 020/7792-5989, www .londonvicaragehotel.com, vicaragehotel@btconnect.com).

Near Holland Park

$ **Norwegian YWCA (Norsk K.F.U.K.)**—where English is definitely a second language—is for women 30 and under only (and men 30 and under with Norwegian passports). Located on a quiet, stately street, it offers a study, TV room, piano lounge, and an open-face Norwegian ambience (goat cheese on Sundays!). They have mostly quads, so those willing to share with strangers are most likely to get a bed (July–Aug: Ss-£36, shared double-£35/ bed, shared triple-£30/bed, shared quad-£26/bed, includes breakfast year-round plus sack lunch and dinner Sept–June, £20 key deposit required, pay Wi-Fi, 52 Holland Park, tel. 020/7727-9346 or 020/7727-9897, www.kfukhjemmet.org.uk, kontor@kfukh jemmet.org.uk). With each visit, I wonder which is easier to get—a sex change or a Norwegian passport?

Other Neighborhoods

North of Marble Arch: $$$ The **22 York Street B&B** offers a casual alternative in the city center, renting 10 stark, hardwood, comfortable rooms (Sb-£89, Db-£120, two-night minimum, Internet access and Wi-Fi, inviting lounge; from Baker Street Tube station, walk 2 blocks down Baker Street and take a right to 22 York Street; tel. 020/7224-2990, www.22yorkstreet.co.uk, mc@22yorkstreet .co.uk, energetically run by Liz and Michael Callis).

$$$ **The Sumner Hotel,** in a 19th-century Georgian townhouse, is located a few blocks north of Hyde Park and Oxford Street, a busy shopping destination. Decorated with fancy modern Italian furniture, this swanky place packs in all the extras (Db-£160–190, 20 percent discount with this book in 2010, extra bed-£30, free Wi-Fi, 54 Upper Berkeley Street just off Edgware Road, Tube: Marble Arch, tel. 020/7723-2244, fax 0870-705-8767, www .thesumner.com, hotel@thesumner.com, manager Peter).

Near Covent Garden: $$$ **Fielding Hotel,** located on a charming, quiet pedestrian street just two blocks east of Covent Garden, offers 24 no-frills rooms and a fine location (Db-£115–140, Db with sitting room-£160, pricier rooms are bigger with better bathrooms, no breakfast, no kids under 6, free Wi-Fi, 4 Broad Court, Bow Street, tel. 020/7836-8305, fax 020/7497-0064, www.thefieldinghotel.co.uk, reservations@the-fielding-hotel.co.uk, manager Graham Chapman).

Near Buckingham Palace: **$$ Vandon House Hotel**, run by Central College in Iowa, is packed with students most of the year, but rents its 32 rooms to travelers from late May through August at great prices. The rooms, while institutional, are comfy, and the location is excellent (S-£46, D-£70, Db-£90, Tb-£99, Qb-£119, only twin beds, elevator, Internet access and Wi-Fi; on a tiny road 3-min walk west of St. James's Park Tube station or 7-min walk from Victoria Station, near east end of Petty France Street at 1 Vandon Street; tel. 020/7799-6780, www.vandonhouse.com, info @vandonhouse.com).

Near Euston Station and the British Library: The **$$$ Methodist International Centre (MIC)**, a modern, youthful Christian hotel and conference center, fills its lower floors with international students and its top floor with travelers. The 28 rooms are modern and simple yet comfortable, with fine bathrooms, phones, and desks. The atmosphere is friendly, safe, clean, and controlled; it also has a spacious lounge and game room (annex S-£85, Sb-£140, deluxe Sb-£150, annex D-£95, Db-£155, deluxe Db-£175, Tb-£195; Sb-£95 and Db-£108 with £115 membership; 3-bedroom annex is great for families, check website for specials, elevator, Wi-Fi; on a quiet street a block west of Euston Station, 81–103 Euston Street—not Euston Road, Tube: Euston Station; tel. 020/7380-0001, www.micentre.com, reservations@micentre.com). In June–August, when the students are gone, they also rent simpler twin rooms (S or D-£50, includes one breakfast, extra breakfast-£12.50).

Hostels

$ London Central Youth Hostel is the flagship of London's hostels, with 300 beds and all the latest in security and comfortable efficiency. Families and travelers of any age will feel welcome in this wonderful facility. You'll pay the same price for any bed in a 4- to 8-bed single-sex dorm—with or without private bathroom—so try to grab one with a bathroom (£20–30 per bunk bed—fluctuates with demand, £3/night extra for nonmembers, breakfast-£4; includes sheets, towel and locker; families or groups welcome to book an entire room, free Wi-Fi, members' kitchen, laundry, book long in advance, between Oxford Street and Great Portland Street Tube stations at 104 Bolsover Street, toll tel. 0870-770-6144 or 0845-371-9154, www.yha.org.uk, londoncentral@yha.org.uk).

$ St. Paul's Youth Hostel, near St. Paul's, is clean, modern, friendly, and well-run. Most of the 190 beds are in shared, single-sex bunk rooms (bed-£22–26 depending on number of beds in room and demand, twin D-£54–61, bunk-bed Q-£96, nonmembers pay £3 extra, cheap meals, open 24 hours, 36 Carter Lane, Tube: St. Paul's, tel. 020/7236-4965 or toll tel. 0845-371-9012, www.yha.org .uk, stpauls@yha.org.uk).

$ A cluster of three **St. Christopher's Inn** hostels, south of the Thames near London Bridge, have cheap dorm beds (£20–25, 161–165 Borough High Street, Tube: Borough or London Bridge, tel. 020/7407-1856, www.st-christophers.co.uk).

Dorms

$ The **University of Westminster** opens its dorm rooms to travelers during summer break, from mid-June through late September. Located in several high-rise buildings scattered around central London, the rooms—some with private bathrooms, others with shared bathrooms nearby—come with access to well-equipped kitchens and big lounges (S-£26–35, Sb-£35–55, D-£47–60, Db-£52–95, apartment Sb-£48–80, apartment Db-£58–90, weekly rates, tel. 020/7911-5181, www.wmin.ac.uk/comserv, unilet vacations@westminster.ac.uk).

$ **University College London** also has rooms for travelers, from mid-June until mid-September (S-£27–30, D-£55, breakfast extra, minimum 3-night stay, www.ucl.ac.uk/residences).

$ **Ace Hotel,** a budget hotel within four townhouses set in a residential neighborhood, has contemporary decor (£18–29 per bed in 3- to 8-bed dorms, bunk bed D-£53–57, bunk bed Db-£57–61, Db with patio-£99, pay Internet access, lounge and garden, 16–22 Gunterstone Road, West Kensington, tel. 020/7602-6600, www .ace-hotel.co.uk, reception@ace-hotel.co.uk).

Heathrow and Gatwick Airports

At or near Heathrow Airport: It's so easy to get to Heathrow from central London, I see no reason to sleep there. But if you do, here are some options.

$$ **Yotel,** at the airport, has small sleep dens that offer a place to catch a quick nap (four hours-£37–64), or to stay overnight (tiny "standard cabin"—£59/8 hours, "premium cabin"—£82/8 hours; cabins sleep 1–2 people; price is per cabin not person, reserve online for free or by phone for small fee). Prices vary by day, week, and time of year, so check their website. All rooms are only slightly larger than a double bed, and have private bathrooms and free Internet access and Wi-Fi. Windowless rooms have oddly purplish lighting (Heathrow Terminal 4, tel. 020/7100-1100, www.yotel .com, customer@yotel.com).

$ **easyHotel** is your cheapest bet, with 53 pod-like rooms on two floors (£25–45, no elevator, no breakfast, pay Internet access and Wi-Fi; Brick Field Lane, take local bus #140 from airport's Central Bus Station or the £4 "Hotel Hoppa" shuttle bus #H8 or #H3 from Terminals 1, 2, or 3—runs 2–3/hr; on-demand shuttle available, tel. 020/8897-9237, www.easyhotel.com, enquiries @heathrow.easyhotel.com).

$$ Hotel Ibis London Heathrow is a chain hotel offering predictable value (Db-£77, Db-£52 on Fri–Sun, check website for specials as low as £45, breakfast-£7, pay Internet access and Wi-Fi; 112–114 Bath Road, take local bus #105, #111, #140, #285, #423, or #555 from airport's Central Bus Station or #555 direct from Terminal 4, or the £4 "Hotel Hoppa" shuttle bus #H6 from Terminals 1, 2, or 3; tel. 020/8759-4888, fax 020/8564-7894, www .ibishotel.com, h0794@accor.com).

$$ Jurys Inn, another hotel chain, tempts tired travelers with 300-plus cookie-cutter rooms (Db-£85–105, check website for deals, breakfast extra; on Eastern Perimeter Road, Tube: Hatton Cross plus 5-min walk; take the £3.20 Tube one stop from Terminals 1, 2, or 3; or two stops from Terminals 4 or 5; or the £4 "Hotel Hoppa" shuttle bus #H9 from Terminals 1, 2, or 3; or buses #285, #482, #490, or #555; tel. 020/8266-4664, fax 020/8266-4665, www.jurysinns.com).

At or near Gatwick Airport: $$ Yotel, with small rooms, has a branch right at the airport (Gatwick South Terminal, see prices and contact info in Heathrow listing, above).

$$ Gatwick Airport Central Premier Inn rents cheap rooms 350 yards from the airport (Db-£75, £67 Fri–Sun, breakfast-£8, £2 shuttle bus from airport—must reserve in advance, Longbridge Way, North Terminal, toll tel. 0870-238-3305, frustrating phone tree, www.premierinn.com). Four more Premier Inns are within a five-mile radius from the airport.

$$ Barn Cottage, a converted 16th-century barn flanked by a tennis court and swimming pool, sits in the peaceful countryside, with a good pub just two blocks away. Its two wood-beamed rooms, antique furniture, and large garden makes you forget Gatwick is 10 minutes away (S-£55, D-£75, cash only, Church Road, Leigh, Reigate, Surrey, tel. 01306/611-347, warmly run by Pat and Mike Comer). Don't confuse this place with others of the same name; this Barn Cottage has no website. A taxi from Gatwick to here runs about £15; the Comers can take you back to the airport or train station for about £10.

$ Gatwick Airport Travelodge has budget rooms about a mile from the airport (Db-£39–57, breakfast extra, Wi-Fi, Church Road, Lowfield Heath, Crawley, £4 "Hotel Hoppa" shuttle bus from airport, toll tel. 0871-984-6031, www.travelodge.co.uk).

For Longer Stays

Staying a week or longer? Consider the advantages that come with renting a furnished apartment—or "flat," as the British say. Complete with a small, equipped kitchen and living room, this option can also work for families or groups on shorter visits. Among the many organizations ready to help, the following have been recommended by local guides and readers: www.perfect placeslondon.co.uk, www.homefromhome.co.uk, www.london33 .com, www.london-house.com, www.gowithit.co.uk, www.aplace likehome.co.uk, and www.regentsuites.com.

Sometimes you can save money by renting directly from the apartment owner (check www.vrbo.com). Readers also report success using Craig's List (http://london.craigslist.co.uk; search within "holiday rentals").

Read the rental conditions carefully and ask lots of questions. If a certain amenity is important to you (such as Wi-Fi or a washing machine in the unit), ask specifically about it and what to do if it stops working. Plot the location carefully (plug the address into http://maps.google.com), and remember to factor in travel time and costs from outlying neighborhoods to central London. Finally, it's a good idea to buy trip cancellation/interruption insurance, as many weekly rentals are nonrefundable.

EATING IN LONDON

England's reputation for miserable food is now dated, and the British cuisine scene is lively, trendy, and pleasantly surprising. (Unfortunately, it's also very expensive.) Even the basic, traditional pub grub has gone "up market," with "gastro pubs" serving fresh vegetables rather than soggy fries and mushy peas.

In London, the sheer variety of foods—from every corner of its former empire and beyond—is astonishing. You'll be amazed at the number of hopping, happening new restaurants of all kinds.

If you want to dine (as opposed to eat), drop by a London newsstand to get a weekly entertainment guide or an annual restaurant guide (both have extensive restaurant listings). Visit www .london-eating.co.uk or www.squaremeal.co.uk for more options.

The thought of a £40 meal in Britain generally ruins my appetite, so my London dining is limited mostly to easygoing, fun, inexpensive alternatives. I've listed places by neighborhood—handy to your sightseeing or hotel. Considering how expensive London can be, if there's any good place to cut corners to stretch your budget, it's by eating cheaply.

London (and all of Britain) is now smoke-free, thanks to a recent smoking ban. Expect restaurants and pubs that sell food to be nonsmoking indoors, with smokers occupying patios and doorways outside.

Budget Eating Tips

You have plenty of inexpensive £8–10 choices: pub grub, daily lunch and early-bird specials, ethnic restaurants, cafeterias, fast food, picnics, fish-and-chips, greasy-spoon cafés, or pizza.

I've found that portions are huge, and with locals feeling the pinch of their recession, **sharing plates** is generally just fine. Ordering two drinks, a soup or side salad, and splitting a £10 meat pie can make a fine and filling meal. If you are on a limited budget, I'd recommend sharing a main course in a more expensive place for a nicer eating experience. Plus, if you split a meal, the price in pounds is cut in half—and you might lose a little weight.

Pub grub is the most atmospheric budget option. Many of London's 7,000 pubs serve fresh, tasty buffets under ancient timbers, with hearty lunches and dinners priced reasonably at £7–9 (see "Pubs," later in this chapter).

Classier restaurants have some affordable deals. Lunch is usually cheaper than dinner; a top-end £25-for-dinner-type restaurant often serves the same quality two-course lunch deals for £10. Look for early-bird dinner specials, allowing you to eat well and affordably (generally two courses-£17, three courses-£20), but early (about 17:30–19:00, last order by 19:00).

Ethnic restaurants from all over the world add spice to London's cuisine scene. Eating Indian or Chinese is cheap (even cheaper if you take it out). Middle Eastern stands sell gyros sandwiches, falafel, and *shwarmas* (lamb in pita bread). An Indian samosa (greasy, flaky meat-and-vegetable pie) costs £2, can be microwaved, and makes a very cheap, if small, meal. You'll find all-you-can-eat Chinese and Thai places serving £6 meals and offering £3.50 take-away boxes. While you can't "split" a buffet, you can split a take-away box. Stuff the box full, and you and your partner can eat in a park for under £2 each—making a take-away box London's cheapest hot meal.

Most large **museums** (and many historic **churches**) have handy, moderately priced cafeterias.

Fast-food places, both American and British, are everywhere.

Cheap chain restaurants, such as steak houses and pizza places, serve no-nonsense food in a family-friendly setting (steakhouse meals about £10, all-you-can-stomach pizza around £5).

Bakeries sell yogurt, cartons of "semi-skimmed" milk, pastries, and pasties (PASS-teez). Pasties are savory (not sweet) meat pies that originated in the Cornish mining country; they had big crust handles so miners with filthy hands could eat them and toss the crust.

Picnicking saves time and money. Fine park benches and polite pigeons abound in most neighborhoods. You can easily get prepared food to go (e.g., see "Ethnic Restaurants," above). Munch a relaxed "meal on wheels" picnic during your open-top bus tour or river cruise to save 30 precious minutes for sightseeing.

Good **sandwich shops** and corner **grocery stores** are a hit with local workers eating on the run. Try boxes of orange juice (pure, by the liter), fresh bread, tasty English cheese, meat, a tube of Colman's English mustard, local eatin' apples, bananas, small

tomatoes, a small tub of yogurt (drinkable), trail mix, nuts, plain or chocolate-covered digestive biscuits, and any local specialties. At **open-air markets** and **supermarkets,** you can get produce in small quantities (3 tomatoes and 2 bananas cost me £1). Supermarkets often have good deli sections, even offering Indian dishes, and sometimes salad bars. Decent packaged sandwiches (£3–4) are sold everywhere. Cheap and cheery chains such as **Pret A Manger, Fresh,** and **Eat** provide office workers with good, healthful sandwiches, salads, and pastries to go. The **Marks & Spencer Simply Food** chain—with fast, fresh, budget meals and free plastic-ware—is ideal for picnics.

Breakfast

The traditional "fry" is famous as a hearty way to start the day. Also known as a "heart attack on a plate," the breakfast is especially feast-like if you've just come from the land of the skimpy continental breakfast across the Channel.

Your standard fry gets off to a healthy start with juice and cereal or porridge. (Try Weetabix, a soggy British cousin of Shredded Wheat and perhaps the most absorbent material known to man.) Next, with tea or coffee, you get a heated plate with a fried egg, Canadian-style bacon or a sausage, a grilled tomato, sautéed mushrooms, baked beans, and toast. Toast comes on edge on a rack (to cool quickly and crisply) with butter and marmalade. This protein-stuffed meal is great for stamina, and tides many travelers over until dinner. Remember: Order only what you'll eat—hoteliers and B&B hostesses don't like to see food wasted. There's nothing wrong with skipping the fry—few locals actually start their day with this heavy breakfast. Many progressive B&B owners offer vegetarian, organic, or other creative variations on the traditional breakfast.

These days, the best coffee is served in a *cafetière* (also called a "French press"). When your coffee has steeped as long as you like, plunge down the filter and pour. To revitalize your brew, pump the plunger again.

For more on breakfast at your B&B, see page 296.

Pubs

Pubs are a basic part of the British social scene, and, whether you're a teetotaler or a beer-guzzler, they should be a part of your travel here. "Pub" is short for "public house." It's an extended living room where, if you don't mind the stickiness, you can feel the pulse of

London. Smart travelers use the pubs to eat, drink, get out of the rain, watch the latest sporting event, and make new friends.

Pub hours vary. Pubs generally serve beer Monday–Saturday 11:00–23:00 and Sunday 12:00–22:30, though many are open later, particularly on Friday and Saturday. As it nears closing time, you'll hear shouts of "Last orders." Then comes the 10-minute warning bell. Finally, they'll call "Time!" to pick up your glass, finished or not, when the pub closes.

A cup of darts is free for the asking. People go to a public house to be social. They want to talk. Get vocal with a local. This is easiest at the bar, where people assume you're in the mood to talk (rather than at a table, where you're allowed a bit of privacy). The pub is the next best thing to having relatives in town. Cheers!

Pub Grub

Pub grub gets better each year. It's London's best indoor eating value. For £6–10, you'll get a basic budget hot lunch or dinner in friendly surroundings. The *Good Pub Guide* is excellent (www .thegoodpubguide.co.uk). Pubs that are attached to restaurants, advertise their food, and are crowded with locals are more likely to have fresh food and a chef—and less likely to be the kind of pub that sells only lousy microwaved snacks.

Pubs generally serve traditional dishes, such as fish-and-chips, vegetables, "bangers and mash" (sausages and mashed potatoes), roast beef with Yorkshire pudding (batter-baked in the oven), and assorted meat pies, such as steak-and-kidney pie or shepherd's pie (stewed lamb topped with mashed potatoes). Side dishes include salads (sometimes even a nice self-serve salad bar), vegetables, and—invariably—"chips" (French fries). "Crisps" are potato chips. A "jacket potato" (baked potato stuffed with fillings of your choice) can almost be a meal in itself. A "ploughman's lunch" is a modern "traditional English meal" of bread, cheese, and sweet pickles that nearly every tourist tries...once. These days, you'll likely find more Italian pasta, curried dishes, and quiche on the menu than traditional fare.

Meals are usually served 12:00–14:00 and 18:00–20:00, not throughout the day. There's often no table service. Order at the bar, then take a seat and they'll bring the food when it's ready (or sometimes you pick it up at the bar). Pay at the bar (sometimes when you order, sometimes after you eat). Don't tip unless it's a place with full table service. Servings are hearty, service is quick, and you'll rarely spend more than £10. (If you're on a tight budget, consider sharing a meal—note the size of portions around you before ordering.) A beer or cider adds another couple of pounds. (Free tap water is always available.) Because pubs make more money selling drinks than food, many stop cooking fairly early.

"Have You Been Caught Short?"

The full pint of beer is under siege...or so claim supporters of the CAMRA (Campaign for Real Ale) movement. They're referring to being "caught short"—ordering a pint and getting less than a full glass of liquid, topped off with some foam. According to research they cite, 8 in 10 pints are short, costing British drinkers £1 million per day. To combat this practice, CAMRA is providing pub-goers with cards to measure the "real price" of their drinks. They're also encouraging pubs to use oversized glasses, marked with pint and half-pint lines, so pouring a 100-percent-full serving is easier and less open to debate. Meanwhile, pub-goers should keep an eye on that costly foam (for more information, see www.camra.org.uk and select "Campaigns").

In a brim measure glass a PINT should come to HERE	HOLD AGAINST THE SIDE OF YOUR NEWLY FILLED PINT GLASS AND READ OFF BY HOW MUCH YOU HAVE BEEN SHORT MEASURED.						
	PRICE PER PINT						
	£1.60	£1.70	£1.80	£1.90	£2.00	£2.10	£2.20
	8p	8.5p	9p	9.5p	10p	10.5p	11p
	14p	15p	16p	16.5p	17.5p	18.5p	19.5p
	21p	22p	23.5p	25p	26p	27.5p	28.5p
	29.5p	31p	33p	35p	36.5p	38.5p	40p
	36p	38.5p	40.5p	43p	45p	47.5p	50p

Prices are rounded to the nearest half pence.
For use with brim measure glasses only. Due to rounding and printing tolerances values should be used as a guide only.

Beer

The British take great pride in their beer. Many Brits think that drinking beer cold and carbonated, as Americans do, ruins the taste. Most pubs will have **lagers** (cold, refreshing, American-style beer), **ales** (amber-colored, cellar-temperature beer), **bitters** (hop-flavored ale, perhaps the most typical British beer), and **stouts**

(dark and somewhat bitter, like Guinness). At pubs, long-handled pulls are used to pull the traditional, rich-flavored "real ales" up from the cellar. These are the connoisseur's favorites: fermented naturally, varying from sweet to bitter, often with a hoppy or nutty flavor. Notice the fun names.

Pub Appreciation

The pub is the heart of the people's England, where all manner of folks have, for generations, found their respite from work and a home-away-from-home. England's classic pubs are national treasures, with great cultural value and rich history, not to mention good beer and grub.

The Golden Age for pub-building was in the late Victorian era (c. 1880–1905), when pubs were independently owned and land prices were high enough to make it worthwhile to invest in fixing up pubs. The politics were pro-pub as well: Conservatives, backed by Big Beer, were in, and temperance-minded Liberals were out.

Especially in class-conscious Victorian times, traditional pubs were divided into sections by elaborate screens (now mostly gone), allowing the wealthy to drink in a more refined setting, while commoners congregated on the pub's rougher side. These were really "public houses," featuring nooks (snugs) for groups and clubs to meet, friends and lovers to rendezvous, and families to get out of the house at night. Because many pub-goers were illiterate, pubs were simply named for the picture hung outside (e.g., The Crooked Stick, The Queen's Arms—meaning her coat of arms).

Historic pubs still dot the London cityscape. The only place to see the very oldest-style tavern in the "domestic tradition" is at **Ye Olde Cheshire Cheese,** which was rebuilt in 1667 (after the Great Fire) from a 16th-century tavern (see description on page 205; open daily, 145 Fleet Street; Tube: Temple or St. Paul's, Blackfriars station is nearest but is closed until 2011; tel. 020/7353-6170). Imagine this place in the pre-Victorian era: With no bar, drinkers gathered around the fireplaces, while tap boys shuttled tankards up from the cellar. (This was long before bar-room taps were connected to casks in the cellar. Oh, and don't say "keg"—that's a gassy modern thing.)

Late Victorian pubs, such as the lovingly restored 1897 **Princess Louise** (open daily 12:00–23:00, 208 High Holborn, see map later in this chapter, Tube: Holborn, tel. 020/7405-8816) are more common. These places are fancy, often with heavy embossed wallpaper ceilings, decorative tile work, fine-etched glass, ornate carved stillions (the big central hutch for storing bottles and glass), and even urinals equipped with a place to set your glass. London's best Art Nouveau pub is **The Black Friar** (c. 1900–1915), with fine carved capitals, lamp holders, and quirky phrases worked into the decor (open daily, Tube: Temple or St. Paul's, across from the Blackfriars Tube station—station closed until 2011—at 174 Queen Victoria Street, tel. 020/7236-5474).

The "former-bank pubs" represent a more modern trend

Historic Pubs

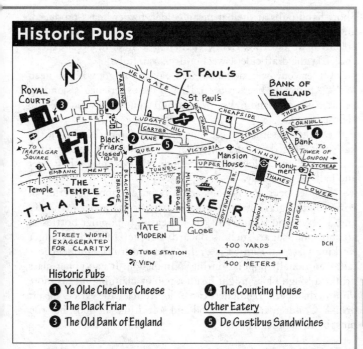

STREET WIDTH EXAGGERATED FOR CLARITY

TUBE STATION
VIEW

400 YARDS
400 METERS

Historic Pubs
1. Ye Olde Cheshire Cheese
2. The Black Friar
3. The Old Bank of England

4. The Counting House

Other Eatery
5. De Gustibus Sandwiches

in pub building. As banks increasingly go electronic, they're moving out of lavish, high-rent old buildings. Many of these former banks are being refitted as pubs with elegant bars and free-standing stillions, providing a fine centerpiece. Three such

pubs are **The Old Bank of England** (closed Sat–Sun, 194 Fleet Street, Tube: Temple, tel. 020/7430-2255), **The Jugged Hare** (open daily, 172 Vauxhall Bridge Road, see map on page 303, Tube: Victoria, tel. 020/7828-1543, also see listing on page 331), and **The Counting House** (closed Sat–Sun, 50 Cornhill, Tube: Bank, tel. 020/7283-7123, also see page 334).

Go pubbing in the evening for a lively time, or drop by during the quiet late morning (from 11:00), when the pub is empty and filled with memories. For more information, see Bob Steel's website, www.aletrails.com. Bob also offers London Heritage pub tours (about £50 per group for a leisurely half-day private walk).

Short-hand pulls at the bar mean colder, fizzier, mass-produced, and less interesting keg beers. Mild beers are sweeter, with a creamy malt flavoring. Irish cream ale is a smooth, sweet experience. Try the draft cider (sweet or dry)...carefully.

Order your beer at the bar and pay as you go, with no need to tip. An average beer costs £3. Part of the experience is standing before a line of "hand pulls," or taps, and wondering which beer to choose.

Drinks are served by the pint (20-ounce imperial size) or the half-pint. (It's almost feminine for a man to order just a half; I order mine with quiche.) Proper English ladies enjoy a half-beer and half–7-Up **shandy.**

Besides beer, many pubs actually have a good selection of wines by the glass, a fully stocked bar for the gentleman's "G and T" (gin and tonic), and the increasingly popular bottles of alcohol-plus-sugar (such as Bacardi Breezers) for the younger working-class set. **Pimm's** is a refreshing and fruity summer cocktail, traditionally popular during Wimbledon. It's an upper-class drink...a rough bloke might insult a pub by claiming it sells more Pimm's than beer. Teetotalers can order from a wide variety of soft drinks. Children are served food and soft drinks in pubs, but you must be 18 to order a beer.

Indian Food

Eating Indian food is "going local" in cosmopolitan, multiethnic London. Take the opportunity to sample food from Britain's former colony. Indian cuisine is as varied as the country itself. In general, they use more exotic spices than British or American cuisine—some hot, some sweet. Indian food is very vegetarian-friendly, offering many dishes to choose from on any given menu.

For a simple meal that costs about £10–12, order one dish with rice and *naan* (Indian bread that can be ordered plain, with garlic, or other ways). Many restaurants offer a fixed-price combination meal that offers more variety, and is simpler and cheaper than ordering à la carte. For about £20, you can make a mix-and-match platter out of several sharable dishes, including dal (lentil soup) as a starter, one or two meat or vegetable dishes with sauce (e.g., chicken curry, chicken *tikka masala* in a creamy tomato sauce, grilled fish tandoori, chickpea *chana masala,* or the spicy vindaloo dish), *raita* (a cooling yogurt that's added to spicy dishes), rice, *naan,* and an Indian beer (wine and Indian food don't really mix) or chai (a cardamom- and cinnamon-spiced tea).

Desserts (Sweets)

To the British, the traditional word for dessert is "pudding," although it's also referred to as "sweets" these days. Sponge cake,

British Chocolate

My chocoholic readers are enthusiastic about British chocolates. As with other dairy products, chocolate seems richer and creamier here than it does in the US, so even the basics like Kit Kat and Twix have a different taste. Some favorites include Cadbury Gold bars (filled with liquid caramel), Cadbury Crunchie bars, Nestle's Lion bars (layered wafers covered in caramel and chocolate), Cadbury's Boost bars (a shortcake biscuit with caramel in milk chocolate), Cadbury Flake (crumbly folds of melt-in-your-mouth chocolate), and Galaxy chocolate bars (especially the ones with hazelnuts). Thornton shops (in larger train stations) sell a box of sweets called the Continental Assortment, which comes with a tasting guide. The highlight is the mocha white-chocolate truffle. British M&Ms, called Smarties, are better than American ones. At ice-cream vans, look for the beloved traditional "99p"—a vanilla soft-serve cone with a small Flake bar stuck right into the middle.

cream, fruitcake, and meringue are key players.

Trifle is the best-known British concoction, consisting of sponge cake soaked in brandy or sherry (or orange juice for children), then covered with jam and/or fruit and custard cream. Whipped cream can sometimes put the final touch on this "light" treat.

Castle puddings are sponge puddings cooked in small molds and topped with Golden Syrup (a popular brand and a cross between honey and maple syrup). Bread-and-butter pudding consists of slices of French bread baked with milk, cream, eggs, and raisins (similar to the American preparation), served warm with cold cream. Hasty pudding, supposedly the invention of people in a hurry to avoid the bailiff, is made from stale bread with dried fruit and milk. Queen of puddings is a breadcrumb pudding topped with warm jam, meringue, and cream. Treacle pudding is a popular steamed pudding whose "sponge" mixture combines flour, suet (animal fat), butter, sugar, and milk. Christmas pudding (also called plum pudding) is a dense mixture with dried and candied fruit served with brandy butter or hard sauce. Sticky toffee pudding is a moist cake made with dates, heated and drizzled with toffee sauce, and served with ice cream or cream. Banoffee pie is the delicious British answer to banana cream pie.

The English version of custard is a smooth, yellow liquid. Cream tops most everything custard does not. There's single cream for coffee. Double cream is really thick. Whipped cream is familiar, and clotted cream is the consistency of whipped butter.

Fool is a dessert with sweetened pureed fruit (such as rhubarb, gooseberries, or black currants) mixed with cream or custard and chilled. Elderflower is a popular flavoring for sorbet.

Scones are tops, and many inns and restaurants have their secret recipes. Whether made with fruit or topped with clotted cream, scones take the cake.

Tipping

Tipping is an issue only at restaurants and fancy pubs that have waiters and waitresses. If you order your food at a counter, don't tip.

If the menu states that service is included, there's no need to tip beyond that. If service isn't included, tip about 10 percent by rounding up. Leave the tip on the table, or hand it to your server with your payment for the meal and say, "Keep the rest, please." Many restaurants in London now add a 12 percent "optional" tip onto the bill—read your bill carefully, and tip only what you think the service warrants.

Restaurants

Central London

Near Trafalgar Square

These places are within about 100 yards of Trafalgar Square.

St. Martin-in-the-Fields Café in the Crypt is just right for a tasty meal on a monk's budget—maybe even on a monk's tomb. You'll dine sitting on somebody's gravestone in an ancient crypt. Their enticing buffet line is kept stocked all day, serving breakfast, lunch, and dinner (£6–8 cafeteria plates, Mon–Wed 8:00–20:00, Thu–Sat 8:00–21:00, Sun 11:00–18:00, profits go to the church, underneath Church of St. Martin-in-the-Fields on Trafalgar Square, Tube: Charing Cross, tel. 020/7766-1158 or 020/7766-1100). Wednesday evenings at 20:00 come with a live jazz band (£5–8 tickets). While here, check out the concert schedule for the busy church upstairs (or visit www.smitf.org).

The Chandos Pub's Opera Room floats amazingly apart from the tacky crush of tourism around Trafalgar Square. Look for it opposite the National Portrait Gallery (corner of William IV Street and St. Martin's Lane) and climb the stairs to the Opera Room. This is a fine Trafalgar rendezvous point and wonderfully local pub. They serve traditional, plain-tasting £6–7 pub meals—meat pies are their specialty. The ground-floor pub is stuffed with regulars and offers snugs (private booths), the same menu, and more serious beer drinking (kitchen open daily 11:00–18:00, order and pay at the bar, 29 St. Martin's Lane, Tube: Leicester Square, tel. 020/7836-1401).

Gordon's Wine Bar, with a simple, steep staircase leading into a candlelit 15th-century wine cellar, is filled with dusty old

Central London Eateries

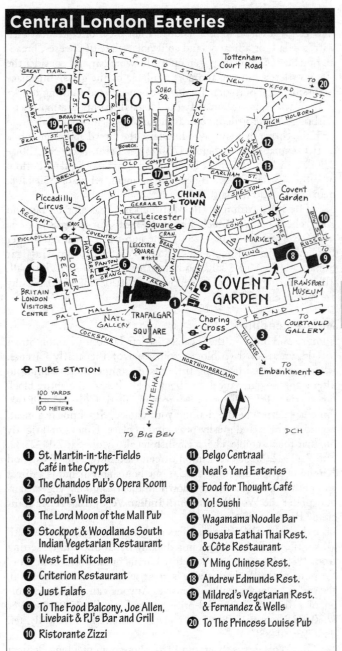

EATING IN LONDON

❶ St. Martin-in-the-Fields
   Café in the Crypt
❷ The Chandos Pub's Opera Room
❸ Gordon's Wine Bar
❹ The Lord Moon of the Mall Pub
❺ Stockpot & Woodlands South
   Indian Vegetarian Restaurant
❻ West End Kitchen
❼ Criterion Restaurant
❽ Just Falafs
❾ To The Food Balcony, Joe Allen,
   Livebait & PJ's Bar and Grill
❿ Ristorante Zizzi

⓫ Belgo Centraal
⓬ Neal's Yard Eateries
⓭ Food for Thought Café
⓮ Yo! Sushi
⓯ Wagamama Noodle Bar
⓰ Busaba Eathai Thai Rest.
   & Côte Restaurant
⓱ Y Ming Chinese Rest.
⓲ Andrew Edmunds Rest.
⓳ Mildred's Vegetarian Rest.
   & Fernandez & Wells
⓴ To The Princess Louise Pub

bottles, faded British memorabilia, and local nine-to-fivers. At the "English rustic" buffet, choose a hot meal or cold meat dish with a salad, or a hearty (and splittable) plate of cheeses, bread, and pickles (£7.50). Then step up to the wine bar and consider the many varieties of wine and port available by the glass. This place is passionate about port. The low carbon-crusted vaulting deeper in the back seems to intensify the Hogarth-painting atmosphere. Although it's crowded, you can normally corral two chairs and grab the corner of a table. On hot days, the crowd spills out onto a leafy back patio (arrive before 17:30 to get a seat, Mon–Sat 11:00–23:00, Sun 12:00–22:00, 2 blocks from Trafalgar Square, bottom of Villiers Street at #47, Tube: Embankment, tel. 020/7930-1408, manager Gerard Menan).

The Lord Moon of the Mall pub has real ales on tap and good, cheap pub grub, including a two-meals-for-the-price-of-one deal (£8 Mon–Fri 14:00–22:00). The pub fills a great old former Barclays Bank building a block down Whitehall from Trafalgar Square (daily 9:00–22:00, no kids after 18:00, 16–18 Whitehall, Tube: Charing Cross or Embankment, tel. 020/7839-7701). Nearby are several cheap cafeterias and pizza joints.

Near Piccadilly

Hungry and broke in the theater district? Head for Panton Street (off Haymarket, two blocks southeast of Piccadilly Circus), where several hardworking little places compete, all seeming to offer a three-course meal for about £8.50. Peruse the entire block (vegetarian, Pizza Express, Moroccan, Thai, Chinese, and two famous eateries) before making your choice. **Stockpot** is a meat, potatoes, gravy, and mushy-peas kind of place, famous and rightly popular for its edible, cheap English meals (Mon–Sat 7:00–23:30, Sun 7:00–22:00, 38–40 Panton Street, cash only). The **West End Kitchen** (across the street at #5, same hours and menu) is a direct competitor that's also well-known and just as good. Vegetarians may prefer the **Woodlands South Indian Vegetarian Restaurant** at #37 Panton Street.

The palatial **Criterion** offers grand-piano ambience beneath gilded tiles and chandeliers in a dreamy Byzantine church setting from 1880. It's right on Piccadilly Circus but a world away from the punk junk. The house wine is great, as is the food. After 19:00, the menu becomes really expensive. Anyone can drop in for coffee or a drink (£17–19 fixed-price meals, Mon–Sat 12:00–14:30 & 17:30–23:30, Sun 12:00–15:30 & 17:30–22:30, 224 Piccadilly, tel. 020/7930-0488).

The Wolseley is the grand 1920s showroom of a long-defunct British car. The last Wolseley drove out with the Great Depression, but today this old-time bistro bustles with formal waiters serving traditional Austrian and French dishes in an elegant black-marble-and-chandeliers setting fit for its location next to the Ritz. Although the food can be unexceptional, prices are reasonable, and the presentation and setting are grand. Reservations are a must (£16.50 plates; cheaper soup, salad, and sandwich menu available; Mon–Fri 7:00–24:00, Sat 8:00–24:00, Sun 8:00–23:00, 160 Piccadilly—see map on page 347, tel. 020/7499-6996). They're popular for their fancy cream or afternoon tea (£9.75–19.75, served Sun–Fri 15:30–18:30, Sat 15:30–17:30).

Near Covent Garden

Covent Garden bustles with people and touristy eateries. Though the area feels overrun, there are some good options.

Just Falafs is a healthy fast-food option in the chaos of Covent Garden. Located in the southeast corner, where rows of outdoor café tables line the tiny shop, they offer falafel sandwiches with yummy vegetarian-friendly extras (£4–6 sandwiches, daily until about 21:00, 27b Covent Gardens Square, tel. 020/7240-3838).

The Food Balcony, with great people-watching overlooking the Jubilee Market Piazza, is a sticky food circus of ethnic places serving £6 meals on disposable plates and wobbly plastic tables (closes at 18:30). A handy Wagamama Noodle Bar is around the corner on Tavistock Street (see description in next section).

Joe Allen, tucked in a basement a block away, serves modern international cuisine with both style and hubbub. Downstairs off a quiet street with candles and white tablecloths, it's comfortably spacious and popular with the theater crowd (meals for about £30, £15 two-course specials and £17 three-course specials 17:00–18:45, open Mon–Fri 8:00–24:45, Sat 11:30–24:45, Sun 11:30–23:45, piano music after 21:00, 13 Exeter Street, tel. 020/7836-0651).

Livebait Restaurant is an upscale fish-and-chips place with an elegant yet simple tiled interior. Their forte is fresh and well-prepared fish (£14–20 main courses, specials before 19:00, Mon–Sat 12:00–23:00, Sun 12:00–21:00, 21 Wellington Street, tel. 020/7836-7161).

Ristorante Zizzi is a fun, top-end Italian chain with a crisp contemporary atmosphere, an open pizza oven adding warmth and action, and a sharp local clientele (£7–10 pizzas, pastas, and salads; great chicken Caesar, daily 12:00–23:00, 20 Bow Street, tel. 020/7836-6101).

PJ's Bar and Grill, a tired diner that seems to be a hit with locals, serves decent "modern European" food. It's family-friendly, with more intimate seating in the back (£10–15 meals, Mon–Sat 12:00–24:00, Sun 11:30–16:00, 30 Wellington Street, 020/7240-7529).

Belgo Centraal serves hearty Belgian specialties in a vast

400-seat underground lair. It's a seafood, chips, and beer empo-rium dressed up as a mod-monastic refectory—with noisy acous-tics and waiters garbed as Trappist monks. The classy restaurant section is more comfortable and less rowdy, but usually requires reservations. It's often more fun just to grab a spot in the bois-terous beer hall, with its tight, communal benches (no reserva-tions accepted). The same menu and specials work on both sides. Belgians claim they eat as well as the French and as heartily as the Germans. Specialties include mussels, great-tasting fries, and a stunning array of dark, blond, and fruity Belgian beers. Belgo actually makes Belgian things trendy—a formidable feat (£10–14 meals; Mon–Sat 12:00–23:00, Sun 12:00–22:30, Mon–Fri £5–6.30 "beat the clock" meal specials 17:00–18:30—the time you order is the price you pay—including main dishes, fries, and beer; no meal-splitting after 18:30, and you must buy food with beer; daily £7.50 lunch special 12:00–17:00; 1 kid eats free for each parent ordering a regular entree; 1 block north of Covent Garden Tube station at intersection of Neal and Shelton streets, 50 Earlham Street, tel. 020/7813-2233).

Neal's Yard is *the* place for cheap, hip, and healthy eateries near Covent Garden. The neighborhood is a tabouli of fun, hippie-type cafés. One of the best is the vegetarian **Food for Thought,** packed with local health nuts (good £5 vegetarian meals, £7.50 dinner plates, Mon–Sat 12:00–20:30, Sun 12:00–17:00, 2 blocks north of Covent Garden Tube station, 31 Neal Street, near Neal's Yard, tel. 020/7836-0239).

Near Soho and Chinatown

London has a trendy scene that most Beefeater-seekers miss entirely. These restaurants are scattered throughout the hipster, gay, and strip-club district, teeming each evening with fun-seekers and theater-goers. Even if you plan to have dinner elsewhere, it's a treat just to wander around this lively area.

Beware of the extremely welcoming women standing outside the strip clubs (especially on Great Windmill Street). Enjoy the sales pitch—but only fools fall for the "£5 drink and show" lure. They don't get back out without emptying their wallet...literally.

Yo! Sushi is a futuristic Japanese-food-extravaganza experi-ence. It's pricey—those plates add up fast—but it's a memorable experience, complete with thumping rock, Japanese cable TV, and a 195-foot-long conveyor belt—the world's longest sushi bar. For £1 you get unlimited green tea or water (from spigot at bar, with or without gas). Snag a bar stool and grab dishes as they rattle by (priced by color of dish; check the chart: £1.75–5 per dish, £1.75 for miso soup, daily 12:00–23:00, 2 blocks south of Oxford Street, where Lexington Street becomes Poland Street, 52 Poland Street,

---

The Soho "Food Is Fun" Three-Course Dinner Crawl

For a multicultural, movable feast, consider enjoying a drink and eating (or splitting) one course at each of these places. Start around 17:30 to avoid lines, get in on early-bird specials, and find waiters willing to let you split a meal. Prices, though reasonable by London standards, add up. Servings are large enough to share. All are open nightly. Arrive at 17:30 at **Belgo Centraal** and split the early-bird dinner special: a kilo of mussels, fries, and dark Belgian beer. At **Yo! Sushi,** have beer or sake and a few dishes, then slurp your last course at **Wagamama Noodle Bar.** For dessert, people-watch at Leicester Square.

---

tel. 020/7287-0443). If you like Yo!, there are several locations around town, including a handy branch a block from the London Eye on Belvedere Road, as well as outlets within Selfridges, Harvey Nichols department stores, and Whiteleys Mall on Queensway.

Wagamama Noodle Bar is a noisy, pan-Asian, organic slurpathon. As you enter, check out the kitchen and listen to the roar of the basement, where benches rock with happy eaters. Everybody sucks. Stand against the wall to feel the energy of all this "positive eating." Portions are huge and splitting is allowed (£7–11 meals, Mon–Sat 11:30–23:00, Sun 12:00–22:00, crowded after 19:00, 10A Lexington Street, tel. 020/7292-0990 but no reservations taken). If you like this place, handy branches are all over town, including one near the British Museum (4 Streatham Street), Kensington (26 High Street), in Harvey Nichols (109 Knightsbridge), Covent Garden (1 Tavistock Street), Leicester Square (14 Irving Street), Piccadilly Circus (8 Norris Street), Fleet Street (#109), and next to the Tower of London (Tower Place).

Busaba Eathai Thai Restaurant is a hit with locals for its snappy service, casual-yet-high-energy ambience, and good, inexpensive Thai cuisine. You'll sit communally around big, square 16-person hardwood tables or in two-person tables by the window—with everyone in the queue staring at your noodles. They don't take reservations, so arrive by 19:00 or line up (£7–10 meals, Mon–Thu 12:00–23:00, Fri–Sat 12:00–23:30, Sun 12:00–22:00, 106 Wardour Street, tel. 020/7255-8686). They have two other handy locations: at 22 Store Street, near the British Museum and Goodge Street Tube; and 8–13 Bird Street, just off Oxford Street and across from the Bond Street Tube.

Côte Restaurant is a contemporary French bistro chain, serving good-value French cuisine at the right prices (£9–13 mains, early dinner specials, Mon–Wed 8:00–23:00, Thu–Fri 8:00–24:00, Sat 10:00–24:00, Sun 10:00–22:30, 124–126 Wardour Street, tel. 020/7287-9280).

Y Ming Chinese Restaurant—across Shaftesbury Avenue from the ornate gates, clatter, and dim sum of Chinatown—has dressy European decor, serious but helpful service, and authentic Northern Chinese cooking (good £10 meal deal offered 12:00–18:00, £7–10 plates, open Mon–Sat 12:00–23:45, closed Sun, 35–36 Greek Street, tel. 020/7734-2721).

Andrew Edmunds Restaurant is a tiny, candlelit place where you'll want to hide your camera and guidebook and act as local as possible. This little place—with a jealous and loyal clientele—is the closest I've found to Parisian quality in a cozy restaurant in London. The modern European cooking and creative seasonal menu are worth the splurge (£25 meals, Mon–Sat 12:30–15:00 & 18:00–22:45, Sun 13:00–15:30 & 18:00–22:30, come early or call ahead, request ground floor rather than basement, 46 Lexington Street in Soho, tel. 020/7437-5708).

Mildred's Vegetarian Restaurant, across from Andrew Edmunds, has cheap prices, an enjoyable menu, and a plain-yet-pleasant interior filled with happy eaters (£7–9 meals, Mon–Sat 12:00–23:00, closed Sun, vegan options, 45 Lexington Street, tel. 020/7494-1634).

Fernandez & Wells is a delightfully simple little wine, cheese, and ham bar. Drop in and grab a stool as you belly up to the big wooden bar. Share a plate of top-quality cheeses and/or Spanish or French hams with fine bread and oil, while sipping a nice glass of wine and talking with Juan or Toby (Mon–Sat 11:00–22:00, Sun 12:00–19:00, quality sandwiches at lunch, wine/cheese/ham bar after 16:00, 43 Lexington Street, tel. 020/7734-1546).

West London
Near Victoria Station Accommodations
I've enjoyed eating at these places, a few blocks southwest of Victoria Station. For locations, see the map on page 303.

Ebury Wine Bar, filled with young professionals, provides a cut-above atmosphere, delicious £13–18 entrées, and a £15.50 two-course special at lunch and 18:00–20:00. In the delightful back room, the fancy menu features modern European cuisine with a French accent; at the wine bar, find a cheaper bar menu that's better than your average pub grub. This is emphatically a "traditional wine bar," with no beers on tap (Mon–Sat 11:00–23:00, Sun 18:00—22:30, reserve after 20:00, at intersection of Ebury and Elizabeth Streets, near bus station, 139 Ebury Street, tel. 020/7730-5447).

Jenny Lo's Tea House is a simple budget place serving up reliably tasty £7–8 eclectic Chinese-style meals to locals in the know. While the menu is small, everything is high quality. Jenny clearly learned from her father, Ken Lo, one of the most famous Cantonese chefs in Britain, whose fancy place is just around the corner (Mon–Sat 11:30–15:00 & 18:00–22:00, closed Sun, cash only, 14 Eccleston Street, tel. 020/7259-0399).

La Poule au Pot, ideal for a romantic splurge, offers a classy, candlelit ambience with well-dressed patrons and expensive but fine country-style French cuisine (£18.75 two-course lunch specials, £25 dinner plates, daily 12:30–14:30 & 18:45–23:00, Sun until 22:00, £50 for dinner with wine, leafy patio dining, reservations smart, end of Ebury Street at intersection with Pimlico Road, 231 Ebury Street, tel. 020/7730-7763).

Grumbles brags it's been serving "good food and wine at non-scary prices since 1964." Offering a delicious mix of "modern eclectic French and traditional English," this unpretentious little place with cozy booths inside and four nice sidewalk tables is *the* spot to eat well in this otherwise workaday neighborhood (£8–16 plates, £11 early-bird specials 18:00–19:00, open Mon–Sat 12:00–14:30 & 18:00–22:45, Sun 12:00–22:30, reservations wise, half a block north of Belgrave Road at 35 Churton Street, tel. 020/7834-0149). Multitaskers take note: The self-service launderette down the street is open evenings.

Chimes English Restaurant and Cider Bar comes with a fresh country farm ambience, serious ciders (rare in London), and very good, traditional English food. Experiment with the cider—it's legal here...just barely (£8–12 meals, £13 two-course specials, hearty salads, Mon–Sat 12:00–15:00 & 17:30–22:15, Sun 12:00–23:15, 26 Churton Street, tel. 020/7821-7456).

The Jugged Hare, a 10-minute walk from Victoria Station, is a pub in a lavish old bank building, its vaults replaced by tankards of beer and a fine kitchen. They have a fun, traditional menu with more fresh veggies than fries, and a plush, vivid pub scene good for a meal or just a drink (£8–10 meals, daily 12:00–21:30, 172 Vauxhall Bridge Road, tel. 020/7828-1543).

Seafresh Fish Restaurant is the neighborhood place for plaice—either take-out on the cheap or eat-in, enjoying a chrome-and-wood mod ambience with classic and creative fish-and-chips cuisine. Though Mario's father started this place in 1965, it feels like the chippie of the 21st century (meals-£5 to go, £6–13 to sit, Mon–Fri 12:00–15:00 & 17:00–22:30, Sat 12:00–22:30, closed Sun, 80–81 Wilton Road, tel. 020/7828-0747).

La Bottega is an Italian delicatessen that fits its upscale Belgravia neighborhood. It offers tasty, freshly cooked pastas (£5.50), lasagnas, and salads at its counter (lasagna and salad meal-£8), along with great sandwiches (£3) and a good coffee bar with pastries. While not cheap, it's fast (order at the counter), and the ingredients would please an Italian chef (Mon–Fri 8:00–18:30, Sat 9:00–18:00, closed Sun, on corner of Ebury and Eccleston Streets, tel. 020/7730-2730). Grab your meal to go, or enjoy the good Belgravia life with locals, either sitting inside or on the sidewalk.

St. George's Tavern is *the* pub for a meal in this neighborhood. They serve dinner from the same fun menu in three zones: on the sidewalk to catch the sun and enjoy some people-watching, in the sloppy pub, and in a classier back dining room (£7–10 meals, proud of their sausages, Mon–Sat 10:00–22:00, Sun until 21:00, corner of Hugh Street and Belgrave Road, tel. 020/7630-1116).

Drinking Pubs that Serve Food: If you want to have a pub meal or just enjoy a drink surrounded by interesting local crowds, consider three pubs in the neighborhood, each with a distinct character: **The Duke of Wellington** is a classic neighborhood pub with forgettable grub, woodsy sidewalk seating, and an inviting interior (food served Mon–Sat 12:00–15:00 & 18:00–21:00, Sun 12:00–15:00 only, 63 Eaton Terrace, tel. 020/7730-1782). **The Belgravia Pub** is a sports bar with burgers, a stark interior, and a little outdoor garden (daily 12:00–21:30, corner of Ebury Street and South Eaton Place at 152 Ebury Street, tel. 020/7730-6040). **The Thomas Cubitt Pub,** packed with young professionals, is the neighborhood's trendy new "gastro pub," great for a drink or pricey meals (44 Elizabeth Street, tel. 020/7730-6060).

Cheap Eats: For groceries, a handy **Marks & Spencer Simply Food** is inside Victoria Station (Mon–Sat 7:00–24:00, Sun 8:00–22:00), along with a **Sainsbury's Market** (daily 6:00–23:00, at rear entrance, on Eccleston Street; a second Sainsbury's is just north of the station on Victoria Street). A larger Sainsbury's is on Wilton Road near Warwick Way, a couple blocks southeast of the station (daily 6:00–24:00). A string of good ethnic restaurants line Wilton Road (near the Seafresh Fish Restaurant, recommended earlier). For affordable if forgettable meals, try the row of cheap little eateries on Elizabeth Street.

Near Notting Hill and Bayswater Accommodations

The road called Queensway is a multiethnic food circus, lined with lively and inexpensive eateries. See the map on page 308.

Maggie Jones, a £40 splurge, is where Charles Dickens meets Ella Fitzgerald—exuberantly rustic and very English with a 1940s-jazz sound track. You'll get solid English cuisine, including huge plates of crunchy vegetables, served by a young and casual staff. It's pricey, but the portions are huge (especially the meat-and-fish pies, their specialty). You're welcome to save lots by splitting your main course. The candlelit upstairs is the most romantic, while the basement is kept lively with the kitchen, tight seating, and lots of action. If you eat well once in London, eat here—and do it quick, before it burns down (daily 12:30–14:30 & 18:30–23:00, reservations recommended, 6 Old Court Place, just east of Kensington Church Street, near High Street Kensington Tube stop, tel. 020/7937-6462).

The Churchill Arms pub and **Thai Kitchens** (same location) are local hangouts, with good beer and a thriving old-English ambience in front, and hearty £6 Thai plates in an enclosed patio in the back. You can eat the Thai food in the tropical hideaway or in the atmospheric pub section. The place is festooned with Churchill memorabilia and chamber pots (including one with Hitler's mug on it—hanging from the ceiling farthest from Thai Kitchen—sure to cure the constipation of any Brit during World War II). Arrive by 18:00 or after 21:00 to avoid a line. During busy times, diners are limited to an hour at the table (daily 12:00–22:00, 119 Kensington Church Street, tel. 020/7792-1246).

The Prince Edward serves good grub in a quintessential pub setting (£7–10 meals, Mon-Sat 11:00–15:00 & 18:00–23:00, Sun 11:00–22:30, plush-pubby indoor seating or sidewalk tables, family-friendly, free Wi-Fi, 2 blocks north of Bayswater Road at the corner of Dawson Place and Hereford Road, 73 Prince's Square, tel. 020/7727-2221).

Café Diana is a healthy little eatery serving sandwiches, salads, and Middle Eastern food. It's decorated—almost shrine-like—with photos of Princess Diana, who used to drop by for pita sandwiches (daily 8:00–23:00, 5 Wellington Terrace, on Bayswater Road, opposite Kensington Palace Garden Gates, where Di once lived, tel. 020/7792-9606).

Royal China Restaurant is filled with London's Chinese, who consider this one of the city's best eateries. It's dressed up in black, white, and gold, with candles, brisk waiters, and fine food (£7–11 dishes, daily 12:00–23:00, dim sum until 16:45, 13 Queensway, tel. 020/7221-2535).

Whiteleys Mall Food Court offers a fun selection of ethnic and fast-food chain eateries among Corinthian columns, and a multiscreen theater in a delightful mall (daily 9:00–23:00; options include Yo! Sushi, good salads at Café Rouge, pizza, Starbucks, and a coin-op Internet place; second floor, corner of Porchester Gardens and Queensway).

Supermarket: **Tesco** is a half-block from the Notting Hill Gate Tube stop (Mon-Sat 8:00–23:00, Sun 11:00–17:00, near intersection with Pembridge Road, 114–120 Notting Hill Gate). The smaller **Spar Market** is at 18 Queensway (Mon–Sat 7:00–24:00, Sun 9:00–24:00), and **Marks & Spencer** can be found in Whiteleys Mall (Mon–Sat 10:00–20:00, Sun 12:00–18:00).

Near South Kensington Accommodations

Popular eateries line Old Brompton Road and Thurloe Street (Tube: South Kensington), and a huge variety of cheap eateries are clumped around the Tube station. For locations, see the map on page 306.

The **Tesco Express** grocery store is handy for picnics (daily 7:00–24:00, 50–52 Old Brompton Road).

La Bouchée Bistro Café is a classy hole-in-the-wall touch of France. This candlelit and woody bistro serves a two-course, £11.50 special weekdays at lunch and from 17:30–18:30, and £17 *plats du jour* all *jour* (daily 12:00–15:00 & 17:30–23:30, 56 Old Brompton Road, tel. 020/7589-1929).

Daquise, an authentic-feeling 1930s Polish time warp, is ideal if you're in the mood for kielbasa and kraut. It's likeably dreary—fast, cheap, family-run—and a much-appreciated part of the neighborhood (£10 meals, weekday lunch special, daily 12:00–23:00, 20 Thurloe Street, tel. 020/7589-6117).

Moti Mahal Indian Restaurant, with minimalist-yet-classy mod ambience and attentive service, serves delicious Indian and Bangladeshi cuisine. Chicken *jalfrezi* and butter chicken are the favorites (£10 dinners, Mon–Sat 11:30–14:30 & 17:30–23:00, Sun 12:00–23:30, 3 Glendower Place, tel. 020/7584-8428).

Beirut Express II has fresh, well-prepared Lebanese cuisine, with barstools for quick service and take-away service in the front, and a sit-down restaurant in the back (65 Old Brompton Road, tel. 020/7591-0123).

The Zetland Arms serves good pub meals in a classic pub atmosphere on its noisy and congested ground floor, and in a more spacious and comfy upstairs—used only in the evenings. Large groups may find it too crowded after 18:00 (same menu throughout, £6–10 meals, food served daily 12:00–21:30, 2 Bute Street, tel. 020/7589-3813).

Elsewhere in London

Between St. Paul's and the Tower: The **Counting House,** formerly an elegant old bank, offers great £8–10 meals, nice homemade meat pies, fish, and fresh vegetables. The fun "nibbles menu" is available 15:00–22:00 (Mon–Fri 11:00–23:00, closed Sat–Sun, gets really busy with the buttoned-down 9-to-5 crowd after 12:15, near Mansion House in The City, 50 Cornhill, tel. 020/7283-7123).

Near St. Paul's: **De Gustibus Sandwiches** is where a top-notch artisan bakery meets the public, offering fresh, you-design-it sandwiches, salads, and soups with simple seating or take-out picnic sacks (great parks nearby), just a block below St. Paul's (Mon–Fri 7:00–17:00, closed Sat–Sun, from church steps follow signs to youth hostel a block downhill, 53–55 Carter Lane, tel.

020/7236-0056; another outlet is inside the Borough Market in Southwark).

Near the British Library: Drummond Street (running just west of Euston Station) is famous in London for very cheap and good Indian vegetarian food. Consider **Chutneys** (124 Drummond, tel. 020/7388-0604) and **Ravi Shankar** (133–135 Drummond, tel. 020/7388-6458) for a good *thali* (both generally open daily until 21:30, later Fri–Sat).

Taking Tea in London

Once the sole province of genteel ladies in fancy hats, afternoon tea has become more democratic in the 21st century. While some tearooms—such as the £37-a-head tea service at the Ritz and the finicky Fortnum & Mason—still require a jacket and tie (and a bigger bank account), most happily welcome tourists in jeans and sneakers.

The cheapest "tea" on the menu is generally a "cream tea"; the most expensive is the "champagne tea." **Cream tea** is simply a pot of tea and a homemade scone or two with jam and thick clotted cream. **Afternoon tea** generally is a cream tea, plus a tier of three plates holding small finger foods (such as cucumber sandwiches) and an assortment of small pastries. **Champagne tea** includes all of the goodies, plus a glass of champagne. For maximum pinkie-waving taste per calorie, slice your scone thin like a miniature loaf of bread. **High tea** generally means a more substantial late-afternoon or early-evening meal, often served with meat or eggs and eaten at a "higher" (i.e., kitchen) table.

Tearooms, which often also serve appealing light meals, are usually open for lunch and close about 17:00, just before dinner. At all the places listed below, it's perfectly acceptable to order one afternoon tea and one cream tea (at about £5) and split the afternoon tea goodies. The fancier places, such as Harrods and The Capital Hotel, are happy to bring you seconds and thirds of your favorites, turning tea into an early dinner.

The Orangery at Kensington Palace serves four different varieties of tea meals, from the £12.50 "Orangery tea" to the £24.95 "Tregothnan tea" in its bright white hall near Princess Di's former residence. You can also order treats à la carte. The portions aren't huge, but who can argue with eating at a princess' house? (Tea served 15:00–18:00, no reservations taken; located on map on page 308, a 10-min walk through Kensington Gardens from either Queensway or High Street Kensington Tube stations to the orange brick building, about 20 yards from Kensington Palace; tel. 020/7938-1406, www.hrp.org.uk.)

The National Dining Rooms, a restaurant/café within the

National Gallery on Trafalgar Square, is both classy and convenient. And though the restaurant can book up in advance, you can generally waltz in for afternoon tea at the café. To play it safe, arrive in the early afternoon to reserve a tea time, then take the self-guided National Gallery Tour (page 113) before or after your appointed time (£4 cakes and tarts, £5.50 cream tea, £14.50 afternoon tea, tea served 15:00–17:00, located in Sainsbury Wing of National Gallery, Tube: Charing Cross or Leicester Square, tel. 020/7747-2525, www.thenationaldiningrooms.co.uk).

The Café at Sotheby's, located on the ground floor of the auction giant's headquarters, is manna for shoppers taking a break from fashionable New Bond Street. There are no windows—just a long leather bench, plenty of mirrors, and a dark-wood room where waiters serve sweet treats and the £5.50 mix-and-match Neal's Yard cheese plate to locals in the know (£3 cakes and creams, £6.50 "small tea," £13.75 afternoon tea must be ordered 24 hours in advance—call 020/7293-5077, café open Mon–Fri only 9:30–11:30 & 12:00–16:45, afternoon tea served 15:00–16:45, located on map on page 347, 34–35 New Bond Street, Tube: Bond Street or Oxford Circus, www.sothebys.com/cafe/restaurant.html).

For a classier experience with an attentive waitstaff, try **The Capital Hotel,** a luxury hotel located a half-block from Harrods. The Capital caters to weary shoppers with its intimate five-table, linen-tablecloth tearoom. It's where the ladies-who-lunch meet to decide whether to buy that Versace gown they've had their eye on. Even so, casual clothes, kids, and sharing plates—with a £2.50 split-tea service charge—are all OK (£18.50 afternoon tea, daily 15:00–17:30, call to book ahead—especially on weekends, see map on page 306, 22 Basil Street, Tube: Knightsbridge, tel. 020/7589-5171, www.capitalhotel.co.uk).

Two famous department stores—Fortnum & Mason and Harrods—serve afternoon tea for sky-high prices. **Fortnum & Mason's St. James's Restaurant,** on the fourth floor, offers plush seats under the elegant tearoom's chandeliers. You'll get the standard three-tiered silver tea tray: finger sandwiches on the bottom, fresh scones with jam and clotted cream on the first floor, and decadent pastries and "tartlets" on the top floor, with unlimited tea. Consider it dinner (about £30–38, Mon–Sat 14:00–18:30, Sun 12:00–16:30, dress up a bit for this—no shorts, "children must be behaved," see map on page 347, 181 Piccadilly, reserve in advance online or at toll tel. 0845-602-5694, www.fortnumandmason.com).

At **Harrods' Georgian Restaurant,** you (along with 200 of your closest friends) can enjoy a fancy tea under a skylight as a pianist tickles the keys of a Bösendorfer, the world's most expensive piano (£21 afternoon tea, includes finger sandwiches and pastries with free refills, served daily from 15:45, last order at 17:15, on Brompton Road, Tube: Knightsbridge, reservations tel. 020/7225-6800, store tel. 020/7730-1234, www.harrods.com).

Having tea is not just for tourists and the wealthy—it's a true English tradition. If you want the teatime experience but are put off by the price, most department stores on Oxford Street (including those between Oxford Circus and Bond Street Tube stations) offer an affordable afternoon tea. **John Lewis** has a mod third-floor brasserie that serves a nice £10 afternoon tea platter (on Oxford Street one block west of the Bond Street Tube station, www .johnlewis.com). **Selfridges'** afternoon tea, served after 15:00 in the Gallery Restaurant, is pricier at £16.50 (www.selfridges.com). Near the Ritz, consider the £9.75 cream tea or the £19.75 afternoon tea at **The Wolseley** (www.thewolseley.com; also see listing on page 326).

Many museums and bookstores have cafés serving afternoon tea goodies à la carte, where you can put together a spread for less than £10—**Waterstone's** fifth-floor café and the **Victoria and Albert Museum** café are two of the best.

The modern **teapod,** near the Tower Bridge, advertises the "best-value afternoon tea in London," serving cream tea for £4.95 and afternoon tea for £9.95, along with sandwiches, soups, salads, and pastries (Mon–Fri 8:30–18:00, Sat 9:00–19:00, Sun 10:00–19:00, 31 Shad Thames, 200 yards from the Tower Bridge on the South Bank, tel. 020/7407-0000).

If you're taking a day trip to Bath, consider afternoon tea in the town's historic, elegant Georgian hall, known as the **Pump Room** (see page 414).

LONDON WITH CHILDREN

The key to a successful family trip to London is making everyone happy, including the parents. My family-tested recommendations have this objective in mind. Consider these tips:

- Take advantage of the local newsstand guides. *Time Out*'s family monthly is called *Kids Out* and the weekly version of *Time Out* has handy kids' calendars listing activities and shows. The *Time Out* guidebook, *London for Children* (£10, www.timeout.com/london/kids, available in bookstores and many newsstands), is chockablock with ideas for the serious parent tour guide in London.

- Ask the Britain and London Visitors Centre on Lower Regent Street about kids' events.

- Most of the big museums—such as the Tate Modern, the Tate Britain, and the National Gallery—schedule children's activities on weekends. Many museums also offer "backpacks" with activities to make the visit more interesting. Ask at museum information desks.

- London's big, budget chain hotels allow two kids to sleep for free in their already reasonably priced rooms (see page 301).

- Eat dinner early (around 18:00) to miss the romantic crowd. Skip the famous places. Look instead for relaxed cafés, pubs (kids are welcome, though sometimes restricted to the restaurant section or courtyard area), or even fast-food restaurants where kids can move around. Picnic lunches and dinners work well.

- Public WCs can be hard to find. Try department stores, museums, and restaurants, particularly fast-food places.

- Follow this book's crowd-beating tips. Kids get antsy standing in a line for a museum. At each sight, ask about a kids' guide or flier.

- Hamleys is the biggest toy store in Britain, with seven floors of toys (Mon–Fri 10:00–20:00, Sat 9:00–20:00, Sun 12:00–18:00, 188–196 Regent Street, Tube: Oxford Circus, toll tel. 0870-333-2455, www.hamleys.com). It's also included in my shopping-oriented "Oxford Circus to Piccadilly Walk," in the Shopping chapter. Hamleys has branches at Heathrow, Gatwick, and Stansted airports, and at St. Pancras International train station.
- Harry Potter fans (and Muggle parents) enjoy visiting places in London where scenes from the movies were filmed (see page 66).

Sights and Activities

East London

Tower of London—The crown jewels are awesome, and the Beefeater tour plays off kids in a memorable and fun way. Avoid the long ticket lines by buying your ticket in advance (must use within seven days) at any London TI, at the gift shop just below the Tower Hill Tube station ticket office, or online at a slight discount (£17, family–£47, audioguide–£4, March–Oct Tue–Sat 9:00–17:30, Sun–Mon 10:00–17:30; Nov–Feb Tue–Sat 9:00–16:30, Sun–Mon 10:00–16:30; last entry 30 min before closing, the long but fast-moving ticket lines are worst on Sun, no photography allowed of jewels or in chapels, Tube: Tower Hill, recorded info toll tel. 0844-482-7777, booking toll tel. 0844-482-7799, www.hrp .org.uk).

   ○ See Tower of London Tour.

Museum of London—The museum has a very kid-friendly presentation that takes you from prehistoric times to the 1600s (the lower galleries covering the 1700s are due to reopen in spring of 2010). The events guide at the entrance lists kids' activities (free, daily 10:00–18:00, last entry at 17:30, until 21:00 first Thu of month, café, Tube: Barbican or St. Paul's, tel. 020/7814-5530, recorded info tel. 020/7001-9844, www.museumoflondon.org.uk).

Unicorn Theatre—This modern complex presents professional theater for children on two stages (show tickets: £10–16 for adults, £7.50–10 for kids, no kids under age 4 unless play is geared for that age group; café, on the South Bank just behind City Hall, 147 Tooley Street; Tube: London Bridge; tel. 020/7645-0560, www .unicorntheatre.com).

Central London

Covent Garden—This is a great area for people-watching and candy-licking. Kids like the **London Transport Museum**, with its interactive zone (£10, kids under 16 free, Sat–Thu 10:00–18:00, some Fri 11:00–18:00, some Fri until 21:00, last entry 45 min before closing, in southeast corner of Covent Garden courtyard, Tube: Covent Garden, tel. 020/7379-6344, recorded info tel. 020/7565-7299, www.ltmuseum.co.uk); see page 55.

Trafalgar Square—The grand square is fun for kids (Tube: Charing Cross). Climb the lions, munch a meal in a crypt (at St. Martin-in-the-Fields, see below), and tour the National Gallery (below).

National Gallery—Begin your visit in the "ArtStart" multimedia room. Your child can list his or her interests (cats, naval battles, and so on) and print out a tailor-made tour map for free. Ask about their children's printed guides, audioguide programs, and events (free, but suggested £1–2 donation; daily 10:00–18:00, Fri until 21:00, no photography or video cameras, cafés, on Trafalgar Square, Tube: Charing Cross or Leicester Square, recorded info tel. 020/7747-2885, switchboard tel. 020/7839-3321, www.national gallery.org.uk).

○ See National Gallery Tour.

St. Martin-in-the-Fields—Next to the church on Trafalgar Square is a pavilion with a brass-rubbing center below that's fun for kids who'd like a souvenir to show for their efforts (£4.50 and up, Mon–Wed 10:00–19:00, Thu–Sat 10:00–22:00, Sun 12:00–19:00; for details, see page 52). The affordable Café in the Crypt has just the right spooky tables-on-gravestones ambience (£6–8 cafeteria plates, Mon–Wed 8:00–20:00, Thu–Sat 8:00–21:00, Sun 11:00–18:00, church tel. 020/7766-1158 or 020/7766-1100, www2 .stmartin-in-the-fields.org).

London Eye—The grand observation wheel is a delight for the whole family (£17, 10 percent discount for booking online, daily July–Aug 10:00–21:30, June and Sept 10:00–21:00, Oct–May 10:00–20:00, closed mid-Jan for annual maintenance, Tube: Waterloo or Westminster, www.londoneye.com). For more specifics, including crowd avoidance, see page 72.).

Changing of the Guard—Kids enjoy the bands and pageantry of the Buckingham Palace Changing of the Guard, but little ones get a better view at the inspection; guards assemble almost daily at 11:00 at Wellington Barracks, and march out at 11:30 for Buckingham Palace (see page 59). For horse-lovers, the Horse Guards change daily at 11:00 (10:00 on Sun) and have a colorful dismounting ceremony daily at 16:00 (on Whitehall, between Trafalgar Square and #10 Downing Street, Tube: Westminster, www.changing-the-guard.com, see page 50).

LONDON WITH CHILDREN

Piccadilly Circus—This titillating district has lots of Planet Hollywood–type amusements, such as the Trocadero Center. Be careful of fast-fingered riffraff. (For more information on the district, see page 53.) Hamleys toy store is just two blocks up Regent Street at 188–196 (hours listed earlier in this chapter).

Shopping—If your teenager wants to bring home a few chic and cheap London fashions, Oxford Street (at the intersection of Regent Street) is a good place to start. Take the Tube to the Oxford Circus stop, and you'll be surrounded by lots of shops selling inexpensive, trendy clothes for teens. Stores include Top Shop (36–38 Great Castle Street), Miss Selfridge (334–348 Oxford Street), Zara (118 Regent Street), two H&M shops (174–176 and 261–271 Regent Street), and music stores like HMV (150 Oxford Street). Sandwich-to-go shops and coffeehouses (including a half-dozen Starbucks) offer easy rest stops for families. Also see the more upscale "Oxford Circus to Piccadilly Walk" (in the next chapter), which begins at the same Tube stop, but goes down Regent Street. Harrods in Knightsbridge, with its over-the-top toy and food departments, can be fun for kids of all ages.

Theater—Long-running shows are kid- and parent-pleasers (see Entertainment chapter).

West London

Hyde Park—London's backyard is the perfect place for museumed-out kids to play and run free. For older kids, the park has a tennis court, horseback riding, and trails for running or biking. Young children will enjoy the Diana, Princess of Wales Memorial Playground in adjacent Kensington Gardens, with its Peter Pan–themed climbing equipment (including a huge wooden pirate ship). Events such as music, plays, and clown acts are scheduled throughout the summer. The Serpentine Lake offers paddleboat rentals and a swimming area with a playground and a shallow kiddie pool (Lido swimming entrance-£4, kids-£1, family-£9, daily May–Sept 10:00–18:00, last entry 30 min before closing, closed Oct–April, tel. 020/7706-3422). The park is open daily from 5:00 in the morning until midnight (www.royalparks.org.uk).

Natural History Museum—This wonderful world of dinosaurs, volcanoes, meteors, and creepy-crawlies offers creative interactive displays (free, possible fee for special exhibits, daily 10:00–17:50, last entry at 17:30, a long tunnel leads directly from South Kensington Tube station to museum, tel. 020/7942-5000, exhibit info and reservations tel. 020/7942-5011, www.nhm.ac.uk).

Science Museum—This museum, next door to the Natural History Museum, offers lots of hands-on fun and IMAX movies (free entry, charge for special exhibits; IMAX shows: adults-£8, kids-£6.25; daily 10:00–18:00, Exhibition Road, Tube: South

Kensington, toll tel. 0870-870-4868, www.sciencemuseum.org
.uk). Both the Natural History and Science museums are kid-
friendly and can be clogged with school groups during the school
year. Check for special events and exhibits (noted at each museum's
entry and on their websites).

North London

Madame Tussauds Waxworks—Despite the lines, the waxworks are popular with kids for gory stuff, pop and movie stars,
everyone's favorite royals, and more (admission £25, kids-£21; save
by purchasing tickets in advance on their website or with other
deals; open Mon–Fri 9:30–17:30, Sat–Sun 9:00–18:00, mid-July–
Aug and school holidays daily 9:00–18:00; Marylebone Road,
Tube: Baker Street, www.madame-tussauds.com).

London Zoo—This venerable animal habitat, with more than
8,000 creatures and a fine petting zoo, is one of the best in the
world (£16.80, children-£13.30, daily mid-July–early Sept 10:00–
18:00, early March–mid-July and early Sept–late Oct 10:00–17:30,
closes earlier in winter, last entry one hour before closing, in
Regent's Park, Tube: Camden Town, then bus #274, tel. 020/7722-
3333, www.zsl.org). Call for feeding and event times.

Pollock's Toy Museum—Kids will wonder how their grand-
parents ever survived without Nintendo, as they wander through
this rickety old house filled with toys that predate batteries and
microchips (£5, kids-£2, generally Mon–Sat 10:00–17:00, closed
Sun, last entry 30 min before closing, 1 Scala Street, near Tube:
Goodge Street, tel. 020/7636-3452, www.pollockstoymuseum.com
or www.pollocksmuseum.co.uk). Call before you come, to make
sure it's open.

Sports—Older kids may enjoy attending a Premier League soccer
game (expensive but memorable and nontouristy; see schedule at
www.premierleague.com).

Greater London

Kew Gardens—These famous 300-acre gardens include the
Rhizotron and Xstrata Treetop Walkway, which lets kids explore
the canopy 60 feet above the ground on a 200-yard-long scenic
steel walkway (£13, discounted to £11 45 min before closing,
kids under 17 free; April–Aug Mon–Fri 9:30–18:30, Sat–Sun
9:30–19:30; closes earlier Sept–March, last entry to gardens 30
min before closing, galleries and conservatories close at 17:30 in
high season—earlier off-season, free 60-min walking tours daily at
11:00 and 14:00; £4 narrated floral 40-min hop-on, hop-off joyride
on little tram departs on the hour from 11:00 from near Victoria
Gate; Tube: Kew Gardens, boats run April–Oct between Kew

Gardens and Westminster Pier; switchboard tel. 020/8332-5000, recorded info tel. 020/8332-5655, www.kew.org).

Fun Transportation

Thames Cruise—Young sailors delight in boats. Westminster Pier (near Big Ben) offers a lot of action, with round-trip cruises and boats to the Tower of London, Greenwich, and Kew Gardens. For details, see page 39.

Hop-on, Hop-off London Bus Tours—These two-hour double-decker bus tours, which drive by all the biggies, are fun for kids and stress-free for parents. You can stay on the bus the entire time, or hop on and hop off at any of the nearly 30 stops and catch a later bus (every 10–15 min in summer, every 20 min in winter), see page 34. The Original London Sightseeing Tour's language bus (marked with lots of flags or a red triangle) has a kids' track on the earphones, but then you miss the live guide.

Day Trip

Legoland Windsor—If your kids are loopy over Legos, they'll love a day trip to Legoland Windsor (adults-£36, £32.40 in

advance online, £34 at Windsor TI; children-£27, £24 online or from TI; free for ages 2 and under; mid-July–Aug daily 10:00–19:00; Sept–Oct and April–mid-July Thu–Mon only, closes 1–2 hours earlier; closed Nov–mid-March except around Christmas, call or check website for exact schedule; toll tel. 0871-

222-2001, www.legoland.co.uk). For details, see "Windsor" in Day Trips in England chapter.

What to Avoid

The London Dungeon's popularity with teenagers makes it one of London's most-visited sights. I enjoy gore and torture as much as the next boy, but this is lousy gore and torture, and I would not waste the time or money on it with my child.

LONDON WITH CHILDREN

SHOPPING IN LONDON

Most stores are open Monday through Saturday from roughly 10:00 to 18:00, and many close Sundays. Large department stores stay open later, until 20:00 or 21:00. If you're looking for bargains, you can visit one of the city's many street markets.

Consider these five ways to shop in London:

1. If all you need are souvenirs, a surgical strike at any souvenir shop will do.
2. Large department stores offer relatively painless one-stop shopping. Consider the down-to-earth Marks & Spencer (Mon–Sat 9:00–20:00, Thu until 21:00, Sun 12:00–18:00, 173 Oxford Street, Tube: Oxford Circus; another at 458 Oxford Street, Tube: Bond Street or Marble Arch; see www.marks andspencer.com for more locations).
3. Connect small shops with a pleasant walk (see "Oxford Circus to Piccadilly Walk," later in this chapter).
4. For flea-market fun, try one of the many street markets.
5. Gawkers as well as serious bidders can attend auctions.

Helpful Hints

Refuse any offers to charge your credit card in dollars. This is called **dynamic currency conversion,** or DCC, and it's offered by some stores (including Harrods) as a "convenience." The very bad exchange rate they use is convenient only for increasing the store's profits.

For information on **VAT refunds** and **customs regulations,** see page 12.

Fancy Department Stores in West London

Harrods—Harrods is London's most famous and touristy department store. With more than four acres of retail space covering seven floors, it's a place where some shoppers could spend all day. (To me, it's still just a department store.) Big yet classy, Harrods has everything from elephants to toothbrushes (Mon–Sat 10:00–20:00, Sun 12:00–18:00, mandatory storage for big backpacks-£3, no shorts or flip-flops, on Brompton Road, Tube: Knightsbridge, tel. 020/7730-1234, www.harrods.com).

Sightseers should pick up the free *Store Guide* at any info post. Here's what I enjoy: On the ground floor, find the Food Halls, with their Edwardian tiled walls, creative and exuberant displays, and staff in period costumes—not quite like your local supermarket back home.

Descend to the lower ground floor and follow signs to the Egyptian Escalator (in the center of the store), where you'll find a memorial to Dodi Fayed and Princess Diana. Photos and flow-

ers honor the late Princess and her lover, who both died in a car crash in Paris in 1997. Inside a small, clear pyramid, you can see a wine glass still dirty from their last dinner and the engagement ring that Dodi purchased the day before they died. True Di-hards can go back up one level to the ground floor and follow signs to Door #3 in Menswear. A huge (and more than a little creepy) bronze statue shows Di and Dodi releasing a symbolic albatross. It was commissioned by Dodi Fayed's father, Mohamed Al Fayed, who owns Harrods.

Back in the center of the store, ride the Egyptian Escalator—lined with pharaoh-headed sconces, papyrus-plant lamps, and hieroglyphic balconies (Al Fayed is from Egypt)—to the fourth floor. From the escalator, make a U-turn left and head to the far corner of the store (toys) to find child-size luxury cars that actually work. A junior Jaguar or Mercedes will set you back about $13,000. The Mini Hummer H3 ($23,000) is as big as my car.

Also on the fourth floor is **The Georgian Restaurant,** where you can enjoy a fancy afternoon tea (see page 336). For non-tea drinkers, 27 other eateries are scattered throughout the store, including a sushi bar, kosher deli, pizzeria, classic pub, and—for the truly homesick—a Krispy Kreme.

Many of my readers report that Harrods is overpriced, snooty, and teeming with American and Japanese tourists. Still, it's the palace of department stores. The nearby Beauchamp Place is lined with classy and fascinating shops.

Harvey Nichols—Once Princess Diana's favorite, "Harvey Nick's" remains the department store *du jour* (Mon–Sat 10:00–20:00, Sun 12:00–18:00, near Harrods, 109–125 Knightsbridge,

Tube: Knightsbridge, tel. 020/7235-5000, www.harveynichols
.com). Want to pick up a little £20 scarf for the wife? You won't
do it here, where they're more like £200. The store's fifth floor is
a veritable food fest, with a gourmet grocery store, a fancy restaurant, a Yo! Sushi bar, and a lively café. Consider a take-away tray
of sushi to eat on a bench in the Hyde Park rose garden two blocks
away.

Oxford Circus to Piccadilly Walk

The walk from Oxford Circus to Piccadilly along Regent Street is
about three-quarters of a mile (only you know how much time—
and money—to allow). If you'd like to stop for afternoon tea at
Fortnum & Mason (Mon–Sat 14:00–19:00, Sun 12:00–16:30),
begin this walk after lunch. Most stores are open Mon-Sat around
10:00–20:00 (or 21:00) and on Sunday around 12:00–18:00.

From the **Oxford Circus Tube stop**, head south on Regent
Street (heading slightly downhill, away from the steeple in the
road). You'll pass a diverse array of places to shop, all on the left-
hand (east) side of the street. Two blocks down, where Regent
crosses Great Marlborough Street, look left to spot **Liberty**—a big,
stately local-favorite department store behind a facade of Tudor-
style half-timbering (Mon–Sat 10:00–21:00, Sun 11:30–18:00, tel.
020/7734-1234 www.liberty.co.uk).

Continuing down Regent Street, turn left on Foubert's Place
and walk a block to reach the once hippie, now hip **Carnaby
Street.** Little remains of its trendsetting '60s-era fashions, but
it's a pleasant, traffic-free shopping street lined with cafés and
boutiques.

Backtrack on Foubert's Place, then continue down Regent
Street to **Hamleys,** Britain's biggest toy store, which in 2010 marks
its 250th anniversary of delighting children. Seven floors buzz with
28,000 toys, managed by a staff of 200. Employees, some dressed
in playful costumes, give demos of the latest gadgets. At the
"Build-a-Bear Factory," kids can pick out a made-to-order teddy
bear and watch while it's stuffed and sewn (Mon–Fri 10:00–20:00,
Sat 9:00–20:00, Sun 12:00–18:00, 188–196 Regent Street, toll tel.
0870-333-2455, www.hamleys.com).

The next few blocks of Regent Street feature familiar names
such as **Levi's, Esprit, Next,** and the American-based men's store
Brooks Brothers, all demonstrating just how globalized shopping
has become.

From Piccadilly Circus, turn right and wander down Piccadilly
Street. On your left, escape from the frenzy of Piccadilly into the
quiet of **Waterstone's,** Europe's largest bookstore (housed in a former men's clothing store). Page through seven orderly floors. The
fifth floor offers a hip bar with minimalist furniture and great views

Oxford Circus to Piccadilly Walk

1. Liberty Dept. Store
2. Carnaby Street
3. Hamleys Toy Store
4. Waterstone's Bookstore
5. St. James's Church & Flea Market
6. Fortnum & Mason Dept. Store & St. James's Restaurant
7. Burlington Arcade
8. Ritz Hotel & Wolseley Bistro
9. Sotheby's Auction House & The Cafe at Sotheby's

of the London Eye, Big Ben, and the Houses of Parliament's towers (Mon–Sat 9:00–22:00, Sun 12:00–18:00, 203–206 Piccadilly, tel. 020/7851-2400, www.waterstones.com).

Next you'll pass Christopher Wren's **St. James's Church** (with free lunchtime concerts at 13:10) and a tiny all-day flea market (Tue—antiques, 10:00–18:00; Wed–Sat—crafts, 11:00–18:00; closed Sun–Mon). One block down is the **Fortnum & Mason** department store, which eschews the glitz of bigger stores and revels in understated, old-school elegance. Consider a traditional afternoon tea in its **St. James's Restaurant** on the fourth floor (see page 336). With rich displays and deep red carpet, Fortnum feels classier and more relaxed than Harrods (Mon–Sat 10:00–20:00, Sun 12:00–18:00, 181 Piccadilly, tel. 020/7734-8040 ext. 2241, www.fortnumandmason.com).

Just past Fortnum & Mason (across the street) is the delightful **Burlington Arcade,** and a block farther is the original **Ritz Hotel,** where the tea is much fancier.

Street Markets

Antique buffs, people-watchers, and folks who brake for garage sales love London's street markets. There's good early-morning market activity somewhere any day of the week. The best are Portobello Road and Camden Market. Any London TI has a complete, up-to-date list. If you like to haggle, there are no holds barred in London's street markets. Warning: Markets attract two kinds of people—tourists and pickpockets.

Portobello Road Market—The flea market, with 2,000 stalls, has three sections: antiques at the top, produce in the middle, and clothing and books and fleas at the other end. Antiques are featured on Saturday, when the market really hops (Mon–Wed and Fri–Sat 8:00–18:30, Thu 8:00–13:00, sparse on Mon, closed Sun, Tube: Notting Hill Gate, near recommended B&Bs, tel. 020/7229-8354, www.portobelloroad.co.uk).

Camden Lock Market—This huge, trendy arts-and-crafts festival has become quite punky to many travelers. Still, it's London's fourth-most-popular tourist attraction (daily 10:00–18:00, Tube: Camden Town, tel. 020/7284-2084, www.camdenlockmarket .com).

Brixton Market—Here the food, clothing, records, and hair-braiding throb with an Afro-Caribbean beat (Mon–Tue and Thu–Sat 9:00–18:00, Wed 9:00–13:00, closed Sun, Tube: Brixton).

Petticoat Lane Market—Expect budget clothing, leather, shoes, watches, jewelry, and crowds (Sun 9:00–14:00, sometimes later; smaller market Mon–Fri 10:00–16:30 on Wentworth Street only; closed Sat; Middlesex Street and Wentworth Street, Tube: Liverpool Street). The Columbia Road flower market is nearby (Sun 8:00–15:00, http://columbiaroad.info).

Spitalfields Market—Housed under an old arcade, this market features more than a hundred merchants. You'll find a lively organic food market, many ethnic eateries, crafts, trendy clothes, bags, and an antique-and-junk market. The antique market is on Thursday, a cutting-edge fashion and art market is held each Friday, and a record and book fair is on the first and third Wednesday of every month (stalls Mon–Fri 10:00–15:00, Sun 10:00–17:00, closed Sat; shops daily 11:00–19:00; restaurants Mon–Sat 11:00–23:00, Sun 9:00–17:00; Tube: Liverpool Street; from the Tube stop, take

East End Walk from Spitalfields Market

The East End, a formerly industrial area, has turned into one of London's trendy spots. Take a 30-minute walk around the Spitalfields Market neighborhood (Tube: Liverpool Street) to see the colorful mix of bustling markets, late-night dance clubs, the Bangladeshi ghetto, and tenements of Jack the Ripper's London.

Start at the **Spitalfields Market.** Across the street (to the east) is **The Ten Bells Pub,** at the intersection of Commercial Street and Brushfield/Fournier. Established in 1753, it was the hangout of one of the Ripper's victims. Across the street from the pub is **Christ Church,** with its impressive 225-foot steeple. Many Ripper witnesses knew the time of the crimes by remembering the church bells' chimes.

Head east one long block on Fournier Street to **Brick Lane,** where you're immediately immersed in "Banglatown," lined with Bangladeshi stores and restaurants—"the curry capital of Europe." At the intersection of Fournier Street and Brick Lane is the not-at-all-obvious neighborhood mosque. Two blocks north on Brick Lane is the former **Truman Brewery,** which now houses a Sunday market and trendy shops (good coffee at Café 1001). A half-block farther north, you'll find the old brewery **smokestack** and two trendy nightclubs: the **Vibe Bar** and **93 Feet East.**

Head south on Brick Lane and turn right (west) on **Fashion Street.** Though it changes names several times, this road leads straight back to the Liverpool Street station. Along the way you'll pass the Islamic-looking **Abraham Davis' Moorish Market,** now housing high-tech businesses. Where Fashion Street becomes White's Row, you could detour a block south to Brune Street to see Industrial Age tenements, the "Soup Kitchen for the Jewish Poor," and a nice view of the modern, bullet-shaped Swiss Re building. Also branching off White's Row is Tenter Ground, the street where weavers once dried cloth "on tenter hooks," giving us the phrase. Continuing west, White's Row becomes narrow **Artillery Passage,** lined with teeny eateries, giving you an idea of how densely packed this neighborhood used to be when it was filled with grimy-faced 19th-century factory workers. At the intersection with Sandy's Row are the **bollards** (black-white-red stakes in the pavement), alerting you that you're officially leaving the East End and entering the City of London. Continue west one block to busy Middlesex Street, with **Dirty Dick's Pub** (the name has a history, but the pub itself doesn't) and the **Liverpool Street** station and Tube stop (to the left).

At 8:45 on July 7, 2005, a Tube train had just pulled out of Liverpool Street station when it was rocked by a terrorist bomb—the first of four to hit London that day. The next day, Londoners were back on the Tube.

Bishopsgate East exit, turn left, walk 2 blocks, and turn right on Brushfield Street; tel. 020/7375-2963, www.visitspitalfields.com). For tips on exploring the surrounding neighborhood, see the "East End Walk" sidebar on the previous page.

Famous Auctions

London's famous auctioneers welcome the curious public for viewing and bidding. You can preview estate catalogs or browse auction calendars online. To ask questions or set up an appointment, contact **Sotheby's** (Mon–Fri 9:00–16:30, closed Sat–Sun, café, 34–35 New Bond Street—see map on page 347, Tube: Oxford Circus, tel. 020/7293-5000, www.sothebys.com) or **Christie's** (Mon–Fri 9:00–17:00, Sat–Sun usually 12:00–17:00 but weekend hours vary—call ahead, 8 King Street, Tube: Green Park, tel. 020/7839-9060, www.christies.com).

ENTERTAINMENT IN LONDON

London bubbles with top-notch entertainment seven days a week: plays, movies, concerts, exhibitions, walking tours, shopping, and children's activities.

For the best list of what's happening and a look at the latest London scene, pick up a current copy of *Time Out* (£3, www .timeout.com). The TI's free monthly *London Planner* covers sights, events, and plays at least as well as *Time Out*. For a chatty, *People* magazine–type website on London's entertainment, check www .thisislondon.co.uk.

Choose from classical, jazz, rock, and far-out music, Gilbert and Sullivan, tango lessons, comedy, Baha'i meetings, poetry readings, spectator sports, theater, and the cinema. In Leicester Square you'll sometimes find movies that have yet to be released in the States—if Hugh Grant is attending an opening-night premiere in London, it will likely be at one of the big movie houses here.

There are plenty of free performances, such as lunch concerts at St. Martin-in-the-Fields (at Trafalgar Square) and summertime events at The Scoop amphitheatre near City Hall (see "Summer Evenings Along the South Bank").

Theater (a.k.a. "Theatre")

London's theater rivals Broadway's in quality and usually beats it in price. Choose from 200 offerings—Shakespeare, musicals, comedies, thrillers, sex farces, cutting-edge fringe, revivals starring movie celebs, and more. London does it all well. I prefer big, glitzy—even bombastic—musicals over serious chamber dramas, simply because London can deliver the lights, sound, dancers, and multimedia spectacle I rarely get back home.

Most theaters, marked on tourist maps, are found in the West End between Piccadilly and Covent Garden. Box offices, hotels,

What's On in the West End

Here are some of the perennial favorites that you're likely to find among the West End's evening offerings. If spending the time and money for a London play, I like a full-fledged, high-energy musical. Generally you can book tickets for free at the box office or for a £2-3 fee by telephone or online. See the map later in this chapter for locations.

Musicals

Billy Elliot—This adaptation of the popular British film is part family drama, part story of a boy who just has to dance set to a score by Elton John (£17.50-50, Mon–Sat 19:30, matinees Thu and Sat 14:30, Victoria Palace Theatre, Victoria Street, Tube: Victoria, toll tel. 0870-895-5577, www.billyelliotthemusical.com).

Chicago—A chorus-girl-gone-bad forms a nightclub act with another murderess to bring in the bucks (£20–59, Mon–Thu 20:00, Fri 17:30 and 20:30, Sat 15:00 and 20:00, Cambridge Theatre, Earlham Street, Tube: Covent Garden, booking toll tel. 0844-412-4652, www.chicagothemusical.com).

Jersey Boys—This fast-moving, easy-to-follow show tracks the rough start and rise to stardom of Frankie Valli and The Four Seasons. It's light, but the music is so catchy that everyone leaves whistling the group's classics (£20–60, Mon–Sat at 19:30, matinees Tue and Sat 14:30, Prince Edward Theatre, Old Compton Street, Tube: Leicester Square, toll tel. 0844-482-5151, www.jersey boyslondon.com).

Les Misérables—Claude-Michel Schönberg's musical adaptation of Victor Hugo's epic follows the life of Jean Valjean as he struggles with the social and political realities of 19th-century France. This inspiring mega-hit takes you back to the days of France's struggle for a just and modern society (£12.50–52.50, Mon–Sat 19:30, matinees Wed and Sat 14:30, Queen's Theatre, Shaftesbury Avenue, Tube: Piccadilly Circus, box office toll tel. 0844-482-5160, www.lesmis.com).

The Lion King—In this Disney extravaganza, Simba the lion learns about the delicately balanced circle of life on the savanna (£30–59.50, Tue–Sat 19:30, matinees Wed and Sat 14:00, Sun

and TIs offer a handy free *London Theatre Guide* and *Entertainment Guide*. From home, it's easy to check www.officiallondontheatre .co.uk for the latest on what's currently playing in London.

Performances are nightly except Sunday, usually with one or two matinees a week (Shakespeare's Globe is the rare theater that does offer performances on Sun, May–Sept). Tickets range from about £11 to £55. Matinees are generally cheaper and rarely sell out.

To book a seat, simply call the theater box office directly, ask about seats and available dates, and buy a ticket with your credit

15:00, Lyceum Theatre, Wellington Street, Tube: Charing Cross or Covent Garden, booking toll tel. 0844-844-0005, theater info tel. 020/7420-8100, www.thelionking.co.uk).

Mamma Mia!—This energetic, spandex-and-platform-boots musical weaves together a slew of ABBA hits to tell the story of a bride in search of her real dad as her promiscuous mom plans her Greek Isle wedding. The production has the audience dancing by the time it reaches its happy ending (£19.50–58, Mon–Thu and Sat 19:30, Fri 20:30, matinees Fri 17:00 and Sat 15:00, Prince of Wales Theatre, Coventry Street, Tube: Piccadilly Circus, box office toll tel. 0844-482-5138, www.mamma-mia.com).

Phantom of the Opera—A mysterious masked man falls in love with a singer in this haunting Andrew Lloyd Webber musical about life beneath the stage of the Paris Opera (£20–55, Mon–Sat 19:30, matinees Tue and Sat 14:30, Her Majesty's Theatre, Haymarket, Tube: Piccadilly Circus or Leicester Square, US toll-free tel. 800-334-8457, London booking toll tel. 0844-412-2707, www.thephantomoftheopera.com).

We Will Rock You—Whether or not you're a Queen fan, this musical tribute (more to the band than to Freddie Mercury) is an understandably popular celebration of their work (£27.50–60, Mon–Sat at 19:30, matinee Sat 14:30, Dominion Theatre, Tottenham Court Road, Tube: Tottenham Court Road, Ticketmaster toll tel. 0844-847-1775, www.queenonline.com/wewillrockyou).

Thrillers

The Mousetrap—Agatha Christie's whodunit about a murder in a country house continues to stump audiences after 58 years (£13.50–36, Mon–Sat 19:30, matinees Tue 15:00 and Sat 16:00, St. Martin's Theatre, West Street, Tube: Leicester Square, box office toll tel. 0844-499-1515, www.the-mousetrap.co.uk).

The Woman in Black—The chilling tale of a solicitor who is haunted by what he learns when he closes a reclusive woman's affairs (£13.50–39, Mon–Sat 20:00, matinees Tue 15:00 and Sat 16:00, Fortune Theatre, Russell Street, Tube: Covent Garden, box office toll tel. 0870-060-6626, www.thewomaninblack.com).

card. You can call from the US as easily as from England. Arrive about 30 minutes before the show starts to pick up your ticket and avoid lines.

For a booking fee, you can reserve online. Most theater websites link you to a preferred ticket vendor, usually www.ticketmaster.co.uk or www.seetickets.com. Keith Prowse Ticketing is also handy by phone or online (US toll-free tel. 800-669-8687, toll tel. 0844-209-0382, www.keithprowse.com).

Although booking through an agency is quick and easy, prices

London's Major Theaters

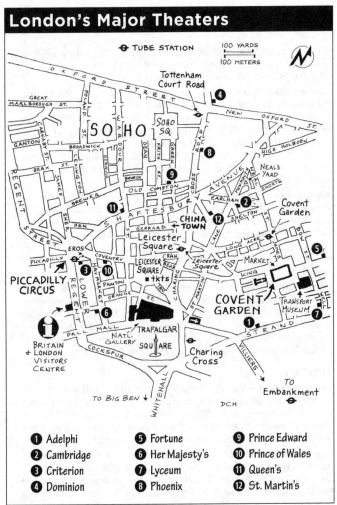

● TUBE STATION

❶ Adelphi	❺ Fortune	❾ Prince Edward
❷ Cambridge	❻ Her Majesty's	❿ Prince of Wales
❸ Criterion	❼ Lyceum	⓫ Queen's
❹ Dominion	❽ Phoenix	⓬ St. Martin's

are inflated by a standard 25 percent fee. Ticket agencies (whether in the US, at London's TIs, or scattered throughout the city) are scalpers with an address. If you're buying from an agency, look at the ticket carefully (your price should be no more than 30 percent over the printed face value; the 17.5 percent VAT is already included in the face value), and understand where you're sitting according to the floor plan (if your view is restricted, it will state this on the ticket; for floor plans of the various theaters, see www.theatre monkey.com). Agencies are worthwhile only if a show you've just got to see is sold out at the box office. They scarf up hot tickets, planning to make a killing after the show is sold out. US booking agencies get their tickets from another agency, adding even more to your expense by involving yet another middleman. Many tickets sold on the street are forgeries. Although some theaters use booking agencies to handle their advance sales, you'll stand a good chance of saving money by avoiding the middleman and simply calling the box office directly to purchase your tickets (international phone calls are cheap, and credit cards make booking a snap).

Theater Lingo: stalls (ground floor), dress circle (first balcony), upper circle (second balcony), balcony (sky-high third balcony), slips (cheap seats on the fringes). Many cheap seats have a restricted view (behind a pillar).

Cheap Theater Tricks: Most theaters offer cheap returned tickets, standing-room, matinee, and senior or student standby deals. These "concessions" (discounted tickets) are indicated with a "conc" or "s" in the listings. Picking up a late return can get you a great seat at a cheap-seat price. If a show is "sold out," there's usually a way to get a seat. Call the theater box office and ask how.

If you don't care where you sit, you can often buy the absolutely cheapest seats—those with an obstructed view or in the nosebleed section—at the box office; these tickets generally cost less than £20. Many theaters are so small that there's hardly a bad seat. After the lights go down, scooting up is less than a capital offense. Shakespeare did it.

Half-Price "tkts" Booth: This famous ticket booth at **Leicester** (LESS-ter) **Square** sells discounted tickets for top-price

seats to shows on the push list—but only on the day of the performance (generally £2.50 service charge per ticket, Mon–Sat 10:00–19:00, Sun 12:00–15:00, matinee tickets from noon, lines often form early, list of shows available online at www.tkts .co.uk). Most tickets are half-price; other shows are discounted 25 percent. Note that the real half-price booth (with its "tkts" name) is a freestanding kiosk at the edge of the garden in Leicester Square. Several dishonest outfits nearby advertise "official half-price tickets"— avoid these.

Here are sample prices: A top-notch seat to *Chicago* costs £59 if you buy directly from the theater; the same seat costs £32.50 at Leicester Square. The cheapest balcony seat is £20 through the theater. Half-price tickets can be a good deal, unless you want the cheapest seats or the hottest shows. But check the board;

ENTERTAINMENT

occasionally they sell cheap tickets to good shows. For example, a first-class seat to the long-running *Les Misérables* (which rarely sells out) costs £52.50 when you go through the theater ticket office, but you'll pay £30.50 at the tkts booth.

West End Theaters: The commercial (nonsubsidized) theaters cluster around Soho (especially along Shaftesbury Avenue) and Covent Garden. With a centuries-old tradition of pleasing the masses, these present London theater at its glitziest. See the "What's On in the West End" sidebar.

Royal Shakespeare Company: If you'll ever enjoy Shakespeare, it'll be in Britain. The RSC performs at various theaters around London and in Stratford year-round. To get a schedule, contact the RSC (Royal Shakespeare Theatre, Stratford-upon-Avon, tel. 01789/403-444, www.rsc.org.uk).

Shakespeare's Globe: To see Shakespeare in a replica of the theater for which he wrote his plays, attend a play at the Globe. In this round, thatch-roofed, open-air theater the plays are performed much as Shakespeare intended—under the sky with no amplification.

The play's the thing from late April through October (usually Mon 19:30, Tue–Sat 14:00 and 19:30, Sun either 13:00 and/or 18:30, tickets can be sold out months in advance). You'll pay £5 to stand and £15–33 to sit, usually on a backless bench. Because only a few rows and the pricier Gentlemen's Rooms have seats with backs, £1 cushions and £3 add-on back rests are considered a good investment by many. Dress for the weather. The £5 "groundling" tickets—which are open to rain—are most fun. Scurry in early to stake out a spot on the stage's edge, where the most interaction with the actors occurs. You're a crude peasant. You can lean your elbows on the stage, munch a picnic dinner (yes, you can bring in food), or walk around. I've never enjoyed Shakespeare as much as here, performed as it was meant to be in the "wooden O." If you can't get a ticket, consider waiting around. Plays can be long, and many groundlings leave before the end. Hang around outside and beg or buy a ticket from someone leaving early (groundlings are allowed to come and go).

For information on plays or £10.50 tours of the theater and museum (see page 76), contact the theater (tel. 020/7902-1400 or 020/7902-1500, www.shakespeares-globe.org). To reserve tickets for plays, call or drop by the theater box office (Mon–Sat 10:00–18:00, Sun 10:00–17:00, stays open one hour later on performance days, New Globe Walk entrance, tel. 020/7401-9919). You can also reserve online (£2 booking fee per transaction). A few non-Shakespeare plays are also presented each year.

The theater is on the South Bank, directly across the Thames

ENTERTAINMENT

over the Millennium Bridge from St. Paul's Cathedral (Tube: Mansion House or London Bridge). The Globe is inconvenient for public transport, but the courtesy phone in the lobby lets you get a minicab in minutes. (These minicabs have set fees—e.g., £8 to South Kensington—but generally cost less than a metered cab and provide fine and honest service.) During theater season, there's a regular supply of black cabs outside the main foyer on New Globe Walk.

Outdoor Theater in Summer: Enjoy Shakespearean drama and other plays under the stars at the **Open Air Theatre,** in leafy Regent's Park in north London. Food is allowed: You can bring your own picnic; order à la carte from the theater menu; or pre-order a £22.50 picnic supper from the theater at least one week in advance (tickets £10–50; season runs late May–mid-Sept, box office open April–late May Mon–Sat 10:00–18:00, closed Sun; late May–mid-Sept Mon–Sat 10:00–20:00, Sun 10:00–until start of play on performance days only; order tickets online after mid-Jan or by phone Mon–Sun 9:00–21:00; £1 booking fee by phone, no fee if ordering online or in person; toll tel. 0844-826-4242, www.openairtheatre.org; grounds open 1.5 hours prior to evening performances, one hour prior to 2:30 matinee, and 30 min prior to earlier matinees; 10-min walk north of Baker Street Tube, near Queen Mary's Gardens within Regent's Park; detailed directions and more info at www.openairtheatre.org).

Fringe Theater: London's rougher evening-entertainment scene is thriving, filling pages in *Time Out*. Choose from a wide range of fringe theater and comedy acts (generally £5).

Classical Music
Concerts at Churches
For easy, cheap, or free concerts in historic churches, check the TIs' listings for **lunch concerts,** especially:
- St. Bride's Church, with free lunch concerts twice a week at 13:15 (generally Tue, Wed, or Fri—confirm by phone or online, church tel. 020/7427-0133, www.stbrides.com).
- St. James's at Piccadilly, with 50-minute concerts on Monday, Wednesday, and Friday at 13:10 (suggested £3 donation, info tel. 020/7381-0441, www.st-james-piccadilly.org).
- St. Martin-in-the-Fields, offering free concerts on Monday, Tuesday, and Friday at 13:00 (suggested £3.50 donation, church tel. 020/7766-1100, www.smitf.org).

St. Martin-in-the-Fields also hosts fine **evening concerts** by candlelight (£6–25, at 19:30 Thu–Sat, sometimes Tue) and live jazz in its underground Café in the Crypt (£5–8 tickets, Wed at 20:00).

Evensong and Organ Recitals at Churches

Evensong services are held at several churches, including:

- St. Paul's Cathedral (Mon–Sat at 17:00, Sun at 15:15).
- Westminster Abbey (Mon–Tue and Thu–Fri at 17:00, Sat–Sun at 15:00; there's a service on Wed, but it's spoken, not sung).
- Southwark Cathedral (Mon–Tue and Thu–Fri at 17:30, Sat at 16:00, Sun at 15:00, no service on Wed or alternate Mon, tel. 020/7367-6700, www.southwark.anglican.org/cathedral).
- St. Bride's Church (Sun at 18:30, tel. 020/7427-0133, www.stbrides.com).

Free **organ recitals** are often held on Sunday at 17:45 in Westminster Abbey (30 min, tel. 020/7222-5152). Many other churches have free concerts; ask for the *London Organ Concerts Guide* at the TI.

Prom Concerts and Opera

For a fun classical event (mid-July–mid-Sept), attend a **Prom Concert** (shortened from "Promenade Concert") during the annual festival at the Royal Albert Hall. Nightly concerts are offered at give-a-peasant-some-culture prices to "Promenaders"—those willing to stand throughout the performance (£5 standing-room spots sold at the door, £7 restricted-view seats, most £22–30 but depends on performance, Tube: South Kensington, tel. 020/7589-8212, www.bbc.co.uk/proms).

Some of the world's best **opera** is belted out at the prestigious Royal Opera House, near Covent Garden (box office tel. 020/7304-4000, www.roh.org.uk), and at the less-formal Sadler's Wells Theatre (Rosebery Avenue, Islington, Tube: Angel, info tel. 020/7863-8198, box office toll tel. 0844-412-4300, www.sadlerswells.com).

Evening Museum Visits

Many museums are open an evening or two during the week, offering fewer crowds. See a list on page 64.

Tours

Guided **walks** are offered several times a day. **London Walks** is the most established company. Daytime walks vary by theme: ancient London, museums, legal London, Dickens, Beatles, Jewish quarter, Christopher Wren, and so on. In the evening, expect a more limited choice: ghosts, Jack the Ripper, pubs, or literary themed. Get the latest from their brochure or website, or call for a recorded listing of that day's walks. Show up at the listed time and place, pay the guide, and enjoy the two-hour tour (£7, cash only, tel. 020/7624-3978, recorded info 020/7624-9255, www.walks.com).

ENTERTAINMENT

To see the city illuminated at night, consider a **bus** tour. A two-hour **London by Night Sightseeing Tour** leaves every evening from Victoria Station and other points (see page 36).

Summer Evenings Along the South Bank

If you're visiting London in summer, consider the South Bank.

Take a trip around the **London Eye** while the sun sets over the city (the wheel spins until 21:00). Then cap your night with an evening walk along the pedestrian-only **Jubilee Walkway,** which runs east–west along the river. It's where Londoners go to escape the heat. This pleasant stretch of the walkway—lined with pubs and casual eateries—goes from the London Eye past Shakespeare's Globe to Tower Bridge (you can walk in either direction; see www.jubileewalkway.com for maps and Tube stops).

If you're in the mood for a movie, take in a flick at the **BFI Southbank,** located just across the river, alongside Waterloo Bridge. Run by the British Film Institute, the state-of-the-art theater shows mostly classic films, as well as art cinema (£8.60, £5 on Tue, Tube: Waterloo or Embankment, box office tel. 020/7928-3232, check www.bfi.org.uk for schedules).

Farther east along the South Bank is **The Scoop**—an outdoor amphitheater next to City Hall. It's a good spot for outdoor movies, concerts, dance, and theater productions throughout the summer—with Tower Bridge as a scenic backdrop. These events are free, nearly nightly, and family-friendly. For the latest event schedule, see www.morelondon.com and click on "The Scoop" (next to City Hall, Riverside, The Queen's Walkway, Tube: London Bridge).

Cruises

During the summer, boats sail as late as 21:00 between Westminster Pier (near Big Ben) and the Tower of London. (For details, see page 39.)

A handful of outfits run Thames River evening cruises with four-course meals and dancing. **London Showboat** offers the best value (£75, April–Oct Wed–Sun, Nov–March Fri–Sat, 3.5 hours, departs at 19:00 from Westminster Pier and returns by 22:30, reservations necessary, tel. 020/7740-0400, www.citycruises.com). Dinner cruises are also offered by **Bateaux London** (£65–120, tel. 020/7695-1800, www.bateauxlondon.com). For more on cruising, get the *River Thames Boat Services* brochure from a London TI.

Winter Diversions

London dazzles year-round, so consider visiting in winter, when airfares and hotel rates are generally cheaper and there are fewer tourists. Despite drearier weather and shorter days, London's museums, theaters, concert halls, and pubs offer a warm, cozy welcome.

London at Christmas is especially appealing, with its buildings dressed in their holiday best. Many holiday traditions have their roots in 19th-century Victorian Britain. Beginning in the 1840s, Queen Victoria's German husband, Prince Albert, popularized the decorating of Christmas trees and the sending of Christmas cards. And what could be more traditional than seeing the setting of Charles Dickens' *A Christmas Carol* come to life? God bless us, every one.

November to January

Pantomimes, or "pantos," are a British holiday tradition. Though they have nothing to do with silent mimes—and they don't mention Christmas—these campy fairy-tale plays entertain with outrageous costumes, sets, and dance numbers. Verbal participation is definitely encouraged and it doesn't take long to learn the lines. Adults will laugh at the more risqué jokes; kids will giggle at the slapstick. Two London theaters that usually stage pantos are the Hackney Empire (northeast London, Tube: Bethnal Green, then 10 min on #106 or #254 bus, tel. 020/8985-2424, www.hackney empire.co.uk) or the Old Vic (southeast of Waterloo Station, Tube: Waterloo, toll tel. 0870-060-6628, www.oldvictheatre.com). For a rundown of all theater events, see www.timeout.com or www .officiallondontheatre.co.uk. For more about pantos and their traditions, see www.its-behind-you.com.

Get some exercise at the **outdoor ice rinks** at Somerset House, Tower of London, Natural History Museum, Hampton Court Palace, and Kew Gardens, among others (£10–15/session, includes skates, generally mid-Nov–mid-Jan 10:00–22:00, can be smart to drop in ahead of time to make reservations).

The **Hyde Park Winter Wonderland** offers kitschy carnival fun with a Ferris wheel, carousel, and other rides, as well as an ice rink and vendors selling silly hats and plenty of food and drink (free entry, rides £2–10, late Nov–early Jan, southeast corner of park, Tube: Hyde Park Corner, www.hydeparkwinterwonder land.com).

Stroll around and enjoy the elaborate **light displays** and store windows on major shopping streets from mid-November to early January, especially on Oxford Street, Bond Street, Regent Street, and Brompton Road. Post-holiday sales start December 26 for many stores; the famous Harrods winter sale begins a day or two later.

The Trafalgar Square **Christmas tree** is given to London every year from the people of Oslo, Norway, in appreciation for British help during World War II (lighting ceremony first Thu in

ENTERTAINMENT

Christmas Travel Strategies

- If arriving on Christmas Day, arrange transport from the airport in advance. Try **Dot2Dot** door-to-door shuttle vans (£19 one-way, Heathrow and Gatwick only, toll tel. 0845-368-2368, www.dot2.com).
- Pick a central location if staying over December 25. There is no public transit (Tube, train, or buses) at all on Christmas Day, and reduced services on Christmas Eve and Boxing Day (Dec 26). For specifics, see www.tfl.gov.uk. Taxis are scarce, so be prepared for a long wait (£4 holiday surcharge, toll tel. 0871-871-8710). Better yet, bundle up and walk.
- To save money and avoid transportation difficulties, stay someplace with a kitchen (such as an apartment, hostel, or hotel room with kitchenette) so you can prepare some of your own meals. Don't forget to buy groceries before stores close on Christmas Eve. For tips on finding apartment rentals, see the "Sleeping" chapter.
- If you plan to eat out December 24–26 without reservations, go ethnic: Indian, Chinese, and Middle Eastern restaurants are usually open in Soho, Chinatown, along Edgware Road, or near the East End's Brick Lane.

Dec, stays up until Jan 6, www.london.gov.uk). Free carol concerts are also held beneath the tree in December.

The **Geffrye Museum's** 12 historic rooms are decorated for Christmas every year, highlighting holiday customs from the 17th century to today (free, see page 71).

Take in a seasonal concert at the grand red-velvet-draped **Royal Albert Hall;** ask about "carols by candlelight" events (tickets as cheap as £12, Tube: South Kensington, box office tel. 020/7589-8212, www.royalalberthall.com).

Instead of visiting Santa Claus at the North Pole, British children see **Father Christmas** in his grotto. In London, the poshest Santas are at Harrods and Selfridges, and it may be worth reserving in advance to avoid long lines (late Nov–Christmas Eve, reservation fee about £2, photos-£10–15; Harrods, Tube: Knightsbridge, tel. 020/7730-1234; Selfridges, Tube: Bond Street or Marble Arch, toll tel. 0845-122-2522).

Nibble your way through **Borough Market**, where you'll find lots of seasonal and gourmet treats (Thu 11:00–17:00, Fri 12:00–18:00, Sat 9:00–16:00; closed Sun–Wed except open daily week before Christmas, closed Dec 25–26; south of London Bridge, where Southwark Street meets Borough High Street; Tube: London Bridge, tel. 020/7404-1002, www.boroughmarket.org .uk). While at the market, be sure and sample traditional favorites

ENTERTAINMENT

such as mulled wine, mince pie, Christmas cake, and Christmas pudding (see page 243).

Don't forget to pick up some **Christmas crackers** to give your holiday meals some extra bang. Not to be confused with something you eat, these fun party favors contain a paper crown, a teeny gift, and a corny joke. Buy them at grocery or department stores, find a friend, and pull hard.

Another popular holiday food event is the German **Cologne Market,** on the South Bank between the London Eye and the Royal Festival Hall (late Nov–late Dec, daily 10:00–22:00, Tube: Waterloo, www.christmasmarkets.com).

Christmas Day

Spending December 25 in London? While almost everything is closed, and there is no public transport, there are still a few options for getting out.

Popular **church services** are held both Christmas Eve and Christmas Day at Westminster Abbey, Westminster Cathedral, St. Paul's, and St. Martin-in-the-Fields, among others. Warning: These draw large crowds, so ask in advance about when to arrive. (For example, you may need to wait in line several hours for the Abbey's 16:00 service on Christmas Eve.)

The Peter Pan Cup **swim race,** held in Hyde Park every Christmas morning since 1864, is named in honor of *Peter Pan* playwright J. M. Barrie, who presented the first cup. You must be a member of the local swimming club to compete, but spectators are welcome (9:00, south side of The Serpentine—a lake in the center of the park). Break the ice by asking a local where to find the nearby Peter Pan statue.

London Walks offers two guided **walking tours** on December 25, with appropriate themes such as "Christmas Morning 1660" and "Charles Dickens' *A Christmas Carol*" (£7, 11:00 & 14:00, meet at Trafalgar Square Christmas tree, tel. 020/7624-3978 or recorded info tel. 020/7624-9255, www.walks.com).

Watch the Queen's annual **Christmas message** on the BBC at 15:00. If you miss it, you can watch it online on Her Majesty's Royal YouTube channel (www.youtube.com).

If your visit extends through the **New Year,** here are two events to be aware of: New Year's Eve **fireworks** from the London Eye attract at least 400,000 revelers to Trafalgar Square and the nearby riverbank, with good viewing spots staked out hours in advance. Public transport is free after the festivities (generally 23:45–04:00). The next day, a **parade** featuring 10,000 performers snakes from Big Ben to Piccadilly Circus (free, grandstand seats-£16, 12:00–15:00, www.londonparade.co.uk).

CONNECTIONS

Airports

Phone numbers and websites for London's airports and major airlines are listed in the appendix. For accommodations at or near the major airports, see page 312.

Heathrow Airport

Heathrow Airport is one of the world's busiest airports. Think about it: 68 million passengers a year on 470,000 flights from 180

destinations riding 90 airlines, like some kind of global maypole dance. Read signs, ask questions. For Heathrow's airport, flight, and transfer information, call the switchboard at 0870-000-0123 (www.heathrowairport.com).

Heathrow has five terminals: T-1 (mostly domestic and Irish flights, with some European); T-2 (mainly European flights; may close in 2010 for renovation), T-3 (flights from North and South America and Asia); T-4 (European and US flights; ongoing renovation may shuffle airlines); and T-5 (British Airways flights only). To travel between terminals, you can take the Heathrow Express and Connect trains (free), buses (free), or the Tube (requires a ticket).

It's critical to confirm which terminal your flight will use (check your plane ticket or call your airline in advance), because if it's T-4 or T-5, you'll need to allow extra time. Taxi drivers generally know which terminal you'll need, but bus drivers may not. If you're

London Airports

taking the Tube to the airport, note that some Piccadilly Line sub-way cars post which airlines are served by which terminals.

Each terminal has an airport information desk (generally daily 6:00–22:00), car-rental agencies, exchange bureaus, ATMs, a pharmacy, a **VAT refund desk** (tel. 020/8910-3682; you must present the VAT claim form from the retailer here to get your tax rebate on items purchased in Britain—see page 12 for details), and **baggage storage** (£8/item for 24 hours, hours vary by terminal but generally daily 5:30–23:00, www.left-baggage.co.uk). Get online 24 hours a day at Heathrow's **Internet access points** (at each terminal—T-4's is up on the mezzanine level) and with a laptop at pay-as-you-go wireless "hotspots"—including many hosted by T-Mobile—in its departure lounges. There's a **post office** on the first floor of T-2. Each terminal has cheap **eateries**.

Heathrow's small **"TI"** (tourist info shop), even though it's a for-profit business, is worth a visit to pick up free informa-tion: a simple map, the *London Planner,* and brochures (daily 6:30–22:00, 5-min walk from T-3 in Tube station, follow signs to Underground; bypass queue for transit info to reach window for London questions).

Getting to London from Heathrow Airport

You have several options for traveling the 14 miles between Heathrow Airport and downtown London. For one person on a budget, the Tube or bus is cheap but slow. To speed things up, though you'll spend a little more, combining the Heathrow Connect train with either a Tube or taxi ride (between Paddington

Station and your hotel) is nearly as fast and less than half the cost of taking a cab the whole way. For groups of four or more, a taxi is faster and easier, as well as cheaper. Some options are better than others for a specific terminal.

By Tube (Subway): For £4, the Tube takes you from any terminal to downtown London in 50–60 minutes on the Piccadilly  Line (6/hr; depending on your destination, may require a transfer, buy ticket at the Tube station ticket window). Note that if you arrive at Terminal 4, you need to take the free Heathrow Connect train to the Heathrow Central terminal (from Terminal 5, take the free Heathrow Express train), which can add 20 minutes to your trip (especially critical if your return plans involve getting back to these terminals). If you plan to use the Tube for transport in London, it may make sense to buy a Travelcard (Zones 1–6) or Oyster card at the Tube station ticket window at the airport. For information on these passes, see page 26.

If you're taking the Tube from downtown London to the airport, note that the Piccadilly Line trains don't stop at every terminal on every run. Trains either go to T-4, T-1, T-2, and T-3 (in that order); or T-1, T-2, T-3, and T-5 (so allow extra time if going to T-4 or T-5). Check before you board.

By Bus: Most buses depart from the outside common area called the Central Bus Station. It serves T-1, T-2, and T-3, and is a 5-minute walk from any of these terminals. To get to T-4 or T-5 from the Central Bus Station, go inside, downstairs, and follow signs to take the Tube to your terminal (free, but only runs every 15–20 min to those terminals).

National Express has regular service from Heathrow's Central Bus Station to Victoria Coach Station in downtown London, near several of my recommended hotels. While slow, the bus is affordable and convenient for those staying near Victoria Station (£4, 1–3/hr, 45–75 min, toll tel. 0871-781-8181, calls are 10p/min, www.nationalexpress.com).

Dot2Dot runs a door-to-door transfer shuttle from Heathrow directly to hotels in central London, with no more than four stops per trip (16/hr, £20 one-way, £38 round-trip, reservation required, toll tel. 0845-368-2368, www.dot2.com).

By Train: Two different trains run between Heathrow Airport and London's Paddington Station. At Paddington Station, you're in the thick of the Tube system, with easy access to any of my recommended neighborhoods—Notting Hill Gate is just two Tube stops away. The **Heathrow Connect** train is the slightly slower, much cheaper option serving T-1, T-2, T-3, and T-4; you can get to T-5 if you transfer at T-1, T-2, or T-3 (£6.90 one-way, 2/hr, 25–28 min, toll tel. 0845-678-6975, www.heathrowconnect.com). The **Heathrow Express** train is fast (15 min to downtown from T-1, T-2, and T-3; 21 min from T-5; not good for T4) and runs more frequently (4/hr), but it's pricey (£16.50 "express class" one-way, £32 round-trip, ask about discount promos at ticket desk, kids under 16 ride half-price, under 5 ride free, buy ticket before you board or pay a £3 surcharge to buy it on the train, covered by BritRail pass, daily 5:10–23:25, toll tel. 0845-600-1515, www.heathrowexpress .co.uk). At the airport, you can use either the Heathrow Express or Heathrow Connect as a free transfer between terminals.

By Taxi: Taxis from the airport cost about £45–70 to west and central London (one hour). For four people traveling together, this can be a deal. Hotels can often line up a cab back to the airport for about £30–40. For the cheapest taxi to the airport, don't order one from your hotel. Simply flag down a few and ask them for their best "off-meter" rate.

Getting to Bath from Heathrow Airport

By Bus: Direct buses run daily from Heathrow to Bath (£19, 10/day direct, 2–3 hrs, more frequent but slower with transfer in London, toll tel. 0871-781-8181, 10p/min, www.nationalexpress.com). BritRail passholders may prefer the 2.5-hour Heathrow–Bath bus/ train connection via Reading (BritRail passholders just pay £15 for bus; otherwise £50–65 depending on time of day, about £10 cheaper when bought in advance; tel. 0118-957-9425, buy bus ticket from www.railair.com, train ticket from www.firstgreatwestern .co.uk). First catch the RailAir Link shuttle bus (2/hr, 45 min) to Reading (RED-ding), then hop on the express train (2/hr, 60 min) to Bath. Factoring in the connection in Reading—which can add at least an hour to the trip—the train is a less convenient option than the direct bus to Bath.

Gatwick Airport

More and more flights land at Gatwick Airport, halfway between London and the South Coast (recorded airport info toll tel. 0870-000-2468).

Getting to London: Gatwick Express trains—clearly the best way into London from here—shuttle conveniently between Gatwick and London's Victoria Station (£16.90, £28.80 round-trip, 4/hr, 30 min, runs 5:00–24:00 daily, purchase tickets on train at no extra charge, toll tel. 0845-850-1530, www.gatwickexpress.com). If you're traveling with two or three other adults, buy your tickets at the station before boarding, and you'll travel for the price of two. The only restriction on this impressive deal is that you have to travel together. So if you see another couple in line, get organized and save 50 percent.

You can save a few pounds by taking Southern Railway's slower and less frequent shuttle between Gatwick's South Terminal and Victoria Station (£10.90, up to 4/hr, 45 min, toll tel. 0845-127-2920, www.southernrailway.com). A train also runs from Gatwick to St. Pancras International Station (£8.90, 8/hr, 60 min, www.firstcapitalconnect.co.uk), useful for travelers taking the Eurostar train (to Paris or Brussels) or staying in the St. Pancras/King's Cross neighborhood.

Getting to Bath: To get to Bath from Gatwick, you can catch a bus to Heathrow and take the bus to Bath from there (10/day, 4–5 hrs, £25 one-way, transfer at Heathrow Airport, www.national express.com—see above). By train, the best Gatwick–Bath connection involves a transfer in Reading (£45–60 one-way depending on time of day, £23 in advance, hourly, 2.5 hrs, www.firstgreat western.co.uk; avoid transfer in London, where you'll have to change stations).

London's Other Airports

Stansted Airport: If you're using Stansted (airport toll tel. 0870-0000-303, www.stanstedairport.com), you have several options for getting into or out of London. The National Express bus runs between the airport and downtown London's Victoria Coach Station (£8, £17 round-trip, 2–3/hr, 1.5 hrs, runs 24 hours a day, picks up and stops throughout London, toll tel. 0871-781-8181, calls are 10p/min, www.nationalexpress.com). Or you can take the faster, pricier Stansted Express train (£18 one-way, £26.80 round-trip, connects to London's Tube system at Tottenham Hale and Liverpool Street, 4/hr, 45 min, 5:00–23:00, toll tel. 0845-850-0150, www.stanstedexpress.com). Stansted is expensive by cab; figure £99 one-way from central London.

Luton Airport: For Luton (airport tel. 01582/405-100, www.london-luton.co.uk), there are two choices into or out of London. The fastest way to go is by rail to London's St. Pancras International Station (£11.50 one-way, 1–5/hr, 25–45 min, check schedule to avoid the slower trains, toll tel. 0845-712-5678, www.eastmidlandstrains.co.uk); catch the 10-minute shuttle bus (£1) from outside the terminal to the Luton Airport Parkway train station. The Green Line express bus #757 runs to London's Victoria Station (£13 one-way, £14.50 round-trip, small discount for easyJet passengers who buy online, 2–4/hr, 1.25–1.5 hrs, 24 hours a day, toll tel. 0844-801-7261, www.greenline.co.uk). If you're sleeping at Luton, consider easyHotel (see listing on page 305).

London City Airport: There's a slim chance you might use

London City Airport (tel. 020/7646-0088, www.londoncityair
port.com). To get into London, take the Docklands Light Railway
(DLR) to the Bank Tube station, which is one stop east of St.
Paul's on the Central Line (£4 one-way, covered by Travelcard,
£2.20–2.70 on Oyster card, 22 min, tel. 020/7222-1234, www.tfl
.gov.uk/dlr).

Connecting London's Airports by Bus

More and more travelers are taking advantage of cheap flights out
of London's smaller airports. The handy **National Express bus**
runs between Heathrow, Gatwick, Stansted, and Luton airports—
easier than having to cut through the center of London—although
traffic can be bad and increase travel times (toll tel. 0871-781-8181,
calls are 10p/min, www.nationalexpress.com).

From **Heathrow Airport** to: **Gatwick Airport** (1–4/hr,
1.25–1.5 hrs, £19.50 one-way, £36.50 round-trip, allow at least
three hours between flights), **Stansted Airport** (1–2/hr, 1.5–1.75
hrs, £22.50 one-way, £29.30 round-trip), **Luton Airport** (hourly,
1–1.5 hrs, £19.90 one-way, £24.50 round-trip).

Discounted Flights from London

London is the hub for many cheap, no-frills airlines, which affordably connect the city with other destinations in the British Isles
and throughout Europe. Although bmi has been around the longest, the other small airlines generally offer cheaper flights. A visit
to www.skyscanner.net, www.mobissimo.com, www.kayak.com,
or www.wegolo.com sorts the numerous options offered by the
many discount airlines, enabling you to see the best schedules for
your trip and find the best deal.

Be aware of the potential drawbacks of flying on the cheap:
nonrefundable and nonchangeable tickets, rigid baggage restrictions (and fees if you have more than what's officially allowed),
use of airports far outside town, tight schedules that can mean
more delays, little in the way of customer assistance if problems
arise, and, of course, no frills. To avoid unpleasant surprises, read
the small print—especially baggage policies—before you book. If
you're traveling with lots of bags, a cheap flight can quickly become
a bad deal, due to per-piece baggage fees.

With **bmi,** you can fly inexpensively from London to destinations in the UK and beyond (fares start at about £45 one-way to
Edinburgh, Dublin, Brussels, or Amsterdam). Call toll tel. 0870-
607-0555 or US tel. 800-788-0555 or check www.flybmi.com.
Book in advance. Although you can book right up until the flight
departs, the cheap seats will have sold out long before, leaving the
most expensive seats for latecomers.

Another low-cost airline, **easyJet** flies from Gatwick, Luton, and Stansted. Prices are based on demand, so the least popular routes make for the cheapest fares, especially if you book early (toll tel. 0905-821-0905, calls are 65p/min, www.easyjet.com).

Ryanair flies from London (mostly Stansted airport, though also Gatwick and Luton) to often obscure airports near Dublin, Glasgow, Frankfurt, Stockholm, Oslo, Venice, Turin, and many others. Sample fares: London–Dublin—£50 round-trip (sometimes as low as £30), London–Frankfurt—£45 round-trip (Irish toll tel. 0818-303-030, British toll tel. 0871-246-0000, calls are 10p/min, www.ryanair.com). However, be warned that Ryanair charges additional fees for nearly everything. They require a mandatory online-only check-in (£5 charge) from 15 days to four hours before your flight (no airport check-in). When checking in, you must also print out your boarding pass; if you show up at the airport without it, there's an additional £40 charge. You can carry on only a small day bag; you'll pay a fee for each checked bag (price depends on number of bags; up to three bags allowed per passenger).

Brussels Airlines is a Brussels-based company with good rates (www.brusselsairlines.com). Brussels Airlines flies from Heathrow or Gatwick. From its hub in Brussels, you can connect cheaply to many cities in Europe.

Trains and Buses

Britain is covered by a myriad of rail systems (owned by different companies), which together are called National Rail. London, the country's major transportation hub, has a different train station for each region. There are nine main stations (see the routes map on next page:

Euston—Serves northwest England, North Wales, and Scotland.

King's Cross—Serves northeast England and Scotland, including York and Edinburgh.

Liverpool Street—Serves east England, including Essex and Harwich.

London Bridge—Serves south England, including Brighton.

Marylebone—Serves southwest and central England, including Stratford-upon-Avon.

Paddington—Serves south and southwest England including Heathrow Airport, Windsor, Bath, South Wales, and the Cotswolds.

St. Pancras International—Serves north and south England, plus Eurostar to Paris or Brussels (see "Crossing the Channel" later in this chapter).

Victoria—Serves Gatwick Airport, Canterbury, Dover, and Brighton.

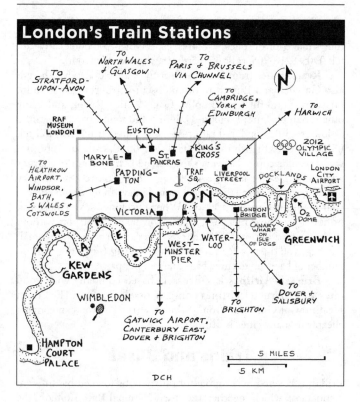

London's Train Stations

Waterloo—Serves southeast England, including Dover and Salisbury.

Any train station has schedule information, can make reservations, and can sell tickets for any destination. Most stations offer a baggage-storage service (£8/bag for 24 hours, look for *left luggage* signs); because of long security lines, it can take a while to check or pick up your bag (www.excess-baggage.com). For more details on the services available at each station, see www.nationalrail.co.uk /stations.

Buying Tickets: For general information, call 0845-748-4950 (or visit www.nationalrail.co.uk or www.eurostar.com; £5 booking fee for telephone reservations).

Railpasses: For train travel outside London, consider getting a BritRail pass. Options include passes that cover England as well as Scotland and Wales, England-only passes, England/ Ireland passes, "London Plus" passes (good for travel in most of southeast England but not in London itself), and BritRail & Drive passes (which offer you some rail days and some car-rental days). For specifics, contact your travel agent or see www.ricksteves.com /rail.

CONNECTIONS

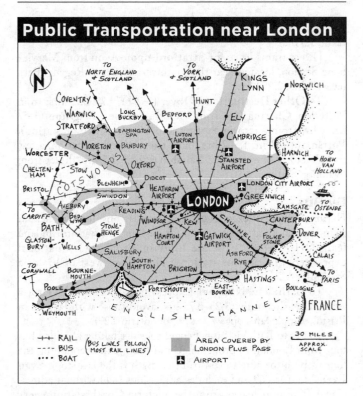

Public Transportation near London

By Train
To Points West
From Paddington Station to: Bath (2/hr, 1.5 hrs; also consider a guided Evan Evans tour by bus—see page 372); **Oxford** (2–5/hr, 1 hr, possible transfer in Reading), **Penzance** (every 1–2 hours, 5–5.75 hrs, possible change in Plymouth), and **Cardiff** (2/hr, 2 hrs).

To Points North
From King's Cross Station: Trains run at least hourly, stopping in **York** (2 hrs), **Durham** (3 hrs), and **Edinburgh** (4.5 hrs). Trains to **Cambridge** also leave from here (2/hr, 1 hr).

    From Euston Station to: Conwy (nearly hourly, 3.25–4 hrs, transfer in Chester or Crewe), **Liverpool** (hourly, 2 hrs, more with transfer), **Blackpool** (hourly, 3 hrs, transfer at Preston), **Keswick** (hourly, 4.5 hrs, transfer to bus at Penrith), **Glasgow** (1–2/hr, 4.5–5 hrs direct, some may leave from King's Cross Station).

From London's Other Stations
Trains run between London and **Canterbury,** leaving from Charing Cross Station and arriving in Canterbury West, as well

as from London's Victoria Station and arriving in Canterbury East (2/hr, 1.5 hrs).

Direct trains leave for **Stratford-upon-Avon** from Marylebone Station, located near the southwest corner of Regents Park (every 2 hrs, 2.25 hrs).

To Other Destinations: Dover (1–2/hr, 1.75–2.25 hrs; from Waterloo, Charing Cross, or Victoria Station), **Brighton** (4–5/hr, 1 hr, from Victoria Station and London Bridge Station), **Portsmouth** (3/hr, 1.5–2 hrs, most from Waterloo Station, a few from Victoria Station), and **Salisbury** (2/hr, 1.5 hrs, direct from Waterloo Station).

By Bus

National Express' excellent bus service is considerably cheaper than the train and a fine option for destinations within England (call 0871-781-8181, calls are 10p/min; or visit www.national express.com or the bus station a block southwest of Victoria Station).

To Bath: The National Express bus leaves from Victoria Station nearly hourly (3.25–3.75 hrs, avoid those with layover in Bristol, sample fares one-way-£19, round-trip-£29).

To get to Bath via Stonehenge, consider taking a guided bus tour from London to Stonehenge and Bath, and abandoning the tour in Bath (be sure to confirm that Bath is the last stop). **Evan Evans'** tour is £69 and includes admissions (£44 without admissions). The tour leaves from the Victoria Coach station every morning at 8:45 (you can stow your bag under the bus), stops in Stonehenge (45 min), and then stops in Bath for lunch and a city tour before returning to London (offered year-round). You can book the tour at the Victoria Coach station or the Evan Evans office (258 Vauxhall Bridge Road, near Victoria Coach station, tel. 020/7950-1777, US tel. 866-382-6868, www.evanevans.co.uk, reservations @evanevanstours.co.uk). **Golden Tours** also runs a Stonehenge–Bath tour (£59, £39 without admissions, check website for seasonal tour days; departs from Fountain Square, located across from Victoria Coach Station, US tel. 800-548-7083, toll tel. 0844-880-6981, www.goldentours.co.uk, reservations@goldentours.co.uk).

To Other Destinations: Oxford (2–4/hr, 1.75–2.25 hrs), **Cambridge** (about hourly, 2–2.5 hrs), **Canterbury** (about hourly, 2–2.5 hrs), **Dover** (about hourly, 2.5–3.25 hrs), **Penzance** (6/day, 9 hrs, overnight available), **Cardiff** (every 1–2 hrs, 3.25 hrs), **Liverpool** (8/day direct, 5.25–6 hrs, overnight available), **Blackpool** (4/day direct, 6.25–7 hrs, overnight available), **York** (4/day direct, 4.75–5.25 hrs), **Durham** (4/day direct, 6–7.5 hrs), **Glasgow** (2/day direct, 8–9 hrs, train is a much better option), **Edinburgh** (2/day direct, 8.75–9.75 hrs, go by train instead).

To Dublin, Ireland: The bus/boat journey takes 9–10 hours (£35–43, 3/day, toll tel. 0871-781-8181, calls are 10p/min, www .nationalexpress.com). Consider a cheap 75-minute Ryanair flight instead (www.ryanair.com).

Crossing the Channel

By Eurostar Train

The fastest and most convenient way to get from Big Ben to the Eiffel Tower is by rail. Eurostar, a joint service of the Belgian, British, and French railways, is the speedy passenger train that zips

you (and up to 800 others in 18 sleek cars) from downtown London to downtown Paris or Brussels (15+/day, 2.25–2.5 hrs) faster and more easily than flying. The actual tunnel crossing is a 20–minute, silent, 100-mile-per-hour non-event. Your ears won't even pop. Eurostar's monopoly expires

at the beginning of 2010, and Air France has already announced plans to start a competing high-speed rail service between London and Paris in late autumn 2010.

Eurostar Fares

Channel fares are reasonable but complicated. Prices vary depending on how far ahead you reserve, whether you can live with restrictions, and whether you're eligible for any discounts (children, youths, seniors, roundtrip travelers, and railpass holders all qualify).

Fares can change without notice, but typically a **one-way, full-fare ticket** (with no restrictions on refundability) runs about $425 first-class and $300 second-class). **Cheaper seats** come with more restrictions and can sell out quickly (figure $80–160 for second class, one-way). Those traveling with a railpass that covers France or Britain should look first at the **passholder** fare ($85–130 for second-class, one-way Eurostar trips). For more details, visit www.ricksteves.com/rail/eurostar.htm.

Buying Eurostar Tickets

Because only the most expensive (full-fare) ticket is fully refundable, don't reserve until you're sure of your plans. But if you wait too long, the cheapest tickets will be gone.

Once you're confident about the time and date of your crossing, you can check and book fares by phone or online in the US and pay to have your ticket delivered to you in the US. (Order online at www.ricksteves.com /rail/eurostar.htm, prices listed in dollars; order by phone at US tel. 800-EUROSTAR). Or you can order in Britain (toll tel. 08705-186-186, £5 booking fee by phone, www.eurostar .com, prices listed in pounds).

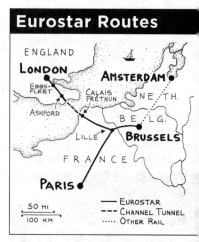

If you buy from a US company, you'll pay for ticket delivery in the US; if you book with the British company, you'll pick up your ticket at the train station. In continental Europe, you can buy your Eurostar ticket at any major train station in any country or at any travel agency that handles train tickets (expect a booking fee). In Britain, tickets can be issued only at the Eurostar office in St. Pancras International Station.

Remember that Britain's time zone is one hour earlier than France or Belgium. Times listed on tickets are local times (departure from London is British time, arrival in Paris in French time).

Departing from London: Eurostar trains depart from and arrive at London's St. Pancras International Station. Check in at least 30 minutes in advance for your Eurostar trip. It's very similar to an airport check-in: You pass through airport-like security, show your passport to customs officials, and find a TV monitor to locate your departure gate. There are a few airport-like shops, newsstands, horrible snack bars, and cafés (bring food for the trip from elsewhere), pay-Internet terminals, and a currency-exchange booth with rates about the same as you'll find on the other end.

Cheap Passage by Tour: A tour company called BritainShrinkers sells one- or two-day tours to Paris, Brussels, or Bruges, enabling you to side-trip to these cities from London for less than most train tickets alone. For example, you'll pay £99 for a one-day Paris "tour" (unescorted Mon–Sat day trip with Métro pass; tel. 207-713-1311 or www.britainshrinkers.com). This can be a particularly good option if you need to get to Paris from London on short notice, when only the costliest fares are available.

Crossing the Channel Without Eurostar

The old-fashioned ways of crossing the Channel are cheaper than Eurostar (taking the bus is cheapest). They're also twice as romantic, complicated, and time-consuming.

Building the Chunnel

The toughest obstacle to building a tunnel under the English Channel was overcome in 1986, when long-time rivals Britain and France reached an agreement to build it together. Britain began in Folkestone, France in Calais, planning a rendezvous in the middle.

By 1988, specially made machines three football fields long were boring 26-foot-wide holes under the ground. The dirt they hauled out became landfill in Britain and a hill in France. Crews crept forward 100 feet a day until June 1991, when French and English workers broke through and shook hands midway across the Channel—the tunnel was complete. Rail service began in 1994.

The Chunnel is 31 miles long (24 miles of it underwater) and 26 feet wide. It sits 130 feet below the seabed in a chalky layer of sediment. It's segmented into three separate tunnels—two for trains (one in each direction) and one for service and ventilation. The walls are concrete panels and rebar fixed to the rock around it. Sixteen-thousand-horsepower engines pull 850 tons of railcars and passengers at speeds up to 100 mph through the tunnel.

The ambitious project—the world's longest undersea tunnel—helped to show the European community that cooperation between nations could benefit everyone.

By Train and Boat

To Paris: You'll take a train from London to the port of Dover, then catch a ferry to Calais, France, before boarding another train for Paris. Trains go from London's Charing Cross, Waterloo, or Victoria stations to **Dover's** Priory station (1–2/hr, 1.75–2.25 hrs; bus or taxi from station to ferry dock). P&O Ferries sail from Dover to Calais; TGV trains run from Calais to Paris. You'll need to book your own train tickets to Dover and from Calais to Paris. The prices listed here are for the ferry only (from £25 one-way or £50 round-trip online, more at dock or by phone, book early for best fares; 22/day, 1.5 hrs, toll tel. 08716-645-645, www.poferries.com).

To Amsterdam: Stena Line's Dutchflyer service combines train and ferry tickets between London and Amsterdam via the ports of **Harwich** and Hoek van Holland. Trains go from London's Liverpool Street station to Harwich (hourly, 1.75 hrs). Stena Line ferries sail from Harwich to Hoek van Holland (7.5 hrs), where you can transfer to a train to Amsterdam or other Dutch cities (ferry—from £32, from £60 with cabin, book at least 2 weeks in advance for best price, 13 hrs total travel time, Dutchflyer toll tel. 0870-545-5455, www.stenaline.co.uk, Dutch train info at www.ns.nl).

For additional European ferry info, visit www.aferry.to. For UK train and bus info, go to www.traveline.org.uk.

By Bus

You can take the bus from London direct to **Paris** (4/day, 8.25–9.75 hrs), **Brussels** (3–4/day, 7.75–9.25 hrs), or **Amsterdam** (4/day, 11.75–12.75 hrs) from Victoria Coach Station (via ferry or Chunnel, day or overnight). Sample prices to Paris for economy fares booked at least two days in advance: £25 one-way, £52 round-trip, book online early for best fares (toll tel. 0871-781-8181, calls are 10p/min; visit www.eurolines.co.uk and look for "funfares").

By Plane

Check with budget airlines for cheap round-trip fares to Paris or Brussels (see "Discounted Flights from London," earlier in this chapter).

DAY TRIPS IN ENGLAND

*Greenwich • Windsor •
Cambridge • Stonehenge • Bath*

Greenwich, Windsor, Cambridge, Stonehenge, and Bath (listed from nearest to farthest) are five of the best day-trip possibilities near London. Greenwich is England's maritime capital, Windsor is home to the Queen and her castle, Cambridge is easily England's best university town, Stonehenge is the world's most famous rock group, and Bath is an elegant spa town dating from Roman times.

Although these five are my top picks, London's convenient public transit can easily whisk you to a wealth of day-trip destinations not covered in this book: Canterbury (cathedral), Dover (castle-crowned chalk cliffs), Portsmouth (treasure trove of maritime history), Stratford-upon-Avon (all things Shakespeare), Warwick (fine medieval castle), Oxford (another classic university town), and Brighton (beach and pier). For details, see *Rick Steves' England*.

Getting Around Southern England

By Bus: Several tour companies take London-based travelers out and back every day. If you're going to Bath and want to stay over-

night, consider taking a day tour to the city, and skipping the trip back to London (for details, see page 372).

By Train: The British rail system uses London as a hub and normally offers same-day round-trip fares that cost virtually the same as one-way fares. For day trips, these "off-peak day return" tickets, available if you depart London outside rush hour (usually after 9:30 on weekdays and anytime

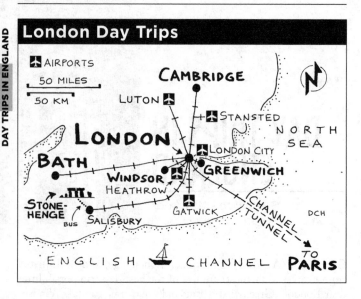

Sat–Sun), are best. You can also save a little money if you purchase tickets before 18:00 the day before your trip.

By Train Tour: London Walks offers a variety of "Explorer Day Tours" year-round by train, with itineraries such as Stonehenge and Salisbury, Oxford and the Cotswolds, Cambridge, and Bath (£12 plus £10–40 for transportation and admissions, cash only, most itineraries run once a week, fewer in winter, pick up their brochure at the TI or hotels, tel. 020/7624-3978, www .walks.com).

Greenwich

Tudor kings favored the palace at Greenwich (GREN-ich). Henry VIII was born here. Later kings commissioned Inigo Jones and Christopher Wren to beautify the town and palace. Yet in spite of Greenwich's architectural and royal treats, this is England's maritime capital, and visitors go for all things salty. While Greenwich's main attraction—the *Cutty Sark* clipper—is closed for restoration through 2010, the town is still worth a visit. It's got the world's most famous observatory, stunning Baroque architecture, appealing markets, a fleet of nautical shops, and hordes of tourists. And where else can you set your watch with such accuracy?

Planning Your Time

Upon arrival, stroll past the *Cutty Sark* dry dock and walk the shoreline promenade. Enjoy a possible lunch or drink in the venerable Trafalgar Tavern, before heading up to the National Maritime Museum and then through the park to the Royal Observatory Greenwich.

Getting to Greenwich

It's a joy by boat, or a snap by Tube.

By Boat: From central London, cruise down the Thames from the piers at Westminster or the Tower of London (2/hr, about one hour; see page 39).

By Tube: Take the Tube to Bank and change to the Docklands Light Railway (DLR), which takes you right to Cutty Sark Station in central Greenwich (one stop before the main—but less central—Greenwich Station, 20 min, all in Zone 2, covered by any Tube pass). Some DLR trains terminate at Island Gardens (from which you can generally catch another train to Greenwich's Cutty Sark Station within a few minutes, though it may be more memorable to get out and walk under the river through the long Thames pedestrian tunnel). Many DLR trains terminate at Canary Wharf, so make sure you get on one that continues to Lewisham or Greenwich.

A fun way to return to London is to ride the DLR back to Canary Wharf and get off there to explore the Docklands area (London's Manhattan, most interesting at the end of the workday, see page 85). When you're done exploring, hop on the speedy Jubilee line and zip back to Westminster in 15 minutes.

By Train: Mainline trains also go from London (Charing Cross, Cannon Street, Waterloo East, and London Bridge stations) several times an hour to Greenwich Station (10-min walk from the sights). Although the train is fast and cheap, the Tube is preferable.

Orientation to Greenwich

(area code: 020)

Covered markets and outdoor stalls make for lively weekends. Save time to browse the town. Wander beyond the touristy Church Street and Greenwich High Road to where flower stands spill onto the side streets, and antique shops sell brass nautical knickknacks. King William Walk, College Approach, Nelson Road, and Turnpin Lane are all worth a look. If you need pub grub, Greenwich has almost 100 pubs, with some boasting that they're mere milliseconds from the prime meridian.

Tourist Information

Until March 2010, the Greenwich TI is located across from Cutty Sark Station at 46 Greenwich Church Street. After that you'll find it back within the Old Royal Naval College, inside the new Discover Greenwich Centre (just east of the closed-for-restoration *Cutty Sark* at 2 Cutty Sark Gardens, Pepys House). Regardless of the location, the hours and phone number are the same (daily 10:00–17:00, toll tel. 0870-608-2000, www.greenwichwhs.org.uk). Guided walks depart from the TI and cover the big sights (£6, daily at 12:15 and 14:15).

Helpful Hints

Markets: Thanks to its markets, Greenwich throbs with day-trippers on weekends. The **Greenwich Market** is an entertaining mini-Covent Garden, located between College Approach and Nelson Road (Wed 11:00–18:00, Thu–Fri 10:00–17:00, Sat–Sun 10:00–17:30, Wed–Fri best for antiques, lots of crafts and food on weekends, tel. 020/7515-7153, www.greenwich market.net). The **Antiques Market** sells old odds and ends at high prices on Greenwich High Road, near the post office (Sat–Sun only 9:30–17:30). The **Village Market** has a little bit of everything—antiques, books, food, and flowers (Sat–Sun only 9:30–17:30, across Nelson Road from the Greenwich Market, enter from Stockwell Street or King William Walk).

Supermarket: If you're picnicking, visit the handy **Marks & Spencer Simply Food** across from the *Cutty Sark* dry dock (Mon–Sat 8:00–21:00, Sun 10:00–21:00, 55 Greenwich Church Street, tel. 020/7228-2545).

Sights in Greenwich

▲▲Cutty Sark—The Scottish-built *Cutty Sark* was the last of the great China tea clippers, and was the queen of the seas when first launched in 1869. With 32,000 square feet of sail, she could blow with the wind 300 miles in a day. The ship is closed for renovation until late 2010—call 020/8858-2698 or check www.cuttysark.org .uk for updates. You may be able to view some of the work through an observation window in the *Cutty Sark* gift shop adjacent to the dry dock (hours vary—call ahead).

Old Royal Naval College—Now that the Royal Navy has moved out, the public is invited to see the college's elaborate Painted Hall and Chapel, grandly designed by Christopher Wren and completed by other architects in the 1700s. You'll also find fine descriptions and an altar painting by American Benjamin West (free, Mon–Sat 10:00–17:00, Sun 12:30–17:00, sometimes closed for private events, choral service Sun at 11:00 in chapel—all are welcome, in the two

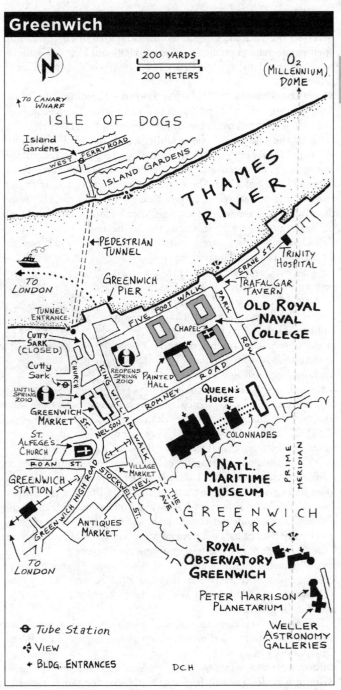

college buildings farthest from river). Guides give 90-minute tours covering the hall and chapel, along with three other places not open to the general public (£5, daily at 11:30 and 14:00, call ahead to check availability, tel. 020/8269-4799, www.oldroyalnaval college.org).

Stroll the Thames to Trafalgar Tavern—From the *Cutty Sark* dry dock, pass the pier and wander east along the Thames on Five Foot Walk (named for the width of the path) for grand views in front of the Old Royal Naval College (see above). Founded by William III as a naval hospital and designed by Wren, the college was split in two because Queen Mary didn't want the view from Queen's House blocked. The riverside view is good, too, with the twin-domed towers of the college (one giving the time, the other the direction of the wind) framing Queen's House, and the Royal Observatory Greenwich crowning the hill beyond.

Continuing downstream, just past the college, you'll see the

Trafalgar Tavern. Dickens knew the pub well, and he used it as the setting for the wedding breakfast in *Our Mutual Friend*. Built in 1837 in the Regency style to attract Londoners downriver, the tavern is popular with Londoners (and tourists) for its fine lunches. The upstairs Nelson Room is still used for weddings. Its formal moldings and elegant windows with balconies over the Thames are a step back in time (food served Mon–Sat 12:00–22:00, Sun 12:00–16:00, elegant ground-floor dining room as well as the more casual pub, Park Row, tel. 020/8858-2909).

From the pub, enjoy views of the former Millennium Dome a mile downstream. The Dome languished for nearly a decade after its controversial construction and brief life as a millennial "world's fair" site. Plans for a casino and hotel project fell through, although it has come in handy as an emergency homeless shelter. It was finally bought by a developer a few years ago and rechristened "The O_2" in honor of the telecommunications company that paid for the naming rights. Currently, it hosts concerts and sporting events, and will see action during the 2012 Summer Olympics. Whatever it's called, locals will no doubt continue to grumble about its original cost.

From the Trafalgar Tavern, you can walk the two long blocks up Park Row, and turn right into the park leading up to the Royal Observatory Greenwich.

Queen's House—This building, the first Palladian-style villa in Britain, was designed in 1616 by Inigo Jones for James I's wife,

Anne of Denmark. All traces of the queen are long gone, and the Great Hall and Royal Apartments now serve as an art gallery for rotating exhibits from the National Maritime Museum. The Orangery is now home to the great J. M. W. Turner painting *Battle of Trafalgar*. His largest (so big that a wall had to be opened to get it in here) and only royal commission, it is surrounded by Christ-like paintings of Admiral Nelson's death (free, daily 10:00–17:00, last entry 30 min before closing, tel. 020/8858-4422, recorded info tel. 020/8312-6565, www.nmm.ac.uk).

▲▲**National Maritime Museum**—Great for anyone remotely interested in the sea, this museum holds everything from a *Titanic*

passenger's pocket watch and Captain Scott's sun goggles (from his 1910 Antarctic expedition) to the uniform Admiral Nelson wore when he was killed at Trafalgar. Under a big glass roof—accompanied by the sound of creaking wooden ships and crashing waves—slick, modern displays depict lighthouse technology, a whaling cannon, and a Greenpeace "survival pod." Kids love the All Hands and Bridge galleries, where they can send secret messages by Morse code and operate a miniature dockside crane.

Note that some parts of the museum, such as the Nelson's Navy gallery, are closed for renovation until 2012 (free, daily 10:00–17:00, last entry 30 min before closing; look for family-oriented events posted at entrance—singing, treasure hunts, storytelling—particularly on weekends; toll tel. 0870-781-5168, www.nmm.ac.uk).

▲▲**Royal Observatory Greenwich**—Located on the prime meridian (0° longitude), the observatory is the point from which all time is measured. However, the observatory's early work had

nothing to do with coordinating the world's clocks to Greenwich Mean Time (GMT). The observatory was founded in 1675 by Charles II to find a way to determine longitude at sea. Today, the Greenwich time signal is linked with the BBC (which broadcasts the famous "pips" worldwide at the top of the hour).

Look above the observatory to see the orange Time Ball, also visible from the Thames, which drops daily at 13:00. (Nearby, outside the courtyard of the observatory, see how your foot measures up to the foot where the public standards of length are cast in bronze.)

In the courtyard, set your wristwatch to the digital clock showing GMT to a tenth of a second, and straddle the prime meridian.

Inside, check out the historic astronomical instruments and camera obscura. In the Time Galleries, see timepieces through the ages, including John Harrison's prizewinning marine chronometers that helped 18th-century sailors calculate longitude (the highlight for fans of Dava Sobel's *Longitude*). The observatory is also home to the state-of-the-art 120-seat Peter Harrison Planetarium, an education center, and the Weller Astronomy Galleries, where interactive displays allow you to guide a space mission and touch a 4.5-billion-year-old meteorite.

Cost and Hours: Free entry to observatory, planetarium shows-£6; observatory open daily 10:00–17:00, last entry 30 min before closing; courtyard open until 20:00; planetarium shows hourly Mon–Fri 13:00–16:00, Sat–Sun 11:00–16:00, fewer in winter, 30 min; tel. 020/8858-4422, www.nmm.ac.uk.

Observatory Grounds and Viewpoint: Before you leave the observatory grounds, enjoy the view from the overlook—the symmetrical royal buildings, the Thames, the Docklands and its busy cranes (including the tallest building in Britain, Canary Wharf Tower, a.k.a. One Canada Square), the huge O_2 (Millennium) Dome, and the square-mile City of London, with its skyscrap-

ers and the dome of St. Paul's Cathedral. At night (17:00–24:00), look for the green laser beam the observatory projects into the sky (best viewed in winter), extending along the prime meridian for 15 miles.

Windsor

Windsor, a compact and easy walking town of about 30,000 people, originally grew up around the royal residence. In 1070, William the Conqueror continued his habit of kicking Saxons out of their various settlements, taking over what the locals called "Windlesora" (meaning "riverbank with a hoisting crane")—which later became "Windsor." William built the first fortified castle on a chalk hill above the Thames; later, kings added on to his early designs, rebuilding and expanding the castle and surrounding gardens.

By setting up primary residence here, modern monarchs increased Windsor's popularity and prosperity—most notably, Queen Victoria, whose stern statue glares at you as you approach the castle. After her death, Victoria rejoined her beloved husband Albert in the Royal Mausoleum at Frogmore House, a mile south of the castle in a private section of the Home Park (house and mausoleum rarely open; check www.royalcollection.org.uk). The current Queen considers Windsor her primary residence, and the one where she feels most at home. You can tell if Her Majesty is in residence by checking to see which flag is flying above the round tower: If it's the royal standard (a red, yellow, and blue flag) instead of the Union Jack, the Queen is at home.

While 99 percent of visitors just come to see the castle and go, some enjoy spending the night. Windsor's charm is most evident when the tourists are gone. Consider overnighting here—parking and access to Heathrow Airport are easy, day-tripping into London is feasible, and an evening at the horse races (on Mondays) is hoof-pounding, heart-thumping fun.

Getting to Windsor

By Train: Windsor has two train stations—Windsor & Eton Central (5-min walk to palace, TI inside) and Windsor & Eton Riverside (5-min walk to palace and TI). First Great Western trains run between London's Paddington Station and Windsor & Eton Central (2/hr, 35 min, change at Slough; £8 one-way standard class, £9–11 same-day return). South West Trains run between London's Waterloo Station and Windsor & Eton Riverside (2/hr, 1 hr, change at Staines; £8.50 one-way standard class, £9–15 same-day return, info toll tel. 0845-748-4950, www.nationalrail.co.uk).

If you're day-tripping into London from Windsor, ask at the train station about combining a same-day return train ticket with a One-Day Travelcard as one ticket (£12–21, lower price for travel after 9:30, covers rail transportation to and from London and doubles as an all-day Tube and bus pass in town, rail ticket may also qualify you for half-price London sightseeing discounts—ask or look for brochure at station, or go to www.daysoutguide.co.uk).

By Bus: Green Line buses #701 and #702 run from London's Victoria Colonnades (between the Victoria train and coach stations) to the Parish Church stop on Windsor's High Street, before continuing on to Legoland (£1–8.50 one-way, £9–12.50 round-trip, prices vary depending on time of day, 1–2/hr, 1.25 hours to Windsor, tel. 01344/782-222, www.rainbowfares.com).

By Car: Windsor is 20 miles from London, and just off Heathrow Airport's landing path. The town (and then the castle and Legoland) is well-signposted from the M4 motorway. It's a convenient first stop if you're arriving at and renting a car from Heathrow, and saving London until the end of your trip.

From Heathrow Airport: Buses #71 and #77 make the 45-minute trip between Terminal 5 and Windsor, dropping you in the center of town on Peascod Street (about £7, 1–2/hr, toll tel. 0871-200-2233, www.firstgroup.com). London black cabs can charge whatever they like from Heathrow to Windsor (and do); avoid them by calling a local cab company, such as Windsor Radio Cars (£20, tel. 01753/677-677).

Orientation to Windsor

(area code: 01753)
Windsor's pleasant pedestrian shopping zone litters the approach to its famous palace with fun temptations. You'll find most shops and restaurants around the castle on High and Thames Streets, and down the pedestrian Peascod Street (PESS-cot), which runs perpendicular to High Street.

Tourist Information

The TI is adjacent to Windsor & Eton Central Station, in the Windsor Royal Shopping Centre's Old Booking Hall (April–Sept Mon–Sat 9:30–17:30, Sun 10:00–16:00; Oct–March Mon–Sat 10:00–17:00, Sun 10:00–16:00; tel. 01753/743-900, www.windsor .gov.uk). The TI sells discount tickets to Legoland for £34.

Arrival in Windsor

By Train: The train to Windsor & Eton Central Station from Paddington (via Slough) will spit you out in a shady shopping pavilion (which houses the TI), only a few minutes' walk from the castle. If you arrive instead at Windsor & Eton Riverside train station (from Waterloo, via Staines), you'll see the castle as you exit—just follow the wall to the castle entrance.

By Car: Follow signs from the M4 motorway for pay-and-display parking in the center. River Street Car Park is closest to the castle, but pricey and often full. The cheaper, bigger Alexandra Car Park (near the riverside Alexandra Gardens) is farther west. To walk to the town center from the Alexandra Car Park, head east through the tour-bus parking lot toward the castle. At the souvenir shop, walk up the stairs (or take the elevator) and cross the overpass to the Windsor & Eton Central Station. Just beyond the station, you'll find the TI in the Windsor Royal Shopping Centre.

Helpful Hints

Internet Access: Get online for free at the **library,** located on Bachelors' Acre, between Peascod and Victoria Streets (Mon and Thu 9:30–17:00, Tue 9:30–20:00, Wed 14:00–17:00, Fri 9:30–19:00, Sat 9:30–15:00, closed Sun, tel. 01753/743-940, www.rbwm.gov.uk).

Supermarkets: Pick up picnic supplies at **Marks & Spencer** (Mon–Sat 9:00–18:00, Sun 11:00–17:00, 130 Peascod Street, tel. 01753/852-266) or at **Waitrose** (Mon–Tue and Sat 8:30–19:00, Wed–Fri 8:30–20:00, Sun 11:00–17:00, King Edward Court Shopping Centre, just south of the Windsor & Eton Central Station, tel. 01753/860-565). Just outside the castle, you'll find long benches near the statue of Queen Victoria—great for people-watching while you munch.

Bike Rental: Extreme Motion, near the river in Alexandra Gardens, rents 21-speed mountain bikes as well as helmets (£12/4 hrs, £17/day, helmets-£1–1.50, £100 credit-card deposit required, bring passport as ID, summer daily 10:00–22:00, tel. 01753/830-220, www.extrememotion.com).

Sights in Windsor

▲▲Windsor Castle

Windsor Castle, the official home of England's royal family for 900 years, claims to be the largest and oldest occupied castle in the world. Thankfully, touring it is simple. You'll see immense grounds, lavish staterooms, a crowd-pleasing dollhouse, an art gallery, and the chapel.

Cost, Hours, Information: £15.50, family pass-£41, daily March–Oct 9:45–17:15, Nov–Feb 9:45–16:15, last entry 1.25 hours before closing, tel. 020/7766-7304, www.royalcollection.org.uk.

Tours: As you enter, ask about the warden's free 30-minute guided walks around the grounds (2/hr). They cover the grounds but not the castle, which is well-described by the included audio-guide (skip the official guidebook).

Other Activities: The **Changing of the Guard** takes place on alternate days at 11:00 (ceremonies begin a little earlier—get there

Windsor

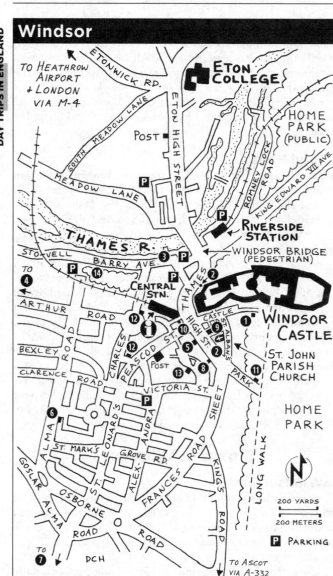

TO HEATHROW AIRPORT & LONDON VIA M-4

ETON COLLEGE

HOME PARK (PUBLIC)

POST

ETON HIGH STREET

ETONWICK RD.

SOUTH MEADOW LANE

MEADOW LANE

ROMNEY LOCK ROAD

KING EDWARD VII AVE

THAMES R.

STOVELL

BARRY AVE.

RIVERSIDE STATION

WINDSOR BRIDGE (PEDESTRIAN)

TO 4

ARTHUR ROAD

CENTRAL STN.

WINDSOR CASTLE

THAMES

CASTLE HILL

ST. ALBANS

HIGH ST.

ST. JOHN PARISH CHURCH

BEXLEY ROAD

CHARLES

PEASCOD ST.

POST

HOME PARK

CLARENCE ROAD

ROAD

VICTORIA ST.

SHEET

PARK

LONG WALK

ST. MARKS

ST. LEONARD'S

GROVE RD.

ALEX-ANDRA ROAD

FRANCES ROAD

KING'S ROAD

N

200 YARDS
200 METERS

GOSLAR

ALMA

OSBORNE

ALMA

ROAD

ROAD

P PARKING

TO 7

DCH

TO ASCOT VIA A-332

1 Castle Tickets & Entry
2 Legoland Bus Stops (2)
3 Boat Trips
4 To Royal Windsor Racecourse
5 Mercure Castle Hotel
6 Langton House B&B
7 To Park Farm B&B & Legoland
8 Cornucopia Bistro
9 The Crooked House Teahouse
10 Wagamama
11 The Two Brewers Pub
12 Grocery Stores (2)
13 Library (Internet Access)
14 Bike Rental

by 10:45), except in very wet weather (and never on Sun). There's an **evensong** in the chapel nightly at 17:15—free for worshippers.

Self-Guided Tour: Immediately upon entering, you pass through a simple modern building housing a **historical overview**

of the castle. This excellent intro is worth a close look—you're basically on your own after this. Inside, you'll find the motte (artificial mound) and bailey (fortified stockade around it) of William the Conqueror's castle. Dating from 1080, this was his first castle in England.

Follow the signs to the state-rooms/gallery/dollhouse. **Queen Mary's Dollhouse**—a palace in miniature (1:12 scale, from 1924) and "the most famous dollhouse in the world"—often has the longest wait. If dollhouses aren't your cup of tea, you can skip that line and go immediately into the lavish **staterooms.** Strewn with history and the art of a long line of kings and queens, they're the best I've seen in Britain—and well-restored after the devastating 1992 fire. Take advantage of the talkative docents in each room, who are happy to answer your questions.

The adjacent gallery is a changing exhibit featuring the **royal art collection** (and some big names, such as Michelangelo and Leonardo). Signs direct you (downhill) to **St. George's Chapel.** Housing numerous royal tombs, it's a fine example of Perpendicular Gothic, with classic fan vaulting spreading out from each pillar (dating from about 1500). The simple chapel containing the tombs of the current Queen's parents, King George VI and "Queen Mother" Elizabeth, and younger sister, Princess Margaret, is along the church's north aisle. Next door is the sumptuous 13th-century **Albert Memorial Chapel,** redecorated after the death of Prince Albert in 1861 and dedicated to his memory.

More Sights in Windsor

Legoland Windsor—Paradise for Legomaniacs under 12, this

huge kid-pleasing park has dozens of tame but fun rides (often with very long lines) scattered throughout its 150 acres. The impressive Miniland has 40 million Lego pieces glued together to create 800 tiny buildings and a mini-tour of Europe; the Creation Centre boasts

an 80 percent-scale Boeing 747 cockpit, made of two million bricks. Several of the more exciting rides involve getting wet, so dress accordingly or buy a cheap disposable poncho in the gift shop. While you may be tempted to hop on the Hill Train at the entrance, it's faster and more convenient to walk down into the park. Food is available in the park, but you can save money by bringing a picnic.

Cost: Adults-£36, £32.40 in advance online, £34 at Windsor TI; children-£27, £24 online or from TI; free for ages 2 and under; optional £10/person "Q-Bot" ride-reservation gadget allows you to bypass lines; coin lockers-£1.

Hours: Mid-July–Aug daily 10:00–19:00, Sept–Oct and April–mid-July Thu–Mon only and closes 1–2 hours earlier, closed Nov–mid-March except around Christmas, call or check website for exact schedule.

Information: Toll tel. 0871-222-2001, www.legoland.co.uk.

Getting There: A £4.50 round-trip shuttle bus runs from opposite Windsor's Theatre Royal on Thames Street, and from the Parish Church stop on High Street (2/hr). If day-tripping from London, ask about rail/shuttle/park admission deals from Paddington or Waterloo train stations. For drivers, the park is on B3022 Windsor/Ascot road, two miles southwest of Windsor and 25 miles west of London. Legoland is clearly signposted from the M3, M4, and M25 motorways. Parking is easy and free.

Eton College—Across the bridge from Windsor Castle you'll find many post-castle tourists filing toward the most famous "public" (the equivalent of our "private") high school in Britain. Eton was founded in 1440 by King Henry VI; today it educates about 1,300 boys (ages 13–18), who live on campus. Eton has molded the characters of 18 prime ministers, as well as members of the royal family, most recently princes William and Harry. The college is sparse on sights, but the public is allowed into the schoolyard, chapel, cloisters, and the Museum of Eton Life (£6, access only by one-hour guided tour at 14:00 and 15:15; tours available mid-April–Sept Wed and Fri–Sun, daily June–July; Oct–Nov Wed and Fri only; closed late Nov–mid-April and about once a month for special events, so call ahead; no photos in chapel, no food or drink allowed; tel. 01753/671-177, www.etoncollege.com).

Boat Trips—Cruise up and down the Thames River for relaxing views of the castle, the village of Eton, Eton College, and the Royal Windsor Racecourse. Relax onboard and nibble a picnic (£5, family pass-£12.50, 40 min; mid-Feb–Oct roughly 2/hr daily 10:00–17:00; Nov Sat–Sun hourly 10:00–16:00, closed Mon–Fri; closed Dec–mid-Feb; tel. 01753/851-900, www.frenchbrothers .co.uk). The same company also offers a longer two-hour circular trip (£8, 1–2/day).

Horse Racing—The horses race near Windsor every Monday evening at the Royal Windsor Racecourse (£8–18 entry, off A308 between Windsor and Maidenhead, tel. 01753/498-400, www .windsor-racecourse.co.uk). The romantic way to get there is by a 10-minute shuttle boat (£5.50 round-trip, see "Boat Trips," previous page). The famous Ascot Racecourse (see below) is also nearby.

Near Windsor

Ascot Racecourse—Located seven miles southwest of Windsor and just north of the town of Ascot, this royally owned racecourse is one of the most famous horse-racing venues in the world. Originally opened in 1711, it is best known for June's five-day Royal Ascot race meeting, attended by the Queen and 299,999 of her loyal subjects. For many, the outlandish hats worn on Ladies Day (Thursday) are more interesting than the horses. Royal Ascot is usually the third week in June (June 15–19 in 2010), and the pricey tickets go on sale the preceding November (see website for details). In addition to Royal Ascot, the racecourse runs the ponies year-round—funny hats strictly optional (regular tickets generally £10–20, online discounts, children 16 and under free; parking-£5–7, more for special races; dress code enforced in some areas and on certain days, toll tel. 0870-727-1234, www.ascot.co.uk).

Sleeping in Windsor

(area code: 01753)

Most visitors stay in London and do Windsor as a day trip. But here are a few suggestions for those staying the night.

$$$ **Mercure Castle Hotel,** with 108 business-class rooms, is as central as can be, just down the street from Her Majesty's weekend retreat (Db-£120–165, nonrefundable online deals,

---

Sleep Code

(£1 = about $1.60, country code: 44)
S = Single, **D** = Double/Twin, **T** = Triple, **Q** = Quad, **b** = bathroom, **s** = shower only. Unless otherwise noted, credit cards are accepted.

To help you sort through these listings easily, I've divided the rooms into three categories based on the price for a standard double room with bath:

$$$ **Higher Priced**—Most rooms £100 or more.
$$ **Moderately Priced**—Most rooms between £60–100.
$ **Lower Priced**—Most rooms £60 or less.

breakfast-£16, air-con, free Wi-Fi, 18 High Street, tel. 01753/851-577, www.mercure.com, h6618@accor.com).

$$ Langton House B&B is a stately Victorian home with three well-appointed rooms lovingly maintained by Paul and Sonja Fogg (Sb-£70, Db-£90, Tb-£110, Qb-£130, 5 percent extra if paying by credit card, family-friendly, guest kitchen, free Internet access and Wi-Fi, 46 Alma Road, tel. & fax 01753/858-299, www.langtonhouse.co.uk, paul@langtonhouse.co.uk).

$$ Park Farm B&B, bright and cheery, is convenient for drivers visiting Legoland (Sb-£65, Db-£85, Tb-£95, Qb-£105, ask about family room with bunk beds, cash only—credit card solely for reservations, free Wi-Fi, pay phone in entry, access to shared fridge and microwave, free off-street parking, 1 mile from Legoland on St. Leonards Road near Imperial Road, 5-min bus ride or 1.25-mile walk to castle, £4 taxi ride from station, tel. 01753/866-823, www.parkfarm.com, stay@parkfarm.com, Caroline and Drew Youds).

Eating in Windsor

Cornucopia Bistro, a favorite with locals, is a welcoming little place two minutes from the TI and castle, just beyond the tourist crush. They serve tasty international dishes with everything made proudly from scratch. The hardwood floors add a rustic elegance (£11 two-course lunches, £10–14 dinner entrées, Tue–Sat 12:00–14:30 & 18:00–21:30, Sun 12:00–14:30, closed Mon, 6 High Street, tel. 01753/833-009).

The Crooked House is a touristy 17th-century timber-framed teahouse, serving fresh, hearty £8–10 lunches and cream teas in a tipsy interior or outdoors on its cobbled lane (Mon–Fri 10:30–18:00, Sat–Sun 10:00–19:00, 51 High Street, tel. 01753/857-534). The important-looking building next door is the Guildhall, which hosted the weddings of both Prince Charles (to Camilla) and Elton John. It's also the home of the town's public WC.

Wagamama offers modern Asian food, mostly in the form of noodle soups. The setting is informal and communal, much like its London siblings (£7–10 main dishes, Mon–Sat 12:00–23:00, Sun 12:00–22:00, just off High Street, on the left as you face the entrance to Windsor Royal Shopping Centre, tel. 01753/833-105).

The Two Brewers Pub, tucked away near the top of Windsor Great Park's Long Walk, serves meals in a cozy Old World atmosphere. Befriend the barman and he may point out a minor royal (open for drinks Mon–Sat 11:30–23:00, Sun 12:00–22:30; lunch served Mon–Sat 12:00–14:00, Sun 12:00–16:00; dinner served Mon–Thu 18:00–22:00, appetizers only Fri–Sat 18:30–21:30, no evening meal on Sun; reservations smart for meals; kids under 18 must sit outside; 34 Park Street, tel. 01753/855-426).

Cambridge

Cambridge, 60 miles north of London, is world-famous for its prestigious university. Wordsworth, Isaac Newton, Tennyson, Darwin, and Prince Charles are a few of its illustrious alumni. The  university dominates—and owns—most of Cambridge, a historic town of 100,000 people that's more pleasant than its rival, Oxford. Cambridge is the epitome of a university town, with busy bikers, stately residence halls, plenty of bookshops, and proud locals who can point out where DNA was originally modeled, the atom was first split, and electrons were initially discovered.

In medieval Europe, higher education was the domain of the Church, and was limited to ecclesiastical schools. Scholars lived in "halls" on campus. This academic community of residential halls, chapels, and lecture halls connected by peaceful garden courtyards survives today in the colleges that make up the universities of Cambridge and Oxford. By 1350 (Oxford is roughly 100 years older), Cambridge had eight colleges, each with a monastic-type courtyard and lodgings. Today, Cambridge has 31 colleges. While students' lives revolve around their independent college, the university organizes lectures, presents degrees, and promotes research.

Planning Your Time

Cambridge is worth most of a day but not an overnight. Arrive in time for the 11:30 walking tour—an essential part of any visit—and spend the afternoon touring King's College Chapel and Fitzwilliam Museum (closed Mon except Bank Holidays), or simply enjoying the ambience of this stately old college town.

The university schedule has three terms: the Lent term from mid-January to mid-March, the Easter term from mid-April to mid-June, and the Michaelmas term from early October to early December. The colleges are closed to visitors during exams—in mid-April and late June—but King's College Chapel and the Trinity Library stay open, and the town is never sleepy.

Getting to Cambridge

By Train: It's an easy trip from London, about an hour away. Catch the train from London's King's Cross Station (2/hr, fast trains leave at :15 and :45 past the hour and run in each direction, 45 min, £19 one-way standard class, £20 same-day return after 9:30, operated by First Capital Connect, toll tel. 0845-748-4950, www.firstcapitalconnect.co.uk or www.nationalrail.co.uk).

By Bus: National Express coaches run from London's Victoria Coach Station to the Parkside stop in Cambridge (hourly, 2–3 hrs, £11.50, toll tel. 08717-818-181).

Orientation to Cambridge

(area code: 01223)
Cambridge is congested but small. Everything is within a pleasant walk. There are two main streets, separated from the river by the most interesting colleges. The town center, brimming with tea-rooms, has a TI and a colorful open-air market (clothes and food Mon–Sat 9:30–16:00; arts, crafts, and food Sun 9:30–16:30; on Market Square).

Tourist Information
An info kiosk on the train station platform dispenses free city maps and sells fancier ones. If it's closed, you can buy a map from a machine using a £1 coin, or get a free one from the nearby bike-rental shop (see "Helpful Hints," below). The official TI is well-signposted, just off Market Square. They book rooms for £5, and sell bus tickets and a £0.30 mini-guide/map (Mon–Fri 10:00–17:30, Sat 10:00–17:00, Easter–Sept also Sun 11:00–15:00—otherwise closed Sun, phones answered from 9:00, Wheeler Street, tel. 01223/464-732 or toll 0871-226-8006, room-booking tel. 01223/457-581, www.visitcambridge.org).

Arrival in Cambridge
By Train: To get to downtown Cambridge from the train station, take a 25-minute walk (any free map can help), a £5 taxi ride, or bus marked *Citi1*, *Citi3*, or *Citi7* (£1.30, every 5–10 min).

By Car: Drivers can follow signs from the M11 motorway to any of the handy and central short-stay parking lots. Or you can leave the car at one of five park-and-ride lots outside the city, then take the shuttle into town (free parking, £2.50 shuttle, buy ticket from machine or driver).

Helpful Hints
Festival: The **Cambridge Folk Festival** gets things humming and strumming (likely July 29–Aug 1 in 2010, www.cambridge folkfestival.co.uk).

Bike Rental: Station Cycles, located about a half-block to your right as you exit the station, rents bikes (£8/half-day, helmets-50p, £50–75 deposit, cash or credit card) and stores luggage (£3–4/bag depending on size; Mon–Fri 8:00–18:00, Wed until 19:00, Sat 9:00–17:00, Sun 10:00–16:00, tel. 01223/307-125, www.stationcycles.co.uk). They have a second location near the center of town (inside the Grand Arcade, on Corn Exchange Street near Wheeler, Mon–Fri 8:00–19:00, Wed until 20:00, Sat 9:00–19:00, Sun 10:00–18:00, tel. 01223/307-655).

Tours

▲▲**Walking Tour of the Colleges**—A walking tour is the best way to understand Cambridge's mix of "town and gown." The walks provide a good rundown of the historic and scenic highlights of the university, as well as some fun local gossip.

The TI offers **daily walking tours** (£10, 2 hrs, includes admission to King's College Chapel if it's open; July–Aug daily at 10:30, 11:30, 13:30, and 14:30, no 10:30 tour Sun; April–June and Sept daily at 11:30 and 13:30; Oct–March Mon–Sat at 11:30 and 13:30, Sun at 13:30; tel. 01223/457-574, www.visitcambridge.org). Drop by the TI (the departure point) one hour early to snag a spot. If you're visiting on a Sunday, call the day before to reserve a spot with your credit card and confirm departure time.

Private guides are also available through the TI (basic 1-hour tour-£3.50/person, £50 minimum; 90-min tour-£4/person, £58 minimum; 2-hour tour-£4.50/person, £65 minimum; does not include individual college entrance fees, tel. 01223/457-574, www.visitcambridge.org).

Walking and Punting Ghost Tour—If you're in Cambridge on the weekend, consider a £5 ghost walk Friday evenings at 18:00, or a spooky £16 trip on the River Cam followed by a walk most Saturdays at 20:00 (book ahead for both, tel. 01223/457-574, www.visitcambridge.org).

Bus Tours—City Sightseeing hop-on, hop-off bus tours are informative and cover the outskirts, including the American WWII Cemetery (£12, 80 min for full 21-stop circuit, departs every 20 min in summer, every 40 min in winter, first bus leaves train station at 10:06, last bus at 17:46, recorded commentary with some live English-language guides, can use credit card to buy tickets in their office in train station, tel. 01223/423-578, www.city-sightseeing.com). Walking tours go where the buses can't—right into the center.

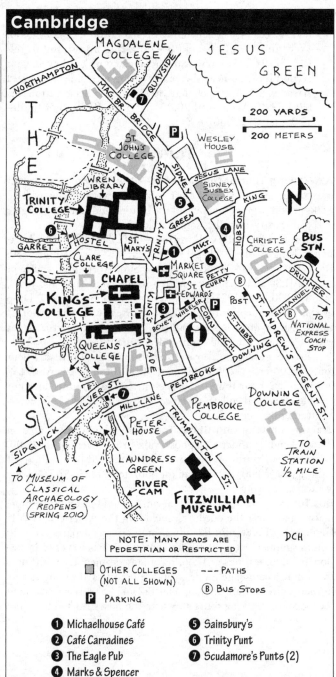

Cambridge

MAGDALENE COLLEGE

JESUS GREEN

NORTHAMPTON

MAG. BR. BRIDGE

QUAYSIDE

7

200 YARDS

200 METERS

T H E

P

WESLEY HOUSE

ST. JOHN'S COLLEGE

WREN LIBRARY

JESUS LANE

SIDNEY SUSSEX COLLEGE

SIDNEY

ST. JOHN'S

TRINITY

KING

5

HOBSON

Trinity College →

6

HOSTEL

GARRET

ST. MARY'S

GREEN

1

4

CHRIST'S COLLEGE

BUS STN.

DRUMMER

CLARE COLLEGE

CHAPEL

MARKET SQUARE

MKT.

2

PETTY CURRY

B

ST. ANDREW'S

EMMANUEL

B

B A C K S

King's College

ST. EDWARD'S

3

POST

TO NATIONAL EXPRESS COACH STOP

KING'S PARADE

BENET

WHEELER

CORN EXCH.

ST. TIBB'S

REGENT ST.

QUEEN'S COLLEGE

i

SILVER ST.

7

MILL LANE

DOWNING

PEMBROKE

DOWNING COLLEGE

SIGWICK

PETER-HOUSE

PEMBROKE COLLEGE

TRUMPINGTON ST.

TO MUSEUM OF CLASSICAL ARCHAEOLOGY (REOPENS SPRING 2010)

LAUNDRESS GREEN

RIVER CAM

FITZWILLIAM MUSEUM

TO TRAIN STATION ½ MILE

DCH

NOTE: MANY ROADS ARE PEDESTRIAN OR RESTRICTED

☐ OTHER COLLEGES (NOT ALL SHOWN)

P PARKING

--- PATHS

B BUS STOPS

1 Michaelhouse Café

2 Café Carradines

3 The Eagle Pub

4 Marks & Spencer

5 Sainsbury's

6 Trinity Punt

7 Scudamore's Punts (2)

Sights in Cambridge

In Cambridge

▲▲**King's College Chapel**—Built from 1446 to 1515 by Henrys VI–VIII, England's best example of Perpendicular Gothic is the single most impressive building in town. Stand inside, look up, and marvel, as Christopher Wren did, at what was the largest single span of vaulted roof anywhere—2,000 tons of incredible fan vaulting. Wander through the Old Testament, with 26 stained-glass windows from the 16th century, the most Renaissance stained glass anywhere in one spot. The windows were removed to keep them safe during World War II, and then painstakingly replaced. Walk to the altar and admire Rubens' masterful *Adoration of the Magi* (£5, erratic hours depending on school schedule and events; during academic term usually Mon–Fri 9:30–15:30, Sat 9:30–15:15, Sun 13:15–14:15; during breaks—see "Planning Your Time," earlier—Mon–Sat 9:30–16:30, Sun 10:00–17:00). When school's in session, you're welcome to enjoy an evensong service (Mon–Sat at 17:30, Sun at 15:30, tel. 01223/331-212, recorded info tel. 01223/331-155, www.kings.cam.ac.uk/chapel).

▲▲**Trinity College and Wren Library**—Nearly half of Cambridge's 83 Nobel Prize winners have come from this richest and biggest of the town's colleges, founded in 1546 by Henry VIII. Don't miss the 1695 Wren-designed library, with its wonderful carving and fascinating original manuscripts. There's a small fee to visit the campus (£2.50), but if you just want to see Wren Library (free), enter from the riverside entrance, located by the Garret Hostel Bridge. The Wren Library should remain open during planned renovation that may close the grounds through July 2010 (otherwise campus open daily 10:00–17:00; library open Mon–Fri 12:00–14:00, Nov–mid-June also Sat 10:30–12:30, always closed Sun and during exams; only 15 people allowed in at a time, tel. 01223/338-400, www.trin.cam.ac.uk). Just outside the library entrance, Sir Isaac Newton, who spent 30 years at Trinity, clapped his hands and timed the echo to measure the speed of sound as it raced down the side of the cloister and back. In the library's 12 display cases (covered with cloth that you flip back), you'll see handwritten works by Sir Isaac Newton and John Milton, alongside A. A. Milne's original *Winnie the Pooh* (the real Christopher Robin attended Trinity College).

▲▲**Fitzwilliam Museum**—Britain's best museum of antiquities and art outside of London is the Fitzwilliam. Enjoy its wonderful paintings (Old Masters and a fine English section featuring Gainsborough, Reynolds, Hogarth, and others, plus works by all the famous Impressionists), old manuscripts, and Greek, Egyptian, and Mesopotamian collections. Watch your step—a visitor tripped a few years ago and accidentally smashed three 17th-century Chinese vases. Amazingly, the vases were restored and are now on display in Gallery 17...in a protective case (free, audio/videoguide-£3, Tue–Sat 10:00–17:00, Sun 12:00–17:00, closed Mon except Bank Holidays, no photos, Trumpington Street, tel. 01223/332-900, www.fitzmuseum.cam.ac.uk).

Museum of Classical Archaeology—Although this museum—reopening after renovation in spring 2010—contains no originals, it offers a unique chance to see accurate copies (19th-century casts) of virtually every famous ancient Greek and Roman statue. More than 450 statues are on display (free, likely Mon–Fri 10:00–17:00, sometimes also Sat 10:00–13:00 during term, closed Sun, Sidgwick Avenue, tel. 01223/330-402, www.classics.cam.ac.uk/museum). The museum is a five-minute walk west of Silver Street Bridge; after crossing the bridge, continue straight until you reach a sign reading *Sidgwick Site*. The museum is in the long building on the corner to your right; the entrance is on the opposite side.

▲Punting on the Cam—For a little levity and probably more exercise than you really want, try hiring one of the traditional flat-

bottom punts at the river and pole yourself up and down (or around and around, more likely) the lazy Cam. Once you get the hang of it, it's a fine way to enjoy the scenic side of Cambridge. It's less crowded in late afternoon (and less embarrassing).

Two companies rent punts and offer tours. **Trinity Punt,** just north of Garrett Hostel Bridge, is run by Trinity College students (£12/hr, £40 deposit, 45-min tours-£30/boat, can share ride and cost with up to 2 others, cash only, ask for quick and free lesson, Easter–mid-Oct Mon–Fri 11:00–17:30, Sat–Sun 10:00–17:30, return punts by 18:30, no rentals mid-Oct–Easter, tel. 01223/338-483). **Scudamore's** has two locations: Mill Lane, just south of the central Silver Street Bridge, and the less convenient Quayside at Magdalene Bridge, at the north end of town (£16–18/hr, £80 deposit required—can use credit card, 45-min tours-£14/person, save £2 by buying at TI, open daily June–Aug 9:00–22:00, Sept–May at least 10:00–17:00, weather permitting, tel. 01223/359-750, www.scudamores.com).

Near Cambridge

Imperial War Museum Duxford—This former airfield, nine miles south of Cambridge, is nirvana for aviation fans and WWII buffs. Wander through seven exhibition halls housing 200 vintage aircraft (including Spitfires, B-17 Flying Fortresses, a Concorde, and a Blackbird), as well as military land vehicles and special displays on Normandy and the Battle of Britain. On many weekends, the museum holds special events, such as air shows (extra fee)—check the website for details (£16, show local bus ticket for discount, daily mid-March–late Oct 10:00–18:00, late Oct–mid-March 10:00–16:00, last entry one hour before closing, tel. 01223/835-000, http://duxford.iwm.org.uk).

Getting There: The museum is located off A505 in Duxford. From Cambridge, you can take the bus marked *Citi7* from the train station (45 min) or from Emmanuel Street's Stop A (55 min, bus runs 2/hr Mon–Sat, www.stagecoachbus.com/cambridge). On Sundays and Bank Holidays, catch the #132 bus, run by private bus operator Myalls, from the train station or the Drummer Street bus station (40 min, first bus around 10:00, then every 2 hours until 18:00, tel. 01763/243-225).

Eating in Cambridge

While picnicking is scenic and saves money, the weather may not always cooperate. Here are a few ideas for fortifying yourself in central Cambridge.

The **Michaelhouse Café** is a heavenly respite from the crowds, tucked into the repurposed St. Michael's Church, just north of Great St. Mary's Church. At lunch, choose from salads, soups, and sandwiches, as well as a few hot dishes and a variety of tasty baked goods (£5–10 light meals, £4 "fill your plate" special available 14:30–15:00, open Mon–Sat 8:00–17:00, breakfast served 8:00–11:30, lunch served 11:30–15:00, hot drinks and baked goods always available, closed Sun, Trinity Street, tel. 01223/309-147).

Café Carradines is a cozy cafeteria that serves traditional British food at reasonable prices, including a Sunday roast lunch for £7 (Mon–Sat 8:00–17:00, Sun 10:00–16:00, down the stairs at 23 Market Street, tel. 01223/361-792).

The Eagle Pub, near the TI, is a good spot for a quick drink or a pub lunch. Look at the carefully preserved ceiling in its "Air Force Bar," signed by local airmen during World War II. Science fans can also celebrate the discovery of DNA—Francis Crick and James Watson first announced their findings here in 1953 (Mon–Sat 11:00–23:00, Sun 12:00–22:30, food served 12:00–14:30 & 17:00–21:30, pleasant patio, 8 Benet Street, tel. 01223/505-020).

Supermarkets: There's a **Marks & Spencer Simply Food** grocery at the train station and a larger store at 6 Sidney Street (Mon–Sat 9:00–18:00, Sun 11:00–17:00, tel. 01223/355-219). **Sainsbury's** supermarket, with slightly longer hours, is at 44 Sidney Street, on the corner of Green Street. A good picnic spot is Laundress Green, a grassy park on the river, at the end of Mill Lane near the Silver Street Bridge punts. There are no benches, so bring something to sit on. Remember, the college lawns are private property, so walking or picnicking on the grass is generally not allowed. When in doubt, ask at the college's entrance.

Connections

From Cambridge by Train to: York (2/hr, 2.5 hrs, transfer in Peterborough), **Oxford** (2/hr, 2.5 hrs, change in London involves Tube transfer between train stations), **London** (3/hr, 1 hr). Train info: Toll tel. 0845-748-4950, www.nationalrail.co.uk.

By Bus to: London (hourly, 2–3 hrs), **Heathrow Airport** (1–2/hr, 2–3 hrs). Bus info: Toll tel. 08717-818-181, www.national express.com.

Stonehenge

As old as the pyramids, and older than the Acropolis and the Colosseum, this iconic stone circle amazed medieval Europeans, who figured it was built by a race of giants. And it still impresses visitors today. As one of Europe's most famous sights, Stonehenge does a valiant job of retaining an air of mystery and majesty (partly because cordons, which keep hordes of tourists from trampling all over it, create the illusion that it stands alone in a field). Although some people are underwhelmed by Stonehenge, most of its nearly one million annual visitors find that it's worth the trip.

Getting to Stonehenge

Stonehenge is about 90 miles southwest of central London. To reach it from London, you can take a bus tour; go on a guided tour that uses public transportation; or do it on your own using public transport, connecting via Salisbury. Given the ease of these options, it's not worth the hassle or expense to rent a car just for a Stonehenge daytrip.

By Bus Tour from London: Several companies offer big-bus day trips to Stonehenge from London, often with stops in Bath, Windsor, Salisbury, and/or Avebury. These generally cost about £40–75, last 10–12 hours, and pack a 45-seat bus. Some include hotel pickup, admission fees, and meals; understand what's included before you book. The more destinations listed for a tour, the less time you'll have at any one stop. Well-known companies are **Evan Evans** (tel. 020/7950-1777 or US tel. 866-382-6868, www.evanevanstours.co.uk) and **Golden Tours** (US toll-free tel. 800-548-7083 or toll tel. 0844-880-6981, www.goldentours .co.uk). **International Friends** runs smaller 16-person tours (tel. 01223/244-555, www.internationalfriends.co.uk). If Bath is your next destination after London, consider taking a multiple-destination bus tour and abandoning it in Bath (for details, see "By Bus" on page 372).

By Bus Tour from Other Cities: For tours of Stonehenge from Bath, see page 412 (Mad Max is best). Note that there is no public transportation between Avebury and Stonehenge.

By Guided Tour on Public Transport: London Walks offers a weekly guided "Explorer Day Tour" to Salisbury and Stonehenge by train and bus (£49, includes all transportation, Salisbury walking tour, and entry fees and guided tours of Stonehenge and Salisbury Cathedral; buy all tickets from guide; cash only, likely Tue only plus a few Sat, meet at 9:45 at Waterloo Station's main ticket office, opposite Platform 16, return to London around 18:45, call or see website to verify price and schedule, advance booking not required, tel. 020/7624-3978, recorded info tel. 020/7624-9255, www.walks.com).

On Your Own on Public Transport: Catch a train to Salisbury, then go by bus or taxi to Stonehenge. Trains to Salisbury run from London's Waterloo Station (£30 same-day return fare leaving weekdays after 9:30, 1–2/hr, 1.5 hrs, toll tel. 0845-748-4950, www.southwesttrains.co.uk or www.nationalrail.co.uk).

Once in Salisbury, you can take **The Stonehenge Tour** bus to the site. Their distinctive red-and-black double-decker buses leave from the Salisbury train station and make a circuit to Stonehenge and Old Sarum (£11, £17.50 with Stonehenge admission; tickets good all day; buy ticket from driver; daily June–mid-Oct 9:30–17:00, 1–2/hr; none on June 21 due to solstice crowds, shorter hours off-season; 30 min from station to Stonehenge; tel. 01722/336-855, check www.thestonehengetour.info for timetable).

A **taxi** from Salisbury to Stonehenge costs about £40 (corral a few fellow tourists and share the cost, call for exact price, includes round-trip from Salisbury to Stonehenge plus an hour at the site, entry fee not included, tel. 01722/339-781 or mobile 07971-255-690, brian@salisburytaxis.co.uk, Brian MacNeillie).

By Car: Stonehenge is well-signed just off A303. It's about 15 minutes north of Salisbury, an hour east of Glastonbury, and an hour south of Avebury.

From **London,** Stonehenge is about 70 miles and 90 minutes east of Heathrow (barring traffic). From the M25 ring road, connect with M3 toward Southampton. Past Basingstoke, exit to A303. Continue west past Andover to Amesbury and follow "From Salisbury" directions from that point (below).

From **Salisbury,** head north on A345 (Castle Road) through **Amesbury,** go west on A303 for 1.5 miles, veer right onto A344, and it's just ahead on the left, with the parking lot on the right.

Orientation to Stonehenge

Cost: £6.60, covered by English Heritage Pass and Great British Heritage Pass (see page 15).

Hours: Daily June–Aug 9:00–19:00, mid-March–May and Sept–mid-Oct 9:30–18:00, mid-Oct–mid-March 9:30–16:00, last entry 30 min before closing.

When to Go: Shorter hours and possible closures June 20–22 due to huge, raucous solstice crowds; £3 parking fee likely in summer—refundable with paid admission.

Information: Entry includes a worthwhile hour-long audioguide—though they sometimes run out (tel. 01980/623-108 or toll tel. 0870-333-1181, www.english-heritage.org.uk/stonehenge).

Reaching the Inner Stones: Special one-hour access to the stones' inner circle—before or after regular visiting hours—costs an extra £14 and must be reserved well in advance. Details can be found on the English Heritage website (look for a link to "Stone Circle Access") or by calling 01722/343-830.

Planned Changes: Future plans for Stonehenge call for the creation of a new visitors center and museum, designed to blend in with the landscape and make the stone circle feel more pristine. Visitors will park farther away and ride a shuttle bus to the site.

Self-Guided Tour

The entrance fee includes a good audioguide, but this commentary will help make your visit even more meaningful.

Walk in from the parking lot, buy your ticket, pick up your included audioguide, and head through the ugly underpass beneath the road. On the way up the ramp, notice the artist's rendering of

what Stonehenge once looked like. As you approach the massive structure, walk right up to the knee-high cordon and let your fellow 21st-century tourists melt away. It's just you and the druids....

England has hundreds of stone circles, but Stonehenge—which literally means "hanging stones"—is unique. It's the only one that has horizontal cross-pieces (called lintels) spanning the vertical monoliths, and the only one with stones that have been made smooth and uniform. What you see here is a bit more than half the original structure—the rest was quarried centuries ago for other buildings.

Now do a slow counterclockwise spin around the monument, and ponder the following points. As you walk, mentally flesh out the missing pieces and re-erect the rubble. Knowledgeable guides posted around the site are happy to answer your questions.

This was a hugely significant location to prehistoric peoples. There are some 500 burial mounds within a three-mile radius of Stonehenge—most likely belonging to kings and chieftains. Built in phases between 3000 and 1000 B.C., Stonehenge's original function may have been simply as a monumental gravestone for a ritual burial site. (So goes one recently popular theory.) But that's not the end of the story, as the monument was expanded over the millennia.

Stonehenge still functions as a remarkably accurate celestial calendar. As the sun rises on the summer solstice (June 21), the "heel stone"—the one set apart from the rest, near the road—lines up with the sun and the altar at the center of the stone circle. A study of more than 300 similar circles in Britain found that each was designed to calculate the movement of the sun, moon, and stars, and to predict eclipses in order to help early societies know when to plant, harvest, and party. Even in modern times, as the summer solstice sun sets in just the right slot at Stonehenge, pagans boogie.

In addition to being a calendar, Stonehenge is built at the precise point where six ley lines intersect. Ley lines are theoretical lines of magnetic power that crisscross the globe. Belief in the power of these lines has gone in and out of fashion over time: They are believed to have been very important to prehistoric peoples, but then were largely ignored until the New Age movement of the 20th century. Without realizing it, you follow these ley lines all the time: Many of England's modern highways are built on top of prehistoric paths, and many churches are built on the site of prehistoric monuments where ley lines intersect. If you're a skeptic, ask one of the guides at Stonehenge to demonstrate the ley lines with a pair of L-shaped divining rods...creepy and convincing.

Notice that two of the stones (facing the entry passageway) are blemished. At the base of one monolith, it looks like someone has pulled back the stone to reveal a concrete skeleton. This is a clumsy repair job to fix damage done by souvenir-seekers long ago, who actually rented hammers and chisels to take home a piece of Stonehenge. On the stone to the right of the repaired one, notice that the back isn't covered with the same thin layer of protective lichen as the others. The lichen—and some of the stone itself—was sandblasted off to remove graffiti. (No wonder they've got Stonehenge roped off now.)

Stonehenge's builders used two different types of stones. The tall, stout monoliths and lintels are made of sandstone blocks called sarsen stones. Most of the monoliths weigh about 25 tons (the largest is 45 tons), and the lintels are about seven tons apiece. These sarsen stones were brought from "only" 20 miles away. The shorter stones in the middle, called "bluestones," came from the south coast of Wales—240 miles away. (Close if you're taking a train, but far if you're packing a megalith.) Imagine the logistical puzzle of floating six-ton stones up the River Avon, then rolling them on logs about 20 miles to this position...an impressive feat, even in our era of skyscrapers.

Why didn't the builders of Stonehenge use what seem like perfectly adequate stones nearby? This, like many other questions about Stonehenge, remains shrouded in mystery. Think again about the ley lines. Ponder the fact that many experts accept none of the explanations of how these giant stones were transported. Then imagine congregations gathering here 4,000 years ago, raising thought levels, creating a powerful life force transmitted along the ley lines. Maybe a particular kind of stone was essential for maximum energy transmission. Maybe the stones were levitated here. Maybe psychics really do create powerful vibes. Maybe not. It's as unbelievable as electricity used to be.

Bath

The best city to visit within easy striking distance of London is Bath—just a 90-minute train ride away. Two hundred years ago,

this city of 85,000 was the trendsetting Hollywood of Britain. If ever a city enjoyed looking in the mirror, Bath's the one. It has more "government-listed" or protected historic buildings per capita than any other town in England. The entire city, built of the creamy warm-tone limestone called "Bath stone," beams in its cover-girl complexion. An architectural chorus line, it's a triumph of the Georgian style. Proud locals remind visitors that the town is routinely banned from the "Britain in Bloom" contest to give other towns a chance to win. Bath's narcissism is justified. Even with its mobs of tourists (two million per year) and greedy prices, Bath is a joy to visit.

Bath's fame began with the allure of its (supposedly) healing hot springs. Long before the Romans arrived in the first century, Bath was known for its warm waters. Romans named the popular spa town Aquae Sulis, after a local Celtic goddess. The town's importance carried through Saxon times, when it had a huge church on the site of the present-day abbey and was considered the religious capital of Britain. Its influence peaked in 973 with King Edgar's sumptuous coronation in the abbey. Later, Bath prospered as a wool town.

Bath then declined until the mid-1600s, languishing to just a huddle of huts around the abbey, with hot, smelly mud and 3,000 residents, oblivious to the Roman ruins 18 feet below their dirt floors. In fact, with its own walls built upon ancient ones, Bath was no bigger than that Roman town. Then, in 1687, Queen Mary, fighting infertility, bathed here. Within 10 months she gave birth to a son...and a new age of popularity for Bath.

The revitalized town boomed as a spa resort. Ninety percent of the buildings you'll see today are from the 18th century. Local architect John Wood was inspired by the Italian architect Andrea Palladio to build a "new Rome." The town bloomed in the Neoclassical style, and streets were lined not with scrawny sidewalks but with wide "parades," upon which the women in their stylishly wide dresses could spread their fashionable tails.

Beau Nash (1673–1762) was Bath's "master of ceremonies."

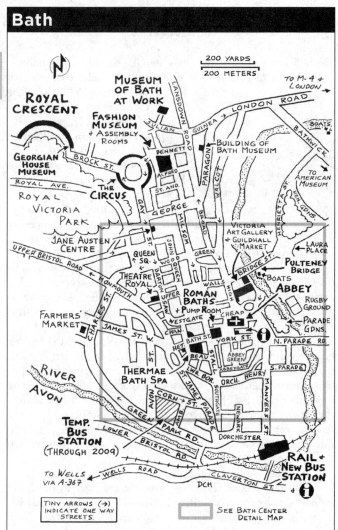

Bath

He organized both the daily regimen of aristocratic visitors and the city, lighting the streets, improving security, banning swords, and opening the Pump Room. Under his fashionable baton, Bath became a city of balls, gaming, and concerts—the place to see and be seen in England. This most civilized place became even more so with the great Neoclassical building spree that followed.

These days, modern tourism has stoked the local economy, as has the fast morning train to London. (A growing number of

Bath professionals catch the 7:13 train to Paddington Station every morning.) With renewed access to Bath's soothing hot springs via the Thermae Bath Spa, the venerable waters are in the spotlight again, attracting a new generation of visitors in need of a cure or a soak.

Planning Your Time

Bath needs two nights, even on a quick trip. There's plenty to do, and it's a delight to do it. On a one-week trip to London, consider spending two nights in Bath with one entire day for the city. Ideally, use Bath as your jet-lag recovery pillow (by flying into Heathrow and taking the bus to Bath from the airport; or maybe even flying into Bristol), then do London at the end of your trip.

Consider starting a London vacation this way:

Day 1: Land at Heathrow. Connect to Bath by National Express bus—the better option—or the less convenient bus/train combination (for details, see page 366). Take an evening walking tour.

Day 2: 9:00–Tour the Roman Baths; 10:30–Catch the free city walking tour; 12:30–Picnic on the open deck of a tour bus; 14:00–Free time in the shopping center of old Bath; 15:30–Tour the Fashion Museum or Museum of Bath at Work. At night, consider seeing a play, enjoy the Bizarre Bath comedy walk, or go for an evening soak in the Thermae Bath Spa.

Day 3: Early train into London.

Orientation to Bath

(area code: 01225)

Bath's town square, three blocks in front of the bus and train station, is a cluster of tourist landmarks, including the abbey, Roman and medieval baths, and the Pump Room.

Tourist Information

The TI is in the abbey churchyard (Mon–Sat 9:30–18:00, Sun 10:00–16:00, closes one hour early Mon–Sat Oct–May, toll tel. 0870-420-1278, www.visitbath.co.uk, note that their 0906 info number costs 50p/min). The TI sells a chintzy £1 city map. The £1.25 map, available in their shop, is much better—or just use the one included in the free *Bath Visitors' Guide and Map*. While you're at the TI, browse through scads of fliers, books, and maps, or ask them to book you a room (£3 charge plus 10 percent deposit). They don't bother to print an events flier, so look at the local paper or their daily events board. You can also buy the Great British Heritage Pass here (see page 15).

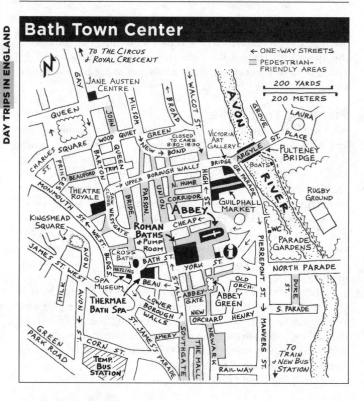

Bath Town Center

Arrival in Bath

The Bath Spa **train station** has a national and international tickets desk and a privately run travel agency masquerading as a TI.

Immediately surrounding the train station is a sea of construction, as Bath gets a new mall and underground parking garage (due to be completed in 2011). To get to the TI from the train station, walk two blocks up Manvers Street and turn left at the triangular "square," following the small TI arrow on a signpost.

The **bus station** is immediately in front of the train station (if you're here in early 2010, you'll find the bus station in a temporary location on Corn Street, a few blocks away).

My recommended B&Bs are all within a 10- to 15-minute walk or a £4–5 taxi ride from the train station.

Helpful Hints

Festivals: The **Bath Literature Festival** is an open book February 27–March 7 in 2010 (www.bathlitfest.org.uk). The **Bath International Music Festival** bursts into song late May to early June (classical, folk, jazz, contemporary; see www.bathmusicfest.org.uk), overlapped by the eclectic **Bath Fringe**

Festival (theater, walks, talks, bus trips; www.bathfringe .co.uk). The genteel **Jane Austen Festival** unfolds in mid-September (www.janeausten.co.uk/festival). Bath's festival box office sells tickets for most events, and can tell you exactly what's on tonight (2 Church Street, tel. 01225/463-362, www .bathfestivals.org.uk). The city's local paper, the *Bath Chronicle*, publishes a "What's On" event listing on Fridays (www.this isbath.com).

Internet Access: You can get online at the Bath library (£1/20 min with free library membership, Mon–Thu 9:30–19:00, Fri–Sat 9:30–17:00, Sun 13:00–16:00, in The Podium shopping centre on Northgate Street near Pulteney Bridge, tel. 01225/394-041, www.bathnes.gov.uk), or ask your hotel or the TI for recommended Internet cafés.

Laundry: Bring lots of £0.20 and £1 coins, as there are no change machines at these launderettes. **Spruce Goose Launderette** is around the corner from the recommended Brocks Guest House, on the pedestrian lane called Margaret's Buildings (self-service daily 8:00–20:00; full-service Mon, Wed, and Fri 9:00–13:00—but book ahead; tel. 01225/483-309). **Speedy Wash** can pick up your laundry before 11:00 anywhere in town for same-day service (£12/bag, Mon–Fri 7:30–17:30, Sat 8:30–13:00 but no pickup, closed Sun, no self-service, most hotels work with them, 4 Mile End, London Road, tel. 01225/427-616).

Car Rental: Enterprise provides a pickup service for customers to and from their hotels (extra fee for one-way rentals, at Lower Bristol Road outside Bath, tel. 01225/443-311, www .enterprise.com). Others include **Thrifty** (pickup service and one-way rentals available, in the Burnett Business Park in Keynsham—between Bath and Bristol, tel. 01179/867-997, www.thrifty.co.uk) and **National Europcar** (one-way rentals available, £7 by taxi from the train station, at Brassmill Lane—go west on Upper Bristol Road, tel. 01225/481-982 or 01761/479-205). Skip **Avis**—it's a mile from the Bristol train station and you'd need to rent a car just to get there. Most offices close Saturday afternoon and all day Sunday, which complicates weekend pickups. Ideally, take the train or bus from downtown London to Bath, and rent a car as you leave Bath.

Parking: Parking in the city center is difficult—short-term street parking is available but pricey (about £2.50/hr, 2-hour maximum, buy Pay & Display tickets from machine), with cheaper parking in parking lots. For more information, visit www .bathnes.gov.uk/bathnes.

Bath at a Glance

▲▲▲**Roman and Medieval Baths** Ancient baths that gave the city its name, tourable with good audioguide. **Hours:** Daily July–Aug 9:00–22:00, March–June and Sept–Oct 9:00–18:00, Nov–Feb 9:30–17:30. See page 413.

▲▲▲**Walking Tours** Free top-notch tours, helping you make the most of your visit, led by The Mayor's Corps of Honorary Guides. **Hours:** Sun–Fri at 10:30 and 14:00, Sat at 10:30 only; additional evening walks offered May–Sept Tue and Fri at 19:00. See page 410.

▲▲**Royal Crescent and the Circus** Stately Georgian (Neoclassical) buildings from Bath's late-18th-century glory days. **Hours:** Always viewable. See page 417.

▲▲**Fashion Museum** 400 years of clothing under one roof, plus opulent Assembly Rooms. **Hours:** Daily March–Oct 10:30–18:00, Nov–Feb 10:30–17:00. See page 418.

▲▲**Museum of Bath at Work** Gadget-ridden circa-1900 engineer's shop, foundry, factory, and office, best enjoyed with a live tour. **Hours:** April–Oct daily 10:30–17:00, Nov–March weekends only. See page 418.

▲**Pump Room** Swanky Georgian hall, ideal for a spot of tea or a taste of unforgettably "healthy" spa water. **Hours:** Daily 9:30–12:00 for coffee and breakfast, 12:00–14:30 for lunch, 14:30–16:30 for afternoon tea (open for dinner during Bath International Music Festival, July–Aug, and Christmas holidays only). See page 414.

Tours

Of Bath

▲▲▲**Walking Tours**—Free two-hour tours are offered by **The Mayor's Corps of Honorary Guides**, led by volunteers who want to share their love of Bath with its many visitors (as the city's mayor first did when he took a group on a guided walk back in the 1930s). Their chatty, historical, and gossip-filled walks are essential for your understanding of this town's amazing Georgian social scene. How else would you learn that the old "chair ho" call for your sedan chair evolved into today's "cheerio" farewell? Tours leave from outside the Pump Room in the abbey churchyard (free, no tips, year-round Sun–Fri at 10:30 and 14:00, Sat at 10:30 only; additional evening walks May–Sept Tue and Fri at 19:00; tel. 01225/477-411, www.thecityofbath.co.uk). Tip for theatergoers: When your guide

▲**Thermae Bath Spa** Relaxation center that put the bath back in Bath. **Hours:** Daily 9:00–22:00. See page 414.

▲**Abbey** 500-year-old Perpendicular Gothic church, graced with beautiful fan vaulting and stained glass. **Hours:** April–Oct Mon–Sat 9:00–18:00, Sun 13:00–14:30 & 16:30–17:30; Nov–March Mon–Sat 9:00–16:30, Sun 13:00–14:30 & 16:30–17:30. See page 415.

▲**Pulteney Bridge and Parade Gardens** Shop-strewn bridge and relaxing riverside gardens. **Hours:** Bridge—always open; gardens—April–Sept daily 10:00–dusk, shorter hours off-season. See page 416.

▲**Georgian House at No. 1 Royal Crescent** Best opportunity to explore the interior of one of Bath's high-rent Georgian beauties. **Hours:** Mid-Feb–Oct Tue–Sun 10:30–17:00, Nov Tue–Sun 10:30–16:00, closed Mon and Dec–mid-Feb. See page 417.

▲**American Museum** An insightful look primarily at colonial/early-American lifestyles, with 18 furnished rooms and eager-to-talk guides. **Hours:** Mid-March–Oct Tue–Sun 12:00–17:00, closed Mon and Nov–mid-March. See page 419.

Jane Austen Centre Exhibit on 19th-century Bath-based novelist, best for her fans. **Hours:** Mid-March–mid-Nov daily 9:45–17:30, July–Aug Thu–Sat until 19:00; mid-Nov–mid-March Sun–Fri 11:00–16:30, Sat 9:45–17:30. See page 419.

stops to talk outside the Theatre Royal, skip out for a moment, pop into the box office, and see about snaring a great deal on a play for tonight.

For a **private tour,** call the local guides' bureau (£60/2 hrs, tel. 01225/337-111). For **Ghost Walks** and **Bizarre Bath** tours, see page 421.

▲▲**City Bus Tours**—City Sightseeing's hop-on, hop-off bus tours zip through Bath. Jump on a bus anytime at one of 17 signposted pickup points, pay the driver, climb upstairs, and hear recorded commentary about Bath. City Sightseeing has two 45-minute routes: a city tour (unintelligible audio recording on half the buses, live guides on the other half—choose the latter), and a "Skyline" route outside town (all live guides, stops near the American Museum—15-min walk). On a sunny day, this is a multitasking tourist's dream come true: You can munch a sandwich, work on a tan, snap great photos, and learn a lot, all at the same time. Save money by doing the bus tour first—ticket stubs get you minor discounts at many sights (£11, ticket valid for 2 days and both tour routes, generally 4/hr daily in summer 9:30–18:30, in winter 10:00–15:00, tel. 01225/330-444, www.city-sightseeing.com).

Taxi Tours—Local taxis, driven by good talkers, go where big buses can't. A group of up to four can rent a cab for an hour (about £20) and enjoy a fine, informative, and—with the right cabbie— entertaining private joyride. It's probably cheaper to let the meter run than to pay for an hourly rate, but ask the cabbie for advice.

To Stonehenge, Avebury, and the Cotswolds

Bath is a good launch pad for visiting Wells, Avebury, Stonehenge, and more.

Mad Max Minibus Tours—Operating daily from Bath, Maddy and Paul offer thoughtfully organized, informative tours that run with entertaining guides and a maximum group size of 16 people. Their **Stone Circles** full-day tour covers 110 miles and visits Stonehenge, the Avebury Stone Circles, and two cute villages: Lacock and Castle Combe. Photogenic Lacock is featured in parts of the BBC's *Pride and Prejudice* and the *Harry Potter* movies; Castle Combe, the southernmost Cotswold village, is as sweet as they come (£30 plus £6.60 Stonehenge entry, tours run daily 8:45–16:30, arrive 10 min early, leaves early to beat the Stonehenge hordes). Their shorter tour of **Stonehenge and Lacock** leaves daily at 13:15 and returns at 17:15, and on some days, leaves at 8:45 and returns at 12:45 (£15 plus £6.60 Stonehenge entry).

Mad Max also offers a **Cotswold Discovery** full-day tour, a picturesque romp through the countryside with stops and a cream tea opportunity in the Cotswolds' quainter villages, including Stow-on-the-Wold, Bibury, Tetbury, the Coln Valley, The Slaughters (optional walk between the two villages), and others (£32.50; runs Sun, Tue, and Thu 8:45–17:15; arrive 10 min early). If you request it in advance, you can bring your luggage along and use the tour as transportation to Stow or, for £2.50 extra, Moreton-in-Marsh, with easy train connections to Oxford.

All tours depart from Bath at the Glass House shop on the corner of Orange Grove, a one-minute walk from the abbey. Arrive 10 minutes before your departure time and bring cash—credit cards are not accepted. It's better to book ahead—as far ahead as possible in summer—for these popular tours. Online or email reservations are preferable to calling (phone answered daily 8:00–18:00, tel. 07990/505-970, www.madmax.abel.co.uk, maddy@madmax.abel .co.uk). Please honor or cancel your seat reservation.

More Bus Tours—If Mad Max is booked up, don't fret. Plenty of companies in Bath offer tours of varying lengths, prices, and destinations. Note that the cost of admission to sights is usually not included with any tour.

Scarper Tours runs a minibus tour to Stonehenge (£14, 10 percent Rick Steves discount if you book direct, does not include £6.60 Stonehenge entry fee, departs from behind the abbey, daily Easter–Sept at 10:00 and 14:00, Oct–Easter at 13:00 only, tel. 07739/644-155, www.scarpertours.com). The three-hour tour (two hours there and back, an hour at the site) includes driver narration en route.

Celtic Horizons, run by retired teacher Alan Price, offers tours from Bath to a variety of destinations, such as Stonehenge, Avebury, and Wells. He can provide a convenient transfer service (to or from London, Heathrow, Bristol Airport, the Cotswolds, and so on), with or without a tour itinerary en route. Allow about £25/hour for a group (his comfortable minivan seats up to 8 people) and £125 for Heathrow–Bath transfers. It's best to make arrangements and get pricing information by email at alan@celtichorizons .com (cash only, tel. 01373/461-784, http://celtichorizons.com).

Sights in Bath

In Bath's Town Center
▲▲▲**Roman and Medieval Baths**—In ancient Roman times, high society enjoyed the mineral springs at Bath. From

Londinium, Romans traveled so often to Aquae Sulis, as the city was called, to "take a bath" that finally it became known simply as Bath. Today, a fine museum surrounds the ancient bath. It's a one-way system leading you past well-documented displays, Roman artifacts, mosaics, a temple pediment, and the actual mouth of the spring, piled high with Roman pennies. Enjoy some quality time looking into the eyes of Minerva, goddess of the hot springs. The included audioguide makes the visit easy and plenty informative. For those with a big appetite for Roman history, in-depth 40-minute guided tours leave from the end of the museum at the edge of the actual bath (included with ticket, on the hour, a poolside clock is set for the next departure time). The water is greenish because of algae—don't drink it. You can revisit the museum after the tour (£11, £14.50 combo-ticket includes Fashion Museum—a £3.50 savings, family ticket available, daily July–Aug 9:00–22:00, March–June and Sept–Oct 9:00–18:00, Nov–Feb 9:30–17:30, last entry one hour before closing, tel. 01225/477-785, www.romanbaths.co.uk). The museum and baths are fun to visit in the evening in summer—romantic, gas-lit, and all yours.

After touring the Roman Baths, stop by the attached Pump Room for a spot of tea, or to gag on the water.

▲**Pump Room**—For centuries, Bath was forgotten as a spa. Then, in 1687, the previously barren Queen Mary bathed here, became pregnant, and bore a male heir to the throne. A few years later, Queen Anne found the water eased her painful gout. Word of its wonder waters spread, and Bath earned its way back onto the aristocratic map. High society soon turned the place into one big pleasure palace. The Pump Room, an elegant Georgian hall just above the Roman Baths, offers visitors their best chance to raise a pinky in this Chippendale grandeur. Above the newspaper table and sedan chairs, a statue of Beau Nash himself sniffles down at you. Drop by to sip coffee or tea or to enjoy a light meal (daily 9:30–12:00 for coffee and £6–9 breakfast, 12:00–14:30 for £6–10 lunches, 14:30–16:30 for £17.50 traditional afternoon tea, tea/coffee and pastries also available in the afternoons; open for dinner July–Aug, during Bath International Music Festival, and Christmas holidays only; live music daily—string trio or piano, times vary; tel. 01225/444-477). For just the price of a coffee (£3), you're welcome to drop in anytime—except during lunch—to enjoy the music and atmosphere.

The Spa Water: This is your chance to eat a famous (but forgettable) "Bath bun" and split a drink of the awful curative water (£0.50). The water is served from the King's Spring by an appropriately attired servant who explains that the water is 10,000 years old, pumped from nearly 100 yards deep, and marinated in 43 wonderful minerals. Convenient public WCs (which use plain, old tap water) are in the entry hallway that connects the Pump Room with the baths.

▲**Thermae Bath Spa**—After simmering unused for a quarter-century, Bath's natural thermal springs once again offer R&R for the masses. The state-of-the-art spa is housed in a complex of three buildings that combine historic structures with controversial (and expensive) new glass-and-steel architecture.

Is the Thermae Bath Spa worth the time and money? The experience is pretty pricey and humble compared to similar German and Hungarian spas. Because you're in a tall, modern building in the city center, it lacks a certain old-time elegance. Jets are very limited, and the only water toys you'll see are big foam noodles. There's no cold plunge—the only way to cool off between steam rooms is to step onto a small, unglamorous balcony. The Royal Bath's two pools are essentially the same, and the water isn't particularly hot in either—in fact, the main attraction is the rooftop view from the top one (best with a partner or as a social experience).

That said, this is the only natural thermal spa in the UK, and a chance to bathe in Bath. If you visit, bring your own swimsuit and come for a couple of hours (Fri night and Sat afternoon are most crowded). Or consider an evening visit, when—on a chilly day—Bath's twilight glows through the steam from the rooftop pool.

Cost: The cheapest spa pass is £22 for two hours, which gains you access to the Royal Bath's large ground-floor "Minerva Bath"; the four steam rooms and the waterfall shower; and the view-filled, open-air, rooftop thermal pool. If you want to stay longer, it's £32/4 hrs and £52/day (towel, robe, and slippers-£9). The much-hyped £37.50 Twilight Package includes three hours and a meal (one plate, drink, robe, towel, and slippers). This package's appeal is not the mediocre meal, but to be on top of the building at a magical hour (which you can do for less money at the regular rate). Thermae also has all the "pamper thyself" extras: massages, mud wraps, and various healing-type treatments, including "watsu"—water shiatsu (£40–70 extra).

Hours: Daily 9:00–22:00, last entry at 19:30.

Location and Information: It's 100 yards from the Roman and Medieval Baths, on Beau Street. Tel. 01225/331-234, book treatments at www.thermaebathspa.com. There's a salad-and-smoothies café for guests.

Cross Bath: This renovated circular Georgian structure across the street from the main spa provides a simpler and less-expensive bathing option. It has a hot-water fountain that taps directly into the spring, making its water temperature higher than the spa's (£13/90 min, daily 10:00–20:00, last entry at 18:30, changing rooms, no access to Royal Bath).

Spa Visitor Centre: Also across the street in the Hetling Pump Room, this free one-room exhibit explains the story of the spa (Mon–Sat 10:00–17:00, Sun 10:00–16:00, £2 audioguide).

▲**Abbey**—The town of Bath wasn't much in the Middle Ages, but an important church has stood on this spot since Anglo-Saxon times. King Edgar I was crowned here in 973, when the church was much bigger (before the bishop packed up and moved to Wells). Dominating the town center, today's abbey—the last great medieval church of England—is 500 years old and a fine example of Late Perpendicular Gothic, with breezy fan vaulting and enough stained glass to earn it the nickname "Lantern of the West." The glass, red-iron gas-powered lamps, and heating grates on the floor are all remnants of the 19th century. The window

behind the altar shows 52 scenes from the life of Christ. A window to the left of the altar shows Edgar's coronation (worth the £2.50 donation; April–Oct Mon–Sat 9:00–18:00, Sun 13:00–14:30 & 16:30–17:30; Nov–March Mon–Sat 9:00–16:30, Sun 13:00–14:30 & 16:30–17:30; handy flier narrates a self-guided 19-stop tour; tel. 0122/422-462, www.bathabbey.org). Posted on the door is the schedule for concerts, services, and **evensong** (at 16:00 or 17:15, check schedule on website). The facade (c. 1500, but mostly restored) is interesting for some of its carvings. Look for the angels descending the ladder. The statue of Peter (to the left of the door) lost his head to mean iconoclasts; it was re-carved out of his once super-sized beard. Take a moment to appreciate the abbey's architecture from the Abbey Green square.

A small but worthwhile exhibit, the abbey's **Heritage Vaults** tell the story of Christianity in Bath since Roman times (free, Mon–Sat 10:00–15:30, closed Sun, entrance just outside church, south side).

▲**Pulteney Bridge, Parade Gardens, and Cruises**—Bath is inclined to compare its shop-lined Pulteney Bridge to Florence's Ponte Vecchio. That's pushing it. But to best enjoy a sunny day, pay about £1 to enter the Parade Gardens below the bridge (April–Sept daily 10:00–dusk, shorter hours off-season, includes deck chairs, ask about concerts held some Sun at 15:00 in summer, www.bathnes.gov.uk). Taking a siesta to relax peacefully at the riverside provides a wonderful break (and memory).

Across the bridge at Pulteney Weir, tour boat companies run **cruises** (£8, £4 one-way, up to 7/day if the weather's good, 60 min to Bathampton and back, WCs on board, tel. 01225/312-900). Just take whatever boat is running—all stop in Bathampton (allowing you to hop off and walk back). Boats come with picnic-friendly sundecks.

Guildhall Market—The little shopping mall, located across from Pulteney Bridge, is a frumpy time warp in this affluent town—fun for browsing and picnic shopping. Its cheap Market Café is recommended in "Eating in Bath."

Victoria Art Gallery—This two-story gallery, next to Pulteney Bridge, is filled with paintings from the late 17th century to the present (free, includes audioguide, Tue–Sat 10:00–17:00, Sun 13:30–17:00, closed Mon, WC, tel. 01225/477-233, www.victoria gal.org.uk).

▲▲**Royal Crescent and the Circus**—If Bath is an architectural cancan, these are its knickers. These first Georgian "condos"

by John Wood (the Elder and the Younger) are well-explained by the city walking tours. "Georgian" is British for "Neoclassical," or dating from the 1770s. As you cruise the Crescent, pretend you're rich. Then pretend you're poor. Notice the "ha ha fence," a drop-off in the front yard that acted as a barrier, invisible from the windows, for keeping out sheep and peasants. The refined and stylish **Royal Crescent Hotel** sits unmarked in the center of the crescent. You're welcome to (politely) drop in to explore its fine ground-floor public spaces and back garden. A gracious and traditional tea is served in the garden out back (£12.50 cream tea, £22.50 afternoon tea, daily 15:00–17:00, sharing is OK, reserve a day in advance in summer, tel. 01225/823-333).

Picture the round Circus as a coliseum turned inside out. Its Doric, Ionic, and Corinthian capital decorations pay homage to its Greco-Roman origin, and are a reminder that Bath (with its seven hills) aspired to be "the Rome of England." The frieze above the first row of columns has hundreds of different panels, each representing the arts, sciences, and crafts. The first floor was high off the ground, to accommodate aristocrats on sedan chairs and women with sky-high hairdos. The tiny round windows on the top floors were the servants' quarters. While the building fronts are uniform, the backs are higgledy-piggledy, infamous for their "hanging loos." Stand in the middle of the Crescent among the grand plane trees, on the capped old well. Imagine the days when there was no indoor plumbing, and the servant girls gathered here to fetch water—this was gossip central. If you stand on the well, your clap echoes three times around the circle (try it).

▲**Georgian House at No. 1 Royal Crescent**—This museum (corner of Brock Street and Royal Crescent) offers your best look into a period house. Your visit is limited to four roped-off rooms, but if you take your time and talk to the docents stationed in each room, it's worth the £5 admission to get behind one of those classy Georgian facades. The docents are determined to fill you in on all the fascinating details of Georgian life...like how high-class women shaved their eyebrows and pasted on carefully trimmed strips of furry mouse skin in their place. On the bedroom dresser sits a bowl of black beauty marks and a head-scratcher from those pre-shampoo days. Fido spent his days in the kitchen treadmill powering the rotisserie (mid-Feb–Oct Tue–Sun 10:30–17:00, Nov Tue–Sun 10:30–16:00, last entry 30 min before closing, closed Mon and Dec–mid-Feb, £2 guidebook available, no photos, "no stiletto heels, please," tel. 01225/428-126, www.bath-preservation-trust .org.uk). Its WC is accessible from the street (under the entry steps, across from the exit and shop).

▲▲**Fashion Museum**—Housed underneath Bath's Assembly Rooms, this museum displays four centuries of fashion, organized by theme (bags, shoes, underwear, wedding dresses, and so on). Follow the included audioguide tour, and allow about an hour—unless you pause to lace up a corset and try on a hoop underdress (£7, £14.50 combo-ticket covers Roman Baths—saving you £3.50, family ticket available, daily March–Oct 10:30–18:00, Nov–Feb 10:30–17:00, last entry one hour before closing, on-site self-service café, tel. 01225/477-173, www.fashionmuseum.co.uk).

The **Assembly Rooms,** which you can see for free en route to the museum, are big, grand, empty rooms. Card games, concerts, tea, and dances were held here in the 18th century, before the advent of fancy hotels with grand public spaces made them obsolete. Note the extreme symmetry (pleasing to the aristocratic eye) and the high windows (assuring privacy). After the Allies bombed the historic and well-preserved German city of Lübeck, the Germans picked up a Baedeker guide and chose a similarly lovely city to bomb: Bath. The Assembly Rooms—gutted in this wartime tit-for-tat by WWII bombs—have since been restored to their original splendor. (Only the chandeliers are original.)

Below the Fashion Museum (to the left as you leave, 20 yards away) is one of the few surviving sets of **iron house hardware.** "Link boys" carried torches through the dark streets, lighting the way for big shots in their sedan chairs as they traveled from one affair to the next. The link boys extinguished their torches in the black conical "snuffers." The lamp above was once gas-lit. The crank on the left was used to hoist bulky things to various windows (see the hooks). Few of these sets survived the dark days of the WWII Blitz, when most were collected and melted down, purportedly to make weapons to feed the British war machine. (Not long ago, these well-meaning Brits finally found out that all of their patriotic extra commitment to the national struggle had been for naught—the metal ended up in junk heaps.)

▲▲**Museum of Bath at Work**—This is the official title for Mr. Bowler's Business, a 1900s engineer's shop, brass foundry, and fizzy-drink factory with a Dickensian office. It's just a pile of meaningless old gadgets—until the included audioguide resurrects Mr. Bowler's creative genius. Featuring other Bath creations through the years, including a 1914 car and the versatile plasticine (proto-Play-Doh), the museum serves as a vivid reminder that there was an industrial side to this spa town. Don't miss the fine "Story of Bath Stone" in the basement (£4.50, April–Oct daily 10:30–17:00, Nov–March weekends only, last entry at 16:30, Julian Road, 2 steep blocks up Russell Street from Assembly Rooms, tel. 01225/318-348, www.bath-at-work.org.uk).

Jane Austen Centre—This exhibition focuses on Jane Austen's tumultuous, sometimes-troubled five years in Bath (circa 1800, during which time her father died), and the influence the city had on her writing. There's little of historic substance here; you'll walk through a Georgian townhouse that she didn't live in (one of her real addresses in Bath was a few houses up the road, at 25 Gay Street), and see mostly enlarged reproductions of things associated with her writing. The museum describes various places from two novels set in Bath (*Persuasion* and *Northanger Abbey*). After a live intro (15 min, 2/hr) explaining how this romantic but down-to-earth woman dealt with the silly, shallow, and arrogant aristocrats' world, where "the doing of nothings all day prevents one from doing anything," you see a 15-minute video and wander through the rest of the exhibit (£7; mid-March–mid-Nov daily 9:45–17:30, July–Aug Thu–Sat until 19:00; mid-Nov–mid-March Sun–Fri 11:00–16:30, Sat 9:45–17:30; between Queen's Square and the Circus at 40 Gay Street, tel. 01225/443-000, www.janeausten .co.uk). Jane Austen–themed walking tours of the city begin at the TI and end at the Centre (£5, 90 min, Sat–Sun at 11:00, July–Aug also Fri–Sat at 16:00, no reservation necessary).

Outer Bath

Building of Bath Collection—This offers an intriguing behind-the-scenes look at how the Georgian city was actually built (£4, mid-April–Oct Sat–Mon 10:30–17:00, last entry 30 min before closing, closed Tue–Fri and Nov–mid-April, north of the city center on a street called "The Paragon," tel. 01225/333-895, www .bath-preservation-trust.org.uk).

▲**American Museum**—I know, you need this in Bath like you need a Big Mac. The UK's only museum dedicated to American history, this may be the only place that combines Geronimo and Groucho Marx. It has thoughtful exhibits on the history of Native Americans and the Civil War, but the museum's heart is with the decorative arts and cultural artifacts that reveal how Americans lived from colonial times to the mid-19th century. Each of the 18 completely furnished rooms (from a plain 1600s Massachusetts dining/living room to a Rococo Revival explosion in a New Orleans bedroom) is hosted by eager guides, waiting to fill you in on the everyday items that make domestic Yankee history surprisingly interesting. (In the Lee Room, look for the original mouse holes, lovingly backlit, in the floor boards.) One room is a quilter's nirvana. You can easily spend an afternoon here, enjoying the surrounding gardens, arboretum, and trails (£8, mid-March–Oct Tue–Sun 12:00–17:00, last entry one hour before closing, closed Mon and Nov–mid-March, at Claverton Manor, tel. 01225/460-503, www.americanmuseum.org). The museum is outside of town and a headache to reach if you don't have a car (10–15-min walk from bus #18 or the hop-on, hop-off bus stop).

Activities in Bath

Walking—The Bath Skyline Walk is a six-mile wander around the hills surrounding Bath (leaflet at TI). Plenty of other scenic paths are described in the TI's literature. For additional options, get *Country Walks Around Bath,* by Tim Mowl (£4.50 at TI or bookstores).

Hiking the Canal to Bathampton—An idyllic towpath leads from the Bath Spa train station, along an old canal to the sleepy village of Bathampton. Immediately behind the station, cross the footbridge and find where the canal hits the river. Turn left, noticing the series of Industrial Age locks, and walk along the towpath, giving thanks that you're not a horse pulling a barge. You'll be in Bathampton in less than an hour, where a classic pub awaits with a nice lunch and cellar-temp beer.

Boating—The Bath Boating Station, in an old Victorian boathouse, rents rowboats, canoes, and punts (£7 per person/first hour, then £3/additional hour, Easter–Sept daily 10:00–18:00, closed off-season, Forester Road, one mile northeast of center, tel. 01225/312-900, www.bathboating.co.uk).

Swimming and Kids' Activities—The Bath Sports and Leisure Centre has a fine pool for laps as well as lots of water slides. Kids have entertaining options in the mini-gym "Active Zone" area, which includes a rock wall and a "Zany Zone" indoor playground (£3.70, Mon–Fri 8:00–22:00, closes earlier Sat–Sun, kids' hours limited, call for open swim times, just across North Parade Bridge, tel. 01225/486-905, www.aquaterra.org).

Shopping—There's great browsing between the abbey and the Assembly Rooms (Fashion Museum). Shops close around 17:30, and many are open on Sunday (11:00–16:00). Explore the antique shops lining Bartlett Street, just below the Assembly Rooms.

Nightlife in Bath

For an up-to-date list of events, pick up the local newspaper, the *Bath Chronicle*, on Fridays, when the "What's On" schedule appears (www.thisisbath.com). Younger travelers may enjoy the party-ready bar, club, and nightlife recommendations at www .itchybath.co.uk.

▲▲▲Bizarre Bath Street Theater—For an immensely entertaining walking-tour comedy act "with absolutely no history or culture," follow Dom, J. J., or Noel Britten on their creative and entertaining Bizarre Bath walk. This 90-minute "tour," which plays off local passersby as well as tour members, is a belly laugh a minute (£8, or £7 for Rick Steves readers, includes some minor discounts in town, April–Oct nightly at 20:00, smaller groups Mon–Thu, heavy on magic, careful to insult all minorities and sensitivities, just racy enough but still good family fun, leaves from The Huntsman pub near the abbey, confirm at TI or call 01225/335-124, www.bizarrebath.co.uk).

▲Theatre Royal Performance—The 18th-century, 800-seat Theatre Royal, newly restored and one of England's loveliest, offers a busy schedule of London West End–type plays, including many "pre-London" dress-rehearsal runs (£15–39, shows generally start at 19:30 or 20:00, matinees at 14:30, box office open Mon–Sat 10:00–20:00, Sun 12:00–20:00, tel. 01225/448-844, www.theatre royal.org.uk). Forty nosebleed spots on a bench (misnamed "stand-bys") go on sale at noon Monday through Saturday for that day's evening performance (£5, pay cash at box office or—for £3 more—call and book with credit card, 2 tickets maximum). Same-day "standing places" go on sale at 18:00 (12:00 for matinees) for £3 (pay cash at box office, 2 tickets maximum). Or you can snatch up any "last minute" seats for £10–15 a half-hour before "curtain up."

A handy, cheap sightseers' tip: During the free Bath walking tour, your guide stops here. Pop into the box office, ask what's playing tonight, and see if there are many seats left. If the play sounds good and plenty of seats remain unsold, you're fairly safe to come back 30 minutes before curtain time to buy a ticket at that cheaper price. Oh...and if you smell jasmine, it's the ghost of Lady Grey, a mistress of Beau Nash.

Evening Walks—Take your choice: comedy (Bizarre Bath, described above), history, or ghost tour. The free city history walks (a daily standard described on page 410) are offered on some summer evenings (2 hours, May–Sept Tue and Fri at 19:00, leave from Pump Room). **Ghost Walks** are a popular way to pass the after-dark hours (£7, cash only, 90 min, year-round Thu–Sat at 20:00, leave from The Garrick's Head pub to the left and behind Theatre

Royal as you face it, tel. 01225/350-512, www.ghostwalksofbath
.co.uk). The cities of York and Edinburgh—which have houses
actually thought to be haunted—are better for these walks.

Pubs—Most pubs in the center are very noisy, catering to a rowdy
twentysomething crowd. But on the top end of town you can still
find some classic old places with inviting ambience and live music.
These are listed in order from closest to farthest away:

The Old Green Tree, the most convenient of all these pubs, is
a rare traditional pub right in the town center (locally brewed real
ales, no children, 12 Green Street, tel. 01225/448-259; also recommended under "Eating in Bath," for lunch).

The Star Inn is much appreciated by local beer-lovers for its
fine ale and "no machines or music to distract from the chat." It's
a "spit 'n' sawdust" place, and its long bench, nicknamed "death
row," still comes with a complimentary pinch of snuff from tins on
the ledge. Try the Bellringer Ale, made just up the road (Mon–Fri
12:00–14:30 & 17:30–23:00, Sat–Sun 12:00–23:00, no food served,
23 The Vineyards, top of The Paragon/A4 Roman Road, tel.
01225/425-072, generous and friendly welcome from Paul, who
runs the place).

The Bell has a jazzy, pierced-and-tattooed, bohemian feel, but
with a mellow older crowd. They serve pizza on the large concrete
terrace out back in summer, and there's some kind of activity nearly
every night, usually involving live music (Mon–Sat 11:00–23:00,
Sun 12:00–10:30, sandwiches served all day, 103 Walcot Street, tel.
01225/460-426).

Summer Nights at the Baths—In July and August, you can
stretch your sightseeing day at the Roman Baths, open nightly
until 22:00 (last entry 21:00), when the gas lamps flame and the
baths are far less crowded and more atmospheric. To take a dip
yourself, consider popping in to the Thermae Bath Spa (last entry
at 19:30; see page 414).

Sleeping in Bath

(£1 = about $1.60, country code: 44, area code: 01225)
Bath is a busy tourist town. Accommodations are expensive, and
low-cost alternatives are rare. By far the best budget option is the
YMCA—it's central, safe, simple, very well-run, and has plenty
of twin rooms available (see "Bargain Accommodations" later in
this chapter). To get a good B&B, make a telephone reservation
in advance. Competition is stiff, and it's worth asking any of these
places for a weekday, three-nights-in-a-row, or off-season deal.
Friday and Saturday nights are tightest (with many rates going up
by about 25 percent)—especially if you're staying only one night, as
B&Bs favor those lingering longer. If staying only Saturday night,

you're very bad news to a B&B hostess. If you're driving to Bath, stowing your car near the center will cost you (though some less-central B&Bs have parking)—see Parking under "Helpful Hints" on page 409, or ask your hotelier. Almost every place provides Wi-Fi at no charge to its guests.

B&Bs near the Royal Crescent

These listings are all a 15-minute uphill walk or an easy £4–5 taxi ride from the train station. Or take any hop-on, hop-off bus tour from the station, get off at the stop nearest your B&B (likely Royal Avenue—confirm with driver), check in, then finish the tour later in the day. The Marlborough Lane places have easier parking, but are less centrally located.

$$$ The Town House, overlooking the Assembly Rooms, is genteel, deluxe, and homey, with three fresh, mod rooms that have a hardwood stylishness. In true B&B style, you'll enjoy a gourmet breakfast at a big family table with the other guests (Db-£95–100 or £115–130 Fri–Sat, 2-night minimum, Wi-Fi, 7 Bennett Street, tel. & fax 01225/422-505, www.thetownhousebath.co.uk, stay @thetownhousebath.co.uk, Alan and Brenda Willey).

$$ Brocks Guest House has six rooms in a Georgian town-house built by John Wood in 1765. Located between the prestigious Royal Crescent and the courtly Circus, it was redone in a way that would make the great architect proud (Db-£79–87, Tb-£99, Qb-£115, prices go up about 10 percent Fri–Sat, Wi-Fi, little top-floor library, 32 Brock Street, tel. 01225/338-374, fax 01225/334-245, www.brocksguesthouse.co.uk, brocks@brocksguesthouse .co.uk, run by Sammy and her husband Richard).

$$ Parkside Guest House has five thoughtfully appointed Edwardian rooms—tidy, clean, and homey, with nary a doily in sight—and a spacious back garden (Db-£77, this price is for Rick Steves readers, 11 Marlborough Lane, tel. & fax 01225/429-444, www.parksidebandb.co.uk, post@parksidebandb.co.uk, Erica and Inge Lynall).

$$ Elgin Villa rents five comfy, nicely maintained rooms (Ss-£40, Sb-£55, Ds-£68, Db-£85, Tb-£99, Qb-£120, more expensive for Sat-only stay, discount for 3 nights, includes substantial un-fried breakfast, Wi-Fi, parking, 6 Marlborough Lane, tel. 01225/424-557, www.elginvilla.co.uk, stay@elginvilla.co.uk, Anna).

$$ Cornerways B&B, located on a noisy street, is simple and well-worn, with four rooms and old-fashioned homey touches (Sb-£45–55, Db-£65–75, 15 percent discount with this book and 3-night stay in 2010, Wi-Fi, DVD library, free parking, 47 Crescent Gardens, tel. 01225/422-382, www.cornerwaysbath.co.uk, info @cornerwaysbath.co.uk, Sue Black).

Bath Accommodations

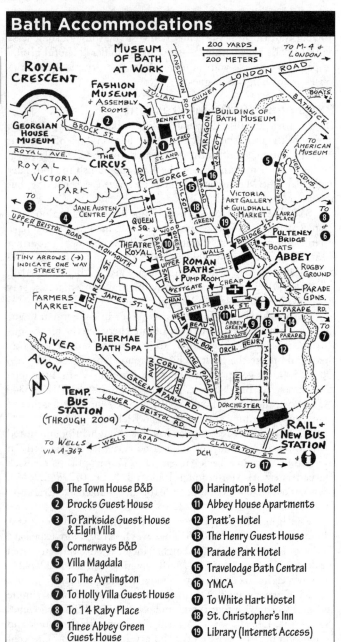

ROYAL CRESCENT

MUSEUM OF BATH AT WORK

FASHION MUSEUM & ASSEMBLY ROOMS

GEORGIAN HOUSE MUSEUM

BROCK ST.

ROYAL AVE.

BENNETT

THE CIRCUS

ST. AND.

200 YARDS
200 METERS

TO M-4 & LONDON

BOATS

BUILDING OF BATH MUSEUM

ALFRED

TO AMERICAN MUSEUM

ROYAL VICTORIA PARK

GEORGE

BROAD

WALCOT

HEN. GDNS.

JANE AUSTEN CENTRE

UPPER BRISTOL ROAD

QUEEN SQ.

JOHN

GREEN

Victoria Art Gallery & Guildhall Market

LAURA PLACE

TO

PULTENEY BRIDGE

THEATRE ROYAL

WOOD

WALLS

BRIDGE ST.

BOATS

ABBEY

RUGBY GROUND

TINY ARROWS (→) INDICATE ONE WAY STREETS.

MONMOUTH

UPPER BORO

WESTGATE

ROMAN BATHS + PUMP ROOM

CHEAP

HIGH

FARMERS' MARKET

CHARLES ST.

JAMES ST. W.

CHAN

HET

BATH ST.

YORK ST.

PARADE GDNS.

N. PARADE RD.

THERMAE BATH SPA

ST. JAMES

BEAU

ABBEY GREEN

ABBEYGATE

ORCH.

HENRY

S. PARADE

TO

RIVER AVON

CORN

ST. JAMES PARADE

SOUTHGATE

MANVERS ST.

NEWARK

GREEN

LOWER BRISTOL RD.

PARK RD.

DORCHESTER

TEMP. BUS STATION
(THROUGH 2009)

TO WELLS VIA A-367

WELLS ROAD

CLAVERTON ST.

DCH

RAIL + NEW BUS STATION

TO

1. The Town House B&B
2. Brocks Guest House
3. To Parkside Guest House & Elgin Villa
4. Cornerways B&B
5. Villa Magdala
6. To The Ayrlington
7. To Holly Villa Guest House
8. To 14 Raby Place
9. Three Abbey Green Guest House
10. Harington's Hotel
11. Abbey House Apartments
12. Pratt's Hotel
13. The Henry Guest House
14. Parade Park Hotel
15. Travelodge Bath Central
16. YMCA
17. To White Hart Hostel
18. St. Christopher's Inn
19. Library (Internet Access)

B&Bs East of the River

These listings are a 10-minute walk from the city center. Although generally a better value, they are less conveniently located.

$$$ Villa Magdala rents 18 stately, hotelesque rooms in a freestanding Victorian townhouse opposite a park. In a city that's so insistently Georgian, it's fun to stay in a mansion that's decorated so enthusiastically Victorian (Db-£95–130, less off-season, fancier rooms and family options described on website, inviting lounge, Wi-Fi, free parking, in quiet residential area on Henrietta Street, tel. 01225/466-329, fax 01225/483-207, www.villamagdala .co.uk, enquiries@villamagdala.co.uk; Roy and Lois).

$$$ The Ayrlington, next door to a lawn-bowling green, has 14 attractive rooms with Asian decor, and hints of a more genteel time. Though this well-maintained hotel fronts a busy street, it's quiet and tranquil. Rooms in the back have pleasant views of sports greens and Bath beyond. For the best value, request a standard double with a view of Bath (twin Db-£80–105, standard Db-£100–130, fancy Db-£120–170, big deluxe Db-£130–195, prices spike 30 percent on weekends, see website for specifics, Wi-Fi, fine garden, easy parking, 24–25 Pulteney Road, tel. 01225/425-495, fax 01225/469-029, www.ayrlington.com, mail@ayrlington.com). If you stay here three weeknights, you get a free pass to the Thermae Bath Spa (worth £22/person).

$$ Holly Villa Guest House, with a cheery garden, six bright rooms, and a cozy TV lounge, is enthusiastically and thoughtfully run by chatty, friendly Jill and Keith McGarrigle (Ds-£60–65, Db-£65–75, Tb-£80–95, cash only, Wi-Fi, free parking; 8-min walk from station and city center—walk over North Parade Bridge, take the first right, and then take the second left to 14 Pulteney Gardens; tel. 01225/310-331, www.hollyvilla.com, jill@hollyvilla .com).

$$ 14 Raby Place is another good value, mixing Georgian glamour with homey warmth and modern, artistic taste within its five rooms. Muriel Guy—a no-high-tech Luddite—keeps things simple and endearingly friendly. She's a fun-loving live wire who serves organic food for breakfast (S-£35, Db-£70, Tb-£80, cash only; 14 Raby Place—go over bridge on North Parade Road, left on Pulteney Road, cross to church, Raby Place is first row of houses on hill; tel. 01225/465-120).

In the City Center

$$$ Three Abbey Green Guest House, with seven rooms, is newly renovated, bright, fresh, and located in a quiet, traffic-free courtyard only 50 yards from the abbey and the Roman Baths. Its spacious rooms are a fine value (Db-£85–135, four-poster Db-£145–175, family rooms-£135–195, 2-night minimum on weekends, Internet access and Wi-Fi, tel. 01225/428-558, www.three abbeygreen.com, stay@threeabbeygreen.com, Sue and Derek). They also rent self-catering apartments (Db-£135–155, Qb-£160–195, higher prices are for Fri–Sat, 2-night minimum).

$$$ Harington's Hotel rents 13 fresh, modern, and newly refurbished rooms on a quiet street in the town center. This stylish

place feels like a boutique hotel, but with a friendlier, laid-back vibe (Sb-£79–130, standard Db-£88–130, superior Db-£98–140, large superior Db-£108–150, Tb-£138–180, prices vary substantially depending on demand, Wi-Fi, attached restaurant-bar open all day, 10 Queen Street, tel. 01225/461-728, fax 01225/444-804, www.haringtons hotel.co.uk, post@haringtonshotel .co.uk). Melissa and Peter offer a 5 percent discount with this book for three-night stays except on Fridays, Saturdays, and holidays. They also rent several self-catering apartments down the street that can sleep up to three (Db-£130, Tb-£150, much pricier on weekends, includes continental breakfast in the hotel, 2-night minimum), and one apartment (with hot tub) that sleeps up to eight.

$$$ Abbey House Apartments consist of three flats on Abbey Green and several others scattered around town—all taste-fully restored by Laura (who, once upon a time, was a San Francisco Goth rocker). The apartments called Abbey View and Abbey Green (which comes with a washer and dryer) both have views of the abbey from their nicely equipped kitchens. These are especially practical and economical if you plan on cooking. Laura

provides everything you need for simple breakfasts, and it's fun and cheap to stock the fridge or get take-away ethnic cuisine. When Laura meets you to give you the keys, you become a local (Sb-£90, Db-£100–175, 2-night minimum, rooms can sleep four with

Murphy and sofa beds, apartments clearly described on website, Wi-Fi, Abbey Green, tel. 01225/464-238, www.laurastownhouse apartments.co.uk, laura@laurastownhouseapartments.co.uk).

$$$ Pratt's Hotel is as proper and olde English as you'll find in Bath. Its creaks and frays are aristocratic. Even its public places make you want to sip a brandy, and its 46 rooms are bright and spacious. Since it's in the city center, occasionally it can get noisy, so request a quiet room, away from the street (Sb-£90, Db-£90–140, check website for specials, drop-ins after 16:00 may get a better rate if room available, dogs-£7.50 but children under 15 free with 2 adults, attached restaurant-bar, elevator, 4 blocks from station on South Parade, tel. 01225/460-441, fax 01225/448-807, www .forestdale.com, pratts@forestdale.com).

$$$ The Henry Guest House is a simple, vertical place, with eight clean rooms. It's friendly, well-run, and just two blocks in front of the train station (S-£40–45, Sb-£55–65, Db-£85–105, extra bed-£15, family room-£135, 2-night minimum on weekends, Wi-Fi, 6 Henry Street, tel. 01225/424-052, www.thehenry.com, stay@thehenry.com). Steve and Liz also rent two self-catering apartments nearby that sleep up to eight with cots and a sleeper couch—email for group prices.

$$ Parade Park Hotel rents 35 modern, basic rooms in a very central location (S-£49, Sb-£69, D-£69, small Db-£85, large Db-£95–105, Tb-£115, Qb-£110–160, no Wi-Fi, lots of stairs, lively bar downstairs and noisy seagulls, 8–10 North Parade, tel. 01225/463-384, www.paradepark.co.uk, info@paradepark.co.uk).

$$ Travelodge Bath Central, which offers 66 American-style, characterless-yet-comfortable rooms, worries B&Bs with its reasonable prices. As it's located over a nightclub, request a room on the third floor—especially on weekends (Db/Tb/Qb-£70 on weeknights, £85–95 Fri-Sat, prices vary widely—as low as £39 on weeknights if you book online in advance, up to 2 kids sleep free, breakfast extra, Wi-Fi, 1 York Building at George Street, toll tel. 08719-846-219, www.travelodge.co.uk). This is especially economical for families of four (who enjoy the Db price). Another Travelodge is located about a mile from the train station (similar prices, free parking, Rossiter Road, toll tel. 08719-846-407).

Bargain Accommodations

Bath's Best Budget Beds: **$ The YMCA,** centrally located on a leafy square, has 200 beds in industrial-strength rooms—all with sinks and prison-style furnishings. The place is a godsend for budget travelers—safe, secure, quiet, and efficiently run. With lots of twin rooms and no double beds, this is the only easily accessible budget option in downtown Bath (S-£28, twin D-£44, T-£60, Q-£72, dorm beds-£16, £1/person more Fri-Sat, WCs and showers down the hall, includes continental breakfast, cooked breakfast-£2.20, cheap lunches, linens, lockers, Internet access and Wi-Fi, laundry facilities, down a tiny alley off Broad Street on Broad Street Place, tel. 01225/325-900, fax 01225/462-065, www.bathymca.co.uk, stay@bathymca.co.uk).

Sloppy Backpacker Dorms: **$-$$ White Hart Hostel** is a simple nine-room place offering adults and families good, cheap beds in two- to six-bed dorms (£15/bed, S-£25, D-£40, Db-£50–70, family rooms, kitchen, fine garden out back, 5-min walk behind train station at Widcombe—where Widcombe Hill hits Claverton Street, tel. 01225/313-985, www.whitehartbath.co.uk). The White Hart also has a pub with a reputation for decent food. **$ St. Christopher's Inn,** in a prime, central location, is part of a chain of low-priced, high-energy hubs for backpackers looking for beds and brews. Their beds are so cheap because they know you'll spend money on their beer (46 beds in 4- to 12-bed rooms-£15–21.50, D-£52–58, higher prices on weekends or if you don't book online, check website for specials, Internet access, laundry, lounge with video, lively "Belushi's" pub and bar downstairs, 9 Green Street, tel. 01225/481-444, www.st-christophers.co.uk).

Eating in Bath

Bath is bursting with eateries. There's something for every appetite and budget—just stroll around the center of town. A picnic dinner of deli food or take-out fish-and-chips in the Royal Crescent Park or down by the river is ideal for aristocratic hoboes. The restaurants I recommend are small and popular—reserve a table on Friday and Saturday evenings. Most pricey little bistros offer big savings with their two- and three-course lunches and "pre-theater" specials. In general, you can get two courses for £10 at lunch or £12 in the early evening (compared to £15 for a main course after 18:30 or 19:00). Restaurants advertise their early-bird specials, and as long as you order within the time window, you're in for a cheap meal.

Romantic French and English

Tilleys Bistro, popular with locals, serves healthy French, English, and vegetarian meals with candlelit ambience. Owners Dawn and Dave make you feel as if you are guests at a special dinner party in their elegant living room. Their fun menu lets you build your own meal, and there's an interesting array of £7 starters. If you cap things off with the cheese plate and a glass of the house port, you'll realize that's a passion of Dave's (Mon–Sat 12:00–14:30 & 18:30–22:30, Sun 18:30–22:30 only, reservations smart, 3 North Parade Passage, tel. 01225/484-200).

The Garrick's Head is an elegantly simple gastro pub right

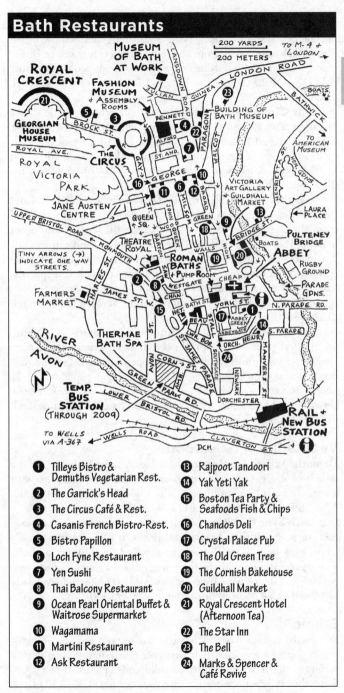

Bath Restaurants

MUSEUM OF BATH AT WORK

ROYAL CRESCENT

FASHION MUSEUM & ASSEMBLY ROOMS

GEORGIAN HOUSE MUSEUM

BROCK ST.

THE CIRCUS

ROYAL AVE.

ROYAL VICTORIA PARK

JANE AUSTEN CENTRE

UPPER BRISTOL ROAD

MONMOUTH

QUEEN SQ.

THEATRE ROYAL

TINY ARROWS (→) INDICATE ONE WAY STREETS.

FARMERS' MARKET

CHARLES ST.

JAMES ST. W.

ROMAN BATHS + PUMP ROOM

WESTGATE

BATH ST.

THERMAE BATH SPA

RIVER AVON

N

TEMP. BUS STATION (THROUGH 2009)

TO WELLS VIA A-367

WELLS ROAD

LOWER BRISTOL RD.

GREEN PARK RD.

CORN ST.

JAMES PARADE

DORCHESTER

NEWARK ST.

RAIL + NEW BUS STATION

CLAVERTON ST.

DCH

200 YARDS
200 METERS

TO M-4 & LONDON

LANSDOWN RD.

JULIAN

GUINEA

LONDON ROAD

BATHWICK

BOATS

BUILDING OF BATH MUSEUM

BENNETT

ALFRED

ST. AND.

GEORGE

PARAGON

WALCOT

TO AMERICAN MUSEUM

HENRIETTA ST.

HEN. GDNS.

VICTORIA ART GALLERY & GUILDHALL MARKET

LAURA PLACE

BROAD

GREEN

BRIDGE ST.

PULTENEY BRIDGE

BOATS

ABBEY

HIGH

WALLS

RUGBY GROUND

PARADE GDNS.

CHEAP

N. PARADE RD.

YORK ST.

ABBEY GREEN

ABBEYGATE

S. PARADE

MANVERS ST.

ORCH.

HENRY

LWR. BOR.

SOUTHGATE

MILSOM

BROAD

JOHN

QUEEN

WOOD

BARTON

SAW CLOSE

CHAN

HET

BEAU

STALL

GAY

① Tilleys Bistro & Demuths Vegetarian Rest.

② The Garrick's Head

③ The Circus Café & Rest.

④ Casanis French Bistro-Rest.

⑤ Bistro Papillon

⑥ Loch Fyne Restaurant

⑦ Yen Sushi

⑧ Thai Balcony Restaurant

⑨ Ocean Pearl Oriental Buffet & Waitrose Supermarket

⑩ Wagamama

⑪ Martini Restaurant

⑫ Ask Restaurant

⑬ Rajpoot Tandoori

⑭ Yak Yeti Yak

⑮ Boston Tea Party & Seafoods Fish & Chips

⑯ Chandos Deli

⑰ Crystal Palace Pub

⑱ The Old Green Tree

⑲ The Cornish Bakehouse

⑳ Guildhall Market

㉑ Royal Crescent Hotel (Afternoon Tea)

㉒ The Star Inn

㉓ The Bell

㉔ Marks & Spencer & Café Revive

around the corner from the Theatre Royal, with a pricey restaurant on one side and a bar serving affordable snacks on the other. You're welcome to eat from the bar menu, even if you're in the fancy dining room or outside enjoying some great people-watching (Mon–Sat 11:00–21:00, Sun 12:00–21:00, 8 St. John's Place, tel. 01225/318-368).

The Circus Café and Restaurant is a relaxing little eatery serving rustic European cuisine. They have a romantic interior, with a minimalist modern atmosphere, and four tables on the peaceful street (£7 lunches, £12 dinner plates, open Mon–Sat 12:00–24:00, closed Sun, reservations smart, 34 Brock Street, tel. 01225/466-020).

Casanis French Bistro-Restaurant is a local hit. Chef Laurent, who hails from Nice, cooks "authentic Provençal cuisine" from the south of France, while his wife Jill serves. The decor matches the cuisine—informal, relaxed, simple, and top-quality. The intimate Georgian dining room upstairs is a bit nicer and more spacious than the ground floor (£11.50 two-course lunch specials, £20 three-course early dinner from 18:00–19:00, closed Sun–Mon, immediately behind the Assembly Rooms at 4 Saville Row, tel. 01225/780-055).

Bistro Papillon is small, fun, and unpretentious, dishing up "modern-rustic cuisine from the south of France." The cozy checkered-tablecloth interior has an open kitchen, and the outdoor seating is on a fine pedestrian lane (£8 lunch plates, £13–15 main courses for dinner, Tue–Sat 12:00–14:30 & 18:30–22:00, closed Sun–Mon, reservations smart, 2 Margaret's Buildings, tel. 01225/310-064).

Vegetarian and Seafood

Demuths Vegetarian Restaurant is highly rated and ideal for the well-heeled vegetarian. Its stark, understated interior comes with a vegan vibe (£15 main dishes, daily 10:00–15:30 & 18:00–21:00, 2 North Parade Passage, tel. 01225/446-059).

Loch Fyne Restaurant, a high-energy, Scottish chain restaurant, serves fresh fish at reasonable prices. It fills what was once a lavish bank building with a bright, airy, and youthful atmosphere. The open kitchen adds to the energy (£10–18 meals, £12 two-course special plus wine from lunch until 19:00 on weekdays, daily 12:00–21:30, 24 Milsom Street, tel. 01225/750-120).

Ethnic

Yen Sushi is your basic little sushi bar—stark and sterile, with stools facing a conveyor belt that constantly tempts you with a variety of freshly made delights on color-coded plates. When you're done, they tally your plates and give you the bill (£1.50–3.50 plates, you can fill up for £12 or so, daily 12:00–15:00 & 17:30–22:30, 11 Bartlett Street, tel. 01225/333-313).

Thai Balcony Restaurant's open, spacious interior is so plush, it'll have you wondering, "Where's the Thai wedding?" While locals debate which of Bath's handful of Thai restaurants serves the best food or offers the lowest prices, there's no doubt that Thai Balcony's fun and elegant atmosphere makes for a memorable and enjoyable dinner (£8 two-course lunch special, £8–9 plates, daily 12:00–14:00 & 18:00–22:00, reservations smart on weekends, Saw Close, tel. 01225/444-450).

Ocean Pearl Oriental Buffet is famous for being the restaurant Asian tourists eat at repeatedly. It offers a practical 40-dish, all-you-can-eat buffet in the modern Podium Shopping Centre and spacious seating in a high, bright dining hall overlooking the river. You'll pay £6.50 for lunch, £13 for dinner, or you can fill up a take-away box for just £4 (daily 12:00–15:00 & 18:00–22:30, in the Podium Shopping Centre on Northgate Street, tel. 01225/331-238).

Wagamama, a stylish, youthful, and modern chain of noodle shops, continues its quest for world domination. There's one in almost every mid-sized city in the UK, and after you've sampled their udon noodles, fried rice, or curry dishes, you'll know why. Diners enjoy huge portions in a sprawling, loud, and modern hall. Bowls are huge enough for light eaters on a tight budget to share (£7–9 meals, Mon–Sat 12:00–23:00, Sun 12:00–22:00, good vegetarian options, 1 York Buildings, George Street, tel. 01225/337-314).

Martini Restaurant, a hopping, purely Italian place, has class and jovial waiters. It offers a very good eating value (£12–16 entrées, £7–9 pizzas, daily 12:00–14:30 & 18:00–22:30, plenty of veggie options, daily fish specials, extensive wine list, reservations smart on weekends, 9 George Street, tel. 01225/460-818; Mauro, Nunzio, Franco, and chef Luigi).

Ask Restaurant is part of a chain of Italian eateries, serving standard-quality pizza and pasta in a big 200-seat place with a loud and happy local crowd (£7 pizza and pasta, good salads, daily 12:00–23:00, George Street but entrance on Broad Street, tel. 01225/789-997).

Rajpoot Tandoori serves—by all assessments—the best Indian food in Bath. You'll hike down deep into a cellar, where the plush Indian atmosphere and award-winning cooking make paying the extra pounds palatable. The seating is tight and the ceilings low, but it's air-conditioned (£8 three-course lunch special, £10 plates, £20 dinners, daily 12:00–14:30 & 18:00–23:00, 4 Argyle Street, tel. 01225/466-833, Ali).

Yak Yeti Yak is a fun Nepalese restaurant, with both

Western and sit-on-the-floor seating. Sera and his wife Sarah, along with their cheerful, hardworking Nepali team, cook up great traditional food (and plenty of vegetarian plates) at prices a sherpa could handle (£6–7 lunches, £4 veggie plates, £7 meat plates, daily 12:00–14:30 & 17:00–22:30, 5 Pierrepont Street, tel. 01225/442-299).

Simple Options

Light Meals: **Boston Tea Party** feels like a Starbucks—if there were only one. It's fresh and healthy, serving extensive breakfasts, light lunches, and salads. The outdoor seating overlooks a busy square (daily 7:30–19:00, 19 Kingsmead Square, tel. 01225/313-901). **Chandos Deli** has good coffee and tasty £6–7 sandwiches made on artisan breads. This upscale but casual eight-table place serves breakfast and lunch to dedicated foodies who don't want to pay too much (Mon–Sat 9:00–17:00, Sun 11:00–17:00, 12 George Street, tel. 01225/314-418).

Pubs: **Crystal Palace Pub** is an inviting place just a block away from the abbey, facing the delightful little Abbey Green. With a focus on food rather than drink, they serve "pub grub with a Continental flair" in three different spaces, including a picnic-table back patio (£8–10 meals, daily 12:00–20:30, last order by 20:00, no kids after 16:30, Abbey Green, tel. 01225/482-666). **The Old Green Tree,** in the old town center, serves satisfying lunches to locals in a characteristic pub setting. As Bath is not a good pub-grub town, this is likely the best you'll do in the center (real ales on tap, lunch Mon–Sat 12:00–15:00 only, no children, can be crowded on weekend nights, 12 Green Street, tel. 01225/448-259).

Fast Food: **Seafoods Fish & Chips** is respected by lovers of greasy fried fish in Bath. There's diner-style and outdoor seating, or you can get your food to go (£4–5 meals, Mon–Sat 11:30–23:00, takeout until 22:00, Sun 12:00–20:00, 38 Kingsmead Square, tel. 01225/465-190). **The Cornish Bakehouse,** near the Guildhall Market, has freshly baked £2 take-away pasties (open until 17:30, off High Street at 11A The Corridor, tel. 01225/426-635). Munch your picnic enjoying buskers from a bench on the Abbey Square.

Produce Market and Café: **Guildhall Market,** across from Pulteney Bridge, has produce stalls with food for picnickers. At its inexpensive **Market Café,** you can slurp a curry or sip a tea while surrounded by stacks of used books, bananas on the push list, and honest-to-goodness old-time locals (£4 meals including fried breakfasts all day, Mon–Sat 8:00–17:00, closed Sun, tel. 01225/461-593 a block north of the abbey, on High Street).

Supermarkets: **Waitrose,** at the Podium Shopping Centre, is great for picnics, with a good salad bar (Mon–Fri 8:30–20:00, Sat 8:30–19:00, Sun 11:00–17:00, just west of Pulteney Bridge and across from post office on High Street). **Marks & Spencer,** near the train station, has a grocery at the back of its department store and the pleasant, inexpensive **Café Revive** on the top floor (Mon–Wed and Sat 8:30–18:00, Thu–Fri 8:30–19:00, Sun 11:00–17:00, 16–18 Stall Street).

Connections

Bath's train station is called Bath Spa (train info: toll tel. 0845-748-4950). The National Express bus office is in front of the train station (bus info toll tel. 08717-818-181, www.nationalexpress .com). If you're here in early 2010, you'll find the bus station west of here—see map on page 406.

From London to Bath: To get from London to Bath and see Stonehenge to boot, consider an all-day organized **bus tour** from London (and skip out of the return trip; see page 372).

From Bath to London: You can catch a **train** to London's Paddington Station (2/hr, 1.5 hrs, £48 one-way after 9:30, cheaper in advance, www.firstgreatwestern.co.uk), or save money—but not time—by taking the National Express **bus** to Victoria Station (direct buses nearly hourly, 3–4 hours, one-way-£19, round-trip-£29).

From Heathrow to Bath: See page 366. Also consider taking a minibus with Alan Price (see "Celtic Horizons" on page 413).

From Bath to London's Airports: You can reach **Heathrow** directly and easily by National Express bus (10/day, 2–3 hrs, £19 one-way, toll tel. 0871-781-8181, 10p/min, www.nationalexpress .com) or by a train-and-bus combination (take twice-hourly train to Reading, catch twice-hourly airport shuttle bus from there, allow 2.5 hours total, £50–65 depending on time of day, about £10 cheaper when bought in advance, BritRail passholders just pay £15 for bus). Or take the Celtic Horizons minibus to Heathrow; see page 413.

You can get to **Gatwick** by train (about hourly, 2.5 hrs, £45–60 one-way depending on time of day, £23 in advance, transfer in Reading) or by bus (10/day, 4–5 hrs, £25 one-way, transfer at Heathrow Airport).

Between Bristol Airport and Bath: Located about 20 miles west of Bath, this airport is closer than Heathrow, but they haven't worked out good connections to Bath yet. From Bristol Airport, your most convenient options are to take a taxi (£35) or call Alan Price (see "Celtic Horizons" on page 413). Otherwise, at the airport you can hop aboard the Bristol International Flyer (city bus #330 or #331), which takes you to the Temple Meads train station in Bristol (£9, 2–4/hr, 30 min, buy bus ticket at airport info counter or from driver, tell driver you want the Temple Meads train station). At the Temple Meads Station, check the departure boards for trains going to the Bath Spa train station (4/hr, 15 min, £6). To get from Bath to Bristol Airport, just reverse these directions: Take the train to Temple Meads, then catch the International Flyer bus.

DAY TRIP TO PARIS

The most exciting single day trip from London is Paris, less than three hours away by Eurostar train. Paris offers sweeping boulevards, sleepy parks, world-class art galleries, chatty crêpe stands, sleek shopping malls, the Eiffel Tower, and people-watching from outdoor cafés. Climb Notre-Dame and the Eiffel Tower, master the Louvre, and cruise the grand Champs-Elysées. Many fall in love with Paris, one of the world's most romantic cities.

This chapter is excerpted from *Rick Steves' France 2010,* by Rick Steves and Steve Smith.

Planning Your Time

Ideally, spend the night in Paris; see the accommodations listed at the end of this chapter.

But if all you have is a day, here's the plan:

About 7:00—Depart London.

About 11:00—Arrive in Paris, take a taxi or the Métro to Notre-Dame.

11:30—Explore Notre-Dame and Sainte-Chapelle.

14:00—Taxi or Métro to the Arc de Triomphe.

14:30—Walk down Champs-Elysées and through Tuileries Garden.

16:00—Tour the Louvre (open until 18:00, until 21:45 Wed and Fri, closed Tue).

18:00—Taxi or Métro to the Trocadéro stop, then walk to Eiffel Tower (if you ascend, allow plenty of time for delays).

19:30—Taxi or Métro back to Gare du Nord train station one hour before departure.

About 20:30—Catch late train back to London (later on Fri—confirm train times when you purchase your ticket).

22:30—Arrive in London.

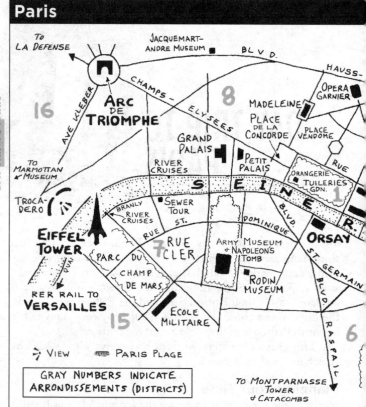

DAY TRIP TO PARIS

Getting to Paris

For information on taking the Eurostar (2.5 hours to Paris), see the Connections chapter. Note that Britain's time zone is one hour earlier than the Continent's; the departure and arrival times listed on Eurostar tickets are local times (i.e., the British time you depart London and the French time you arrive in Paris). Air France plans to start a competing rail service through the Chunnel in late 2010.

Orientation to Paris

(€1 = about $1.40; €1 = about £0.90; country code: 33)

Paris is split in half by the Seine River. You'll find Paris easier to navigate if you know which side of the river you're on, and which subway stop (abbreviated "Mo") you're closest to. If you're north of the river (above on any city map), you're on the Right Bank *(rive droite).* If you're south of it, you're on the Left Bank *(rive gauche).*

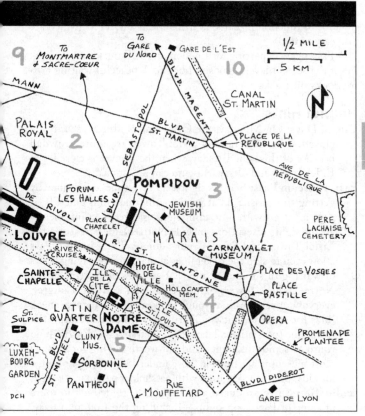

Tourist Information

Avoid the Paris TIs—long lines, short information, and a charge for maps. This chapter and a map (cheap at newsstands or free from any hotel) are all you need for a short visit. If you're staying longer than a day, pick up a copy of *Pariscope* (or one of its clones, €0.40 at any newsstand, in French), which lists museum hours, concerts, plays, movies, nightclubs, and art exhibits.

If you really need a TI, try the one at the **Pyramides** Métro stop between the Louvre and Opéra (daily 9:00–19:00). Paris' TIs share a single phone number: 08 92 68 30 00 (from Britain, dial 00 33 8 92 68 30 00) and the same website (www.parisinfo.com).

Arrival in Paris

Paris has six major train stations, each serving a different region. The Eurostar train departs from London's St. Pancras International Station and zips you to Paris' **Gare du Nord** train station. Change offices, the Métro, and taxis are easy to find. You'll need currency in euros to function in Paris, available from any ATM (which are also easy to find).

Passengers departing for London on the Eurostar must check in on the second level, opposite track 6. A peaceful waiting area overlooks the tracks.

Helpful Hints

Closed Days: On Monday, the Orsay and Rodin Museums are closed. The Louvre and Eiffel Tower are more crowded because of this. On Tuesday, when the Louvre is closed, the Eiffel Tower and Orsay Museum can be jammed.

Paris Museum Pass: Serious sightseers save time and money by getting this pass. Sold at participating museums and TIs, it pays for itself with four admissions and gets you into nearly all the sights (exceptions include Notre-Dame's treasury, the Eiffel Tower, and Sacré-Cœur's dome). The Museum Pass allows you to skip the ticket lines at many sights, saving hours of waiting in summer. Note that at a few sights (including Notre-Dame's tower, Sainte-Chapelle, and the Louvre), everyone must shuffle through slow-moving baggage-check lines for security, but you'll still save time by avoiding the ticket line (pass prices: 2 days/€32, 4 days/€48, 6 days/€64; no youth or senior discounts, and not worth buying for kids, as most museums are free for those under 18; if the sight is free for kids, they can skip lines with passholder parents).

Audio Tours: I've produced a series of self-guided audio tours of some of Paris' top sights—including the Louvre, Orsay, Historic Paris Walk, and Palace of Versailles. These free tours are available through iTunes and at www.ricksteves.com. Simply download them onto your computer and transfer them to your iPod or other MP3 player.

Getting Around Paris

By Taxi: Parisian taxis are reasonable, especially for couples and families. Two people with only one day should taxi everywhere. You'll save lots of time and spend only a few bucks per ride (a 10-min ride costs about €10; €5.60 minimum per ride). Parisian cabs are comfortable and have hassle-free meters. You can try waving down a taxi, but it's easier to ask for the nearest taxi stand ("*Où est une station de taxi?*"; oo ay ewn stah-see-ohn duh "taxi").

By Métro: In Paris, you're never more than a 10-minute walk from a Métro station (runs daily 5:30–24:30 in the morning, later on Fri–Sat). One ticket (€1.60) takes you anywhere in the system with unlimited transfers. These are your essential Métro words: *direction, correspondance* (transfer), *sortie* (exit), *carnet* (cheap set of

10 tickets for €11.40), and *Donnez-moi mon porte-monnaie!* (Give me back my wallet!). Thieves thrive in the Métro.

Sights in Paris

Start your visit where the city began—on the Ile de la Cité ("Island of the City"), facing Notre-Dame.

▲▲Notre-Dame Cathedral—This 700-year-old cathedral is packed with history and tourists. Study its sculpture and windows, eavesdrop on guides, and walk all around the outside of the

church. The cathedral facade is worth a close look. The church is dedicated to "Our Lady" (Notre-Dame). Mary is center-stage, cradling Jesus and surrounded by the halo of the rose window. Adam is on the left, and Eve is on the right. Below Mary and above the arches is a row of 28 statues known as the Kings of Judah. During the French Revolution, these biblical kings were mistaken for the hated French kings. The citizens stormed the church, crying, "Off with their heads!" All were decapitated but have since been recapitated (church—free entry, daily 7:45–19:00; treasury—€3.50, not covered by Museum Pass, Mon–Sat 9:30–18:00, Sun 1:30–18:30; audioguide–€5; ask about free English tours, normally Wed and Thu at 14:00, Sat at 14:30; Mo: Cité, Hôtel de Ville, or St. Michel; tel. 01 42 34 56 10, www .cathedraledeparis.com). Climb to the top for a great gargoyle's-eye view of the city; you get 400 steps for only €8 (covered by Museum Pass but no bypass line for passholders, daily April–Sept 10:00–18:30—also June–Aug Sat–Sun until 23:00, Oct–March 10:00–17:30; last entry 45 min before closing). Free WCs are in front of the church near Charlemagne's statue. Two blocks west of Notre-Dame is the...

▲▲▲Sainte-Chapelle—This tri-umph of Gothic church architecture is a cathedral of glass like no other. It was speedily built from 1242 to 1248 for Louis IX (the only French king who is now a saint) to house the supposed Crown of Thorns. Its architectural harmony is due to the fact that it was completed under the direction of one architect in only five years—unheard of in Gothic times. (Notre-Dame took more than 200 years to build.) Climb

DAY TRIP TO PARIS

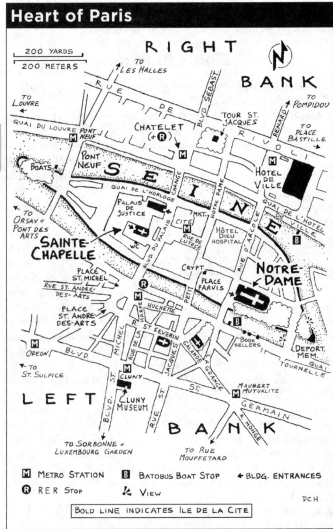

Heart of Paris

RIGHT BANK

200 YARDS
200 METERS

TO LES HALLES

TO LOUVRE

RUE DE

BLVD SEBAST.

TOUR ST. JACQUES

RENARD

TO POMPIDOU

TO PLACE BASTILLE

QUAI DU LOUVRE   PONT NEUF

CHATELET (+R)

M

RIVOLI

M

PONT NEUF

BOATS

S E I N E

QUAI DE L'HORLOGE

CHANGE

M

NOTRE DAME

Hôtel DE Ville

TO ORSAY + PONT DES ARTS

PALAIS DE JUSTICE

CITÉ

MKT.

M

RUE DE LUTECE

Hôtel DIEU HOSPITAL

QUAI DE L'HOTEL DE VILLE

RUE D'ARCOLE

B

SAINTE-CHAPELLE

WC

BLVD. DU PALAIS

CRYPT

RUE DU PALAIS

NOTRE-DAME

PLACE ST. MICHEL

R

PETIT

PLACE PARVIS

RUE ST. ANDRE-DES-ARTS

HUCHETTE

PLACE ST. ANDRE DES-ARTS

RUE DE LA HARPE

ST. SEVERIN

GALANDE

Book SELLERS

B

M

ODEON

BLVD

RUE ST. MICHEL

RUE DE LA

ST. JACQUES

GRANGE

DEPORT. MEM.

TOURNELLE QUAI

TO ST. SULPICE

M

CLUNY

MAUBERT MUTUALITE

L E F T

BLVD.

CLUNY MUSEUM

RUE ST. JACQUES

ST.

M

GERMAIN

MONGE

B A N K

TO SORBONNE + LUXEMBOURG GARDEN

TO RUE MOUFFETARD

M METRO STATION   B BATOBUS BOAT STOP   ◄ BLDG. ENTRANCES

R RER STOP   ⚓ VIEW

DCH

BOLD LINE INDICATES ILE DE LA CITE

the spiral staircase to the Chapelle Haute and "let there be light." There are 15 separate panels of stained glass (6,500 square feet—two-thirds of it 13th-century original), with more than 1,100 different scenes, mostly from the Bible (€8, free for kids under 18, covered by Museum Pass, daily March–Oct 9:30–18:00, Nov–Feb 9:00–17:00, last entry 30 min before closing, Mo: Cité, tel. 01 53 40 60 80, http://sainte-chapelle.monuments-nationaux.fr).

▲▲▲**Arc de Triomphe**—Napoleon commissioned the magnificent Arc de Triomphe to commemorate his victory at the battle of

Austerlitz. There's no triumphal arch bigger (165 feet high, 130 feet wide). And, with 12 converging boulevards, there's no traffic circle more thrilling to experience—either from behind the wheel or on foot (take the underpass). The 284 steps lead to a cute museum about the arch, sweeping skyline panoramas, and a mesmerizing view down onto

the traffic swirling below (outside-free, always open; inside-€9, free for kids under 18, covered by Museum Pass, daily April–Sept 10:00–23:00, Oct–March 10:00–22:30, last entry 30 min before closing, Mo: Charles de Gaulle-Etoile, tel. 01 55 37 73 77, http://arc-de-triomphe.monuments-nationaux.fr).

▲▲**Champs-Elysées and Place de la Concorde**—This famous boulevard, which carries the city's greatest concentration of traffic, came about because Catherine de Medici wanted a place to drive her carriage. She had the swamp that would become this boulevard drained. Napoleon added the final touches, and it's been the place to be seen ever since. The Tour de France bicycle race ends here, as do all parades (French or foe) of any significance. Although the boulevard has become a bit hamburgerized, a walk here is a must. Take a taxi or the Métro to the Arc de Triomphe (Mo: Etoile) and saunter down the Champs-Elysées (Métro stops are located every few blocks along the boulevard: Etoile, George V, FDR). The Champs-Elysées leads to the city's largest square, place de la Concorde. Here the guillotine took the lives of thousands—including King Louis XVI and Marie-Antoinette. Back then it was called place de la Révolution. Continuing past this square and through the Tuileries Garden brings you to the...

▲▲▲**Louvre**—This is Europe's oldest, biggest, greatest, and second-most-crowded museum (after the Vatican in Rome). Housed in a U-shaped, 16th-century palace (accentuated by a 20th-century glass pyramid), the Louvre is Paris' top museum and one of its key landmarks. It's home to *Mona Lisa, Venus de Milo,* and hall after hall of Greek and Roman masterpieces, medieval jewels, Michelangelo statues, and paintings by the greatest artists from the Renaissance to the Romantics (mid-1800s).

Pick up the free English-language Louvre Plan Information at the information desk under the pyramid as you enter. Touring the Louvre can be overwhelming, so be selective. Focus on the Denon wing (south, along the river), with Greek sculptures, Italian paintings (by Raphael and Leonardo da Vinci), and—of course—French paintings (Neoclassical and Romantic). For extra credit, tackle the Richelieu wing (north, away from the river), with works from ancient Mesopotamia (today's Iraq), as well as French, Dutch, and Northern art; or the Sully wing (connecting the other two wings), with Egyptian artifacts and more French paintings.

Cost: €9, €6 after 18:00 on Wed and Fri, free on first Sun of month, covered by Museum Pass. Tickets good all day and reentry allowed. Optional additional charges apply for temporary exhibits.

Hours: Wed–Mon 9:00–18:00, closed Tue; most wings open Wed and Fri until 21:45, galleries start closing 30 minutes early, last entry 45 minutes before closing; crowds worst on Sun, Mon, Wed, and mornings; tel. 01 40 20 53 17, recorded info tel. 01 40 20 51 51, www.louvre.fr.

Tours: The 90-minute English-language **guided tours** leave three times daily except Sun from the *Accueil des Groupes* area, under the pyramid between the Sully and Denon wings (usually at 11:00, 14:00, and 15:45, €5 plus your entry ticket, tour tel. 01 40 20 52 63). Digital **audioguides** give eager students a directory of about 130 masterpieces (€6, available at entries to the three wings, at the top of the escalators).

Getting There: The Métro stop Palais Royal-Musée du Louvre is closer to the entrance than the stop called Louvre-Rivoli. From the Palais Royal-Musée du Louvre stop, you can stay underground to enter the Louvre, or exit above ground if you want to enter the Louvre through the pyramid (possibly longer lines; see below).

There is no grander entry than through the main entrance at the pyramid in the central courtyard, but metal detectors (not ticket-buying) create a long line at times. There are two ways to avoid the line:

If you have a Museum Pass, you can use the group entrance in the pedestrian passageway (labeled *Pavilion Richelieu*) between the pyramid and rue de Rivoli. It's under the arches, a few steps north of the pyramid; find the uniformed guard at the entrance and take the escalator down.

Otherwise, you can enter the Louvre from its (usually less-crowded) underground entrance, accessed through the Carrousel du Louvre shopping mall or the Métro stop. Enter the mall at 99 rue de Rivoli (the door with the red awning) or directly from the

Métro stop Palais Royal-Musée du Louvre (stepping off the train, exit to the left, following signs to *Musée du Louvre-Le Carrousel du Louvre*).

▲▲▲**Eiffel Tower (La Tour Eiffel)**—It's crowded and expensive, but this 1,000-foot-tall ornament (6 inches taller in hot weather) is worth the trouble. The Eiffel Tower covers 3.5 acres and requires 60 tons of paint. Its 7,300 tons of metal are spread out so well at the base that it weighs no more per square inch than a linebacker on tiptoes.

Built a hundred years after the French Revolution (and in the midst of an industrial one), the tower served no function but to impress. To a generation hooked on technology, the tower was the marvel of the age, a symbol of progress and of human ingenuity.

There are three observation platforms—at 200, 400, and 900 feet; the higher you go, the more you pay. One elevator will take you to the first or second level (just stay on after the first stop), but the third level has a separate elevator and line. Plan on at least 90 minutes if you go to the top and back. While being on the windy top of the Eiffel Tower is a thrill you'll never forget, the view is actually better from the second level because you're closer to the sights, and the monuments are more recognizable.

It costs €8 to go to the first and second levels, and €13 to go to the top (not covered by Museum Pass, daily mid-June–Aug 9:00–24:45 in the morning, last ascent to top at 24:30 and to lower levels via elevator at 23:00 or by stairs at 24:00; Sept–mid-June 9:30–23:45, last ascent to top at 22:30 and to lower levels via elevator at 23:00 or by stairs at 18:00; Mo: Bir-Hakeim, Trocadéro, or Champ de Mars-Tour Eiffel RER stop—each about a 10-min walk away, tel. 01 44 11 23 23, www.tour-eiffel.fr). To avoid most crowds, go early (get in line by 8:45, before it opens) or late in the day (after 20:00 May–Aug, after 18:00 in off-season). Weekends and holidays are the worst. A new online reservation system may be available by 2010, allowing you to book a half-hour time slot for your visit—check their website.

The best place to view the tower is from the **Trocadéro** square to the north. It's a 10-minute walk across the river, a happening scene at night, and especially fun for kids. Consider arriving at the Trocadéro Métro stop for the view, then walking toward the tower. Another great viewpoint is the long, grassy field called **Champ de Mars,** to the south (great for dinner picnics). However impressive the Eiffel Tower may be by day, it's an awesome thing to see at twilight, when the tower becomes engorged with light, and virile Paris lies back and lets night be on top. When darkness fully envelops the city, the tower seems to climax—with a spectacular light show—at the top of each hour...for five minutes.

▲▲▲Orsay Museum—The Musée d'Orsay (mew-zay dor-say) boasts Europe's greatest collection of Impressionist works. It's housed in a former train station (Gare d'Orsay) across the river and a 15-minute walk downstream from the Louvre (Mo: Solférino, 3 blocks south of Orsay).

This museum picks up where the Louvre leaves off: the second half of the 19th century. Begin on the ground floor, featuring Conservative art of the mid-1800s. Then glide up the escalator to the late 1800s, when the likes of Manet, Monet, Degas, and Renoir jolted the art world with their colorful, lively new invention, Impressionism. You'll also see the works of their artistic descendants, Vincent van Gogh, Paul Cézanne, and other Post-Impressionists (Rousseau, Gauguin, Seurat, and Toulouse-Lautrec). On the mezzanine level, waltz through the Grand Ballroom, Art Nouveau exhibits, and Rodin sculptures. The second floor has a pricey but *très* elegant restaurant, serving tea and coffee 15:00–17:30. A simple fifth-floor café is sandwiched between the Impressionists; above it is an easy self-service place with sandwiches and drinks.

Cost: €8, €5.50 Fri–Wed after 16:15 and Thu after 18:00; free on first Sun of month, also see "Free Entry near Closing" below; covered by Museum Pass. As you face the front of the museum from rue de la Légion d'Honneur (with the river on your left), passholders enter on the right side of the museum (Entrance C), and ticket purchasers enter along the river side (Entrance A). The booth inside the entrance gives free floor plans in English. Tel. 01 40 49 48 14, www.musee-orsay.fr.

Free Entry near Closing: Right when the ticket booth stops selling tickets (Tue–Wed and Fri–Sun at 17:00, Thu at 21:00), you're welcome to scoot in free of charge. (They won't let you in much after that, however.) The Impressionist galleries upstairs start shutting down 45 minutes early, frustrating unwary visitors, so go there right away.

Hours: Tue–Sun 9:30–18:00, Thu until 21:45, last entry one hour before closing (45 min before on Thu), closed Mon. Tuesdays are particularly crowded, because the Louvre is closed that day.

Tours: Audioguides are €6. English guided tours usually run daily (except Sun) at 11:30 (€7.50/90 min). Tours are occasionally offered at other times (inquire when you arrive).

▲▲**Army Museum and Napoleon's Tomb (Musée de l'Armée)**—The emperor lies majestically dead inside several coffins under a grand dome glittering with 26 pounds of gold—a goose-bumping pilgrimage for historians. Napoleon is surrounded by the tombs of other French war heroes and fine military museums in the Hôtel des Invalides. Follow signs to the "crypt" to find Roman Empire–style reliefs that list the accomplishments of Napoleon's administration. The Army Museum's WWI exhibit is well-presented in English and complements its interesting and worthwhile WWII rooms. The section on French military history ("Louis XIV to Napoleon I") had a complete makeover before reopening in the spring of 2009.

Cost: €8.50, covers Napoleon's Tomb, audioguide for tomb, and entry to all museums within Les Invalides complex; price drops to €6.50 one hour before closing time; covered by Museum Pass; always free for all military personnel with ID.

Hours: Daily April–Sept 10:00–18:00, museum open Tue until 21:00; July–Aug tomb stays open until 18:45; Oct–March closes at 17:00; last entry 30 min before closing, Oct–May closed first Mon of every month.

Location: At Hôtel des Invalides at 129 rue de Grenelle; Mo: La Tour-Maubourg, Varenne, or Invalides (tel. 01 44 42 37 64, www.invalides.org).

▲▲**Rodin Museum (Musée Rodin)**—This user-friendly museum is filled with passionate works by the greatest sculptor since Michelangelo. See *The Kiss, The Thinker, The Gates of Hell*, and many more. Don't miss the room full of work by Rodin's apprentice and lover, Camille Claudel (€6, free on the first Sun of the month and for kids under 18, covered by Museum Pass; €1 for gardens only—perhaps Paris' best deal, as many works are well displayed in the beautiful gardens; €4 audioguides, mandatory baggage check; April–Sept Tue–Sun 9:30–17:45, gardens close 18:45; Oct–March Tue–Sun 9:30–16:45, gardens close 17:00; last entry 30 min before closing, closed Mon; near Army Museum and Napoleon's Tomb, 79 rue de Varenne, Mo: Varenne, tel. 01 44 18 61 10, www.musee-rodin.fr).

▲**Latin Quarter**—The Left Bank neighborhood just opposite Notre-Dame is the Latin Quarter, named for the scholarly language of the neighborhood's university. This was a center of Roman Paris, but its touristic fame relates to the Latin Quarter's intriguing artsy, bohemian character. This was Europe's leading university district in the Middle Ages—home, since the 13th century, to the prestigious Sorbonne College. In more recent times, this was the center of Paris' café culture. The neighborhood's main

boulevards (St. Michel and St. Germain) are lined with cafés—
once the haunts of great poets and philosophers, but now just
places where tired tourists can hang out. Though still youthful and
artsy, the area has become a tourist ghetto filled with cheap North
African eateries. The neighborhood merits a wander, but you're
better off focusing on the area around boulevard St. Germain and
rue de Buci, and on the streets around the Maubert-Mutualité
Métro stop.

▲▲Sacré-Cœur and Montmartre—This five-domed, Roman-
Byzantine-looking church, while only about 90 years old, is
impressive. It was built as a "praise the Lord anyway" gesture after
the French were humiliated by the Germans in a brief war in 1871.
The church is free and open daily from 6:00 until 22:30 (€5 to climb
dome, not covered by Museum Pass, daily June–Sept 9:00–17:45).
One block from the church, the place du Tertre was the haunt of
Henri de Toulouse-Lautrec and the original bohemians. Today, it's
mobbed by tourists and unoriginal bohemians, but it's still fun. To
beat the crowds, go early in the morning.

To get to Montmartre, take the Métro to the Anvers stop (one
more Métro ticket buys your way up the funicular and avoids the
stairs) or the closer but less scenic Abbesses Métro stop. A taxi to
the top of the hill saves time and avoids sweat (costs about €10,
€20 at night).

Sleeping in Paris

In the Rue Cler Neighborhood
(7th district, Mo: Ecole Militaire or La Tour-Maubourg)
Rue Cler, a village-like pedestrian street, is safe, tidy, and makes
me feel like I must have been a poodle in a previous life. How such
coziness lodged itself between the high-powered government/
business district and the expensive Eiffel Tower area, I'll never
know. Staying here ranks with the top museums as one of the city's
great experiences.

The street called rue Cler is the glue that holds this pleasant
neighborhood together. On rue Cler, you can eat and browse your
way through a street full of tart shops, cheesemongers, and colorful outdoor produce stalls.

$$$ Hôtel Relais Bosquet* is an excellent value with
generous public spaces and comfortable rooms that are large by
local standards and feature effective darkness blinds. The staff are
politely formal and offer free breakfast (good buffet, including eggs
and sausage) to anyone booking direct with this book in 2010 (stan-
dard Db-€185, bigger Db-€210, check website for special discounts,
extra bed-€30, 19 rue du Champ de Mars, tel. 01 47 05 25 45, fax 01
45 55 08 24, www.relaisbosquet.com, hotel@relaisbosquet.com).

Sleep Code

(€1 = about $1.40, country code: 33)
S = Single, **D** = Double/Twin, **T** = Triple, **Q** = Quad, **b** = bathroom, **s** = shower only, ***** = French hotel rating system (0–4 stars). Unless otherwise noted, credit cards are accepted, hotel staff speak basic English, and breakfast is not included (but is usually optional).

To help you easily sort through these listings, I've divided the rooms into three categories based on the price for a standard double room with bath:

$$$ Higher Priced—Most rooms €150 or more.
$$ Moderately Priced—Most rooms between €100–150.
$ Lower Priced—Most rooms €100 or less.

If you're calling Paris from the US, dial 011-33 (from Britain dial 00-33), and then dial the local number without its initial zero.

$$$ Hôtel du Cadran***, perfectly located a *boule* toss from rue Cler, is daringly modern with a chocolate-shop lobby, efficient staff, and stylish rooms featuring cool colors, mood lighting, and every comfort (Db-€210–240; 10 percent discount and free, big breakfast by entering the code "RickSteves" when you book by email or on their website, discount not valid for promotional rates on website; 10 rue du Champ de Mars, tel. 01 40 62 67 00, fax 01 40 62 67 13, www.hotelducadran.com, info@cadranhotel.com).

$$$ Hôtel de la Motte Picquet***, at the corner of rue Cler and avenue de la Motte-Picquet, is an intimate little place with plush rooms at fair prices (Sb-€150, standard Db-€160, bigger Db-€200, 30 avenue de la Motte-Picquet, tel. 01 47 05 09 57, fax 01 47 05 74 36, www.hotelmottepicquetparis.com, book@hotelmottepicquetparis.com).

$$ Hôtel Beaugency***, a good value on a quieter street a short block off rue Cler, has 30 small rooms with standard furnishings and a lobby you can stretch out in (Sb-€120, Db-€145–155, 21 rue Duvivier, tel. 01 47 05 01 63, fax 01 45 51 04 96, www.hotel-beaugency.com, infos@hotel-beaugency.com). Occasional discounts are possible for Rick Steves readers.

Warning: The next two hotels are super values, but very busy with my readers (reserve long in advance).

$$ Grand Hôtel Lévêque** faces rue Cler with red and gray tones, a singing maid, and a sliver-sized slow-dance elevator. This busy hotel has a convivial breakfast room but no real lobby. Half the rooms have been renovated and cost more; those on rue Cler come with some noise (S-€75–80, Db-€105–115, Tb-€145–150, 29 rue Cler, tel. 01 47 05 49 15, fax 01 45 50 49 36, www.hotel-leveque .com, info@hotel-leveque.com, helpful Christophe).

$ Hôtel du Champ de Mars,** with adorable pastel rooms and serious owners Françoise and Stephane, is a cozy rue Cler option. This plush little hotel has a small-town feel from top to bottom. The rooms are snug but lovingly kept, and single rooms can work as tiny doubles. It's an excellent value despite the lack of air-conditioning. This popular hotel receives an overwhelming number of reservation requests, so please be patient (Sb-€95, Db-€100, 30 yards off rue Cler at 7 rue du Champ de Mars, tel. 01 45 51 52 30, fax 01 45 51 64 36, www.hotelduchampdemars.com, reservation@hotelduchampdemars.com).

Connections

To London: The sleek Eurostar train makes the trip in 2.5 hours, with frequent departures daily in each direction. For details and prices, see the Connections chapter. The cheapest tickets sell out early—book as soon as you can.

To Other Destinations: Paris is Europe's transportation hub. The city has six central rail stations, each serving a different region. You'll find trains (day and night) to almost any French or European destination. For schedule information, check Germany's excellent all-Europe website: http://bahn.hafas.de/bin/query .exe/en.

ENGLISH HISTORY AND CONTEMPORARY POLITICS

Four Millennia in Four Pages

Invasions (2000 B.C.–A.D. 1066)

The mysterious Stonehenge builders were replaced by the Celts, whose druid priests made human sacrifices and worshipped trees.

The Romans brought 500 years of peace and stability, establishing London (Londinium) as a major city. Then civilization fell for a thousand years, to German pirates (Angles and Saxons), Danish Vikings, and, finally, William the Conqueror (A.D. 1066). During these Dark Ages, Christians battled pagan gods for supremacy of the island.

Notables

People: Boadicea, Julius Caesar, "King Arthur," "Beowulf," Alfred the Great

Sights: Boadicea statue, Roman Wall, Lindisfarne Gospels

Wars with France, Wars of the Roses (1066–1500)

French-speaking kings ruled England, and English-speaking kings invaded France as the two budding nations defined their modern borders. In the 1400s, feuding English nobles duked it out for control of the country.

Notables

People: Richard the Lionhearted, Robin Hood, Eleanor of Aquitaine, Chaucer, Joan of Arc

Sights: Tower of London, Magna Carta, Westminster Abbey, Temple Church

The Tudor Renaissance (1500s)

Powerful Henry VIII thrust England onto the world stage by defying the pope and sparking a century of Protestant/Catholic warfare. His daughter, Elizabeth I, reigned over a cultural renaissance of sea exploration, scientific discovery, and literature known as the "Elizabethan Age."

Notables

People: Anne Boleyn, Thomas More, Bloody Mary, William Shakespeare, Sir Francis Drake, Sir Walter Raleigh

Sights: Shakespeare folios and Shakespeare's Globe, Tower of London execution site, Chapel of Henry VII and Elizabeth I's tomb in Westminster Abbey, portraits of Henry VIII's wives and daughter Elizabeth in the National Portrait Gallery

Kings vs. Parliament (1600s)

The "Virgin Queen" Elizabeth died without heirs, and the Crown passed to the Stuart family. Their arrogant, divine-right management style sparked a civil war, led by the commoner Oliver Cromwell, who beheaded the king and briefly established the commonwealth. The monarchy returned, along with back-to-back disasters—first the Great Plague (1665), and then the Great Fire (1666) that leveled London.

Notables

People: King James I (Bible), Charles I (headless), Christopher Wren (St. Paul's Cathedral), Isaac Newton (apple)

Sights: St. Paul's and other Wren churches, Fire Monument, City of London, Banqueting House, crown jewels, King James Bible

Colonial Expansion (1700s)

Britannia ruled the waves and became a world power, exploiting the wealth of India, Africa, Australia, and America...at least until the Yanks revolted in the "American War."

Notables

People: King George III, James Cook, Handel, Admiral Nelson, Duke of Wellington

Sights: Portraits by Reynolds and Gainsborough in the Tate Britain

Victorian Gentility and the Industrial Revolution (1800s)

Britain under Queen Victoria reigned supreme, steaming into the modern age with railroads, factories, electricity, telephones, and the first Underground. Meanwhile, Romantic poets longed for the innocence of nature, Charles Dickens questioned the social order, and Rudyard Kipling criticized the colonial system.

HISTORY AND POLITICS

Notables

People: Byron, Wordsworth, Keats, Shelley, Coleridge, Blake, Brontë Sisters, Jane Austen, James Watt, Charles Darwin, Tennyson, "Sherlock Holmes," Jack the Ripper

Sights: Big Ben and Halls of Parliament, Buckingham Palace, The Mall, Hyde Park, the Tube, writers' manuscripts in the British Library, Poets' Corner in Westminster Abbey

World Wars and Recovery (20th Century)

Two world wars whittled Britain down from a world empire to an island chain struggling to compete in a global economy. The German Blitz in World War II leveled eastern London. Colonies rebelled and gained their independence, then flooded London with immigrants. Longtime residents fled on the Tube for London's suburbs.

In the 1960s, "Swinging London" became a center for rock music, film, theater, youth culture, and Austin Powers–style joie de vivre. The 1970s brought massive unemployment and a conservative reaction in the 1980s and early 1990s.

Notables

People: T. E. Lawrence (of Arabia), Winston Churchill, Edward VIII and Wallis Simpson, T. S. Eliot (American-turned-British), Virginia Woolf, Dylan Thomas, John/Paul/George/

Ringo, The Rolling Stones, The Who, Elton John, David Bowie, Margaret Thatcher, John Major, Martin Amis

Sights: Cabinet War Rooms, Cenotaph, Westminster Abbey's Poets' Corner, Blitz photos at St. Paul's, Beatles memorabilia in British Library

London Today

London is one of the world's major cultural capitals, an exporter of art, science, and technology. The city is gearing up to host the 2012 Olympics.

Notables

People: Gordon Brown, Tony Blair, Hugh Grant, soccer star David Beckham and wife (former "Posh" Spice Girl) Victoria Beckham, Helen Mirren, Anthony Hopkins, J. K. Rowling, Tom Stoppard, Prince William, Daniel Craig, Daniel Radcliffe.

Sights: The London Eye, West End theaters, Tate Modern contemporary art exhibits

Timeline of London History

c. 1700 B.C. Stone slabs erected to create ceremonial site... Stonehenge.

A.D. 43 Romans defeat the Celtic locals and establish Londinium as a seaport. They build the original London Bridge and a city wall, encompassing one square mile, which sets the city boundaries for 1,500 years.

c. 60 Boadicea defies the Romans and burns Londinium before the revolt is squelched.

c. 200 London is the thriving, river-trading, walled, Latin-speaking capital of Roman-dominated England.

410 The city of Rome is looted by invaders, and the Europe-wide Roman infrastructure crumbles. England is soon overrun by "barbarian" Anglo-Saxon invaders from Germany. This begins 500 years of Viking invasions, poverty, ignorance, superstition, and hand-me-down leotards—the Dark Ages.

886 King Alfred the Great liberates London from Danish Vikings; he helps reunite England, re-establish Christianity, and encourage learning.

1052 King Edward the Confessor builds his palace and abbey a mile and a half from London at Westminster.

Typical Church Architecture

Knowing a few simple terms will make your church visit a lot richer. Note that not every church will have every feature, and that a "cathedral" isn't a type of church architecture, but rather a governing center for a local bishop.

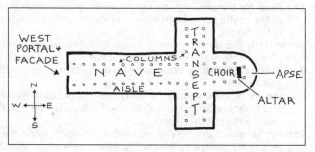

Aisles: The long, generally low-ceilinged arcades that flank the nave.

Altar: The raised area with a ceremonial table (often adorned with candles or a crucifix), where the priest prepares and serves the bread and wine for Communion.

Apse: The space beyond the altar, generally bordered with small chapels.

Choir: A cozy area, often screened off, located within the church nave and near the high altar where services are sung in a more intimate setting.

Cloister: A square-shaped series of hallways surrounding an open-air courtyard, traditionally where monks and nuns got fresh air.

Facade: The outer wall of the church's main (west) entrance, viewable from outside and generally highly decorated.

Groin Vault: An arched ceiling formed where two equal barrel vaults meet at right angles. Less common usage: term for a medieval jock strap.

Nave: The long, central section of the church (running west to east, from the entrance to the altar) where the congregation stood through the service.

Transept: The north–south part of the church, which crosses (perpendicularly) the east–west nave. In a traditional Latin cross-shaped floor plan, the transept forms the "arms" of the cross.

West Portal: The main entry to the church (on the west end, opposite the main altar).

Typical Castle Architecture

Castles were fortified residences for medieval nobles. Castles come in all shapes and sizes, but knowing a few general terms will help you understand them.

The Keep (or Donjon): A high, strong stone tower in the center of the castle complex that was the lord's home and refuge of last resort.

Great Hall: The largest room in the castle, serving as throne room, conference center, and dining hall.

The Yard (or Bailey or Ward): An open courtyard inside the castle walls.

Loopholes: Narrow slits in the walls (also called embrasures, arrow slits, or arrow loops) through which soldiers could shoot arrows at the enemy.

Towers: Tall structures serving as lookouts, chapels, living quarters, or the dungeon. Towers could be square or round, with either crenellated tops or conical roofs.

Turret: A small lookout tower projecting up from the top of the wall.

Moat: A ditch encircling the wall, often filled with water.

Wall Walk (or Allure): A pathway atop the wall where guards could patrol and where soldiers stood to fire at the enemy.

Parapet: Outer railing of the wall walk.

Crenellation: A gap-toothed pattern of stones atop the parapet.

Hoardings (or Gallery or Brattice): Wooden huts built onto the upper parts of the stone walls. They served as watch towers, living quarters, and fighting platforms.

1066	England is conquered by Norman invaders under William the Conqueror, beginning two centuries of rule by French-speaking kings. London reasserts itself as a trade center.
1209	London Bridge—the famous stone version, topped with houses—is built. It stands until 1832.
1215	King John, under pressure from barons and London's powerful trade guilds, signs the Magna Carta, establishing that even kings must follow the rule of law.
1280	Old St. Paul's Cathedral is finished.
1337	Start of the Hundred Years' War with France.
1348	The Black Death (bubonic plague) kills half of London.
1415	British victory over the French at Battle of Agincourt.

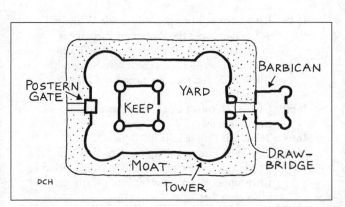

Machicolation: A stone ledge jutting out from the wall, fitted with holes in the bottom. If the enemy was scaling the walls, soldiers could drop rocks or boiling oil down through the holes and onto the enemy below.

Barbican: A fortified gatehouse, sometimes a stand-alone building located outside the main walls.

Drawbridge: A bridge that could be raised or lowered, using counterweights or a chain-and-winch.

Portcullis: A heavy iron grille that could be lowered across the entrance.

Postern Gate: A small, unfortified side or rear entrance used during peacetime. In wartime, it became a "sally-port" used to launch surprise attacks, or as an escape route.

HISTORY AND POLITICS

1455–1485	Prosperous London plays kingmaker in the Wars of the Roses, helping determine which noble becomes king.
1500	London's population swells to 50,000.
1534	Henry VIII breaks with Rome and dissolves monasteries, bringing religious strife. Generally speaking, London leans to the Protestant side.
1558	Elizabeth I is crowned, with London's backing. Her reign brings a renaissance of theater (Shakespeare), literature, science, discovery, and manners to the city.
1588	England's navy defeats the powerful Spanish Armada and starts to rule the waves. Overseas trade brings the world's wealth directly to London's wharves.
1600	London, population 200,000, is Europe's largest city, expanding beyond the medieval walls,

stretching westward along the river to Charing Cross.

1649 King Charles I is beheaded outside Whitehall as London backs the Protestant Parliament in England's Civil War (1642–1648). Oliver Cromwell heads a democratic commonwealth (1649–1653) and then becomes Lord Protector (1653–1659).

1660 Charles II, son of Charles I, is invited to restore the monarchy.

1665 The Great Plague kills 100,000.

1666 The Great Fire rages for four days, destroying the wooden city. The city is rebuilt in stone, including Christopher Wren's new St. Paul's Cathedral and other churches.

1700 London's population is 500,000 and growing fast. One in seven Brits lives in London.

1702 London's first daily newspapers hit the streets.

1776 Britain fights one of its colonies in the American War of Independence (1775–1783).

1789 The French Revolution sparks decades of war with France.

1805 Admiral Nelson defeats the French navy at Trafalgar (Spain), ending the threat of invasion by Napoleon.

1815 The Duke of Wellington defeats Napoleon for good at Waterloo (Belgium). Britain becomes Europe's No. 1 power.

c. 1830 Railroads lace the country together. The Industrial Revolution kicks into high gear.

1837 Eighteen-year-old Victoria becomes queen, soon marries Prince Albert, and presides over an era of peace and middle-class values.

1851 With Britain at the peak of prosperity from its worldwide colonial empire, London—population one million—hosts a Great Exhibition in Hyde Park, trumpeting the latest triumphs of science and technology.

1863 First Underground (Tube) line is built.

1914–1918 World War I. Britain, France, and other allies battle Germany from trenches dug in the open fields of France and Belgium. A million British men die.

1936 King Edward VIII abdicates to marry an American commoner.

1939–1945 World War II.

1940–1941   The Blitz. Preparing to invade the Isle, Nazi Germany air-bombs Britain, particularly London. Despite enormous devastation, Britain holds firm.

1945   Postwar recovery begins, aided by the United States. Many cheap, concrete (ugly) buildings rise from the rubble. Britain begins granting independence to many foreign colonies.

1964   The Beatles tour America, spreading "Swinging London" hipness to the world.

1970s   Labor strikes, unemployment, and recession.

1973   Britain joins what is now called the European Union, but maintains her distance.

1980s   The Conservative government of Margaret Thatcher rules.

1981   Prince Charles marries Lady Diana Spencer.

1982   Britain battles Argentina over the Falkland Islands. Britain claims victory.

1994   Channel Tunnel ("Chunnel") opens, linking London with Paris and Brussels.

1997   Tony Blair becomes prime minister, signaling a shift toward moderate liberalism. Princess Diana dies in a car crash in Paris. The nation—and the world—mourn.

2000   London hosts big millennium celebration, building a Ferris wheel, the Millennium Bridge, and the Millennium Dome exhibition.

2002   Many EU nations adopt the euro currency, but Britain sticks with the pound sterling. Queen Elizabeth II celebrates her 50-year Jubilee.

2003   Britain joins America's "Coalition of the Willing," and invades Iraq, dividing the British people.

2005   Four terrorist bombs rock London on "7/7."

2007   Tony Blair steps down as prime minister, and Gordon Brown takes over. In September, a bank run on Northern Rock, the country's fifth-biggest mortgage lender, marks beginning of an economic downturn.

2010   You visit Britain and make your own history.

London's History Is Britain's History

When Julius Caesar landed on the misty and mysterious Isle of Britain in 55 B.C., England entered the history books. The primitive Celtic tribes he conquered were themselves invaders, who had earlier conquered the even more mysterious people who built Stonehenge. The Romans built towns and roads and established their capital at Londinium. The Celtic natives in Scotland and

Royal Families: Past and Present

Royal Lineage

802–1066	Saxon and Danish kings
1066–1154	Norman invasion (William the Conqueror), Norman kings
1154–1399	Plantagenet (kings with French roots)
1399–1461	Lancaster
1462–1485	York
1485–1603	Tudor (Henry VIII, Elizabeth I)
1603–1649	Stuart (civil war and beheading of Charles I)
1649–1653	Commonwealth, no royal head of state
1653–1659	Protectorate, with Cromwell as Lord Protector
1660–1714	Restoration of Stuart monarchy
1714–1901	Hanover (four Georges, Victoria)
1901–1910	Edward VII
1910–present	Windsor (George V, Edward VIII, George VI, Elizabeth II)

The Royal Family Today

It seems you can't pick up a London newspaper without some mention of the latest scandal or oddity involving the royal family. Here is the cast of characters:

Queen Elizabeth II wears the traditional crown of her great-great grandmother, Victoria. Her husband is Prince Phillip, who's not considered king.

Their son Prince Charles (the Prince of Wales) is next in line to become king. In 1981, Charles married Lady Diana Spencer (Princess Di) who, after their bitter divorce, died in a car crash in 1997. Their two sons, William and Harry, are next in line to the throne after their father. In 2005, Charles married his longtime girlfriend, Camilla Parker Bowles, who is trying to gain respectability with the Queen and the public. But she's not allowed to call herself a princess—her title is the Duchess of Cornwall.

Prince Charles' siblings are occasionally in the news: Princess Anne, Prince Andrew (who married and divorced Sarah "Fergie"

Wales, consisting of Gaels, Picts, and Scots, were not subdued so easily. The Romans built Hadrian's Wall near the Scottish border as protection against their troublesome northern neighbors. Even today, the Celtic language and influence are strongest in these far reaches of Britain.

As Rome fell, so fell Roman Britain, a victim of invaders and internal troubles. Barbarian tribes from Germany and Denmark,

Ferguson), and Prince Edward (who married Di look-alike Sophie Rhys-Jones).

But it's Prince Charles' sons who generate the tabloid buzz these days. Handsome Prince William (b. 1982), a graduate of Scotland's St. Andrews University and an officer in both the Royal Air Force and Royal Navy, serves as the royal family's public face at many charity events. There's endless speculation about his romantic interests, especially about his longtime on-again-off-again girlfriend, Kate Middleton (a commoner he met at university). Whoever he marries may eventually become Britain's queen.

Red-headed Prince Harry (b. 1984) made a media splash as a bad boy when he wore a Nazi armband (as an ill-advised joke) to a costume party. Since then, he's proved his mettle as a career soldier. His combat deployment to Iraq was cancelled because of fears his presence would endanger fellow troops, but he served two months in Afghanistan (early 2008). In 2008, he and his regiment did charity work in Africa and since then he's been training to become a pilot with the Army Air Corps. Harry's love life, like his brother's, is a popular topic for the tabloids.

For more on the monarchy, see www.royal.gov.uk.

Royal Sightseeing

You can see the trappings of royalty at Buckingham Palace (the Queen's residence) with its Changing of the Guard; Kensington Palace, where members of the extended royal family keep apartments (now a Diana shrine); St. James's Palace, the London home of Prince Charles and sons; Althorp Estate (80 miles from London), the childhood home and burial place of Princess Diana; Windsor Castle, a royal country home near London; and the crown jewels in the Tower of London.

Your best chances to actually see the Queen are on three public occasions: Opening of Parliament (late October), Remembrance Sunday (early November, at the Cenotaph), or Trooping the Colour (one Saturday in mid-June, parading down Whitehall and at Buckingham Palace).

Otherwise, check *The Times* newspaper for the "Court Circular," which lists all public engagements of the royal family.

called Angles and Saxons, swept through the southern part of the island, establishing Angle-land. These were the days of the real King Arthur, possibly a Christianized Roman general fighting valiantly, but in vain, against invading barbarians. The island was plunged into 500 years of Dark Ages—wars, plagues, and poverty—lit only by the dim candle of a few learned Christian monks and missionaries trying to convert the barbarians. The sightseer sees little from this Saxon period.

Modern England began with yet another invasion. William the Conqueror and his Norman troops crossed the English Channel from France in 1066. William crowned himself king in Westminster Abbey (where all subsequent coronations would take place) and began building the Tower of London. French-speaking Norman kings ruled the country for two centuries. Then followed two centuries of civil wars, with various noble families vying for the Crown. In one of the most bitter feuds, the York and Lancaster families fought the Wars of the Roses, so-called because of the white and red flowers the combatants chose as their symbols. Battles, intrigues, kings imprisoned and nobles executed in the Tower of London—it's a wonder the country survived its rulers.

England was finally united by the "third-party" Tudor family. Henry VIII, a Tudor, was England's Renaissance king. He was handsome, athletic, highly sexed, a poet, a scholar, and a musician. He was also arrogant, cruel, gluttonous, and paranoid. Henry married six wives in 40 years, and divorced, imprisoned, or beheaded five of them when they no longer suited his needs. Henry's last wife (Catherine Parr) was fortunate enough to outlive him.

Henry also "divorced" England from the Catholic Church, establishing the Protestant Church of England (the Anglican Church) and setting in motion years of religious squabbles. He also "dissolved" the monasteries (about 1540), leaving just the shells of many formerly glorious abbeys dotting the countryside and pocketing their land and wealth for the crown.

Henry's daughter, Queen Elizabeth I, who reigned for 45 years, made England a great trading and naval power (defeating the Spanish Armada) and presided over the Elizabethan era of great writers (such as Shakespeare) and scientists (such as Sir Francis Bacon).

The long-standing quarrel between England's divine-right kings and the nobles in Parliament finally erupted into a civil war (1642). Parliament forces under the Protestant Puritan farmer Oliver Cromwell defeated—and beheaded—King Charles I. This civil war left its mark on much of what you'll see in England. Eventually, Parliament invited Charles' son to take the throne. This "restoration of the monarchy" was accompanied by a great colonial expansion and the rebuilding of London (including Christopher Wren's St. Paul's Cathedral), which had been devastated by the Great Fire of 1666.

Britain grew as a naval superpower, colonizing and trading with all parts of the globe. Admiral Horatio Nelson's victory over Napoleon's fleet at the Battle of Trafalgar secured her naval superiority ("Britannia rules the waves"). Ten years later, the Duke of Wellington stomped Napoleon on land at Waterloo. Nelson and

Wellington—both buried in London's St. Paul's Cathedral—are memorialized by many arches, columns, and squares throughout England.

Economically, Britain led the world into the Industrial Age with her mills, factories, coal mines, and trains. By the time of Queen Victoria's reign (1837–1901), Britain was at the zenith of her power, with a colonial empire that covered one-fifth of the world.

The 20th century was not kind to Britain. Two world wars devastated the population. The Nazi blitzkrieg reduced much of London to rubble. The colonial empire dwindled to almost nothing, and Britain was no longer an economic superpower. The "Irish Troubles" were constant, as the Catholic inhabitants of British-ruled Northern Ireland fought for the independence their southern neighbors had won decades ago. The war over the Falkland Islands in 1982 showed how little of the British Empire was left—and how determined the British were to hang on to what remained.

But the tradition (if not the substance) of greatness continues, presided over by Queen Elizabeth II, her husband, Prince Philip, and their son Prince Charles. With economic problems, the turmoil between Charles and the late Princess Diana, and a relentless popular press, the royal family has had a tough time. But the Queen has stayed above it all, and most British people still jump at an opportunity to see royalty. The massive outpouring of grief over the death of Princess Diana made it clear that the concept of royalty was still alive and well when Britain entered the third millennium.

Queen Elizabeth marked her 50th year on the throne in 2002 with a flurry of Golden Jubilee festivities. While many wonder who will succeed her, the case is fairly straightforward: The Queen sees her job as a lifelong position, and, legally, Charles (who wants to be king) cannot be skipped over for his son William. Given the longevity in the family (the Queen's mum, born in August of 1900, made it to 101 before she died in April 2002), Charles is in for a wait.

Thumbnail Sketches of Famous Brits

Albert, Prince (1819–1861)—German-born husband of Queen Victoria, whose support of the arts and sciences enriched London. (See National Portrait Gallery Tour.)

Arthur, King (c. 600?)—A character of legend, perhaps based on a Roman Christian general battling barbarians after the Fall of Rome.

Beatles (1960s)—Rock music quartet (John Lennon, Paul McCartney, George Harrison, Ringo Starr) whose worldwide popularity brought counterculture ideas to the middle class. (See British Library Tour.)

Boadicea (d. 61)—A queen of the Isle's indigenous people, who defied Roman occupation, burning Londinium to the ground before being defeated. (See Westminster Walk.)

Charles I (1600–1649)—King beheaded after England's Civil War, which pitted a Catholic aristocracy against a Protestant Parliament. Parliament won. (See Westminster Walk, National Gallery Tour, and National Portrait Gallery Tour.)

Charles II (1630–1685)—Son of Charles I who was invited to restore the monarchy under supervision by the Parliament. (See National Portrait Gallery Tour.)

Chaucer, Geoffrey (c. 1340–1400)—Poet, author of *The Canterbury Tales*, which popularized common English. (See Westminster Abbey Tour and Bankside Walk.)

Churchill, Sir Winston (1874–1965)—As prime minister during World War II, his resolve and charismatic speeches rallied Britain during its darkest hour. (See "Churchill Museum and Cabinet War Rooms" on page 49, plus Westminster Walk, St. Paul's Tour, and The City Walk.)

Constable, John (1776–1837)—Painter of the English countryside, specializing in cloudy skies. (See Tate Britain Tour and National Gallery Tour.)

Cromwell, Oliver (1599–1658)—Leader of the Protestant Parliament that deposed the king in England's Civil War, briefly establishing a Parliament-run commonwealth. (See National Portrait Gallery Tour and Westminster Walk.)

Dickens, Charles (1812–1870)—Popular novelist, bringing literature to the masses and educating them about Britain's harsh social and economic realities. (See Bankside Walk, National Portrait Gallery Tour, and Westminster Abbey Tour.)

Edward the Confessor (c. 1002–1066)—The English king who built Westminster Abbey, his death prompted the Norman invasion by William the Conqueror. (See Westminster Abbey Tour.)

Elizabeth I (1533–1603)—Daughter of Henry VIII and Anne Boleyn, she ruled England when its navies gained mastery of the seas, bringing prosperity and a renaissance of the arts (Shakespeare). (See National Portrait Gallery Tour and Tower of London Tour.)

Garrick, David (1717–1779)—Actor and theater manager whose naturalism on the stage—and business sense off it—greatly enhanced the blossoming theater scene. (See National Portrait Gallery Tour and The City Walk.)

Henry VIII (1491–1547)—Charismatic king during an era of expansion whose marital choices forced a break with the pope in Rome, leading to centuries of religious division. (See National Portrait Gallery Tour and Tower of London Tour.)

Hogarth, William (1697-1764)—Painter of realistic slices of English life. (See Tate Britain Tour.)

Holmes, Sherlock (late 1800s)—Fictional detective living at fictional 221-B Baker Street, who solved fictional crimes that the real Scotland Yard couldn't.

Jack the Ripper (late 1800s)—Serial killer of prostitutes in east London; his or her identity remains unknown.

Johnson, Dr. Samuel (1709-1784)—Writer of a magazine column on everyday London life, compiler of the first great English dictionary, known to us today for witty remarks captured by his friend and biographer, James Boswell. (See The City Walk and Westminster Abbey Tour.)

Keats, John (1795-1821)—Romantic poet (in the company of Percy Shelley, Lord Byron, and William Wordsworth) who pondered mortality before dying young. (See National Portrait Gallery Tour.)

Nelson, Horatio (1758-1805)—Admiral who defeated the French navy at Trafalgar (Spain), ending Napoleon's plans to invade England. (See Westminster Walk, National Portrait Gallery Tour, St. Paul's Tour, and National Maritime Museum in Greenwich—on page 383.)

Pepys, Samuel (1633-1701)—Not a famous man himself, Pepys (pronounced "peeps") chronicled London life and the Great Fire in a diary that, even today, makes that time come alive. (See The City Walk.)

Richard the Lionhearted (1157-1199)—Not a great king, he preferred speaking French and spent his energy on distant Crusades.

Robin Hood (1100s)—Fictional (or perhaps real) bandit.

Shakespeare, William (1564-1616)—Earth's greatest playwright. Born in Stratford, he lived most of his adult life in London, writing and acting. (See Bankside Walk, British Library Tour, National Portrait Gallery Tour, and Westminster Abbey Tour.)

Thatcher, Margaret (b. 1925)—Prime minister during the conservative 1980s, known as the "Iron Lady." (See Westminster Walk and National Portrait Gallery Tour.)

Victoria, Queen (1819-1901)—During her 64-year reign, the worldwide British Empire reached its height of power and prosperity. "Victorian" has come to describe the prim middle-class morality of the time. (See National Portrait Gallery Tour.)

Wellington, Duke of (1769-1852)—General who defeated Napoleon at Waterloo and later served as a domineering prime minister. (See National Portrait Gallery Tour and St. Paul's Tour.)

William the Conqueror (c. 1027-1087)—Duke of Normandy in northern France, he invaded England (1066), built the Tower of London, and initiated two centuries of rule by French-speaking kings. (See Tower of London Tour.)

Wren, Christopher (1632–1723)—Architect who rebuilt London after the Great Fire of 1666, designing more than 20 churches, including his masterpiece, St. Paul's Cathedral. (See St. Paul's Tour and The City Walk.)

What's So Great About Britain?

Regardless of the revolution we had 200 years ago, many American travelers feel that they "go home" to Britain. This most popular tourist destination has a strange influence and power over us. The more you know of Britain's roots, the better you'll get in touch with your own.

Geographically, the Isle of Britain is small (about the size of Idaho)—600 miles long and 300 miles at its widest point. Its highest mountain is 4,400 feet, a foothill by our standards. The population is a fifth that of the United States. At its peak in the mid-1800s, Britain owned one-fifth of the world and accounted for more than half the planet's industrial output. Today, the empire is down to the Isle of Britain itself and a few token, troublesome scraps, such as the Falklands, Gibraltar, and Northern Ireland.

Economically, Great Britain's industrial production is about five percent of the world's total. After emerging from a recession in 1992, its economy enjoyed its longest period of expansion on record. But in 2008, the global economic slowdown, tight credit, and falling home prices pushed Britain back into a recession.

Culturally, Britain is still a world leader. Her heritage, culture, and people cannot be measured in traditional units of power. London is a major exporter of actors, movies, and theater, of rock and classical music, and of writers, painters, and sculptors.

Ethnically, the British Isles are a mix of the descendants of the early Celtic natives (like Scots and Gaels in Scotland, Ireland, and Wales), of the invading Anglo-Saxons who took southeast England in the Dark Ages, and of the conquering Normans of the 11th century. Cynics call the United Kingdom an English Empire ruled by London, whose dominant Anglo-Saxon English (49 million) far outnumber their Celtic brothers and sisters (8 million).

Politically, Britain is ruled by the House of Commons, with some guidance from the mostly figurehead monarch and House of Lords. Just as the United States Congress is dominated by Democrats and Republicans, Britain's Parliament is dominated by two parties: Labour and Conservative ("Tories").

The prime minister is the chief executive. He or she is not elected directly by voters, but, rather, assumes power as the head of the party that wins a majority in parliamentary elections. Instead of imposing term limits, the Brits allow their prime ministers to choose when to leave office. The ruling party also gets to choose

Get It Right

Americans tend to use "England," "Britain," and "United Kingdom" interchangeably, but they're not quite the same:

- England is the country occupying the southeast part of the island.
- Britain is the name of the island.
- Great Britain is the political union of the island's three countries: England, Scotland, and Wales.
- The United Kingdom adds a fourth country, Northern Ireland.
- The British Isles (not a political entity) also includes the independent nation of Ireland.
- The British Commonwealth is a loose association of possessions and former colonies (including Canada, Australia, and India) that profess at least symbolic loyalty to the Crown.

You can call the modern nation either the United Kingdom ("the UK") or simply "Britain."

HISTORY AND POLITICS

when to hold elections, as long as it's within five years of the previous one—so prime ministers carefully schedule elections for times that (they hope) their party will win.

In the 1980s, Conservatives were in charge under Prime Ministers Margaret Thatcher and John Major. As proponents of traditional, Victorian values—community, family, hard work, thrift, and trickle-down economics—they took a Reaganesque approach to Britain's serious social and economic problems.

In 1997, a huge Labour victory brought Tony Blair to the prime ministership. Labour began shoring up a social-service system (health care, education, the minimum wage) undercut by years of Conservative rule. Blair's Labour Party was "New Labour"—akin to Clinton's "New Democrats"—meaning they were fiscally conservative but attentive to the needs of the people. Conservative Party fears of old-fashioned, big-spending, bleeding-heart, Union-style liberalism have proved unfounded. The Labour-controlled Parliament has proved to be more open to integration with Europe.

Tony Blair—relatively young, family-oriented, personable, easygoing, and forever flashing his toothy grin—started out as a respected and well-liked PM. But after he followed US President George W. Bush into an unnecessary and costly war with Iraq, his popularity took a nosedive. The 2005 elections were a virtual referendum on whether Blair could be trusted. His Labour party won by only a slim majority. In May of 2007, Blair announced he would resign his post; a few weeks later, his chancellor of the exchequer,

Gordon Brown, was sworn in as Britain's new prime minister. Burdened with an economic crisis and lacking Blair's charisma, Brown will find it challenging to keep Labour in power through the next parliamentary elections (which must be held by June of 2010).

Meanwhile, London has been coping with its own string of terrorist threats. On the morning of July 7, 2005, London's commuters were rocked by four different bombs that killed dozens across the city. The bombers (who died in the attacks) were British citizens of Pakistani descent, and the incident has caused the country to ponder how well it has incorporated its Muslim population. On June 29, 2007—just two days after Gordon Brown became prime minister—two car bombs were discovered (and defused) near Piccadilly Circus. But Londoners, who seem to have retained the can-do survival spirit of the bleak Blitz days, are determined not to let these scares dampen their enthusiasm for their city. The same goes for the recent economic downturn. Though Britain's financial sector was hit especially hard, you wouldn't know it in London, which remains a vibrant place. Looking to the future, London is gearing up to host the 2012 Olympic Games.

APPENDIX

Contents

Tourist Information

London has a fine tourist information office, called the **Britain and London Visitors Centre** (see page 24). Note that tourist information offices are abbreviated "TI" in this book.

Websites: Start with the TI's official website, www.visit london.com. Other helpful sites include www.timeout.com /london and www.londontown.com. For information on London and beyond, go to try www.visitbritain.com.

Communicating

Telephones

Smart travelers get comfortable using the telephone to reserve or reconfirm rooms, get tourist information, reserve restaurants, confirm tour times, or phone home. Generally the easiest, cheapest way to call home is to use an international phone card purchased in Britain. This section covers dialing instructions, phone cards,

European Calling Chart

Just smile and dial, using this key:
AC = Area Code, LN = Local Number.

European Country	Calling long distance within ...	Calling from the US or Canada to ...	Calling from a European country to ...
Austria	AC + LN	011 + 43 + AC (without the initial zero) + LN	00 + 43 + AC (without the initial zero) + LN
Belgium	LN	011 + 32 + LN (without initial zero)	00 + 32 + LN (without initial zero)
Bosnia-Herzegovina	AC + LN	011 + 387 + AC (without initial zero) + LN	00 + 387 + AC (without initial zero) + LN
Britain	AC + LN	011 + 44 + AC (without initial zero) + LN	00 + 44 + AC (without initial zero) + LN
Croatia	AC + LN	011 + 385 + AC (without initial zero) + LN	00 + 385 + AC (without initial zero) + LN
Czech Republic	LN	011 + 420 + LN	00 + 420 + LN
Denmark	LN	011 + 45 + LN	00 + 45 + LN
Estonia	LN	011 + 372 + LN	00 + 372 + LN
Finland	AC + LN	011 + 358 + AC (without initial zero) + LN	999 + 358 + AC (without initial zero) + LN
France	LN	011 + 33 + LN (without initial zero)	00 + 33 + LN (without initial zero)
Germany	AC + LN	011 + 49 + AC (without initial zero) + LN	00 + 49 + AC (without initial zero) + LN
Gibraltar	LN	011 + 350 + LN	00 + 350 + LN
Greece	LN	011 + 30 + LN	00 + 30 + LN
Hungary	06 + AC + LN	011 + 36 + AC + LN	00 + 36 + AC + LN
Ireland	AC + LN	011 + 353 + AC (without initial zero) + LN	00 + 353 + AC (without initial zero) + LN
Italy	LN	011 + 39 + LN	00 + 39 + LN

European Country	Calling long distance within ...	Calling from the US or Canada to ...	Calling from a European country to ...
Montenegro	AC + LN	011 + 382 + AC (without initial zero) + LN	00 + 382 + AC (without initial zero) + LN
Morocco	LN	011 + 212 + LN (without initial zero)	00 + 212 + LN (without initial zero)
Netherlands	AC + LN	011 + 31 + AC (without initial zero) + LN	00 + 31 + AC (without initial zero) + LN
Norway	LN	011 + 47 + LN	00 + 47 + LN
Poland	LN	011 + 48 + LN (without initial zero)	00 + 48 + LN (without initial zero)
Portugal	LN	011 + 351 + LN	00 + 351 + LN
Slovakia	AC + LN	011 + 421 + AC (without initial zero) + LN	00 + 421 + AC (without initial zero) + LN
Slovenia	AC + LN	011 + 386 + AC (without initial zero) + LN	00 + 386 + AC (without initial zero) + LN
Spain	LN	011 + 34 + LN	00 + 34 + LN
Sweden	AC + LN	011 + 46 + AC (without initial zero) + LN	00 + 46 + AC (without initial zero) + LN
Switzerland	LN	011 + 41 + LN (without initial zero)	00 + 41 + LN (without initial zero)
Turkey	AC (if no initial zero is included, add one) + LN	011 + 90 + AC (without initial zero) + LN	00 + 90 + AC (without initial zero) + LN

- The instructions above apply whether you're calling a land line or mobile phone.
- The international access codes (the first numbers you dial when making an international call) are 011 if you're calling from the US or Canada, or 00 if you're calling from virtually anywhere in Europe (except Finland, where it's 999).
- To call the US or Canada from Europe, dial 00, then 1 (the country code for the US and Canada), then the area code and number. In short, 00 + 1 + AC + LN = Hi, Mom!

and types of phones (for more in-depth information, see www
.ricksteves.com/phones).

How to Dial

Calling from the US to Britain, or vice versa, is simple—once you
break the code. The European Calling Chart on page 468 will
walk you through it.

Dialing Domestically Within Britain

Britain, like much of the US, uses an area-code dialing system.
To make domestic calls anywhere within Britain, if you're dialing
within an area code, you just dial the local number to be connected;
but if you're calling outside your area code, you have to dial both
the area code (which starts with a 0) and the local number.

Area codes are listed in this book and by city on phone-booth
walls, and are available from directory assistance (dial 118-500,
64p/min). It's most expensive to call within Britain between 8:00
and 13:00, and cheapest between 17:00 and 8:00. Still, a short call
across the country is inexpensive, so don't hesitate to call long
distance.

Dialing Internationally to or from Britain

If you want to make an international call, follow these steps:

1. Dial the international access code (00 if you're calling from
Europe, 011 from the US or Canada).

2. Dial the country code of the country you're calling (see
European calling chart on page 468).

3. Dial the area code (London's area code is 020) and the
local number, keeping in mind that if you're calling Britain, drop
the initial zero of the area code (the European calling chart lists
specifics per country).

Calling from the US to Britain: To call from the US to a
recommended London hotel, dial 011 (the US international access
code), 44 (Britain's country code), 20 (London's area code without
its initial 0), then 7730-8191 (the hotel's number—in this example
the Lime Tree Hotel).

Calling from Britain to the US: To call from Britain to my
office in Edmonds, Washington, I dial 00 (Europe's international
access code), 1 (the US country code), 425 (Edmonds' area code),
and 771-8303.

Note: You might see a + in front of a European number.
When dialing the number, replace the + with the international
access code of the country you're calling from (00 from Europe,
011 from the US or Canada).

The English Accent

In the olden days, an English person's accent indicated his or her social standing. Eliza Doolittle had the right idea—elocution could make or break you. Wealthier families would send their kids to fancy private schools to learn proper pronunciation. But these days, in a sort of reverse snobbery that has gripped the nation, accents are back. Politicians, newscasters, and movie stars have been favoring deep accents over the Queen's English. While it's hard for American ears to pick out all of the variations, most English can determine where a person is from based on their accent...not just the region, but often the village, and even the part of a town.

Public Phones and Hotel-Room Phones

British public pay phones are easy to find and easy to use, but relatively expensive. They take major credit cards (which you insert into the phone—minimum charge for a credit-card call is 50p) or coins. Phones clearly list which coins you can use (usually from 10p to £1, with a minimum toll of 40p; some new phones even accept euro coins), and a display shows how your money supply's doing. Only completely unused coins will be returned, so put in biggies with caution. (If money's left over, rather than hanging up, push the "make another call" button.)

The only tricky public pay phones you'll use are the expensive, coin-op ones in bars and B&Bs. Some require money before you dial, while others wait until after you're connected. Many have a button you must push before you begin talking. And some might just eat your money.

Hotel-Room Phones: Calling from your room can be cheap for local calls (before you dial, get a clear explanation from the hotel staff of the charges, even for local and—supposedly—toll-free calls). If you want to make affordable international calls from your hotel room, use an international phone card (described next). However, increasingly, hotels are blocking the toll-free numbers used for international phone cards, so you end up paying certain hotel charges.

Incoming calls are free, making this a cheap way for friends and family to stay in touch (provided they have a good long-distance plan for calls to Britain—and a list of your hotels' phone numbers).

International Phone Cards: These are the cheapest way to make international calls from Britain (less than 10 cents a minute to the US) as long as you don't call from a phone booth. British Telecom charges a hefty surcharge for using international phone cards from a pay phone (so instead of 100 minutes for a £5 card, you'll get less than 10 minutes—a miserable deal). But they're still a good deal if you use them when calling from mobile phones or fixed-line phones such as hotel-room phones (check to make sure that your phone is set on tone instead of pulse).

To use the card, dial a toll-free access number, then enter your scratch-to-reveal PIN number. (If you have several access numbers listed on your card, you'll save money overall if you choose the toll-free one starting with 0800, rather than 0845, 0870, or 0871, which cost around 10p per minute.) To call the US, see "Dialing Internationally to or from Britain," above. To make calls within Britain, see "Dialing Domestically within Britain," above; when using an international calling card, the area code must be dialed even if you're calling across the street. These cards work only within the country of purchase (e.g., one bought in Britain won't work in France).

To make numerous, successive calls with an international calling card without having to redial the long access number each time, press the keys (see instructions on card, usually ##) that allow you to launch directly into your next call. Remember that you don't need the actual card to use a card account, so it's sharable. You can write down the access number and code in your notebook and share it with friends. If you have a still-lively card at the end of your trip, give it to another traveler.

US Calling Cards: These cards, such as the ones offered by AT&T, Verizon, or Sprint, are the worst option. You'll nearly always save a lot of money by using a local phone card instead.

Mobile Phones

Many travelers enjoy the convenience of traveling with a mobile phone.

Using Your Mobile Phone: Your US mobile phone works in Britain if it's GSM-enabled, tri-band or quad-band, and on a calling plan that includes international calls. For example, with a T-Mobile phone, you'll pay about $1 per minute to make or receive a call, and about $0.35 apiece for text messages.

You can save money if your phone is electronically "unlocked"— then you can simply buy a British **SIM card** (a fingernail-sized chip that stores the phone's information) in Britain. SIM cards, which give you a British phone number, are sold at mobile-phone stores and some newsstand kiosks for about $5–10. When you buy the card, you'll also buy some prepaid calling time. Simply insert the SIM card into your phone (usually in a slot behind the battery), and it'll work like a British mobile phone. When buying a SIM card, always ask about fees for domestic and international calls, roaming charges, and how to check your credit balance and buy more time.

Many **smartphones,** such as the iPhone or BlackBerry, work in Britain—but beware of sky-high fees, especially for data downloading (checking email, browsing the Internet, watching videos, and so on). Ask your provider in advance how to avoid unwittingly "roaming" your way to a huge bill. Some applications allow for cheap or free smartphone calls using a Wi-Fi connection.

Using a British Mobile Phone: Local mobile-phone shops all over Britain sell basic phones with prepaid calling time, which you can "top up" as you use up your credit. (For example, Britain's Carphone Warehouse sells pay-as-you-go mobile phones for as little as £10 plus £10 for calling time.) Incoming calls are generally free, and outgoing domestic calls generally run about 15–20p per minute—less than from a pay phone. You'll also need to buy a SIM card (explained above). If you remain in the phone's home country, domestic calls are reasonable, and incoming calls are generally free. You'll pay more if you're "roaming" in another country. If your phone is "unlocked," you can swap out its SIM card for a new one in other countries. Some London hotels will lend you a free mobile phone, but you'll pay a usage fee of 50 cents a minute. Ask your hotel about this if you're interested. For more information on mobile phones, see www.ricksteves.com/phones.

Americans, who generally pay the same no matter how many local calls they make, think nothing of asking a stranger (or B&B owner) if they can use their phone. But most British people pay for each local call (whether from a fixed line or a mobile phone), and rates are expensive. To be polite, ask to use someone's phone only in an emergency—and offer to use an international calling card or to pay for the call.

Calling over the Internet

Some things that seem too good to be true...actually are true. If you're traveling with a laptop, make calls using VoIP (Voice over Internet Protocol). With VoIP, two computers act as the phones, and the Internet-based calls are free (or you can pay a few cents to call from your computer to a telephone). The major providers are Skype (www.skype.com) and Google Talk (www.google.com /talk).

Useful Phone Numbers

Understand the various prefixes—numbers starting with 09 are telephone-sex–type expensive. As mentioned earlier, 0800 numbers are toll-free, but numbers with prefixes of 0845, 0870, and 0871 cost around 10p per minute. If you have questions about a prefix, call 100 for free help.

Embassies and Consulates

US Consulate and Embassy: tel. 020/7499-9000, passport services available Mon–Fri 8:30–12:30 (24 Grosvenor Square, Tube: Bond Street, www.usembassy.org.uk)

Canadian High Commission: tel. 020/7258-6600, passport services available Mon–Fri 9:30–13:30 (Trafalgar Square, Tube: Charing Cross, www.unitedkingdom.gc.ca)

Emergency Needs

Police and Ambulance: tel. 999

Dialing Assistance

Operator Assistance: tel. 100 (free)

Directory Assistance: toll tel. 118-500 (64p/min, plus 23p/min connection charge from fixed lines)

International Directory Assistance: toll tel. 118-505 (£1.99/min, plus 69p connection charge)

Trains

Train information for trips within England: toll tel. 0845-748-4950 (www.nationalrail.co.uk)

Eurostar (Chunnel Info): toll tel. 08705-186-186 (www.eurostar.com)

Trains to all points in Europe: toll tel. 08705-848-848 (www.raileurope.com)

Airports

For online information on the first three airports, check www.baa.co.uk.

Heathrow (flight info): toll tel. 0870-000-0123

Gatwick (general info): toll tel. 0870-000-2468 for all airlines, except British Airways—toll tel. 0870-551-1155 (flights) or 0870-850-9850 (reservations)

Stansted (general info): toll tel. 0870-000-0303

Luton (general info): tel. 01582/405-100 (www.london-luton.com)

London City Airport (general info): tel. 020/7646-0088 (www.londoncityairport.com)

Airlines

Aer Lingus: toll tel. 0870-876-5000 (www.aerlingus.com)

Air Canada: toll tel. 0871-220-1111 (www.aircanada.com)

Alitalia: toll tel. 08714-241-424, (www.alitalia.com)

American: tel. 020/7365-0777 (www.aa.com)

bmi: toll tel. 0870-607-0555 (www.flybmi.com)

British Airways: toll tel. 0844-493-0787, flight info toll tel. 0844-493-0777 (www.ba.com)

Public Transportation Routes in Britain

Continental Airlines: toll tel. 0845-607-6760 (www.continental.com)

easyJet: toll tel. 0905-821-0905 (65p/min, www.easyjet.com)

KLM Royal Dutch/Northwest Airlines: toll tel. 0870-507-4074 (www.klm.com)

Lufthansa: toll tel. 0871-945-9747 (www.lufthansa.com)

Ryanair: toll tel. 0871-246-0000 (www.ryanair.com)

Scandinavian Airlines (SAS): toll tel. 0871-521-2772 (www.flysas.com)

United Airlines: toll tel. 0845-844-4777 (www.unitedairlines.co.uk)

US Airways: toll tel. 0845-600-3300 (www.usairways.com)

Heathrow Airport Car-Rental Agencies

Avis: toll tel. 0844-544-6000 (www.avis.co.uk)

Budget: toll tel. 0844-544-4600 (www.budget.co.uk)

Enterprise: tel. 020/8897-2100 (www.enterprise.co.uk)

Europcar: tel. 020/8564-3500 (www.europcar.co.uk)

Hertz: toll tel. 0870-846-0006 (www.hertz.co.uk)

APPENDIX

The Internet

The Internet can be an invaluable tool for planning your trip (researching and booking hotels, checking train schedules, and so on). It's also useful to get online periodically as you travel—to reconfirm your trip plans, check the weather, catch up on email, blog or post photos from your trip, or call folks back home (explained earlier, under "Calling over the Internet").

Many hotels offer a computer in the lobby with Internet access for guests. Smaller places may sometimes let you sit at their desk for a few minutes just to check your email, if you ask politely. For those traveling with a laptop, your hotel may have Wi-Fi (wireless Internet access) or a port in your room where you can plug in a cable to get online. Some hotels offer Internet access and/or Wi-Fi for free; others charge a fee.

If your hotel doesn't have access, your hotelier can direct you to the nearest place to get online. Internet cafés are easy to find in London; for specific listings, see page 25.

Mail

Get stamps at the neighborhood post office, newsstands within fancy hotels, and some mini-marts and card shops. While you can arrange for mail delivery to your hotel (allow 10 days for a letter to arrive), phoning and emailing are so easy that I've dispensed with mail stops altogether.

Resources

Resources from Rick Steves

Rick Steves' London 2010 is one of more than 30 titles in a series of **books** on European travel, which includes country guidebooks

(including Great Britain), city and regional guidebooks (including England), and my budget-travel skills handbook, *Rick Steves' Europe Through the Back Door.* My phrase books—for French, Italian, German, Spanish, and Portuguese—are practical and budget-oriented. My other books are *Europe 101* (a crash course on art and history, newly expanded and in full color), *Travel as a Political Act* (a travelogue sprinkled with tips for bringing home a global perspective), *European Christmas* (on traditional and modern-day celebrations), and *Postcards from Europe* (a fun memoir of my travels). For a complete list of my books, see the inside of the last page of this book.

My **TV series**, *Rick Steves' Europe,* covers European destinations in 100 episodes, with 10 episodes on Great Britain. My weekly public **radio show,** *Travel with Rick Steves,* features interviews with travel experts from around the world, including several hours on Great Britain and British culture. All the TV scripts and radio shows (which are easy and free to download to an iPod or other MP3 player) are at www.ricksteves.com.

Take advantage of my free self-guided **audio tours** of the major sights in London (coming in early 2010). Simply download them from www.ricksteves .com or iTunes (search for "Rick Steves' tours" in the iTunes Store), then transfer them to your iPod or other MP3 player. If your travels take you beyond Britain to France or Italy, I also offer audio

tours of the major sights in Paris, Florence, Rome, and Venice.

Maps

The black-and-white maps in this book, drawn by Dave Hoerlein, are concise and simple. Dave, who is well-traveled in London and Britain, designed the maps to help you orient yourself quickly and get where you want to go painlessly. The color city maps and Tube map at the front of this book are also useful.

For more detail, buy a city map at a London newsstand—the red *Bensons Mapguide* (£3) is excellent. Even the vending-machine maps sold in Tube stations are good. The *Rough Guide* map to London is well-designed (£5, sold at London bookstores). The *Rick Steves' Britain, Ireland & London City Map* has a good map of London ($6, www.ricksteves.com). Many Londoners, along with obsessive-compulsive tourists, rely on the highly detailed *London A–Z* map book (generally £5–7, called "A to Zed" by locals, available at newsstands). Before you buy a map, look at it to make sure it has the level of detail you want.

Other Guidebooks

If you're like most travelers, this book is all you need. But if you'll be exploring beyond my recommended neighborhoods and destinations, $30 for extra maps and books can be money well spent.

The following books are worthwhile, though not updated annually, so check the publication date before you buy. *Michelin Green Guide to London,* which is somewhat scholarly, and the more readable Access guide for London, are both well-researched. *Let's Go: London* is youth-oriented, with good coverage of nightlife, hosteling, and cheap transportation deals. *Secret London* by Andrew Duncan leads the reader on unique walks through a less-touristy London.

London's TIs hand out a useful, free monthly *London Planner* (includes a listing of sights and lots of London tips). Newsstands sell the excellent weekly entertainment magazine *Time Out,* which has good maps and a concise and opinionated rundown on sightseeing, shopping, entertainment, and eats (£3, www.timeout.com /london).

If you'll be traveling elsewhere in Britain, consider *Rick Steves' England 2010* or *Rick Steves' Great Britain 2010.*

Recommended Books and Movies

To get a feel for London past and present, check out a few of these books or films.

Nonfiction

A History of London (Inwood), topping out at a thousand pages, covers two thousand years. *London* (Ackroyd) takes the form of a biography rather than a conventional history. *Elizabeth's London* (Picard) re-creates 16th-century life in the era of England's first great queen.

Originally published in the *New Yorker* magazine, *Letters from London* (Barnes) captures life in the city in the early 1990s. The book *84, Charing Cross Road* is a collection of letters between a stiff-upper-lip London bookseller and a witty writer, Helene Hanff, in the post-WWII years. (Also worth reading is the sequel, *The Duchess of Bloomsbury Street.*) Although not specific to

Begin Your Trip at www.ricksteves.com

At our travel website, you'll find a wealth of free information on European destinations, including fresh monthly news and helpful tips from thousands of fellow travelers. You'll also find my latest guidebook updates (www.ricksteves.com/update) and my travel blog.

Our **online Travel Store** offers travel bags and accessories specially designed by Rick Steves to help you travel smarter and lighter. These include Rick's popular carry-on bags (roll-aboard and rucksack versions), money belts, totes, toiletries kits, adapters, other accessories, and a wide selection of guidebooks, journals, planning maps, and DVDs.

Choosing the right **railpass** for your trip—amidst hundreds of options—can drive you nutty. We'll help you choose the best pass for your needs, plus give you a bunch of free extras.

Rick Steves' Europe Through the Back Door travel company offers **tours** with more than three dozen itineraries and more than 300 departures reaching the best destinations in this book...and beyond. We offer several tours that include London, such as our seven-day in-depth London city tour; our eight-day Paris and London tour, featuring the highlights of both great cities; and our 15-day Best of Britain tour. You'll enjoy great guides, a fun bunch of travel partners (with small groups of around 28), and plenty of room to spread out in a big, comfy bus. You'll find European adventures to fit every vacation length. For all the details, and to get our Tour Catalog and a free Rick Steves Tour Experience DVD (filmed on location during an actual tour), visit www.ricksteves.com or call the Tour Department at 425/608-4217.

London, consider *Notes from a Small Island,* which is chock-full of Bill Bryson's witty observations about Great Britain. Dava Sobel's *Longitude* tells the story of the clockmaker who solved a problem that had thwarted previous geniuses. Kids of all ages enjoy the whimsical and colorful impressions of the city in Miroslav Sasek's classic picture-book *This Is London.*

Fiction

Describing the classics of British literature is a book in itself. But some favorites that feature London include *Pygmalion* (Shaw), the story of a young Cockney girl groomed for high society; *Persuasion,* a beloved Jane Austen book partially set in Bath; and Charles Dickens' tale of a workhouse urchin, *Oliver Twist.*

Dating from the turn of the century, P. G. Wodehouse's Jeeves series, with a problem-solving valet as the lead character, have endured. *A Study in Scarlet* (Doyle) introduced the world to detective Sherlock Holmes.

Edward Rutherfurd's *London,* which begins in ancient times and continues through to the 20th century, is as big and sprawling as its namesake. *The Jupiter Myth* (Davis) takes place in the days when the city was called Londinium. In *The Great Stink* (Clark), the sewer system is also a metaphor for the blight that plagued the city.

Lucia in London (Benson) sends the protagonist of this 1920s series to the big city. Helen Fielding created another well-loved heroine in her *Bridget Jones* books, which began in the late 1990s as a newspaper column (and inspired two fun films). *Confessions of a Shopaholic* (Kinsella) continues the Bridget Jones formula. Nick Hornby explores a young male perspective of life and love in *Fever Pitch, High Fidelity,* and *About a Boy.*

London's movers and shakers commit bad deeds in the detective story *In the Presence of the Enemy* (George). *Murder in Mayfair* (Barnard) is based on a true crime from the 1980s. *Rumpole of the Bailey,* created by Sir John Mortimer, is a popular detective series, spawning both books and television shows.

Ian McEwan's highly praised post-9/11 novel, *Saturday,* takes place over the course of a day all over the sprawling city. Many recent works feature the city's thriving immigrant communities, including *The Buddha of Suburbia* (Kureishi), *White Teeth* (Smith), and *Brick Lane* (Ali, also a 2007 film).

Films

For a taste of Tudor-era London, try *Shakespeare in Love* (1999), which is set in the original Globe Theatre. In *A Man for All Seasons* (1966), Sir Thomas More faces down Henry VIII. For equally good portraits of Elizabeth I, try *Elizabeth* (1998), its sequel *Elizabeth:*

The Golden Age (2007), and *Elizabeth I* (2005, a BBC/HBO miniseries).

Written and set in the early 19th century, the works of Jane Austen have fared well in film. *Persuasion* (1995) was partially filmed in Bath.

Equally genteel was the Edwardian era of the early 20th century. *Howard's End* (1992) captures the stifling societal pressure underneath the gracious manners. In *The Elephant Man* (1980), the cruelty of Victorian London is starkly portrayed in a black-and-white film.

Wartime London was captured in many fine movies, including *Waterloo Bridge* (1940), a story of lost love between a woman and a WWI officer. In *Passport to Pimlico* (1949), an explosion in a Tube station is the source of riches and comedy in a time of post-WWII rationing.

In the 1960s, two blockbuster Hollywood musicals were set in London: *Mary Poppins* (1964) and *My Fair Lady* (1964). British acts were all the rage in the States, thanks to a little band called the Beatles, whose *A Hard Day's Night* (1964) is filled with wit and charm.

During this time, "swinging London" also exploded on the international scene, with films such as *Alfie* (1966), *Blowup* (1966) and *Georgy Girl* (1966). (For a swinging spoof of this time, try the Austin Powers comedies.) In *To Sir, with Love* (1967), Sidney Poitier brings order to his undisciplined students.

For more recent films, watch Hugh Grant charming the ladies in *Four Weddings and a Funeral* (1994) and *Notting Hill* (1999); Gwyneth Paltrow living two lives in *Sliding Doors* (1998); and *A Fish Called Wanda* (1988), in which John Cleese is embroiled in love, revenge, and exotic fish.

For something completely different from the typical Hollywood fare, see *My Beautiful Laundrette* (1986), a gritty story of two gay men (one of whom is played by Daniel Day-Lewis). For another portrayal of urban London—and the racial tensions found in its multiethnic center—look for *Sammy and Rosie Get Laid* (1987). *Lock, Stock and Two Smoking Barrels* (1998) is a violent crime caper set in the city.

In the last decade, *Billy Elliot* (2000), about a young boy ballet dancer, and *Bend It Like Beckham* (2003), about a young Punjabi soccer player, were both huge crowd-pleasers. In *The Queen* (2006), Helen Mirren expertly channels Elizabeth II during the days after Princess Diana's death.

Shaun of the Dead (2004) combines comedy and horror, when the city's residents turn into zombies. The same team more recently merged cop/action films and comedy in *Hot Fuzz* (2007). *V for Vendetta* (2006), based on a British graphic novel, shows a sci-fi future of a London ruled with an iron fist. *Sweeney Todd* (2007) captures the gritty Victorian milieu.

If you're traveling to London or Great Britain with children, consider watching *Mary Poppins* (1964), *My Fair Lady* (1964), *A Little Princess* (1995), the *Wallace & Gromit* movies, Rowan Atkinson's *Mr. Bean* television series and movies, and the *Harry Potter* films.

Holidays and Festivals

This list includes major festivals in London, plus national holidays observed throughout Great Britain. Many sights and banks close on national holidays—keep it in mind when planning your itinerary. Note that this isn't a complete list; holidays often strike without warning.

Included in this list are events in the nearby towns of Bath, Windsor, and Cambridge. Each of these towns is an easy train ride from London (see Day Trips in England chapter).

For specifics and a more comprehensive list of festivals, check the websites recommended earlier in this chapter: www.visit london.com, www.timeout.com/london, www.londontown.com, and www.visitbritain.com.

Jan 1	New Year's Day
Feb (one week)	London Fashion Week (www.london fashionweek.co.uk)
Feb 27–March 7	Literature Festival, Bath (www.bathlit fest.org.uk)
April 2	Good Friday
April 4–5	Easter Sunday and Monday
May 3	Early May Bank Holiday (first Monday in May)
May 25–29	Chelsea Flower Show, London (book tickets ahead for this popular event at www.rhs.org.uk/chelsea)
Late May–early June	International Music Festival, Bath (www.bathmusicfest.org.uk)
Late May–early June	Fringe Festival, Bath (alternative music, dance, and theater; www.bathfringe .co.uk)
May 31	Spring Bank Holiday (last Monday in May)
June 13	Trooping the Colour, London (military bands and pageantry, Queen's birthday parade)

APPENDIX

2 0 1 0

JANUARY
S	M	T	W	T	F	S
					1	2
3	4	5	6	7	8	9
10	11	12	13	14	15	16
17	18	19	20	21	22	23
24/31	25	26	27	28	29	30

FEBRUARY
S	M	T	W	T	F	S
	1	2	3	4	5	6
7	8	9	10	11	12	13
14	15	16	17	18	19	20
21	22	23	24	25	26	27
28						

MARCH
S	M	T	W	T	F	S
	1	2	3	4	5	6
7	8	9	10	11	12	13
14	15	16	17	18	19	20
21	22	23	24	25	26	27
28	29	30	31			

APRIL
S	M	T	W	T	F	S
				1	2	3
4	5	6	7	8	9	10
11	12	13	14	15	16	17
18	19	20	21	22	23	24
25	26	27	28	29	30	

MAY
S	M	T	W	T	F	S
						1
2	3	4	5	6	7	8
9	10	11	12	13	14	15
16	17	18	19	20	21	22
23/30	24/31	25	26	27	28	29

JUNE
S	M	T	W	T	F	S
		1	2	3	4	5
6	7	8	9	10	11	12
13	14	15	16	17	18	19
20	21	22	23	24	25	26
27	28	29	30			

JULY
S	M	T	W	T	F	S
				1	2	3
4	5	6	7	8	9	10
11	12	13	14	15	16	17
18	19	20	21	22	23	24
25	26	27	28	29	30	31

AUGUST
S	M	T	W	T	F	S
1	2	3	4	5	6	7
8	9	10	11	12	13	14
15	16	17	18	19	20	21
22	23	24	25	26	27	28
29	30	31				

SEPTEMBER
S	M	T	W	T	F	S
			1	2	3	4
5	6	7	8	9	10	11
12	13	14	15	16	17	18
19	20	21	22	23	24	25
26	27	28	29	30		

OCTOBER
S	M	T	W	T	F	S
					1	2
3	4	5	6	7	8	9
10	11	12	13	14	15	16
17	18	19	20	21	22	23
24/31	25	26	27	28	29	30

NOVEMBER
S	M	T	W	T	F	S
	1	2	3	4	5	6
7	8	9	10	11	12	13
14	15	16	17	18	19	20
21	22	23	24	25	26	27
28	29	30				

DECEMBER
S	M	T	W	T	F	S
			1	2	3	4
5	6	7	8	9	10	11
12	13	14	15	16	17	18
19	20	21	22	23	24	25
26	27	28	29	30	31	

APPENDIX

June 15–19	Royal Ascot Horse Race (www.ascot.co.uk), Ascot (near Windsor)
Late June–early July	Wimbledon Tennis Championship, London (www.wimbledon.org)
July 29–Aug 1	Cambridge Folk Festival, Cambridge (buy tickets early at www.cambridgefolkfestival.co.uk)
Late Aug	Notting Hill Carnival, London (costumes, Caribbean music, www.londoncarnival.co.uk)
Aug 30	Late Summer Bank Holiday (last Monday in August; England only, not Scotland)
Sept (one week)	London Fashion Week (www.londonfashionweek.co.uk)
Mid-Sept	Jane Austen Festival, Bath (www.janeausten.co.uk)

Nov 5	Bonfire Night (bonfires, fireworks, effigy burning of 1605 traitor Guy Fawkes)
Nov 14	Remembrance Sunday (royals lay wreaths at Cenotaph for WWI dead)
Dec 24–26	Christmas holidays (many sights close; limited or no public transport)

Conversions and Climate

Britain uses a mix of the metric system and "our" Imperial system. That, and a few other little differences, can cause visitors to stumble. Here are the basics, along with a snapshot of the weather you can expect.

Numbers and Stumblers

- The British write a few of their numbers differently than we do. 1 = 1, 4 = 4, 7 = 7.
- In Europe, dates appear as day/month/year, so Christmas is 25/12/10.
- What Americans call the second floor of a building is the first floor in Britain.
- On escalators and moving sidewalks, Brits keep the left "lane" open for passing. Stand to the right.
- When pointing, use your whole hand, palm down.
- When counting with fingers, start with your thumb. If you hold up your first finger to request one item, you'll probably get two.
- To avoid the British version of giving someone "the finger," don't hold up the first two fingers of your hand with your palm facing you. (It looks like a reversed victory sign.)
- And please...don't call your waist pack a "fanny pack" (see the British-Yankee Vocabulary list at the end of this appendix).

Metric Conversions (approximate)

Weight and volume are typically calculated in metric: A kilogram is 2.2 pounds, and a liter is about a quart. The weight of a person is measured by "stone" (one stone equals 14 pounds). On the road, Brits use miles instead of kilometers. Temperatures are generally given in both Celsius and Fahrenheit.

1 foot = 0.3 meter	1 square yard = 0.8 square meter
1 yard = 0.9 meter	1 square mile = 2.6 square kilometers
1 mile = 1.6 kilometers	1 ounce = 28 grams
1 centimeter = 0.4 inch	1 quart = 0.95 liter
1 meter = 39.4 inches	1 kilogram = 2.2 pounds
1 kilometer = 0.62 mile	32°F = 0°C

Weights and Measures
1 British pint = 1.2 US pints
1 imperial gallon = 1.2 US gallons or about 4.5 liters
1 stone = 14 pounds (a 168-pound person weighs 12 stone)
Shoe sizes = about .5 to 1.5 sizes smaller than in the US

Clothing Sizes
When shopping for clothing, use these US-to-UK comparisons as general guidelines (but note that no conversion is perfect).
- Women's dresses and blouses: Add 4 (US women's size 10 = UK size 14)
- Men's suits and jackets: US and UK use the same sizing
- Men's shirts: US and UK use the same sizing
- Women's shoes: Subtract 2½ (US size 8 = UK size 5½)
- Men's shoes: Subtract about ½ (US size 9 = UK size 8½)

London's Climate
First line, average daily high; second line, average daily low; third line, days of no rain. For more detailed weather statistics for destinations throughout England (as well as the rest of the world), check www.worldclimate.com.

J	F	M	A	M	J	J	A	S	O	N	D
43°	44°	50°	56°	62°	69°	71°	71°	65°	58°	50°	45°
36°	36°	38°	42°	47°	53°	56°	56°	52°	46°	42°	38°
16	15	20	18	19	19	19	20	17	18	15	16

Temperature Conversion: Fahrenheit and Celsius

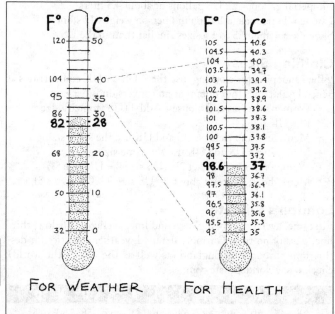

Britain uses both Celsius and Fahrenheit to take its temperature. For a rough conversion from Celsius to Fahrenheit, double the number and add 30. For weather, remember that 28°C is 82°F—perfect. For health, 37°C is just right.

APPENDIX

Essential Packing Checklist

Whether you're traveling for five days or five weeks, here's what you'll need to bring. Remember to pack light to enjoy the sweet freedom of true mobility. Happy travels!

- ❑ 5 shirts
- ❑ 1 sweater or lightweight fleece jacket
- ❑ 2 pairs pants
- ❑ 1 pair shorts
- ❑ 1 swimsuit (women only—men can use shorts)
- ❑ 5 pairs underwear and socks
- ❑ 1 pair shoes
- ❑ 1 rainproof jacket
- ❑ Tie or scarf
- ❑ Money belt
- ❑ Money—your mix of:
  - ❑ Debit card for ATM withdrawals
  - ❑ Credit card
  - ❑ Hard cash in US dollars
- ❑ Documents (and back-up photocopies)
- ❑ Passport
- ❑ Printout of airline e-ticket
- ❑ Driver's license
- ❑ Student ID and hostel card
- ❑ Railpass/car rental voucher
- ❑ Insurance details
- ❑ Daypack
- ❑ Sealable plastic baggies
- ❑ Camera and related gear
- ❑ Empty water bottle
- ❑ Wristwatch and alarm clock
- ❑ Earplugs
- ❑ First-aid kit
- ❑ Medicine (labeled)
- ❑ Extra glasses/contacts and prescriptions
- ❑ Sunscreen and sunglasses
- ❑ Toiletries kit
- ❑ Soap
- ❑ Laundry soap
- ❑ Clothesline
- ❑ Small towel
- ❑ Sewing kit
- ❑ Travel information
- ❑ Necessary map(s)
- ❑ Address list (email and mailing addresses)
- ❑ Postcards and photos from home
- ❑ Notepad and pen
- ❑ Journal

If you plan to carry on your luggage, note that all liquids must be in three-ounce or smaller containers and fit within a single quart-size baggie. For details, see www.tsa.gov/travelers.

Hotel Reservation

To: _____   _____
        hotel   *email or fax*

From: _____   _____
          name   *email or fax*

Today's date: _____ / _____ / _____
                  day   *month*   *year*

Dear Hotel _____ ,
Please make this reservation for me:

Name: _____

Total # of people: _____ # of rooms: _____ # of nights: _____

Arriving: _____ / _____ / _____ My time of arrival (24-hr clock): _____
              day *month* *year*   (I will telephone if I will be late)

Departing: ____ / ____ / ____
               day *month* *year*

Room(s): Single ____ Double ____ Twin ____ Triple ____ Quad ____

With: Toilet ____ Shower ____ Bath ____ Sink only ____

Special needs: View ____ Quiet ____ Cheapest ____ Ground Floor ____

Please email or fax confirmation of my reservation, along with the type of room reserved and the price. Please also inform me of your cancellation policy. After I hear from you, I will quickly send my credit-card information as a deposit to hold the room. Thank you.

_____
Name

_____
Address

_____
City   *State*   *Zip Code*   *Country*

Before hoteliers can make your reservation, they want to know the information listed above. You can use this form as the basis for your email, or you can photocopy this page, fill in the information, and send it as a fax (also available online at www.ricksteves.com/reservation).

British–Yankee Vocabulary

advert–advertisement

afters–dessert

anticlockwise–counterclockwise

aubergine–eggplant

banger–sausage

bangers and mash–sausage and mashed potatoes

bank holiday–legal holiday

bap–small roll

bespoke–custom-made

billion–a thousand of our billions (a million million)

biro–ballpoint pen

biscuit–cookie

black pudding–sausage made from dried blood

bloody–damn

blow off–fart

bobby–policeman ("the Bill" is more common)

Bob's your uncle–there you go (with a shrug), naturally

boffin–nerd, geek

bollocks–testicles (used in many colorful expressions)

bolshy–argumentative

bomb–success or failure

bonnet–car hood

boot–car trunk

braces–suspenders

bridle way–path for walkers, bikers, and horse riders

brilliant–cool

brolly–umbrella

bubble and squeak–cabbage and potatoes fried together

builder–construction worker

bum–butt

candy floss–cotton candy

caravan–trailer

car boot sale–temporary flea market, often for charity

car park–parking lot

casualty–emergency room

cat's eyes–road reflectors

ceilidh (KAY-lee)–informal evening of song and folk fun (Scottish and Irish)

cheap and cheerful–budget but adequate

cheap and nasty–cheap and bad quality

cheers–good-bye or thanks; also a toast

chemist–pharmacist

chicory–endive

chippie–fish-and-chip shop; carpenter (see also "joiner")

chips–French fries

chock-a-block–jam-packed

chuffed–pleased

cider–alcoholic apple cider

clearway–road where you can't stop

coach–long-distance bus

concession–discounted admission

concs (pronounced "conks")–short for "concession"

cos–romaine lettuce

cotton buds–Q-tips

council estate–public housing

courgette–zucchini

craic (pronounced "crack")–fun, good conversation (Irish and spreading to England)

crisps–potato chips

cuppa–cup of tea

curry–any Indian meal flavored with curry, popular with all Brits

dear–expensive

dicey–iffy, risky

digestives–round graham cookies

dinner–lunch or dinner

diversion–detour

donkey's years–ages, long time

draughts–checkers

draw–marijuana

dual carriageway–divided highway (four lanes)

dummy–pacifier

elevenses–coffee-and-biscuits break before lunch

elvers–baby eels

engaged tone–busy signal

estate car–station wagon

face flannel–washcloth

faff–bumble (about)

fag–cigarette

fagged–exhausted

faggot–meatball

fairy cake–cupcake

fancy–to like, to be attracted to (a person)

fanny–vagina

fell–hill or high plain (Lake District)

first floor–second floor

fixture–sports schedule

fizzy drink–pop or soda

flat–apartment

flutter–a bet

football–soccer

force–waterfall (Lake District)

fortnight–two weeks

fringe–hair bangs

Frogs–French people

fruit machine–slot machine

full Monty–whole shebang; everything

gallery–balcony

gammon–ham

gangway–aisle

gaol–jail (same pronunciation)

gateau (or gateaux)–cake

gear lever–stick shift

geezer–dude (slang for young man)

ginger-haired–redhead

give way–yield

glen–narrow valley (Scotland)

goods wagon–freight truck

green fingers–green thumbs

grizzle–grumble, fuss (especially by a baby)

gutted–deeply disappointed

half eight–8:30 (not 7:30)

hash sign–pound sign, as on a phone

heath–open treeless land

hen night–bachelorette party

High Street–Main Street (in a generic sense)

hire–rent, as in a car or bike

hire car–rental car

hob–stove burner

holiday–vacation

homely–homey or cozy

hoover–vacuum cleaner

ice lolly–Popsicle

interval–intermission

ironmonger–hardware store

ish–more or less

jacket potato–baked potato

jelly–Jell-O

Joe Bloggs–John Q. Public

joiner–carpenter (see also "chippie")

jumble sale–rummage sale

jumper–sweater

just a tick–just a second

kipper–smoked herring

knackered–exhausted
(Cockney: cream
crackered)

knickers–ladies' panties

knocking shop–brothel

knock up–wake up or visit
(old-fashioned)

ladybird–ladybug

lady fingers–flat, spongy
cookie

lady's finger–okra

lager–light, fizzy beer

left luggage–baggage check

lemon squash–lemonade, not
fizzy

lemonade–lemon-lime pop,
fizzy

let–rent, as in property

licenced–restaurant authorized
to sell alcohol

lie-in, having a–sleeping in
late

lift–elevator

listed–protected historic
building

loo–toilet or bathroom

lorry–truck

mac–mackintosh raincoat

mangetout–snow peas

main–entrée

mains–electrical outlet

Marmite–yeast paste, spread
on sandwiches

marrow–summer squash

mate–buddy (boy or girl)

mean–stingy

mental–wild, memorable

mews–former stables converted
to two-story rowhouses
(London)

mince–hamburger meat

mobile (MOH-bile)–cell
phone

moggie–cat

M.O.T.–mandatory annual car
safety certificate

motorway–freeway

naff–dorky

nappy–diaper

natter–talk on and on

neep–Scottish for turnip

newsagent–corner store

nought–zero

noughts & crosses–tic-tac-toe

O.A.P.–old-age pensioner,
retiree

off-licence–liquor store

on offer–for sale

one-off–unique; one-time
event

panto, pantomime–fairy-
tale play performed at
Christmas (silly but fun)

pants–underwear, briefs

paracetamol–acetaminophen,
Tylenol

pasty (PASS-tee)–crusted
savory (usually meat) pie
from Cornwall

pavement–sidewalk

people mover–minivan

pear-shaped–messed up, gone
wrong

pensioner–senior citizen,
retiree

petrol–gas

pillar box–mailbox

pissed (rude), **paralytic,
bevvied, wellied, popped
up, merry, trollied,
ratted, rat-arsed, pissed
as a newt**–drunk

pitch–playing field

plaster–Band-Aid

pram–baby carriage

publican–pub manager (old-fashioned)

public school–private "prep" school (e.g., Eton)

pudding–dessert in general

pull, to be on the–looking for love

punter–customer, especially in gambling

pushchair–stroller

put a sock in it–shut up

queue–line

queue up–line up

quid–a pound (money)

randy–horny

rasher–slice of bacon

redundant, made–laid off

Remembrance Day–Veterans' Day

return ticket–round trip

ring up–call (telephone)

rocket–arugula

roundabout–traffic circle

rubber–eraser

rubbish–bad

salad cream–mayo, mustard, and vinegar dressing

Sat Nav–GPS device

sausage roll–sausage wrapped in a flaky pastry

Scotch egg–hard-boiled egg wrapped in sausage meat

scrumpy–type of hard cider

self-catering–accommodation with kitchen

Sellotape–Scotch tape

services–freeway rest area

serviette–napkin

settee–couch

shag–intercourse (cruder than in the US)

shandy–lager and 7-Up

silencer–car muffler

single ticket–one-way ticket

skip–Dumpster

sleeping policeman–speed bumps

smalls–underwear

snogging–kissing, making out

sod–mildly offensive insult

sod it, sod off–screw it, screw off

soda–soda water (not pop)

solicitor–lawyer (a.k.a. barrister)

spanner–wrench

sparkie–electrician

spend a penny–urinate

stag night–bachelor party

starkers–buck naked

starters–appetizers

state school–public school

sticking plaster–Band-Aid

sticky tape–Scotch tape

stone–14 pounds (weight)

stroppy–bad-tempered

subway–underground walkway

suet–fat from animal rendering (sometimes used in cooking)

sultanas–golden raisins

surgical spirit–rubbing alcohol

suspenders–garters

suss out–figure out

swede–rutabaga

ta–thank you

take the mickey–tease

tatty–worn out or tacky

taxi rank–taxi stand

telly–TV

tenement–stone apartment house (not necessarily a slum)

tenner–£10 bill

theatre–live stage

tick–a check mark

tight as a fish's bum–
    cheapskate (watertight)

tights–panty hose

tin–can

tip–public dump

tipper lorry–dump truck

top hole–first rate

top up–refill a drink

torch–flashlight

towel, press-on–panty liner

towpath–path along a river

trainers–sneakers

Tube–subway

twee–quaint, cute

twitcher–bird watcher

Underground–subway

verge–grassy edge of road

verger–church official

way out–exit

wee (adj)–small (Scottish)

wee (verb)–urinate

Wellingtons, wellies–rubber
    boots

whacked–exhausted

whinge (rhymes with hinge)–
    whine

wind up–tease, irritate

witter on–gab and gab

yob–hooligan

zebra crossing–crosswalk

zed–the letter Z

INDEX

INDEX

MAP INDEX

MAP INDEX

EUROPEAN TOURS

ADRIATIC • ATHENS & THE HEART OF GREECE • BARCELONA & MADRID • BELGIUM & HOLLAND • BERLIN, VIENNA & PRAGUE BEST OF EUROPE • BEST OF ITALY • BEST OF TURKEY • EASTERN EUROPE • ENGLAND FAMILY EUROPE • GERMANY, AUSTRIA & SWITZERLAND • HEART OF ITALY IRELAND • ISTANBUL • LONDON • PARIS PARIS & HEART OF FRANCE • PARIS & SOUTH OF FRANCE • PORTUGAL • PRAGUE ROME • SAN SEBASTIAN & BASQUE COUNTRY SCANDINAVIA • SCOTLAND • SICILY SOUTH ITALY • SPAIN & MOROCCO ST. PETERSBURG, TALINN & HELSINKI VENICE, FLORENCE & ROME • VILLAGE FRANCE • VILLAGE ITALY • VILLAGE TURKEY

VISIT **TOURS.RICKSTEVES.COM**

Great guides, small groups, no grumps

Free information and great gear

▸ Plan Your Trip

Browse thousands of articles and a wealth of money-saving tips for planning your dream trip. You'll find up-to-date information on Europe's best destinations, packing smart, getting around, finding rooms, staying healthy, avoiding scams and more.

▸ Eurail Passes

Find out, step-by-step, if a rail p... makes sense for your trip—and ... how to avoid buying more than y... need. Get a bunch of free extras!

▸ Graffiti Wall & Travelers' Helpline

Learn, ask, share—our online community of savvy travelers is a great resource for first-time travelers to Europe, as well as seasoned pros.

rn your travel dreams into affordable reality

Free Audio Tours & avel Newsletter

et your nose out of this guide-
ok and focus on what you'll be
eing with Rick's free audio tours
the greatest sights in Paris,
me, Florence and Venice.
Subscribe to our free *Travel
ews* e-newsletter, and get monthly
ticles from Rick on what's
ppening in Europe.

▶ Great Gear from Rick's Travel Store

Pack light and right—on a
budget—with Rick's custom-
designed carry-on bags, roll-
aboards, day packs, travel
accessories, guidebooks, journals,
maps and DVDs of his TV shows.

130 Fourth Avenue North, PO Box 2009 • Edmonds, WA 98020 USA
Phone: (425) 771-8303 • Fax: (425) 771-0833 • www.ricksteves.com

Rick Steves

www.ricksteves.com

TRAVEL SKILLS
Europe Through the Back Door

EUROPE GUIDES
Best of Europe
Eastern Europe
Europe 101
European Christmas
Postcards from Europe

COUNTRY GUIDES
Croatia & Slovenia
England
France
Germany
Great Britain
Ireland
Italy
Portugal
Scandinavia
Spain
Switzerland

CITY & REGIONAL GUIDES
Amsterdam, Bruges & Brussels
Athens & The Peloponnese
Budapest
Florence & Tuscany
Istanbul
London
Paris
Prague & The Czech Republic
Provence & The French Riviera
Rome
Venice
Vienna, Salzburg & Tirol

PHRASE BOOKS & DICTIONARIES
French
French, Italian & German
German
Italian
Portuguese
Spanish

RICK STEVES' EUROPE DVDs
Austria & The Alps
Eastern Europe
England
Europe
France & Benelux
Germany & Scandinavia
Greece, Turkey, Israel & Egypt
Ireland & Scotland
Italy's Cities
Italy's Countryside
Rick Steves' European Christmas
Spain & Portugal
Travel Skills & "The Making Of"

PLANNING MAPS
Britain, Ireland & London
Europe
France & Paris
Germany, Austria & Switzerland
Ireland
Italy
Spain & Portugal

JOURNALS
Rick Steves' Pocket Travel Journal
Rick Steves' Travel Journal

NOW AVAILABLE

ICK STEVES APPS FOR THE iPHONE OR iPOD TOUCH

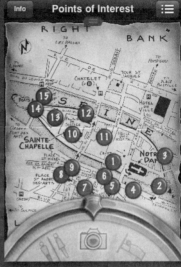

'ou're standing at the center of France,
he point from which all distances are
neasured. It was also the center of Paris
,300 years ago, when the Parisii tribe
shed where the east—west riv   Info

With these apps you can:

Spin the compass icon to switch views between sights, hotels,
and restaurant selections—and get details on cost, hours, address,
and phone number.

Tap any point on the screen to read Rick's detailed information,
including history and suggested viewpoints.

Get a deeper view into Rick's tours with audio and video segments.

Go to iTunes to download the following apps:

Rick Steves' Louvre Tour

Rick Steves' Historic Paris Walk

Rick Steves' Orsay Museum Tour

Rick Steves' Versailles

Rick Steves' Colosseum & Roman Forum Tour

Rick Steves' St. Peter's Basilica Tour

**Once downloaded, these apps are completely self-contained on your iPhone
or iPod Touch, so you will not incur pricey roaming charges during use
overseas.**

Rick Steves books and DVDs are available at bookstores and through online booksellers.
Rick Steves guidebooks are published by Avalon Travel, a member of the Perseus Books Group.
Rick Steves apps are produced by Übermind, a boutique Seattle-based software consultancy firm.

Credits

Researchers

To help update this book, Rick and Gene relied on...

Cathy McDonald

Cathy, an editor and researcher for Rick Steves, enjoys England's natural history and how it affects its people. She lives in Seattle, where she has written about the Pacific Northwest for more than 15 years as a free-lancer for the *Seattle Times*.

Lauren Mills

Lauren, a map editor and in-house search engine at Rick Steves, was an ardent Anglophile even before bringing home her British husband as a souvenir. They live in Seattle with their cat Keswick.